AN AFRICAN PEOPLE'S QUEST FOR FREEDOM AND JUSTICE

ALEMSEGED TESFAI

An African People's Quest for Freedom and Justice

A Political History of Eritrea, 1941–1962

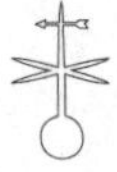

HURST & COMPANY, LONDON

First published in the United Kingdom in 2025 by
C. Hurst & Co. (Publishers) Ltd.,
New Wing, Somerset House, Strand, London, WC2R 1LA

Distributed in the United States, Canada and Latin America by
Oxford University Press, 198 Madison Avenue, New York, NY 10016,
United States of America.

Partially funded by the Miles Morland Foundation and/or Winner of the Morland African
Writing Scholarship Award, 2017.

A Cataloguing-in-Publication data record for this book
is available from the British Library.

ISBN: 9781911723790

www.hurstpublishers.com

Printed and bound in Great Britain by Bell & Bain Ltd, Glasgow

This book is dedicated to the memory of our son Temesgen, whose tragic death at the age of sixteen in 2009 threw us into the depths of grief and desperation, only for his spirit to return to us as the inspiration that he has become.

Also, to Matyas and Abrehet, for their love, comfort and patience.

CONTENTS

PART THREE
THE ROAD TO THE ERITREAN REVOLUTION

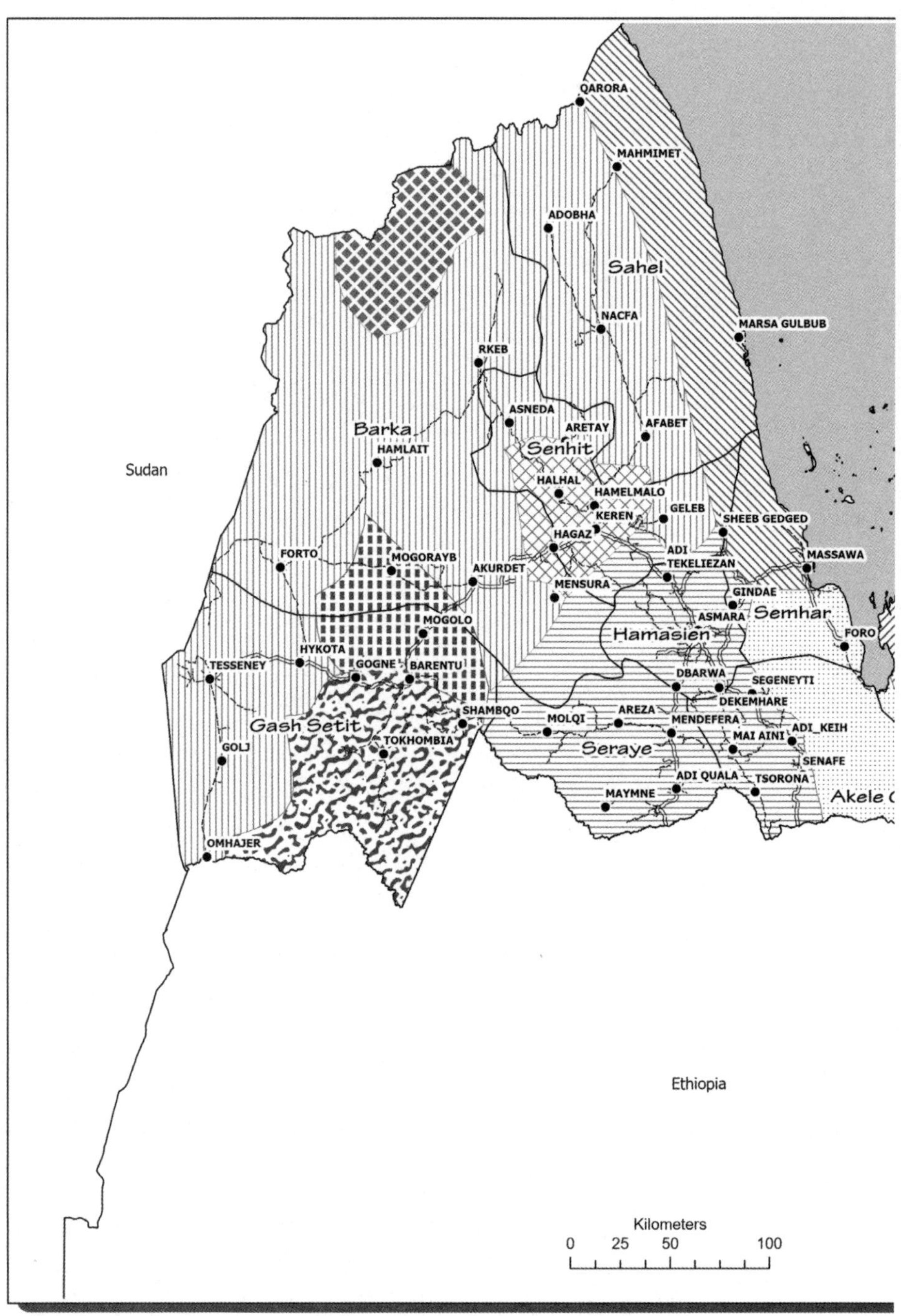

Pre–independence Eritrea: Ethnic Distribution and Administrative Structure.

Courtesy of Office of National Statistics Office, Ministry of Planning and Development, Asmara, Eritrea.

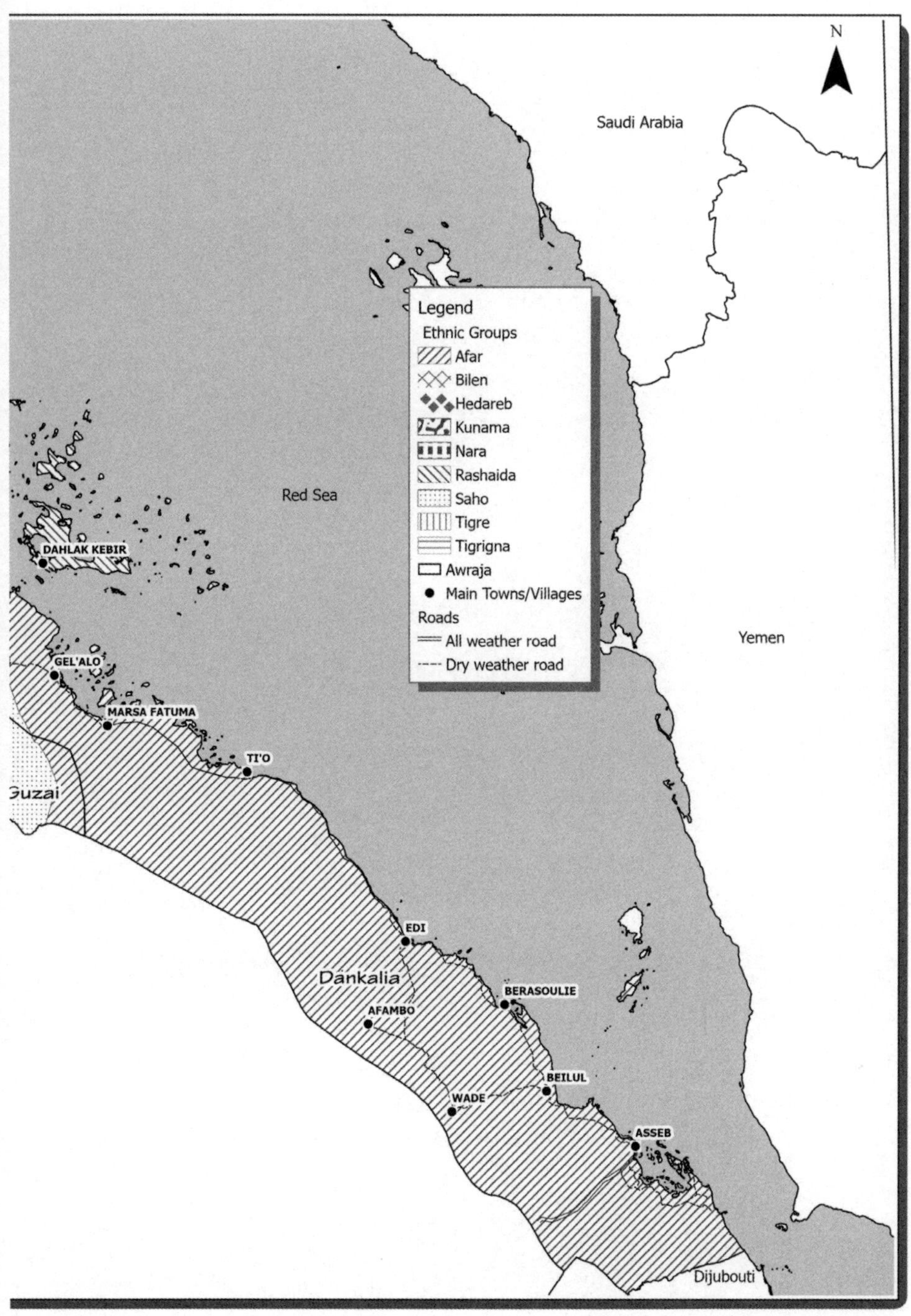

N
Saudi Arabia
Legend
Ethnic Groups
Afar
Bilen
Hedareb
Kunama
Nara
Rashaida
Saho
Tigre
Tigrigna
Awraja
Main Towns/Villages
Roads
All weather road
Dry weather road
Red Sea
Yemen
DAHLAK KEBIR
GEL'ALO
MARSA FATUMA
TI'O
Guzai
EDI
Dankalia
BERASOULIE
AFAMBO
BEILUL
WADE
ASSEB
Dijubouti

PREFACE

There is a Tigrinya word, *aynfelale*, which means 'let us not separate' or 'let us stay or stick together'. This was the slogan of the Independence Bloc of Eritrea, formed in the wake of a failed British–Italian plan to partition Eritrea along religious lines by awarding the predominantly Christian parts to Ethiopia and the Muslim areas to Sudan. As a symbol of the Eritrean people's decades-long struggle to maintain their unity against supreme odds, I have chosen it as the most appropriate emblem for the story in my book. It also honours the pioneers of Eritrean independence, who gave so much to live up to the challenges of their own slogan.

I am a lawyer by training but turned to writing history as a result of an unintended shift in my academic focus. In 1970, when I was a graduate law student at the University of Illinois at Champaign-Urbana, I chose as the topic for my master's thesis the legal basis for the handling of the Eritrean case by the victors of World War II, the Four Great Powers, and the General Assembly of the UN. In my research on the historical background to the problem, I remember being dismayed by the paucity of written material representing the Eritrean side of the story. I also recall spending days at the University of Illinois library searching, in vain, for anything written by Eritreans on their own history. My interest in Eritrean history, especially the formative years of the British and Federal periods, started at that time.

In the course of examining the mid-nineteenth-century works of Werner Munzinger and Leo Reinisch on the region that was to become Eritrea, Bairu Tafla and Eva Schmidt explain the reason behind the dearth of published Eritrean history:

> [The] research launched by the pioneers continued with relative intensity for half a century or so until scholarship eventually gave way to the politics of grandeur. Italian colonial rule had to extend to Ethiopia, and for that very purpose, Eritrean historiography had to be sacrificed. Eritrean studies thus subsided into more or less insignificance, not figuring even as a regional area of focus within *Africa Orientale Italiana* and still less under the Ethiopian Empire, which equally aspired to centralism and grandeur. In the 1960s and 70s in fact, historicizing Eritrea became a taboo the breach of which was dangerous for Ethiopians as well as Eritreans and unamenable to foreigners.[1]

Scholarship on Eritrea and Ethiopia has suffered major setbacks as a result of this official policy of denial and suppression. Significantly, exponents of Ethiopian history who write on Eritrea, whether Ethiopians or expatriates, generally do so without referring to Eritrean sources or without conducting serious research inside Eritrea itself. The Imperial Ethiopian narrative assigned to Eritrea has generally been deemed adequate enough not to warrant any further inquiry. The hold of this narrative has been so strong, especially in the Horn region, that attempts at presenting an alternative history are often met with alarming hostility.

The official denial or suppression of a people's history does not necessarily mean it ceases to exist. The sense of a suppressed identity will often find a means or voice of self-expression that will assure its continuity. Whether that voice will develop into a material force, as it did in Eritrea, or peter out into submission and obscurity will always depend on the strength of the historical and social factors that created that identity. It will also depend on the conscious efforts of the forces that act on the reconstruction of these historical and social factors.

In this work, I have tried to trace that 'something' that 'engaged the imagination of a significant portion of the [Eritrean] population', to borrow Benedict Anderson's famous phrase, and moved it to make untold sacrifices to establish its separate identity. No understanding of Eritrea's hard journey to its present independent existence can ever be attained if the internal dynamics that made it happen are not properly examined. Arguably, in no other African independence movement was the issue of a people's identity fought to consummation as it was in Eritrea. All the other African movements had, at the time, an easily identifiable European coloniser as an adversary. For Eritreans, the decolonisation process was disrupted when Ethiopia took over as Italy's successor on the strength of a carefully designed 'Eritrean history' that was current in the Imperial court and was readily adopted by the Great Powers that decided their future in 1950.

Eritrean history has been analysed by various scholars in many ways but rarely are these analyses based on the most important factor in the whole context—the people of Eritrea. What is manifestly lacking in most of these writings is the actual actions, intentions, expectations and preferences of the people and their leaders. For example, on what evidence was the assumption based that no sense of Eritrean nationalism arose under Italy? What was the depth of the 'Ethiopian irredentist movement', identified by the British as the sole 'nationalism' in Eritrea? What did the unionists (seeking union with Ethiopia), and especially their youth wing, Andinet, really mean by their slogan 'Ethiopia or death'? Why did Eritrean Muslims seeking independence feel obliged to establish the Muslim League of Eritrea? Was it indicative of an irreconcilable difference with Christians, as is often surmised? The same questions may be posed about the other major groups, chiefly the Liberal Progressive and Pro-Italy parties. Answers to such questions can only be obtained from the words and actions of the main protagonists of the day. I have been fortunate to have either met some of the most prominent personalities on both sides of the political divide or gained access to the documents, newspaper articles, correspondence and similar sources that help to define major issues.

Facts, therefore, are what this work is mostly about. With the introductory sections as a background, it attempts to tell the Eritrean story of the 1940s to the 1960s in a chronological narration, an approach that I feel best helps fill the factual gaps in most previous works. But the story will also be told within the context of existing literature and scholarly work on the country and on the period. Hopefully, it will provide some of the missing links that have plagued scholarship on Eritrea for so long.

Alemseged Tesfai
August 2023

ACKNOWLEDGEMENTS

At the end of 2018, as I was starting work on this book, I was diagnosed with a life-threatening kidney disease and I had to be evacuated from Asmera. With characteristic concern and generosity, my old friend and schoolmate Tsegai Tesfatsion (Dinish), Eritrea's Ambassador to China, invited me to Beijing where, under the care of Professor Ying Su of Peking Union Medical College Hospital, I was brought back to full health. The major part of this book was written during my ten-month recovery period at the hospital and his residence in Beijing. Words of thanks cannot measure up to Tsegai's role in the making of this book.

I thank Professor Su for her dedication, professionalism, and inspiring grace and treatment. Professor Negassi Leake of Orotta Hospital, also a friend of over twenty years, continues to play no less of a role in keeping me healthy and functional. A person who, at his own request, will remain anonymous helped in arranging the coverage of a great part of my medical expenses in Beijing.

Zemhret Yohannes's stubborn belief that, despite my advancing age and health issues, I could write this book was the main force behind the project. My lifelong friend in joy and adversity, Teame Beyene, and my neighbour and friend, Yemane Dawit Ghide, also pushed me all the way to the finishing line. All three read the manuscript and made pertinent comments.

Professor Fouad Mekki of Cornell University went through the initial draft and made significant suggestions on the main themes of the book. I have followed as much of his advice as I could. Dr Gebrehiwet Tesfagiorgis, an old friend from my student days at Madison, Wisconsin, and an emeritus professor at Iowa State University, read the whole manuscript twice, and his sharp comments have helped me consider some fundamental issues. Similarly, Cornell University emeritus professor Kiflai Gebremedhin gave me some candid and valuable advice on language usage and manner of presentation.

Deep appreciation to all my colleagues, past and present, at the History Project. Azeb Tewolde, head of the Research and Documentation Centre, and her staff opened the doors of their vast archives to enrich the contents of this book. Freminatos Estifanos, as always with my other books, is my main advisor on form and design.

My siblings, along with their partners, children and grandchildren, too many to list here, have always been there for my family and myself. I need not say thank you, as each one knows the depth of my love and gratitude.

I thank all those who granted interviews, and offered documents, photographs and other relevant material; they are listed in the bibliography. If this book claims originality, it is thanks to their contributions. Those who deserve recognition are, again, too numerous to list here. I therefore will have to confine myself, with due apologies, to a collective expression of gratefulness and appreciation.

Last, but most important, is the Miles Morland Foundation. In 2017, I won a special Miles Morland Foundation Writing Scholarship Award for a non-fiction entry. Miles Morland himself took a personal interest in my work and, with his assistant at the foundation, Mathilda Edwards, extended the Award's fifteen-month deadline in consideration of my health and recovery issues. In addition, Miles has gone the extra mile to help me meet extra publishing expenses incurred by my publisher to accommodate the size of my book. When I designate this volume a Miles Morland Foundation book, it is in appreciation of Miles's and the Foundation's generosity.

The Foundation's creative writing editor, Giles Foden, who read the first chapters of my manuscript, and Michela Wrong, a foundation trustee, have given their unreserved support all the way through to the end. Professor Awet T. Weldemichael took the initiative to introduce my manuscript to Hurst Publishers and dedicated much of his time to seeing the process to fruition. Dr Senai Woldeab, head of the Department of Law at the College of Business and Social Sciences, Eritrea, has handled all the legal issues involved with amazing speed and professionalism. I am thankful to Russell Martin and Niamh Drennan for their cooperation and excellent editorial contributions, and express appreciation and respect for Michael Dwyer, Hurst Publisher and Managing Editor, who identified an 'intrinsic value' in my manuscript.

Thank you all.

GLOSSARY

abba	father; mainly reserved for monks and hermits
abujadid	traditional cloth
abune	bishop
ad/adi	village
askari	Eritrean soldier of the Italian army; also, servant
ato	title, similar to Mr
azmatch	literally, one who leads a military campaign; old Ethiopian title, below *dejazmatch*, used by the Italians
balambaras	Ethiopian military and civilian title for fort, artillery or similar commanders; used by Italy for lower ranks in Eritrea
bashai	military and civilian title, often of lower rank
bayto	assembly (village or national), parliament
bedew	nomad, Bedouin (often derogatory)
biet (Tigre), *bet* (Tigrinya)	literally, house; used to distinguish between sub-groups belonging to a *kebila* or *enda*
bitweded	literally, beloved or favoured; high-level Ethiopian title given to the Emperor's favourites
blata	Ethiopian civilian title
buluqbash	Turkish title for mid-level military officers used by Italy for Eritrean soldiers
carabinieri	Italian police
dejazmatch	army commander, equivalent to the rank of general; second-highest Ethiopian title

deqebat	original members of a village or community with a common ancestry and attendant rights
deqeQti	literally, small in size; commoners, the masses
diessa	ownership of land periodically distributed among village residents with an ancestral claim
diglel	leader of the Beni Amer of western Eritrea
enda	clan
Federalisti	members of AFYA who advocated the preservation of the Federation and the Eritrean flag
fitawrari	front commander; a rank below *dejazmatch*
grazmatch	commander of the left flank of an army
gulti	feudal levies imposed on farmers or pastoralists by local or regional rulers
hebret	union
hidmo	traditional quadrangular village house with thatched roof
kebessa	highland Eritrea, where the majority of the Tigrinya-speaking people live
kebila	a community of several *biets* or those with a common ancestry
kegnazmatch	commander of the right flank; also a civilian rank below *fitawrari*
kentabai (Tigre), *kentiba* (Tigrinya)	feudal title awarded to a local chief; today, mayor
Medri Bahri	earlier name for most of present-day Eritrea
ma'ekelai aliet	village residents (latecomers) with no ancestral claims, who have to satisfy various residential and other requirements to acquire the rights of the *deqebat*
melake selam	literally, messenger of peace; a religious title of the Orthodox Church
membir	teacher, equivalent to the Arabic *ustaz*
Mereb Mellash	literally, 'beyond Mereb'; a later name for Medri Bahri

metahit	lowlands; usually refers to the western lowlands of Eritrea
mislene	traditional district chief, often accountable to a government-appointed district officer
mufti	Muslim legal expert
muntaz	Turkish title equivalent to corporal, a rank below *buluqbash*
naib	deputy or representative; title of Turkish and Egyptian representatives, based in Hirgigo, who administered Massawa on their behalf
nazir	traditional district or area chief in lowland Eritrea, equivalent to a *mislene* of the *kebessa*
Nebure Ed	high-level Orthodox Church official who administers the Holy Church of Zion in Axum
negadras	merchant chief
Negarit Gazeta	Ethiopian official bulletin containing proclamations, orders and decrees
notabili	Eritrean elders and knowledgeable persons appointed by the Italians to advise on local affairs
qadi	judge of the Sharia court
ras	highest Ethiopian military and civilian title, equivalent to field marshal or duke
risti	right pertaining to ownership of land by a village or extended family or clan
saidna	prophet or saint
salat	prayers
shaleka	military title equivalent to major
sheka	lower-level military title given to the Eritrean rank and file
shifta	outlaws, often intent on righting a wrong or protesting an injustice; also, organised armed robbers
shum	traditional *kebila* chiefs of the lowland areas

shumagille	feudal lords mainly of the Sahel and Barka regions
shumbash	highest military honour bestowed on a native (originally Turkish)
Tigre	the name of the people inhabiting the coastal plains and a significant area of the western lowlands of Eritrea, who speak the Tigre language
tigre	tenant or serf of the Sahel and Barka regions who had been subjugated by the feudal lords of the area
tsehafe te'ezaz	high Ethiopian court and government official who transmitted the Emperor's messages and orders; later known as the Minister of the Pen
tsilmi	inheritable ownership of land by members of an extended family unit or clan; a variety of *risti*, it contrasts with *diessa*, which extends the right to village membership regardless of family or *enda* membership
umda	village chief
ustaz	teacher or leader
zaptia	indigenous (native) police force during the Italian colonial period

LIST OF ABBREVIATIONS

AEFTU	Association of Eritrean Free Trade Unions
AUEE	Association for the Unity of Eritrea with Ethiopia
BA/BAE	British Administration of Eritrea
BMA	British Military Administration
CIE (United Nations)	Commission of Inquiry on Eritrea, UN
CPA	Central Personnel Agency
CPO	chief political officer
CRIE	Comitato Rappresentativo degli Italiani dell'Eritrea
DOJ	Department of Justice, US
DOS	Department of State, US
EA	Eritrean Administration
EDF	Eritrean Democratic Front
EFYA	Eritrean Federalist Youth Association (known as Federalisti)
ELF	Eritrean Liberation Front
ELM	Eritrean Liberation Movement
EPF	Eritrean Police Force
EPLF	Eritrean People's Liberation Front (prior to 1977, Eritrean People's Liberation Forces)
EPRP	Eritrean People's Revolutionary Party
ESG	*Nai Ertra Semunawi Gazeta* (Eritrean Weekly News)
FHC	Federal High Court
FO	Foreign Office, UK
FPC	Four Power Commission of Inquiry
GOE	Government of Eritrea
IB/IBE	Independence Bloc of Eritrea
ICFTU	International Confederation of Free Trade Unions

IEG	Imperial Government of Ethiopia
IES	Institute of Ethiopian Studies, Addis Ababa
IFC	Imperial Federal Council
JCS	Joint Chiefs of Staff
LPP	Liberal Progressive Party
MFH	Maher Fiqri Hager (Love of Country Association Eritrea with Ethiopia—One Ethiopia)
ML	Muslim League of Eritrea
ML-WP	Muslim League–Western Province
NSC	National Security Council, US
OETA	Occupied Enemy Territory Administration
UK	United Kingdom
UN	United Nations
UNCIE	United Nations Commission of Inquiry on Eritrea
UP	Unionist Party (commonly used to refer to Mahber Fiqri Hager)
US	United States
USSR	Soviet Union (Russia)
WO	War Office, UK

LIST OF ILLUSTRATIONS

Every effort has been made to identify copyright holders and obtain their permission for the use of copyright material. Notification of any additions or corrections that should be incorporated in future reprints or editions of this book would be greatly appreciated.

INTRODUCTION

History Matters

Literature on the Horn of Africa is replete with the theory that Eritrean nationalism first made its appearance in the 1950s and that there is no discernible attachment to that identity in previous decades. Based on the Imperial claim that Eritrea had formed an integral part of Ethiopia from time immemorial, the narrative enforcing it was never seriously challenged until the emergence of the Eritrean nationalist movement of the 1940s and 1950s and the subsequent thirty-year armed struggle for independence. Such has been its power, however, that scholars, researchers and political analysts have since attempted to 'discover' a turning point at which a new Eritrean identity emerged.

The Tigrayan writer Alemseged Abbay argues that, especially in the Christian highlands, or *kebessa*, 'the primordially-based trans-Mereb (Tigrayan) identity' previously prevailed in Eritrea. An Eritrean identity manifested itself only when the 'ethnocidal policy of Amharization' and Ethiopia's move to abrogate the UN-sponsored federation between Eritrea and Ethiopia in the 1950s aroused Eritrean sensitivities. Contact with the Amhara of Ethiopia further created a sense of subjugation by a less developed people and led to the Eritrean armed struggle of 1961.[1]

Another Ethiopian academic, Shumet Sishagne, states that Eritrean nationalism developed more in response to Italian and British provocation than as an internal evolution. Pointing to the initial political split between predominantly Christian support for union with Ethiopia and largely Muslim demand for independence in the 1940s, he contends that the decisive forces in Eritrean politics 'negated the existence of a separate Eritrean entity'.[2] The Eritrean armed struggle was, therefore, a reaction to Ethiopian suppression of Eritrean rights and 'so-called Amhara domination' in the period between 1956 and 1959, which led to the disappointment of expectations.[3] Like Alemseged Abbay, Sishagne pays little attention to the independence struggle of the various forces of the 1940s. Furthermore, he totally discounts any element of nationalism in the Muslim League of Eritrea's quest for independence.

For Haggai Erlich, the 1952 elections to the Eritrean Assembly of the Federal period, in which unionists won a majority of seats, is proof that Eritrean nationalism had not yet made its appearance. It emerged, he argued, in the second half of the 1950s when the rise of pan-Arabism in neighbouring countries encouraged Eritrean Muslims to initiate separatist activities; while, at the same time, 'many Eritrean Christians, frustrated by Ethiopian methods of doing away with their autonomy, slowly started identifying with Eritreanism'.[4] To Erlich, 'Eritreanism' was 'a negation of Ethiopianism rather than a historically rooted supratribal, supralinguistic and suprareligious sense of Eritrean affiliation'.[5]

Christopher Clapham also stresses that the 1952 election results showed that no 'composite Eritrean nationalism' had emerged till that point. Two factors brought this about—the 'incapacity of the imperial system of government' of Ethiopia; and the appointment of Andargatchew Mesai, a 'nobleman with a hectoring manner', to govern Eritrea.[6]

Patrick Gilkes sees Eritrean nationalism as a development of the 1960s that began with an armed struggle against Amhara–Tigrayan privileges, not as a 'real expression of anticolonialism'. But he identifies as a landmark the events of January 1975, when government atrocities in response to an attack on Asmera (also known as Asmara) by Eritrean liberation movements induced thousands of youths to join the armed struggle. 'In fact,' he concludes, 'there is a strong case for believing that the attack and the response to it marked the first real appearance of Eritrean nationalism'.[7] Other writers have assigned different dates to the phenomenon.[8]

Such attempts to attach specific dates or events to the rise of Eritrean nationalism raise serious questions about the nature of nationalism. Is nationalism a sudden happening? Can an election result (Erlich), frustration over bad governance (Clapham, Alemseged Abbay, Shumet Sishagne) or Ethiopian atrocities in response to guerrilla attacks on Asmera in 1975 (Gilkes) independently create a new nationalism or convert a people from a previous identity? Or is it a historical process whose beginning and end one can neither determine nor predict?

As a relatively new social phenomenon of the last two hundred years or more, nationalism has defied scientific definition or even rational explanation. As Eric Hobsbawm has noted, nationalism gets more complicated when it creates a myth that 'sometimes takes pre-existing cultures and turns them into nations, sometimes invents them, and often obliterates pre-existing cultures'.[9] Such was the case with what E.H. Carr called the 'unpolitical' and 'unhistorical' conglomerate of nations, potential nations and peoples of the Habsburg Empire, who 'once they began to have aspirations for the future, discovered or invented histories of their past'.[10]

Similarly, of all the nations of the Greater Horn, and probably Africa too, none has been more successful than Imperial Ethiopia in the manipulation of a past to bolster its present nationalism. By extending its modern, centrally administered national existence back to the ancient Axumite Empire, it succeeded in creating a myth of 3,000 years of uninterrupted history under the hegemony of an Amhara ruling aristocracy, and even imposed this myth upon the peoples that it had put under its rule by conquest. However, modern Ethiopia, although the product of centuries of shifting centres of feudal power, mainly in Tigray, Gondar, Wello and Showa, and of attempts at conquest and unification by the emperors Tewodros and Yohannes in the 1860s to 1880s, actually took shape with Menelik's establishment of the Empire of Ethiopia at the end of the 1800s, during the Scramble for Africa.

As Clapham has pointed out elsewhere, the history of the feudal wars and alternating dominance, primarily between Tigray, Showa and Gondar, from the mid-sixteenth to the mid-nineteenth centuries 'did not foster the growth of any "national" sentiment, because it was almost entirely internal rather than external: there was no significant "other", against which a national identity could be defined'.[11] Nevertheless, the myth of an ancient Ethiopian nationhood held sway nationally, regionally and internationally throughout the first four decades of the twentieth century.

The Eritrea Factor

When the British dislodged Italy from Eritrea, Somalia and Ethiopia in 1941, initial Eritrean uncertainty about their political status and direction eventually crystallised into two diametrically opposed preferences for the territory's future—independence versus union with Ethiopia. Ethiopian and unionist claims that Eritrea had—historically, culturally and politically—been inseparable from Ethiopia were met with an Eritrean counter-narrative that tended to dismiss or render irrelevant the precolonial historical ties between the two countries.

The issue, however, is not whether the precolonial history of the peoples of Eritrea was or was not connected to that of Ethiopia of the same period. There is no question that, especially since the mid-eighteenth century, historical contacts of varying degrees and frequency existed between the two populations—closer and more frequent in the proximate *kebessa*, also known as Mereb Mellash; intermittent in the Bogos–Habab areas of the north; and virtually non-existent (except for raids and invasions) in the western lowlands, the *metahit*. The Red Sea coastline had been under the control of the Ottoman Empire and, later, Egypt since 1557. The real question in relation to the emergence of Eritrean nationalism, therefore, is what those historical contacts meant for the peoples whom Italy assembled together in one colonial territory. How were they affected by them? Were they of a kind that could create a common, unshakable identity, or was it one that militated against such a development?

Both Eritrean and Ethiopian studies need to come to grips with the historical events and landmarks that have been at the root of the costly conflicts between the two peoples. To start with, the deep-rooted belief, dominant in the literature of the Horn until today, that the territory constituting Eritrea formed part and parcel of an Ethiopian polity and Ethiopian national identity demands an objective re-examination. Similarly, an Eritrean tendency that, in reaction to this claim, denies the major historical links between the two countries and attempts to find the roots of the Eritrean nation state in that period also needs to be scrutinised.

The Precolonial Experience in Eritrea

From the mid-eighteenth until the end of the nineteenth century, precolonial Eritrea was peripheral to the centres of political and military power in the region, which mainly alternated between Tigray and Gondar in today's Ethiopia, and also involved Turkish and Egyptian incursions from the Red Sea and Sudan. Mereb Mellash, the combined *kebessa* (highland) provinces of Hamasien, Seraye and Akeleguzai, was itself never a united entity, but was often in turmoil as a result of internal squabbles and clashes. With the exception of *Ras* Alula's control of the *kebessa* from 1877 to 1889, the territory was never centrally administered from Tigray or Amhara, south of the Mereb River. On the contrary, powerful warlords in such centres as Tse'azega (a few kilometres west of Asmera) developed bigger ambitions of their own. The tribute to kings and warlords across the Mereb was thus never regular, and their authority could only be imposed through local appointees and periodic invasions.[12]

From the mid-eighteenth till the end of the nineteenth century, the peoples of future Eritrea suffered persistent campaigns of pillage, enslavement and annihilation by successive warlords from south of the border. Beginning with Mikael Sehul's first invasion in mid-1750's, successive Tigrayan and Amhara warlords, namely, *Ras* Weldeselassie, *Dejazmatch* Subagadis, *Dejazmatch* Wubie, *Dejazmatch* Neguse and *Ras* Alula turned Eritrea into a war zone for a century and a half.[13] Alula's 'greatest [act of] plunder in the history of the Baria tribes', in which two-thirds of the people and cattle of the Baria and the Kunama north of the Gash River were destroyed during November 1886, is but one example of the campaigns suffered by the people of the territory.

Moreover, in the 1830s, Turkish, Sudanese dervish and Egyptian campaigns of conquest and Islamisation also brought the peoples of western, northern and eastern Eritrea to the limits of desperation; so much so that, by the mid-1860s, people in the Keren area sought protection from the governments of Britain and France.[14] In addition, between 1875 and 1895, six major wars were fought between the forces of Emperor Yohannes IV and Egyptian, Mahdist and Italian invaders on Eritrean soil.[15]

Local rivalries, often aligned with Tigrayan–Amhara or Turkish–Egyptian forces, also played a significant role in destabilising the region. The attempt by the Hazega chief *Ras* Weldemikael Solomon to unify the *kebessa* and parts of the *metahit* under his control failed when he fell victim to an ostensible peace deal with Alula, who arrested him and had him sent into exile in Axum, where he died in 1906.[16]

The great famine of 1888–92, which decimated the population and forced a large section to migrate, coincided with Italy's march up the eastern escarpment from

Massawa to conquer the *kebessa* and the *metahit*. For the most part, Italy occupied deserted villages and took control of an impoverished population with virtually no will to resist.[17]

The Italian Colony of Eritrea

With the exception of *Ras* Alula's failed attempt to stop the Italian advance at Sehatit and his defeat of an Italian regiment at Dogali in 1887, Italy faced little resistance in the conquest of its future colony. People speaking different languages and professing different faiths flocked to the protection of an alien force to secure their life and property. It is significant that this submission to Italy was confined to people north of the Mereb—the victims of the scourge of famine and war. Neither the Tigrayans nor the Amhara followed that path. If, as Isaiah Berlin has stated, nationalism is 'an inflamed condition of national consciousness' which 'can be caused by wounds, some form of collective humiliation',[18] then this fact of Eritrean history deserves more serious consideration.

The submission of *kebessa* and *metahit* chieftains to the Italians, which began with *Kentabai* Hamid of Sahel during Alula's period of rule, became total upon his evacuation to Tigray in 1888. As if in a coordinated move, the chiefs of the entire territory went over to the Italians in a quest to obtain safety for their people. It is important to note that Italy's easy occupation of Eritrea was greatly facilitated by the future Emperor Menelik's alliance with Italy against Emperor Yohannes of Tigray.[19]

Italy's Colonial Land Policy

Once Italy declared Eritrea a colony in 1890, it wasted no time in implementing its colonial policies. Ignoring or underestimating the strong links between land rights and identity in Eritrea, the Italians arbitrarily declared thousands of acres of fertile land *demaniale* (public lands) and enclosed them for Italian settlement.[20] The land confiscation policy provoked many Eritreans to rebel in several areas. Prominent among the uprisings were those led by *Kentabai* Hamid of the Habab in 1889; *Balambaras* Kafel and his son Yilma between 1889 and 1891; Beyene Biru of Adi Quala in 1892; Zemat wed Ekud of Barka c.1889–90; *Dejazmatch* Aberra Kassa of Tse'azega in 1892; and the much-celebrated Bahta Hagos of Akeleguzai, whose defeat of an Italian garrison at Halai in 1894, where he was killed, is seen as the precursor to subsequent anti colonial uprisings and wars both in Eritrea and Ethiopia. Like other rebellions preceding and following it, Bahta's attempt was thwarted by Tigrayan collaboration under Menelik's leadership.[21]

Eritrean Askaris and the Battle of Adwa

A hallmark of colonial Italian policy in Eritrea was the recruitment or conscription of Eritrean askaris to fight its colonial wars in Libya, Somalia and Ethiopia. These included Italy's attempt to invade Ethiopia, which led to its devastating defeat at the hands of Emperor Menelik in the celebrated Battle of Adwa in 1896. Menelik chased what remained of the retreating Italians into Eritrea, but he chose not to pursue his advantage. Instead, he retreated with his victorious army back to Showa in central Ethiopia, from where he continued his conquests to the south, east and west of his old dominions.[22]

Of the estimated 17,000 or more Italian 'effectives' who faced Menelik's army of 80,000–100,000 at Adwa, about half were askaris, recruited or conscripted from Eritrea. Of these, 2,000 were killed and hundreds wounded; a total of 3,000 Italian and Eritrean soldiers were captured.[23] While using the Italian prisoners as a bargaining chip in his peace negotiations with Italy, Menelik subjected about 800 Eritrean captives to horrifying treatment by amputating their right hands and left feet.[24] Raymond Jonas, who characterises the act as 'Menelik's worst decision', has this to say on its lasting impact:

> [Menelik] was unable to prevent the further shedding of blood, blood that was now carving a chasm between these men and his own ... The resentments of the askari would stand between any easy reconciliation of Ethiopia and Eritrea, a point Augustus Wylde presciently observed in the immediate aftermath of the battle. The antipathy generated that day poisoned Eritrean–Ethiopian relations for years to come.[25]

Survivors of that carnage, with wooden stumps replacing their lost limbs, remained a common sight in the streets of Asmera until the 1950s and early 1960s, and their fate would form part of the political initiation of the generation that launched the Eritrean independence struggle.

The Beginnings of a New Identity

A major consequence of Adwa was the demarcation of a border between colonial Eritrea and Menelik's Ethiopia at the Mereb–Belesa–Muna line. It was precisely the same line that had demarcated the Mereb Mellash, or the Medri Bahri, from Tigray in past centuries.[26] The establishment of Eritrea within defined borders inevitably meant the creation of a new Eritrean identity, which, even at the rudimentary level, soon started to manifest itself. Thus, the aftermath of the Battle of Adwa saw further attempted rebellions against Italian land confiscation policies. Among them were those led by Abubeker Ahmed and Mohammed (Ahmed) Nuri of the Assaorta (Saho) in 1901–2; Osman Buri, the leader of a prison breakout from Nakhura with 107 fellow prisoners in November 1899; and Buri's comrade *Dejazmatch* Mahrai in 1899–1906.[27] The efforts of these rebels were again thwarted, ironically, with the assistance of Ethiopia's Emperor Menelik, especially through the direct intervention of Tigray's Governor, *Dejazmatch* Gebreselassie. Following an agreement in 1904 between himself and the Governor of Eritrea, Ferdinando Martini, Italian troops were allowed to pursue the Eritrean rebels into his territory or else he himself captured and extradited them to the Italians.[28]

The rebellions were also indicative of the deep attachment of diverse sections of the population to their traditional and customary rights to life and property. The Italian violations, which the British adopted half a century later, assumed that such values did not exist in their newly acquired colony and that its social fabric was loose and easy to dismantle. Denying a British officer's depiction of Eritrea as an Italian creation with no history of unity, statehood or name,[29] Bairu Tafla has argued:

> The assumption that history should necessarily be associated with a polity of a particular form was fallacious as civil or political organization was but ... one of many aspects of history, and there is no exigent reason to give priority to that particular aspect. The society at large, regardless of its political and economic forms, constitutes the historical quintessence and any activities of its members provide the historical substance. The daily life of the inhabitants, their beliefs and institutions, their laws and traditions, their trade and industry, their concerted actions for war or peace—in short, all spheres of activities of the society—make up the history of that human community living in a given territory.[30]

Bairu's contention is that Italy did not occupy a void when it colonised Eritrea. It was, on the contrary, a society of autonomous communities, most of which had sets of customary laws—some of them written down several centuries earlier—governing the essential issues arising out of their everyday dealings.[31]

Thus, although Italy took over a population with no state formation, they were still a people whose intricate web of kinship relations spanned potential ethnic, linguistic, religious and regional divides. Besides, despite the endless precolonial internal conflicts over land and power between contending forces, no single power had ever previously emerged to impose its will or physically subjugate the peoples of both the *kebessa* and the *metahit*. To that extent, Italy united a population with no significant home-grown conflict or deeply ingrained mutual resentments, especially of an ethnic or religious nature, arising from past relationships of dominance. According to Isaiah Berlin, nationalism 'can be, and has on occasion been, tolerant and peaceful'.[32] Eritrea seems to prove the veracity of Berlin's statement.

Socio-economic Changes

The changes introduced by Italy inevitably spilled over into the traditional economy. Here the exposure of the countryside to the cash economy was the primary cause.[33] As Zemhret Yohannes has pointed out, the main agent in this respect was conscription into the Italian army. By 1907, the army had recruited 5,125 askaris. During the invasion of Libya and Somalia, the numbers shot up to 21,715, compared with 11,320 Italian soldiers. By 1935, when Fascist Italy's invasion of Ethiopia began, about 60,000 men, or more than a tenth of the entire Eritrean population, had been inducted into the Italian army. In 1939, the Polizia dell'Africa Italiana in Eritrea numbered 428 Italians and 1,030 Eritreans in all ranks. In addition, the *carabinieri* and the *zaptia* consisted of 339 Italians and 600 Eritreans respectively, giving a grand total of 767 Italians and 1,630 Eritreans in the police forces.[34]

The transition from subsistence to cash crop production was preceded by land reform measures that expanded the state domain (*demaniale*), mainly in the *metahit*, but also in large parts of the *kebessa*. Urban expansion also encroached on ownership and use rights held by *kebila* communities, powerful families, villages and the Orthodox Church, thus forcing large numbers of pastoralists and farmers into the growing cash economy.[35]

Construction work became a major employment sector. Beginning in 1888, over 350 kilometres of railway line linking Massawa, Asmera, Keren, Akurdet and Bisha were laid and completed by 1932. During the same period, 550 kilometres of all-weather roads were built connecting Asmera to Senafe, Adi Quala, Keren and Massawa. A network of seasonal roads, totalling 2,264 kilometres, branching off the main roads and extending to the far corners of the colony, was also completed by 1941. The port of Massawa was enlarged and modernised; it could handle, at its peak, as much as 1.1 million tons of freight in 1936 alone. A 71-kilometre-long cable line between Asmera and Massawa, the longest in the world at the time, managed 720 tons of freight a day.

Urbanisation also drew a significant portion of the rural population into Asmera, Massawa, Keren, Asseb (also known as Assab) and several other emerging towns, where the urban population grew threefold, from 27,837 in 1893 to over 100,000 in 1939. Asmera alone counted 60,000 Eritreans and 40,000 Italians among its population in 1940. By 1931, Massawa had developed into a modern port inhabited by 10,572 Eritreans and 676 Italians. With the growth of the Italian population from about 5,000 before 1935 to over 75,000 in 1939, urbanisation in Eritrea showed a marked increase. The general population grew more than threefold, from 191,127 in 1893 to 614,353 in 1939.[36]

Industrialisation, especially in the manufacturing, mining, agricultural and construction sectors, took off from 1933 onwards. Despite Britain's destruction of Eritrea's industrial base after World War II, the Four Power Commission of Inquiry (FPC) found in 1947 that Italian industries had left a significant workforce of 39,300 Eritreans. Manufacturing held the lion's share, with 23,900 Eritrean and 5,000 Italian workers.[37]

Italian Policy of Segregation

The Italian policy of segregation was evident in all sectors of the economy, the army, the administration, and the industrial workplace. Uoldelul Chelati identifies several key elements in this policy: Italy's codification of the customary laws of the country; the retention, with some modifications, of the traditional land tenure and distribution system; the respect and protection accorded the two major religions, Orthodox (Coptic) Christianity and Islam; the adoption of Arabic and Tigrinya as the main languages of the colony; and toleration of the country's ethnic identities and diversity.[38] A society fragmented into competing ethnic, linguistic and religious communities was, obviously, easier to govern than one that was nationally cohesive.

Italy took parallel measures to bolster its policy. Eritrea was divided into seven provinces (*commissariati*), with a *commissario*, answerable to the *Governatore dalla Colonia Eritrea* in Asmera, administering each province. The provinces were in turn divided into districts and sub-districts that corresponded to the ethnic, linguistic and religious divides in the country. Amenable traditional or appointed chiefs—known as a *mislene* in the highlands and a *nazir* in the lowlands—were installed in each sub-district. These were the highest administrative positions that Eritreans could occupy. Although subordinate to a lowly Italian *residente* at the district level, they were invested with enough rank and authority to implement commands and maintain order over their subjects. In the civil service, segregation was enforced by a discriminatory ranking and salary system that kept Eritreans below Italians of equal or lesser abilities. Eritreans filled the lowest levels of government employment as interpreters, bookkeepers and messengers.[39] Similarly, factory employment for Eritreans was also restricted to menial jobs. Later in the Fascist period, laws barring Eritreans from special skills were enforced. They were forbidden, for example, to drive trucks, a profession considered beyond their ability to learn and master.[40]

The army was arguably the most segregated institution in which to serve. Separate battalions (*bande*, sing. *banda*) were organised specially for natives under Eritrean commanders, who were accountable to Italian officers. Known as askaris, Eritrean troops were subjected to a different system of military administration and hierarchy from their Italian counterparts. Their uniforms were more Turkish or Egyptian in design. They wore tarbushes (rather than the Italian army caps) and sandals—army boots being reserved for Italians. The ranks of *muntaz*, *buluqbash* and the highest military honour for a native, *shumbash*, were also Turkish in origin. Although prestigious in the Eritrean communities, none of them measured up to an Italian regular. No askari could cross over into the Italian military ranks.

But more consequential socially and politically was Italy's suppression of higher educational standards for Eritreans. With the advent of Fascism and the legal institutionalisation of racism, a ceiling of four years of schooling was imposed during which Eritreans were allowed to learn only basic Italian, arithmetic, hygiene and rudimentary Italian history. Holding Eritreans to such low levels of education was meant to limit the emergence of a class of educated elites that might form and lead a nationalist movement.

Along with this policy, the further segregation within the system between 'Arabic' and 'Tigrinya' schools for Muslims and Christians, respectively, compounded the ethnic, linguistic and religious differences already in existence. In addition, the denial to Eritreans of all forms of political organisation and participation and the absence of any journalistic or literary outlets of self-expression, except religious, gave the appearance of a static society, fragmented into ancient traditional communities with very little in common.[41] Nevertheless, segregation had the unintended effect of drawing the society into a common psychological and cultural resistance that would contribute to the nationalist movement of later years.

PART ONE

THE BRITISH PERIOD

1

THE BRITISH IN ERITREA

On 10 June 1940, Italy declared war on the Allies. The next day, British planes flew over Asmera, Keren and other Eritrean population centres, showering the areas with propaganda leaflets. The pamphlets urged Eritrean soldiers of the Italian army to abandon their positions and the people at large to forsake the enemy who had confiscated their lands. They accused Italy of sending Eritrean youths to endless wars as cannon fodder, promised them the right to fly their own flag and to earn military rank, commands and honours, and encouraged them to dare consider themselves a nation. 'Stop being slaves to the Italians,' one leaflet read, 'you will command battalions, drive tanks and fly airplanes.' Another pamphlet carried the name of Emperor Haile Selassie of Ethiopia, who was still in exile in Britain following his country's invasion by Italy in 1936; he touted Ethiopia's historical and cultural ties to Eritrea and promised an 'Ethiopian liberation'.[1] Inevitably, the messages raised Eritrean hopes to levels never felt before. They had had enough of Italy's stifling and alienating policies in every aspect of their lives and activities. They were longing for change, and that was what the British promised to deliver.

'The First to Be Freed'

The period from 1 April 1941 to 15 September 1952 encompasses the near-dozen years of the British Administration of Eritrea (BAE). Despite its brevity, British occupation enabled Eritreans to emerge from confinement under Fascist Italy into the international arena in a dramatic fashion. Italy had denied Eritreans any meaningful education and the right to political participation at any level. Their role in the colonial administration had been too marginal to enable them to acquire experience in modern government. In short, this was a period of great challenges and events for Eritreans—full of action and reaction, anticipation and disappointment, acrimony and reward. In those dozen years, Eritreans came to know each other better, but they also came to know the world through Britain. The impact of the British Administration, therefore, was tremendous. In many ways, it shaped the course of Eritrean history as we know it today.

Paradoxically, Eritrea's entry into World War II had very little to do with concern over its fate or the condition of its people under Italian Fascist rule. Except for the propaganda leaflets promising Eritrean rights to self-rule and nationhood that the RAF distributed all over the country, there is no official evidence indicating prior consideration by the British of such intentions.

The actual events leading to the British invasion of Eritrea, Ethiopia and Somalia started less than a month after Italy's declaration of war on Britain. On 4 July 1940, Italian forces made incursions from western Eritrea and Ethiopia and captured the British-controlled eastern Sudanese towns of Kassala and Galabat. On 4 August, the Italians invaded and subsequently conquered British Somaliland. With Djibouti under the control of the Vichy Government in France, the western coastline of the Red Sea, including the strategic entry into the Indian Ocean, the Bab-el-Mandeb, fell into the sphere of the Axis powers.[2]

One month later, on 9–16 September, the Italian army in Libya pushed 85 kilometres into Egypt and captured the north-western port of Sidi Barani, securing a foothold for the invasion of that country.[3] Both the Mediterranean and the Red Sea were thus in imminent danger of becoming an Axis stronghold and, in view of their strategic interconnections, East Africa, North Africa and Europe constituted 'the foot, the belly and the head, respectively, of the same body of conflict'.[4] Sandwiched on the 'belly' that was North Africa, Britain's position was indeed untenable. The danger of Britain being squeezed out of Egypt and the Middle East looked real and imminent. To avert this, the British army launched a major counterattack into Libya, dislodged the Italians from Sidi Barani, and pushed deeper to rout their fleeing troops and capture the port of Tobruk.[5] This took place in mid-December.

Italian defeat in North Africa provided only a temporary respite for the British, as it also opened the way for military intervention by the German army in support of their ally. Foreseeing this probability, General Archibald Wavell, Commander of the Allied Forces in North Africa and the Middle East, ordered the withdrawal of the 4th Indian Division from North Africa for deployment in Sudan. There, it joined the 5th Indian Division and some more reinforcements from Burma and South Africa. General William Platt was put in command of the British campaign in Eritrea.[6]

On 18 January, British forces captured Kassala without a fight. With Italian resistance crumbling and thousands of Eritreans abandoning their posts or surrendering to the British, Barentu and Akurdet followed suit within two weeks. On 18 February 1941, Italian troops withdrew to the fortress town of Keren, landmined its only access from the south and held off the British for several weeks. The Battle of Keren, the greatest battle on African soil at that time, began on 15 March and ended with a British victory on 1 April 1941. An official UK Government report put the casualties of the two Indian divisions at between 4,000 and 5,000 men.[7] On the Italian side, of the 12,417 dead, 3,000 were Italians and 9,000 Eritrean askaris; 1,700 Italians and 20,000 Eritreans were wounded.[8]

After the capture of Keren, General Platt ordered his troops to march to Asmera the same day. However, the expectation of Italian resistance on the escarpment to Adi Tekelezan, 40 kilometres from Asmera, did not materialise. Instead, the Vice Governor of Eritrea, accompanied by the Catholic Bishop Marinoni, travelled to Adi Tekelezan in a small Fiat, waving a white flag, and escorted the surprised British army to Asmera.[9]

With the capture of Massawa on 8 April, the Italian defeat in Eritrea was final and complete. In the meantime, British forces had liberated British Somaliland in late March. On 6 April 1941, Ethiopia was liberated too.

Weeks of Anticipation and Frustration

The British entry into Asmera on 1 April 1941 was smooth and leisurely. Army vehicles approaching 'on the wrong side of the street' confirmed to a stunned Asmera population that Italian rule had actually come to an end. The city erupted into instant celebration.[10]

Brigadier Kennedy-Cooke was named the Military Administrator of what was called the Occupied Enemy Territory Administration (OETA) in Eritrea. Despite jubilation, the atmosphere in Asmera was tense. The 70,000 Italians in the city, many of them armed and Fascist in their leanings, were restive. General Rommel's sweeping successes against British forces took place in the very week that Kennedy-Cooke was setting his administrative priorities. The expectation that Italian power would soon be reinstated with a German victory added to Italian confidence. David Cracknell, who was to become the Commissioner of Police during the Federal years, talks about Italian abrasiveness in those months. 'They dared to shove British officers off the pavement and would not apologise for it,' as he put it in an interview.[11]

There were 120,000 Eritreans in Asmera, many of them former askaris who had hidden their arms in safe places. Scarcity of food, medicines and drinking water brought the threat of famine and disease to the Eritrean quarters. The housing problem forced families to crowd in makeshift shelters or squat on public grounds. If living conditions were 'pitiful and seemingly hopeless' for the Italians, they were squalid and desperate for Eritreans.[12]

In the interest of stability, Kennedy-Cooke's administration chose a policy of Italian appeasement and allowed the Italian bureaucracy and Italian officers to continue in their former positions and functions. Although known Fascist individuals in both the government and the police force were interned, the old *carabinieri* were left in charge of law and order. G.K.N. Trevaskis, a British official, explained that this was intended to cool Italian tempers as they still had access to 'secret caches of arms and ammunition ... and a number of hot-headed young fascists were still at large'.[13]

Naturally, Eritreans did not sympathise with the British Administration's logic and pragmatism. They had been promised major political concessions in return for cooperation with the British, and that was their expectation. In a later interview, Weldeab Weldemariam, an icon of the Eritrean struggle for independence, was scathing in his appraisal of Kennedy-Cooke. He accused him not only of having gone back on promises made to Eritreans, but also of having imposed sanctions more rigorous than those of Fascist Italy. 'Kennedy-Cooke knew that the Italians were blaming Eritrean defections for their defeat and that they were waiting for the chance to vent their anger and grudge on Eritreans at the first opportunity for revenge. For two years, the English forsook and betrayed Eritreans. They put them at the mercy of vengeful Italians who now saw them as enemies. Eritreans resented these developments deeply.'[14]

It took a few weeks for Weldeab and others similarly inclined to realise that Eritreans were likely to be pushed aside in the emerging OETA policies and administrative framework. As the Italian journalist Enrico Mania has put it, 'The English were administering an enemy territory. They needed to avail themselves of collaboration from Italian officials, judges, doctors, the *carabinieri* and the tax officials.' Other Italians and the Eritreans who had worked under them were considered part of the enemy camp.[15]

The Eritreans mentioned, who consisted of former interpreters, teachers, *mislenes* (sub-district administrators), businessmen, judges and officers of the native army under Fascist Italy, started to arrange secret meetings to discuss the British attitude and the breach of their promises. The prominent Muslim Jeberti leader Mohammed Aberra Hagos's Pearl of the Red Sea restaurant was the initial venue. Except for parity in Muslim and Christian representation, there were no apparent criteria for attendance at the meetings. According to Mania, the discussions focused on self-rule under British protection; the issue of union with Ethiopia was not even raised as a possibility.[16] Weldeab too has consistently claimed that political differences or discussions did not figure prominently in those initial consultations.

The clandestine discussions were still under way when an incident in Asmera spurred the participants to concrete action.

Mahber Fikri Hager

In May 1941, a little over a month after the British takeover, about twenty members of the former native police force, the *zaptia*, marched to the Asmera police headquarters to present their grievances. They demanded retroactive pay for three months of service under Italy and one month under the OETA, which had extended their term of service. An Italian officer together with a *carabiniere* received them at the entrance to the office. Angry that one of the *zaptia* could dare accuse Italy of such an act so soon after its defeat, he ordered the *carabiniere* to shoot at the unarmed demonstrators. One native policeman died on the spot and the rest dispersed for safety's sake. The officer and his man pursued them to the Church of Kidane

Mehret, a good kilometre north of the police headquarters, and shot another native policeman right at the gates of the church. As word of the killing spread throughout the town, crowds converged on the church where the Italians had taken refuge. If British soldiers had not arrived to put the culprits under their protection, the crowd would certainly have avenged the murder of their compatriots.[17]

That very evening, a meeting took place at the Pearl of the Red Sea, where the participants discussed their course of action. Probably to take advantage of the emotions aroused by the killings, they called for a public demonstration for the next day, 5 May 1941. The call was heard throughout Asmera, and thousands of residents showed up in support.[18] It was a peaceful protest, made also to look like a welcoming party for the British. Accompanied by drums, ululation and dancing, the crowd marched to Kennedy-Cooke's offices across the street from the Palace in Asmera.

Kennedy-Cooke, formerly the Governor of Kassala in Sudan, declined to come out to meet his well-wishers. At his instruction, a committee was selected to represent the demonstrators. Since he could speak Arabic, Abdelkader Kebire, a merchant and former interpreter at the Italian mission in Yemen, was assigned to address the Administrator. Weldeab Weldemariam was present as a committee member.

Kebire expressed words of welcome and thanks for the British sacrifices made to free Eritrea. He then reminded Kennedy-Cooke that Eritreans were expecting Britain to fulfil its promises to deliver their country and grant freedom to them. Kennedy-Cooke did not address Kebire's demands directly. His reply was terse, and his attitude detached. 'I have heard you,' he told Kebire. 'The demonstration that you have just staged is contrary to police regulations. It is illegal. Since the regulations have not been publicly proclaimed yet, you will not be held accountable. Now, disperse, go home. I order you that, from this moment on, you are never to hold meetings not specifically permitted by the police.' He dismissed the committee unceremoniously.[19]

The humiliation and disappointment of the moment, according to Weldeab, served as a rude awakening to the committee, which decided to ignore Kennedy-Cooke's order to disband, and they continued to lead the demonstration into the centre of Asmera. Disregarding the insults hurled at them by angry Italians, they visited the Grand Mosque and the Orthodox, Catholic and Protestant churches to offer prayers of gratitude. That evening, the activists met at Aberra Hagos's place. Weldeab recalled:

> It was a large gathering in a big hall. We decided to form an association that at least would appeal Italian excesses to the new authority. We named it Mahber Fikri Hager. We assigned a committee of twelve people to lead the Association—six Muslims and six Christians. *Fitawrari* Gebremeskel Weldu was elected chairman. I remember *Blata* Demsas Weldemikael, *Grazmatch* Zere Bekhit, *Dejazmatch* Hassen Ali, *Haji* Imam Musa ... to have been among the first members of the committee; I too was elected on that day.

Neither the Mahber Fikri Hager (MFH—Love of Country Association) nor the committee had a political agenda or mandate. Its purpose was to appeal to the British authority for redress for the wrongs perpetrated by the Italians. People were dying and property was being confiscated by armed Italians. The MFH was an advocacy group meant to protect Eritrean interests.[20]

The day of the MFH's formation, 5 May, was also the date of Emperor Haile Selassie's return to Addis Ababa. We shall see later that the simultaneous events in Asmera and Addis Ababa were to raise the controversial issue of whether they had been pre-planned and linked. It was to be one of the central issues in the split that subsequently divided the MFH into two antagonistic camps.

On the day after the demonstrations, Kennedy-Cooke issued an order banning public demonstrations, unauthorised meetings of more than three or four persons, and the carrying of sticks and clubs above specified sizes. Thus began the uneasy relationship between the Eritrean people and the power that had promised to liberate them.

OETA Attitude towards Eritrea

Kennedy-Cooke, according to Trevaskis, knew Italy well, 'liked Italians and delighted in the colour, charm and culture of Italian life'. Thus, while other military officers sought to maintain a tough stance towards Italian Fascists and their sympathisers, Kennedy-Cooke chose a 'civilized' approach that could 'wean them away from the Fascist minority'. This policy of 'fraternization' during which, 'in time, Italian sullenness and British frigidity began to thaw out,'[21] could only come at the cost of alienating Eritreans, although the experience also prompted them to reflect on their status. Even small matters, upon reflection, acquired enormous significance, and the OETA was not slow in exacerbating Eritrean discontent.

In April 1942, the *Eritrean Daily News* issued a notice from the police ordering 'natives' not to occupy seats on buses reserved for Europeans and vice versa. This was a return to the laws of segregation of Fascist Italy proclaimed in the mid-1930s. Other racist Italian laws and practices were also neither changed nor challenged.[22] A survey of British Administration documents reveals that, for the British, as for the Italians before them, Eritreans were collectively referred to as 'natives' or 'indigenous', or 'Copts' and 'Muslims' whenever an identification was required. Military uniforms and civilian and military titles remained different for natives from those for Europeans—with Ethiopian titles for Christians, and Turkish ones for Muslims. Furthermore, popular indignation notwithstanding, British reference to Eritreans as 'natives' or 'indigenous', or as 'Moslems' and 'Christians' for clearer identification, continued throughout their tenure. By 1934-38, even Italy had abandoned those appellations and recognized its subjects as 'Eritrean.'[23]

Italians held a commanding position over the Eritreans during Kennedy-Cooke's administration. Apart from the killings and arbitrary imprisonment, Eritrean villages were harassed by a regime of collective fines imposed for causes real or imagined. Goats and sheep were forcibly taken and slaughtered to feed Italians incarcerated in towns like Mendefera, Dekemhare and Keren. Cows were similarly milked to feed Italian children in various shelters. Worse still, as some Fascist laws re-emerged by proclamation, the MFH's appeals and protestations fell on deaf ears. According to Weldeab, Kennedy-Cooke took all the blame. 'But it was English policy, really. He was just a front man. When the British realised their mistakes, they sent him away. He became the sacrificial lamb.'[24]

Kennedy-Cooke's tenure ended in May 1942, and he was replaced as head of OETA by Brigadier Stephen Longrigg, whom Trevaskis described as 'cold of eye and sharp of tongue ... not easily humoured'. Longrigg, who later wrote *A History of Eritrea*, was an accomplished scholar with vast experience of Arab affairs. In two years at the helm, he 'could claim to have been both the author of British policy and the architect of the Administration itself'.[25]

Barely six months after assuming responsibility, Longrigg submitted his first six-monthly report to his superiors. He began by describing Eritrea as dry, unproductive and incapable of meeting its own agricultural demands. He was equally dismissive of the Eritrean people, whom he judged to be ill-equipped to build an administration or to be groomed for positions of high authority. For this reason, he said, he could employ only a handful of Eritreans, leaving the most important positions in Italian hands. British officers kept the superior, supervisory roles.

The war in North Africa was intensifying as General Rommel's army advanced towards Egypt at the time Longrigg assumed responsibility. Eritrea, with its modern port facilities, strong industrial base, reasonably well-maintained network of rail and road communications, and, above all, highly skilled Italian labour force, had become an important base for Britain's war efforts in North Africa and the Middle East. Its location, close to Egypt and the Middle East, made it ideal as a repair centre for damaged ships and aeroplanes and for sheltering and treating the wounded. Longrigg argued that, since necessity dictated the optimal utilisation of Italian labour, giving priority to catering to their needs was justified. After all, a major factor in choosing Eritrea as a base was the availability of their skills and technical know-how.

Longrigg was aware that his policy drew criticism from many corners. Nevertheless, he argued that improving Italian livelihoods and protecting them from local people's hostility took precedence over other considerations. His sweeping view of Eritreans was already set even in those early days. Fifty years of Italian rule, he claimed, had taught Eritreans to love and, at times, respect Italians. It was unfortunate that the British 'could not keep the promises and half-promises' that they had made before the occupation. However, he expected that improvements in the economy would keep Eritreans quiet, and that their loyalty would follow the victor and whoever provided them with cash. Eritreans, he concluded, were more docile and less inclined to violence than other Africans, and he expressed gratitude for their low level of political consciousness.

On the economy, Longrigg's report concentrated more on the activities and productivity of Italian factories and concession farms. At this time, former askaris and people displaced by the war were returning to their villages. Changes to land use and possession were creating disputes, especially in the *kebessa* (highlands), and this was leading to banditry and violence. Although Longrigg acknowledged the problem, he admitted that the appropriate legal steps for a more permanent solution were not being taken by his Administration. Nor was aid provided to people in Akeleguzai when a regional drought caused famine and the migration of hundreds of people into Tigray. The Barka was being rocked by an armed conflict between the Beni Amer of Eritrea and the Hadendowa of Sudan. In Sahel, a simmering tension between feudal masters and their serfs was waiting to boil over. Here, too, Longrigg admitted that little had been done to find lasting solutions for these major problems.[26]

Longrigg's report was never translated into fundamental changes throughout the time of the British presence in Eritrea. However, as we shall see, within the general direction spelt out in the report, Longrigg and subsequent administrators did introduce reforms that were to bring about transformations in the political, social and economic life of Eritreans.

Initial British Views of Eritrea's Future

Britain came to Eritrea with a preconception. In its official statements, it often declared that, as caretaker on behalf of the Allies, it had neither the interest nor the authority to influence the course of Eritrea's future. The truth, however, was different.

In June 1942, Ethiopia submitted to the British Government its first formal claim to Eritrea. In response, the Foreign Secretary, Anthony Eden, instructed the British Ambassador to Ethiopia, Robert Howe, to tell the Ethiopians that the question of Eritrea's future would be decided at a peace conference at the end of the war. He added confidentially that although Britain had its own designs on Eritrea, these were not to be revealed in 1942.[27]

Howe wrote in another message that there was no visible Eritrean sentiment in favour of incorporation within Ethiopia in 1942. However, he predicted that Ethiopia's claims would probably gain momentum as the years went by. In case they did, he asked to be informed of any sign of irredentism in Eritrea.[28] Trevaskis, too, observing events from inside the country, asserted that there was no significant preference for Ethiopia in the early 1940s. On the contrary, he wrote, 'Ethiopian irredentism had never caused the Italians a moment's serious concern. No Ethiopian fifth column had emerged in Eritrea after the Italian defeat at Adowa; and when the Italians invaded Ethiopia in 1935, they had received the most loyal and wholehearted Eritrean cooperation ... If they were not to lose their case by default, the Ethiopians had to arouse some Eritrean support.'[29]

We will see later how that 'Eritrean support' was obtained by Ethiopia; but nothing that Ethiopia did or could do in Eritrea was possible without the acquiescence or active support of the British administrators. At the same time, Britain was not ready to accommodate Ethiopian demands except in so far as they fitted into or did not interfere with their own designs for the region at large. After all, upon liberating Ethiopia, the British still treated it almost like an occupied territory. Emperor Haile Selassie was reinstated on his throne, but his sovereign authority was not restored to him, as the British kept running Ethiopian affairs themselves. Thus, in addition to the former colonies of Eritrea and Italian Somaliland, even Ethiopia's affairs and future were subordinated to the requirements of British strategy for the region.

On 31 March 1943, one month after the cessation of the OETA and its replacement by the British Military Administration of Eritrea (BMA) on 28 February 1943, Ambassador Howe wrote to Anthony Eden suggesting three ways in which British interests could be established in the three former Italian possessions. These were the imposition of British influence over Ethiopia through British advisors; frontier modifications along the borders of the three territories; and, in exchange for the fulfilment of British designs, the accommodation of the Ethiopian Emperor's demands.[30] Doubts about Ethiopia's ability to effectively administer Eritrea were simply set aside, giving way to Ethiopia's demands by partitioning Eritrea. Where did these ideas come from?

On 18 April 1943, Ethiopia appealed to Britain, renewing its claims to Eritrea. On 18 May, the British Committee on Ethiopia met in London. This was a high-level committee led by the Deputy Foreign Secretary, Lord Moyne, and it included Eritrea's Administrator, Stephen Longrigg, and General William Platt, the commander who had masterminded Italy's defeat in Eritrea. After agreeing in principle on border modifications affecting Eritrea and Ethiopia, the committee made the following proposals: the BMA was to occupy Massawa and the Asmera Plateau and to open a free line of transport with Sudan. Denkalia and the Tigrinya-speaking southern parts of Eritrea were to be ceded to Ethiopia, but the Orthodox Christian parts of southern Eritrea were to form part of a united Tigray under the protection of Britain. The rest of Eritrea was to merge with Sudan. The Ogaden was to form part of a united Somalia composed of the Italian and British Somaliland. Kenya was to cede the border region (presumably to the proposed united Somalia). And Ethiopia was to give up the Baro Valley, including Gambela, to Sudan.[31]

This early partition proposal would go through a number of changes in future versions. However, what remained constant was the idea of partitioning Eritrea and treating the *kebessa* as compensation for Ethiopia's potential loss of Ogaden to Britain's Greater Somalia project. What was remarkable about these proposals was the casual manner in which they were formulated. Even the on-the-ground studies that preceded them had at times been cursory and superficial. One month after the meeting of the Committee on Ethiopia, a British researcher was put on an aeroplane to examine and identify Eritrea's possible lines of partition. After a sweeping flight that took him to Asseb, Keren and Nakfa, in northern Eritrea, he was able to submit his views. He had acquired, he said, a substantive knowledge of central and northern Eritrea and of how those areas could be partitioned. Although Sudan had not claimed any land, he continued, it would, if so requested, be willing to take the two provinces of Keren–Nakfa and Akurdet–Barentu, 'that is, the Muslim-Beja' sections. After recommending the Tigrinya-speaking Christian areas be given to 'other claimants', he turned to the port city of Asseb. He described it as a sparsely populated, unproductive and dreary area of depressions, ruined houses and wrecked ships. He exclaimed, 'Let the Emperor take it!'[32]

Such hasty assessments were not limited to the issue of partition. Another study undertaken by an official, H.B., started out with the emphatic statement that, ethnographically and historically, the unity of Eritrea was 'artificial' and that the territory did not possess 'the makings of a state'. Writing about a month before the Committee on Ethiopia meeting, H.B. also suggested that, regardless of what the Atlantic Charter of 1943 declared about people's right to self-determination and the need to gain the consent of the people concerned for territorial changes, Eritrea should be partitioned.

H.B. did not stop there. He also commented on an idea making the rounds at the time regarding the establishment of a Jewish colony in Eritrea, which 'may or may not be linked to the Jewish State in Palestine'. H.B. himself was sceptical about the proposal. Since Eritrea would eventually be awarded to Haile Selassie, he argued, the Emperor would not allow the formation of a Jewish state within his own.[33] The idea, however, had its supporters. One of them, Eritrea's Administrator, Stephen Longrigg, wrote a long letter exploring the possibilities. Longrigg ruled out the *kebessa* as candidate for a Jewish settlement on the basis that it was already occupied by settled, Christian farmers. The western and eastern lowlands, too, he deemed unsuitable for European settlement. That left the area north of Keren, which he thought could be considered. Although scarcity of water could pose a problem, he said, it could be tackled by building dams and expanding terraced agriculture. The mobile, nomadic livelihoods of the inhabitants of the area would also be an impediment as cheap labour would not be readily available to the settlers. Should a decision be made in spite of the obstacles detailed, the Chief Administrator of Eritrea declared the Keren area open for Jewish settlement.[34]

The proposal was taken seriously enough to arouse interest in London, Cairo and Asmera, where officials scrutinised the issue for several months. By 28 August 1943, though, the interest had tapered off. On that date, Longrigg wrote a review of all the correspondence on the subject. He then suggested that, should Keren be dropped from view, Jimma in Ethiopia could be considered as an alternative settlement.

We should note here that Eritreans were kept totally in the dark about both the partition and the Jewish settlement proposals at the time of these discussions. They came to know about the idea of partition only in 1944 when Longrigg publicised it. Even today, the great majority of Eritreans are unaware that part of their country had once been considered for Jewish settlement.

The Story of a Partition Policy

Gerard Trevaskis's book *Eritrea: A Colony in Transition* is a scholarly work still regarded as a leading analysis of British rule in Eritrea. He also wrote a book of memoirs, *The Deluge*, published in 2019, in which he adopted a freer style and revealed more information that in his previous work. As a result, he has left a rare glimpse into the thinking behind some of the puzzling acts and decisions of the British authorities in Eritrea. One of these is the origin and development of Britain's partition policy.

Trevaskis's first serious assignment was in Keren as a junior political officer when Kennedy-Cooke was still in office in 1941. Like most of his colleagues, he had already formed his opinion about Eritrea, which he referred to as a 'chimera ... a hotchpotch', and thought it should be transferred to Ethiopia. However, to protect Muslims from oppression under Ethiopia, he was inclined to seek a separate solution for them.

While still in his first months at Keren, Colonel Hugh Boustead (who was later knighted) entered the town with a battalion of Sudanese soldiers, part of the victorious British army that had defeated Italy. A 'colourful and bulldoggish soldier', by Trevaskis's account, Boustead was intent on ensuring that Sudan got a lion's share of the spoils of the war in North Africa. For Boustead, whoever stood in the way of that objective, such as the 'Abyssinians' (Christian Eritreans) in Keren, was an enemy. As soon as they garrisoned in Keren, Boustead's soldiers went on the rampage, looting and raping in the Christian sectors of the town. When the residents complained, Boustead proposed to 'cane the bloody Habesh' for lying. The Christians for their part took revenge, not on the Sudanese, but on some fellow Eritrean Muslims, whom they accused of collaboration. Boustead was about to pour oil on troubled waters by taking punitive measures against the 'Habesh' when Eritrean elders on both sides brought the incident to a resolution.

Although dismayed by Boustead and his Sudanese battalion, Trevaskis regarded the incident in another light. He wrote:

> The disturbing little incident was an eye-opener. The apparent sectarian harmony created by years of orderly government seemed to justify Italian claims that Muslims and Christians looked on each other as brothers and it was in any event easy enough to believe that religious sectarianism was a thing of the past in this increasingly secular

> present. Now I knew that sectarian harmony was a façade behind which old fears and passions still lived malevolently on.[35]

Soon after Trevaskis's 'eye-opening' experience, he took medical leave for treatment and recuperation in Khartoum, where he was surprised to receive an invitation to a meeting with Sir Douglas Newbold, head of the Sudan Administration at the time. When they met, Newbold informed him that Haile Selassie was claiming Eritrea on the grounds that the Italians had taken it away from Ethiopia; and that the Allies would likely let him have it 'if only to ease their consciences for letting him down at the time of the Italian invasion'. As a man who lived in Keren where Christians and Muslims coexisted, Trevaskis was asked if he thought the 'Muslems would give three cheers that they had been taken over by the fiercely militant Ethiopian Christian regime which had fought Islam for centuries'. Responding to his own question, Newbold predicted that the Muslims would revolt and that their co-religionists in Sudan would help them with cash and arms. Since Ethiopia would retaliate by 'egging the non-Muslem Southern Sudanese to revolt against the Government in Khartoum ... it would mean civil war for Sudan'. Newbold told Trevaskis that he was preparing Sudan for independence; hence his concern over the possibility of a civil war.

Trevaskis asked if the Sudanese were ready for independence. 'If you will forgive the cliché,' Newbold replied, 'politics is the art of the possible and it will be impossible to carry on as we are for very much longer.' Newbold expected that, at the end of the war, colonial peoples would rise up and demand independence. Britain faced a choice: whether to encourage those demands and gain the friendship of the independent states or 'to fight for a hopeless cause and be left with nothing but enemies'. Based on this logic, if Sudan were to achieve early independence and Ethiopia took Eritrea, Newbold said, trouble would come from Eritrean Muslims. But there was a way out: 'partition Eritrea, giving the Muslims of western Eritrea to the Sudan and the mainly Christian Abyssinian eastern half of the country to Ethiopia ... the only rational way of dealing with Eritrea'.

Newbold's main worry was that the Allies might not see it the way he did, unless 'it was put right under their noses by the Muslims of the West themselves. Would the Muslims clamour for partition or would they just sit back and do nothing?' he asked Trevaskis. 'Having seen Cain and Abel in action,' wrote Trevaskis, referring to the skirmishes provoked by Boustead and his men, 'I could not believe that the Muslims would meekly submit to what would be a Christian-Abyssinian take-over. Given an escape route to Sudan, I would have thought that they would tumble over themselves to use it. "Fair enough," Newbold said with a chuckle. "That would be the reasonable thing for them to do, but are they reasonable?" We would have to wait and see. I promised to keep him posted.'[36]

From those days on, we find Trevaskis ascribing irreconcilable differences to any dispute, big or small, that involved the two religions. In 1943–4, he was briefly transferred to Seraye province in the *kebessa*, where a movement called Tigray-Tigrigni was actively lobbying to unite the Tigrinya-speaking peoples of Eritrea and Ethiopia. When he found out that the Muslim Jeberti people of the province were threatening to demand Italy's return to Eritrea in opposition to the movement, Trevaskis started to consider Newbold's proposal more seriously.[37]

For Trevaskis, slicing off western Eritrea and giving it over to Sudan was not a problem. The problem was 'letting Ethiopia take over the Muslims in other parts of Eritrea'. These included, he said, the Muslims of the coastal regions of Massawa and Denkalia, the Saho peoples of Akeleguzai province, and the Jeberti: all in all, almost a third of Eritrea's Muslims. He wrote to Newbold airing his concerns. Newbold wrote back to say that 'to exclude Ethiopia from other Muslim areas would mean "excluding her from the Port of Massawa and, were that to happen, we could say goodbye to peace for anyone, the Muslims of Western Eritrea included". In an avuncular postscript he warned me that I would have to learn to swallow on the unpleasant truths: that politics is the art of the possible.'[38]

As the war approached its end, the question of Eritrea's future started to gain prominence. In Britain itself, supporters of Ethiopia's claim, led by Sylvia Pankhurst, organised a powerful lobby and gained a great deal of public and parliamentary support. Concerned that the issue of Eritrea's Muslims might be pushed to the side, Trevaskis asked both Longrigg and Newbold to inform him of their latest stands. 'To protect Muslims from Ethiopia, Eritrea should be partitioned,' they reiterated to him.

By 1945, several events of significance had taken place—Longrigg had publicised his proposals for partition; the serf movement for emancipation had shaken the Tigre areas of Sahel and Barka; and political discussions on Eritrea's future were receiving international attention. In early January 1945, Trevaskis was visiting London when he was invited to the Eritrea section of the Foreign Office. 'The Italian colonies were likely to become pawns in the game of diplomatic chess which would be played once the war is over,' he was told by an official. This meant that 'Eritrean, let alone Eritrean Muslim, wishes were unlikely to count for very much'. As for the question of Eritrea's future, it would be a straightforward contest between Italy and Ethiopia, the official told him. And the Atlantic Charter, self-determination, and all that? 'My guess is as good as yours,' smiled the official and showed Trevaskis to the door.

Intent on saving the partition plan, Trevaskis met the prominent Africanist and writer Dame Margery Perham who, Newbold had informed him, was sympathetic to the idea. Perham told him that Newbold's partition plan was not perfect, but since it was the best that they could make for Eritreans, she would do what she could to push it along. She then told him that Sir Douglas Newbold had just died in London.

On Perham's recommendation, Trevaskis next met Rita Hinden, secretary to the Colonial Bureau of the influential Fabian Society, which had helped to found the

Labour Party. After obtaining as much inside information as she needed on Eritrea, Hinden gave her views to Trevaskis.

> 'Yes, yes,' she said, 'partition seemed to be the only feasible solution to the Eritrean problem. With the great majority of Abyssinians so ardently pro-Ethiopia, it would be madness to deny them union with Ethiopia. Equally, it would be madness to let Ethiopia take over the great bloc of Muslim tribes in Western Eritrea. So, what are we left with? Partition.'[39]

Hinden got in touch a little later to say that Arthur Creech Jones, who was then the Labour Party's recognised colonial expert, had agreed that partition was the right answer and had asked her to produce a paper on the subject for publication.[40]

A few weeks later, the war ended. With the Labour Party's victory in the British elections in 1945 and Ernest Bevin's appointment as Foreign Secretary, the Fabian Society's proposals for the partition of Eritrea became official British policy.

2

POLITICAL RUMBLINGS IN ERITREA, 1941–1945

Urban Eritrea

Eritrea's economy boomed between 1933 and 1941, when Italy's war against Ethiopia spurred it to grow at a rapid pace. The construction business exploded as military installations, residential houses, factories, workshops and stores were built to accommodate the expanded activities as well as the sudden increase of the Italian population. The influx of military officers and men, investors, entrepreneurs and experts of every description raised the number of Italians in the colony tenfold, from 5,000 earlier in the century to 50,000 by the end of the 1930s.[1] But with Italy's defeat, the economy came to a virtual standstill. Italian soldiers and Eritrean askaris returning from the war suddenly filled Asmera and other towns. Their chief concerns were employment, food and shelter.

With guns from the war falling into people's hands, there was a spate of banditry and armed robbery in the very first weeks of the British Administration. Armed *kebessa* farmers attempted to reclaim land from the hands of Italian concession farmers. British troops had to use force to protect the concessions, whose vegetable and dairy products they needed for their soldiers (mainly Sudanese) and the European community. The main trouble spots were Asmera and Massawa. Although a curfew was often imposed, especially in Asmera, clashes and scuffles between Eritreans and Sudanese troops kept disrupting peace in the urban centres. One British publication reported a major confrontation in Massawa at the beginning of August 1941. In a street fight that involved the use of knives and bayonets between Eritrean residents and Sudanese soldiers, fifteen people were killed. A few days later, on 7 August, an Italian ammunition depot caught fire; 8,000 hand grenades and 1,200 mines and booby-traps exploded, destroying several dwellings, and thereby further exacerbating the housing problem. The Administration suspected sabotage, but there were no arrests.[2]

It was at this point, about six months after the British occupation, that General Rommel's army scored big successes in North Africa. The Middle East was threatened and British strategic installations there needed to be moved to a safer place—

Eritrea. Beginning in the summer of 1941, and through 1942, the Americans built a major aircraft repair and reconstruction centre for the British Overseas Airways Corporation (BOAC) in Asmera. They also rebuilt and equipped the Massawa naval base, a big 'rest-camp' and a naval ammunition depot at Ghinda'e, 'amalgamated a dozen workshops in Asmera and enlarged, improved and equipped Gura'e airport as a great American centre of aircraft maintenance'.[3]

Within a short time, the Eritrean economy showed great improvement. Italian investors used the opportunity to finance the production of commodities needed in the war zones. Soap, beer, household utensils, oil, oxygen, paper, glue and margarine were among the products that Eritrea could export. The value of exported commodities jumped from £494,000 in 1943 to £1,678,000 in 1945.[4] The new economic boom also created jobs for Eritreans, leading to some improvement in their living conditions. However, compared to those of the Europeans and Arabs, it fell far short of expectations. Unemployment was widespread. Most Eritreans still led a hand-to-mouth existence, occupying the lowest levels of skilled labour and government positions. Trade licences, which were the preserve mostly of Arab and Italian merchants, were not open to Eritreans until about 1944. In 1942, two prominent Asmera businessmen, Abdelkader Kebire and Abdella Gonafer, were denied trade licences. The decision was strongly contested both by the affected persons and by the MFH.[5]

The MFH, whose activities stretched from May 1941 to October 1943, succeeded in bringing people's grievances to the attention of the BMA. Besides the denial of business licences to Eritreans, the MFH also strongly protested against the continuation of the racist laws of Fascist Italy. One egregious example was an official directive ordering taxi drivers not to allow natives into their vehicles. The penalty for disobeying included withdrawal of the licence. The MFH also fought against the confiscation of choice land for distribution to Italian concessionaires. Concession agriculture in several villages of the *kebessa* and the forested northern escarpment, Semienawi Bahri, descending to the Red Sea coastline north-west of Massawa, was also off-limits to Eritreans. There was concern that clearing woods for commercial farming and felling trees for use in Italian enterprises were deforesting the land. Taxes and duties strained the peasants' meagre resources. All these issues were consistently taken up by the MFH.[6]

Thanks to the MFH's efforts, the British established a Native Affairs Council to help them in administrative matters. Prominent figures, such as Tedla Bairu, future Chief Executive of Eritrea, and Beyene Beraki, Hassen Ali and Abraha Tessema, each a well-known *dejazmatch* during the Italian period, were among the first to be appointed as Native Advisors at the national level. Every *commissariato* (province) in the country also appointed provincial advisors. In parallel, Native Courts were set up to adjudicate cases involving Eritreans primarily in the rural areas. Italian judges still adjudicated cases in the urban centres. Provincial *commissari* were replaced by British political officers as provincial administrators. Eventually, district administration was taken away from the Italian *residenti* and reserved for British junior officers. However, Italian functionaries continued to occupy key positions in the provincial offices, still blocking Eritrean advance or promotion. There was very little change here too.

Regardless of the economic benefits and the few administrative positions that trickled down to urban Eritreans, their inferior social and political status aroused in them resentment against the Italians, hitherto publicly unexpressed. Arabs, who dominated commerce and trade, also became targets of Eritrean indignation. Sometimes this pent-up frustration led to acts of violence with grave consequences. Thus, in January 1943, a scuffle between two Yemeni groups resident in Massawa expanded into an armed confrontation between Sudanese soldiers of the British army and Eritrean citizens of Massawa. On 8 January, armed clashes raged for several hours, leaving eleven Eritreans and three Sudanese dead and twenty more wounded, including three Sudanese soldiers and five Eritrean policemen. Five days later, shooting broke out again, causing the deaths of six Eritreans, including a sergeant of the Eritrean Police Force (EPF).[7]

The causes of the clashes were mostly minor. But they indicated that a sense of betrayal was leading Eritreans to unplanned, spontaneous violence. They had wanted to see Italy go, but there had been no visible attempt to speed up its exit. Weldeab has described the situation:

> [Towards the end of Italian rule] we used to gather in great secrecy. Seven, eight, up to fifteen of us would meet to listen to the radio ... The businessman Werede Beyin was the only person in our neighbourhood to own a radio. The BBC was our main source of news. The Fascists considered listening to that radio a crime punishable by death. We met all the same and exchanged information ... Above all, we prayed. We cursed the Italians with all our hearts. We hoped and pleaded with the Lord for salvation. We could do nothing more. That was the only course available to us.[8]

There was a genuine belief among Eritreans that the British had come to them by divine intervention, in answer to their hopes and prayers, and that the incoming administration would keep its promises. Trevaskis devoted a whole section of his book *Eritrea: A Colony in Transition* to how the disappointment of expectations led urban Eritreans, especially 'Christian Abyssinians', to intense hatred of foreigners and 'urban xenophobia'. But he attributed these sentiments to envy, fear and jealousy of Italian, Arab and Jeberti advantages and privileges in the political and economic life of the country. Although Trevaskis admitted that British discriminatory practices did arouse Eritrean rage, he justified them by detailing Eritrean shortcomings in education, work experience, skills and management as the real reasons for their subordination. Even the Eritreans' 'proficiency in the use of Italian counted for little in an Administration that now worked in English', Trevaskis said in explaining the denial of higher official positions to Eritreans. That was a fallacy, as the Italians who kept those same positions had themselves no knowledge of the English language. In a tone of innocent surprise, Trevaskis noted:

> Xenophobia is seldom a selective quality. Hatred for Italians, Arabs, Jeberti and Sudanese was accompanied by a growing suspicion of British intentions. Under the nagging ache of poverty and unredressed grievances, the sophisticated Eritreans began to suspect the British of favouring their enemies ... In an Administration of such recent origin there was no tradition to cast its stamp on its servants and, though the Administration was, for the most part, surprisingly well served, there was some poor material at the lower levels.

Insulated from direct contact with Eritreans, the British were content to let 'native anger' be directed primarily at the Italians. If any Briton was to be held accountable, it would be 'poor materials at the lower levels', as Trevaskis intimated. This situation gave the Administration the freedom to put its broader regional plans into practice and assign blame to others as the need arose.[9]

Longrigg, who soon played a leading role in the British partition plan, repeatedly claimed that the law on the administration of occupied territories constrained the British from making fundamental changes in the social structure of Eritrea. The Administrator was required, he wrote, to 'govern the territory in accordance with existing [Italian] laws; ... to show humanity and reason in his dealings with all classes and races; ... [and to use] all the surplus resources of the territory in men and supplies'. In this endeavour, the Administration was to operate with 'care and maintenance', which, he asserted, was 'interpreted with reasonable generosity both by administrators on the spot and the War Office. In fact, the indirect needs of the war effort, as well as considerations of policy and common sense in the territory, led the Administration to adopt standards—and even to initiate reform and improvement—well above the theoretically possible minimum.'[10] Despite this, Eritreans were not the prime beneficiaries of the 'reasonable generosity' and the 'standards of common sense' that Longrigg highlighted. On the contrary, under the excuse of 'governing the territory in accordance with Italian laws', they were relegated to the lowest level of the social structure, where they had first been placed under Fascist Italy.

By Longrigg's admission, 'a number of the British administrators had knowledge of African races, but none of Eritrea or its people; all was to be learnt'. Yet he deemed it possible for the British to contribute something positive to native administration; and he went on to list the changes in the administrative, judicial, educational, health and other sectors introduced for the benefit of Eritreans.[11] However, the 'learning' that Longrigg mentioned took place within the framework of preconceptions of a divided Eritrea with no claims to nationhood. There is no evidence that an objective study was ever attempted to test whether this was true. Nor was attention given to the possibility that Eritrean anger and hatred could have deeper causes than mere envy arising from their comparative disadvantage in the competition for available jobs and opportunities in the administrative and business sectors; that Eritreans could be claiming not just jobs, administrative position and business licences, but their land and their country back from an occupying foreign power.

Longrigg and Trevaskis, who left substantial bodies of literature on the subject, as well as other administrators and officials in the British War and Foreign Offices, never went beneath the surface to determine if some nascent sense of Eritrean nationalism had not already gestated in some Eritrean minds. They all took it for granted that fifty years of a common experience under Italian colonialism had gone over the heads of Eritreans, leaving no trace of a common identity. Longrigg's words may describe more fittingly the attitude of the occupying power. Thus far, he wrote in 1945, 'the Eritrean has fared ill under British occupation; but he has had sympathy and justice, and been treated as a man who may hope to rise. Towards the British, the Eritrean attitude has been, by great majority, as friendly as the exigencies of a military administration and an uncertain future could permit.'[12] In fairness, Longrigg was also known as a reformer who brought about major changes in the areas of agriculture, health and education, as well as in the introduction of a national press and of political debate. However, his statement that the Eritrean was treated as 'a man who may hope to rise' paints a picture of a people in need of treatment and guidance to break out of their abject condition.

Rural Eritrea: The Metahit

Lowland Eritrea is generally known as the *metahit*, indicating a lower elevation. The western lowlands today form the Gash–Barka area while the eastern lowlands constitute the stretch of the arid Eritrean coastline running for over 1,300 kilometres from Ras Kassar in the north to Ras Dumeira on the border with Djibouti. The lowlands together constitute about four-fifths of Eritrea's land surface. Although Islam is the dominant religion, the population is ethnically diverse, especially in the western lowlands, where the Tigre and the Beni Amer, the Bidawyet (Hidareb), the Kunama and the Nara have cohabited for centuries.

As the gateway to both the *metahit* and *kebessa* (highlands), Keren, which is actually at the edge of the highlands but is culturally more akin to the *metahit*, is strategically located. For most of the British period, Keren provided the seat of administration for its own province of Senhit, for Sahel to the north, and for the huge expanse of the western lowlands. These are criss-crossed by the seasonal rivers of the Barka, the Gash, extensions of the Mereb, and the Setit rivers. (The Setit is the Eritrean name of the Tekeze, which flows north from Ethiopia and demarcates the south-westernmost border between Eritrea and Ethiopia.)

Keren is probably the most diverse town in the country. Four languages, Tigre, Blin, Tigrinya and Arabic, are either spoken or understood by most of its inhabitants.

Islam and Christianity—Orthodox, Catholic and Protestant—coexist within villages and family units, thus obliterating religious divides. This is particularly the case with the Blin- and the Tigre-speaking Mensa'e, who, although divided between Christianity and Islam, still maintain a remarkable level of family and kinship harmony.

When the British took over the *metahit*, they initially divided it into the Keren division, which included the two provinces of Senhit and Sahel, and the Akurdet division, comprising the Barka and Gash areas. They found both divisions embroiled in conflicts whose consequences far outweighed the local issues that had given rise to them.

Serfs (Tenants) and Masters

In the province of Sahel, up on the Roras (mountains) of Habab and Baqla, a severe and highly structured feudal regime had taken root over the centuries. Sahel is the land of the Tigre, an ancient people whose language, also called Tigre, is closer to the original Semitic Geez than are its related tongues of Tigrinya and Amharic. They are primarily a pastoral people who, unlike the peoples of Semhar and Denkalia further south, were less inclined to adopt a maritime livelihood, despite the fact that a sizable portion of the Red Sea coastal area was within their province.

About four hundred years ago, families belonging to the Bet Asghede of Adi Nefas (themselves originally from Tsen'adegle in Akeleguzai), just five kilometres north of Asmera, migrated to Sahel and settled on the plateaus of Baqla and Habab. Over the years, and under the influence of Ad Sheik, a religious family that claimed descent from the Prophet Muhammad's line in Arabia, they abandoned their Tigrinya language and Christian religion to adopt the language and faith of their hosts. They established villages where remains of the *hidmo* (traditional dwelling) of the *kebessa* along with internal decorative patterns and crosses can still be found. But they also subjugated the original Tigre-speaking Muslim inhabitants and set up a feudal regime enforced by a remarkable system of taxation, forced labour and machinery for coercion.[13] The word 'serf' will here be used interchangeably with 'tenant' to indicate that the laws of servitude imposed on the *tigre* (their vernacular name) by the ruling *shumagille* (feudal lords) practically rendered the land rights of the former non-existent. The system was more akin to Russian feudal bondage than other, less stringent tenancy relationships.

The Ad Sheik, which operated under the sponsorship of the *naib* of Hirgigo, the powerful representative of the Ottoman and, later, the Egyptian rulers, soon grew in number and stature, and were able to convert the neighbouring Tigre peoples of the Marya, the Bejuk, and part of the Mensa'e. One part of the Blin too followed suit. Not stopping there, the Ad Sheik and the Egyptians also converted tenant or Tigre *kebilas* (communities) subject to the *shumagille* of the Bet Asghede, thus 'undermining the master–serf structure of Tigre-speaking pastoralist societies'.[14]

Like the Bet Asghede, the Mensa'e, the Marya, the Bejuk and the Blin were mixed pastoralist and agro-pastoralist communities with a social structure clearly divided between *shumagille* masters and majority serfs.

Parallel to the spreading influence of the Ad Sheik, another holy order, the Khatmiya, originating in Sudan, made initial incursions into western Eritrea in the early to mid-1820s. It scored initial successes when it recruited followers among the Halenga, Beni Amer, Sebderat, Algheden, Nara (Barya) and parts of the Marya. Soon its influence spread far and wide to reach the Massawa area and the Saho-speaking parts of Akeleguzai. The competition with Ad Sheik must have been fierce and contentious. Jonathan Miran notes that among the Marya, for example, Khatmiya incursions into Ad Sheik disrupted the *tigre–shumagille* divide previously in place.[15] Even the *shumagille* of the Habab joined the order of the Khatmiya,[16] presumably to avoid being cast in the same league as their Ad Sheik-adhering tenants.

Although by preaching equality, harmony and peace, both the Ad Sheik and the Khatmiya created awareness among the serfs of their own plight, the feudal system stayed in operation throughout the Italian period and into the British Administration of the 1940s. Bet Asghede's feudal system must have been the harshest of the lot. The Italian scholar Alberto Pollera lists thirteen different categories of duties and services imposed on the serfs. For every conceivable event—the birth of a child, the master's illness, a religious feast, the dry season, the wet season, the lord's travelling expenses, his wife's apparel—the serfs were obliged to give away crops, cows, sheep, goats, camels and cash, depending on the charge tagged to each obligation. This was in addition to the physical labour that the *tigre* had to provide on different occasions.[17]

It was a humiliating system in which the serfs were regarded as chattels whose deaths at the hands of their master or another did not bear any legal consequences. Ironically, apparently in earlier times, a tenant who killed a master was not held responsible for the crime, in the same way that a bull who gored its owner to death would not be liable. Instead, the *tigre* and his family were simply condemned or sold into slavery.[18]

It is not surprising, therefore, that the first rumblings of a serf emancipation movement should be heard from the *tigre* of the Bet Asghede. In the 1920s, the Almeda, a Tigre *kebila*, had risen against its Habab masters, prompting the Italian Governor, Gasparini, to introduce some reform. However, even after those measures, the serfs were still obliged to pay a cow for every 24 head of cattle they owned, a goat for every *eid* (religious feast), and a camel for every *shumagille* journey: half-hearted reforms that the serfs refused to accept. With the intensification of their protests, excessive duties such as those enumerated above were banned. Nevertheless, what was allowed to continue remained a burden that the serfs could not carry. They still had to pay taxes for every animal they sold, and the obligation to give gifts at their masters' weddings, funerals and anniversaries and at births, holy feasts and harvest time continued to drain their resources.[19]

The Serf Uprising

On his return from Sudan and his meetings with Douglas Newbold, Gerard Trevaskis went back to resume his duties in Keren. At the end of 1941 or the beginning of 1942, Trevaskis took a police unit to Nakfa, in response to a request from *Kentabai* Osman Hidad, chief of the Habab. He had been told that the serfs of Bet Ibrahim refused to pay taxes. Accompanied by the *kentabai*'s son Hidad, he found about fifty men and women relaxing by their tents. From the often angry exchanges between Hidad and the head of the Ad Ibrahim, Trevaskis realised that the amount that the *ad* (village) was being asked to pay exceeded tenfold the total due to the Administration. They owed £20 but were being asked to pay £200, that is, £1 for every man, woman and child, as customary dues. At that rate, whereas the collective government tax for 30,000 subjects of the Habab totalled £3,000, they were being asked to pay £30,000. The difference was to be pocketed by the *kentabai* and his fellow *sheiks* of the Bet Asghede. Trevaskis pointed out the discrepancy to *Sheik* Hidad, who simply replied, 'It is our custom.' When Trevaskis refused to commit his police force to carry out what he saw as 'daylight robbery', *Kentabai* Osman was livid. He saw the British officer off, 'prophesying revolt and ruin'.[20]

The *kentabai* was right. A few weeks later, a reproachful and agitated *Sheik* Ali, head of the Bet Asghede branch of Ad Tekles, approached Trevaskis for immediate help as his tenants were in open revolt. Trevaskis travelled to Sahel once again to face an assembly of 300 serfs who showed no sign of trouble. Their spokesman was a turbaned man from Keren named Mohammed Hamid Tahge (Trevaskis spelled his name as Taiyeh).[21] Tahge, who flatly refused to recognise the *sheik*'s authority, used the platform to give a spirited explanation of why the serfs were revolting. The picture of servitude that he expounded, Trevaskis wrote, was reminiscent of 'the sort of tenants that there had been in Russia during the bad old Tsarist days. Tenants, that is to say, who had to part with so many goats, sheep and even camels when their masters celebrated births, circumcisions, marriages and deaths.'[22]

What differentiated Tahge's remonstrance from the previous rebellion by Bet Ibrahim was that it went much further than the mere refusal to pay excessive dues. By refusing to acknowledge the *sheik* as his chief, Tahge and his followers were, in effect, 'issuing a unilateral declaration of independence'. They were trying 'to put the clock back to the status quo ante, before *Sheik* Ali's ancestors carved it up. This was not the little storm in a pipkin that I had expected. It was a king-size hurricane blowing up.'[23]

The system that Tahge confronted was not confined to the Bet Asghede alone. The same system, often with different variations, prevailed among the *shumagille* of Sahel, the *diglel* (leader) of the Beni Amer, and the *shums* (traditional chiefs) of Marya and Mensa'e, who had abandoned all forms of physical labour to live off the toil of their subjects, while they were 'robed and turbaned in manicured and scented ease'.[24] As Joseph Venosa has pointed out, not all of the *shumagille* were so fortunate, as many of them had fallen into abject poverty and were dependent on their serfs for sheer survival.[25] However, Tahge and his followers could not be expected to sympathise with the lot of the fallen *shumagille*, as their survival came at their serfs' expense.

Tahge's bold challenge alarmed Trevaskis, who warned him of the consequences should he persist in his refusal to accept his authority. '"Never!" the little man shouted,' Trevaskis wrote. 'I coaxed, wheedled and threatened but drew a blank. There was nothing for it but to resort to my ultimate deterrent—prison bars. "Amen!" said Mohammed Taiyey [*sic*], deadpan and unblinking. "Do as you please!" I gaoled him. His followers promptly caved in and that was that.'[26]

Despite Trevaskis's claim, the troubles did not subside. Complaints from the *kentabai* of Bet Asghede continued to flow as more and more serfs followed Tahge's line of protest. As Trevaskis kept refusing to recognise customary dues as legitimate, the Bet Asghede presented him with an ultimatum. Weeks after Tahge's incarceration, *Sheik* Hidad came to him with yet another case of disobedience. 'Were the tenants being allowed to defy their chiefs?' he asked before making his point. 'Either you support chiefs, or you don't. If you do not, the responsibility for the consequences is yours.' Hidad left Trevaskis in serious doubt about the course that he was adopting.

Trevaskis complained that, up to the time of the Tahge protests, his superiors had shown only a token interest in the troubles. This changed when Stephen Longrigg replaced Kennedy-Cooke as Administrator and the BMA took over the role of OETA. Right from the start, Longrigg took a no-nonsense approach to the Ad Tekles incidents and visited Keren soon after assuming control in early 1942. Trevaskis recalled their encounter in the following words,

> 'You are, I suppose, aware that we are fighting a war?' he asked. 'And you would, I imagine, agree that this is hardly the time to upset established institutions and so weaken authority?' His cold eye, long contemptuous nose and curling lip pronounced me guilty of unbelievable folly. The upshot of this visit was that there must be a stop to 'this nonsense.' The chiefs were to be given the fullest support and the tenants were to be kept in their customary places. There was to be no more tinkering about with the feudal system.[27]

Trevaskis was still seething at Longrigg's humiliating rebuke when Sir Douglas Newbold appeared in Keren a few days later. 'Longrigg is one hundred percent right,' he told Trevaskis. 'There was no possible way of disentangling the chiefs without undermining their authority and ending up with anarchy.' The alternatives, Newbold argued, were either to keep the present system intact or to scrap it and replace it with something else; and scrapping it would be risky with the war going on. He suggested that the time be used for studying its replacement and that the plan be postponed until after the end of the war.[28]

It took the BMA up to June 1943 to settle on a policy that recognized *shumagille* authority while promising 'security and tenure for the *tigre*'. With serf demands for total emancipation still spreading, the BMA did manage to get *tigre* and *shumagille* representatives to sit together and confer in Keren. However, with Tahge and his followers still influencing opinion, and with other movements popping up in various areas, the BMA's efforts could not achieve a reasonable compromise.[29]

Earlier in 1943, an incident sparked an uprising far more potent than anything seen thus far. At a place called Tselim Dengel one morning, Hummed Shentub of the Rigbat, a Tigre *kebila* of the Bet Asghede, was ploughing a plot he had inherited from his father when his master came to evict him for having reneged on a payment. Shentub refused to comply and, since he was not well, several of his friends from the neighbouring *kebilas* came to help him the following morning. The master brought his *shumagille* followers and friends and, since they were armed with knives and swords, a violent confrontation ensued.

Shentub, who arrived late, joined in the fracas by throwing a rock and breaking his master's leg. The master died on the way to the local clinic. Shentub was put under custody, and soon a British court sentenced him to three years' imprisonment and ordered him to pay blood money. Obviously, practices had changed and, rather than selling *shumagille* killers into slavery, masters had started to accept blood money.

The issue that shook the whole region, however, was not Shentub's prison sentence or the payment of blood money. Since a *shumagille*'s life was worth considerably more, the *kentabai* of Bet Asghede demanded that Shentub and his clan pay a hundred camels in settlement for the killing. When the *diglel* of Beni Amer, the *shums* of Marya and the *naib* of Semhar supported the *kentabai*'s claims, Shentub's case grew into a regional issue embroiling the whole of the lowlands of Eritrea.

The matter grew so intense that the struggle of the tenants started to draw relatively more educated people like Tahge into the picture. One of these was Ibrahim Sultan Ali, a former translator with a good command of Italian and Arabic, an entrepreneur and an activist who was then employed at the Native Affairs Office in Keren. Never afraid of controversy, he immersed himself in the struggle by taking a leading role. He was from the Rigbat, a *kebila* found both in Sahel and Barka. Taking advantage of his connections, Ibrahim launched a vigorous campaign in support of Shentub's refusal to pay the amount demanded. His slogan, *Egl sheik shekshiko, egl shum shemshmo* (literally, poke the *sheik* and smash the *shum*), was a deliberate play on words meant to reduce the feudal and religious lords' esteem in the eyes of the lower classes. According to the testimony of oral historians, the effect was dramatic.[30]

Tenant communities in the land heard the call, and offered rebellion and open defiance against the feudal system as a whole.[31] The incident stands out as the first social issue to cut across previous clan, *kebila* and regional divides and unite Eritreans across the board. Inasmuch as it provided the basis for the emergence of the strongest political organisation seeking independence, the Moslem League of Eritrea, its historical significance cannot be underestimated. Of similar national significance was the emergence of Ibrahim Sultan as a leader of serf emancipation.

The British response was predictable and may be summarised in Longrigg's words: 'The abolition by a "stroke of the pen" of all feudal dues, much as we may recommend it on general grounds, cannot be upheld. Such a change, which would have far-reaching repercussions, must go hand in hand with a general reorganization of tribal society—its tributary system, political representation, etc. The present time is hardly suitable for such far-reaching schemes.'[32]

The Beni Amer–Hadendowa Conflict

In the western expanses of Barka, an armed conflict was already raging between the Beni Amer of Eritrea and the Hadendowa of Sudan. At issue was grazing land between the Sudanese border and the Barka River coveted by the Hadendowa. The immediate cause of the conflict was a Beni Amer claim early in 1942 that the Hadendowa had stolen one of their camels. In retaliation, the former crossed the Sudanese border and rustled a sizable number of Hadendowa cattle.[33]

According to oral history, there was more to the story. In early 1941, women returning from the funeral of the *diglel* of Beni Amer, Mustafa Alamin, claimed to have been harassed and humiliated by Hadendowa youth. Armed Beni Amer units under the leadership of a former corporal of the Italian army, Ali *Muntaz*, and his deputy, Mohammed Hamid Shileshi, organised themselves to avenge the transgression; the camel allegedly stolen from them provided the immediate excuse.[34] Apart from Ali *Muntaz*, one of the rising figures in the *shifta* (outlaw) upsurge was Hamid Idris Awate, whom we will come across later.

For three years, the conflict raged with no visible resolution. In a series of raids and counter-raids, lives were lost, property destroyed, and social life disrupted on both sides. The Beni Amer, who were better armed and organised, had the upper hand. In time, the conflict took on a regional dimension as it pitted the Kunama in armed confrontations against the Nara and Beni Amer settlers in the Gash–Setit area. The arrival of Tigrinya-speaking highlanders to settle in the Kunama areas of the Badme Plains further enlarged the conflict zone.[35] By 1945, the BMA had not managed to control the situation. It therefore sought military intervention from Sudan.

A brigade of Sudanese troops took over key positions in Barka. At the helm was none other than Hugh Boustead, the same officer who had stirred up religious troubles in Keren in 1941. As we shall see later, by this time Longrigg had long left the service and Brigadier Benoy was now Chief Administrator. Benoy, in turn, had merged the Keren and Akurdet divisions under one 'Western Province' and appointed Trevaskis as the senior political officer.

According to Trevaskis, Boustead regarded his mission as a punitive measure to avenge the Hadendowa. An experienced colonial officer, he knew better than to engage 'bedouins' in the parched vastness of the plains of Barka. He thus decided to hit the Beni Amer where it would hurt them most—their cattle, camels, goats and sheep. Within a short time, companies of Sudanese troops raided every grazing field, water well and *ad* (village) to dispossess the Beni Amer of their very sources of wealth and survival. The troops were also given a free hand to deal with the animals as they saw fit. In the meantime, Boustead announced that those rebels who laid down their arms and surrendered would be allowed to retrieve their cattle.[36]

The effect was magical. Hundreds of armed Beni Amer rushed to save their possessions, thus greatly reducing Ali *Muntaz*'s army. Ali *Muntaz* himself and his deputy, Mohammed Hamid Shileshi, also surrendered. In a regional peace conference at Sawa that also included representatives of the Kunama, Nara and neighbouring *kebilas* of the Tigre, the BMA secured an agreement that put an end to the conflict.

With the British contingent garrisoned at Sawa, the Beni Amer were forced to bear further responsibility for the damages incurred during the armed confrontations. They agreed to pay a large amount of cash and 700 guns to the Hadendowa. In return, they procured amnesty for 250 armed men still at large.[37] Not all of them returned, as many felt that, as victors in the conflict, they had been robbed of their rightful claims. Besides, the people at large, especially Beni Amer tenants, held a grudge against Boustead and his Sudanese troops for their high-handedness. Soon, Barka entered into a new phase of unrest.

To remedy what Boustead had undone, Trevaskis approached the *diglel* of Beni Amer for help to secure the return of the outlaws to a peaceful life. To his surprise, the *diglel* demanded that the BMA pay the amount due the Hadendowa from the British Administration's coffers. It took a lot of arguments and threats for the *diglel* to agree to call on the rebels to accept British authority. The popular response was swift and decisive. The *diglel* was condemned for complicity. 'Both of us lost,' wrote Trevaskis, the *diglel* for having breached his people's trust, and the Administration for having ridden on his back and gone back on its promises.[38]

Initially, Ali *Muntaz*'s rebellion was linked to the Nabtab, the ruling Beni Amer *kebila* of which the *diglel* was the head. The class character of the conflict only came to the surface after the convention at Sawa and when the people of Barka held the *diglel* and his Nabtab followers responsible for their humiliation. Since many of the rebelling *kebilas* of the Beni Amer of Barka were also extensions of the *kebilas* of Sahel, the tenant rebellion in Sahel inevitably spread into Barka. By 1945, the groundwork for a broad-based political movement was in place.

Rural Eritrea: The Rural Kebessa

The situation in the rural *kebessa*—the provinces of Akeleguzai, Hamasien and Seraye—was different from that in the *metahit*. Here, class stratification was not as clear-cut. Access to land, in the form of *risti*, *tsilmi* or *diessa* holdings, was an inalienable birthright, upheld by codified customary laws, and available to chiefs and commoners in equal measure.

Although communities often chose their own leaders from among their ranks, political authority in precolonial times was often conferred by appointment by the kings and princes of Abyssinia. During the Italian period, it came by way of government appointment or recognition. Claims to royalty and aristocratic heritage in Eritrea are, therefore, often fictitious or tangential. As the Hamasien elders told Conti Rossini, personal servitude, dispossession of landed property and disenfranchisement of the type that we saw in the *metahit* was not the rule in the *kebessa*. In those cases where dispossession did take place for some reason, the party affected retained the right to reclaim the land.

Nothing provokes a *kebessa* peasant into action as much as the land question. Returning Eritrean askaris who found their land occupied by Italian concession farmers were prone to take personal action if litigation failed to right a perceived wrong. So too were the *ma'ekelai aliet*, village residents with no ancestral claims in the village but who, by customary law, were entitled to full access after forty years. Along with Italian concessionaires, they became the targets of unending litigation and forced eviction. The province of Seraye, where the *tsilmi* or family ownership was most prevalent, became a hotspot of violent land disputes.

In 1942, for example, a concession farm belonging to an Eritrean called *Kentiba* Tesfamariam was totally destroyed. Trevaskis also described the case of the grizzly hacking and dismemberment of an Italian couple near Mendefera by armed peasants when he was briefly on assignment in Seraye.[39] Individual acts of vengeance or anger and desperation like these became a destabilising factor in the maintenance of law and order. However, there was no pattern to them, no common cause of the type we saw in the *metahit*.

The net effect of this difference in the social structure between the *metahit* and *kebessa* was that, whereas the tenants of the lowlands had identifiable common enemies in the shape of *shumagilles*, *sheiks* and *shums*, the common people of the *kebessa* had to deal with individual chiefs, often within their respective *endas* or clans. Loyalty to the *enda* generally meant that members were pressured to give priority to *enda* issues, thus blocking the emergence of common interests to unite *endas* in the pursuit of broader regional objectives. By the time of the British arrival, therefore, land disputes pitting family against family, *enda* against *enda*, and village against village were fragmenting communities at large. It was inevitable that such a fragmented base would give rise to an equally fragmented political process. In the initial stages, family, marriage and kinship ties would play a significant role in political association. This was clearly manifest in the first attempt at an organised political movement in the *kebessa*, the Tigray-Tigrigni movement, which proposed to unite the Tigrinya-speaking peoples of Eritrea and Ethiopia in one nation.

The Tigray-Tigrigni Movement

Two events may have contributed to the development of the Tigray-Tigrigni movement. When Italy invaded Ethiopia, it created a separate region based in Asmera that joined the whole of Eritrea and of Tigray under one administration. With the appointment of the Eritrean *Abune* Markos as Patriarch of both Eritrea and Tigray, the Italians also united the Orthodox churches of the two regions. Secondly, as we have seen, the British Committee on Ethiopia that convened in London in May 1943 suggested that Tigray and Eritrea should unite under the sovereignty of the Emperor of Ethiopia.

The leaders of the Tigray-Tigrigni movement were *Dejazmatch* (later *Ras*) Tessema Asberom and his son *Fitawrari* (later *Dejazmatch*) Abraha Tessema. Born in 1870 in the village of Ma'ereba, in Akeleguzai, Tessema Asberom achieved great fame as a warrior, administrator and judge under the Italians.[40] An able adjudicator in land and civil disputes, he was as revered for his even-handedness and incorruptibility as he was feared for his severe treatment of recalcitrants. His son Abraha Tessema, who was born in 1901, was the main force behind the movement. A well-known administrator in his own right, he gained greater prominence when the BMA appointed him as an advisor on native affairs.

Little is known about how exactly Tigray-Tigrigni was organised or how large a following it developed. The Ethiopian writer Alemseged Abbay regards it as a natural development since, 'until the 1960s, the *Kebessa* had entertained no sense of identity than the primordially-based trans-Mereb identity'.[41] Alemseged describes how *kebessa* elites 'watched with sadness the suffocation of the Tigrayan aristocracy, whom they regarded as their own rightful leaders'; how they lamented the 'confinement of *Ras* Seyoum, the grandson of Emperor Yohannes IV ... [whom they] considered as the one who could have been the leader of Tigray-Tigrigni'; and how 'their identification with Tigray was so profound that they mourned the death of members of the Tigrayan aristocracy'.[42] Alemseged claims that sentiments like these lay behind Tigray-Tigrigni activities and that they found full expression when the peasant uprising in western Tigray, the Weyane revolt, erupted in 1943 under the leadership of *Blata* Hailemariam Redda. Yet, he says, the idea was not as well received in Tigray as in Eritrea, except with some 'disgruntled Tigrayan elites such as Seyoum Mengesha and Haile Selassie Gugsa, grandson of Emperor Yohannes and the husband of one of Emperor Haile Selassie's daughters, Princess Zenebewerk, respectively'.[43] According to Alemseged, Haile Selassie Gugsa, who betrayed the Emperor to the Italians and escaped to Asmera to seek British protection upon the Emperor's return, had a hand in the Weyane uprising. In fact, some of the leaders of the Weyane were his men. Presumably, it was through this channel that the Tigray-Tigrigni movement worked in coordination with the Weyane uprising.[44]

Alemseged's depiction of an intense trans-Mereb Tigrayan identity in Eritrea gives little attention to the history of bitterness experienced by the people of Eritrea before the colonial era. We have discussed in some detail the deep scars that the campaigns of raid and pillage by Tigrayan or affiliated warlords such as Mikael Sehul, Subagadis, Wubie and Alula left in the minds of Eritreans. Even after the Battle of Adwa, *Dejazmatch* Gebreselassie, Governor of Adwa under Menelik, seized and deported potential Eritrean rebels seeking to fight the Italians from Tigray. Many of these were either summarily executed or exiled to the island of Nakhura by the Italians.[45] Such stories and memories, repeated in every Eritrean home in the 1940s and 1950s, formed part of the Eritrean national narrative.

Living side by side and sharing the bonds of a common language, religion and culture has been the rule in the common experience of both peoples. Intermarriage between the two peoples was also a common occurrence. However, to suggest that Tessema Asberom and his followers wished to come under Tigrayan lords requires more proof than Alemseged has provided. *Ras* Tessema, given his proud and unbending nature, and his son Abraha, by virtue of his relatively higher education, were more likely to harbour ambitions of leadership of the Tigray-Tigrigni movement. As we shall see, Trevaskis alluded to this when he discussed Abraha's acute awareness of how, within the proposed union, Tigray would need to start from scratch.

Gebru Tareke, another Ethiopian scholar who has written extensively on peasant revolts in Ethiopia, presents a different explanation. He suggests that the idea of forming a 'Greater Tigray' state was a British initiative which attempted to stop the unionist leanings that were growing inside Eritrea. Gebru rejects the notion that the Weyane uprising was the brainchild of the British, though he says that British policy on Tigray-Tigrigni was unclear. He also asserts that Tigray-Tigrigni was mainly an Eritrean affair, which was not as widely supported in Tigray.[46]

But what in fact were the men who initiated the movement really thinking? *Grazmatch* Seyoum Maasho, who was a merchant in Tigray in the early 1940s, was a close ally of Tessema Asberom. He describes the main reason for starting the movement:

> Many prominent Tigrayans were at the time opposed to the government in Showa. Some of these were entertaining the possibility of forming their own government. We started talking to them. We began to feel that we too could think as they did. Thus, we took the initiative; but we were not intent on uniting with Tigray. Nor were they considering uniting with Eritrea. We said to each other, 'If we declare separately that we are seeking our respective independence, we will not get the necessary support. So, let us spread the word that we will join into a union. That will give us strength.' I was myself part of this discussion. *Blata* Kidanemariam Aberra and *Shaleka* Kassa were among the people I used to contact.[47]

In his book *The Deluge*, Trevaskis, who was transferred to Seraye at the peak of Tessema's and Abraha's activities, provides a first-hand account of the progress of the initiative. He confirms Seyoum Maasho's contention that the move was an Eritrean initiative, whose author, Abraha Tessema, 'was a man of the twentieth century with an education in metropolitan Italy'. In his endeavours, he had the support of the senior political officer of Akeleguzai, Basil Lee, and the Chief Administrator himself, Stephen Longrigg. Lee's support derived from his belief that, with some education and training, Eritreans could administer themselves and be saved from a forced association with Ethiopia, a country he believed was unfit to govern Eritrea. Longrigg was happy with the idea because it fitted into his partition plan.

Trevaskis also asserted that, through his family connections, Abraha Tessema was involved in the Weyane uprising. The possibility of Ethiopia taking over Eritrea, therefore, was 'a matter of political life or death' for him and his father: Ethiopia had to be kept out. Abraha knew enough not to demand immediate independence for Tigray-Tigrigni. To allay British sensitivities, therefore, he proposed that the union come into effect only after a period of trusteeship under Italy. It was the first time, according to Trevaskis, that the notion of trusteeship was introduced into Eritrea.[48]

With active support from Lee and Longrigg, Tigray-Tigrigni made dramatic progress within Eritrea between 1942 and 1943. With the exception of *Dejazmatch* Ghebrai Teklu of Dekemhare,[49] almost all the Tigrinya-speaking chiefs of the Akeleguzai, as well as those of the Seraye leadership related to them by blood or marriage, rallied around the Tessema plan. Even after the defeat of the Weyane uprising by Ethiopian forces supported by the British RAF in September 1943, Longrigg still continued to support Tessema and Abraha by singling them out for awards and promotion. Thus, on 17 February 1944, *Dejazmatch* Tessema was invested with the highest military and civilian rank of *Ras*. At the same time, by appointing another advocate of the Tigray-Tigrigni plan, Weldeab Weldemariam, as the editor of the weekly Tigrinya newspaper *Nai Ertra Semunawi Gazeta* (*ESG*), Longrigg's administration encouraged an intense propaganda campaign to popularise it further.

However, the movement could not make any further headway. First, many in the Administration believed it was a futile attempt, as Ethiopia could not be expected to let Tigray, considered its most ancient province, be severed from its territory without objecting. Secondly, suspicion that the Administration was planning to name *Ras* Tessema overlord of the *kebessa* provoked fierce opposition from rivals even in his own camp. Trevaskis mentions instances where chiefs formerly averse to unionist propaganda began changing sides and signing up for union with Ethiopia. Third, and more important, Muslim opposition to the movement was gaining momentum.

In regard to Muslim opposition, while in Seraye, Trevaskis was paid a visit by *Dejazmatch* Hassen Ali, the venerable leader of the Jeberti in the province, together with his followers. He told Trevaskis that the Tigray-Tigrigni proposal was better than others on the table because of the initial spell of British trusteeship. However admirable,

> it had one grave defect. If Eritrea and the Tigray are united, the Christians would have an overwhelming majority and Christians being Christians, that would bode no good for the Muslims. Did I want the truth, he asked. I nodded. The truth was this, he continued. If the British did not want Eritrea, he and his brothers wanted the Italians back. That was the first time that I had heard an Eritrean say that.[50]

With such formidable forces arrayed against it, and with lukewarm support from Tigray itself, Tigray-Tigrigni had no chance of progressing forward. To top it all, as Gebru Tareke correctly points out, the officials of the British Administration were neither clear about their approach to the movement nor in agreement within their ranks about it. Later, an official document, *Contemporary Politics*, downplayed the movement as a form of 'Tigrinya nationalism' that had gained some prominence in 1942–3 but that was motivated by a common Eritrean and Tigrayan 'hatred' for Showan rule. The document also characterised the movement as a 'conservative and reactionary' collection of leaders seeking British sympathy and help.[51]

The net result of Tigray-Tigrigni was that, in the race to control the MFH, of which Tessema and Abraha were prominent leaders, the independence movement lost precious time. However, the side benefit for *Ras* Tessema and *Dejazmatch* Abraha was that they became recognisable national figures with a loyal following. On the other hand, by the end of 1944, the movement for broader union with Ethiopia, which had taken big strides especially in the *kebessa*, had turned into a force to reckon with.

The Fight over MFH and the Roots of 'Ethiopian Irredentism'

The MFH, as we saw previously, was an advocacy body more concerned with the human and civil rights of Eritreans. Until late 1943, no political differences or separate groupings were discernible among its forty committee members. Nor did its executive body, which had equal Muslim and Christian representation, show any signs of division. This did not mean an absence of diversity in political opinion, but it was kept outside the sphere of the MFH, and this enabled the organisation to maintain its internal cohesion.

All that changed in October 1943 when Stephen Longrigg participated in an exhibition on agricultural products staged at Adi Qeih, the capital of Akeleguzai. Addressing Eritrean dignitaries invited from all over the country, Longrigg announced that the ban on political discussion and organisation had been lifted and that Eritreans were now entitled to present their views on their country's future. Significantly, Longrigg's timing came after the defeat of the Tigray uprising and the decline of Tigray-Tigrigni as a movement. This factor supports the contention that the BMA had been the force behind that movement.

In late 1942, British officials were reporting that there was no significant pro-Ethiopian sentiment in Eritrea.[52] Longrigg too made similar observations when he discussed the deep divisions among 'Coptic highlanders' in their political sentiments. He wrote:

> The elements among them who favour some form of union of all or part of Eritrea with Ethiopia are the young race-conscious and usually Mission-educated intelligentsia of Asmera; the Coptic priesthood who favour the Emperor in the hope that he will favour them; a small proportion of the chiefs and village heads; and a very few of the merchant class. The idea of union is opposed by most merchants who value principally security; by a majority of the chiefs; by all who value the progress made by Eritrea in the last half-century and contrast its present condition with that of northern Ethiopia; and all ranks of the Muslims.[53]

One of the earliest open supporters of union with Ethiopia was *Abune* (Bishop) Markos of the Eritrean Orthodox (Coptic) Church. When Italy occupied Ethiopia, Governor Rodolfo Graziani instituted his own synod and appointed Markos as the bishop of a combined Eritrea–Tigray diocese in 1937. Since the OETA continued the merger for six months, Markos continued to retain his enlarged domain. However, his congregation shrank back to its old Eritrean base when the British returned Tigray to Ethiopia. Discontented by the decision, he started to raise issues of concern to his church. Chief among these was land, mainly on the fertile eastern escarpment towards the Red Sea and throughout the Eritrean plateau, that had traditionally belonged to the Orthodox Church and to the monastery at Debre Bizen, of which he had been the abbot. When his repeated pleas to the British authorities for their reinstatement failed, he started to turn towards Ethiopia in the hope that the Emperor would be sympathetic.[54] Others have contended that, as the appointee of an illegal synod set up by Graziani and the Fascists, Markos lived in fear of persecution as a collaborator and censure from the Ethiopian Patriarchate, of which the Eritrean Orthodox Church had been part before Italian interference. By plumping for Ethiopia, he was clearing the way for his exoneration and the return of his Eritrea–Tigray diocese.[55]

With his easy and continuous access to Orthodox believers, Markos used the pulpit to openly campaign for Ethiopia. In February 1942, at the Feast of the Epiphany, he referred to Ethiopia as 'the weaning mother' and urged thousands of church-goers to 'know her as she already knows you'.[56] In a British list of Eritrean personalities prepared in the mid-1940s, Markos is described as 'poorly educated, conceited, ambitious and deceitful'. Yet, the document admits, '[although] he is hated and despised by the more enlightened of his followers who are however few in number, he has considerable influence amongst the Coptic masses'.[57]

The entry of *Abune* Markos into the Ethiopian fold was nothing short of a godsend for Ethiopia. Its attempts to win over Eritrean support had actually started in the later years of Italian rule. One of the first people sent for that purpose was Lorenzo Ta'ezaz, an Eritrean from the Adi Qeih area, who had escaped Italian rule in 1922 to seek refuge in Ethiopia, where he was well received and from where he was sent to France for higher studies. During Emperor Haile Selassie's exile in Britain in 1936–41, Lorenzo became his close and efficient aide and is credited by some with collaborating with John Spencer to author the Emperor's famous speech at the League of Nations in Geneva. From 1938 to 1940, he acted as the main link between Haile Selassie and Ethiopian patriots fighting Italian occupation by slipping into Ethiopia and consulting with them. During these trips, he also contacted Eritreans who had abandoned Italy to fight on the side of the patriots, using this means to spread word of unionism into Eritrea.[58]

After Italy's defeat, Lorenzo paid a series of visits to Eritrea on the same mission. Among the Eritrean officials of the Ethiopian Government who helped him in his endeavours were Ephrem Teweldemedhin, Dawit Okbazghi, Gebremeskel Habtemariam, Kiflezghi Yehdego, Abraha Weldetatios and Asfaha Weldemikael—all of them in prominent positions in Ethiopia, who used their prestige and advantage to lure Eritreans to their side.[59] The idea of union with Ethiopia therefore entered Eritrea from Ethiopia; it did not, as is often alleged, originate and take root solely in Eritrea.

This is not to say that there was no affinity for Ethiopia, especially in the *kebessa*. Ethiopia was the symbol of black pride and resistance throughout black Africa and wherever black people were to be found in that age of colonialism—and not just for Eritreans under Fascist Italy. Haile Selassie was an inspiration for Marcus Garvey's Back to Africa movement, and the Rastafarians elevated him to a religious icon. When Mussolini invaded Ethiopia, Nelson Mandela, who was then seventeen, said that the event 'spurred not only my hatred for that despot but of fascism in general'. Ever afterwards, wrote Mandela, Ethiopia held a special place in his imagination, and the prospect of visiting Ethiopia in the early sixties 'attracted me more strongly than a trip to France, England and America combined. I felt I would be visiting my own genesis, unearthing the roots of what made me an African. Meeting the Emperor himself would be like shaking hands with history.'[60]

Kwame Nkrumah, future leader of independent Ghana, was on a London street when he saw the newspaper headline 'Mussolini Invades Ethiopia'. At that moment, he said, 'It was almost as if the whole of London had declared war on me personally. For the next few minutes, I could do nothing but glare at each impassive face, wondering if those people could possibly realize the wickedness of colonialism. And praying that the day might come when I could play my part in bringing about the downfall of such a system.'[61]

Given Ethiopia's proximity to Eritrea and the cultural and historical ties that existed between them, the reaction in Eritrea was even more intense. Throughout the colonial period, Ethiopia had been a refuge for Eritreans at odds with Italy, just as

Italian Eritrea provided an outlet for Ethiopians seeking jobs and better opportunities. Both peoples had always welcomed and hosted each other. Thus, Italy's invasion of Ethiopia was a painful event for Eritreans of all walks of life. Ibrahim Sultan was so vocal in his opposition that it cost him his job and personal security.[62] Scores of askaris abandoned the Italian army to join the fight for freedom against the invasion.

Did all this translate into the rise of Ethiopian nationalism in the hearts of Eritreans, as many have claimed? Were Eritreans taking refuge in Ethiopia because of an inherent belief that Ethiopia was their motherland? Weldeab Weldemariam is unequivocal in his rejection of this line of thinking. He argues that running away from Fascist Italy 'was an expression of Eritrean anger and sense of wrong and injustice rather than a manifestation of their attachment to Ethiopia, as many Eritreans were also escaping to Kenya, Tanganyika and Uganda for the same reasons'.[63]

It was thus mainly as a result of *Abune* Markos's overtures of 1942–4 that Ethiopia acquired the support base that it so much desired. The assumption that the first Eritreans to follow his lead, especially from within the MFH, were Orthodox Christians is not entirely true. Ethiopia's most significant prize was *Fitawrari* Gebremeskel Weldu, president of the MFH. Born in 1907 into a prominent Catholic family in the Segeneiti area, he was educated at the Keren *seminario*, from where he proceeded to higher studies in Khartoum and Rome. Known as an honest and straightforward man, he was one of the intellectual luminaries of the time.[64] Most of his peers testify that Gebremeskel's preference for Ethiopia was based mainly on his hatred of and principled opposition to white rule. His understanding of the consequences of union with Ethiopia being limited, he adopted a cautious approach. This ambivalence in his thinking was to create problems for him at a later time. At this early stage, however, he influenced a large section of the *kebessa* members of MFH to follow him into *Abune* Markos's camp.

Among the important public figures who followed Gebremeskel's footsteps were *Blata* Demsas Weldemikael, a Hamasien Protestant and district chief of Aba Shawl; *Dejazmatch* Hagos Ghebre and *Fitawrari* Hadgu Ghilagaber, both Catholics and district chiefs from Hamasien; and *Fitawrari* Haregot Abbay, a prominent Orthodox businessman and native of Arba'te Asmera, the original village that gave its name to Asmera. From this time on, the term 'nationalist' was applied to this group in all subsequent British documentation. Later, the independence faction earned the label of 'separatist', an appellation still in use in some studies (a misnomer, obviously), in view of the rise of Eritrean nationalism in the 'separatist' direction.

Of equal significance to Gebremeskel's move was Tedla Bairu's induction into the same cause. Hardly thirty years of age at the time, he was the interpreter and advisor to Stanley-Parker, chief political officer in charge of Asmera. Politically, it was the most important and influential position in the country. Just as Abraha Tessema had Basil Lee under his influence in opposing union to Ethiopia, so too Tedla Bairu, according to Trevaskis, had Stanley-Parker under his spell but in the opposite cause. In *The Deluge*, in which Trevaskis has little good to say of many of the people he wrote about, he showers praise on Tedla. 'A very gifted man he was,' he says, and adds:

> A former protégé of the Swedish Evangelical Mission, this exceptional young man was one of the very few Eritreans to have had anything in the way of higher education. Neat, well-spoken, superbly mannered, he was a gem. He knew the district [Hamasien] inside out like the back of his hand. Ask him the most out of the way question, and back would come the answer as if he were reading it off a computer. Nothing was too much trouble for this Admirable Crichton and, when it came to explaining how passionately Eritreans of every class and creed yearned for union with their Ethiopian Mother Country, he did not stint himself. 'That is what is so splendid about him,' Stanley-Parker would say. 'He is totally selfless, totally dedicated.'[65]

Using his strategic position in the office of the chief political officer, Tedla became the contact person for the unionist faction of the MFH with the Administration. As mentioned earlier, most influential supporters of union among the intelligentsia were either Catholics or Protestants, with a sprinkling of Orthodox Christians.[66] This is probably because their relative educational advantage enabled them to seek alternatives to European rule. But why union with Ethiopia and not independence?

Gebreyohannes Tesfamariam, later *Dejazmatch*, was one of the most effective polemicists on behalf of union with Ethiopia. He later described the romanticised image of Ethiopia that he had grown up with in Da'ero Paulos, a village in the suburbs south of Asmera. At the age of fourteen, he attempted to run away to what he considered the Promised Land. 'The idea of independence?' he asked rhetorically.

> Thanks to Italian meanness and malice, how could our minds entertain that way of thinking? Independence, self-sufficiency, self-government ... those remote ideas could not come to us. The mind-set of the colonised, the spirit of submission was etched in our brains. Our opinions about union with Ethiopia or independence were more expressions of hatred for colonialism than anything else. No one that I know of was thinking or contemplating deeply and dispassionately. Egypt was claiming us from way up there. Italy was trying to reassert its old dominion. The Englishman was using his politics to divide us. The only choice that we thought most plausible was union with Ethiopia.[67]

The split within the MFH came at the cost of great divisions in the emerging political life of the country. After the decline of the Tigray-Tigrigni movement, that faction started to lose a large proportion of its following to the aggressive campaigns of *Abune* Markos and his formidable allies. It was apparently a patchy grouping to begin with. Most of the Seraye traditional chiefs who had been behind it were no match for the type of enlightened persons rooting for union. Unionist propaganda lauding Ethiopia began to increase, in which feudal Ethiopia was presented as a

Christian nation where the 'Habesha' reigned supreme over Italians, Arabs and even the British. Leaflets secretly left on the streets or posted on public buildings attacked Italian, Arab and Jeberti businessmen as usurpers who would have no place in Ethiopia. Although still in its initial stages, the propaganda accompanying the unionist agenda gave the impression that the movement was larger and more widespread than its actual size.

Most devastating, though, was Markos's unscrupulous use of the pulpit and the thousands of monks and priests around the country to instil fear among the mass of Orthodox believers. According to Weldeab, Markos had been vociferously anti-Ethiopian during his time as bishop under Italy. After he fell out with the British, his courtship of Ethiopia and Haile Selassie went beyond anything expected of a religious leader. By equating unionism with salvation, Weldeab said,

> the monasteries and the clergy became the largest and most effective instruments of Ethiopian interests. The holy communion, funerals and weddings were denied believers who would not raise the slogan 'Ethiopia or death!' Even attendance at the weddings and funerals of 'renegades' or tasting food prepared by them became a religious trespass. They were denied burial inside the church compound, a punishment reserved for the most evil transgressors. Father confessors made absolution conditional on loyalty to union with Ethiopia. The spiritual pressure on the Orthodox congregation was immense.[68]

The religious tone of the unionist agenda and the open attacks on Arabs and Jeberti naturally alienated prominent Muslims within the MFH. Members of the committee such as *Dejazmatch* Hassen Ali, *Kegnazmatch* Berhanu Ahmeddin, *Blata* Mohammed Omer Kadi and Ibrahim Sultan himself, founding members of MFH, were thus sidelined to the extent that they began to think of finding new paths for themselves. As Weldeab puts it, 'It was unthinkable for Eritrean Muslims to even consider submission to a nation that was openly ruled by the Holy Cross, that openly called itself a "Christian State".'[69]

As usual, the BMA officers were not in agreement on the issue of the religious divisions that were deepening under their very noses. Stanley-Parker saw nothing wrong in Markos's frequent visits to Addis Ababa to brief the Emperor on the latest developments in Eritrea and to come back with instructions for further action. He saw the Eritrean Orthodox Church as an indivisible part of the Ethiopian Church and, therefore, Markos was within his rights to maintain a close relationship. For his part, Longrigg dismissed Stanley-Parker's reasoning, telling him that he had only to see how the tempo of agitation quickened following the bishop's return from a visit to Addis Ababa to know that he had come back with orders and cash. As far as Longrigg was concerned, 'the Bishop was the Root of all Evil'.[70]

At the beginning, Longrigg consulted with Markos, advising him to tone down his provocative sermons. Markos gave promises but went straight back to his old ways. Thereupon,

> Longrigg issued a proclamation forbidding public gatherings and the 'flying of foreign flags'. Regardless, pro-Ethiopian demonstrations continued as before but under ecclesiastical cover. The honouring of the Church's innumerable saints and the celebration of its limitless holy days were now devoted to preaching, praying and cheering for union with Ethiopia ... since the Church's flag was the Ethiopian flag, it flew proudly over the celebrants on all such lively occasions. That looked like checkmate for Longrigg.[71]

Eritrean politics were thus strewn with the seeds of division right at their infancy. It was a challenge that would threaten Eritrean unity and encumber the progress of Eritrean nationalism for years to come. However, other events, both internal and external, would further compound the process.

3

REFORMS, INTERVENTIONS AND RESISTANCE

British Reforms

The British Military Administration (BMA) can be credited with the formation of an Eritrean police force, following the dismantlement of the *carabinieri* and the *zaptia*; the introduction of local newspapers and press freedom; and the creation of space for political debate and organisation. But its most outstanding reform was in the field of education. According to the British official Gerard Trevaskis, the Italians left a mere 24 elementary schools for natives scattered throughout the country.[1] An Ethiopian document puts the number at nineteen elementary schools with a total of 1,530 Eritrean pupils and 38 teachers. In contrast, there were twenty Italian schools (twelve elementary and intermediate, seven secondary and a university) catering to 4,995 Italian students.[2] (Italo-Eritreans were treated differently.)[3] In 1932, the Italians closed down the Swedish Evangelical schools, which had provided relatively higher-quality education to Eritreans.

In 1942, the BMA appointed Major Kynaston-Snell, a highly motivated advocate for the advancement of education for all, as its educational officer. His Eritrean assistant was *Memhir* (Teacher) Yishak Teweldemedhin, already a legend as a teacher and wit, who helped in the transformation of the Italian system.[4] One of the first issues that needed attention was the medium of instruction. Although Yishak Teweldemedhin and his aides translated English texts into Tigrinya for use in all classes, British officials, like Trevaskis in Keren, objected, arguing that Muslims would prefer Arabic over the Geez script, as they would associate Geez with the Orthodox Christian Church of Ethiopia. The counter-argument that Tigrinya was the only written language in Eritrea was overruled. Eventually, the BMA adopted Arabic as the medium in all predominantly Muslim schools. Books for that purpose could be acquired from Cairo and elsewhere in the Arab world.

Kynaston-Snell's budget was so inadequate that he proposed that local communities should bear school construction costs. The public response was immediate and enthusiastic. Soon, several villages were requesting the Administration to supply teachers and teaching material for the newly constructed buildings. A hastily devised teacher training programme produced the first batch of over thirty Eritrean teachers in 1943. This led to the establishment of the Teacher Training Institute, from where many renowned teachers and future lawyers, judges, administrators, sportsmen and women, nationalists and revolutionaries would graduate.[5]

By the end of British rule, the number of schools in Eritrea had risen to about 100. Whereas under Italy no Eritrean could rise above the fourth grade, there were 1,200 students at the middle school level and 167 at the secondary school level in 1952 alone.[6] This means that in the nine or ten years of active British involvement in education, hundreds of relatively well-educated Eritreans entered the job market. Of major significance was the entry of women into the teaching profession.

The spread of education naturally brought new issues and challenges to the fore. However, the Administration was slow in opening meaningful employment opportunities to Eritrean nationals, for whom the newly established police force, where they could rise to the rank of inspector, remained the most lucrative. But the police force could not by itself be the answer to the demands for placement and position that education brought about. Nevertheless, the British kept stalling on opening up the civil service to Eritrean candidates. It is significant that the first open competition for government employment announced by the Administration was made in the first week of August 1947, almost six and a half years after the British takeover. Of 83 candidates, 25 were shortlisted for the final examination.[7]

At the beginning of his duties as education officer, Kynaston-Snell had warned that 'if you educate, you educate for discontent'.[8] It was a warning and prediction whose accuracy was soon to be revealed.

The third major British reform was the introduction of a local press for Eritreans, whose only means of self-expression had hitherto been through the Native Affairs Council. In August 1943, the BMA printed the first issue of a weekly newspaper, *Nai Ertra Semunawi Gazeta* (Eritrean Weekly Gazette—henceforth *ESG*), written in Tigrinya. It was a significant event for a nation that had been allowed only token participation in Italian-directed Tigrinya and Arabic publications. Yet even that limited experience had produced the likes of *Blata* Gebregziabher Gilamariam (Gilai), one of the so-called Nakhura Breakers, who went on to introduce the craft of journalism to Ethiopia under Menelik.[9] *ESG* began under the supervision of Edward Ullendorff, a scholar of Semitic languages.

Since political discussions were still restricted, the early opinion columns were confined to topics of local and global history, culture, lessons on morality, adherence to traditional values, and current news about the world war. Despite the prevailing educational and journalistic limitations, the clarity of thinking and effective use of language of many of the contributors were highly impressive. Under the capable editorship of Weldeab Weldemariam, articles of reasonable breadth and depth made the *ESG* a valuable source of information. Eventually, an Arabic section was included under the editorship of Mahmoud Iraba'e.

Articles on the correct usage of written Tigrinya were among the first serious topics to appear in the paper. These drew on lectures and seminars organised by the Information Department under Edward Ullendorff, who had established a Tigrinya Language Council. Composed of church representatives and the 'most experienced practitioners of the language', the committee functioned well for a year or two. 'But later on,' according to Ullendorff, 'political considerations began to enter the picture, the initial enthusiasm flagged, and the committee became moribund.'[10] The *ESG* never published the content of those 'political considerations'. However, a participant in those sessions, *Bashai* Fesseha Weldemariam (Gandhi), recalled that signs of impending political differences already began appearing in those discussions. Some future unionists heaped praise on the wealth and expressive powers of Amharic and Geez while belittling Tigrinya, the preference of Eritrean nationalists. The discussions were thus significant as much for their linguistic content as for their political undertones.[11]

Before political discussions came to dominate the columns of *ESG*, Eritrean unity remained the issue on which some of the most memorable and impassioned articles were centred. The words of an anonymous writer who decried the slavishness of the colonial era summarised the mood of the time. Referring to a famous comment from an Italian general disparaging Eritreans as 'Habesha in need of bread and the whip', the writer urged:

> Let us prove by our noble character that what that cowardly and spineless (*Codardo e Vigliaco*) general said is not true. Yes, we are young and need to learn, but we are not cattle. We are, rather, like the eagle that, although he has wings, has been tied up for so long that he has forgotten how to fly and appears to look like a chicken. True, we need someone to get us started, but we are not like the cattle that cannot learn ... Let us march towards knowledge, towards wisdom.[12]

The resumption of political discussions brought about a major shift in the hitherto moderate discourse of innocent civility and reaching out across potential dividing lines. More significantly, with increasing outside intervention, what had once been simple, naturally evolving matters arising in both the *metahit* and the *kebessa* started to become complex and wide-ranging issues for a population ill-equipped and unprepared to deal with ideas beyond its national and local context. By 1944, Eritreans were entering a new era in terms of regional and international strategy. This marked a major development in their progress. From here on, their understanding of who exactly they were or what they wanted for themselves would develop along a painful and rocky road.

ESG played a significant role at this time. Ullendorff was partly right when he claimed that the 'cultural gains' obtained from a free press, 'together with Kyanston-

Snell's devoted work for Eritrean education, represent some of the principal achievements of eleven years of British rule in Eritrea. That an essentially short-lived military and caretaker administration should have done so much must surely tip the balance in its favour when the definitive history of the period comes to be written.'[13] But the British were active in other spheres as well, and they cannot be judged only on their achievements in the fields of education and the press, laudable though these were.

Ethiopia's Claims

On 6 April 1941, British forces under General Alan Cunningham captured Addis Ababa. On the same day, a British force under Colonel Orde Wingate led Emperor Haile Selassie into Debre Markos, the capital of the Ethiopian province of Gojam. Haile Selassie had assumed that, as Emperor of Ethiopia, he would immediately enter Addis Ababa at the head of Cunningham's army. To that end, he asked for an aircraft to transport him to the capital. Cunningham turned the request down, citing some security excuse, and the Emperor had to wait until 5 May, a full month later, to return to Addis Ababa.

Within days, it became clear that the British were not about to restore his authority and sovereignty. Attempts to lure Cunningham to his palace with an award of the Empire's highest medal were fruitless, as was his proposal for a head-to-head talk with the general. In defiance, just five days after his return, he announced the appointment of his own cabinet of seven ministers and various governors to the provinces.

Harold Marcus points to the appointment of ministers as evidence of Haile Selassie's success in rebuffing British attempts at neutralising him.[14] In contrast, in his book *Yeqedamawi Haile Selassie Mengist* (The Government of Haile Selassie I), Zewde Retta reveals from primary sources the depths of desperation into which the Emperor fell because of British attitudes and actions. His detailed narration of the indignity suffered by Haile Selassie in person at the hands of an officer of lower rank, Brigadier Morris Lash, provides telling evidence of the Emperor's situation.[15]

Haile Selassie's strong protests and appeals to the British Government received a prompt response when Sir Philip Mitchell, the chief political officer for the British Command in East Africa, paid him a visit on 23 May 1941. The Emperor demanded that the British lift their designation of Ethiopia as occupied enemy territory and that a treaty recognising its sovereignty be signed between his government and the UK. He also complained of the British army's plunder of 'enemy property', which it was shipping to its colonies.[16]

Mitchell responded that all that was taking place, including the confiscation of enemy property, was consistent with the rules and necessity of war. On the other demands, he promised action upon notification to the authorities in London and their deliberation on the matter. It took Mitchell eight months to return to Ethiopia. To a stunned Haile Selassie and his advisors, Mitchell read out a non-negotiable twelve-point list of proposals that transferred virtually all form of authority and sovereignty in Ethiopia into the hands of British administrators. Ethiopia's internal and external dealings as well as the Emperor's correspondence and senior appointments had to be approved by British officers. Ethiopia was denied the right to set up its own police and military force and the right to raise taxes. The British even took over the administration of the old Franco-Ethiopian Railway Company and the post, telegram and telephone services. The agreement was to last for two years.[17]

Ethiopia was thus virtually an 'occupied enemy territory' when it claimed Eritrea in 1942 and again on 18 May 1943. In exile, Haile Selassie had nevertheless garnered widespread public support and sympathy, and there was a strong lobby of British MPs, writers and influential figures rooting for him in Parliament and in public debate. One of them, Sylvia Pankhurst, was a great advocate for the 'return of Eritrea to Ethiopia'. Many Ethiopian officials believed that the country's predicament was due to the intransigence of the British military. Churchill and his administration were, they felt, sympathetic to the Ethiopian cause but were unable to overturn the military's adherence to old colonial principles and mentality.[18]

Clearly, the lobby in Britain and the Churchill administration were unlikely to rescue Ethiopia from the grip of the British military. Haile Selassie and his colleagues thus decided to take their case to the United States. In his previous dealings with Haile Selassie, President Franklin D. Roosevelt had shown sympathy for Ethiopia's plight during the Emperor's difficult time with the League of Nations. The US, however, had not gone beyond its refusal to give recognition to Italy's colonial rights in Ethiopia.[19] Ethiopia could, however, appeal to the American conscience by playing the victim. But with all its foreign relations in the hands of the British military, how to reach Roosevelt became a major issue.

American Involvement

In spite of the virtual quarantine imposed on Haile Selassie's government, the British could not stop some contacts from taking place. Thus, on 11 February 1943, a US military delegation led by General Russell Maxwell and including the American Consul General in Eritrea, E. Talbot Smith, met with the Emperor in Addis Ababa. Although he said little in the formal meeting, he was able to pass a letter clandestinely to the delegation detailing his government's suffering under the British. Talbot Smith, for his part, wrote to his superiors in the State Department criticising British treatment of Ethiopia and arguing that recognition of Ethiopian sovereignty would present the Allies as defenders of the rights of nations still under Axis control in Europe and elsewhere.[20]

In June 1943, Haile Selassie was able to smuggle a message to Roosevelt requesting that Ethiopia become the beneficiary of the US's Lend-Lease policy, which supplied food, oil and war materiel, including warships and planes, to its allies during the war years. To the delight of the Ethiopians, Roosevelt responded positively and even gave hints that his government would be willing to contribute to Ethiopia's defence outside the Lend-Lease programme.[21] But these were token contacts that could not guarantee the kind of American sponsorship that Ethiopia was seeking.

By a stroke of luck, an opportunity presented itself in June 1943, in the form of an invitation for the Government of Ethiopia to attend an international conference on food and agriculture in the US state of Virginia. Inadvertently, the British gave their permission as they saw no harm in Ethiopia's attendance at the conference. The Ethiopians on their side conferred secretly, carefully constructed their list of complaints and requests, and assigned one of the rising stars in the regime, the British-educated economist Yilma Deressa, to deliver a message to Roosevelt. Yilma presented his case directly to Roosevelt when the president granted him an audience. In addition to the usual demands for the return of Ethiopian rights in accordance with the Atlantic Charter, Yilma raised the issue of his country's right of access to the sea. Eritrea, he told Roosevelt, was the name given by the Italians to the old 'Ethiopian province of Hamasien', whose population 'formed an integral part of the racial, cultural, religious and linguistic unity of Ethiopia'.

Yilma's mission was a triumph for Ethiopia. Over the heads of the British military in Addis Ababa, Haile Selassie's government procured the benefits of the Lend-Lease policy. In an exchange of ambassadors, the US soon sent John Caldwell to Ethiopia and received the Eritrean-born Ephrem Teweldemedhin as Ethiopia's ambassador in Washington. John Spencer, who had been advisor to the Ethiopian Government before the Italian occupation, was chosen by the US to help Ethiopia in the imminent resumption of negotiations with the British. Another American, George Blowers, was also assigned to Addis Ababa to head the National Bank of Ethiopia. On top of this, Ethiopia obtained a substantial amount of US dollars to pay for the printing of its own currency, thus freeing itself from the forced use of the British-backed East African shilling. The British could not go beyond voicing their opposition to what amounted to a fait accompli.[22]

Apparently, Roosevelt and his Secretary of State, Cordell Hull, had refrained from entering into any commitment on Yilma's other major proposal, that of handing Eritrea over to Ethiopia. Having been deeply involved in the war effort in Eritrea, the US was well aware of the issues involved. There are hints that it may even have toyed with its own design for the territory. How did the US interest in Eritrea come about?

Project 19

As we have seen, in the heat of the war in North Africa in November 1941, Britain requested American help in enlarging its war base in Eritrea. A Lend-Lease contract was signed and Project 19, a 'mission most secret', was launched. The Douglas

Aircraft Corporation and Johnson, Drake and Piper Inc. were charged with setting up an aircraft repair and assembly centre in Gura'e, south-east of Asmera; an ammunition depot in Ghinda'e, down the escarpment on the way to Massawa; and the enlargement of the Massawa port for the repair of warships. At the peak of its activities in August 1942, Project 19 employed about 16,200 people, of whom approximately 320 were US officers and enlisted men, 2,800 US civilians, 5,600 Italians, almost 7,400 Eritreans and some twenty Arabs.[23] By the time of the German defeat in North Africa on 8 November 1942, six ships, a floating dock, and about a hundred warships and boats had been repaired in Massawa.[24]

American interest in Eritrea was not confined to Project 19. In April 1943, seven US communications experts arrived at Radio Marina, the former Italian naval headquarters in Asmera. By May, they had set up their antennas and were in direct contact with Washington. In December, ten US officers and 50 communications personnel began the establishment of an American base in Asmera. In a few years, the base expanded to Kagnew Station, which became the largest overseas US communications centre from the early 1950s to 1976.[25]

Such was the US background in Eritrea. Roosevelt's silence on Ethiopia's claim to Eritrea did not, however, necessarily indicate lack of sympathy over the issue. At the same time, a State Department official suggested that a 'fairly strong case could be made in support of the Ethiopian contention that Eritrea, or part of it, should be incorporated into Ethiopia'.[26] We can assume from this that the US had still not formulated a policy on Eritrea and that, as Marcus puts it, Yilma Deressa's pleas were heard 'with equanimity'.[27] On the other hand, Yilma had succeeded in registering the claim at the highest level of US policy-making.

However, in a book published by one of the major companies that operated in Eritrea from 1942 to 1943, Johnson, Drake and Piper, there is a strange statement that indicates that the US may initially have had other plans for Eritrea.

> The ultimate aim of the American effort in Eritrea, taken from the General Directive of the President of the United States, the Secretary of War and the War Department through the North African Mission in Cairo and thence through the Army Engineer Corps Officers down to our own working organization, was to make Eritrea the 'American Arsenal of Democracy' in Africa. In conformance with this general plan—even before the arrival of any special personnel or equipment—we were directed to start work on the great Massawa Naval Base on the Red Sea.[28]

Unless this was a figment of the company's imagination, it may partly explain the US's continuous ambivalence and changing attitudes towards Eritrea in the years that followed. Without a doubt, Eritrea was becoming a pawn in the calculations of superpower strategic interests and eventual rivalry.

Early Calls for Union with Ethiopia

The end of the war in North Africa and the Allies' success in securing the safety of the Middle East and the Red Sea region greatly reduced Eritrea's role as a military base and main supplier of necessities for the Allied war effort. By the end of 1943, the Americans had dismantled their installations in Gura'e, Ghinda'e and Massawa, and shipped them elsewhere. As the Middle East economy recovered, Italian agricultural and industrial firms in Eritrea were forced to close down or greatly reduce their operations. Eritrean workers were the hardest hit. Rampant unemployment forced people to flock to urban centres, where fertile ground was laid for unrest.

After Longrigg gave the green light for the resumption of political debate on Eritrea's future, *Abune* Markos and his Coptic clergy took immediate steps to exploit the opportunity. On 20 January 1944, Markos repeated his Epiphany sermon of 1942, exhorting Eritreans to welcome Ethiopia as their mother. On the same day, about twenty youths, working clandestinely, hung the Ethiopian flag on the main streets of Asmera. In the meantime, in a well-planned and coordinated move, activists had drafted a petition for immediate union to submit to the BMA. Markos spearheaded the drive for signatures by threatening spiritual reprisals, including excommunication, against believers who would not sign. British sources reported that in Asmera alone, about 5,000 people, mainly the unemployed, signed the petition. The influential president of the Mahber Fikri Hager (MFH), Gebremeskel Weldu, and Eritrean officials of the Ethiopian Government also worked hard to foster opposition to British policies in Eritrea, including their wilful neglect and subsequent destruction of the Eritrean economy.[29]

By either design or coincidence, the BMA put in place a measure that ignited an already volatile situation. In January 1943, it announced that, henceforth, Eritrean members of the police force (EPF) were to wear sandals rather than the boots that had been part of their attire. The reason given was that the Administration wanted to cut costs. Trevaskis describes the reaction as follows: 'Sandals! Every tavern in town exploded in outrage at this insult to Eritrean honour. Sandals were for the ignorant and uncivilized. To accept them was to accept the humiliation of racial inferiority. No constable with an ounce of natural pride could possibly submit to the indignity of being debooted. Inflammatory words led to action.'[30]

On 20 January, members of the Asmera police went on strike and took to the streets to demonstrate their opposition. On 5 February, hundreds joined them, refusing to work under Italian superiors and demanding an end to the British adoption of fascist laws.[31] Stanley-Parker and his aide Tedla Bairu in Asmera were inclined to agree with the striking police and grant their demands. Longrigg took a tougher stance. While promising to reintroduce boots, he identified two inspectors and a sergeant as ringleaders and put them behind bars.[32] Not stopping there, he had five prominent Asmerans arrested on charges of having incited the police. At least one of these was a founding member of the MFH; all of them were known supporters of union with Ethiopia.[33]

Stanley-Parker's and Tedla Bairu's warnings that the clampdown would create an upheaval did not materialise. Eventually, Longrigg agreed to have the five 'agitators' released on bail. The measure, however, visibly cowed the emerging unionists into silence. Even Markos's loud objections and call to arms failed to bring out his followers. Trevaskis, who was in Asmera during the strike, observes: 'To the surprise, perhaps even disappointment of Stanley-Parker, Eritrea did not explode with outrage at Longrigg's old-fashioned handling of the police mutiny ... as if at a signal, the entire pro-Ethiopia circus closed down. There were no more demonstrations, no more strikes, no more protests. The Bishop went to Addis Ababa, the Eritrea Committee went into retreat.'[34]

A British document of the time characterised the unionist agitators as politicians not willing to pay sacrifices for their cause. Their political activities were limited to corresponding with their Ethiopian and English propagandists, occasionally distributing some leaflets, staging lukewarm demonstrations during religious festivals, and sending one telegram to the conference of Allied foreign ministers in London. Their hope was that Sylvia Pankhurst's campaign in Britain and the activities of Eritreans in Ethiopia would soon show a more concrete result. They were thus banking on help from outside.[35]

Unionist Push from Ethiopia

On 14 February 1944, an Eritrean named *Blata* Weldemikael Teferi presented his idea for the formation of an association working towards the union of Eritrea with Ethiopia at the home of *Blata* Dawit Okbazghi, then deputy mayor of Addis Ababa. This led to a follow-up meeting on the 27th of the same month, at Addis Ababa's Hager Fikir Theatre (Love of Country Theatre). The venue was obviously chosen to create a symbolic link with the Love of Country Association (MFH) of Eritrea. Here, *Blata* Weldemikael's proposal found general acceptance and it was decided to form the association.[36]

It took several months before the formal inauguration of the organisation took place. Apparently, the BMA were not aware of the developments in Addis Ababa until mid-1944. As late as 7 June, four months after its formation, the Chief Administrator of Eritrea was still asking the British Ambassador, Robert Howe, in Addis Ababa if an association called 'Free Eritrea' or 'Free Hamasien' had been formed. Was it also true, he wanted to know, if Haile Selassie's own secretary, *Tsehafe Te'ezaz* Weldegiorgis, and the Eritrean officials Dawit Okbazghi and Gebremeskel Habtemariam, a director general at the Ministry of Posts, Telegraphs and Telephones, were the main sponsors of the proposed association?[37] The chargé d'affaires in Addis Ababa, F.G. Cook, confirmed to the Administrator that such an association had indeed been formed and that the 'intriguer and ... xenophobe' Weldegiorgis was at the helm. Cook revealed that, initially, the cover for the association had been some self-help project. The real purpose, however, was to finance pro-union propagandists to lobby Eritreans at home.

Cook was of the opinion that the majority of Eritreans in Ethiopia were opposed to the idea of their country coming under Showan domination. He also wrote that capable Eritreans were being sidelined by design. He mentioned as a prime example Lorenzo Ta'ezaz, foreign minister in Haile Selassie's 1941 cabinet, who had been 'exiled' to the embassy in Moscow. He also viewed Ephrem Teweldemedhin's appointment as ambassador to Washington in a similar light. After the abortive rebellion in Tigray the year before, Cook concluded, Eritreans had become suspicious.

Cook's overall judgement was that, since most Eritreans residing in Ethiopia had no confidence in Ethiopia's administrative efficiency and judicial fairness, they generally chose self-government or independence. The only issue that gave some life to the 'Free Eritrea' movement in Addis Ababa was its slogan against the return of Italy to Eritrea. People could and did rally around that cause. Otherwise, there was no consensus on the association's proposal for immediate union.[38]

On 8 October 1944, the Association for the Unity of Ethiopia and Eritrea (AUEE) was formally inaugurated at a big meeting in the Cinema Empire in Addis Ababa. The aim of the association was to work towards the full and immediate integration of Eritrea with Ethiopia. Gebremeskel Habtemariam (not to be confused with Gebremeskel Weldu, president of MFH in Eritrea) was elected president. An all-Eritrean committee was also set up to run the association's everyday affairs.[39]

Ambassador Howe of the UK was present at the meeting as an invited guest. Also in attendance were several Ethiopians, both Amhara and Tigrayans, many of whom spoke after Gebremeskel Habtemariam's address. *Blata* Kidanemariam Aberra, a Tigrayan who had served as Ethiopia's consul in Eritrea prior to Italy's invasion of Ethiopia, impressed Howe the most. He was also one of the Tigrayans who had been in contact with Eritreans about the Tigray-Tigrigni movement.

Although not a member of the association, Kidanemariam got up to say that all the talk about the racial and cultural similarities especially between the peoples of the highlands of Eritrea and Ethiopia was fine and true. The real issue, however, was whether Ethiopia was fit to administer Eritrea. Could Ethiopia convince the Four Great Powers, he asked, of its capacity to take more territory than it already had, and manage it efficiently? If Ethiopia was to deserve Eritrea, it needed to work hard on establishing an adequate and efficient system of administration and justice. For Howe, Kidanemariam's speech was significant because it substantiated Cook's assertion that the Eritrean leadership of the association was divided over some fundamental issues. What surprised Howe most was that such a difference of opinion was apparent even among the Ethiopians.[40]

Many years later, Asfaha Weldemikael, subsequently Chief Executive of Eritrea, confirmed that the AUEE was divided on some basic issues. The association's French-educated president, Gebremeskel Habtemariam, was a director at the Post Office, a position that did not fairly recognise his calibre. He had lived in exile in Cairo and Khartoum during the war and had joined a British force commanded by Brigadier Sandford in its push through Gojam. According to Asfaha's own admission, Gebremeskel was an uncompromising patriot with little regard for people like Asfaha who had served the Italians and were going to extremes to ingratiate themselves with Emperor Haile Selassie. On his election as president of AUEE, Gebremeskel soon started to clash with Weldegiorgis and his Eritrean aide, *Fitawrari* Abraha Weldetatios, whom he accused of behind-the-scenes interference in the affairs of the AUEE. At issue was Gebremeskel's opposition to a hasty and unconditional merger and his advocacy of a union that would respect the culture, languages, religions and history of Eritrea.

In time, Weldegiorgis prevailed and Gebremeskel was ousted from the association's presidency. He even lost his directorship at the Post Office and spent several years idle.[41] Nevertheless, he would not abandon his advocacy of conditional union. In later years, he was given the lofty rank of *Dejazmatch* and sent off to Haiti as ambassador. After Lorenzo Ta'ezaz, he was the second high-profile Eritrean to be sidelined in this manner.

Following Gebremeskel's ouster, the AUEE became Ethiopia's main instrument for guiding and leading unionist activities in Eritrea. As an immediate neighbour, Tigray became the main springboard for the intense, organised Ethiopian campaign to gain a strong foothold in Eritrea. To this end, the Eritreans Dawit Okbazghi and Colonel (later General) Isaias Gebreselassie succeeded each other throughout most of the 1940s as governors of Adwa, the district adjacent to the Eritrean border. From that vantage point, they followed up and directed Ethiopia's plans and strategy.

Besides these two, another Eritrean named Gebremeskel Yebio was appointed head of the powerful Orthodox Church in Axum with the prestigious title of *Nebure Ed*. Like *Abune* Markos, the *Nebure Ed* put his substantial spiritual authority at the service of the unionist agenda. Lastly, *Tsehafe Te'ezaz* Weldediorgis's friend Abraha Weldetatios, who was named chairperson of the Tigray branch of AUEE, shuttled between Adi Grat and Mekele, fully employed as troubleshooter for the association.[42]

Axum, Adwa and Adi Grat all had easy access to Eritrea. With Eritreans themselves running the show from there, Ethiopia had every reason to expect that its plans would meet with rapid success.

The MFH in Turmoil

On 3 August 1944, *ESG* published an article in Tigrinya entitled 'Some Thoughts on the Future of Eritrea' by 'An Eritrean'. For a long time, people suspected that

Weldeab Weldemariam had been the author of the article; in 1995, the late Tiquabo Arese'e attributed it to him in his compilation of Weldeab's articles and speeches. Weldeab has, however, revealed that he was merely the translator; the author was none other than Stephen Longrigg himself. (The quotations included below are from the original English version.)

It was a strange article where, much as he tried, even deliberately corrupting his grammar and sentence construction, Longrigg could not conceal some of the prejudices typical of the British view of Eritreans. Some of the words he employed were not of the kind that Eritreans would use to describe or demean themselves. 'In my country,' he stated, 'my people do not have any political views ... very few have learnt already the importance of education and knowledge ... the Eritrean is very docile ...' On the country's future, he said that Eritreans were confused and that 'we shall have very little saying in what is going to happen to our country. Our feelings, our sympathies and our aversions will be of little interest.' He dismissed Italy's claims to Eritrea and stated that Ethiopia was 'physically and spiritually not in a position to "swallow" Eritrea'. Ethiopia was so immersed in its own problems that its future was uncertain and Eritrea would be a perpetual source of unrest to it.

Following this analysis, the article went straight to Longrigg's proposals for solving 'the Eritrean problem'. Since it became a highly controversial article that shaped the Eritrean political discourse, we will quote extensively from its contents. The article continued:

> Eritrea is a melting pot of races, languages, tribes and religions. Some superficial distinction allows us to divide the country into two main parts: the so-called *Bassopiano* [*metahit*] inhabited by Moslems and mostly Tigre or Arabic speaking, and the *Altopiano* [*kebessa*] populated by the sedentary Coptic Tigrinya speaking block.
>
> It is a fact that the *Bassopiano* [*metahit*] wishes some kind of incorporation into the Sudan which can represent best their commercial, religious and cultural interests. There are already today numerous ties which connect the *Bassopiano* population with that of Sudan.
>
> My main concern, however, as an Eritrean of the high plateau, is the fate of the vast Coptic Christian Tigrinya speaking population. The Eritrean and Northern Abyssinian high plateau is one block, racially, religiously and culturally. The Tigre [Tigray] province—the source of all Abyssinian civilization—cannot be divided into two ... Therefore, I cannot see any solution of the redistribution and regrouping of former Italian East Africa, unless the old Tigre province—i.e. the Eritrean high plateau and all the Tigrinya speaking parts of Northern Ethiopia—are united in one state—and in my opinion most suitably—under some form of British mandate.
>
> Nominally, the British-Tigre-province-mandate could form part of the Ethiopian Empire, the Emperor could also be King of the province, but technically it is administered by Britishers and Tigreans. After a certain period—25 years or so—a plebiscite could be held, then the population could decide whether they wish the mandate to continue or to be directly part of the Ethiopian Empire.[43]

This was the first time that the British partition plan, or a variation of it, had been made public to the people of Eritrea. Naturally, it sent shock waves across the spectrum of the emerging Eritrean political tendencies. Within weeks, articles responding to the unnamed 'Eritrean' poured into the *ESG*. Many criticised the author of such a provocative piece for hiding behind a pseudonym. Some openly expressed their doubt that he could be an Eritrean at all. The first person to comment on the article was the president of MFH, Gebremeskel Weldu. He had, as we saw, just joined the unionist camp. In a series of articles entitled 'Deliver Us from Evil', Gebremeskel rejected the article's suggestion that Ethiopia could not 'swallow' Eritrea. 'To separate Eritrea from Ethiopia', he wrote, 'would be like separating a suckling from its mother—Eritrea is inseparable from Ethiopia.' A person in a crouching position who spreads his limbs far and wide will still be the same person, he argued. Similarly, 'If Ethiopia reaches out to gather an integral part of its body, Eritrea, she will only be stretching out her limbs. By no means can this be regarded as expanding to a new colony.' Gebremeskel saw nothing out of the ordinary in the diversity of the people of Eritrea. Yes, the majority of the people of the *metahit* were Muslim, he explained, but they were not Arabs, nor did they speak Arabic. 'They are all ours; we are of the same stock. They are racially akin to the Muslims and Christians who inhabit the highlands and the escarpment.'[44] He therefore rejected the very idea of partition.

Like Gebremeskel Habtemariam in Addis Ababa, Gebremeskel Weldu was wary of the dangers of immediate and unconditional union. In a second article published a few weeks later, he wrote extensively on the mentality and capabilities of the Eritrean people, whom he classified as *fruyat* and *deqeQti*, roughly meaning 'the heavyweights' and 'the commoners'. Eritrea's future, he declared, was not the concern only of the chiefs and notables, the *fruyat* or heavyweights. The commoners, the *deqeQti*, too had an equal say. The fate of Eritrea could only be decided by a consensus of those two classes of Eritreans.[45]

The second major debater was *Dejazmatch* Abraha Tessema, whose father, Tessema Asberom, had just been elevated to the rank of *Ras* by the BMA. In Longrigg's proposal, Abraha saw the chance to rekindle his old Tigray-Tigrigni project, which, he claimed, had the full support of the chiefs of the Akeleguzai province. Abraha wrote plainly and directly. He condemned Emperor Menelik for having abandoned Eritrea in his hour of great victory. He reminded his readers that Eritreans—the gentry, the clergy, the interpreters and the armed fighters—had helped Italy defeat Ethiopia. 'The Ethiopians hold a grudge against us; they will give us no peace.' He rebuked the unionists for their unconsidered and emotional leap to embrace a choice whose repercussions they could not foresee. He warned that the new rulers would bring with them an alien language and wondered, 'Are we to go back to the dreadful days of interpreters, this time with masters who look like us?' Like Gebremeskel Weldu, Abraha rejected the partition plan in very strong terms. Seeing a chance for the revival of his old Tigray-Tigrigni project, he suggested that the whole of Eritrea and the whole of Tigray form one united nation and detailed the advantages that the merger would bring about.[46]

The debate between Gebremeskel and Abraha grew so contentious, acrimonious and divisive that other voices of reason intervened to cool tempers down. One of these, the future Secretary of Finance of Eritrea, *Grazmatch* Teklehaimanot Bokru, called for a convention of representatives elected by the people and sanctioned by the Administration. Endless debate between individual writers was not producing any tangible result. What was needed was a convention that would consider public opinion and come up with a mature assessment of the will of the people. 'We know what the few who write think. What about the majority who do not write?'[47]

Finally, *Ras* Tessema, the emerging leader of the independence camp, also said his bit. He decried the unfettered war of words between Gebremeskel Weldu and his son Abraha. 'It cannot benefit us Eritreans,' he said.

> If anything, it makes us look petty and inconsequential. Even if the two were to join hands, not to mention being divided into two camps, they could not represent the people of Eritrea. What the people of Eritrea need ... is what the Europeans do. They elect great and wise people to deliberate and agree on matters pertaining to their country. Eritreans need that kind of process. Everything that is decided by consensus is beneficial to all.

Tessema then proposed that fifteen Muslims and fifteen Christians be elected from all over the country and convene to discuss Eritrea's future in a neutral venue.[48]

No party showed any willingness to accept these proposals of moderation and dialogue. Indeed, even if they had been accepted, the chances of their effective implementation would have been very slim, if not non-existent. The ball was not in the Eritrean court; and the BMA was not in any way inclined to help create harmony when the growing division within the MFH and the country at large favoured its plans for partition.

Significantly, Muslim activists remained silent during those highly charged debates. Although Ibrahim Sultan did not give a specific date, he later confirmed that the MFH had been hijacked by the unionists at a meeting called by *Abune* Markos in the Orthodox Cathedral of St Mary. Present at the meeting were Gebremeskel Weldu, *Blata* Demsas Weldemikael, *Dejazmatch* Hagos Gebre and other luminaries of the MFH. According to Ibrahim, it was at that gathering that the unionists decided to adopt the name of Mahber Fikri Hager (MFH). But they added the words *Ertra ms Ityopia—Hanti Ityopia* to it. Literally translated, the whole name meant 'Love of Country Association: Eritrea with Ethiopia—One Ethiopia'. More popularly it became known as Mahber Hibret, or the Unionist Party (UP), the name we will use from here on. Muslim leaders of the old MFH, particularly Ibrahim himself, Abdulkader Kebire and Mohammed Aberra Hagos, were invited to attend the meeting when all had been decided. 'We voiced our opposition and announced our withdrawal from the association,' Ibrahim recalled. The original MFH was no more.[49]

How could all this have happened? How did the other side allow the takeover of the association by the unionist faction? Weldeab explains as follows:

> They stole it; we were outpaced ... we were pre-empted. They rushed to take it in '44 when the British granted us the right to discuss Eritrea's future. They added the words 'With Ethiopia' to the original MFH of Eritrea. They turned it into an association that begged for union with Ethiopia. When we saw that we had been outsmarted, we met to organise ourselves around a new name and a new organisation. We named it Ertra n'Ertrawyan, Eritrea for Eritreans. What enabled them to succeed was Gebremeskel Weldu's decision to go to their side. As president of MFH, he facilitated the transition for them. They embraced him, only to trip him over later.

Weldeab never questioned Gebremeskel's integrity. 'In those difficult days, Eritrean hearts were filled with hatred of Italians and foreigners. People expected nothing from them, except poverty, oppression and betrayal.' For this reason, many started to look to union with Ethiopia as the only way out of foreign domination. Gebremeskel Weldu, according to Weldeab, fell into that category.[50]

From this point on, Eritrean politics took two irreconcilable paths. Except for the issue of partition, which both parties rejected with equal determination, there was no other matter on which they could see eye to eye. Unionist propaganda was swift and effective enough to attract people, mainly former askaris and the unemployed, who readily believed that Ethiopia was a land of freedom, prosperity and justice. Eritrean officers of the Ethiopian army who came back in gabardine uniforms with stars and epaulettes on their shoulders dazzled the Eritrean police and former *zaptia* still fighting for boots instead of sandals. The Lorenzos, Ephrems and Dawits, currently Haile Selassie's favourites, tantalised Eritreans with the illusory prospect of the heights to which Ethiopia could elevate them.

As a movement born of anger, hatred and frustration over white rule, the sheer emotion and aggressiveness manifested by the newly recruited members of the Unionist Party alarmed the independence and allied groups. Most frightening was the spiritual legitimacy that the movement gained from the Orthodox Church and its leadership. The other half of the MFH, led by Abraha Tessema, Weldeab, Hassen Ali and Berhanu Ahmeddin from Asmera, and Omer Sefaf from Ghinda'e, sought to counter what they saw as an emotional movement entering uncharted territory with one that would be more representative of the nature and diversity of Eritreans. Weldeab described how they set out to do this:

> We first went to Saleh Kekia's house and spent a whole day in consultation. We vowed to work together with no regard for religious, racial or regional differences. Kekia slaughtered a chicken and we all dined from his plate. We swore on the Koran to seal our agreement. Some days later, we went to *Dejazmatch* Abraha's house at Mai Edaga,

> near Dekemhare. We repeated the process by dining on a chicken slaughtered by the *Dejazmatch* and swearing by the Bible to stay true to our principles. We then sent representatives to all the provinces and the sub-district chiefs, the *mislenes*, to collect signatures of support for 'Eritrea for Eritreans'. We started with western *metahit* and proceeded to Massawa and the coastal area, Akeleguzai and Seraye. We were able to gather support and signatures from thousands of people.[51]

Saleh Kekia Pasha, a native of Hirgigo with wide business interests in Ethiopia, was entrusted with the safekeeping of the signed documents but somehow he lost them. Moreover, probably to protect his businesses in Ethiopia, he joined the Unionist Party and eventually became its vice president.[52] Nevertheless, 'Eritrea for Eritreans' kept up a fruitful campaign for support and signatures. Its main concern at this initial stage was the maintenance of Eritrean unity and opposition to Ethiopian rule. Like the Unionist Party, it had no clear programme of action or statement of principles.

Both parties started out, in fact, as very loose movements. 'Love of Country: Eritrea with Ethiopia—One Ethiopia' was a slogan indicating a feeling or an attachment, as was 'Eritrea for Eritreans'. There was no political meaning in those appellations. One party felt that Eritrea needed Ethiopia to survive as a united country; the other side thought differently—that Eritrea could survive as an independent entity. Behind both movements was the conviction that each side held the key to the issue of what was best for Eritrea. For many activists, 'what was best for Eritrea' often changed with time, altered circumstances and reassessment of political positions based on new information or some new revelation. Changing alliances and allegiances between one side and the other, and the flow of members between the two movements, were to remain common. In those days, Eritrean nationalism passed through a highly confusing stage.

Ethiopia's Intensified Claims

As the war wound down in favour of the Allies, Ethiopia increasingly argued its claim to Eritrea. In the 19 December 1944 agreement between Britain and Ethiopia, the latter extracted important concessions regarding rights pertaining to its sovereignty. With regard to the Ogaden region, which Britain insisted on continuing to administer, Ethiopia was satisfied with recognition, in principle, of its sovereignty over the territory.[53] In other respects, Haile Selassie's situation under the British remained the same and, just as previously, he found a way to appeal to President Roosevelt for help. On his way back from the Yalta summit in February 1945, Roosevelt agreed to meet Haile Selassie in Egypt. The Emperor had to be smuggled out of Addis Ababa in an American aircraft one morning before dawn.

At the meeting, on a ship docked in the Suez Canal, Haile Selassie asked for American help to obtain Eritrea and secure its own access to the sea. On regaining control of the Addis Ababa–Djibouti railway and Ogaden region, he promised to give concessions to American firms seeking to run the railway or explore for oil in the Ogaden. He also requested Roosevelt's intervention to secure Ethiopia's participation in the drafting of the UN Constitution and at the peace conference projected to take place at the end of the war.

A period of uncertainty followed for Haile Selassie when Roosevelt died a few months after their meeting and was succeeded by Harry Truman. But the war ended in May 1945. On 2 August, the leaders of the Allied powers met in Potsdam and, among other issues, agreed that their Council of Foreign Ministers would deal with the fate of the former Italian colonies of Eritrea, Somalia and Libya.[54] Membership of the proposed conference was restricted to those countries that had fought against Italy. With support from the US, Ethiopia qualified for membership in view of the war waged by Ethiopian patriots against Italy. Since this put it in a strategic position to influence conference members in respect of its claims to Eritrea, it was a major triumph for Ethiopian diplomacy.

At the first London Conference, Ethiopia's detailed claims to Eritrea, which it presented in its 'Green Memorandum', failed to impress the Great Powers.[55] Instead, after the US proposed UN trusteeship before the granting of independence to all the former colonies except Italian Somaliland, the powers failed to reach any consensus. A second conference, held in Paris between 25 April and 16 May 1946, produced the same result: France and the USSR supported Italy's resumption of control of its former colonies; the British proposed partition for Eritrea; and the US repeated its previous position.[56]

For the next phase of the Paris Conference, Ethiopia came better prepared. To highlight its treatment of Eritreans, it even recalled the Eritreans Lorenzo Ta'ezaz from his semi-exile in Moscow and Ephrem Teweldemedhin from New York to attend the conference as Prime Minister Aklilu Habtewold's aides. None of that produced the expected result. France, Belgium and Brazil wanted Italy back in Eritrea. Citing its former administrative control of Massawa, Egypt laid claim to the whole of Eritrea.[57] On the other side, Ethiopia had a number of supporters: Greece and India, which had sizable communities in Ethiopia; Yugoslavia, with its well-known enmity towards Italy; and Canada came out strongly in favour of granting Ethiopia's claims to Eritrea.[58]

In view of such divergent views and conflicting strategic interests, especially those of the Great Powers, the conference avoided issues specific to the former Italian colonies. Instead, they settled on three major points on which they could agree. First, Italy was to renounce all 'title to territorial possession' over its former colonies of Eritrea, Italian Somaliland and Libya. Secondly, the former Italian colonies would continue to be administered by the current powers, pending their final disposal. And thirdly, the final disposal of the former colonies was to be decided by the US, the UK, France and the USSR within one year. In an appendix to the main agreement, the

Four Powers agreed that, in the event of their failure to agree on a common solution, the question of the Italian colonies would be transferred to the United Nations.[59]

The Paris Conference ended a full two years after the first London Conference in early 1945. As we shall see, during that period Eritrea went through a tumultuous series of developments, none of whose local consequences had any impact on the way its affairs were discussed in Paris. Ethiopia, on the other hand, had a free hand throughout the process. As Prime Minister Aklilu's reminiscences show, Ethiopia used its membership of the Paris Conference to present its case on Eritrea fully and adequately. Although Ethiopia still had a long way to go before succeeding in its quest to possess Eritrea, the Paris Conference definitely enabled it to advance closer to its coveted prize.[60]

In effect, the fate of Eritrea was discussed and decided not in Eritrea and by Eritreans, but by the representatives of nations who had little or no idea of who Eritreans were and what they wanted. For their part, the majority of Eritreans were unaware of the drama being played in a faraway European capital that affected their future.

4

TOWARDS PARTY FORMATION IN ERITREA

Further Economic Ruin

With the end of World War II and the return of relative stability to the Middle East and North Africa, Eritrea lost its vital economic role in the region. The problem did not stop there. When the Paris Conference decided to hand the fate of the former Italian colonies to the Four Great Powers, Britain's already lukewarm interest in Eritrean affairs declined considerably. Nowhere was this more manifest than in the BMA's systematic destruction of the industrial and social infrastructure already in place.

The BMA's dismantlement and shipment of Italy's war installations actually started in 1941. By 1945, industrial plants were being closed down or dismantled for sale to other countries. The excuse was that their products could not compete with those of newly revived firms in Europe. The once thriving Eritrean industrial base was thus confined to such local agricultural activities as livestock and cash crop production and to marine and mining businesses.[1] Within months, the hangars and prefabricated residential and entertainment structures left behind by the Americans in Gura'e, Ghinda'e and Massawa were torn down and sold abroad.

In anticipation of an Ethiopian takeover of Eritrea, Sylvia Pankhurst wrote a book entitled *Why Are We Destroying Ethiopian Ports?*, in which she detailed the damage that the British were causing to the Eritrean economy. In Massawa alone, 75 buildings, including residential houses and hostels, had been ripped to pieces. Corrugated iron sheets, steel beams and tiles were piled at the docks for shipment. Bridges and even parts of the world's longest cable transport at the time were not spared. Floating docks and cranes from Italian colonial times met a similar fate. One floating dock was sold to Pakistan for £500,000. Sixteen large boats were also sold to Pakistani businesses. Pankhurst estimated that the sale of the installations left intact by the Americans alone brought $20 million to the coffers of the British Government.[2] 'They did not even leave rusty nails behind' is how Eritreans summarise what they still see as an act of state vandalism by a major European power. Lobbyists for Ethiopia did succeed in having the issue raised in the British parliament. The excuse given by government officials was that the cost of maintaining and administering facilities in Eritrea was becoming a burden on the British taxpayer.[3]

The cynicism inherent in Britain's pillage of property that Eritrea could use for its future development further exasperated Eritreans. Nothing that the BMA did by way of administrative and social reform could compensate for its active role in the destruction of the Eritrean economy. In November 1944, Stephen Longrigg was replaced by Brigadier C.D. McCarthy as Military Administrator. Some months before his departure, Longrigg had persuaded his London superiors that after the incarceration of hardline Fascists, moderate ones be employed to fill vital posts.[4] For Eritreans, this meant living and working under their former Fascist tormentors, a situation that they were united in opposing.

McCarthy, whose tenure extended only up to August 1945, sought to employ Eritreans in a restructured administrative set-up of six provinces centred on the towns of Akurdet, Keren, Asmera, Massawa, Adi Ugri (Mendefera) and Adi Qeih. McCarthy also instituted a military tribunal composed of British judges and a criminal appeals court staffed by Italian jurists. At the same time, about 250 Eritreans were assigned to various parts of the country as district judges and administrators.[5] A group of prominent figures from the provinces were also appointed as *notabili* and tasked with settling local disputes and representing their respective provinces at ceremonial events. For the first time, Eritreans could deal with their own compatriots in their local district offices. With the language barrier removed, Tigrinya and Arabic started to take over as working languages in predominantly Christian and Muslim areas, respectively. Other local languages also began to be used frequently for official purposes.

McCarthy's reforms were generally appreciated as a move in the right direction. At the beginning, the people appointed to positions of responsibility came from the traditional leadership of chiefs and *shums*. After 1947, this gave way to the recruitment of younger and better-educated citizens who started to form the core of an emerging Eritrean bureaucracy. The political consequence of this new development was that many hitherto uncommitted traditional chiefs, who felt sidelined by the new breed of judges and administrators, began to move to the unionist camp in opposition to the BMA's reforms.[6]

The civil service, which functioned with efficiency until its decline and virtual abandonment upon Eritrea's annexation by Ethiopia in the 1960s, was, by itself, no answer to the people's main demands for employment and improvement in their living conditions. Class conflict in the *metahit*, especially Sahel, was still raging. Although the Beni Amer–Hadendowa armed conflicts were settled in late 1945, disgruntled Beni Amer youths still roamed the expanses of the Barka and Gash areas as armed *shifta* (bandits). In the *kebessa*, unresolved land issues pitted villages against one another, and resentment at Italian and Arab domination of trade in the urban areas threatened to boil over.

In April 1946, the BMA formed a Native Advisory Committee for Asmera and Hamasien to assess the economic situation and come up with proposals for its improvement. It included sixteen high-profile figures from the political and business communities of the country. Most notable among them were the unionists *Dejazmatch* Araia Wassie and Gebremeskel Weldu; *Haji* Imam Musa and Said Ahmed Hayoti from the independence camp; and Abdella Gonafer and *Bashai* (later *Dejazmatch*) Bemnet Tessema from the business sector. All major religions were fairly represented. The findings of the committee summarised the economic story of the British period. *Risti* (communally owned land) was being confiscated contrary to customary law and practice. Italian concessionaires, especially in Semienawi Bahri (the eastern escarpment), were holding on to areas of former community property that they could not utilise properly. Many were renting it to former owners on terms disadvantageous to the latter. Unresolved land disputes, lack of basic necessities and exorbitant commodity prices brought disruption to the lives of the people. Heavy British customs duties and robbery by thieves and the *shifta* rendered the free movement of trade with Ethiopia impossible, leading to price hikes and scarcity of basic commodities.

Taxation was another major problem that the committee identified as causing economic harm. It complained that, while taxation had increased 5–10 per cent on most commodities, salaries and wages had remained the same. Besides, two taxation categories that the committee could not understand or justify—'arrears in tax payments' and '*contributo di guerra*'—were compounding the problem. 'We know that we are not considered as enemies of the British Government,' the committee commented with regard to the 'war contribution' requirement.

The BMA's failure to rectify the situation by, for example, providing agrarian credit to farmers for procuring seeds, implements and oxen, giving back unutilised concession land to dispossessed owners, or introducing changes to the land tenure system,[7] was causing massive rural and urban unemployment, and leading to petty theft, robbery and the rise in *shifta* activity. Eritreans, the committee noted, 'are disciplined and God-fearing by nature. But nowadays, because of unemployment and hunger, they are falling into thefts and cheating.' It therefore recommended that greater employment opportunities be opened for Eritreans in the industrial, commercial and public sectors. It also called for reform in the security and judicial systems, where police and security practices lacked fairness and the requirements of due process.

One surprising recommendation by the committee was that the repatriation of Arabs should be an emergency concern of the BMA. 'The Arabs have made of themselves a real danger to the natives,' it contended, 'The acute economic deterioration experienced among the Eritreans has two causes: locust to the farmer, Arab to the merchant ... We recommend ... that commercial licences in Arab hands be given to the natives ... that the work done by the poors [*sic*] among the Arabs be done by the poor natives of the country.'[8] The committee's recommendation on the Arab issue was accompanied by a petition signed by 237 Muslim and Christian Eritreans, demanding Arab repatriation. It was a significant event in Muslim–Christian relations, indicating the prioritisation, especially within the Muslim community, of national over religious interests, a development that the British downplayed throughout their time in Eritrea. The BMA rejected the wholesale repatriation of Arabs and insisted that a distinction should be made between legal residents and illegal migrants. Those who entered the country illegally after 1941 were therefore liable for repatriation, along with those who transgressed the immigration laws of Eritrea.[9]

The attempt to take the economy away from foreign hands did not stop with the committee's recommendations. In July 1946, 93 major political and business leaders, almost evenly divided between Muslims and Christians (47 and 46 respectively), formed a business association, Società Anonima Commerciale per l'Economia Eritrea. Nine board members—five Muslim and four Christian—were elected, under the presidency and vice presidency of *Haji* Ahmed Abdulrahman Hilal and Haregot Abbay, respectively. Among the councillors were Araia Wassie and Abdella Gonafer. The association began with a capital of 100,000 shillings, and its concern was importing and exporting grain, textiles, hides and skins, coffee, meat and marine products. Its life span would extend to 31 December 1950.[10] There is no documentation to show how the association fared. But it constituted one more example of how Eritreans attempted to pull together towards common national goals and to insert themselves into the economic life of the country.

Social Unrest and Banditry

Rather than resolving the problems already mentioned, some of the BMA's measures aggravated the situation. Its tacit support for the divisive Tigray-Tigrigni movement in 1942–4 is a case in point. In 1945, when organised political activities were still banned, it allowed the president of AUEE, Gebremeskel Habtemariam, to enter Eritrea and agitate on behalf of union with Ethiopia. In February 1946, the BMA opened the door for Ethiopian intervention by receiving the Ethiopian military officer Colonel Nega Haileselassie as liaison officer for Haile Selassie's government. Soon Nega's office became the meeting place for unionist leaders, propagandists and unemployed Eritreans and Tigrayans seeking cash in return for unionist errands.[11] It was no coincidence that these events were accompanied by the resurgence of the *shifta* movement.

Beginning in 1943, deteriorating economic conditions encouraged the *shifta* to create havoc in the countryside. In that year, 108 cases of robbery were registered in police situation reports while there were 85 such cases in the following year. In the beginning, the BMA tried to dismiss the problem by calling them occasional thefts by peasants armed with sticks and clubs. Pressure from their superiors in Cairo forced the Administration's officials to admit that some of the activities were being perpetrated by organised armed bands.[12]

British statistics showed that in 1943 two people were killed and eight wounded in ten instances of armed robbery at night. In 1944, armed *shifta* incidents jumped to eighteen, while the number of dead and wounded rose to eleven and eight, respectively. The main targets of these attacks were Italians and their concession farms. In the 1944 incidents, six Italian concession farms and a bar were robbed and five Italians killed. In parallel incidents, two Eritrean policemen and a civilian met similar fates.[13]

At the end of 1944, *shifta* bands put a roadblock on the Asmera–Massawa road and made away with loot from a bus. Two police officers and an Italian civilian died in the ensuing shootings. Since this daring act took place in broad daylight, it became a cause of deep concern for the BMA and people in general. Nor were the *shifta* activities confined to the countryside, as they also carried out nightly raids into Asmera, Mendefera and Dekemhare to harass and kill Italians. Although the economy was the chief reason, *shifta* activity did have some political undertones. Targeting Italians was a direct response to the economic and political privileges Italians held under the British. Thus, albeit at a rudimentary stage, there was already a yet unarticulated political motivation built into the movement. The rise of a violence-prone unionist movement would soon change the *shifta*'s political direction.

Violence was in the air, especially in Asmera, Massawa and other major towns. On 18 February 1945, an argument between Eritreans and members of the Sudanese army at Edaga Hamus in Asmera deteriorated into verbal and physical fighting. By the time the British police arrived, one Sudanese soldier had been killed and nine Sudanese and Eritrean police officers injured. The BMA imposed a curfew in the city.[14]

It was generally believed that such sporadic flare-ups of violence were instigated by unionists who, in spite of Longrigg's ban on open political agitation, used their Ethiopian connections to stir up trouble. On 23 September 1945, about 150 well-organised demonstrators, including several children, marched to the BMA headquarters in Asmera and insisted on an audience. They presented a written petition addressed to the Council of Foreign Ministers meeting in London, demanding immediate union with Ethiopia. By this time, McCarthy had already been replaced by Brigadier J.M. Benoy as Chief Administrator. Although Benoy thought it inappropriate for the group to claim to represent the people of Eritrea, he still complied with the request of the demonstrators.[15]

Soon, petitions opposing Benoy's accommodation of the unionist demonstrators flooded into his office. On 3 January 1946, *mislenes*, *nazirs* and *notabili* from the Keren division presented signed appeals to the Council turning down the unionists' demands and their claim to represent the people of Eritrea. Rejecting Ethiopia as 'an uncivilised country, unable to govern itself', they requested UN trusteeship under British administration. Even the *shums*, *kentabais* and *diglels*, feudal masters of Sahel and the western lowlands, signed the petition.[16] Similar petitions came from the Massawa and Akeleguzai provinces. Led by *Ras* Tessema Asberom, 29 chiefs of Akeleguzai demanded that the voices of the Eritrean people, and not of 'outsiders', should be heard. Their petition claimed that Muslims and Christians spoke with one voice; they also demanded that, under British trusteeship, their tradition of electing their own leaders and being administered by their own people should be respected.

British documents confirm that the five major petitions opposing union with Ethiopia represented about 268,800 people.[17] In a memo he wrote at the time, Brigadier D.C. Cumming, future Chief Administrator of Eritrea, noted that the petitions came from the same source and that the claim to represent the districts mentioned was authentic. Unionist support, he wrote, was confined to the Hamasien province and in the Seraye districts adjacent to Hamasien.[18]

In these early days, Benoy tried to be even-handed in his dealings with both sides. However, the growing hostility between the two camps became so toxic that the unionists kept accusing the Administration of bias against them. Defending the neutrality of his Administration, Benoy declared that the temporary nature of Britain's tenure did not allow it to interfere in Eritrea's internal affairs. The unionists had had their say earlier. What he found objectionable were the unionist pamphlets, highly provocative and insulting in content, that were being secretly distributed around town.

Encouraged by Benoy's accommodating approach, political debate revived once again in the *ESG*. At its heart were Gebremeskel Weldu, Weldeab Weldemariam and other figures from both sides. Vitriol and acrimony characterised those exchanges. Gebremeskel's unconditional love of and praise for Ethiopia often met with bitter criticism and protest. One writer complained that Gebremeskel's 'audacity' would throw the country 'down a deep precipice ... it would be more appropriate for him to acknowledge that he was elected by a few disciples and cronies.'[19] Things reached a point where any topic could easily raise tempers. An exchange between two protagonists on the proximity of Tigrinya and Amharic to the parent Geez language ended up in an unnecessarily abusive war of words. Moderate leaders like *Dejazmatch* Hassen Ali had to intervene to call a truce.[20]

The Paris Peace Conference and the arrival of Colonel Nega Haileselassie coincided with this highly charged political atmosphere in Eritrea. The following weeks saw a dramatic increase in unionist activity and daring. More petitions demanding the expulsion of Arabs and the removal of Italians from policy and administrative positions rained down on the Administration. The previous March, unionist supporters had attacked some Arabs and destroyed their properties in Keren and Massawa.

In what seemed a coordinated move, Ethiopia started to take steps against Arabs and Italians resident in that country. In June 1946, it confiscated the property of about 130 Arabs, brought them to the border and expelled them into Eritrea. Over the objection of the Chief Administrator, Ethiopia again took the same step with 98 Italians and 145 Yemenis the following August.[21] 'This action, which was taken without the consent of the Administration,' said Trevaskis, 'scarcely accorded with the normal rules of international behaviour but, to the Eritrean Abyssinian, it was effective proof of Ethiopia's determination and ability to deal with undesirable aliens ... This campaign of calculated xenophobia was supported by a number of Nationalist [*sic*] demonstrations and processions in the principal towns.'[22]

Ethiopia's no-nonsense stance on aliens aroused awe and admiration among Eritrean unionists. On 28 July 1946, 200 unionists with 50 schoolchildren among them staged yet another demonstration demanding immediate union with Ethiopia. From the headquarters of the Chief Administrator, they marched to Nega Haileselassie's office and conferred with him. Not stopping there, they continued into the heart of Asmera, where the Asmera chief of police detained a few of their number for questioning. Violence broke out on the streets of the town, and Arab shops and property were looted or set on fire. The crowd even broke into the police station and freed their detained compatriots. When their re-arrest led to serious rioting that threatened to overwhelm the available police force, a platoon of the Sudan defence force intervened. Order was restored when shots were fired, killing four demonstrators.[23]

The BMA imposed a curfew, banned further demonstrations and issued a directive regulating the manner of submitting petitions. But violence was taking root within the politics of Eritrea. In an article, Weldeab tried to rationalise the aggressiveness and violent tendencies among the youth:

> I am in no doubt that Eritrean youths have arisen in the spirit of liberation. This is something to rejoice. But these enlightened young people have not found a correct and proper leadership. For this reason, the warm and healthy blood surging inside them is often swerving out of course to leakage and waste. These youths should not be suppressed. Instead, they should be encouraged to rise up and be given appropriate leadership. They need to be protected from the evil spirit that comes to them camouflaged as the love of country, while paving the way for its own self-interest. This is not a force that will stand for them.[24]

While writing this article, Weldeab was deeply involved in discussions with like-minded people in the other camp in search of a middle-ground solution that would bring the unionist and independence blocs to a common agreement. Meanwhile, in the *metahit*, events of momentous importance for Eritrean history were taking place.

The Road to the Moslem League of Eritrea

When Trevaskis returned in early 1945 from his visit to London, Benoy was already in charge in Eritrea. Before assigning him back to Keren, Benoy voiced his misgivings about the way matters were being managed in Eritrea. Trevaskis reported their conversation as follows:

> First, Eritrea was not a British colony. We were caretakers and our job was to hand it over as we found it. Nothing more, nothing less. Secondly, we had to 'play fair' and keep our noses clean. We were British officers and had to behave as British officers should. He took a poor view of Eritreans being bullied and badgered for saying that they wanted union with Ethiopia and, as for that childish tomfoolery about a Greater Tigray, the less said about it the better. 'Do I make myself plain?' he asked, pinning me down with a pair of unblinking eyes. If he had drawn a straight line on a clean sheet of paper, he could not have presented me with anything plainer.[25]

Armed as he was with Douglas Newbold's partition plan, Trevaskis was not happy with Benoy's directive. In his previous tours of duty in Keren, he had gained the reputation of being friendly to the Muslim and *tigre* (serf) causes. According to his account, on his return, protests and defiant refusal to obey the *shumagille* flared up. Within weeks, all tax payments stopped. Whereas previously rebellion had been confined to one or two *kebilas*, this time it spread to a dozen simultaneously. The problem became so intractable that the *kentabai* and his followers confronted Trevaskis, asking whether the Administration saw them as 'chiefs worthy of support' or as 'mere nobodies to be insulted and humiliated'. The meeting ended with the *kentabai* threatening to seek other arrangements and walking out on Trevaskis.[26]

Soon after this, Benoy decided to merge the Akurdet and Keren divisions into one administrative unit called the Western Province. He appointed Trevaskis as chief political officer (CPO) of the new division. 'What this meant was that I was to be in charge of Eritrea's Muslim West, the very region which Newbold had earmarked for the Sudan,' he wrote. '"You don't seem very pleased," sniffed Benoy. Not pleased! I was over the moon!'[27]

Following the settlement of the Beni Amer–Hadendowa conflict, in which Trevaskis had played a role as the newly appointed CPO, Keren was plunged in a new state of anxiety and apprehension. With Benoy's tacit permission, busloads of unionist agitators—abbots, priests, peasants and proletarians included—invaded Keren for a demonstration and a spectacle that the town had never seen before. The greatest surprise for Keren residents, however, was the announcement that the *kentabai* of Bet Asghede and a number of *shumagille* chiefs had crossed over to the unionist camp. Unionist celebration at their newly acquired gains and their encroachment into Muslim strongholds reached ecstatic levels when the *diglel* of Beni Amer followed the *kentabai* in the same direction.[28] The unionist 'coup' had the direct result of jolting tens of thousands of *tigre* serfs into a 'frenzy of anti-Ethiopian passion ... By publicly conferring their patronage on the Muslim chiefs, the unionists had aligned themselves with them against their rebellious Tigray [*tigre*].'[29]

In the wake of what they saw as a unionist invasion, more educated and enlightened members of the various *kebilas* resident in Keren and other urban centres descended on *tigre* villages with anti-unionist and anti-Ethiopian messages. In one of his trips into the Keren countryside, Trevaskis came across meetings where merchants and teachers of the Asfeda lectured their fellow *kebila* members on the dangers looming at them. Their message was that, since the *shumagille* had chosen to side with the Abyssinian unbelievers, they could not be considered Muslim. They were 'Kaffirs' who had to be confronted in the name of Islam.[30]

Condemnation of the *kentabai* and his *shumagille* allies spread throughout the serf areas, and the feudal system of administration began to weaken. According to Trevaskis, the Native Courts were barely functioning; taxes were not being collected; schools, health clinics and schemes were suffering from neglect. 'Every rule in the book, from deforestation to smuggling, was being broken with impunity ... I should have been overwhelmed by depression. In fact, I could not have been happier. The seemingly impossible had happened. The Muslims had come to political life.'[31]

Trevaskis was confident that the serf uprising could be directed towards the partition project with which he was becoming obsessed. When the *qadi* (religious judge) of Keren, Musa Umron, arrived at his office at the head of a delegation of Tigre leaders and elders, he received them graciously. The *qadi* told him that they had come to voice their concerns about the unionist (Abyssinian) invasion of Keren and the propaganda that Eritrea would be handed over to Ethiopia. They needed assurances from him that Britain would not betray Muslim Eritreans and deliver them to Ethiopian control. Trevaskis replied that he did not have the authority to give such assurances; Eritrea's fate was to be decided by the Allies and it was possible that they could decide in Ethiopia's favour. 'Every face in the room except one registered wild-eyed consternation,' Trevaskis wrote. He then described what the odd man out did next.

> 'You hypocrites!' a personage named Ibrahim Sultan raved. 'You say you respect the Atlantic Charter and yet you look on us as nothing more than a baggage in the caravans of our feudal oppressors!' A good deal more followed in tones of stinging insolence. I stood as much of it as I could and then rose to my feet, bade the Qadi a curt good-bye and stalked off in dudgeon.[32]

After an hour, Musa Umron, and Ibrahim Sultan came back to offer an apology, which Trevaskis accepted. Ibrahim then went straight down to business and asked for a small favour in return for the establishment of an 'anti-Ethiopian Muslim party', whose desirability Trevaskis had hinted at. The favour was for the Administration to commit itself to the emancipation of the *tigre* from the rule of the *shumagille*. What Ibrahim proposed was the restoration of the old Tigre tribes (*kebilas*) to the status they had held before being 'conquered, carved up and distributed as serfs amongst the ancestors of the *Kentabai*, *Diglel* and all the rest of the feudal chiefs'. To allay Trevaskis's scepticism, Ibrahim assured him that all the preparatory work had been taken care of, apparently, by the *kebila* meetings.

Ibrahim's plan was nothing short of a revolution. The Tigre *kebilas* were to have their own chiefs. To avoid fragmentation, smaller *kebilas* would join larger, related ones or merge with *kebilas* of corresponding size in some loose union. The old *shumagille* houses would then be reduced to mere *kebilas* minus the feudal powers they had wielded over their serfs.

When Trevaskis presented the proposal to Benoy, he omitted Ibrahim's plan to use it as a basis for the establishment of a Muslim political party. Instead, he presented it as a possible solution to the chaos and unrest that was gripping the *metahit.* Benoy was unconvinced, arguing that supporting the *shumagille* and maintaining the status quo would be more of a guarantee of stability than the drastic changes being proposed. Instead of an outright rejection, he demanded a complete and detailed account of the proposal.[33]

Benoy's directive would have led to an impasse. However, events in the *kebessa* were having a direct impact on developments in the *metahit.* Unionist demonstrations and attacks on Arab and Jeberti shops, as well as the intervention by Sudanese troops already mentioned, were fuelling religious sensibilities. Above all, the blood spilled by the Sudanese in the July riots had earned them the hatred of Christian activists in the unionist camp and the resentment of the population in general. The conflict between the two could only escalate.

A Massacre in Asmera

On 28 August 1946, a simple argument over a game of cards between Eritreans and some Sudanese soldiers led to a fight in which one of the latter was killed. About an hour later, a company of fully armed Sudanese soldiers left their barracks in Asmera, ran to where they believed Christian Eritreans lived, and started shooting anyone in sight. About seventy Eritreans, three of them Muslims caught in the crossfire, and three Sudanese died that afternoon. Several Sudanese were also injured. The Administration declared three days of mourning and Benoy announced that he was setting up a fund to help the families of the victims.[34]

The most bizarre aspect of the BMA's behaviour on the day of the massacre was that neither the Eritrean police nor British troops were sent to intervene and stop the carnage. Sergeant Major (*Shambel Basha*) Kidane Kelib was on duty that day. When fist fights broke out over the card game, he said,

> someone ran to the barracks and told Sudanese soldiers that one of their members had died. The English called us, all the Eritreans on duty, to a building near St Mary's Church belonging to the Arab businessman, Bahubeshi. There were about two

> hundred of us. From there, we could hear shots being fired from the direction of Aba Shawl. People running away from the shooting told us that the Sudanese were killing innocent people. This was in mid-afternoon. The shooting continued until dusk. We were under orders to sit it through. There was nothing that we could do.[35]

Police inaction, which the Asmera population regarded as a deliberate move to fuel religious tensions, sent a wave of anger throughout the country. The funeral ceremony for sixty victims at the St Mary cemetery attracted tens of thousands of 'highly excited mourners'. The atmosphere was menacingly hostile when an apprehensive Chief Administrator Benoy arrived accompanied by Hugh Senior, the political secretary, and his assistant, Edward Ullendorff. According to Ullendorff, *Abune* Markos delivered a funeral oration in which he addressed Benoy directly:

> We Abyssinians had longed for the British to come and liberate us from the Fascist yoke. We had trusted you to lead us to freedom. But what have you done? You have given us the freedom to die ... Neither the Italians nor the British, in whom we had believed, will help us. So, we must return to our Mother Ethiopia who will receive her Eritrean children with open arms. The only demand we make of you now is: kill sixty Sudanese troops as they have killed our innocent brethren. Will you promise that?

In the ensuing exchange of words, Benoy tried to explain publicly that guilt had to be determined before the death sentence could be carried out on any of the perpetrators. Observing that the crowd was getting hostile, Benoy suddenly gave a military salute to the coffin nearest to him. With Senior and Ullendorff following suit, he repeated the gesture at every coffin. 'This exceptional mark of respect by a red-tabbed general and Governor to a humble Abyssinian, indeed to all the anonymous victims,' wrote Ullendorff, 'made a deep impression on the Abuna and the large concourse of people. By a hardly perceptible gesture, the Abuna signalled to those nearest to us to let us go ... we breathed a sigh of relief.'[36]

The next day, Benoy invited the Asmera community leadership for consultations. *Abune* Markos and Ibrahim Mukhtar, *Mufti* of Eritrea, were among those invited. Benoy expressed his regret at the incident and offered his condolences to the bereaved families. *Dejazmatch* (later *Ras*) Beyene Beraki, the emerging senior leader of the unionists, demanded that the perpetrators be brought to justice. Weldeab Weldemariam, editor of *ESG* at the time, told Benoy that what had happened the day before was neither spontaneous nor surprising; as the outcome of a biased administration, it was to be expected. He continued:

> I don't believe that the Administration ordered the killings directly. But I cannot help wondering why a month ago British troops ran to the rescue of Arab shops from stone-throwing crowds; and why the English chose not to be so prompt and decisive when innocent Eritrean blood was being shed without restraint. If peace is to reign in our country, stop administering us by aliens and parasites. Let us manage ourselves under your guidance.[37]

Given his position in the Administration, this was probably as far as Weldeab could go. As adamant as the day before, Markos said, 'This is not how you repay a people who cheered and ululated to welcome you. We know how you care for pheasants and partridges; how come you denied safety and defence to human beings created in God's image?'[38] Markos did not stop there. Although he contributed 300 shillings to the fund established by Benoy, he issued secret directives to members of his church and the victims' families not to accept 'blood money from their killers'. Once again, Benoy was on the defensive. 'The fund we have established has not been accepted. I have noted the reasons for this. I feel that the persons who have ordered the boycott are hurting those who stand to benefit from the assistance.' He repeated his denial that his Administration had been involved in the killings.[39]

Markos's tough action was probably coordinated with the Ethiopian liaison officer. In October 1946, Emperor Haile Selassie sent 40,000 shillings to be distributed to the 'families of those who had died or sustained injuries in the incident'. Benoy accepted the grant on behalf of the victims.[40] As Nega handed out money in the name of his emperor, Benoy and his Administration were left out in the cold. Ethiopia thus consolidated its foothold, enabling it to expand its activities inside Eritrea.

Later, a commission of inquiry was set up and eight Sudanese were charged with murder. An additional sixty were detained for acts endangering public security. The Military Court was chaired by Major General Steiner, Commander of the Sudan Defence Force. In its verdict of 19 December 1946, the court concluded that the perpetrators of the killings could not be identified individually. Seven of the accused were acquitted. The rest were sentenced to prison terms ranging from nine months to fifteen years.[41] The tribunal's verdict never measured up to the seriousness of the crimes committed. Even the removal of Sudanese soldiers from Eritrea and their replacement by British contingents who had fought under General Montgomery in North Africa could not rectify the damage that had already been done.[42]

Benoy did not last much longer in his job. Although his apology and personal show of sorrow and sympathy did help in cooling Eritrean tempers, his colleagues and superiors in Khartoum and Cairo felt that he had compromised British dignity. As Trevaskis put it, 'Poor Benoy earned no marks for "playing fair" by Abyssinians—they were not "our chaps".' He was removed at the end of the year.[43]

Serf Emancipation

Back in Keren, the shock waves of the August massacre in Asmera reverberated for a long time. Ibrahim Sultan was vocal in declaring openly, even to Trevaskis, that the whole event had been a British plot. Trevaskis did not seem much concerned with the issue of who was to blame for what had happened. Benoy's departure, and his replacement by an acting officer of lower rank pending the arrival of a successor, gave him the opportunity to lay out the basis for the reorganisation of the Tigre *kebilas*.

Along with Ibrahim, who had already taken care of most of the preliminary tasks of identifying and grouping the *kebilas*, he employed as assistants Omer Hassano and Saleh Hinit, who were to become prominent figures in the Eritrean and Ethiopian governments, respectively, in the years to follow.

Kebila reorganisation was a daunting task, as 123 separate units claimed equal status. If splinter groups and clans were added to them, the number could rise to 230. To reduce such fragmentation, it was proposed that a group had to consist of at least 1,000 souls for it to be accepted as a viable social or political unit. Only a few could meet this criterion. By joining smaller groups together and merging others into larger units, the number was reduced to 23 *kebilas* of over 1,000 people each. The largest *kebila* became the 23,328-strong Almeda of Barka. The former *shumagille kebila* of Ad Tekles in Sahel was the smallest with only 1,050 individuals. Spread out as they were in Sahel, Barka and Semhar, the Almeda numbered in total 41,401 persons. The Asfeda, another *kebila* with a presence in the three provinces, numbered 18,007.[44] Although the reorganisation was worked out over the next two years, Ibrahim and his friends had already galvanised popular support for the idea.

Kebila consent was quickly achieved on the basic issues. Once the removal of *shumagille* rule was assured, however, the question of *kebila* leadership threatened to disrupt the process. Saleh Hinit suggested that the teachers, businessmen and other urban dwellers who had been campaigning for serf freedom should be appointed by the Administration. Surprisingly, this found acceptance by the *kebila* leadership. With that hurdle out of the way, serf emancipation and the relegation of *shumagille kebilas* to the level of their former serfs started in earnest.

As he was the driving force behind serf freedom, Ibrahim's prestige and acceptability within the Tigre communities rose considerably. Since the persons slated for appointment as *kebila* chiefs were his friends and messengers, his leadership became indisputable. Sometime in the second half of 1946, Ibrahim informed Trevaskis of his intention to form a Muslim League of Eritrea and said he was organising it in imitation of Ali Jinnah's movement of the same name in Pakistan. Jinnah was then working for the separation of Pakistan from India. Ever on the lookout for Muslim moves that smacked of partition, Trevaskis gave his consent.[45]

Ibrahim and his followers spent most of 1946 criss-crossing Eritrea to whip up Muslim support for their movement. They generally met with success, but lack of funds began to threaten their progress. When Ibrahim's attempt to obtain British financing failed, he travelled to Egypt for the same purpose. The Egyptians turned him away with nothing more than words of encouragement and political support.

Fortunately for the Muslim League, the unionists unwittingly provided the elusive financial source. Just as they had driven *tigre* serfs to the independence camp by winning the *shumagille* over to their side, unionist attacks on the persons and property of the Jeberti drove a majority of their businessmen to sign up for membership in the League. They provided most of the funds that Ibrahim and colleagues were looking for.[46] Finally, the Muslim League of Eritrea (MLE) could be formally inaugurated.

Thus far, BMA officials had not received any confirmation from the founders that the Muslim League would spearhead their partition plan. In late 1946, Trevaskis called on Ibrahim to ask him bluntly what the objective of the League was. '"Independence!" he said with a touch of defiance in his eyes,' wrote Trevaskis. '"Yes, yes!" he went on as if I had disagreed with him.'[47] Not only did Ibrahim mean what he told Trevaskis, but he was then actually making preparations for a huge inaugural congress of his newly formed organisation. That should have ended any hopes for the British partition plan. But Trevaskis was so committed to the old Newbold project that he immediately began to seek ways of dividing the League's base right at the outset.

Meanwhile, other events in Eritrea had a direct bearing on the progress of the formation of the Muslim League.

The Bet Giorgis Convention

Prelude to the Wa'ela

The August massacre led to more violence on the streets and neighbourhoods of Asmera. At the same time, the imminent establishment of the Muslim League (ML) predictably aroused the unionists into a state of agitation and extreme anger. Barely two weeks after the Sudanese shootings, on 10 September 1946, the Jeberti leader *Dejazmatch* Hassen Ali survived a bomb attack. In the same week, another prominent Jeberti personality, *Haji* Imam Musa, survived a similar attempt on his life.[48]

These attacks were the direct product of a furious propaganda campaign launched against the ML by unionist leaders. One of these, Tedla Bairu, who left his senior advisory position in the BMA to join the leadership of the unionists sometime in September, demanded 'the immediate proscription of the League on the grounds that Ibrahim was exploiting religion for his own malign political purposes'.[49] Perhaps the best-educated and best-qualified person of his time, Tedla Bairu was a significant catch for the unionists. Although his condemnation of Ibrahim for playing the religious card fell flat in the face of his own 'shameless campaign under the banner of the Coptic Church', he was still a voice to reckon with.[50] In the frenzied atmosphere of ethnic and religious contention and acrimony that gripped Eritrean politics, his words could only fire up his followers.

Two successive events helped electrify the highly charged political atmosphere. First, was the Paris Peace Conference, which decided to refer the case of the former Italian colonies to the Four Great Powers on 25 September 1946, just one month after the Asmera massacre. The second factor was Benoy's tour of the country in the following October, announcing the BMA's decision to allow Eritreans to form political organisations working towards the country's future.

The ever-widening gap between the unionist and independence camps, and the violent reaction towards the impending establishment of the ML, prompted moderate politicians from both sides to seek a middle ground. As the editor of *ESG* and the translator of Longrigg's article on the partition of Eritrea, Weldeab Weldemariam was well aware that the irreconcilability of unionism and independence and the threat of a Muslim–Christian division would eventually serve British designs. Weldeab approached Gebremeskel Weldu, president of MFH, a committed unionist who was uncomfortable with the idea of an immediate and unconditional union. He sought a more dignified union, one that gave due consideration to Eritrea's history and colonial experience. They agreed that the preservation of Eritrea as a unitary country was non-negotiable. 'Now is the time to salvage Eritrea or lose it,' they said to each other. They then discussed the possibility of both sides sacrificing some part of their respective positions—for full independence and unconditional union—and meet halfway. They drafted a thirteen-point proposal fashioned after the Canadian and Australian models of a commonwealth and took it to their colleagues for consultation.

Leaders from both sides accepted the idea with enthusiasm. The mood and tone of the political dialogue softened considerably from vitriol to a polite exchange of views. In a thoughtful article published in *ESG* on 17 October 1946, *Blata* Mohammed Omer Qadi, one of the most ardent advocates of conditional union with Ethiopia, re-set the tone of the discussion. He advised that politics and political participation demanded deeper knowledge and education. In an apparent hit at traditional chiefs who were clamouring for leadership, he wrote that proper leadership could only come from a free people exercising their democratic rights in free elections. He was particularly critical of the manner in which political parties were being established and the unhealthy relationship developing between them.[51] Stressing the importance of tolerance for the other point of view, Omer Qadi wrote, 'The politics of a nation or a people is not based on the deeds and privileges of the self-serving few, who would use it for personal gain. Only if the participation of members of the parties and associations is guaranteed will politics benefit the people and obtain a national character.'[52]

Weldeab echoed Omer Qadi's appeal for unity. In one of his most eloquent pieces of writing, he called for the cohesion and unity of the people and territory of Eritrea to be maintained. He argued that Ethiopia's main aim was not the acquisition of the land and resources of Eritrea, as it had wider expanses of land and far richer assets than Eritrea had to offer. He enumerated, instead, what he thought Ethiopia was really after—the people of Eritrea, whose attributes he claimed were those of lawfulness, cooperation, a sense of sympathy and empathy; a spirit of liberty born of a genuine hatred of domination and enslavement; a sense of sacrifice for the common good; and the quality of mercy and self-restraint. Such a people, he argued, should not be denied the right of weighing the advantages and disadvantages of the choices open to them. They should not be forced to accept union with Ethiopia as the 'one and only' political solution.

Like Omer Qadi and Gebremeskel Weldu, Weldeab would not trust traditional chiefs with responsibility for Eritrea's future. Over the previous half a century, the people of Eritrea had created 'one belongingness, one history, and one name. If this history continues, it will serve the country's greatness and honour.' Like most *kebessa* activists, however, Weldeab was alarmed by the emergence of the Muslim League. In the same article, he wrote:

> We hear and read allegations that Muslim rights and dignity have been curtailed; that there is no body that would protect those interests. This is the kind of thinking that throws the road to destruction wide open. I believe that, up to now, the people of Eritrea are sharing whatever they possess without showing any sign of splitting. If the apprehension is that such partiality may come in the future, the better option is for the people of *metahit* to work towards the institution of a parliament that will guarantee their rights. As for the elders and prominent personalities who are resigned to accept 'whatever fate dictates', they should know that that is not an honourable stand and that God or Allah will one day take them to task.[53]

This opinion was shared by a majority of those involved in the discussions preceding the *wa'ela* or convention at Bet Giorgis. Besides Gebremeskel, Weldeab and Omer Qadi, *Blata* Demsas, chief of Aba Shawl; *Kegnazmatch* Berhanu Ahmeddin, chief of Geza Berhanu; *Dejazmatch* Abraha Tessema; *Fitawrari* Hadgu Ghilagaber, chief of Seharti district; and the businessman and future mayor of Asmera, *Fitawrari* Haregot Abbay, were involved in the preparations. On 16 November 1946, a preliminary meeting was held between them amid the trees of the Bet Giorgis park. A draft agreement for presentation at the projected convention was approved without much disagreement. This contained provisions that guaranteed Eritrea's autonomy within a union with Ethiopia; the right of its citizens to exercise their respective religions and develop their various languages; the rights to a free press, the establishment of political parties and the preservation of democratic rights; and the rule of law. The convention was scheduled for the morning of 24 November.[54]

Trouble at Bet Giorgis

In the eight days between the preparatory meeting and the convention, major changes took place within the unionist camp. Both Weldeab and Trevaskis have said that the move for a united stand by both contending Eritrean parties alarmed the Ethiopians into quick and decisive action. Nega Haileselassie, who had been away in Addis Ababa, immediately returned to Asmera, where he was followed by *Tsehafe Te'ezaz* Weldegiorgis's friend and representative in Tigray, Abraha Weldetatios. Weldeab has claimed that the latter came with luggage stuffed with money and hand grenades.[55]

On the night of Saturday, 23 November, the eve of the convention, the unionists held a secret meeting where they entered into a long and bitter discussion. Present at this meeting were all the major leaders of the faction, including Nega and Abraha Weldetatios. All eyes focused on Gebremeskel Weldu, joint organiser of the following day's convention. After having delivered the MFH to the unionists and, by means of his erudition and powerful writing, articulated the philosophy of unionism, he was severely criticised for his new stance. A convention for 'conditional union', he was told, was a betrayal of the principles for which he had been elected president. As a reprimand for his 'transgression', Gebremeskel was ordered not to address the convention the next morning. That honour and responsibility was awarded to the rising star, Tedla Bairu. No one, including those who had supported him throughout the past weeks, came to Gebremeskel's rescue.[56]

The next day, neither Weldeab nor his colleagues in the independence camp were aware of the events of the previous night. They were first to arrive at the appointed time. The majority were Muslim, but with the addition of a sizable Christian presence. The unionists came well past the appointed hour of 10 am. They were led by their honorary leader, Beyene Beraki, followed by Demsas, Gebremeskel and Tedla Bairu. Besides the agreed number of participants, the unionists brought with them about thirty young men, members of the newly organised unionist youth movement called Andinet—Amharic for 'unity' or 'oneness'.

As soon as they took their assigned seats, Demsas, one of the main supporters and organisers of the convention, rose to speak. 'Our brothers,' he begun, 'you who claim to be the sons of independence, you are making a big mistake. When you join your parents, you don't enter into a contract or convention with them. Ethiopia is our father and mother. Abandon this idea of independence. Come join us; unite with us. This is all we have to say to you.'

'One by one they rose and repeated Demsas's words,' Weldeab said. 'At last, when Gebremeskel Weldu himself joined in the chorus, we realised that things had gone terribly wrong. Next arose friction between Tedla and myself. Andinet youths had surrounded us. They were armed and in a state of agitation. We felt that trouble was imminent. My independence friends pushed me away into a car and drove me to the meadows of Adi Nefas nearby. We ran away, really. We returned home after dark.'[57]

In his interviews, Weldeab never disclosed the background to his quarrels with Tedla. In 1976, he told this writer that he and Tedla had met in Sweden in the sixties and agreed never to speak ill of each other. Both kept that promise. Luckily for the history books, their heated exchange at Bet Giorgis, expressing their respective versions, was published in subsequent issues of *ESG*.

According to Weldeab's version, following Demsas, Gebremeskel and a few others, Tedla Bairu rose to declare that, as an Eritrean by birth, it was his right to speak out. Addressing Weldeab directly, he continued, 'You, *Ato* Weldeab Weldemariam, you are from Tigray. You are a Tigrayan. We all know that. Why do you keep proposing first trusteeship and now conditional union for our country, Eritrea! As if Eritrea is a toy to play with!'

Weldeab was a seasoned writer and an effective orator who could charm audiences and disarm opponents. He was also a polemicist with a tongue and pen that could spit back as much venom as was directed against him. As he paused before responding to Tedla, he wrote, he could see Tedla beaming with a sense of triumph. 'But I was wondering at the kind of spirit that was possessing some people ... I was saying to myself, "If not the people assembled here, then who would be the right person to speak on behalf of Eritrea?"' He rose to speak:

> If a 'Tigrayan' means a man who is not under the pay of two masters; if it means a man who does not betray his comrades or speak with two tongues; and since a 'Tigrayan' is the offspring of kings, dukes and noblemen; then, I told him, I would accept the 'insult' happily and with pride. In case he wanted to partake of the bounties of my ancestors, I detailed for him the origin and expanse of my paternal and maternal lines. However, I also pointed out the inappropriateness of discussing mundane topics of race and origin in a meeting where great men and dignitaries were assembled to discuss national issues. Digging into race and origin may unearth some unpleasant details that are best left aside for the moment.[58]

Weldeab's words contained a veiled attack on Tedla's character, integrity and even the veracity of his ancestral claims. They obviously angered his armed followers, who made a move to harm him, thereby disrupting the convention.

A few days later, an indignant Tedla Bairu told his side of the story, contradicting Weldeab's account of what happened between them at the convention.

> What I said was as follows, '*Ato* Weldeab Weldemariam, we all know that your country is in Ethiopia, in Tigray. You have your own flag and king, and you are independent. We too are Ethiopians, but we live under the administration of a government and a king who do not belong to us. As an Ethiopian, why don't you wish for us the privileges of freedom and flag that you enjoy? Why don't you tell us to obtain our freedom without preconditions? Why do you keep creating obstacles with your constant shifts between trusteeship and conditional union?'[59]

However that exchange is recalled in the history books, it sounded the death knell for any hopes of a reconciliation between the antagonistic parties. Soon after the convention, and under instructions from Nega Haileselassie, Gebremeskel Weldu was replaced by Tedla Bairu as secretary general. As Trevaskis put it, 'The party leaders were no longer free agents. They had become servants of the Ethiopian Government.'[60]

5

ERITREAN POLITICAL PARTIES

The Muslim League

In a major interview he gave in 1982, Ibrahim Sultan recalled that he and his colleagues arrived late at the convention at Bet Giorgis. They were sitting on the sidelines when the quarrel between Tedla and Weldeab flared up. As they rose to leave, he said, Demsas and Hagos Gebre ran up to them to apologise.

> 'We made a mistake,' they told us. 'We should have asked our Muslim brothers to speak. Now, Ibrahim, please say something.'
>
> 'I have nothing to say,' I told them. 'We just arrived from our journey; we do not represent Muslims. The Muslims are not here. The *kentabai* of Bet Asghede, the *kentabais* and *shums* of the Bilen, Mensa'e and Marya are not here; the *diglel* of Beni Amer, the *shums* of the Nara and Kunama and the *naib*s of Massawa and Semhar are not present; neither are the chiefs of the Saho—the Assaorta and the Minifere—amongst you; the same with the *shums* of Denkalia and the Jeberti. We can only speak for ourselves. Suspend this convention and call another meeting where everyone may be represented.'
>
> As the elders were listening quietly, a young man nearby sprang up to me and shouted, '*Wedi* [son of] Sultan, this is all *fesseria*, pure nonsense. How many Muslims, cattle and camel herders; how many *bedew* [derogatory term for nomads] are we to entertain here? Whatever we decide, the Muslims will accept by force. Whatever we say, they follow; whatever we do, they also do!'
>
> 'Right now, I cannot exchange insults with you, I am overpowered,' I answered. 'We are only ten or twenty, you are hundreds. Do as you see fit. Then come and try to stuff your will down our Muslim throats. I wish you good luck.'[1]

None of the former unionists who were interviewed for this book would confirm that such an exchange took place at Bet Giorgis. While they would not rule out the possibility of some overzealous youths overstepping the mark, they rejected the suggestion that unionist leaders would condone such gross behaviour. First, major Muslim figures like Ahmed Kekia Pasha, *Sheik* Suleiman Aldin and others were sitting right there at the convention, on the unionist side. Secondly, they were courting the likes of Ibrahim to join them and so would not possibly tolerate such behaviour. As we will see, Andinet youths were also badgering the unionist elders.

Whatever the case, Ibrahim recounted how, after his experience at the convention, he went straight to an office he kept at the Asmera Chamber of Commerce. Beginning with the holy phrase *Bismillah al Rahman al Raheem* (In the name of Allah, the Most Gracious, the Most Merciful), he wrote the draft programme of Al Rabita al Islamia al Eritrea (henceforth, Al Rabita or the Muslim League (ML)). He took his draft for comments to Abdelkader Kebire and *Sheik* Suleiman Ahmed, brother of *Mufti* Ibrahim Mukhtar. Together, they met the *mufti* himself and *Dejazmatch* Hassen Ali, both of whom gave their blessing. The idea of a Muslim movement had been brewing, not only among the *tigre* of Sahel and Barka as we have seen, but also among Muslim youths in Asmera. In 1944, for example, they had formed a self-help association and held secret discussions on the status and future of Eritrean Muslims. In an article he wrote in 1947, Hassen Ali confirmed that such an association had existed and that the name of Al Rabita al Islamia had been suggested at the time and also gained the approval of Muslim leaders in Asmera.[2]

At Ibrahim's suggestion, a meeting of Muslim representatives from all over the country was scheduled for 3 December 1946 in Keren, where the programme of the ML was approved. *Said* Bekri al Mirghani, spiritual leader of the Khatmiya, was elected president and Ibrahim Sultan became the secretary general. A date was set for an enlarged conference of Muslim representatives and the formal inauguration of the league on 20–1 January 1947.[3]

As expected, it did not take long for Muslim leaders to be besieged by nervous calls and appeals to desist from taking measures that would fuel religious discord. Many argued that a separate Muslim party could easily play into the hands of the British with their partition plan. In one of its earliest issues, the ML's paper, *Saut al Rabit*a, stated that 'the propaganda of the mid-1940s for delivering Eritrea to Abyssinia had been too powerful' for Muslims to take lightly. The call by wise leaders for a 'correct and balanced vision' had not been heeded. Instead, the paper explained, 'The activists, whose political stand does not allow debate and progress, kept pressuring Muslims to fall into line. They tried to pull them along. That is why Muslims decided to take their own stand. As a result, Al Rabita was formed in Keren.' Besides internal pressure, continued the paper, the most frightening aspect of unionism for Muslims came from their perception of the treatment of Muslims in Ethiopia. They were a 'degraded and neglected' people with only one Muslim sitting in the Ethiopian parliament. 'They have no representation, no Muslim ministers, governors or any high official. No Muslim at all.'[4]

Perhaps the people most concerned were the protagonists of the Eritrea for Eritreans movement, in which Muslims formed a majority. Alarmed that a Muslim split would greatly curtail the power and effectiveness of the independence camp, a group of their leaders, including *Ras* Tessema, approached Ibrahim for an explanation. Ibrahim gave his assurances.

> Let us do what *Abune* Markos did. He said in our very presence, 'My people, the Muslims are after your rank, status, honour and seat. They are seeking to share and take away the saddle on which you rode for three thousand years. Beware, Christians ...'
>
> I say, let us do as he did. The unionists brought the Coptic Church and *Abune* Markos and called for union. We do the same. We call our party Al Rabita al Islamia and bring all the *tigre* to our side. In the name of Islam, we line up the Mirghanis [a powerful Sunni Muslim family] and the *sheiks* in our ranks.[5]

According to Ibrahim, the blessing that his side received from Tessema and his followers became the basis for the future alliance and unity between the parties. The Muslim–Christian alliance for independence was certainly strongest in the Akeleguzai province, where the Saho and their Christian neighbours lived alongside each other. Seyoum Maasho, later secretary general of Eritrea for Eritreans, or the Liberal Progressive Party (LPP) as it became known, recalled how Muslim leaders of the province came to their Christian counterparts to explain why they were joining the ML.

> 'We are using Islam as a rallying cause, not to separate ourselves from you,' they told us. 'We have already vowed to each other, eaten meat from the same plate, for unity. We have no reasons to separate. Religious division is coming to us from Ethiopia. We need Al Rabita to strengthen our common cause.'
>
> We told them, 'We cannot tell you what to do or not to do. As long as we are still within the same principle, we are in no position to interfere with your decision.'[6]

Ultimately, the leadership of Eritrea for Eritreans, albeit reluctantly, resigned itself to the ML's existence. It was, after all, in the process of growing into the largest and most powerful independence movement in the country.

The Muslim League Inaugurated

On 20–21 January 1947, the Muslim League of Eritrea was officially inaugurated at a rally in Keren. Ibrahim Sultan had promised the British official Trevaskis that he would give the unionists in Asmera 'something to think about'. He was as good as his word, Trevaskis wrote:

> He put on a Hollywood style spectacular. Two thousand sword-waving, camel-borne Bedouin led a procession of ten thousand slowly round the streets of Keren chanting 'Hurya, Hurya—Independence, Independence!' It was the right thing to shout, even if those who shouted it meant independence from their feudal overlords ... There was only one minor hiccup. The Mirghani, who had been elected President of the League out of respect for his name and position, did not turn up.[7]

Bekri al Mirghani, whom Trevaskis alludes to, did not last long as president of the ML. There would come a time when he defected to the unionists, only to return later to the ML.

In the opposing camp, the ML became the focus for unionists determined to nip it in the bud. A strong propaganda campaign depicting it as an anti-nationalist, religious and sectarian movement dominated the discourse of those weeks and months in 1946 and early 1947. Leaders of the ML were portrayed as traitors ready to sell Eritrea to the Arabs and as jihadists bent on Islamising the people. The invective reached a peak with the publication of ML's programme. The main tenets of the programme were maintenance of the territorial integrity of Eritrea; UN trusteeship under a British Administration, pending independence after ten years; categorical rejection of any form of union with Ethiopia; free election of 'the learned and the wise' to help administer the trusteeship; and the presentation of the programme to their 'Christian brothers' for consent.

The fourth of the seven articles of the programme became the most controversial as it called for 'Muslim brothers who have been separated from Eritrea, to return to it with their land'.[8] Confusion spread throughout the unionist and independence camps. Which 'Muslim brothers' were being invited to return with their land? Was the ML, asked the polemicist and future editor of the unionist paper *Ethiopia*, *Azmatch* Gebremikael Gurmu, 'opening Eritrean borders for Arab invasion? Are we to welcome in snakes and pythons? ... Are we to share our little plots of land with them and will they leave our descendants in peace?'[9]

The ML's ambiguous explanations about what their controversial article really meant were not helpful. Even Weldeab Weldemariam voiced his discomfort, not only with article 4, but also with the idea of a separate Muslim organisation in principle. Teaming up with Gebremeskel Habtemariam, leader of the unionists in Addis Ababa, he attempted to set matters straight at Bet Giorgis. Writing under various pen names, Weldeab not only expressed his fears that ML might be playing the partition game, but as a result of his own ambivalence in those testing days, he also appeared to lean towards the unionists.[10] In a series of five articles entitled '*Ertra Nmen*—Eritrea for Whom?' which appeared in the *ESG* from 17 April to 19 May 1947, he made a ringing defence of the factors that justified Ethiopia's claims to Eritrea, thus exasperating his friends and delighting the unionists. Only in the last article of the series did he dispel any notion of betrayal when he declared that any consideration of union with Ethiopia had to be preceded by Eritrea's full independence and a free referendum by its people to choose that path. Should that not succeed, he concluded, then Tigray and Eritrea should be given administrative, political and cultural autonomy within an Ethiopian union.[11]

Both sides were infuriated by what many saw as Weldeab's deliberate and provocative shifts between the two positions; the Muslim League above all. His colleague at Bet Giorgis, Berhanu Ahmeddin, voiced the ML's sentiments when he made a scathing criticism of Weldeab's use of pseudonyms to attack the league. Berhanu wrote:

> No one believes you when you call us 'a Muslim Government' ... We are a league, not a government. If we write in Arabic, it is only because we studied in Arabic; it is just like you using the European calendar for your dates. We have no dirt to conceal ... We have devised nothing aimed at establishing an Islamic government or ceding land to Sudan. However, if there are land and people across our borders that belong to us, we will not hesitate to claim them.[12]

The meaning of article 4 of the ML's programme remained unclear until the league's representatives clarified it before the Four Power Commission of Inquiry at the end of 1947. They said they had been referring all along to the Beja peoples living across the border in Sudan. As extensions of the Beni Amer and the Hidareb, the ML was seeking their inclusion in an expanded Eritrea.[13] This was a naive idea that showed the ML leadership's lack of understanding of international law, and, if anything, the clarification played into the hands of the ML's critics who denounced it as expansionist and bent on increasing the Muslim population to secure domination over Christians.

The ML's explanations would not dispel the suspicions and accusations directed against it. Perhaps the most eloquent and convincing defence of the ML's intentions came in a letter that Abdelkader Kebire wrote to a friend in Australia in 1948. This only came into the public domain in 1997 when the news website Dehai published an English translation of the original. As a private communication between Muslim friends, the credibility of its contents cannot be impugned. The aim of the ML, Kebire wrote,

> is not to repress our Christian compatriots or to expand Islam. It is rather to reject the very idea of a federal union with Ethiopia in all its forms and shapes. When the All-Hearing Allah has provided us with the power to reason, how can we unite with the oppressive and tyrannical Ethiopia?
>
> Are we not witnessing the condition of the 10 million alienated and muffled Ethiopian Muslims? We have, therefore, united as one and are determined to demand and defend our rights to the death. We will neither apologize for nor compromise our principles. God forbid, should we not succeed, at least, our objective will be known to Allah and his creatures and history will duly record it ...
>
> ... [Muslims] will pay a price; but it will not be the price of a cheap commodity. It will be their dearest and priceless possession, blood. It will be paid to occupy a page in the chapters of the international struggle for justice. The ultimate objective is to secure justice or to die in the process.
>
> Please, do not forget the following Italian proverb, '*Meglio vivere un giorno da leone che cent'anni da pecora* (Better live one day a lion than a hundred years a lamb).'[14]

Subsequent measures taken by the ML to ensure the unity of the independence camp bear out Kebire's assertions. In view of what he was to face in less than two years' time, his words were chillingly prophetic.

The Unionist Party

There is a tendency in some nationalist Eritrean literature to dismiss the unionist leadership and the Unionist Party (UP) in general as a collection of people motivated by personal interest. Whereas personal interest is often difficult to separate from principled political positions, such blanket judgements do not help in understanding the unionist phenomenon, a fact of Eritrean history that decided the fate of the nation for the following half a century.

Fifty years of Italian rule had completely cut off Eritreans from Ethiopia. The great majority of Eritreans thus had very little knowledge of what life in that country was like or would be like. The few who escaped from Italian rule into Ethiopia had mostly been accepted warmly and given education, rank and position and, as we saw earlier, they served Haile Selassie as leading agents and propagandists. A large part of the *kebessa* Christians swallowed the propagandists' image of a holy Ethiopia, led by a holy man, whose only motivation was the welfare of his people, including Eritreans. The UP produced polemicists like Gebremikael Gurmu, Gebreyohannes Tesfamariam and Teweldeberhan Gebremedhin (Zekios), who never refrained from vouching for Ethiopia in a manner that even the Ethiopians found hard to emulate. In almost every article written by unionists, Ethiopia, religion and spiritual salvation were synonymous.

On 5 December 1946, the unionist leadership met for the formal institution of the party. Just back from another visit to Addis Ababa, *Abune* Markos read out the names of 42 persons whom he installed as members of the higher council of the UP. *Ras* Kidanemariam of Areza, in the province of Seraye, was made honorary president. Already in his mid-eighties, he had distinguished himself as an Italian askari commander in the Battle of Adwa. *Dejazmatch* (later *Ras*) Beyene Beraki of Asmera was named president and Saleh Kekia Pasha vice president. Kekia was the same businessman from Hirgigo who had collaborated with Weldeab, Abraha Tessema, Omer Sefaf and others in the initial formation of Eritrea for Eritreans. They were all handpicked; no election was held.[15]

In his maiden speech, Kidanemariam likened Eritrea to the mosquito that appealed to God for the restoration of its clipped wing. Rejecting God's offer of a bounty of wealth and gold in lieu of its severed part, it won its wing back and flew away happily. Eritrea, he said, was in the same position. As a clipped-off wing of Ethiopia, it was seeking nothing more than reattachment to the body of which it had been part.[16]

On 29 December, the three top leaders of the UP met to name Tedla Bairu secretary general.[17] On 4 January 1947, the first issue of the unionist newspaper,

Ethiopia, was published. Tedla Bairu himself edited the first fourteen issues of the paper until Gebremikael Gurmu took over. In one of his earliest articles as editor of *Ethiopia*, Tedla Bairu, himself an Evangelical Protestant, surpassed even *Abune* Markos in appealing to the majority Orthodox believers by using their language and exploiting their spiritual fears. Deliberately referring to Eritrea as 'Mereb Mellash', the ancient name for part of the territory, he explained why love of Ethiopia also meant love of religion.

> People of Mereb Mellash, beware! Religion is the true love of country. Faith is its base. If they tell you that they are the real country lovers, but that you are a sycophant, tell them, 'May God have mercy on you.' If they tell you that they are the learned, the philosophers who know when to hold conventions or how to separate, stand firm, dear people, tell them, 'May God have mercy on you.' If they come to you as prophets [of trusteeship], don't budge from your Ethiopianness, just tell them, 'May God have mercy on you.' If we hate Satan or the Devil as the father of lies and evil, we should equally hate everything that is the product of evil; we should hate the very thought of evil with all our might.[18]

Given his Protestant faith and more enlightened background, it is reasonable to ask if Tedla really believed his own pronouncements. He knew the Bible too well to swallow the notion that spiritual salvation could only come to his people if they joined Ethiopia or, as he stated in another article, that 'where the Kingdom of Ethiopia reigns, so does Democracy'.[19] It was rather the political style of those days to make the most outlandish claims in order to win one's argument.

As the date of the arrival of the Four Power Commission of Inquiry approached, the UP mouthpiece *Ethiopia*'s depiction of Ethiopia rose to incredible heights. In an advertisement entitled 'Good Tidings!', it committed a whole page to the announcement that oil—kerosene and benzene—had been discovered in Ogaden, Ethiopia. The well was limitless, it claimed. A city larger than Addis Ababa was to be built on the site and only 600,000 Ethiopians would be allowed to work there.[20] In the desperate days of economic distress and despair about an uncertain future, many Eritreans fell for that kind of propaganda. Some even crossed the border into Ethiopia, in search of the Ethiopian Eldorado, only to meet with disappointment. However outlandish such claims, they generally found their mark. As the better organised and better financed party, the UP used every trick at its disposal to instil hope and awe in a population with little means of verifying information.

Above all, the UP also proved capable of employing violence as a means of imposing its will. This it achieved through the establishment of the unionist youth movement, the Mahber Andinet.

Mahber Andinet

Andinet is an Amharic word that means 'oneness', and is different from *hebret* or union, the Tigrinya name of the UP. In view of the Andinet Party's involvement in acts of violence and terrorism, its office and those of the UP were the object of constant raids and confiscation by British security officers. As a result, their original documents have been lost. We know from interviews with various former members of the party that it was formed on 9 September 1945, at Mai Anbessa, the foot of the Hazhaz Hill in Asmera. The founders, a core group of about ten highly motivated young residents of Asmera's Aba Shawl district, were led by Haile Abrehe, who became Andinet's first president. Habtom Araia, Bahta Iyoab and Tewelde Fesseha were among his fellow founders. According to Bahta, the young activists had been holding meetings in various places, pretending to be students studying together.

According to the documents of its branch office in Massawa,[21] the party was highly organised and structured. It had a constitution whose preamble stated that it was committed to the objective of joining 'Ethiopia and no other culture or people'. It had a secretariat, a central council, and a membership organised into units and teams like a military regiment. Members were obliged to pay monthly fees, attend all meetings, and carry out the orders of the secretariat as transmitted to unit and team leaders. Renegades and recalcitrant members were dealt with by imposing penalties including, in extreme cases, ejection from the party and a total ban on any personal contact with party colleagues.[22] In the initial phases, Andinet called itself the Youth Association of Eritrea and Ethiopia—One Ethiopia, and posed as a wing of the UP. However, one of its internal directives clearly stated that, pending its formal recognition by the British Administration, its real identity and purposes would remain a secret even from the UP, of which it claimed to be a part.[23]

Many activists interviewed for this book asserted that their party's aim was not limited to immediate and unconditional union with Ethiopia. Andinet youths were at the same time dissatisfied with the way the unionist agenda was being carried out by traditional leaders of the UP. Many believed that the older dignitaries were there for personal gain and position, not to cater to the real needs of the population. They found the way that they bent and kowtowed in front of the Ethiopian Nega Haileselassie, a mere liaison officer, demeaning and shameful. They wanted a more dignified approach, enabling them to enter the Ethiopian union as a force to be reckoned with; not as bootlickers and sycophants trying to ingratiate themselves with yet another ruler.[24]

A style full of zeal and naiveté, it had very little substance. It took little note of whether Ethiopia would accept an assertive population joining it on its own terms. Nor did the leadership or general membership pause to consider whether the image of 'Mother Ethiopia' etched in their minds would actually match up to the reality. A few, like Berhe Mesgun, Andinet's second president, were teachers or people of some education. The majority, however, were former askaris, factory workers, the unemployed and similar people whom life under the British had driven to the limits of despair and extremism. Andinet helped them vent their anger and frustration.

Every member was sworn to secrecy about each piece of information, event or plan pertaining to the party. The teams, usually containing fifteen members each, were answerable to team leaders who could create and execute plans and operations without first informing the top leadership of the organisation. At least four types of teams were identifiable—assassination squads, propaganda units, fundraising groups, and security staff in charge of overseeing the safety of the offices and members of the party. These worked independently of each other but followed the general directives of the secretariat and the central council. As we shall see later, even assassination squads were not obliged to clear their plans with the party leadership. As long as they operated within the general directives of the party, the manner of execution of individual tasks was left to their discretion. This decentralisation was to be instrumental in throwing British security forces off the track whenever acts of terrorism were carried out and the actual perpetrators could not be pinned down.[25]

Andinet was open to both Eritreans and Tigrayans resident in Eritrea. This was true of the UP too. According to the files of the Massawa branch, for example, at least five or six of the fifteen members of every team were Tigrayans or other Ethiopians. The Massawa women's sub-branch consisted almost entirely of Tigrayan members; only one was Eritrean. Of 24 Andinet 'heroes' recommended for rank and position by the party leadership after the institution of the Ethio-Eritrean Federation in 1952, seven were Ethiopians from Tigray. Significantly, the most effective assassination missions—the murders of Kebire and Vittorio Longhi and the attempts on Weldeab's life—were attacks by Tigrayan terrorists.[26] Presumably, Eritrean terrorists preferred to attack Italians, as killing Eritreans brought with it the risk of retaliation by the victims' families.

A second significant aspect of Andinet was its targeting of UP members whom it suspected of deviating from the objectives of union with Ethiopia. As we will see, many UP leaders became the targets of propaganda and armed attacks on a par with members of the independence camp, the main enemy. 'We were obsessed with Ethiopia, it was madness,' said Bahta Iyoab, the leader of one of the main assassination squads in Asmera. 'We had very little suspicion that Ethiopia would betray us once we had delivered Eritrea to it.'[27]

Andinet was created with the seeds of discord gestating inside it. The presence of Ethiopians within its ranks, the unrealistic expectations of a bountiful Ethiopia, issues of religion and regionalism temporarily submerged under the wave of unionism: all these features would come back and haunt the party and its members.

Eritrea for Eritreans: The Liberal Progressive Party

After its campaign for signatures in favour of independence in 1945, Eritrea for Eritreans seems not to have made any headway in consolidating its earlier advantages. First, the establishment of the ML, albeit bearing a similar political programme, greatly diminished the formidable impetus with which it had started. Second, with the more organised and aggressive campaign of the UP, many of its former adherents were, either willingly or by coercion, lured to the other side. This was particularly true in Akeleguzai, the main home of Eritrea for Eritreans, where the majority of the 29 district chiefs who had signed up for it abandoned it to join the ML or the UP.

As a result, by the time of its institution as a recognised political party in February 1947, its influence was restricted to a few centres, mainly Ma'ereba in Hadegti district, Halai in Aret, Adi Quita in Deqi Digna and Adi Angefom in Degra.[28] Similarly, in Seraye province, where the UP had a commanding presence, Eritrea for Eritreans was mainly confined to three highly contested districts—Tekela, Mai Tsa'eda and Damba Mitch. In Tekela and Mai Tsa'eda, the chiefs affiliated to the party were relatives of *Ras* Tessema by marriage, thereby raising the cry that Eritrea for Eritreans was nothing more than a family affair.[29] Only Hamasien was predominantly and incontestably in the unionist camp. Except for some pockets of dissension consisting of independence sympathisers in Tse'azega and a few other places, there was no meaningful support for Eritrea for Eritreans in the whole province, excluding Asmera.[30]

On 18 February 1947, delegates of the party met at Adi Qeih, capital of Akeleguzai province, for its inaugural congress. Present at the meeting were all the major figures of the party and three specially invited guests, Ibrahim Sultan, Hassen Ali and Abdelkader Kebire of the ML. *Ras* Tessema was elected president; *Dejazmatch* Maasho Zeweldi of Aret vice president; and his son Seyoum Maasho secretary general. At this meeting, Eritrea for Eritreans adopted a new name, the Liberal Progressive Party (LPP). As Weldeab explains: 'We found Eritrea for Eritreans too limited in meaning. If Eritrea was to be an independent country, then it had to accommodate everyone without discrimination. Eritrea for Eritreans sounded too much like the current Negro nationalism in America. Liberal Progressive had a political meaning. That is why it was chosen.'[31]

At the low-key ceremony, Tessema stressed that Eritrea had been a Muslim and Christian country for thousands of years. 'We have lived in love and cooperation while honouring our respective religions,' he said. He also underlined that the idea of independence was not new, as all of Akeleguzai had supported it only a year before. The Administration had been duly informed that 'our desire was, and is today, the attainment of independence so that our country is administered by its own citizens'.

The keynote speaker was his son Abraha Tessema, who blamed the deep political and religious divisions in the country on the 'disruptors of the Bet Giorgis Convention'. Abraha continued:

> Some will say that Al Rabita have been baptised or that the independence party have converted to Islam. We should leave such talk to blow away with the wind. The correct way is for Christians and Muslims to follow the faith and tradition of their ancestors. Religion should never enter into our discourse. It is best left to the sermons of the churches and mosques. It should never determine national issues.[32]

A difference of opinion between the leaders of the LPP surfaced at the inauguration of its branch office in Mendefera. Here, too, Abraha Tessema was the main speaker. In a departure from the main theme of the Adi Qeih meeting, he attempted to rekindle his old Tigray-Tigrigni project. Tigray-Tigrigni, he claimed, was an ancient unit that included the peoples of Tigray, the *kebessa* and the Tigre, whose name had been 'Midre Ag'azi or Tigray-Tigrigni'. He went on to blame the British for not having followed the Italian lead by joining Eritrea and Tigray into one unit. He even listed the raids and atrocities of the Tigray warlords of past centuries as proof of the unity of the two peoples.[33]

The response by the vice president of the Seraye branch of LPP, *Azmatch* Berhe Gebrekidan, was tantamount to a rebuke of Abraha Tessema's position. In an article he wrote in May, Berhe explained why Eritrea could never join Ethiopia or any part of it:

> The mutual killings and the blood shed between the two peoples at the battles of Koatit, Adwa, Alaje and Mekele will not permit such union. It is a barrier cemented by the blood and bones of both sides. Therefore, Eritrea can never be a part of Ethiopia. It can only be a neighbour, like Kenya, Sudan, Tanganyika ... It is good to be a genuine lover; but to pretend to love is unacceptable. To pretend that one is a lover of Ethiopia, while yearning to reinstate oneself to old *risti, gulti* and title rights is a futile dream.[34]

The Tigray-Tigrigni project was always fraught with elements of division. The ML was especially apprehensive that Christian domination, the main reason for its total opposition to union with Ethiopia, would find another avenue through which to reign in Eritrea. In spite of the alliance formed with the LPP, therefore, an element of suspicion would characterise the relationship between the two organisations.

For the UP, Abraha's attempts to revive the Tigray-Tigrigni idea provided a welcome line of attack. Tedla Bairu was at the forefront of the campaign. Comparing the programmes of the ML and the LPP, he noted that the former was seeking independence for Eritrea within its old borders. However, 'Eritrea for Eritreans wants to slice a chunk of land from the legally constituted and internationally blessed Ethiopia. In other words, it seeks to snatch Tigray away from Ethiopia. Where then is the common programme and principles that they claim to have?'[35]

When the newspaper exchanges turned nasty, Gebremeskel Weldu, now sidelined from the UP, attempted to calm the storm. In a series of articles in which he expressed his pain and sorrow, he severely criticised the arrogance and aggressive behaviour taking root within his party. 'We cannot attain independence [union] through gossip, defamation, lies and insults,' he stated. 'God may forgive us if we proceed with love, humility, compassion and prayers ... This is the only way to salvage the honour of our party. For better or for worse, let us follow our own conscience, not that of aliens. If we really mean to serve our people, let us understand their plight. Let us stop pursuing our individual benefits.' He punctuated every point he made with sighs of sorrow and despair equivalent to 'alas, alas'.[36]

No unionist was willing to pay any heed to Gebremeskel's moderation and personal pleas. He soon became one of the earliest of a long list of Ethiopia-loving Eritreans to be thrown to the side once his usefulness had come to an end. His colleague in the Bet Giorgis conciliatory approach, Mohammed Omer Qadi, a member of the UP central council, also became increasingly apprehensive of the uninhibited praise and longing for Ethiopia. All along, he had insisted on a union that would respect Eritrean, especially Muslim, rights, culture and history. In mid-1947, he and likeminded Muslim members of the UP from the Massawa area decided to withdraw from the party and establish one that would represent their line of thinking. They named it the Independent Muslim Party for Union of Eritrea with Ethiopia. Omer Qadi explained why: 'When we say we are self-contained and independent, we mean that our party of Massawa, although still a party for union with Ethiopia, seeks to effect that union upon the satisfaction of conditions that need to be met ... The convention that our party is demanding is for the benefit of our nation and people. It is our party's own original plan.'[37]

The split within the UP was welcome news to the ML, but it helped ratchet up political tensions to higher levels. Barely a month after the split, a bomb which was thrown into Weldeab's car as he drove out of his house in Geza Kenisha exploded and wounded him seriously. It was the second attempt on his life. An earlier bomb had been tossed through a window of his house into the dining room where he was eating lunch with his wife and two young children; it had rolled harmlessly into a corner. Three days later, on 9 August 1947, a bomb exploded inside the compound of *Dejazmatch* Hassen Ali, causing no harm to the ML leader or his family. This was also a second attempt on his life. In the previous month, a British prison official had been wounded in a separate bomb attack.[38]

Although Tedla Bairu expressed his indignation and dismay at the attempts on Weldeab's life, a British report nevertheless pointed a finger at some elements within the UP. Three suspects, one of whom boasted of having carried out the attempt 'for the cause', were apprehended.[39] Two of these readily admitted that Weldeab and Hassen were targeted because they were believed to be an obstacle to the unionist agenda. Identified as members of the newly formed Andinet Party, they were sentenced to death. The third received a twenty-year sentence. None of the sentences were carried out.[40]

As the date of arrival of the Four Power Commission of Inquiry drew near, the emergence of a Pro-Italy movement added yet another dimension to a political situation.

Pro-Italy Party

In spite of its protestations that, as a caretaker government, it had no private stake in Eritrea's future, Britain still pushed for the creation of a Greater Somalia that included Ethiopia's Ogaden region. For the loss of that huge chunk of territory, Ethiopia was to be awarded the *kebessa* and the Red Sea coast of Eritrea. This was a project, as we saw, that Britain had neither discussed nor cleared with its war allies. Its partners had their own individual ideas of how not only Eritrea but also all the former Italian colonies should be disposed of. Thus, for example, France and the USSR were, for separate reasons, considering the return of Italy as a trustee to Italian Somaliland.

Worried about this prospect, the British Foreign Secretary, Ernest Bevin, met his Ethiopian counterpart, Aklilu Habtewold, on 13 June 1946. Bevin suggested that Ethiopia and Britain should take a common stand to thwart the possibility of Italy's return to the region in any capacity. He then presented the British plan for a Greater Somalia and the partition of Eritrea as the ultimate solution for the threat posed by Italy.

Aklilu was quick to point out that any talk of excising the Ogaden from Ethiopia was offensive to his country. Instead, he proposed that Eritrea and the ancient port of Zeila in the north-western Adal region of Somalia be ceded to Ethiopia. Ethiopia would then be willing to agree to a British takeover of pastureland adjacent to British Somaliland for the Greater Somalia project. The meeting ended inconclusively with Bevin pointing out that the issue would finally be settled by the United Nations.[41]

In the meantime, the British Administration changed its original policy of accommodating Italian interests. Part of the reason for the change of heart had to do with Britain's adamant opposition to Italy's return to Eritrea. In Italy itself, the fall of Fascism had opened the door for the emergence of various parties vying for power. Many of them desired the restoration of Italy's glory and wanted to see the Italian flag flying over Eritrea once again. Besides, the safety of Italians in Eritrea, already deteriorating under the British, could only worsen with an Ethiopian takeover of Eritrea. The Italians, therefore, were as adamantly opposed to the union of Eritrea with Ethiopia and to the idea of its partition as Britain and Ethiopia were to Italy's return as a trustee.[42]

In spite of this debacle, Italian political activity in Eritrea remained low-key and inconsequential up to the beginning of 1947, when the ever-bickering Italian residents announced the creation of CRIE—Comitato Rappresentativo degli Italiani dell'Eritrea—to speak on their collective behalf. Curiously, the committee's formation came immediately after its president, Dr Vincenzo di Meglio, returned from a visit to Italy. CRIE's first declarations showed that it was to act as the Italian Government's mouthpiece in Eritrea. They lauded Italy's 'civilising mission' in the former colony and advocated its return to oversee that mission to fruition.[43] In a departure from the usual Italian submission to British rule, CRIE accused the British Administration of deliberately destroying the Eritrean economy and introducing a policy of ethnic and religious discord aimed at dividing Eritreans, particularly the thousands of former Eritrean askaris who had fallen on hard times. Soon, this approach bore some fruit.

In March 1947, a group calling itself the Association of Former Italian Askaris, or the Askari Association, headquartered near the Asmera abattoir in Aba Shawl, announced its formation. Its stated purpose was strictly limited to seeking compensation for its members from the Government of Italy, and accordingly it invited former askaris and their families to register for the proposed benefits. In July of that year, the Italian Government communicated its intention to send a committee to study the demands of the Askari Association, thus giving rise to suspicions that the association was Italian-instigated and that it aimed at the creation of a party friendly to Italy.[44]

As with the other parties and associations, the askaris had their own internal squabbles. On 7 August, the president of the association, *Azmatch* Asfaha Hambir, accused ten Italian and about thirty Eritrean residents of Keren of having knocked on the doors of former askaris, urging them to register for a new party. While distributing the Italian flag and offering sums of money to those willing to comply, the old *Azmatch* charged, they urged the askaris and others to swear not to betray the Italian flag. He condemned these actions and reasserted that the Askari Association was engaged in fighting for the rights of its members and was not a body associated with any political organisation.[45]

Similar protests came to the Administration from within the association, but it soon became obvious that the formation of a pro-Italy party was inevitable. Reaction from the UP and ML was swift and categorical. Both sides condemned the emerging party and charged the organisers with treason and the sale of Eritrea. They also demanded the banning of the Askari Association.[46] The British gave in to the demands and closed down the Askari Association only to allow the leaders to change the name of their association to the Nuova Eritrea—Pro-Italy Party. This came after a period of delay on the part of the British in deference to the fierce opposition of the ML and UP. To further appease the latter, the Administration also allowed Pro-Italy, at least for the initial stages, to operate only in Keren.[47]

Pro-Italy ('Burro Italia'—Italian butter—to its detractors) added to the increasing congestion of political organisations. We have seen that Mohammed Omer Qadi had hived off from the UP to organise the small Independent Unionist Party in Massawa. To complicate the picture, another group calling itself the National Islamic Party withdrew from the ML and registered itself to operate in Massawa. By the time of the arrival of the Four Power Commission of Inquiry, Eritrea was, politically speaking, very divided.

6

THE FOUR POWER COMMISSION OF INQUIRY

Preparations for the Commission's Visit

The Paris Peace Conference of 1947 had stipulated that, should the Four Great Powers fail to reach an agreement on the disposal of the former Italian colonies within the year, the matter would be referred to the United Nations General Assembly. Any agreement was a distant hope, as on the issue of the disposal of Eritrea alone there were four competing positions.

Britain proposed that Tripolitania and Cyrenaica in Libya be placed under Italian and British trusteeship, respectively. With regard to East Africa, it sought to administer, as a trustee under the UN, all of Italian, French and British Somaliland as well as the Ogaden region of Ethiopia as one unit. On Eritrea, Britain stuck to its old partition plan, with the *kebessa* and the Red Sea coast going to Ethiopia and the western *metahit* staying within the UN trusteeship system, pending a future solution.

France rejected the British proposal. Fear of losing its North African colonies of Tunisia, Algeria and Morocco would not allow it even to consider independence for any colony. It therefore came up with the proposal that Italy should be restored to its old dominions as a trustee under international supervision, with the exception of Tripolitania, which it claimed for itself, and the Eritrean port of Asseb, which it suggested should be handed over to Ethiopia as an outlet to the sea.

The Americans shifted positions. As the self-proclaimed opponents of colonialism, they first proposed a joint Four Power trusteeship for all the colonies with the exception of Asseb, which would be assigned to Ethiopia. After ten years of trusteeship, the US suggested that the rest of Eritrea and Libya should be granted independence. However, when the Soviet Union rejected its proposal, the US joined France in the Italian trusteeship plan.

The USSR too was not consistent in its views. First, it suggested that the Four Powers take a colony each. Later, encouraged by the apparent successes at the polls of the Italian Communist Party, it advocated the return of Italy as a trustee of all its former colonies.[1]

Since France, the US and the USSR were proposing Italian trusteeship for their own individual reasons, there was no real unity in their approach. Even if there had been, the three would always have had to deal with Britain's refusal to allow any possibility of Italy returning as a colonial power. In accordance with their previous agreement, the Four Great Powers decided to send a commission of investigation to determine the 'wishes of the populations' involved.

Britain was given the task of facilitating the work of the commission in Eritrea. For this purpose, the British authorities assigned a colonial officer, Brigadier Frank Stafford, to determine the agenda and modus operandi of the commission. Stafford, who had served in the Middle East and East Africa, had also done a tour of duty as advisor to the Ethiopian Government from 1941 to 1944. A writer and researcher, he was variously described as a man of great skills and secrecy. According to Weldeab Weldemariam, Stafford's appointment was designed to give him and Britain a decisive voice in the proceedings of the commission.[2]

In the months before the arrival of the commission, Stafford submitted his findings and report on the commission's manner of investigation, the political inclinations of the people, and Britain's stand on the matter. Eritrean Muslims, Stafford wrote, were nomads living off the land, who could not comprehend simple matters; the concept of government was beyond their capacity to grasp. The Christians too he saw as being below even the lowest levels of political maturity. Based on this assessment, he ruled out the idea of allowing Eritreans to decide their fate through a referendum. Instead, he proposed that each district, *kebila* and community in the country should elect its own representatives, who would then speak on behalf of the province concerned. Where, for any reason, the commission found the depositions of the representatives unacceptable or inconclusive, it could then go to the villages to determine the wishes of the people directly.

Stafford was categorical in his conclusion that the Eritrean people as a whole were totally opposed to the return of Italy in any form. On the contrary, he asserted that Britain was more acceptable because it had introduced a system of higher education and concepts and practices of democracy. True, he admitted, there was some resentment in Barka arising from the harsh measures taken against the people of the area following the Ali *Muntaz* uprising. Similarly, the killings of innocent citizens by Sudanese troops on the streets of Asmera were still fresh in the minds of the inhabitants. Nevertheless, British popularity was high enough for such resentments not to fester.

When comparing popular preferences for union with Ethiopia with those for Italian trusteeship, Stafford came up with detailed statistical data. The bulk of unionist support was in Hamasien and Seraye, where he estimated that 75% and 85%, respectively, of the populations in both provinces supported the Unionist Party (UP). The rest of Eritrea was in favour of British trusteeship—98% in Barka, 66% in Senhit or the Keren area, 98% in the Red Sea division, and 80% in Akeleguzai.

Of a population totalling 957,000, he estimated that 538,100, or over 56%, were supporters of independence.

Stafford did not indicate how he had come to those detailed figures. However, in spite of the thousands of petitions that he admitted were reaching him in favour of independence and against partition, he still ruled out Eritrean independence as impractical and untenable. In an open endorsement of his government's long-held position, he concluded that Britain's partition plan stood a better chance of success with the commission than Italian trusteeship.[3]

The Work and Decisions of the Commission

About a month before the arrival of the Four Power Commission (FPC), the Muslim League (ML) and the Liberal Progressive Party (LPP) announced that they were aligning their programmes and forming an alliance called the Liberal League. Their stated aim was to appear before the FPC as one body, united in the cause of independence after a period of British trusteeship. The Liberal League would have been a formidable force for anyone to contend with had it built on its advantage. But, for unspecified reasons, there was no follow-up on the organisational and strategic merger nor the kind of coordination that such an alliance demanded. Having failed to capitalise on their huge advantage, the ML and the LPP went ahead with making their respective preparations for appearance before the commission.

The FPC arrived at Asmera on 12 November 1947. Two days later, the ML called a press conference which correspondents of the BBC, Associated Press and some major British newspapers attended. Despite its best efforts to promote its agenda, it failed to impress any of the invitees. The *Manchester Guardian* recognised the sensitivity of the Eritrean case but suggested that the best solution to the issue was to hand the *kebessa* and the coastal areas over to Ethiopia while reserving the *metahit* for trusteeship, 'assuming anyone would be willing to administer such a territory'. The *Glasgow Herald* rejected the claims that Egypt, Italy and Ethiopia were making over Eritrea and voiced its support for British trusteeship. 'It is clear', the paper concluded, 'that Eritreans do not possess the capacity to administer themselves.'[4]

The FPC's attitude was no different from that of the journalists present. To begin with, three of the heads of the delegation had no prior knowledge of Eritrea. J.A. Utter of the US was a bank executive; Étienne Burin of France had served as a diplomat in European capitals; and A.F. Fedorov of the USSR was a military officer who had served in Manchuria. Britain assigned Brigadier Frank Stafford, the officer already involved in designing the commission's programme and itinerary on behalf of the British Military Administration (BMA), to double as head of the British delegation. He became the expert in the group.[5]

The FPC stayed in Eritrea from 12 November 1947 to 3 January 1948—a total of 52 days. During this period, it received the leaders of Eritrea's political parties and associations; it also travelled to some parts of the country to meet with groups selected by the BMA (by Frank Stafford, in other words) as representatives of the people. At the end of its mission, it was able to produce some valuable documentation on the socio-economic history and formation of Eritrea. However, it could not and, indeed, was not meant to come to an agreement on its main mission—viz., determining the wishes of the people of Eritrea.

It may not be fair to put the blame for this inconclusiveness entirely on the commission or the powers that sent it. Eritreans were themselves hopelessly divided, and both mentally and organisationally unprepared to challenge the attitudes and prejudices of the delegates poised to decide their future. There was, for example, no difference in content between the statements that the ML and the LPP presented to the commission. Both asked for independence after a period of British trusteeship; and both vehemently rejected union with Ethiopia and the partition of Eritrea. They chose to speak separately, thus losing the chance to impress the delegates.[6]

As if this was not enough of a drawback, the ML itself showed cracks in its unity. While the main body wanted British trusteeship under UN supervision, a splinter group, the National Muslim League of Massawa, wanted British trusteeship with no UN supervision. Such hair-splitting differences often camouflaged underlying local rivalries or religious and regional differences. For example, some have pointed out that the only reason for the Massawa split was that Afars in the area wanted their own representation.[7] With most of the *shumagille* appearing on the UP's side, this additional defection from the ML's ranks made it look vulnerable.

The same could be said of the LPP, which paraded three of its luminaries, *Ras* Tessema, his son Abraha and *Dejazmatch* Sebhatu (a former interpreter to Governor Graziani) of the Mendefera area, in front of the commission. In the ensuing exchange, Tessema made a strong case for independence and against union, including conditional union with Ethiopia or any form of partition. Under cross-examination, members of the LPP delegation asserted that they would support independence for Tigray, if there was such a possibility. They also stressed that the issue of serf emancipation should be postponed until after the resolution of the whole Eritrean question.

The ML too sent its top leadership composed of Ibrahim Sultan, Abdulkader Kebire, Hassen Ali and *Qadi* Musa of Keren, among others. There was very little difference in what they and the LPP leaders presented. Unfortunately for their common cause, the FPC found gaping discrepancies in the claims they made. For example, the number of followers that they claimed sometimes surpassed the estimated population of the country as a whole. Their position on serf emancipation and details about their preferences on trusteeship would not support their assertion of a common stand on issues. In other words, they had failed to hold even cursory preliminary consultations on how to challenge or pre-empt the agenda of the UP. It was the same with the party and associations that advocated the return of Italy.[8]

In contrast, the UP came united and coordinated. Weldeab Weldemariam, a master coiner of Tigrinya phrases and quotable utterings, used to say of the discrepancy between unionist cohesion and the disunity on the other side that 'While angels bickered on the best way to salvation, devils always united around a project of evil'. Flanked by suitably adorned and decorated chiefs of the *kebessa* and *metahit*, Tedla Bairu made a grand appearance before the commission. He presented Ethiopia as a land where even the rights of serfs would be protected. Pointing to the *shumagille* chiefs on his side, he claimed that both the *kebessa* and *metahit* were united in the unionist cause. He also asserted that the demand of the entire population of Eritrea was for an unconditional union with Ethiopia.[9]

It was obvious that the commission could not come to a common agreement based on its findings and the presentations of the party leaders. It therefore set out to visit the sites prearranged by Stafford and his aides. In UP-controlled areas, the public gatherings were orderly and accompanied by the pomp and pageantry of religious processions, hymns and dances especially by Orthodox priests. It was not the same in the rallies organised by the ML, the LPP and the Pro-Italy Party.

Organised bands of Unionist Party and Andinet youths and thugs, many of them recognisable at every event, were moved by trucks from one rally to the other to block independence supporters from reaching the rally sites or disrupt the rallies themselves, often in the very presence of the commission members. In the village of Tse'azega, a few kilometres west of Asmera, the LPP tent prepared for the commission was dismantled and the arriving LPP representatives were forced to scatter under a barrage of stones thrown by unionist youths. The car of the LPP leader in the area, *Azmatch* Kahsu Milkes, was overturned and the *azmatch* himself detained and prevented from attending the rally. Rallies scheduled to be held in the village of Dekemhare, on the road to Keren, had to be cancelled for similar reasons.

The worst of these incidents took place in Tera Emni, a village some twenty kilometres north of the town of Mendefera, on 30 November 1947. Very early that morning, supporters of Pro-Italy started to gather in anticipation of the arrival of the commission. However, unionist youths had already placed themselves in key positions of attack. By 7 am, their rally had been completely routed and their leader had to be carried to hospital with an injury. A police sergeant was also injured in the fracas. The same afternoon, at the place where the ML and the LPP had scheduled a huge joint rally, the same youths repeated their earlier stone-throwing campaign. Although the rally holders attempted to fight back, they could not match the aggression and determination of the attackers. The LPP regional secretary, Asmerom Weldegiorgis, was hospitalised with a severe injury, and the rally was disrupted. A similar rally was also dispersed in the Seraye town of Adi Quala. Neither the Eritrean police force nor British troops in the area attempted to intervene.[10]

On 17 December, a joint ML–LPP appeal to the commission accused Ethiopian and Eritrean notables and officials of the Ethiopian Government of having carried out open campaigns for union prior to the troubles in Tse'azega, Dekemhare and Tera Emni. They also alleged that the UP had secretly smuggled about 1,000 Tigrayan peasants from across the border to disrupt the Adi Quala rally.[11] Stafford and his US colleague Utter dismissed the claims as baseless. They also rejected allegations that the Orthodox clergy were threatening potential attendees of the independence rallies with punitive measures, including excommunication.[12]

There was no way for the FPC to reach a consensus on any of the issues under consideration. Nevertheless, after plenty of wrangling and acrimony, it arrived at a statistical breakdown of Eritrean preferences. The UP, it claimed, commanded the support of 44.8% of the population; the ML, 40.5%; the LPP, 4.4%; Pro-Italy, 9.2%; and the National Muslim League, 1.1%. By the FPC's computation, while 44.8% supported union, 55.2% came up for independence after some form of trusteeship.[13]

The commission's figures were not based on any scientific survey or any form of vote or referendum. Indeed, in a nation where no census had ever been taken, it is difficult to understand how the commission could come to such estimates, complete with percentages and decimals. It turned out that members of the commission were themselves in disagreement as to how the figures reached should be analysed. The French and the Russians imputed the Pro-Italy Party's poor showing to its late formation. The British and Americans insisted that the only meaningful parties were the UP and ML, which had divided the country along clear religious lines. By the time that the commission submitted its findings to the Council of Ministers, it was far further from a consensus than it had been at the outset. This set the stage for the ministers to deliberate on the Eritrean issue on the basis of their existent strategic policies.

The Council of Ministers' Deliberations

The FPC left Eritrea on 3 January 1948, to continue a similar mission in Libya. In the interim, Britain started to put forward new ideas that further complicated the problem. In a memorandum that he submitted on 4 February 1948, the British Foreign Secretary wrote that the need for British trusteeship giving it 'strategic facilities in Cyrenaica' was paramount; this could only be realised if Britain obtained trusteeship over the whole of Libya. The Foreign Secretary expected that such a plan would meet with strong objections at least from France and Italy, which was claiming Tripolitania. To appease such concerns, he proposed, first, support for Italy to return to its former colonies in East Africa as a trustee; and second, a guarantee to safeguard Italian interests in Tripolitania. As regards the first proposal, he suggested that the whole of Italian Somaliland be placed under Italian trusteeship and that a considerable part of Eritrea, including 'as much as possible of the Coptic highlands behind Asmera, and the Danakil Coast with the port of Asseb as an outlet to the sea', be ceded to Ethiopia.[14]

This departure from Britain's former adamant rejection of Italy's return to its former colonies provoked a sharp retort from Haile Selassie. His government would not hesitate, he warned, 'to condemn the shocking international transgression over an ally and a fellow member of the UN ... an act unworthy of the Great Powers'.[15] In spite of its tough posturing, Ethiopia was worried that Britain might succeed with its new proposals.[16] Besides Haile Selassie, the three major Eritrean parties, the ML, the LPP and the UP, also voiced their alarm and dismay at the idea of Italian trusteeship over parts of Eritrea. Furthermore, they demanded permission to send representatives to London to present their objections, a request the BMA refused to grant.[17] Yet the BMA authorities were themselves fearful that Italian trusteeship would arouse violence in Eritrea and that it would be defeated by a combination of internal uprisings and Ethiopian attacks. They thus asked for an additional British battalion to be garrisoned in Eritrea.[18]

Although the BMA doubted whether Ethiopia would have the capacity to effectively administer Eritrea or preserve its modernised industrial and transportation infrastructure, they still preferred an Ethiopian takeover to the Italian alternative. Perhaps Sir Philip Mitchell, a major figure in British East Africa, put the BMA's sentiments most clearly. On 2 April 1948, he wrote to the Foreign Secretary:

> Friendly Ethiopia in possession of Asmera/Massawa area is strategically probably best for us short of British occupation because (i) it would enjoy general support in UNO; (ii) there would be no one in position to attempt their expulsion; (iii) they would be unlikely ever to possess air and sea resources sufficient to menace traffic in Red Sea which any resolute power holding those bases could disrupt and probably prevent altogether; (iv) in event of war with communist or other revolutionary powers in Mid-East area, would almost certainly be at our disposal and might assume great importance as forward base and repair shop and transit airfield especially for central and south Arabia; (v) although it would of course be in essence a Colony, colonial power would be black, which in UNO circles would no doubt make it respectable.[19]

Mitchell's memorandum indicated that Britain was abandoning its latest inclination to support some form of Italian trusteeship over Eritrea. BMA officials were quick to capitalise on this gradual shift of policy. Frank Stafford wrote that, should Italy return to Eritrea, *shifta* bands armed by Ethiopia would threaten its control. In Addis Ababa, he noted, Eritrea's future was a burning issue; and Ethiopia would not hesitate to do all it could to prevent the eventuality of an Italian return.[20]

Similar opinions voicing often exaggerated predictions of an Ethiopian reaction visibly weakened Italy's chances for trusteeship over Eritrea. As usual, only a few officials cared to make some passing remarks on the Eritrean response. R.W. Mason, political advisor to the Chief Administrator, wrote that Eritreans were too divided along religious lines and lacking in arms, organisation and leadership to form a viable force. He predicted that, should Italy return as a trustee, they would fall on each other in vying for whatever jobs and positions that would become available.[21]

When the Council of Ministers of the Four Great Powers and their allies met in September 1948 to deliberate on the future of the former Italian colonies, these attitudes on Eritrea and Eritreans had gained dominance. Yet Britain found no opening to persuade its allies of the position it was adopting. After their victory over the Axis powers, the Allies had turned into competitors for global control. As Trevaskis rightly puts it, had the Allies maintained their level of wartime unity, they would have had no problems in coming to a common solution to the problem of the former Italian colonies. But that had changed. The Soviet Union was in control of socialist Eastern Europe. Furthermore, its meddling in the internal affairs of Greece and its occupation of half of Berlin put it at loggerheads with its former Western allies. All the elements of a new global confrontation were firmly in place.

As we pointed out earlier, for Britain, the Eritrean issue had become part of its new ambitions in Libya. The acquisition of the wide expanse of flat lands in Cyrenaica and Tripolitania, conducive for building airstrips, was still of paramount importance for its Mediterranean strategy, and it saw Eritrea as a bargaining chip for the attainment of that aim. It was an ambition that especially the French and the Soviets, albeit for their own separate reasons, would not support.

As a result, the FPC could only come up with a diverse and contradictory set of recommendations. In a joint statement, Britain and the US explained that the religious divisions in Eritrea justified the old partition plan. In separate proposals, the Soviet Union and France argued that none of the political groupings had a clear majority over the rest. They therefore came out in support of Italian trusteeship. When the Council of Ministers met to issue its final verdict on Eritrea, the FPC's proposals could not provide any meaningful input for its deliberations. On 15 September 1948, the four delegations came up with the following mutually exclusive proposals that reflected each nation's strategic interests. France proposed that the southern Red Sea coastline south of the Gulf of Zula (in other words, the whole of Denkalia, including the port of Asseb) be ceded to Ethiopia; the rest of Eritrea would be administered by Italy as a trustee. Britain, having abandoned its old plans, even that of partition, proposed that Ethiopia administer Eritrea for ten years under UN supervision and that a UN advisory commission be set up for the purpose. The US, in yet another change of position, advocated the cession of Hamasien, Seraye, Akeleguzai and Denkalia to Ethiopia; the fate of Asmera, Massawa and the rest of Eritrea would be postponed for a year to arrange for protection of the US military bases in Asmera and Massawa. The Soviet Union, for its part, shifted positions in the space of a few days: first, it proposed Italian trusteeship, only to later recommend a joint Four Power administration for ten years at the end of which Eritrea was to be granted its independence.[22]

The Four Powers failed to agree, not only on the Eritrean issue, but also on the disposal of the former Italian colonies as a whole. In accordance with their previous agreement, they transferred the whole question to the UN General Assembly for deliberation and final recommendations.

The Aftermath of the FPC Investigation

The Rise of a Unionist *Shifta* Movement

The FPC had raised high hopes among Eritreans of an end to their period of internal conflict and state of perpetual uncertainty. Thus its failure to come up with a generally acceptable solution sent a wave of disappointment and frustration throughout the country. One of the most direct consequences of this was the sharp rise in terrorist and *shifta* activity in the urban and rural areas of the country. *Shifta* activity in East Africa, especially in Eritrea, Ethiopia and Somalia, was an old practice whereby individuals or groups took to lawlessness and banditry for reasons ranging from common brigandage for personal gain to the rectification of injustices or social wrongs. But it was during the period of British rule in the 1940s that the Eritrean countryside fell under the virtual control of minor warlords out to take advantage of the availability of small arms and ammunition left over from the war and the gaps created by an overstretched British security system.

At the peak of the *shifta* troubles in 1950, Trevaskis was assigned to come up with an analysis of the genesis and growth of the movement. In this study, Trevaskis found that there had been no significant *shifta* activity until the Italian defeat in 1941. Trouble started in 1942 on the border between Seraye and Tigray, when the authorities replaced the chief of the district of Adi Quala with a rival, causing his relatives and supporters in Eritrea and Tigray to take up arms in protest.[23] The year 1942 also saw Ethiopian *shifta* raids on the Kunama of the Barentu area, as well as the resumption of the Beni Amer–Hadendowa clashes that, as we have seen, rocked the Gash–Barka region for over three years.[24] But the problem was still limited in scope and intensity.

Unemployment and the physical displacement of thousands of people following the decline of the war economy became a major factor in the further growth of the *shifta* problem. At the same time, the BMA's reduction of the number of districts in the country by a third displaced a number of influential chiefs from their traditional positions. Resentment over such dismissals, the appointment of new chiefs unacceptable to some parties, and the BMA's continued expropriation of agricultural land to give to Italians in concession contracts were additional factors in the growth of *shifta* activity.[25]

In the second half of the 1940s, a crop of *shifta* leaders with large followings started to behave like warlords with territorial claims. Most notable among these was Asresehey Embaye, out to rectify his uncle's dismissal from the chieftainship in the Areza district of Seraye, where he moved freely in the escarpments leading to the plains of Barka.[26] Another warlord who emerged was Gebre Tesfatsion (later

Fitawrari), a man with definite connections with Ethiopia. Having escaped from an Italian prison in Tesseney in 1936, he had joined the British forces in Sudan, ran errands to lure Eritrean askaris away from the Italian army, fought with the British at Metema, and accompanied Haile Selassie back to Ethiopia as a patriot. While there is no evidence that he was planted in the *shifta* movement by Ethiopia, we can assume that he was the only leader well placed to introduce an Ethiopian political agenda. He shared his area of control in Hamasien and parts of Barka with Hagos Temnewo, a rebel against Italy since the 1920s.[27]

The four Mossazghi brothers, natives of Akeleguzai, formed the fourth major force to emerge in the 1940s. In the 1920s, when they were still children, their father had died in prison at Nakhura for having opposed the Italian appointment of a chief over a mentor of his. In the early 1940s, the brothers avenged their father's death by killing the Italian-appointed chief and then took to the bushes. Initially, they had no discernible political agenda, and their campaign against the Italians was, as we shall see, a later development.

Mention should also be made of two of the most notorious *shiftas*, Debessai Dirar and Tekeste Haile, who terrorised the Seraye and Akeleguzai areas. These were not as powerful as those already mentioned, but were most feared for the terror and damage they inflicted on the peasantry.[28]

Of special interest to the present history of Eritrea was the story of Hamid Idris Awate, the *shifta* most wanted by the BMA. His was a lone campaign against British officers and their Sudanese troops, one that became intertwined with the transition of the Eritrean struggle for independence to armed revolution. We will deal with Hamid's case later.

The *Shifta*–Andinet Connection

Andinet was such a secretive organisation that very few of its surviving members were willing to break its code of silence half a century later. For this reason, it has been difficult to establish the timing and circumstances of its and the *shifta*'s allegiance to union with Ethiopia. As a development of momentous significance for the outcome of the political struggle of the 1940s, it deserves closer scrutiny.

British documents often pointed an accusatory finger at the Ethiopian liaison officer in Eritrea, Nega Haileselassie, and his deputy, Tekola Gebremedhin. There was even a time when they considered the latter's expulsion to Addis Ababa, only to be ruled out by Foreign Office officials in Cairo and London for the problems it would create in Ethiopian–British relations.[29] Other sources indicate that Ethiopia's hand in the promotion and spread of terrorism also came directly from Haile Selassie's Minister of the Pen, Weldegiorgis Weldeyohannes. He was known to have created a line of contact through the Eritrean Abraha Weldetatios, which Nega and Tekola could not control. When exactly this started is not clear, but UP leaders have indicated that in the late 1940s, Abraha came to Eritrea with a pile of money to be transferred to *shifta* leaders. When the UP declined the offer, Abraha chose to make direct contacts with the *shifta* through the offices of the governorship at Adwa, occupied at the time by Colonel Isaias Gebreselassie, and through the head of the Axum Church, *Nebure Ed* Gebremeskel Yebio, both Eritreans by birth.[30]

In the meantime, and especially after the FPC's failure to solve the Eritrean issue, terrorism gripped practically every part of the country. It started in Keren on 1 January 1948, when Andinet youths attacked a group of Muslims, killing one. During the same week, an Italian estate at Elabered was raided and 300 head of cattle stolen. At the end of the week, a band of *shifta* carrying an Ethiopian flag stopped a train and robbed its passengers of their belongings. As the first indication of some form of Ethiopian involvement, this caused the BMA to impose collective fines on villages found aiding or supplying the *shifta*.[31] The penalty made very little difference.

Shifta daring and boldness increased by leaps and bounds. In the months of February and April alone, raids targeting Italians resulted in several deaths and the destruction of property. In some of these raids, the *shifta* left well-written notes calling themselves 'Ethiopian patriots' and even listing their names for clearer identification. Hagos Temnewo's band was generally identified as the perpetrator of these acts, although Gebre Tesfatsion also moved in the same area. British concern grew when one of their officers was attacked in the Keren area and a patrol of British troops engaged in armed confrontation with a *shifta* band. In May 1948, the BMA issued a reward of 1,000 EA shillings to anyone who would hand over an outlaw. It also requested the deployment of four Tempest aircraft to frighten the *shifta* into submission.[32] The latter request was turned down by Major General D.C. Cumming of the Cairo command, advising caution in such matters, as Ethiopian supporters of Eritrea, particularly Sylvia Pankhurst, were likely to make trouble in London.[33]

In spite of Cumming's objections, the BMA's anti-terrorist measures, supported by a few sorties by the Tempest aircraft, bore some fruit when Hagos Temnewo's band was dealt a heavy blow, resulting in several deaths and the surrender of over twenty of his members. Hagos himself sought refuge in Ethiopia, where he regrouped and resumed his campaign of scourging the Keren and Barka countryside.[34]

Regardless of mounting evidence pointing to some form of Ethiopian involvement, British authorities still avoided holding the Ethiopians responsible at least for providing refuge and free cross-border passage to Eritrean outlaws. Ethiopian designs, argued one document, was not aimed at procuring the whole of Eritrea. The expectation was that Ethiopia would be content with gaining access to the sea through the cession of Asseb and Denkalia. Therefore, Britain saw no reason to make the Eritrean *shifta* connection a point of contention with Ethiopia.[35]

The Eritrea–Ethiopia border remained porous throughout this period, encouraging Ethiopian *shifta* to move in and out at will. In one incident alone, 40 Ethiopian *shifta* raided the village of Mai Alba in Seraye. On the same day, Hagos

Temnewo, just back and rearmed from his refuge in Ethiopia, entered Korokon in the Gash area and killed three Beni Amer men and stole 600 head of cattle.[36]

Despite British prevarication, evidence of an Ethiopian *shifta* connection was becoming clearer. In June 1948, the UP secretary general Tedla Bairu, who developed a friendship with Haile Selassie's Minister of the Pen, Weldegiorgis, returned from a visit to Addis Ababa. At a meeting of the central council of the UP, he declared that, in the event of an Italian return to Eritrea, Ethiopia would be willing to supply arms to the Eritrean resistance. He emphasised further that, rather than wait for some unwanted UN decision, it would be better to take measures into one's own hands.[37]

The authorities did nothing more than report Tedla's open declaration of the use of force. Barely two months after Tedla's speech, Hagos Temnewo was in action again, this time attacking a train station on the Asmera–Keren road and killing two Italian employees. The note attached to the murdered men was no longer in the usual *shifta* calligraphy, indicating that it had been written by abler hands seated at a proper table. Again, Hagos claimed to be the author. It was a telling note indicative of the anger that was building against an eventual Italian return. After detailing his suffering under Italian imprisonment in Nakhura, Hagos declared:

> Therefore, it is my wish to kill and slaughter Italians. Yes, these people denied us our freedom, whipped us with cruelty, confiscated our land, named us 'moschi' [mosquitoes] and refused to consider us better than a grain of mustard. I will peck on their flesh like the eagle and suck their blood like the tiger. Beyond that, I have no quarrel with the English. I assert that my hatred is against Italians.[38]

The BMA's suspicion quickly turned to the leadership of the UP itself. While celebrating Haile Selassie's birthday on 23 July 1948, its president, Beyene Beraki, declared that his organisation was 'committed to active opposition to anyone coming with aims other than union with Ethiopia' and that Eritrea had clearly expressed its rejection of an Italian return. 'We will manifest by our actions our hatred and opposition to that possibility,' he concluded.[39] This was what was reported in the unionist newspaper *Ethiopia*. In the actual speech, he also added that, in order to create 'disorder in this world', one needed to 'take the ultimate step of picking up the gun'.[40] Beyene Beraki and the editor of the *Ethiopia* newspaper, Gebremikael Gurmu, were charged and sentenced to one and a half years' and six months' imprisonment, respectively, for incitement to violence; the punishment was later commuted to suspended sentences of two years and one year, respectively.

Convinced that Beyene's speech and Hagos Temnewo's declaration were the direct result of Tedla's visit to Addis Ababa, BMA's Chief Secretary, G.W. Kenyon-Slaney, warned that he would arrest Tedla if the acts of violence did not stop. Again, London turned down the idea on the ground that the BMA should not resort to old Italian laws of detention without due process. Besides, with Britain leaning towards the unionist agenda, they expected the UP to change course. Arresting Tedla would therefore be counterproductive.[41]

In the meantime, other *shifta* bands were becoming politicised by events and confrontations not themselves politically motivated. The Mossazghi brothers, for example, had no known inclinations other than vengeance. All that changed when two of the brothers, Beyene and Fessehaye, were killed in a shootout with a police patrol on the Segeneiti–Adi Qeih road. Since the gunman was identified as an Italian officer known simply as Barba, the remaining brothers, Weldegabriel and Berhe, began to attack Italians wherever they were found. The terror that their band unleashed may have surpassed that of the veteran Hagos.[42]

Towards the end of 1948, on an unspecified date, a meeting of *shifta* leaders and their deputies took place at Ubel, western Seraye, an area controlled by Asresehey Embaye. How exactly that meeting was organised and by whom has not been verified. It has been speculated that, given the previous contacts that Gebre Tesfatsion had with Ethiopia, he could have provided the link and that Abraha Weldetatios may have been the chief agent of contact. One of Asresehey's deputies, *Grazmatch* Gebrai Meles, spoke more broadly in an interview about the deliberations at that meeting. According to his recollection, this was how the meeting proceeded:

> We said to each other, 'All of us are rebelling, going to the wilderness, harassing people, dispossessing them of their belongings and slaughtering their cattle. At this rate, everyone will choose this way of life. There is no peace in this land and we are not giving any service to our fatherland. Let us therefore protect the honour of our people. Let the merchant trade; let us not frighten our women; let us swear never to procure food without our hosts' permission. Let us make this pact.

According to Gebrai, the prime purpose of the meeting was to agree on this principle. It was only at a later stage that they raised the issue of how best to promote the interests of the people. According to Gebrai,

> We said to each other, 'The Englishman wants to continue living here by dividing us and Italy is claiming that Eritreans love it and that it should be allowed to come back. The issue is too heavy for us; it is beyond our capacity. The Englishman is increasing his attacks on us. We can only gain strength if we lean on Ethiopia and seek what we want.' That is how we chose Ethiopia.[43]

Other sources confirm that Ethiopia's role in initiating and organising the *shifta* was minimal. *Kegnazmatch* Tesfaselassie Kidane, an Eritrean by birth who served as a district official in the Adyabo area of Tigray in the 1940s and 1950s, lived and worked among the *shifta*. His rejection of the idea of an Ethiopian hand guiding the Eritrean *shifta* movement was straightforward and categorical: 'A blind hatred of Italy and grave suspicions over British intentions drove Eritrean Christians towards Ethiopia,' he stressed. 'Fear of Muslim domination was also there. But the Ethiopians had very little to do in *shifta* plans and actions. They did not possess that kind of thinking. True, we provided the *shifta* with free passage, gave them refuge and treated their wounded. But they ran their own affairs.'[44]

There is much more evidence of *shifta* meetings with Ethiopian officials for the period following the Ubel meeting. In one of these, Gebrai Meles accompanied his leader, Asresehey, to Shire in Tigray where they met *Nebure Ed* Gebremeskel Yebio of Axum. The cleric drove them to Axum for a meeting with the Adwa Governor, Isaias Gebreselassie. They returned to Eritrea with guns and money. At one point, Asresehey and Gebrai travelled to Gondar in great secrecy to be presented to Haile Selassie. They came back with arms and cash.[45]

In his interview, Hagos Temnewo described a meeting he had with the Emperor himself, who sent him away with guns and cash.[46] Gebre Tesfatsion too was known to have made several trips to Addis Ababa to meet Weldegiorgis. Gebrai Meles recalled two instances where Gebre Tesfatsion came back from Gondar with 2,000 birr and Asresehey with 5,000 birr. As the treasurer of the Asresehey band, he remembered disbursing Asresehey's share to 250 *shiftas* at 20 birr apiece.[47]

Other than such sketchy details, more concrete evidence of Ethiopian leadership of the Eritrean *shifta* movement is hard to come by. In the Andinet files of the Massawa branch, we find consistent appeals by the leadership for arms made to *Ras* Seyoum Mengesha of Tigray, Nega Haileselassie, and the Emperor himself. These went largely ignored, but those in need never ceased to knock on these doors, consistently airing their frustration at the lack of response.[48] With all the information available to him, even John Spencer, legal advisor to the Ethiopian Government, never went beyond suspecting Nega as the man behind the *shifta* phenomenon. He admitted he could find no connecting evidence.[49]

The irredentism of the 1940s is, in many ways, a conundrum for the study of nationalism in an African context. Here were young urban and rural Eritreans, who had been born and raised inside a tightly controlled colony with no form of contact with Ethiopia, willing to kill and die for it. It was an emotional attachment of immense intensity, not based on a clearly identifiable historical process. The old feudal ties with Abyssinia, intermittent and conflictual for the large part, had taken place prior to the emergence of modern Ethiopian and Eritrean nationalisms. During the long period of alienation and deprivation under Italy, Ethiopia naturally became their beacon of hope, a refuge and escape from a reality they could not handle. It is significant, however, that the most ardent unionists were those who knew Ethiopia from a distance. As we mentioned in earlier chapters, the majority of Eritrean residents in Ethiopia had enough personal reasons and experience to oppose the idea.

7

THE ERITREAN CASE AT THE UN GENERAL ASSEMBLY

The Assassination of Abdelkader Kebire

On 12 February 1949, armed men shot and killed *Blata* Kahsai Malu, *mislene* of the Tsillima district of Seraye. The killers were never apprehended, but since Kahsai Malu was a major Liberal Progressive Party (LPP) leader in the province, his murder was seen as politically motivated.[1] It was amid the tension that this act of violence generated that the United Nations Political Committee on the disposal of the former Italian colonies expressed its intention to invite representatives of these colonies to present their cases to the world body. Eritrean political discussion and activity started back to life from a temporary slumber.

The Unionist Party (UP) quickly called on all parties to form a common Eritrean platform in order to avert the possibility of chaos following a British exit. The Muslim League (ML) responded by issuing a statement rejecting any idea of a link with Ethiopia, 'which itself needs a trustee, and cannot administer Eritrea', it declared. The LPP, for its part, got down to drafting its vision of a free Eritrea and renewed its request for attendance at the UN deliberations.

In March 1949, the UN Political Committee sent a formal invitation to Eritrean political representatives. The BMA, which felt that the Eritrean case had been adequately studied by the Four Power Commission, argued that a UN repetition of the same process was unnecessary and redundant. Besides, it saw the committee's direct contact with Eritrean parties as trespassing on its authority.[2]

Not impressed by the BMA's objections, the committee renewed its invitations, and the ML named a delegation consisting of four of its leaders, led by Ibrahim Sultan.[3] British officials mulled over whether to impose a ban on their travel permits, but to avoid the bad image that such a move could create, they attempted to stop the delegation's progress from Cairo. R.W. Mason, advisor to the Administrator, wrote to his superiors in Egypt, saying that Ibrahim and his friends, who spoke no English, were politically immature. Since they had never left Eritrea, he suggested that they would be content with a 'two or three weeks' stay in Cairo'. He recommended that visas to the US should be denied them there.[4]

The UN Committee overruled these objections and the ML delegation completed its preparations for the journey. A few nights before their scheduled flight, on the evening of 27 March, gunmen shot and wounded Abdelkader Kebire, prominent nationalist leader and vice president of the ML, across the street from Mohammed Aberra Hagos's tearoom in Via Cagliari (Godena Seraye today). He died on 29 March 1949 and was buried in the Muslim cemetery in Asmera the next day.

Police immediately searched the offices of the UP and Andinet, where they found evidence that could incriminate Nega and Tekola of the Ethiopian Liaison Office and Tedla Bairu of the UP. This included documents and weapons—90 machetes, 50 swords and 20 hatchets—the latter at the offices of Gebreselassie Garza and Habtom Araia, the top Andinet leaders at the time. They were both arrested immediately.[5]

An unsigned document containing directives for a variety of tasks, administrative matters and terrorist targets gave a rare glimpse into the internal workings of both organisations. The instructions included killing Italian leaders, bribing Eritreans in Italian employment, planting spies inside government and party offices, compromising members of opposing parties, and possessing firearms and grenades.[6]

A second document, signed with the words 'On Behalf of Union', was more specific. Ibrahim Sultan, it read, was shuttling between Keren and Asmera, and was being actively helped by the British. 'We are ready to face death in pursuit of our objective,' concluded the first part of the letter. The second part dealt with Abdelkader Kebire. After pointing out that Kebire was up to something with Italians in the Ghinda'e area, the writer continued, 'If you give your approval, I will arrange all that is necessary to have him killed. As you well know, we are loyal ... On behalf of all my followers, I pledge my full cooperation.'[7]

A third document, this time involving daily reports by Andinet leader Gebreselassie Garza, told of a meeting between him and Abraha Weldetatios, at the Albergo CIAAO in Asmera, where Gebreselassie said he discussed his party's financial problems and its plans of action. Abraha promised to inform Nega of the situation.[8]

Based on this evidence, the BMA's Chief Administrator, Brigadier Drew, declared Andinet a terrorist organisation and closed its offices. He also had about thirty members from its Asmera and Massawa branches arrested, although he soon released them for lack of evidence. However, further investigation revealed to Drew that the Andinet leader was in contact with UP secretary general Tedla Bairu even while in prison—thus compromising Tedla's credibility. From a combination of these leads and documents, Drew came to the conclusion that Nega, Tekola, Tedla and even Weldegiorgis were all involved in Andinet's activities. As to the murder of Kebire, he was uncertain, as the document suggesting the fatal measure gave no source. He therefore dropped Tedla as a leading suspect and concentrated on

Nega and Tekola, both of whom he accused of being the main driving force behind Andinet. His suspicions were later reinforced by the discovery of a piece of paper at the Andinet office requesting the assignment of two 'bold and dependable members to carry out a special mission'. Drew suspected that the mission referred to was Kebire's assassination. It was written by Tekola.[9]

Drew told his superiors that Nega and Tekola were exceeding their designated roles as liaison officers, and that they should be expelled and replaced. He also warned that Andinet was in contact with the 'intriguer' *Tsehafe Te'ezaz* Weldegiorgis through Abraha Weldetatios; he thought that link should be cut too.[10] George Clutton, head of the African Department at the Foreign Office in London, rejected Drew's charges against Nega as unreasonable and inconclusive as they were based on anonymous letters. Besides, since negotiations on a settlement were under way with Ethiopia for an outlet to the sea, taking steps against Nega would create problems for Britain's plans in the region. Britain was also seeking another Ethiopian concession on the use of Lake Tana and the Blue Nile. In other words, dismissing Ethiopian officials was neither timely nor convenient.[11] Drew had no choice but to express his disappointment and drop the issue altogether.[12]

Like all issues pertaining to events inside Eritrea, Kebire's assassination, a landmark in the upsurge of Eritrean nationalism, was submerged within Britain's regional power plan. His identified killer, a hitman from Tigray called Gebremedhin Abraha, was smuggled out by his Andinet and *shifta* colleagues to Adwa, where he was known to have bragged of his exploits openly. Gebreselassie Garza and Habtom Araia received prison sentences, later commuted, for possession of dangerous arms. No one was charged for Kebire's assassination.[13]

Kebire was an icon of the Eritrean struggle for independence. More than an ML leader, he was an exponent of Eritrean unity and nationalism, a man who crossed lines and barriers to reach out to a national base. In July 1947, he had given one of his most memorable speeches on the meaning of freedom:

> We are not gathered here today for a cause that does not include truth and justice, because our objective is founded on a rationality based on truth and justice. Our desire is to let the world know that we are a people with a separate livelihood and the right to claim what is ours. We hold no grudge or ill will against any monarch or any people. What we are demanding are merely the rights accorded to other peoples and nations. We should not be regarded as criminal for harbouring such dreams. Gentlemen, we demand freedom and liberty. We are ready to attain them by shedding our blood.[14]

So Kebire died as he promised to do in his often-repeated prophetic words about shedding his blood for his country. Forty days after his funeral, friends and colleagues in the ML, the LPP and the Italo-Eritrean Association held a large commemorative ceremony in his honour at Asmera's Cinema Impero. His fellow exponent of Eritrean nationalism, Weldeab, delivered the eulogy. Apparently, the UP leaders were not in attendance. Weldeab said:

> This august body has gathered here today to honour Abdelkader Kebire the Eritrean; not merely Kebire the politician. We are here to honour the father of a large family, not merely the leader of the Muslim League. Since this is a commemoration of our brave and steadfast Eritrean brother, no distinction between Muslim and Christian should be tearing us apart at this moment ...

After that pointed reference to the absent, chiefly Christian UP leadership, Weldeab commented that no side or party could ever stand to benefit from Kebire's fall. He then gave an impassioned plea:

> If a person's thoughts and ideas are sound and correct, they cannot be killed. Ideas have wings; they have muscles with which to fight. *Sheik* Abdelkader Kebire has bequeathed his thoughts and ideas to us. Our duty is to take them to their logical conclusion. Should we fail to do so because of our own weaknesses, we will be found guilty of having killed his ideas and objectives. To make sure that his ideas and objectives are not dead, therefore, let us struggle to pursue them to final victory. Let us obtain for Eritrea full and immediate liberty and progress.[15]

Kebire is still celebrated as the first martyr of Eritrea's decades-long struggle for independence.

Background to the Bevin–Sforza Agreement

In the meantime, the disposal of the former Italian colonies became the central focus of the UN's Political Committee. Although Italy had been part of the vanquished Axis powers, Mussolini and his Fascists had been toppled towards the end of the war and Italy made a last-minute switch to the Allied camp. This qualified it for full participation in the UN deliberations, and its foreign minister, Count Sforza, launched a strong campaign for Italy's return to Eritrea as a trustee. He was careful in his approach, mainly arguing that Ethiopia's fears of another invasion from Eritrea were unfounded, as that could not possibly happen under the UN's supervision. Italy sought to resume its development plans in Eritrea and continue 'the good work' about to be terminated by the British.[16]

Despite contradictory claims and counter-claims between them,[17] both Ethiopia and Italy were actually privately attempting to court Britain's favour by leaning towards its renewed plan of partition. Britain, in turn, sought US support for partition at the General Assembly. As we saw earlier, the US had been vacillating between different positions, especially on the Eritrean question. Towards the end of 1948, it started to favour the British position, but for its own reasons. As the emerging undisputed leader of the Western world, its opinion mattered, and with characteristic cunning, Ethiopia sought to secure superpower patronage from the US.

In November 1949, Prime Minister Aklilu met US Secretary of State George C. Marshall and suggested that, if the US supported Eritrea's 'return' to Ethiopia, the latter would agree to the extension of the lease of the American base, Radio Marina, for an indefinite period of time. Marshall approved but also added into the bargain the free use by the US of Asmera airport and the port of Massawa. Despite Aklilu's request that he put the agreement in writing, Marshall preferred that it remained an oral accord for the time being.[18]

The US's turnaround from trusteeship for Eritrea to its cession to Ethiopia was based on its emerging global policy. On 5 August 1948, the US Joint Chiefs of Staff (JCS) held a meeting where they developed their military policy for the broader Middle East. No rival party or power would be allowed to establish itself in the Middle East. An alliance with the peoples of the region would be assured through the provision of social and economic help and the establishment of a common defence pact. The oil in the region should only be exploited by the US and its allies. In the case of a resumption of war, US military intervention would be guaranteed. The JCS declared that these decisions were also necessitated by Britain's concerns in the Middle East. Just as with Tripoli for the British, Asmera airport and the port of Massawa were essential for the US. As for the US communications base in Asmera, since no other spot could equal the quality of service it provided, the US's rights in Eritrea were not negotiable.[19]

The US had thus already come to the conclusion that Italy's return to Eritrea as a trustee would stand in the way of its domination of the Middle Eastern region. One day before the meeting of the JCS, the American Assistant Secretary of Defence met his British counterpart to say that the US stood against an Italian return to Eritrea. Instead, his government supported the cession of the *kebessa* and the Red Sea coast of Eritrea to Ethiopia; western Eritrea should be annexed to Sudan.[20]

Other considerations may have prompted the US change of mind. According to Okbazghi Yohannes, the US was apprehensive of an Ethiopian move to the Soviet camp if its demands were not met. US investment in Ethiopia was also growing. Above all, the political mood in Eritrea was so unstable that even the UP's strong presence could dissipate with changing conditions. It was in the US's interest, therefore, to come out in support of the British partition plan.[21]

By the time of the presentation of the Eritrean case before the UN committee, the two powers were already in agreement over partition. As a concession to Italian demands and sensitivities, the US suggested that Italian residents of Eritrea be allowed to maintain their Italian citizenship; run their own schools, hospitals and religious establishments; and express themselves freely through publications in their own language.[22] Judging from Italy's subsequent change of direction, it must have regarded the concessions as satisfactory.

On 6 April 1949, the Political Committee started its deliberations on the Italian colonies. The head of the US delegation, John Foster Dulles (later Secretary of

State), was the first to give indications of the points the US and Britain had already agreed upon. On Libya, he generally suggested that Britain's interests should be given due consideration. He recommended Somalia be placed under Italy's trusteeship. Eritrea, he declared, was lacking in unity and was not ready for independence; it posed a threat to Ethiopia, which deserved an outlet to the Red Sea. He therefore recommended that the eastern parts of the country, including Asmera and the port of Massawa, should be merged with Ethiopia. A separate solution would be arranged for Eritrea's Western Provinces.[23]

Dulles's intention was to pre-empt other positions, and he succeeded, as the points he raised became the focus of all the discussion that followed. In its often-heated debate, the committee split in competing directions: the Anglo-American proposal for partition; French insistence on Italian trusteeship, with Ethiopia taking Asseb; the Soviet bloc's similar stance on Italian trusteeship followed by independence or a joint UN trusteeship; and what Okbazghi Yohannes called 'the third way'. This group, which consisted of several Arab, Eastern European and Asian states, tried to push the interests of the people of the former colonies to the fore. Did the territories under consideration have populations and did they matter? The delegate from the Philippines, for example, mused that only in Antarctica was it possible to carve up land the way the powers were suggesting. He also expressed his objection to the word 'disposal' as inappropriate for land inhabited by human beings. The issue was not land or territory, but the future and fate of the people who populated it. They had the right to be consulted.[24]

Such calls to reason and justice usually fell on deaf ears. Arguments were often furious and full of hostility. Britain and Ethiopia presented such a bleak picture of Eritrea's poverty and lack of self-sufficiency that it provoked a Soviet rebuke. Britain, Andrei Gromyko of the USSR pointed out, might have registered a deficit of £1.9 million over the previous six years in Eritrea, but he reminded the committee that it had plundered £85 million worth of property from the same country.[25] Most of these exchanges were expressed more out of rivalry than real concern for the people in the colonies. It was in the middle of such bickering that the Political Committee decided to hear from representatives of Eritrea, Somalia and Libya. The ML, Pro-Italy, the UP, CRIE and the Italo-Eritrean Association were allowed their time before the committee.

First up was Ibrahim Sultan of the ML. He spoke in detail to disprove Ethiopian claims that Eritrea had historically been part and parcel of Ethiopia. He denied that Muslim Eritreans had ever had anything to do with the ethnicity, religion, history or economy of Ethiopia. Referring to Kebire's recent assassination, he argued that, given the chance, Ethiopia would oppress Muslims and cause them suffering. He further stressed that 80% of the Eritrean people stood against the partition of the country and that, if trusteeship was the final decision, the ML preferred the UN itself to assume responsibility. Having made his point, he turned from his well-known nationalistic approach to speak as a Muslim. His claim that, of a total population of 1.25 million, 75%, or close to one million Eritreans, were Muslim was highly exaggerated. He also reiterated that there was not much unity among the non-Muslim population, as it was divided along ethnic and religious lines.[26] His testimony, which gave Aklilu Habtewold the chance to expose his inaccuracies, failed to impress the committee.[27]

Tedla Bairu and his UP colleagues had little more to tell the committee beyond what the Ethiopians had been saying to it for months on the historical, religious, cultural and geographical unity between the two countries. He claimed that the UP spoke for the majority of the people, including one-third of the Muslim population of the country. He rejected Italian trusteeship and underlined that Eritrea's interests as a whole could only be safeguarded within a union with Ethiopia and turned down any form of partition.[28]

The Pro-Italy's *Blata* Mohammed Abdallah gave his party's reasons for preferring Italian trusteeship, to be followed by independence. Filippo Casciani, representing the Italo-Eritrean Association, argued that Eritrea's network of kinship ties and the spirit of cooperation and good-neighbourliness among its people provided a sound base for Eritrean independence. He suggested that Ethiopia's need for access to the sea could be accommodated by allowing it the use of port facilities or the creation of a free zone, but he vehemently rejected Eritrea's partition.[29]

Overall, it was not a good session for the Eritrean nationalists. They were too divided and ill-prepared to argue complicated issues in an international forum. Perhaps to galvanise the strong support of the fifteen Arab and Muslim states, even Ibrahim Sultan sounded more like a Muslim leader than the inclusive nationalist he actually was.[30] Ibrahim and his colleagues thus failed to capitalise on their first appearance before the world body. It was a lesson that they would learn from over the following few days. This is not to suggest that an impressive presentation by Ibrahim or others would have influenced the outcome. However, in the slow and painful progress towards a cohesive approach to the protection of Eritrea's national interests, the disappointing performance by the advocates of Eritrean independence would have a sobering effect on them.

The Bevin–Sforza Agreement

In the Political Committee, two contending views confronted each other. A clause in the American-backed British plan of partition, known as A/C.1/446, provided for a special charter for the administration of Asmera and Massawa, which was meant to protect Italian interests there. On the other side, a majority of the members, including France, the Soviet Union and most Latin American delegations, argued, albeit from different perspectives, that the interests of the people of the colonies should be given top consideration. Mexico, for example, proposed a joint trusteeship for Eritrea to be followed by eventual independence, with Britain, the US, Italy, France and Ethiopia as administering powers. The USSR came out with its own alternative proposal of joint trusteeship with itself, the US, Britain and Italy as caretakers.[31] India and Iraq suggested that the whole matter should be removed from the sphere of superpower competition and based instead on the interests of the populations concerned. With regard to Eritrea, they proposed the holding of a referendum to determine the true wishes of its people. Iraq also proposed setting up a five-nation commission to carry out the task.[32]

When this proposal appeared to hold sway within the committee, Dulles intervened once again and suggested the establishment of a fifteen-member subcommittee to examine all the proposals thus far put forward, including possible new ideas that could be entertained. This was on 9 May, and the subcommittee was instructed to come back with its findings on the 12th of the same month.

The very next day, 10 May, Associated Press announced that foreign ministers Ernest Bevin of Britain and Carlo Sforza of Italy had reached a settlement on the former colonies in secret side meetings. The surprise announcement proposed British and French trusteeship over Cyrenaica and Fezzan, respectively, with Tripolitania to be placed under Italian charge after 1951. There was no change on Eritrea. Except for the Western Provinces, which they assigned to Sudan, Bevin and Sforza proposed that Eritrea should join Ethiopia, provided the latter agreed to a UN-sponsored special status for Asmera and Massawa and guarantees for the safety of Italian residents in the country. Italy, according to the plan, was to administer Italian Somaliland.

The most difficult obstacle that Bevin–Sforza purported to remove was the deadlock between Britain and Italy over Britain's refusal to recognise any Italian rights over Tripolitania and Italy's equally strong resistance to accepting any Great Power involvement in Eritrea except its own. This was initially hailed as the possible solution to a difficult problem. Some foresaw it gaining the two-thirds majority vote needed for adoption in the UN General Assembly.[33]

Of great significance was Ethiopia's furtive shift from its long-held, adamant claim to the whole of Eritrea to one of acceptance of the partition plan. In his book *Ye-Ertra Gudai* (The Eritrea Matter), Zewde Retta has described Ethiopia's reaction during the discussions leading up to the agreement and the agreement itself. In view of the American preference for the accord, Ethiopia's Aklilu Habtewold knew that his country would have little chance of putting up a successful resistance. He therefore sent a message to Haile Selassie suggesting that it would be wiser for Ethiopia to be satisfied with the Eritrean territory assigned to it by Bevin–Sforza and fight for the rest later. He made an exception with the special charter for Asmera and Massawa, insisting that such a decision would infringe on Ethiopia's rights and that he would argue against it. He also asked for advice on where to stand on the trusteeship proposals for Libya and Somalia, more because he feared reprisals for taking the side of the Great Powers.

Haile Selassie wrote back to Aklilu to say that, although the Bevin–Sforza agreement was not to his liking, 'We agree with your suggestion to possess the half and fight for the rest in the future. We give you our permission to go ahead.' He had cautioned Aklilu earlier not to be too harsh on the agreement as it might jeopardise Ethiopia's warm relations with Britain. Haile Selassie's instructions to Aklilu were so vague that he needed further explanations, this time from Weldegiorgis. The latter's message was terse. 'During the discussions,' Weldegiorgis wrote, 'avoid lining up on the forefront in criticising our friends and infringing on their interests is what the Emperor is telling you.'[34] Thus, Ethiopia had already accepted the partition of Eritrea even before the agreement was presented for the full committee's consideration.

Soon it became clear why Dulles had insisted on creating the subcommittee of fifteen members. At its first meeting, it accepted Bevin–Sforza as a package and, relegating all the other proposals to secondary votes, adopted the accord by a majority of ten for, four against and one abstention. This decision was duly submitted to the full committee on its appointed date of 12 May.[35]

Opposition from the full committee was immediate. Several members put up a serious challenge to the manner in which Bevin–Sforza was passed to the subcommittee without the full committee's approval, a requirement for the competing proposals. Furthermore, unrest was flaring up on the ground in the former colonies. Anti-Italian riots and demonstrations rocked Tripolitania, causing the full committee to back down and, over the objection of the British delegation, recall representatives of the former colonies to restate their case once again.[36] 'Death with honour!' would be better than another hour of subjugation under Italy, exclaimed a spokesman from Libya in front of the committee. He went on to declare a state of passive resistance against the British Administration and asserted that the agreement was in breach of the Atlantic Charter, characterising it as an imposition that could only be rejected by force of arms.

Ibrahim Sultan too had his hour at the meeting, and this time he did not disappoint. In a hastily constructed merger named the Eritrean Popular Front, the ML, LPP and Pro-Italy chose him to speak on their behalf. Here is how *The Times* of London reported Ibrahim's performance:

> The spokesman ... was equally vehement in condemning the Bevin–Sforza agreement as detrimental to the aspirations of the whole Eritrean people for immediate independence. He asked that a neutral United Nations Commission be sent to the territory to ascertain their views. They were opposed both to partition and to annexation by any country, and if immediate independence were not granted them, they asked for direct United Nations trusteeship ...[37]

Had Ibrahim's impressive presentation come before Bevin–Sforza, it might have made some difference. But, with Italy's acceptance of partition, many of the Latin

American delegations had already relaxed their former stance on Italian trusteeship and Eritrean independence. Ecuador, for example, came out clearly on the side of partition.[38] Not all hope was lost. Pakistan and the Soviet bloc led the fight against the implementation of the accord, with tangible results.

On 13 May, the committee adopted Bevin–Sforza and passed it on to the UN General Assembly for final ratification. The latter took up the matter on 17 May. In the meantime, violent demonstrations took place in Tripolitania, and strong messages of protest and petitions flowed in from Eritrea and Somalia. Arab and socialist states joined in the chorus.[39]

The voting process was complicated. First, the General Assembly had to vote on the proposals for each former colony individually. At the second stage, the agreement as a package had to be approved by a two-thirds majority. Only the partition of Eritrea gained a majority vote on the first ballot. However, since the package as a whole was defeated in the second round, the Bevin–Sforza plan was abandoned.[40]

Bevin–Sforza was a wake-up call for Eritreans, who saw it as a sinister plot not only against themselves, but also against the committee. When news of the General Assembly's vote to partition reached Eritrean ears, notices of protest meetings and permission to hold public demonstrations filled the Chief Administrator's office in Asmera. The ML led the drive for an independent commission of inquiry to determine the extent of the Eritrean people's total aversion to any form of partition or Ethiopian rule. This was a move coordinated with the three parties—ML, Pro-Italy and CRIE—that formed the Eritrean Popular Front. All three parties had in fact circulated an appeal among members of the General Assembly voicing their opposition in the strongest of terms; a petition they also copied to independence-seeking parties in Eritrea. 'It is not our wish or that of our people to see our blessed and fertile land, which has never been divided, to be so dissected against our will,' the petition concluded.[41]

Although the BMA was well aware of the strong resistance to partition, it still attempted to convince the petitioners that a second commission of inquiry could not possibly bring about a different solution. On the other hand, in one of its reports, the BMA let it be known that, since partition was opposed by all parties, it had felt relief at the final outcome of Bevin–Sforza. It also underlined that the establishment of the Eritrean Popular Front was the direct result of that debacle. It admitted that British betrayal had caused much pain in Eritrea and that, although the Administration's ban on public demonstrations denied them a chance of self-expression, they would allow them at some future time.[42]

Unionist reaction in the aftermath of Bevin–Sforza was vague. Ethiopia's acceptance of partition created doubts among members who had opposed the plan from the start. In spite of public declarations by the leadership of biding their time and going prepared to the impending fourth session of the General Assembly, their tone had moderated considerably. This led to a temporary abatement of violence and active political confrontation. A different atmosphere was actually taking shape within the UP. The BMA noted that this had come about with the appearance of groups within the UP shifting to an acceptance of conditional union as opposed to direct merger with Ethiopia.[43]

It was probably the calm before the storm. Across the border from Ethiopia, *shifta* bands were regrouping after a lull. In May, Hagos Temnewo, Gebre Tesfatsion, Asresehey Embaye and Weldeselassie Adal met to coordinate and plan joint activities. They duly sent messages signed by all four leaders, warning chiefs and *mislenes* in the Seraye province that any form of resistance or collusion against union would be punished. The scene was set for a new wave of violence.[44]

In the meantime, in spite of its failure at the UN, the spectre of partition, opposed thus far by unionists and nationalists alike, was to haunt Eritreans during yet another round of British pressure.

Eritrean Response to Bevin–Sforza

Political activity sprang back to life when Ibrahim returned from Lake Success. The BMA authorities reported that he had come back transformed in stature, while still acknowledging his sharpness of mind and ability to change a situation through his sheer will and personality.

On 19 June 1949, the leaderships of ML, LPP, Pro-Italy and the Veterans Association of former Eritrean askaris convened a meeting. Here, Pro-Italy and the Veterans agreed to change their demand for Italian trusteeship and merge into a new party, Nuova Eritrea, to work for full independence. Together, they all formed the Eritrean Bloc for the Independence of Eritrea, or the Independence Bloc (IB). Later, the Italo-Eritrean Association joined the bloc, thus increasing its political and numerical strength.[45] An immediate British assessment gave the IB a two-thirds majority over the rest of the parties. However, nervousness in the unionist camp was leading to a return to violence.[46] In June alone, when the Mossazghi brothers murdered two Italians in Senafe and another *shifta* attack resulted in two more deaths around Mendefera, Tigrayan *shifta* bands confronted the Eritrean police force in the Adwa border area.[47]

Extreme political pressure on Italian Eritreans added to the growing tension. In a scathing attack, the unionist polemicist Teweldeberhan Gebremedhin (Zekios) characterised them as 'unbaptised by their parents; stateless people who, forgetful of fascist neglect over their fates, are attempting to whiten their tanned skins'.[48] Ibrahim and Weldeab also filled unionist propaganda pages with unrelenting vitriol from the same polemicist and his colleagues. They were often referred to as '*i due inganni*', meaning deceitful or fraudulent.

As the IB's relentless growth continued, the possibility of independence started to look and sound real. However, British officials downplayed the notion as impractical. Not one native can sit in a position of responsibility, declared a Foreign

Office official; nor could the country sustain itself economically. He predicted that an independent Eritrea would soon be invaded by Ethiopia or become an Italian backyard. Others invoked Eritrea's ethnic and religious diversity as impediments to its survival as a free country.[49]

On 4 July, the IB's five parties—ML, LPP, Veterans, Nuova Eritrea and CRIE—met to create a coalition of political parties seeking the independence and territorial integrity of Eritrea within existing borders. They underlined their firm stand against any form of partition or annexation of the country.[50] A new group calling itself Association of Eritrean Intellectuals threw its support behind the bloc. It was composed mostly of better-schooled citizens who had been on the unionist side or remained neutral.[51]

The IB was a hastily regrouped coalition none of whose components could claim to possess the discipline, control and adherence to principles that characterise political parties. Its membership was so wide open that movement in and out of its ranks became an immediate problem. Nevertheless, to the dismay and concern of British officials, the tide was on its side, and the possibility of Eritrean independence standing a fair chance of prevailing at the UN could not be ruled out.

Such fears intensified when the UP started to show cracks within its leadership. Frustrated by the advances of the IB and its incursions into UP membership, even Tedla Bairu's enthusiasm was increasingly put to the test. Just as in 1944, after Brigadier Longrigg's crackdown on the mutinying Eritrean police, the UP caved in to months of low-key *shifta* and terrorist activities, mainly on Italians by the Mossazghi band. Again, just as in 1944, Ethiopia sent its officials to the rescue, this time led by the Finance Minister, Yilma Deressa, and including the Health Minister, Ephrem Teweldemedhin, and Judge Kiflezgi Yehdego (both Eritreans) and Kidanemariam Aberra (a Tigrayan). Although they gave different excuses, including health, for their visit, Chief Administrator Drew soon found out that they had come to breathe some life into the declining unionists.

Ethiopia had cause to be alarmed. Prior to Yilma's arrival, the UP sent a telegram to the Ethiopian Government, warning it that, unless it came up with concrete proposals on what Eritrea was to expect from the union, the whole UP membership could defect to the IB. The UP wanted to know how many Eritreans would occupy places in the Ethiopian cabinet, what proportion of seats would be reserved for Eritreans in the Ethiopian parliament and the central government itself, and so on.[52] These were preconditions previously unheard of.

It was obvious that the UP was losing its hold.[53] Aklilu too joined Yilma to avert the danger. Significantly in terms of a later event, he met with Abraha Tessema, a major leader of the LPP who had spearheaded the Tigray-Tigrigni movement, giving rise to some speculation. In his meeting with Drew, he voiced his deep concern over the IB's gains and his fears that Eritrea would deny his country access to the sea. Drew tried to allay Aklilu's fears by stating that, eventually, a poor Eritrea would fall into Ethiopian dependency, but privately he concluded that Eritrea's independence movement had indeed become a major problem for Ethiopia.[54]

August 1949 ended in favour of the IB, and it was with great anticipation that its leaders prepared to head to Lake Success for the fourth session of the UN General Assembly, scheduled to begin on 28 August. Even in the judgement of the British, Ibrahim was riding high above all the politicians of those days. Brushing aside rumours that he was a paid Italian agent, he set his sights on broadening his contacts abroad—with Arab, Asian and Latin American countries—to gain support at the UN, where he expected the Eritrean case to be settled.[55] But his home base was still fractious.

At the beginning of September, the ML faced its biggest setback yet. Mohammed Omer Qadi, one of the chief organisers of the Bet Giorgis Convention on conditional union with Ethiopia, announced his withdrawal from the ML to set up a new party that he named the Independent Muslim League—Massawa Division. In the preamble to its declaration, his group acknowledged, somewhat apologetically, that its move would divide the ML in two. However, in view of British rejection of trusteeship over Eritrea, they considered the IB as good as dead and feared a return to the old Italian rule. For this reason, it concluded, 'We have come to realise that the best way is to join Ethiopia, the land most proximate to us by land and interest. However, the union should be based on equal or mutual rights and obligations and should be presented at the UN.'[56]

Both Ethiopia and the UP warmly accepted Omer Qadi, a man of stature and influence in Eritrea. His highly exaggerated figure of a 60,000 membership notwithstanding, the UP shelved its severe stand against conditional union to include him in its delegation to Lake Success. Omer Qadi's damaging move left a sour taste as the IB made its high-spirited preparations for the fourth session of the General Assembly.

The Fourth Session of the General Assembly

The fourth session started on 20 September. At the very beginning, US Secretary of State Dean Acheson announced that his government supported the independence of an undivided Libya, following a period of UN trusteeship.[57] Suddenly, the issue of the former Italian colonies was no longer to be treated as a package: each case would stand on its own peculiarities and merits. When the general consensus leaned towards an Italian return to Somalia as a trustee, Eritrea remained the outstanding issue.

After the Political Committee created a 16th Ad Hoc Committee, the IB, UP, Independent Muslim League and CRIE appeared before the latter committee. Most of their presentations were a repeat of their former positions. According to Weldeab, who was there as an IB delegate, they could do no more, as only fifteen minutes was allotted per speaker. The major deliberations were meanwhile taking place in the corridors of the UN.

Ibrahim made an impassioned speech for independence. Rejecting the often-repeated allegation that Eritrea's ethnic and religious diversity would stand in the way of nation-building, he denounced any plan that aimed to place his country or any part of it under foreign rule. He reiterated Ethiopia's inability to govern a country that occupied a higher level of social and economic development.

In a major departure from the old unionist stand for the annexation of the whole of Eritrea by Ethiopia, Tedla Bairu appeared before the committee to openly support the already defunct Bevin–Sforza plan. According to Weldeab, the UP delegation had been met upon arrival at Lake Success by Aklilu Habtewold himself, and he had instructed it to support partition. The delegation was so stunned by the new development, recalled Weldeab, that its leader, Beyene Beraki, had to be treated for a nervous breakdown.[58] It was indeed an embarrassing change of principle from the abrasive and aggressive stance that the UP had taken thus far. Any pretence that it was an independent party seeking to join Ethiopia of its own volition was now compromised. Tedla's explanation that his party would not insist on forcing Eritreans unwilling to join Ethiopia into the bargain was not carefully considered beforehand, as it threw the field wide open for other groups of people to demand separate treatment. Tedla further expressed to the committee his fears that, should the UN declare Eritrea an independent state, the people of the *kebessa* would be severed from Ethiopia and be subjected to rule under the IB against their will. It was to avoid this possibility that the UP was reluctantly agreeing to the partition plan.[59]

Encouraged by Ethiopia's support, Britain raised its pitch for partition to much higher levels. Eritrea, one of its statements claimed, 'is not the result of an organic political growth', but the legacy of disjointed clans and religions put together by old commercial groups.[60] Britain's depiction of Eritrea's poverty, disunity and deprivation was so off the mark that it prompted a biting criticism from Zafarullah Khan of Pakistan, who spearheaded the argument that the wishes of the people of Eritrea should be examined by a commission. If, as the British delegation was claiming, Eritrea was poor, destitute and a hopeless ruin, he mused, would Britain be justified in asking Ethiopia to carry such a heavy burden?[61]

The idea of sending a commission of inquiry to Eritrea gained ground when Latin American and Asian countries put their support behind it. In those weeks, nothing that Ethiopia could do would turn the tide in its favour. In frustration, its delegate, Ephrem Teweldemedhin, attempted to prick the Western conscience by accusing the world body of a second round of betrayal of Ethiopia in favour of Italy. He even threatened that Ethiopia would invoke its right to self-defence as stipulated in the Atlantic Charter.

As we have noted, the US had developed the habit of injecting new ideas whenever matters got out of hand. In October 1949, its delegate, Philip Jessup, suggested the creation of a federation between Eritrea and Ethiopia. It was a vague formula whereby Eritrea would, as a state, form a federal partnership with Ethiopia, under the sovereignty of the Ethiopian Crown. Such an arrangement would last for ten years, after which the people of Eritrea could freely choose whether they wanted to continue the partnership or go their separate way.[62]

After rejecting the Jessup proposal, the 17th Ad Hoc Committee agreed to send a commission of inquiry to Eritrea. Its task was to determine the wishes of the Eritrean population; to guarantee their safety; and, upon studying the question of its final disposal, to submit its assessments and recommendations to the Secretary General of the UN. At the same time, the Ad Hoc Committee recommended independence for Libya and Italian trusteeship for Somalia.[63] The larger Political Committee not only adopted the Ad Hoc Committee's recommendations, but it also named the five UN members that would constitute the commission of inquiry for Eritrea—Pakistan, Guatemala, Burma, South Africa and Norway. Of these, Norway was the only country that had supported Ethiopia's claims throughout the proceedings; the rest had opposed Eritrea's cession to Ethiopia. Norway's inclusion was obviously made to accommodate Ethiopia's fears and sensitivities.[64]

On 12 November 1949, the Political Committee submitted its recommendations to the General Assembly of the UN. The proposal was carried with forty-eight votes for, one against and nine abstentions.[65] Preparations then got under way for the commission's visit to Eritrea.

8

THE INDEPENDENCE BLOC

GAINS AND VULNERABILITIES

Eritrean Reaction to the UN's Recommendations

Philip Jessup's 'federal' proposal may have been brushed aside at the UN, but it produced quite an effect inside Eritrea. In view of the acceptance of partition by the Unionist Party (UP) and Ethiopia, many unionists started to question Ethiopia's real motives in claiming Eritrea. Was it territory, especially ports, that Ethiopia was after or did it seek, as they had been led to believe, a people bonded with it in history and culture? Suddenly, the base on which unionism had been presumed to flourish, the much-heralded 'irredentist movement' that every British document had christened 'Ethiopian nationalism in Eritrea', revealed signs of further crumbling. If a federal arrangement could be devised, UP members already leaning towards some form of conditional union started to entertain that idea, and even to join the Independence Bloc (IB) in great numbers.

Alarmed by the new development, the UP leadership, headed by its president, old *Ras* Kidanemariam himself, and *Abune* Markos, met British Administration of Eritrea (BAE) authorities and demanded permission to hold public demonstrations to protest against any solution for Eritrea except immediate and unconditional union. Their request was turned down, but their demands and petitions were duly sent to Lake Success.[1] A few days later, the IB also sent some forty delegates to the authorities putting forward its own demands that rejected any solution other than full independence.[2] Such local demands and petitions were largely ignored by the UN Ad Hoc Committee, which at the time had already chosen its course of action. Frustrated by the results and fearful of what the Commission of Inquiry on Eritrea (CIE) might have in store for it, the UP raised the level of its propaganda campaign throughout the country.

Although the IB had formed a central council and set up regional offices, delays in starting serious political work caused it to lose valuable time that could have been used to prepare for an appearance before the CIE. Ibrahim Sultan was still in Italy and the Middle East, galvanising international support, and nothing of substance could be done in his absence. By the end of 1949, the IB had not been formally inaugurated, nor its top leadership named. As a new party, it had no formal newspaper of its own, and its strategy and tactics were not yet in place. The UP, on the other hand, had all those advantages, and it used them to effect. Following the UN decision, its newspaper, *Ethiopia,* started issuing chilling propaganda pieces, chiefly targeting Ibrahim and Weldeab as agents of Italy. It accused the IB of treason and of seeking to return Eritrea to Italian slavery. 'Your country, your property, your land and your *risti* will be confiscated. Your genes and lineage will be obliterated,' it warned. Referring to Italy, one of its articles declared:

> A wolf may change its skin, but it cannot change its character, evil and wickedness. Understand that Italy will not stop its old bloody deeds and actions. Should you be compromised by its money and promises, then start to feel sorry for yourself, your offspring and your descendants. As for you, children, who are being condemned through no fault of yours, denounce your parentage.[3]

Parallel to this propaganda campaign, a sustained and relentless campaign of *shifta* activity gripped the countryside. On 25 September, Asresehey and the Mossazghi brothers joined forces to attack a police post at Beraqit Abay in Akeleguzai. Between 50 and 75 *shifta* participated in the incident, in which a police officer was killed and five more captured.[4] On 5–6 October, five armed men attacked a railway station on the Asmera–Massawa line, killing two Italian employees. They left a note identifying themselves as unionists. One month later, eight men entered Mendefera one evening and murdered an Italian and a Greek in a bar on the main street. They too left notes urging the British to keep their promises and warning Italians to desist from supporting Eritrean independence. A few days later, an Indian and two more Italians suffered the same fate in Embatkala, on the Massawa road and in the Dekemhare area.[5]

The linkages between the UP campaign of words and the increasing *shifta* activity became too obvious for the BAE to keep ignoring them. Thus, after the Mendefera incident, the BAE detained two of the major UP leaders of the Seraye province, *Melake Selam* Dimetros Gebremariam, a cleric whom we will meet in subsequent pages, and *Azmatch* Tesfai Beraki, a *mislene*. They were both exiled to the town of Tesseney.[6]

Yet, in spite of all the attempts to harass the IB and frighten off further defections from the UP, the IB's progress continued. Upon his return from Lake Success, Tedla Bairu, already frustrated by the proceedings of the fourth session of the General Assembly, put the blame squarely on Britain's refusal to consider the US's federal proposal. Was the die-hard unionist leaning towards a 'federal' solution? This ambiguity on the issue of federation was to haunt Tedla throughout the rest of his political career. Furthermore, by being coerced to accept partition at the UN, he and his colleagues had bent to the will of Ethiopia, thus compromising the UP's claims to an independent line and existence.

In the meantime, other developments were brewing that rendered the months prior to the arrival of the CIE very complicated indeed.

The Shuban (Youth) al Rabita

Ever since its inception as a political organisation, the Muslim League (ML) had sought the active participation of young Muslims from all over the country. According to Ahmed Mohammed Seid, a founder of the Shuban al Rabita, the youths had consistently demanded arms to protect themselves from their Andinet antagonists. Ibrahim Sultan resisted the idea for very practical reasons. 'Andinet have a base area in Ethiopia,' he kept telling them. 'Where can you go for refuge? You can't go to Ethiopia. Sudan is British territory. Our only alternative is to drown in the Red Sea.'[7]

However, the idea of organising a separate youth organisation continued with a core of active young Muslims leading the drive. At an unspecified date, possibly in late 1948, a meeting took place in Mohammed Aberra Hagos's tearoom, the Pearl of the Red Sea, where the Shuban (Youth) held their inaugural meeting. Chairing the meeting were Ahmed Mohammed Seid, Mohammed Seid Aberra of the Aberra Hagos family, Said Sefaf of Ghinda'e, and Mahmoud Omer Ibrahim, a qualified engineer from Keren.

Shuban offices were subsequently opened in selected centres of the country where veterans were assigned to run them and recruit new members. An executive committee was also named with Mohammed Seid Aberra elected president. Shuban al Rabita—Youths of the (Muslim) League—was essentially a volunteer organisation that had little financial support from either the ML or the IB. Ahmed Mohammed Seid asserted that, throughout its active existence, its day-to-day running had to be covered from the contributions of its membership. Yet, by 1949, it had managed to grow into an impressive group recognisable by its white uniform, capes and the ML flag and insignia. It was an all-male group, women being excluded from public activities in accordance with Sharia practice. Inevitably, the Shuban's formation heightened the tension between Andinet and Muslim youths that would later culminate in a major violent confrontation.

Parallel to the establishment of the Shuban, a more potent Muslim force was asserting itself in the Hazemo Plains, along the Akeleguzai side of the Mereb River. Inhabited by the Eritrean Assaorta, the numerically dominant Saho group, this area had been the target of Ethiopian *shifta*, crossing the border to harass them. In 1948, the Assaorta had suffered several deaths and inflicted some in turn on the Tigrayans. To add insult to injury, Tigrayans of the Ahse'a region started to demand the removal of the Assaorta from the border areas, thus arousing the anger and indignation of the Assaorta as a whole.

Sheik Saleh Musa Abudawd, who was to represent the Assaorta in the Eritrean Assembly in 1952, was deeply involved in the events that followed. According to him, the Assaorta, under the leadership of their paramount chief, Nasser Abubeker Pasha, demanded that the BAE supply them with arms and ammunition for self-defence. The British demurred, saying that the move would only worsen the situation. *Sheik* Ibrahim and the ML were then approached for help. Ibrahim too was against the idea. 'If Al Rabita arms the Assaorta,' he told them, 'it will be inviting Ethiopia to come in with all its force. We have neither the capacity nor the resources to enter into an armed race with Ethiopia. Let us concentrate on our political struggle.' Luckily for the Assaorta, the BAE saw the justice of their demands and gave its approval, provided the arms were not used to disrupt trade, attack neighbours and peaceful citizens, or target British police and troops. Nasser Abubeker himself oversaw the arming of his people. Thus was formed a group that called itself the Guards of al Rabita.

Out of this group emerged Saho leaders who gained notoriety as independence fighters or *shifta* leaders whose feats still form part of the folklore of the local population. Omer Guduf, the first designated leader of the Guards, was succeeded in that role by the celebrated Ali Shum, Omer Alula, Osman Haji Nasser and Saleh Suleiman. Under their leadership, the armed Assaorta were able to organise and maintain a disciplined regime of self-defence that allowed the people of the area to return to a peaceful life, while checking any further attempts by Tigrayan *shifta* to resume their old attacks. The ML could also justifiably boast of a period of armed resistance to Ethiopian and Andinet domination.

But this essential balance did not continue for long. For some inexplicable reason, unidentified armed Saho bands scaled the escarpment up to the highlands of eastern Seraye on 31 December 1949, and burned several villages, destroyed property, looted livestock and even desecrated churches. In most prior confrontations involving Muslims and Christians, churches and mosques had usually been spared. Taking it as an affront to Christianity, the Mossazghi and Asresehey bands joined forces, followed the culprits in hot pursuit, and unleashed a campaign of retaliation on the Saho of the Hazemo Plains. It was an ugly confrontation in which innocent lives were lost. Probably because the Guards of al Rabita were at hand to protect their people, the Mossazghi band suffered the most on the battlefield. The incident would have taken a religious turn had the two senior leaders of Akeleguzai, *Ras* Tessema Asberom and Nasser Abubeker Pasha, not intervened to arrange a truce between the warring parties. Their mediation is still hailed as an example of local wisdom and sound traditional practice in conflict resolution.[8]

Both Ethiopian and local sources were quick to blame the British for having instigated the troubles over the new year. Indeed, in every interview carried out in the area, the names of two British officers come up as agents playing one side against the other. According to eyewitnesses, a British officer, L.M. Brans, was seen in the company of UP *shiftas*, while one Lorimer paid visits to the Saho militia.[9] We have not found documented evidence to prove Lorimer's contacts with the Saho, but a British police report reveals a telling conversation between Superintendent L.M. Brans and *shifta* leader Gebre Tesfatsion in 1951, a year of excessive violence and *shifta* activity throughout the country.

In the 1951 encounter, Gebre expressed his acceptance of a possible official pardon. 'But I would not consider it a pardon, but my demobilization from the British army ... I have always served the British,' he told Brans and apologised profusely for having killed a British officer in one of his confrontations with police troops. He talked of his quarrel with the Italians and his service for the British, with whom, as we saw previously, he had fought at Metema.

> Brans: How many Italians have you killed, Gebre?
> Gebre: I have not kept count; they are not worth it.
> Brans: Didn't you kill an Italian woman in 1941 on the road to Keren?
> Gebre: Yes, Italian women breed fascists.
> Brans: Are you still bitter towards Italians?
> Gebre: ... Let's not talk anymore about Italians because I am starting to tremble.
> Brans: ... If all *shifta* are pardoned, do you think they will all come in?
> Gebre: Yes, I think so. A few thieves may stay out, but we can deal with them ...
> Brans: Do not commit any offences until you hear from the British Administration.
> Gebre: That is easy, too easy. I will go to Korea and fight with the British if I am sent.[10]

Such indulgence of a *shifta* leader by an officer of the British police gives credibility to charges of British involvement in sponsoring violence and armed internal conflict in those crucial years.

The Independence Bloc Inaugurated

As mentioned earlier, the IB lost valuable time waiting to resume activities. By December 1949, the British were calling it an organisation built on sand and rent apart by internal conflict and contradictions. Nevertheless, they admitted that it was maintaining its hold. Referring to their own impending plans of interference, they added that the real test for the IB was imminent.[11] Indeed, there was little sense of purpose in the IB's course of action. It was only on 28 January 1950 that it was able to print the first issue of its own newspaper, *Hanti Ertra*, with Weldeab Weldemariam as the editor. Following this, the IB was at last able to convene meetings of representatives in the town of Dekemhare between 3 December 1949 and 1 January 1950. It had taken seven months for the IB to declare itself a formal political organisation.

The convention started on a positive note. The octogenarian *Ras* Tessema, who chaired it, gave one of his most memorable speeches. He said:

> We regret that the organisation that is opposing us is using weapons contrary to the laws of God and that of our ancestors. We warn that this cannot be to the benefit of Eritrea. We could employ similar methods. But we prefer to obtain our quest for independence through our traditional laws, the laws of God and the laws of the United Nations. We do not seek to spread chaos in this country that we love. We seek to found a free and independent state, administered by its educated citizens; a state devoid of partiality and oppression ...[12]

When the actual proceedings began, the issue of election to the presidency became contentious, so much so that the majority of the delegates decided to take a break for consultation with their respective parties. They met again on 10 February. When the issue threatened to disrupt the convention, Ibrahim Sultan came up with a compromise. The presidency, he proposed, would rotate between a Muslim and a Christian every year. He also suggested that the first presidency go to a Christian. As the leader of ML, the majority party, he could have legitimately claimed the post for his group, but he chose statesmanship over partisanship and the problem was averted. Tessema was elected to lead the IB for the following year.[13]

As the convention ended on a note of goodwill and camaraderie, Ibrahim Sultan, newly elected secretary general, called the youths in attendance inside the hall and addressed them:

> You may have heard our enemies call our independence party a tool of foreign powers, especially of Italy. But you will no doubt understand that such talk and allegations have no basis whatsoever. We are fighting for our freedom and liberty. Our independence is for us, our children and the generations to come ... not for others. We fight for Eritrean independence, not for Italy or the English or Ethiopia or Egypt. We love those who love Eritrea, but we cannot love those who do not.
>
> Youths of Eritrea, since we are advancing in age, you are the beneficiaries of your country's independence. If Eritrea attains independence, your lot will improve. If it does not, you will suffer. We therefore urge you to participate in this struggle for your freedom, your honour, your *risti* and the history of your ancestors.
>
> Reject the evil and deceitful campaign of the enemy. Put it aside, throw it away! We are fighting for independence. These words cannot be minced, retracted, rephrased or compromised ... May a free and independent Eritrea live forever![14]

The IB convention was generally praised for breaking the religious and regional divide in the country, and for bringing together all the ethnic and linguistic groups at one table and for one objective. In addressing the youths, Ibrahim was actually targeting wavering Andinet members, urging them to shift their allegiance and join the Shuban in forming a united front. Anticipating the move, the unionists had already prepared their own strategy to block that possibility.

After the ban imposed on it following Abdelkader Kebire's assassination, Andinet had gone underground, and its effectiveness had been compromised. However, in December 1949, the president of the Asmera–Hamasien section of UP, Gebreyohannes Tesfamariam, joined forces with the Orthodox Church to convene what he called Bayto Hamasien, or the Hamasien Assembly. Consisting of UP members of the province, it also included a core group of young people called the Hamasien Youth Association.[15] Why the British Administration acquiesced in the formation of an alternative to Andinet is not clear. But Bayto Hamasien was allowed to print the following religious ban on the people of the province as a whole:

> No Hamasien resident is to come in contact with a member of the IB for any reason whatsoever.
>
> Betrothals arranged with IB families are to be terminated immediately.
>
> No Hamasien resident is to attend wedding ceremonies hosted by IB members—no financial or material help is to be offered to them.
>
> Should an IB member or one of his family die, no Hamasien resident is to visit his house or sit in mourning with his family. However, to protect the village from disease, his corpse should be buried by four pall-bearers and three gravediggers designated for the purpose. He is to be buried as an infidel, no Holy Cross or funeral rights are to be allowed in the process.
>
> A priest who has joined the Bloc is automatically expelled from his post; believers are forbidden to be baptised, blessed or absolved by him, nor will they confess to him.[16]

In its second editorial, *Hanti Ertra* issued a direct attack on the Orthodox Church of Eritrea, something it had never dared do before. Since the Church had blessed Italy's invasion of Ethiopia in 1935, the editorial accused it of having subjected the youths of Eritrea and Tigray to extreme spiritual pressure in favour of the invading army. And now, *Hanti Ertra* continued,

> It is denying its holy benedictions to honest believers and condemning them to be buried like animals ... These are not people who have reneged on the religions of their forefathers. These are faithful believers who happen to hold different views from the political line that it is the leader of ... The Honourable Mufti [Ibrahim al Muktar], who protects the followers of the Prophet Mohammed, is leading his followers with equality and justice; with no form of discrimination between those who follow Al Rabita and those who have chosen other parties.[17]

Neither Bayto Hamasien nor indeed the Church itself could take such an affront lightly. On the day of the publication of the editorial, Weldeab survived a bomb attack, the third on his life since 1946, on the streets of Asmera. Earlier, the Hamasien Youth Association had published a stern warning and ultimatum to the youths of the province, to be ready for action or else face condemnation and exclusion.

A series of terrorist acts followed the establishment of the youth association. On 12 December, a week after the group was formed, three leaders of Nuova Eritrea (formerly Pro-Italy) narrowly missed being hit by bombs at 2.15 pm, as they emerged from a coffee shop on a main street.[18] On the same evening, an Italian, Dr Muti, was murdered on what was then known as Via Lorenzini. The BAE imposed a dusk-to-dawn curfew following the killing.

Gebreyohannes Tesfamariam, who sponsored the youth organisation, admitted in his interview for this work that the young people were a highly motivated group with no clear aims or programme of action. Upon the imposition of the curfew, twenty-three to thirty of them, led by their president, Kidane Habtetsion, approached Gebreyohannes and told him that they were joining the *shifta* to try to dissuade them from acts of pillage and vandalism, which had become common practice. 'Union with Ethiopia is not robbery,' they told him. Nothing that Gebreyohannes could say would stop them in their resolve. They sealed a written statement explaining their motive inside a bottle and buried it at a spot that Gebreyohannes could not remember in later years.[19]

There was so much hatred of Italy, Gebreyohannes explained, that the young activists did not seriously understand the alternative loyalty they were adopting. It took only a week for Kidane Habtetsion to be captured in the vicinity of Asmera, on 19 December 1949. He was sentenced to death, but survived until the federal years.[20] Confirming the confused state of the youth of those crucial years, Kidane and many of his colleagues later regretted their former stance and either vacillated between the UP and the IB or became ardent defenders of Eritrea's federal status.

Nor did their aim of 'humanising' or 'politicising' the *shifta* have any success. In the first weeks of 1950, the *shifta*, with the active participation of the Hamasien group, targeted political figures for kidnapping and harassment and continued with their pillaging.[21] All the moral and physical pressures and attacks on the IB began to have an effect. Some prominent figures within the IB started to waver under duress and looked for some excuse to move back to the UP.[22]

Although such individual and group reversions to the UP testified to the IB's vulnerability, they did not succeed in weakening the advantages it had already obtained. By the time of the arrival of the UN commission, British officers were admitting that, if a referendum were to be held in Eritrea, 75% of the population would back the IB. If the battle for political control had been left to Eritreans themselves, the British assessments might have been proved right. But, as we saw earlier, the British had undertaken their own 'test' of the IB's viability as a united force.

Frank Stafford and the Independence Bloc

Breaking Up the ML

After his mission as head of the British delegation to the Four Power Commission (FPC), Brigadier Frank Stafford came back to Eritrea in September 1949 for a 'preliminary study'. In his conclusions, he stated that the major political tendencies in the country could be divided into those who sought union with Ethiopia and accepted partition and those who demanded independence and rejected both union and partition. He admitted that the Unionist Party had no form of support in the western lowlands and the coastal regions. On the other hand, party support in the highlands had not decreased from what it had been at the time of the FPC visit. If the western lowlands were cut off from Eritrea, he asserted, 65% of the population would choose union.

How he got to that figure, he did not elaborate. But moving to his main focus, the IB, he said that it was a collection of people with no common programme and little mutual trust, whose only uniting factor was the independence of a united Eritrea. He stressed that the ML–LPP alliance was easy to break and thus urged Britain to keep pushing for partition as the only viable option. Should this fail to find acceptance, he warned, the *kebessa* would be embroiled in violence by unionists.[23]

Stafford's mission did not end there. On 27 January 1950, as the newly appointed head of the British delegation to the UN Commission of Inquiry on Eritrea, he met Emperor Haile Selassie. Their conversation was telling. Haile Selassie expressed his pleasure at Stafford's appointment as it showed British support for Ethiopia's interests. He assured him of Colonel Nega's full cooperation in Stafford's attempts to penetrate the Eritrean political parties and influence their courses of action. Stafford, for his part, reminded the Emperor that dependence only on Christian support would not deliver Eritrea to Ethiopia; and that serious efforts were needed to bring Muslims into the fold.[24]

Stafford was, at the same time, working closely with Prime Minister Aklilu. As a starter, they arranged for Omer Qadi and his Independent Muslim League to visit Addis Ababa, where the Emperor granted him an audience. Ever the optimist, Omer Qadi presented his programme and demands for a conditional union with Ethiopia. These involved equal treatment and equal rights for Eritreans in all matters, including participation in the Ethiopian administration; a guarantee of religious equality; the protection of Eritrean cultures and traditions; the introduction of Arabic as one of Eritrea's official languages; and the implementation of Sharia law.[25]

Aklilu assured Omer Qadi that all his demands were already guaranteed by the Ethiopian Constitution that the Emperor had graciously granted to his people in 1931. As for equal treatment for Eritreans, did Ethiopia not practise it even when they were under Italian rule? Omer Qadi went back home satisfied with Aklilu's promises and also with having secured a place in the UP delegation at Lake Success.[26]

As we saw earlier, Omer Qadi's splinter group made a dent in the ML's unity, but the bigger blow was yet to come.

As the arrival date of the UN commission drew nearer, Stafford and his team started to move quickly against the ML. Every effort that they had expended to cause Ibrahim to change the direction of the ML towards partition had been frustrated by his principled stand on a united Eritrea. At one point, a British officer, D.C.E. Cook, told of a stormy exchange of words with Ibrahim on the subject. Although he accused Ibrahim of 'megalomania', he admitted at the same time that he was 'a force that is still very much to be reckoned with, and that he has an amazing knack of getting himself out of tight corners'.[27]

Stafford was aware that, as the undisputed leader of the ML and the emancipation movement among the Tigre, Ibrahim also faced some competition within his own camp. Stafford moved quickly to exploit that opening. On 9 February, the day after the arrival of the commission in Eritrea, he wrote to George Clutton at the Foreign Office in London:

> In the Western Province, I look for interesting developments ... There is a considerable potential disruptive force within the ML, and the Independence Bloc generally, composed of people who dislike the way in which the ML has been hitched on to an Italian wagon by our mutual and slippery acquaintance, Ibrahim Sultan. This movement has continued underground to such an extent that there is reason to believe that it might be able to butter a majority of the important tribal chiefs in the Western Province. I have been in touch with the leader of the movement. He and his friends are bothered by the fact that they swore an oath when the Muslim League was formed that they would work for the independence of Eritrea ... but I think that that can be got over by interpreting 'independence' as being what they demanded in their original manifesto, i.e., immediate independence or British trusteeship ...[28]

Playing to the level of political consciousness among the people of the region, Stafford was able through his skilful manoeuvres to avoid potential stumbling blocks. In working to exploit this vulnerability to the detriment of ML unity, Stafford teamed up with G.K.N. Trevaskis, who was still chief political officer of the Keren division in the early 1950s. Trevaskis had for long aired his dismay at Ibrahim's behaviour even towards him. He had placed himself above the *kentabais*, he complained in his book *The Deluge*. Ibrahim even went to the extent of ordering him to carry out his will, appointing someone or dismissing another—'treating me like a messenger'. He therefore refrained from engaging in open confrontation with the power and influence that Ibrahim had accumulated and chose to weaken his base by working on Ibrahim's potential rivals within the ML.

Through his aide, Saleh Hinit, Trevaskis came in contact with the kind of man he had been looking for, the man Stafford was already in touch with, *Sheik* Ali Musa Rad'ai (Ali Rad'ai). Born in the Keren area in 1913, Ali Rad'ai had been trained as a carpenter at the Keren Salvago Raggi School and became a successful businessman in the 1930s. With the founding of the ML, he was elected secretary for the Keren division.[29] Trevaskis described Ali Rad'ai as a man of great influence with his own personal ambitions. 'He is ideal for my purposes,' he wrote. Whenever he invited Rad'ai for tea to his residence, Trevaskis added, Ibrahim began to tone down and even to obey: 'Divide and rule? Yes, I suppose you could call it that.'[30]

Stafford and Trevaskis also secured the services of another influential man, *Qadi* Hamid Abu Alama. A roving politician who had registered as a member of Pro-Italy, the UP and the ML at different times, he joined Ali Rad'ai to bolster the Stafford–Trevaskis plan. By concentrating more on the Barka area, Stafford and Trevaskis used the two men to meet with the more amenable *kebila* leaders among the Tigre and worked on setting them against Ibrahim and his party. They presented him as an Italian agent who, sooner or later, would overturn their newly acquired positions for his own benefit, just as he had done to the *shumagille*.[31]

Sheik Omer Adem Nashih, later a member of the Eritrean Assembly, was at the meeting of the heads of those *kebilas* that followed the Ali Rad'ai–Abu Alama lead. One dark evening, he said, Trevaskis assembled them in a secluded place and addressed them. Here is how *Sheik* Omer remembered that crucial meeting:

> Ibrahim had completely turned down all of Trevaskis's efforts to change the ML into a party for *teqsim* [partition]. Ibrahim had said to Trevaskis, 'Have you ever seen a dog barking and jumping at the moon in an attempt to catch it? I am the moon; you cannot catch me.' Ibrahim was like that, he was strong.
>
> At the meeting, Trevaskis told us, 'Will you stand for *teqsim* or do you prefer to go back to your old rule under the *kentabais* and the *diglels*?' We were all shocked. Going back to the old *shumagille* rule was death to us. We told him, 'The whole of the Tigre is with Ibrahim. We represent only parts of ten *kebilas* in Barka. How can we call for *teqsim* when all of the others are still with Ibrahim?'
>
> Trevaskis said, 'Ten are enough for us. But don't call yourselves "*teqsim*". Call yourselves the Muslim League of the Western Province.' This was how *teqsim* was formed. When everyone else was with the big Al Rabita, we, the *nazirs* assembled that night, chose *teqsim* out of fear of the return to *kentabai* and *diglel* tyranny. Trevaskis did this in the dark. This is the truth.[32]

Abu Alama became president and Ali Rad'ai secretary general of the new party. As *Sheik* Omer said, the formation of the ML-Western Province (ML-WP) may not have affected the ML's numerical advantage, but the damage it caused to the unity of the party was significant. Ever since Douglas Newbold's initiative, the British had been keen to secure the region's partition through indigenous people and voices. That was precisely what they got, numbers and statistics notwithstanding. As long as the ML appeared before the UN commission looking diminished in their political and territorial unity, it would serve the purpose. And it did. Having seen his designs on the ML achieve fruition, Stafford turned to the LPP on a similar mission.

Stafford and the LPP

In a message that he sent to Aklilu, Stafford admitted that his attempts to sway *Ras* Tessema and the LPP had failed. But he had found an influential group within the party that was dissatisfied with its own position inside the organisation and what it saw as the dependence of the IB on Italian aid. In his letter to George Clutton, Stafford wrote:

> I am still unable to give you a considered forecast as to how the wishes of the people over the country will be recorded, but I have hopes that my efforts to detach the LPP, the only dissident Christians on the Plateau, from the Independence Bloc, may meet with success and bring them out in support of conditional union with Ethiopia. This would be an important gain because it might weaken the allegiance to the 'bloc' of certain of the Muslim chiefs on the Plateau, with whom I have also been in contact. The position on the Plateau would then be assured.[33]

The dissident group within the LPP that Stafford was working on was led by none other than Abraha Tessema, the *Ras*'s own son, whom Stafford described as honest and efficient. He and his followers, he told Aklilu, were forming a Liberal Unionist Party, asking for conditional union with Ethiopia. On Stafford's suggestion, the three top leaders of the splinter group—*Dejazmatch* Abraha; *Dejazmatch* Gebrezghi Guangul, vice president of the LPP and Tessema's son-in-law; and *Grazmatch* Seyoum Maasho, secretary general of the party—flew to Addis Ababa as invited guests. The British Government facilitated the trip so that the group could return to Asmera in time for the start of the UN commission's operations.[34]

On 16 February 1950, just one week after the arrival of the UN commission in Asmera, the unionist newspaper *Ethiopia* published a notice announcing the formation of the Liberal Unionist Party. The party was being formed in accordance with the principles laid down at the Bet Giorgis Convention in 1946. It called, among other things, for Eritrea's territorial integrity; the adoption of Arabic and Tigrinya as Eritrea's official languages; the introduction of the UN principles of human rights; the institution of an Eritrean parliament; equality of Eritrean participation in the central government; guarantees that the head of the Eritrean administration would be an Eritrean citizen; and assurances that no Ethiopian armed personnel would enter Eritrea without the express permission of Eritrea's administrator.[35]

Why Abraha chose this path has always been a matter for speculation. The points listed in the Liberal Unionist programme resembled those that the American Philip Jessup had presented to the UN General Assembly's fourth session. Seyoum Maasho has denied having been aware that the British and the Americans promised Abraha leadership of an Eritrean administration.[36] On the other hand, information was reaching the British that some Tigray traditional leaders along the Eritrean border sought an autonomous status for their region, similar to Abraha's proposals. This was especially prevalent in northern Tigray and the Adyabo area, where the village of Badme is located.[37] There were widespread but unsubstantiated suspicions that

Abraha was in secret discussions with the Tigray elements to rekindle his old Tigray-Tigrigni plan.

The LPP reaction to the splinter group was predictably one of anger and dismay. Seyoum Maasho was summarily dismissed from his position of secretary general and replaced by Asmerom Weldegiorgis of Adi Quala. In subsequent editorials of *Hanti Ertra*, the defectors were condemned for an inexplicable decision that smacked of haste and immaturity. 'Liberal union?' mused the paper in one of its issues. 'If this means a "free union", could they not wait until independence and then freely unite with a free Ethiopia? ... Was it necessary to form a new party for this? ... Let Ethiopia first accept and bless an independent Eritrea. We can then talk about conditional union or other matters.'[38]

The article was a pained response to the blow the LPP had suffered by losing three of its top-level leaders and luminaries. Stafford's attack had indeed hit its intended target. At every turn, as Eritreans attempted to manage their own affairs, the British seemed to frustrate their moves. In all the major political events of the past decade affecting their future, Eritreans had proved unable to put their mark on matters directly affecting them. Resentment of the high-handed treatment Eritrea had endured at the hands of the British started to grip especially the younger generation of Eritreans. The realisation that the process that they had been going through had been a sham, that they had been duped at every step, could not escape a sizeable number of them. This understanding was to shape the course of Eritrean politics.

Stafford's Debacle with the Saho

In the Foreign Office dossier that documents Stafford's surprising disclosures about his mission to dismantle the IB, we find there is a blank file—FO 371/80876 62366, JT 1015/165. It comes immediately after the memo in which Stafford wrote about his moves to block dialogue between Ibrahim and Ali Rad'ai and where he expressed his feelings about both men. Written on the blank page are the words 'Following document(s) retained in the Department of origin under Section 3(4) of the Public Records Act, 1958'. The decision to impound it was taken in March 1980. Article 3(4) allows retention by departments of origin of material still in use or of special sensitivity, such as matters of intelligence.[39] Assuming that the impounded file dealt with Stafford's activities in the early days of 1950, what could be so sensitive to warrant the kind of measure taken? Stafford was never shy about his designs against the IB. Something else must have taken place which the British Government did not want known; and unless the document is declassified, we may never know. It remains a puzzle. The author's attempts to try to retrieve the document have failed so far.[40]

This is not to suggest that the following story, which Stafford probably left out of his reports, provides the contents of the missing document. It is rather an example of the kinds of resistance that his efforts faced from various quarters of the Eritrean political spectrum. *Balambaras* Mehretab Asfaha, who served as Chief of Protocol at the Asmera Imperial Palace in the 1960s, was a junior district officer at Senafe, Akeleguzai, in 1950. One morning, he was summoned to the district office where Stafford himself was waiting for him. Since he spoke English, Stafford wanted him as an interpreter. 'Everything we say and do here is a secret,' he told him as they headed to the home of Nasser Abubeker Pasha, paramount chief of the Assaorta. Mehretab recalled the meeting as follows:

> Nasser Pasha, the son of Abubeker, was a courageous man; no fear whatsoever. When we sat with him, Stafford said, 'This man Ibrahim Sultan is being shunned and sidelined by his own brothers. Why are you still following his footsteps? Let me give you my advice. It would be better for you not to do so.'
>
> Nasser Pasha replied calmly, 'We know what we want. You cannot come here to teach us about our preferences. We are Al Rabita and Al Rabita means independence. We want our independence.'
>
> 'I don't think that you understand,' Stafford said turning to me. 'Explain to him,' he ordered me, and I repeated his words to the Pasha.
>
> 'That's the word, cousin,' Nasser gave as his final answer.

Disappointed by the outcome of the meeting, Stafford next took Mehretab to Ali Bey, leader of the Minifere, who, on the excuse of old age and illness, delegated his son, Mohammed Said Ali Bey, to meet the brigadier on his behalf. 'If he is here to speak about Al Rabita,' he instructed his son, tell him we are Al Rabita and Al Rabita we shall remain.' Mohammed Said delivered his father's message.

To complete his list of meetings with the major Saho leaders, Stafford next approached Ona Ali, head of the Hazo. The Ona told him, 'Our party is Al Rabita; Ibrahim Sultan is our secretary general, the leader of Al Rabita. If some Barka leaders have their internal cases, it does not concern us. We are Al Rabita.'

In a last-ditch attempt to go back to Asmera with something more tangible, Stafford decided to revisit Nasser Abubeker. This time, said Mehretab, the Pasha got upset.

'I have told you of my decision,' he told Stafford angrily. 'I don't want you to visit my house in the dark, like a thief. Don't ever come to me again. This is my last word.' He was wielding a long stick. I even feared that he might use it. We were herded out of his house without ceremony.[41]

Stafford seemed to take personal pleasure from his mission of destroying a fledgling nationalist coalition. He boasted to Clutton that his success in weakening the IB was achieved 'by the expenditure solely of fair words.'[42] Yet, on 6 June 1950, Deputy Foreign Secretary Strang chaired a top secret meeting in London to discuss payment of £720 incurred by ML-WP leader Ali Rad'ai, to dissuade him from defecting back to the ML if his demands were not met. Setting aside possible accusations of bribery, the committee agreed that 'since the political party had been actively encouraged by His Majesty's Government ... We should have to be prepared to defend the payment in public, e.g. in Parliament.[43] Stafford's 'fair words' was thus not the sole 'expenditure'.

Stafford is still remembered in Eritrea as the man who led the counterattack against a united Eritrean front for independence.

9

THE UN'S FINAL VERDICT ON ERITREA

The UN Commission of Inquiry on Eritrea

Fighting on the Streets of Asmera

Members of the United Nations Commission of Inquiry on Eritrea (UNCIE) started to arrive in Asmera on 8 February 1950. Barely two weeks later, fighting broke out on a scale never witnessed before or since in the city. On 21 February, *Bashai* Nesredin, an Independence Bloc (IB) member and railway station master near Asmera, was gunned down by a *shifta* band. According to Islamic practice, a funeral is ordinarily held on the day and in the place of death of the believer. But, against the advice of the Muslim League (ML) leadership, the Shuban chose to turn the incident into a procession of protest and show of force. They thus made arrangements for an afternoon burial at the Muslim cemetery on the northern flanks of Edaga Hamus, at the foot of the Hazhaz Hills. The procession, two to three thousand strong by official estimates, began at the Regina Elena (today's Orotta) Hospital.

The Shuban in their white uniforms, carrying the blue and green flag of the ML and traditional swords and daggers, led the procession, followed by schoolchildren and elders accompanying Nesredin's body. They made a detour to the centre of town, past the Asmera electricity station from the Asmera Cathedral, and tried to cross to Edaga Hamus by way of the Asmera abattoir. In order to do so, they had to pass in front of the Unionist Party (UP) headquarters nearby. The trouble began right at that spot when Andinet supporters, who had thus far been jeering and gesticulating along the way, threw a few stones at the procession. The Shuban responded by wielding their swords and threatening to retaliate. Things got out of control and fighting broke out. Suddenly, a bomb thrown from the crowd exploded against the walls of the UP offices without causing any damage. The court of inquiry that Chief Administrator Drew instituted on 24 February identified the bomb-thrower as a certain Khelifa, a Muslim member of Andinet, whom it called an agent provocateur, though it never specified who exactly had given him the order.

A curfew was imposed on the first day, but the fighting resumed between Edaga Hamus and Akria early on the 22nd with frightening ferocity. As the day progressed, it spread to Amba Galliano, Aba Shawl, Haddish Adi and Geza Banda Habesha. By the evening of the 22nd, 27 people (9 Andinet and 18 Shuban) had been killed; 73 (34 Andinet and 39 Shuban) were admitted to hospital; and 69 (45 Andinet and 13 Shuban) were treated for lighter wounds. The court, which gave these details, tallied only the losses of the first two days of fighting. But the troubles continued until the 26th, and by that time the number of deaths had risen to 47 (16 Andinet and 31 Shuban), 100 (51 Andinet and 49 Shuban) were hospitalised, and 121 (72 Andinet and 49 Shuban) were treated for minor wounds. Two women and a child were among the victims.[1]

The imbalance in the number of casualties – more Shuban dead and more Andinet wounded – was attributable to the fact that Andinet were armed with guns and bombs, while the Shuban fought mainly with swords, clubs and stones, thus gaining the upper hand only in hand-to-hand confrontations. It was found later that ten of those killed had fallen to bullets fired by the police, who claimed that the Andinet had been shooting at them and that they had responded in self-defence.[2] Predictably, the court of inquiry reached the same conclusion. After ruling that the police officers, British and Eritrean, had discharged their duties properly, no charges were laid against them. Only one British soldier was identified as having fired at a gathering where a woman passer-by was killed. He was exonerated on the ground of 'lack of experience'.[3] On the other side, a total of 154 Eritrean civilians were arrested and put on trial.[4]

Both sides to the conflict denounced the police failure to stop the killings. Gebreyohannes Tesfamariam, active in the conflict on Andinet's side, recalled: 'Our aim had been to frighten the Muslim League into submission. But when the fighting spread beyond our control, we started to hope for British intervention. We panicked when we saw them joining in the carnage. Wise elders from both sides started to meet and call for a truce.'[5]

On the afternoon of 24 February, the third day of the conflict, conferring Asmera elders met with *Mufti* Ibrahim Mukhtar and *Abune* Markos for their blessing and approval, which they were granted. They then nominated 62 citizens, 31 Muslims and 31 Christians, to work as a joint committee in securing a truce. Two chairmen were elected to lead the effort, *Dejazmatch* Asresehey Beraki of Arba'te Asmera and *Blata* Ahmed Nuru, also of Asmera. Leaving the task of passing judgement and sentences to the court of inquiry, the people's committee defined its role as persuading the still-battling parties to end the conflict. After securing the necessary legal approval from the Administration, it set to work.[6]

News of the formation of the committee and its campaign for peace had an immediate effect of halting the troubles by 26 February. Since no further violent incident took place in the month of March, the committee used that breathing space to bring the parties to agree to peace. On 25 March, it was able to convene a large gathering of reconciliation where prominent representatives from the UP, ML, Shuban and Andinet were represented. At the meeting held at the home of Abdella Gonafer, the usual venue for such major gatherings, the words uttered by some of the prominent elders drew on the wisdom and traditional art of Eritrean conflict resolution. All the speakers criticised and condemned, directly or by implication, the Administration's failure to intervene in a meaningful way. *ESG* printed the whole proceedings in its issue of 30 March. The following are some of the memorable words of conciliation uttered on the occasion:

> Let us accept with an open heart, the reconciliation charted for us by our elders. Ultimately, we were the victims. Let us settle this by ourselves, let us not invite mediators. Above all, let us reject harmful attitudes and gossip. (*Fitawrari* Hagos Adem)
>
> Our problem so far has been that we bowed to aliens too low; we allowed ourselves to stoop whichever way they willed us. Let that be our lesson, lest we become the laughingstock of strangers. They are the ones who are now rejoicing at the blood we have shed. (*Fitawrari* Haregot Abbay)
>
> The time has come for us to wipe each other's tears. There is no doubt that our innocent victims have already met in the heavens and are embracing each other. But their happiness can only be complete if we, who are still here on earth, also reconcile in a manner acceptable to God. True, we differ in our preferences. But that comes from our perception of what is best for our country. No one among us can consciously advocate doom and damnation. (*Sheik* Suleiman Aldin of the UP leadership)
>
> It is possible that God willed this to happen in consideration of our future fortunes and prosperity. Not only should the blood of a sibling not flow for nothing, but the reason for such bloodletting should also not exist. To come to this realization is of vital importance for our truths. Let us beware of becoming the instruments of Satan. May God have mercy on us. (*Abba* Kidanemariam of the Roman Catholic Church)[7]

Following the meeting, the committee approached the *Mufti* of Eritrea and *Abune* Markos to lead a procession of peace and reconciliation through the streets of Asmera. With portable loudspeakers blaring out the tidings, the two religious leaders led a procession of an estimated 20,000 Asmera citizens of both religions. They marched to both the Muslim and Christian cemeteries at Edaga Hamus and Enda Mariam, respectively, and laid wreaths of flowers on the graves of the victims of the previous month.[8]

This bipartisan act of reconciliation ended the tragic events of February 1950. It is significant that the violence left no residue of resentment or feelings of revenge. Life simply picked up from where it had rudely been interrupted. Gebreyohannes Tesfamariam explained why: 'It was basically a political conflict between union and independence, especially the Shuban and Andinet. It was not a Muslim–Christian conflict. There was no base for that kind of broader confrontation in our history, no entrenched hatred between the religions. After the reconciliation, we saw the last of it.'[9]

But the court of inquiry did not see it in that light. Its constant reference to 'Copts' and 'Muslims' as the conflicting parties was challenged by the likes of Ibrahim Sultan and Tedla Bairu, who came before it to give their testimonies. Tedla made a strong deposition, arguing that the troubles were political in nature. He stressed that the people of Eritrea had not inherited any home-grown religious hatred from their history. Besides, he told the court, since both religions were represented in both political groups, the court's references were patently wrong and inappropriate.[10]

Although the court still kept its 'Muslim' and 'Coptic' references in its final report, it did admit that the conflict had mainly been political in nature. It found that almost all of the casualties were members of Shuban or Andinet, giving support to claims that the attacks had been targeted by antagonists who knew whom to hit. The court also assigned more blame to the 'Copts', who had used live ammunition and hand grenades and, therefore, had come prepared for trouble. Except for an insignificant number, the Shuban's biggest weapon had been the sword.[11]

The general population in Asmera chose to sit out the conflict without taking sides. Women were especially in the forefront of the attempt to stop the killings. Seidi Hassen Ali, the ML leader's daughter, confirmed in an interview that the women of Akria sheltered their Christian neighbours and their children inside their homes from possible Shuban attack. The women of Aba Shawl and other predominantly Christian zones did the same to hide their Muslim neighbours from the scourge of the Andinet. The killings would otherwise have been more widespread.[12]

The UNCIE was a witness to all the carnage of February 1950. How those incidents may have influenced the thinking of the commission as a whole or its individual members cannot be known. But, on 22 February, the commission issued a statement in which it expressed its sadness at the incident. It declared at the same time that its mission would not be compromised or swayed by the events. It condemned the violence as an act of bloodletting, with no value whatsoever. It urged the people not to follow that dangerous path.[13]

The Commission of Inquiry's Findings

The commission started its mission on 14 February, a week before the skirmishes began. Whatever individual impressions or prejudices the troubles may have evoked in the minds of its members were not reflected in the stands of their respective governments. In the course of the UN General Assembly's fourth session, Pakistan and Guatemala had favoured Eritrean independence; Burma, an inquiry into Eritrean wishes; Norway, Ethiopian annexation; while South Africa stood against any form of independence or self-government for any African colony. Britain was obviously not happy that there was no commission member country that supported partition. Reinforced by a strong lobby led by Sylvia Pankhurst, Brigadier Frank Stafford of the British Administration attempted to sway the commission to adopt his plans. By his own admission, Pakistan and Guatemala rejected his proposal outright, but he gained some ground with the remaining three members.[14]

Ethiopia and the UP were by now in open collusion with Britain in its quest for partition; and this, as we saw, created much resentment within the ranks of the UP. That adverse turn of events against unionism had to be curbed and, upon the resumption of the commission's operations, a sharp surge in terrorist and *shifta* activity marred its inquiry at practically every step of the way. According to a British report, *shifta* support and involvement from across the border in Ethiopia could neither be hidden nor denied. *Shifta* leaders Asresehey Embaye and Gebre Tesfatsion were reported to be in direct contact with the *Nebure Ed* of Axum and the Governor of Tigray, coordinating activities with them. Hagos Temnewo was also known to have procured three sacks of hand grenades from Axum. Asresehey was in particular mentioned as having placed himself and his band under the direct command of the Governor of Adwa, the Eritrean-born Colonel (later General) Isaias Gebreselassie. The Mossazghi brothers had their own launching ground and safe haven in Ahse'a, Tigray. The report concluded that if Tigrayan administrators did not refrain from such subversive acts, the situation would get out of control.[15]

In fact it had already got out of control. IB-leaning villages and districts had fallen victim to unrelenting campaigns of *shifta* intimidation and spiritual terror unleashed by the Orthodox clergy. *Abune* Markos must have surpassed his own well-known enthusiasm to elicit the following personal attack by a contributor to *Hanti Ertra*:

> *Abune* Markos is the man who is attempting to strike fire in Muslim and Christian relations. He is listening to the advice of infidels. What are we to say about a bishop who urges his followers not to bury the dead and visit the sick: or who incites killings on behalf of a [political] organization? ... His rhetoric may, for now, succeed in shedding some Muslim and Christian blood. But he cannot understand that the Showans are observing him closely and judging him to be a worthless person. If he thinks that his sermons will reinstate his [the Orthodox Church's] *risti*, it is a dream.[16]

It was in this atmosphere that the commission carried out its inquiry from 14 February to 6 April 1950, 51 days in all. It visited 37 centres and met with representatives of 64 different sections of the population, far fewer than the number that its predecessor, the Four Power Commission (FPC), had reached. According to G.K.N. Trevaskis, the FPC was overall more organised and thorough in its methodology and deliberations. The UNCIE acted only as a disinterested observer of contending meetings, where it met people whose identity and credentials it could not properly ascertain.[17]

Moreover, truckloads of Andinet activists were transported daily from Asmera to wherever IB rallies were being visited by the commission, to prevent pro-independence representatives from appearing before it. On the other hand, the same truckloads would whisk the same activists to UP rallies to bolster their numbers and sizes.[18] The Pakistani and Guatemalan delegates, who noted this (and could identify the same faces at every UP rally), pointed to the unfairness of this practice. They also argued that, as a result, they could not estimate the real size of the followings of the opposing parties. Burma, South Africa and Norway either rejected their colleagues' claims or maintained they had no problem in estimating crowd sizes.[19]

A poignant encounter with the Liberal Progressive Party (LPP) leader in Seraye, *Azmatch* Berhe Gebrekidan, was to prove the Pakistan and Guatemala delegates right. Appearing before the commission on 10 April, Berhe accused Ethiopia of sponsoring *shifta* terrorism, and described how 970 members of the LPP and 1,350 of the ML in his district alone were physically blocked by *shifta* bands controlling the main routes to the commission's venue. After reminding the commission that the IB could not show its full force under the circumstances, he confided to the members that his own life was in danger.[20] Neither the commission nor the British Administration took any steps to ensure his safety or that of the IB representatives.

On 16 May 1950, at dawn, a band of *shifta*, sixty strong, led by Asresehey himself, surrounded the home of Berhe Gebrekidan at Damba Mitch, where the nationalist was saying his morning prayers. He was killed under a hail of bullets on the threshold of his house. Two other people died by his side.[21] After Abdelkader Kebire, Berhe Gebrekidan is regarded as the second national martyr for the cause of Eritrean independence.

Nothing that took place in Eritrea and to Eritreans made an impact on the entrenched thinking of the foreign powers and their representatives. The commission's disagreements were not limited to the political implications of the points raised by Berhe and the IB in general. The same kind of split arose on other issues, such as economics. The Burmese, Norwegian and South African delegates accepted the oft-repeated British and Ethiopian position that Eritrea depended on Ethiopia even for pasture for its livestock and crops for its inhabitants. They argued that eventually the people of highland Eritrea would inevitably migrate to Ethiopia and that, economically, Eritrea would forever be dependent on Ethiopia. Meanwhile, their Pakistani and Guatemalan counterparts rejected the argument that economic self-sufficiency was a precondition for independence. They insisted that most of Eritrea's problems had been exaggerated by its uncertain future; the breakdown of security, especially in the countryside; and the continuing exodus of Italians and their economic enterprises from the country.[22]

There was, in truth, not much that could be new or ground-breaking in the commission's deliberations. It left Eritrea on 8 April 1950 to consult with Ethiopia, Egypt, France, Italy and Great Britain, and wrap up its mission. Here too nothing emerged that was new or revealing, as the delegates resorted to their original positions. They split three ways. In their joint statement, Pakistan and Guatemala proposed that Eritrea become an independent and sovereign state within its existing borders. Its independence would come into effect ten years after approval by the UN General Assembly. During those ten years, Eritrea would be placed under international UN trusteeship, administered by Great Britain on behalf of the UN, assisted by an Advisory Council consisting of the US, Ethiopia and Italy, a Muslim state and a Latin American state; with a Muslim and a Christian to represent Eritrean citizens and an Italian to look after Italian and Italo-Eritrean interests.[23]

Burma, Norway and South Africa rejected any suggestion of independence for Eritrea owing to its economic non-viability. They contended that, with the formation of the ML-Western Province, the independence camp had lost its majority. They recognised Ethiopia's right to an outlet to the sea and declared that the similarities between Ethiopians and Eritreans called for their unity. As for the details, Burma and South Africa proposed a federal solution whereby Eritrea would constitute an autonomous unit with Ethiopia as the other partner, under the sovereignty of the Ethiopian Crown. Each partner would be governed by its own internal laws and authority, with matters pertaining to defence, foreign affairs, finance and foreign trade being reserved to the federal government. They also called for the creation of a customs union between the partners and a common federal nationality.[24] Norway alone proposed the unconditional merger of Eritrea with 'its mother Ethiopia', a measure that its delegate stressed should have been put into effect much earlier.[25]

Eritrea after the UN Commission's Departure

The comings and goings of the UNCIE had no visible positive effect on Eritrea's internal political situation. The divisions between the political parties widened and the uncertainty about the country's future became even more pronounced. Above all, the shifts in individual and group loyalty between the parties continued unabated. Rivalry between Abu Alama and Ali Rad'ai, for example, threatened to disrupt Stafford's hastily instituted ML-Western Province. Talk of a possible dialogue between Ali Rad'ai and Ibrahim Sultan to bridge the issues that divided them thus brought Stafford back to the scene for yet another act of disruption. He wrote to the British Foreign Office to say that any dialogue between Ali Rad'ai and Ibrahim would be to the benefit of the latter. And if, as Ali Rad'ai was intimating, they arrived at a common demand for British trusteeship, Stafford warned that they could go to Lake Success on that joint platform. F.G. Cook of the Foreign Office agreed that the possibility was undesirable. He even met both Ibrahim, with whom he said he had 'a stormy meeting', and Ali Rad'ai, whom he apparently dissuaded from coming to any agreement with Ibrahim.[26]

Ten days after his communication with Cook, Stafford showered praises on Ali Rad'ai as the moving force behind the 'movement' and as an honest and sincere man. On Ibrahim, he had this to say:

> I would not touch Ibrahim Sultan, whom I regard as a political toad, with a pointed stick. He has a sinister influence but, in my opinion, it is on the wane and it would be

> wrong for us to foster or promote a conciliation between him and either of the two people I have mentioned [Rad'ai and Abu Alama] in this paragraph or to pay him any more attention than necessary.
>
> As regards the present-day value to us of the Muslim League of the Western Province, I maintain the opinion that I expressed at the time a political truce was suggested in Eritrea, i.e., that those who favour our policy in any way should be kept in being, fully organized, and be given support where necessary. The greater the influence of the Muslim League of the Western Province in that Province, the better it is for us. I would like to see it grow.[27]

Wanton British interference in every aspect of Eritrean politics never ceased to be a source of pain and consternation within the IB. Referring specifically to Stafford's obsession with Eritrea, *Hanti Ertra* printed an editorial attacking his character and his meddling:

> From the political point of view, it is the Eritrean who is being branded with red-hot iron; but, strangely, it is the British envoy, Mr Stafford, who screams with pain. Every time the Eritrean is branded, he holds his head in agony.
>
> If the Eritrean says, 'I will not partition my country,' he says, 'Never, it has to be partitioned.' He argues that unless Eritrea is partitioned, it will never attain health and happiness ... When some people in the Western Province requested the UN Commission for British trusteeship, pending independence after ten years, Brigadier Stafford would not indulge them. 'No,' he told them, 'the people of the Western Province must merge with Sudan, Britain cannot administer them.' He chills the hearts even of his own supporters.
>
> The government of the English is big and strong. Its democratic system is well known throughout the world. It is hard for us to know by what rationality Brigadier Stafford is attempting to handle the Eritrean case.[28]

Anger and desperation mounted in the independence camp. On 14 May 1950, a hand grenade was thrown into the UP headquarters where it exploded harmlessly. Suspecting that the act could have been carried out by the Nuova Eritrea party in retaliation for the murder of eight Italians in as many months, the British Administration rounded up suspects and jailed them in Tesseney.[29] Italian objection to the incarcerations brought a quick response from Britain, which was then courting Italy to secure support for the implementation of its regional plans in return for safety guarantees for Italians in Eritrea. Between 26 May and 5 June, Britain sent several battalions of British troops to clear Eritrea of the *shifta*. In a message, apparently meant to appease the Italians, Cook reported the details of substantial *shifta* casualties to the Italian Undersecretary for Foreign Affairs, Giuseppe Brusasca.[30]

However, at the end of June, the *shifta* came back in greater numbers to virtually control much of rural Eritrea. In reaction, a high-level meeting in London decided to add a trained anti-*shifta* 'striking force' of 300 troops to the Eritrean police force. British officers were put in command of the new contingent and Spitfire fighters were deployed as air support.[31] Despite this, the overt participation of Ethiopian *shifta* backed by Tigrayan chiefs and warlords aggravated the problem.[32] Equally significant were raids for territorial possession and cattle rustling carried out on the Kunama people of the Barentu and the Gash River areas. The British were aware that these raids were motivated by the desire on the Tigrayan side 'to control the land between the Gash and Setit rivers'.[33]

As Spitfire planes attacked *shifta* positions in early July, the British Administration issued a proclamation condemning murderers to death by hanging. Consequently, one person was hanged publicly as a warning to others.[34] Still, terrorism activity did not subside. On 15 June 1950, an 85-year-old former chief of Geza Berhanu in Asmera and a prominent elder of both ML and IB, *Azmatch* Abdelkader Jabir, was murdered at his home in Arba'te Asmera by unionist *shifta*.[35] Five days later, one of the most senior leaders of the Italo-Eritrean Association and an activist for Italian trusteeship and Eritrean independence, Vittorio Longhi, was assassinated on one of the main streets of Asmera.[36] His killer was identified as a discharged Eritrean police member who had just returned from a visit to Addis Ababa.[37]

These high-profile assassinations were accompanied by *shifta* attacks targeting Muslim individuals and Muslim villages in many parts of the country, including Keren and western Seraye. On 2 August 1950, the Muslim village of Zeban Seb'o was raided by the Asresehey band, which left four villagers dead and twelve wounded. The attack was generally seen as a deliberate unionist provocation to inflame Muslim–Christian relations.

However, through the medium of *Hanti Ertra*'s Arabic version, *Wehdet Eretria*, and its own weekly, *Saut al Eretria*, the ML put the blame on the British Administration and the police 'striking force', whom it accused of idling around town in their new uniforms.[38] But the threat of a potential religious conflict was not confined to the areas already mentioned or to the initiative of the unionists only. On 2 August, the day of the Zeban Seb'o attack, a Saho band of 25 members, led by the *shifta* Mohammed Saleh Suleiman, confronted 40 armed and 120 unarmed *shifta* under the command of Berhe Mossazghi and Debessai Dirar at Mehemad, on the escarpment of eastern Seraye. In the ensuing battle, Berhe Mossazghi, along with several of Debessai's men, lost their lives. Debessai himself took refuge in Tigray.[39]

It was a defeat that neither the UP nor the *shifta* could accept and, consequently, tensions began to rise. Probably to avoid retaliatory measures, Mohammed Saleh Suleiman led 32 of his followers to surrender to the Administration.[40] This move practically ended the Saho armed resistance to unionist aggression, which continued to provoke religious confrontations by targeting Muslims. The notorious *shifta* leader Tekeste Haile, for example, took pleasure in cutting off the ears of Muslim traders. Debessai Dirar too avenged Berhe Mossazghi's death by the random killing of innocent Muslims. Even the Keren region, which had been relatively safe from the *shifta*, started to suffer a similar fate.[41]

Remarkably, the breakdown in law and order did not generate religious strife among the common people. According to Gebreyohannes Tesfamariam, sectarian violence came with Britain's partition policy of promoting religious division. Prior to that, the people had no history of entrenched mutual ill-feeling, especially of a religious nature. This helped them avoid falling for British machinations.[42] Chief Administrator Drew acknowledged this fact of Eritrean history when he wrote that the civil strife of February 1950 had 'broken out on a clear-cut politico-religious line and is the more regrettable that, so far as I know, it is the first occasion in this territory of inter-communal strife on a religious cleavage. It bodes ill for the future.'[43]

Drew's bleak prediction of a doomed Muslim–Christian relationship within Eritrea has never materialised, confirming Gebreyohannes's assertion that religious discord did not have a home-grown historical or social base on which to grow. In the meantime, the Eritrean case took centre stage at the United Nations.

Eritrea and the Fifth Session of the General Assembly

Months before the UNCIE's submission of its recommendations to the UN Secretary General on 13 July 1950, the US and Britain formed a joint committee to seek common ground on Eritrea's future. Although the Americans had occasionally toyed with Britain's partition plans, they had never adopted it seriously. For them, Philip Jessup's federal proposal was an adequate alternative to Eritrea's independence. Seeking to bring Italy and Ethiopia closer on the issue, therefore, they included them in their dialogue with the British.

An Italian–Ethiopian rapprochement required each side to give up its original demands – Ethiopia on its annexation ambitions, and Italy on its trusteeship or independence preferences. Insisting that the federal formula would satisfy both parties' demands, the Americans consistently put pressure on Ethiopia, in particular, to refrain from disrupting the work and progress of the UNCIE. In January 1950, a month before the UNCIE's arrival in Eritrea, they promised that the US and Britain would pre-empt the commission's recommendations, once it had completed its task.

In the face of the progress that the IB was making at the time, Ethiopia could not agree to the idea of keeping its hands off Eritrea even temporarily. On the other hand, since the American 'alternative' proposal would preclude independence as a possibility, Italy also became reluctant to go along with it. The first attempt at an Ethio-Italian rapprochement did not succeed.[44] Nevertheless, the Americans pushed for acceptance of their formula by meeting key delegates in the UN and attempting to win them over to their side. They told the Pakistani representative, for example, that Eritrea's economic problems denied it the possibility of becoming an independent country. They also warned that an independent Eritrea could become the gateway for Soviet and communist intervention in Africa and the Red Sea region.

Italian leftists had indeed distributed a newspaper, *La Carroccio*, during the colonial period but it seems to have made little political impact. After the British takeover, Italian communists attempted to organise themselves and even printed a few issues of a newspaper called (like that of the mainland Italian Communist Party) *L'Unità*. But it folded after a few issues and sold its rights to the Independence Bloc's *Hanti Ertra* and *Wehdet Eretria*. Apart from these publications of not much significance, there was no trace of Soviet activity inside Eritrea at the time. At one point, US Secretary of State Dean Acheson himself raised the issue with his Italian counterpart, Carlo Sforza, persuading him of the danger. This was the communication that led Sforza to refer to the possibility of Eritrean independence as a *lettera morta* (dead letter).[45]

In spite of Sforza's statement, Italy's position was still not secure, as the US formula denied Eritrea the powers and privileges due a partner state within a federation, an option that Italy opposed. At the beginning of May 1950, some days before the UNCIE's submission of its report, British and American delegates met with their Italian counterparts once again to break Italian resistance. Normalising relations with Ethiopia, they told the Italians, meant getting access to a large market and investment opportunities. They also raised the Soviet threat as an added reason for Italian compliance with the American proposal. In addition, Italian rights and safety in Eritrea would be guaranteed.

Italian vacillation threatened to lead to another deadlock. The problem for the Americans was that Italy still had strong Latin American backing in the UN and its demands had a fair chance of winning in a General Assembly vote, as Pakistan and many of the Arab states were also likely to be supportive. They thus pressured Italy to at least agree to two conditions – that it refrain from actively advocating Eritrean independence in front of the UN Political Committee; and, secondly, that it accept, in principle, a federal solution whose specifics would be clarified later. Italy accepted.

All three conspiring powers knew that they were also deceiving each other. Britain had no intention of dropping its partition plan. But it promised that its delegate to the Political Committee would speak in support of viable alternatives. The Ethiopian delegation was told not to use the aggressive and boastful language that had become a trademark of its presentations. Other countries, such as Norway and South Africa, were also approached and instructed on what to say. At the same time, the attempt to bring Italy and Ethiopia closer was to continue.[46]

On 11 September 1950, just two days before the commission's submission of its report, Dean Acheson warned his diplomats not to magnify the differences in opinion between Britain and the US on the Eritrean issue. They were rather to initially propose support for the partition plan and, later, retreat to their own federal proposal as a compromise. Acheson also instructed his aides to find a link between the Eritrean question and the highly charged Korean crisis that was raging at the time, and press for a quick resolution of the former issue.[47]

On 13 July, the Political Committee of the General Assembly had named an Ad Hoc Committee to look into the Eritrean case. The US and Britain wasted no time in presenting their proposal to it. However, a Burmese version of the federal solution consisting of two equally empowered states had been making the rounds at the UN, and it seemed to stand in the way of their formula. Besides, since Italy had agreed to the formula only in principle, it revealed that it had no intention of approving an arrangement that denied Eritrea wide administrative and economic powers.[48] The US and Britain therefore decided to get their way 'under the table', to borrow Frank Stafford's phrase. For this, they solicited the help of the Brazilian Ambassador, João Carlos Muniz, chairman of the Ad Hoc Committee on Eritrea, who agreed to act as a mediator and facilitator. Muniz brought along his Mexican counterpart, Luis P. Nervo, to assist him. Charles Noyes of the US, Frank Stafford as part of the British delegation, the Italian Leonardo Vitetti, and Aklilu Habtewold, along with his American advisor, John Spencer, completed the circle of schemers. Eritrean representation was nowhere in the picture.

When they proposed to consider the Burmese proposal as the basis for discussion, Aklilu rejected the very suggestion roundly. Ethiopia, a nation that had preserved its independence and sovereignty for hundreds of years, he told them, was not about to compromise its existence in order to unite with a country that had never known freedom and that was one-twentieth of its size. If Ethiopia's historical and international continuity was not guaranteed, the Eritrean case would never be resolved; and Italy's return to Eritrea would provoke Ethiopia to use all in its power to oppose it.[49]

Muniz came up with an idea that broke the impasse. He agreed with Aklilu that Ethiopia should not be federated with Eritrea. But Eritrea could be federated to Ethiopia under the sovereignty of the Ethiopian Crown. In that arrangement, Eritrea would be the 'federated' state, while Ethiopia would constitute the 'federal government'. It was a new interpretation, unheard of in constitutional history or theory. John Spencer mused that Charles Noyes and Frank Stafford were obliged to set aside the knowledge and principles of constitutionality they had grown up with to go along with Muniz's amendment.[50]

It was a very vague proposal whose details the circle of schemers could not clearly articulate. They had no problem assigning areas like foreign affairs, defence, finance, international and federal commerce, and communications to Ethiopia or the federal government. They made no provision for the existence of an Eritrean parliament, merely suggesting that Eritrea would be represented in the Ethiopian parliament in proportion to its population. That would make it just another province of its partner in the Federation. As a compromise, they provided for the formation of a federal council consisting of an equal number of Ethiopian and Eritrean representatives, but gave it only advisory powers. The same happened with the justice system: Eritrean courts were to fall under the judicial review of their Ethiopian counterparts. They also proposed a federal citizenship to obtain throughout the Federation and an Eritrean citizenship to be recognised inside Eritrea only. There could of course be no federal citizenship, as no federal government would be established: 'federal citizenship' simply meant Ethiopian citizenship.

After agreeing on most points, the group came up with a new problem when Muniz, as advised by the Italians, suggested that the proposal be approved by the people of Eritrea. Aklilu and Spencer opposed the idea. Noyes and Stafford then brought up the possibility of establishing an Eritrean parliament and leaving the task of approving the federal arrangement to it. Another impasse was broken.[51]

Next, Muniz showed the draft to selected delegates thought to be sympathetic to the proposal as well as to the Latin American representatives. But Italy reneged once again on the grounds that the American plan would not find acceptance in Italy and declared that, should the Soviet Union propose independence for Eritrea, Italy would not object. At the same time, Latin American delegates went along with Italy in opposing the US–British initiative.[52] This constant change of mind on the part of the Italians encouraged Britain to go back to its old partition plan. According to Okbazghi Yohannes, Eritrea's Chief Administrator, Brigadier Drew, had never taken the federal idea seriously and was, on the contrary, preparing the ground for the division of the country.[53]

By September, it looked as if the US agenda had died when Ethiopia stepped in. At the time a US-led United Nations force was engaged in war on the Korean Peninsula. Openly declaring its support for the US invasion, Ethiopia expressed its readiness to send troops to fight against the communist advance. As we may recall, Dean Acheson had wanted a link to be created between the Korean War and the Eritrean issue, for a quicker solution to the latter. Conveniently, Ethiopia opened that way and the Americans were happy to accept a black African country that would fight on their side – a boost, indeed, to their new status as a superpower.

From this point on, Acheson took personal charge of the Eritrean issue and moved to put a stop to Britain's revival of its partition plan. To this effect, he called on the foreign ministers of Britain and Italy to support the American initiative. On his instructions, Noyes and Spencer came up with a plan that put to rest Ethiopian opposition to Italian trusteeship of Somalia and also opened the way for the elusive Ethio-Italian rapprochement.[54] With Italy's acceptance of the Acheson initiative, Latin American resistance to the federal formula crumbled. The US could now present its plan without much opposition, and it did so when the Ad Hoc Political Committee on Eritrea took up the matter on 8 November 1950.

Ibrahim Sultan Faces the Political Committee

Italy was probably the first nation to accept the US–British proposal upon its presentation to the Political Committee. Several Latin American countries followed in its footsteps. Even Syria and Iraq, led by Egypt, pledged their support, and what glimmer of hope there had been for Eritrean independence dimmed. The US then solicited the support of about thirteen other countries and formally presented its proposals to the committee on 20 November 1950.

Every competing proposal on Eritrea had its sponsor at the UN – partition was Britain's idea; federation, in the US, Burmese and South African variations, had various advocates; while annexation was an Ethiopian scheme, with Norway its chief supporter. No one rooted for independence at the Political Committee. Even the Soviet Union and its Eastern European allies, which had supported Italian claims to Eritrea in the hope of a communist victory at the Italian polls, had lost their initial enthusiasm. Not only Eritrean independence as an agenda, but the Eritreans themselves had been absent from all the processes that led to the Ad Hoc Political Committee's consideration of their case from 8 to 26 November.

To fill this glaring absence, the committee sent an invitation to the IB to attend a hearing. Ibrahim Sultan and Yasin Batok of the ML and Asmerom Weldegiorgis of the LPP were among the delegates that started for Lake Success. The British delegation at the UN were unhappy about the invitation and, as they had done with the ML's first visit, they attempted to stop it. The British representative at the UN, Sir Gladwyn Jebb, even wrote to the Foreign Office to say that the arrival of Ibrahim would be an obstacle to the acceptance of the federal arrangement and that he should be dissuaded from taking the trip.[55] Stafford was equally opposed, as he saw the invitation as an opening for 'old intrigues and false representations' to reappear and complicate matters.[56]

Despite opposition, Ibrahim and his colleagues obtained their required visas and arrived at Lake Success on 16 November, eight days after the debate on Eritrea had started and three days after the US had presented its proposal to the committee. Their opportunity came on 21 November, by which time opinions had already been formed, deals cemented and votes secured. It was also unfortunate for Ibrahim and his delegation that his presentation came in the week when the Korean crisis dominated all proceedings at the UN. There was a general tendency at the world body to want to get rid of the Eritrea question as quickly as possible and focus on the issue of global consequence. Nevertheless, Ibrahim gave an impassioned explanation of why Eritrea should be granted its independence. He may not have changed the minds of the powers that were deciding Eritrea's future. But, even more than seventy years after its deliberation and more than thirty years after Eritrea's hard-won independence, his words and predictions still resonate.[57]

Ibrahim summarised the demands of his party as follows. They sought effective independence; a democratic government; and the territorial integrity of Eritrea within its present geographical borders. They also opposed any project for the partition of Eritrea or the annexation of any part of it to Ethiopia or the Sudan, or any scheme of annexation or subordination to any other country; any project for union or federation with Ethiopia; and any postponement in solving the Eritrean problem.

Addressing the allegation, widely circulating at the UN, that independence was a Muslim demand that was not supported by Eritrea's Christian population, Ibrahim listed the five parties constituting the IB whose majority membership was Christian.[58] To Ethiopia's claims that Eritrea had always constituted an integral part of Ethiopia and that Italy had forcibly carved it out of its territory, Ibrahim gave the following answer:

> Our country has never been subject to Ethiopia even in ancient times. On the contrary, the Eritreans were forced on many occasions to hurl back attempted invasions by the Ethiopians ... for the sake of robbery and plunder.
>
> As for our modern history, it is a well-known fact that our country consisted of small principalities until it was occupied by the Abbasids, and later by the Ottoman Turks, then by the Egyptians, later by the Italians, who seized our country from the Egyptians and not the Ethiopians as claimed by the Ethiopian Foreign Minister and those whom he inspires and who support him.

After listing the history of armed resistance by the people of Eritrea against centuries of Ethiopian raids and invasions, Ibrahim continued:

> Was not this armed opposition exclusively for preventing it from occupying our country? If you realize this fact, do you still wish to hand Eritrea over to its historical enemy under the pretext of union or federalization? And why should division be considered when the country unanimously refuses such an idea? Is it because we are weak and a peace-loving nation?
>
> To take such a decision will be against the wishes of the country and would be incompatible with the lofty principles for which the Allies fought this war and the principle for which this great international organization has been founded, and whose foundation has been hailed by the weak and the strong alike.

His strongest words were reserved for the notion that Eritreans did not constitute a united people and hence needed to be divided. He characterised the claim as a shameful ploy meant to accommodate Ethiopia's expansionist policy and continued:

> We should like to know at what point in our history there was any manifestation of national differences and friction between Muslims and Christians. Failing this knowledge and in the absence of discord between the religious elements of the Eritrean nation, we obviously cannot approve of any scheme for partition. Such an idea has been opposed and fought by all Eritrean parties and we cannot believe that this Commission would consent to the employment of such a coercive measure to achieve an artificial condition.
>
> ... I now come to the federation issue ... a federal union, as we understand it, can only come willingly between two independent states with equal sovereign rights, and not between an independent state and one that is being denied independence. Such a compulsory federation, which we are being ordered to accept against our wishes, does not signify any respect for liberty and the democratic principles of self-determination.

> We demand, first, complete independence. Later, when this independence will ensure the proper functioning of a constitutional democratic government, it would be feasible to submit to our independent nation the proposal of federation.

On 27 November, Ibrahim was recalled by the commission for clarification of some of the issues regarding political and religious representation and the question of Eritrea's economic viability, to which he gave his measured responses. But he took the opportunity to appeal to the reason and conscience of his audience:

> We would like to ask the members of this Commission, how many of them have in the past had their countries subjected to colonialism and only earned their independence after shedding the precious blood of their sons and sacrificing the flowers of their youth ... Why are we, therefore, being deprived of this independence which is the natural right of all nations of the world? Is it because of the existence and presence here of a little group which calls for unity with a foreign country?
>
> ... Our country is the neighbour of a large country which wants to annex us to it, in spite of the wishes of our people. We have an Administration governing our country which wants to divide our country and to annex part of it at least to Ethiopia. Both parties object to our idea of independence. This is how this group mushroomed and it is in fact a minority.
>
> I ask the members of the Committee, why is European colonialism being fought and opposed? Is it in order to replace it by an African form of colonialism? ... Ethiopia asked for Somaliland to be annexed to it ... [and] we are glad to see that Somaliland has had its right to independence recognized. Why, therefore, are we being deprived of this natural right that has been given to Libya and Somaliland?
>
> The members of this Committee are responsible for what may take place in this part of East Africa in the way of skirmishes and uprisings in case a mistaken decision is made which will force us to resist it in order to earn and maintain our independence and preserve our being. Up to now, we have suffered difficulties and tolerated hardships only to maintain peace and order in our country and in the hope that we shall get from this Committee justice and an unbiased attitude towards our natural rights.

Ibrahim's prophetic warnings may not have changed many minds at the Ad Hoc Political Committee, but they were to prove accurate in the years that followed. For Eritreans, they form part of the history that set them off on the arduous and bloody journey towards self-determination.

UN Resolution 390-A(V)

The US–British proposal for federation had come before the Ad Hoc Committee two days before Ibrahim's second address to that body. On the afternoon of Ibrahim's address on 27 November, the proposal came to the vote. No time was allotted for a discussion of the points that he had raised; nor was there time to digest his pleas. His appearance had been just a formality.

Four other proposals were waiting for a vote on the committee's table. The Soviet Union demanded the withdrawal of British troops and the immediate independence of Eritrea. Poland suggested independence after three years of transitional administration under the supervision of a council composed of Eritrea, Ethiopia and some Arab countries. Pakistan set a specific date, 1 January 1953, as Eritrea's day of independence, and proposed a UN commissioner to manage the transition period. Iraq wanted to refer the whole question to an Eritrean parliament that would be formed to decide between federation with Ethiopia or independence with an Ethiopian outlet to the sea. All of these proposals were defeated. That left the federal plan as the only viable option.

Thirty-eight nations, including Ethiopia, Liberia, Egypt, Yemen and Lebanon, supported the US federal plan. All Western European countries, except Sweden which abstained, and all countries of the British Commonwealth voted likewise. Fourteen countries, including Pakistan, Saudi Arabia, Syria, Iraq, and the Soviet Union and its Eastern European allies, voted against the plan. Seven countries abstained.[59]

On 2 December 1950, the General Assembly sat in session to deliberate on the final resolution of the Eritrean question. By this time, the outcome was not in doubt. But, probably as a gesture of benign indulgence, the supporters of Eritrean independence were called upon to speak first. The Cuban delegate complained that the proposal at hand closed every door to Eritrean independence. Like Pakistan, his country preferred the decision to be left to the people of Eritrea. He stressed that granting Somalia and Libya their independence and denying Eritrea an equal chance was unfair. El Salvador, for its part, insisted that the wishes of the people of Eritrea had not really been determined, and that a plebiscite should have been conducted; the UN, its delegate stressed, was deciding on the fate of the people of Eritrea. The Guatemalan delegate dismissed the plan as a 'compromise' solution and questioned the motives and sincerity behind it. So did his Uruguayan colleague.

Members of the Soviet alliance took the same position. The Czech delegate characterised the design as the camouflaged annexation of Eritrea by its bigger and much more populous neighbour. He wondered how the representatives of one million Eritreans would fare in a parliament dominated by the representatives of sixteen million Ethiopians. How were the rights of the Eritrean people to be protected in this unbalanced arrangement?[60]

The supporters of the US plan fell mostly silent as the opposing views were expressed one by one. There were a few undecided delegations that could still be swayed. Aklilu Habtewold took that moment to make a crucial intervention. Although the federal alternative was not Ethiopia's request or idea, he told the General Assembly, his government would accept it in the 'spirit of compromise' and in deference to the urgent crisis in Korea. He vowed that Ethiopia would spare no effort in respecting and implementing the terms of the federal plan. No distinction would be made between a majority and a minority, Muslims and Christians, and former friends and enemies. In Ethiopia's struggle to write a new chapter based on the principles on which the UN had been built, he promised that there would only be Eritreans who cooperated with Ethiopians and friends who had been former enemies.[61]

Aklilu's words had an electrifying effect on all the delegates. One by one they rose to shower their praises on the seasoned, French-educated diplomat. Iran, which had abstained earlier, announced that it had changed its mind. Expressing his faith in Aklilu's time-tested leadership and Ethiopia's adequate explanations, the Lebanese delegate also voiced his support. Others followed suit.[62]

Yet, some misgivings and unease still lingered. The UN was in its fifth year of existence, and it was in the middle of a global crisis. Many delegations were uncomfortable at the way the Eritrean issue was being rushed by the Korean conflict. The Chilean delegate, for example, clarified that her country's support for the federal solution did not indicate its abandonment of the principle of the right of self-determination of nations and peoples. It was an admission that Chile was bowing to the pressures of the day and doing so unwillingly.

It was in this atmosphere of big power pressure that Eritrea's future was decided, not in Eritrea, but at Lake Success. For all intents and purposes, the Eritrean people were invisible and non-existent for most of the delegates. Aklilu acted as their representative and the delegations, genuinely or for the sake of convenience, believed every word he uttered.

On 2 December, the US–British federal proposal came to the vote: 46 countries voted for, 10 opposed and 4 abstained. Resolution 390-A(V) of the General Assembly of the United Nations, known also as the Federal Act, was passed by a great majority. It provided that Eritrea was to 'constitute an autonomous unit federated with Ethiopia under the sovereignty of the Ethiopian Crown'. The Assembly chose September 1952 as the month for the formation of the Federation. A UN commissioner, tasked with drafting an Eritrean constitution and implementing the federal arrangement, was also to be appointed.

The Peace Congress

Ever since Philip Jessup's federal proposal at the fourth session of the UN, Eritreans had been following its progress and discussing its meaning. Two opposing interpretations surfaced as the argument heated up. As early as June 1950, the UP had taken a different path. Commenting on the Burmese proposal, its newspaper, *Ethiopia*, had this to say:

> Realizing that Eritrea cannot survive politically and economically, and that it would also have no life without Ethiopia, they have reached the chapter where it will be granted 'internal independence' inside Ethiopia. Although it is a change of

> procedure, Eritrea is for Ethiopia. As they say, 'Where there is space in which to crouch, one can always stretch out.' Dear Reader, you don't need to ask for more at this moment.[63]

Hanti Ertra dismissed this comment as an open call for Ethiopia to take over Eritrea once it had secured the territory under the 'federal' system. In that case, the Government of Ethiopia would be 'one that does not adhere to its own vows and agreements, that has no concern for international laws and system of rules, and that does not even understand the meaning of democracy. We do hope that the Ethiopian Government is not such a government. We hope that these childish thoughts are simply the musings of the writer himself.'[64]

The differences in interpretation widened further after the UN's resolution on Eritrea was announced on 2 December. The IB stuck to the Burmese model. It seemed that the likelihood that the UN resolution was a camouflaged cession of Eritrea to Ethiopia had not sunk in yet. The UP's jubilation was summed up by its president Beyene Beraki's acceptance speech in which he declared, 'Let us rejoice for now that the way to union with Ethiopia ... and the administration of His Imperial Majesty has opened up.'[65]

A few days later, an alarmed *Hanti Ertra* stated that by granting to Eritrea an autonomous status, the UN was recognising the ability of Eritreans to manage their affairs. It then tried to find solace in the following words:

> [The UN Resolution] has completely removed the danger of partition that had been looming over Eritrea and against which the Independence Bloc fought singlehandedly, paying with dear life and property in the process ... Obviously, we did not achieve our demand for full independence. But we are the ones who have been able to preserve the unity of the country ... and who have enabled the people of Eritrea to be recognized as the masters in their own land.[66]

IB president *Ras* Tessema was more practical and conciliatory in his approach. The victory that had been achieved, he said in addressing his party members,

> should be for our common benefit. Thanks to it, the unity of our country has not been disrupted; and our people have not been divided. Let us keep in mind that many have died for this cause and be thankful. The fact that we, the children of Eritrea, have withstood the religious divisions that had threatened to stumble and falter us and have struggled to preserve our country's cohesion and our people's unity, must have earned us the praises of the whole world.[67]

With these words, Tessema pledged full cooperation by his party in all forthcoming efforts to implement the UN resolution, a call that was echoed by the UP leadership and all the remaining parties as well as by the British Administration. On 31 December 1950, British officials, the leaders of all political parties, religious leaders and the representatives of the consular offices in Asmera came together at the Cinema

Impero for what is known as the Peace Congress. Around 4,000 people filled the main hall and the entrance to the cinema.

The ceremony began with the main protagonists of the previous ten contentious years, Tessema of the IB and Kidanemariam of UP, embracing in a spirit of reconciliation. It was a moment of nostalgia, according to *Hanti Ertra*, that brought tears to the eyes of many participants. Ibrahim Sultan cautioned the gathering that the suffering of the past years would take time to heal. In a gesture of goodwill and 'to contribute to the success of the plan of the United Nations resolution', he said, 'we, the Independence Bloc of Eritrea, have taken the initiative to change our name to the Eritrean Democratic Front.' He expressed his hope that the move would express the Eritrean people's longing for liberty and that the other parties would reciprocate.[68]

Ibrahim's speech was followed by that of *Azmatch* Zerom Kifle, newly installed secretary of the UP. He too acknowledged that the confrontations that had pitted Eritreans against one another had taken place between brothers and compatriots, and that 'the UN plan demands that we cast stones on what has passed and open a new chapter of Eritrean history', in which Eritrea and Ethiopia 'will attain modernity and progress under the dynasty of our own Imperial Majesty Haile Selassie I'.[69]

***

Eritrean history of the 1940s was characterised by two processes that were, to all intents and purposes, mutually exclusive. The first one involved the efforts and demands of Eritreans, unionists, nationalists, pro-Italians, partitionists and others in respect of their future. The other process involved Britain, the United States, Ethiopia and various others in a collaboration to impose a future that none of the Eritreans had asked for. The latter process prevailed, leaving Eritreans with the hollow feeling that they had been betrayed and rendered irrelevant. Weldeab Weldemariam may have accurately depicted the Eritrean reaction when he described how the UN's federal solution was accepted in Eritrea:

> As a big betrayal, a major travesty of justice by great powers on a small nation. Without their knowledge, without being asked, when they were expecting fairness in good faith, it was done by coercion, manipulation and treachery. The independence people regarded it with exceptional regret and sorrow. But they could not reject it. Rejecting the federal solution would have resulted in a conflict between Muslims and Christians. It would have opened the way for the triumph of the *shifta* movement. Eritrea would have died economically and even as an entity.[70]

New thinking was entering Eritrean politics. A gradual realignment of political forces would alter the old ethno-religious divisions that had plagued the 1940s. The ground for the forthcoming bitter struggle of the people of Eritrea for independence, which they were to attain forty years later, was laid at this momentous juncture of the nation's history.

We conclude this part of our narrative back at Cinema Impero, where the Peace Congress concluded with a resolution to which every political party in the country put its signature. It was perhaps the last time that Eritreans came together to give peace and a common fate a chance. The agreement may be summarised as follows: To respect and implement the content, letter and spirit of the decision of the General Assembly of the United Nations federating Eritrea to Ethiopia. To cooperate fully and sincerely with the commissioner of the United Nations in his mission to set up the Eritrean Government. To assist the British Administration and facilitate its assigned duty to secure peace and stability in the country. To pledge the pooling of available Eritrean strengths and capabilities and harness them into a common campaign for the growth and progress of Eritrea in the shortest time possible.

On 9 February, Bolivia's Ambassador to the UN, Anze Matienzo, arrived in Eritrea to lead the task of implementing the UN resolution in cooperation with the British administering authority. His duties included drafting an Eritrean constitution, supervising the election of a representative constitutional assembly, defining the respective powers of the Eritrean and Ethiopian governments, and ratifying the Eritrean constitution.

PART TWO

THE FEDERAL YEARS

10

UN RESOLUTION 390-A(V)

The Federal Act

We have already familiarised ourselves with the type of 'federation' envisaged by UN Resolution 390-A(V). As the UN Commissioner in Eritrea later described it, it was 'a new departure in constitutional history ... [where] Eritrea ... [was to be] a member of a Federation whose organs had not yet been fully created'.[1] That was an understatement, as the designers of the formula in Lake Success, especially the US, Britain and Ethiopia, had ruled out the creation of a federal organ separate from the Imperial Government of Ethiopia, following Aklilu Habtewold's vehement dismissal of the Burmese proposal.

Of the fifteen articles that made up Resolution 390-A(V), the first seven constituted 'the Federal Act' and contained the principles on which the federal arrangement was to be based. The remaining eight dealt with procedural matters of the resolution's implementation.

Eritrean popular reaction to the UN resolution came mainly after the political parties had accepted the plan and upon closer reading of and reflection on its tenets. Article 1 of the Act read, 'Eritrea shall constitute an autonomous unit federated with Ethiopia under the sovereignty of the Ethiopian Crown.' But what did 'autonomous unit' mean? Article 2 seemed to hint at a definition with the provision that 'The Eritrean Government shall possess legislative, executive and judicial powers in the field of domestic affairs'. Initially, Eritreans may have been pleased with the idea of forming and running their own government, albeit in a limited local jurisdiction. That jurisdiction, according to article 2, was to extend to all matters 'not vested in the Federal Government, including the power to maintain the internal police, to levy taxes to meet the expenses of domestic functions and services, and to adopt its own budget'. These capacities would have been acceptable since they were, with variations, commonly awarded to states within a federal system. Ever since the days of the Bet Giorgis Convention, many of the Eritrean political leaders had familiarised themselves with the federal and commonwealth systems of the US and Canada. Some, like Weldeab, Gebremeskel Weldu, Omer

Qadi and Abraha Tessema, had already advocated the same or similar formulas as a solution to the Eritrean question.

But, despite article 2, which gave ultimate sovereign rights and powers to the Federal-cum-Ethiopian Government, the creation of an Eritrean Government within a 'federation' created the illusion of equality between the Eritrean and Ethiopian governments. Many in the independence camp thus wanted to read more into the resolution than it actually offered. They had struggled for independence, but what lay before them appeared to be the wholesale cession of their country under federal disguise. The question of guarantees of the survival of the 'federation', even as formulated, also began to surface.

Resolution 390-A(V), like many other UN resolutions, was issued as a recommendation, which, unlike a decision, regulation or directive, appealed to UN members to adhere to it.[2] As sovereign states, members cannot be coerced into acceptance of UN decisions. Adherence to recommendations is thus left to the discretion of each member state and no sanctions are attached to those that choose not to observe them. Besides, the Federal Act did not include guarantees whereby the Eritrean Government and its people could protect their autonomous status in case the Federal Government trespassed on their rights and powers in whole or in part. Neither was a process of appeal to the UN or any other body put in place in case of a unilateral abrogation of the Federal Act by the Ethiopian Government. The only assurance on the issue was Aklilu Habtewold's solemn declaration at the fifth session of the General Assembly that his country would respect and protect the federal arrangement. Later in the year, the Panel of Legal Consultants on Eritrea addressed the crucial question of the force of the UN recommendations, only to confirm the rising fears in the country. Here is how they put it:

> 1. The General Assembly's recommendation is binding upon the Four Great Powers which are parties to the Treaty of Peace with Italy, since in that Treaty they agree to accept the recommendation.
> 2. The Governments which voted for the recommendation have a political and moral duty to comply with it; if they fail to comply, they would be going back on their decision and jeopardising the conduct of international affairs. Yet they are not legally bound by the mere fact of their vote, since for the Members of the United Nations as such, the General Assembly's resolution only formulates a recommendation.
> 3. If Ethiopia refuses to ratify the Federal Act or the Constitution adopted by the Eritrean Assembly, the whole question of the disposal of Eritrea would have to come before the General Assembly again. Hence the importance ... of consulting the Government of Ethiopia when preparing the draft Constitution.[3]

On 5 December 1950, Emperor Haile Selassie gave a short talk to express his acceptance of the Federal Act. He singled out the US, Britain and France for praise and gratitude in helping the UN realise that Eritrea and Ethiopia should live together.

After stressing that the federal arrangement was not what Ethiopia had fought for, he continued:

> Before the implementation of the idea, the Federal Act and the Eritrean administrative law ought to be studied closely and given our ratification. This study will require several months. Nevertheless, since the principle has been agreed upon, we have accepted it. Since the time has come for the peoples of Ethiopia and Eritrea to become one Ethiopian people, Ethiopia is now assured of its long-denied outlet to the sea.[4]

This was probably one of the very few times that the Emperor ever uttered the word 'federation' in relation to Eritrea. 'The Eritrean administrative laws' that he mentioned referred to the Eritrean Constitution, another term that neither he nor his officials nor the Ethiopian media were ever to mention. Other terms of the Federal Act that were to be avoided in Ethiopia were the Eritrean Assembly, which to Ethiopians became the 'Eritrean Council'; the Eritrean Government, often referred to as the 'Eritrean Administration'; and the Chief Executive, renamed 'Chief Administrator'.

As Zewde Retta has observed, the Emperor gave no hint of the fact that Eritrea was joining Ethiopia as an autonomous unit within a federal relationship.[5] This was a deliberate policy, formulated in those early stages, to promote the notion that, after having been forcibly snatched away from Ethiopia, 'the long-lost province of Eritrea was finally re-merging with its mother'. It was the narrative that generations of Ethiopians, especially those who fought against Eritrean freedom fighters, were served and that they actually believed.

Within Eritrea, Unionist Party (UP) leaders continued to support the Ethiopian tendency to downplay the 'federal' aspects of the UN resolution and influence opinion before the arrival of the UN Commissioner. Gebremikael Gurmu, editor of UP's *Ethiopia*, argued that the UN chose the formula because the members 'found no fundamental difference between union with Ethiopia (*anesione*) and federal union with Ethiopia (*federazione*) ... It is just a variation in names ... and those who reject this interpretation ... can only be anti-peace elements ... and worthless individuals who serve foreigners. No one else can ever reject this peaceful judgement of the Lord.'[6]

During these initial stages, the restrained response of the Eritrean Democratic Front (EDF, formerly the Independence Bloc) stood in sharp contrast to the aggression of the UP. EDF leader Tessema Asberom, who characterised the federal formula as the opening of a new dawn, called instead for the end to all resentment, grievance and vengefulness. He stressed that love of Eritrea, which gave rise to disagreements on what was best for its future, had been the main cause of the political divisions of the past. That love, he hoped, would still serve as a motivating factor in 'the struggle for the greater benefits and better livelihood of the people of Eritrea', provided that, while past mistakes were owned and recognised as lessons for the future, the imputation of guilt was ended.[7]

Eritrean politics was thus entering a new phase centred on the preservation or abrogation of its newly found 'federal' status, but with more far-reaching implications. That status could not be altered without infringing on the Eritrean sense of identity, which itself was enhanced by the Federal Act's recognition of Eritrea as an autonomous entity with wide domestic powers. This was perhaps an unintended result of the UN resolution that Eritreans, including unionists, began to take seriously enough to defend and guard jealously.

Thus far, Eritrean nationalism had been in a state of flux, with political parties taking it in different directions. Now all those parties were coming under the umbrella of Imperial Ethiopia as Eritreans with certain rights, not as nationalists or irredentists seeking more or similar rights. The whole picture, the paradigm even, had changed; so too, inevitably, would the alliance of forces and the perception of what really constituted Eritrean identity and Eritrean nationalism. Our narrative turns in that direction.

UN Commissioner Matienzo

Born in 1902, Eduardo Anze Matienzo of Bolivia studied political science in France and served his country in various capacities before being assigned as Bolivia's UN representative. His main task as UN Commissioner in Eritrea was 'the preparation of a constitution which, in conformity with resolution 390-A(V), would firmly establish the foundations of autonomy for Eritrea federated with Ethiopia under the sovereignty of the Ethiopian Crown'.[8] Appointed to assist him was a team of four highly qualified legal experts: the American expert on Roman law Arthur Schiller; the French constitutional lawyer Emil Giroud; the British lawyer and professor of constitutional law Sir Ivor Jennings; and Swiss scholar and International Court of Justice judge Paul Guggenheim.

Since, as a Latin American nation, Bolivia had supported the right of the people of Eritrea to be respected during the General Assembly's deliberations, Ethiopia was not happy with Matienzo's appointment. To deal with any eventuality, it replaced the unpopular Nega Haileselassie with a new liaison officer, Amdemikael Dessalegn. Having served the Italians during their occupation of Ethiopia, he was chosen for his knowledge of the Italian language and the leverage his Italian contacts would give him in his task.[9]

Matienzo arrived in Asmera on 9 February 1951. In his introductory speech, he described the UN resolution as a 'middle-of-the-road plan' which should give equal satisfaction to the advocates of union with Ethiopia and those of independence for Eritrea. He appealed to Eritreans to accept the spirit of 'conciliation and compromise' that was the basis of the Federal Act and set their differences aside to serve their country 'during the momentous period when the foundations would be laid for the autonomy of Eritrea'.[10] Before starting his formal consultations, Matienzo spent seven weeks visiting as much of Eritrea as he could. Although, wherever he went, people voiced approval for the UN resolution, he got the impression that 'the population was mainly pessimistic, particularly on account of the insecurity caused by brigandage', and that 'part of the population had no real confidence in the idea of federation or in the possibility of applying it'.[11]

The brigandage Matienzo mentioned involved an upsurge in *shifta* activity which had risen sharply in early 1951, after a lull following the UN resolution. To the old political *shiftas* who were still at large had been added common bandits out to take advantage of the confusion created by the transitional period. What was most alarming this time was the size of the *shifta* bands, sometimes numbering forty to fifty men in each unit, moving freely in the countryside, and sometimes even daring to enter towns and attacking police posts.[12] The British Administration attributed the *shifta* explosion to the combined factors of economic distress, the easy availability of guns and ammunition, anger over choice land granted to Italian farmers, and uncertainty about Eritrea's future caused by the UN resolution's ambiguity. While introducing fundamental concepts of democracy, the resolution at the same time empowered traditional bases of power and privilege, and this in turn rekindled old clan and *kebila* rivalries, thereby preparing fertile ground for *shifta* activity.[13] Politically, the UK Government's final report stated, 'the twin theses of independence and union were the articles of faith of contending political parties and had sown bitter political and racial dissension among the population ... Moreover, the years of uncertainty as to the country's political future had produced unrest and partisan animosities which could not be expected to give way immediately to national harmony.'[14]

In January 1951, when the number of *shifta* attacks reached about 130 a month, the British Administration announced a conditional amnesty to those who had not committed homicide and who were willing to confess to their crimes and surrender their arms. By April, only 296 had surrendered, some of whom had a 'tendency to recidivism'. The major leaders of the pro-Ethiopian *shifta* ignored the amnesty.[15]

When Matienzo concluded his eleven-week preliminary tour of Eritrea, he had planned to start the consultations mandated by the UN with the Eritrean population; he was also duty-bound to consult with the Ethiopian Government and the British Administration. However, Matienzo refused to meet with a population threatened by violence. In March 1951, he pointed out to the Administration:

> Although such activity might for the time being be due to common banditry, [he feared that] during the consultations, or when the Eritrean Assembly was convoked, it could again be politically exploited as it had been in the past. The elections must be preceded by a period of electoral campaigning, during which it was particularly important that the atmosphere of insecurity caused by banditry should be dissipated.[16]

Matienzo demanded a broader amnesty or more tangible results, which would involve clemency even for those who had committed multiple murders, something the British were reluctant to give. Frustrated by lack of progress on the matter, Matienzo announced the postponement of all consultations while the population was in danger. Nor would it be proper 'for a United Nations Commissioner to travel over roads along which the victims of the terrorists were falling ... under the protection of an armed escort while the inhabitants ran the risk of *shifta* attacks when they came to meet him'.[17]

The Administration tried to argue in reply that the lives and property of the population were not at such great risk and that 'banditry was generally considered to have lost the political complexion formerly attributed to it'.[18] But pressure built up on the British. Everywhere he went, Matienzo was reminded in public meetings that nothing short of a drastic change in the Administration's policy would work. Local newspapers, Tigrinya, Arabic and Italian, published daily articles demanding a similar solution. Even Emperor Haile Selassie sent a delegation of five of his Eritrean-born officials and supporters, led by the future Eritrean Chief Executive, Asfaha Weldemikael, to advise and assist the British in curbing the *shifta* menace.[19] In view of Ethiopia's previous role in supporting the *shifta*, its new stance could be questioned. However, there was the danger that Matienzo's postponement of consultations could jeopardise the whole process, an eventuality the Ethiopians were keen to avoid. Okbazghi Yohannes has suggested that the *shifta* upsurge was a deliberate move by Ethiopia to intimidate Eritrean nationalists and give the impression that the country could not govern itself.[20] With all the disruptions and delays caused by the *shifta*, the Ethiopians may have felt that their objective had been fulfilled.

Thanks to Matienzo's stern warnings, the British relented. On 19 June 1951, the Administration issued a proclamation declaring a general amnesty extending for one month only. As a result, 903 *shiftas*, including 45 known leaders, surrendered within the appointed time.[21] By September, 1,300 had surrendered. *Shifta* incidents also dwindled to about six a month by September, from around 300 in April.[22]

Consultations with the Government of Ethiopia

On 29 June, Matienzo announced that he was ready to resume consultations with the Eritrean population. But in the interim Ethiopia had taken advantage of the delay and resumed preliminary consultations with him in May. He had by then presented to the Ethiopians his outline and vision of the Eritrean Constitution and the democratic principles on which the Eritrean government was to be based. He had also drawn up a structure for the three branches of the Eritrean government. The Ethiopians were working on their response when Matienzo made his 29 June announcement.

The very next day, 30 June, Prime Minister Aklilu arrived in Asmera to continue his consultations. From Matienzo's previous meetings with Eritrean people, the Ethiopians were aware of the demands in various sections of the country for a broader interpretation of Eritrean autonomy and of Matienzo's sympathy for those demands. Aklilu hastened to Asmera to forestall that possibility. Objecting to

Matienzo's broad interpretation of the Federal Act, Aklilu argued that the powers granted to Eritrea over internal security, the budget and taxation were so broad that they could weaken respect for federal laws within the autonomous region. The powers of the Eritrean Assembly, in particular, needed to be reduced. Eritrea was an autonomous unit incapable of governing itself, not a state, Aklilu argued, and Matienzo's whole approach needed reconsideration. To solve the problem, Aklilu proposed that a closer link between the executive branches of both Ethiopia and Eritrea should be established. In concrete terms, he put forward the following ideas. The Eritrean Chief Executive should be elected from outside the Eritrean Assembly (so as to be free from the Assembly) and appointed by the Emperor of Ethiopia. Since Eritrea was to be represented by Ethiopia in all international affairs, there should be a close link between its educational, health and labour affairs and those of Ethiopia. Amharic should be the official language of Eritrea and the Ethiopian flag should be adopted as Eritrea's national flag.[23]

Matienzo reminded Aklilu that his proposals would alter the content and principles of the UN's Federal Act, which Ethiopia had accepted at the General Assembly and which he had no mandate to modify or revise. He also refused to accept Aklilu's repeated claims that Eritrea was incapable of administering itself, as the resolution specifically recognised that capacity by providing for the formation of an Eritrean government to be run by the Eritreans themselves. Although he rejected the idea of the Emperor appointing Eritrea's Chief Executive, Matienzo showed willingness to consider creating a link between the Emperor and the Chief Executive of Eritrea, a proposal that had not been provided for by the Federal Act.

Determined to emerge with some tangible gains from the consultation, Aklilu kept pushing Matienzo to adopt provisions in the Eritrean Constitution that would curb the powers of the Eritrean Assembly. He suggested, for example, that the definition of powers between the Eritrean and Ethiopian governments (article 2 of the Federal Act) not be included in the Eritrean Constitution.[24] While refusing to accept such arbitrary amendments to a binding UN resolution, Matienzo voiced his frustration at the pressure being imposed on him by the Ethiopians and even threatened to abandon his mission.[25]

Aklilu presented a threat of his own. It so happened that, after Matienzo's assumption of his duties in Eritrea, the Bolivian government that had appointed him UN representative was ousted from power and Matienzo was consequently replaced at the UN. Through Amdemikael Dessalegn's contacts, Aklilu had come to know that Matienzo was feeling insecure in his position as commissioner. He thus bluntly told Matienzo that Ethiopia would launch a campaign to have him removed as commissioner since he had lost his UN base. Matienzo relented. He went as far as promising to reconsider his position on many of the issues, including acceptance of the presence of the Emperor's representative in Eritrea, an inclusion not sanctioned by the Federal Act.[26]

Later, upon consultations with his UN-appointed legal authorities, Matienzo went back on his promises to Aklilu and resumed his old stance. No agreement could be reached between them on such issues as the powers and responsibilities of the Eritrean Government vis-à-vis the Federal Government, the issue of languages and other problems that were soon to become contentious at the national level. The only concession that Aklilu was able to secure was the appointment of a representative of the Emperor in Eritrea. Considering the crucial role that the office was to play during the federal period, this was a victory for Aklilu. Matienzo for his part must have felt satisfied for having stopped what would have amounted to the reduction of Eritrean autonomy to virtual annexation. However, as Okbazghi Yohannes has intimated, Aklilu's objection to broader Eritrean autonomy carried with it a dangerous trend for the future.[27]

Discussion on Matienzo's Draft

Matienzo's consultations with the people of Eritrea could only start on 11 July, almost two months after his original schedule. Prior to this, he made public his draft proposals and the specific issues that he sought to raise with the people and their political parties. Should there be one or two Assemblies? Should universal suffrage be adopted? Should the Emperor of Ethiopia be represented in the executive and should he take part in constituting the Eritrean Government? How should the powers and responsibilities of the Chief Executive be defined? What should be the official languages of Eritrea, and should Eritrea have its own separate flag? These were some of the main topics on which the commissioner sought the public's opinion.[28]

Matienzo's draft proposals inevitably aroused a heated debate both in print and in public debate. In a speech on 4 July, he stated that the Ethiopian Government would constitute the Federal Government, and that it would maintain its external structure and identity. Eritrea, he added, formed part of that identity.[29] The EDF's *Hanti Ertra* responded by addressing Matienzo directly: 'The Government of Ethiopia cannot become the Federal Government. The Federal Government that wears the Imperial Crown can neither be the Eritrean nor the Ethiopian Government; it can only be the "Federal Government". Your words or interpretation cannot be corroborated by any part of the Articles 1–7, decided upon and delineated by the UN resolution.'[30] After pointing out that this arrangement was an open invitation to Ethiopia to interfere in Eritrea's internal affairs, the paper continued: 'The existing Ethiopian Government did not come about in a democratic manner; it was not installed by the people. The Government and Assembly that are being formed in Eritrea, on the other hand, are by the people, for the people and from the people. It will be inappropriate for the Ethiopian Government to tamper with the Eritrean Government.'

In reaction, the UP wrote, 'Yes, they have always been voicing their opposition to any kind of union with Ethiopia. They even rejected the federal resolution when it was decided at the UN. This is recent memory. They are people who are led by alien minds. They are seeking to extract chunks of meat from the limbs of an insect.[31] Indeed, the UP had a point there. The EDF knew very well that the Ethiopian Government was to be the Federal Government. But they felt that Matienzo's choice of words, as translated into Tigrinya, removed the vestiges of Eritrean autonomy. A few days later, they again addressed Matienzo to ask for further explanation:

> You know that the internal autonomy granted to the people of Eritrea is narrow and limited. It can even be regarded on a level with municipal authority. Since this is the case, why are you designing to diminish it further? The people of Eritrea are already encircled by the five major functions assigned to Ethiopia. What harm will the Eritrean people cause if they assume internal authority? What are you afraid of?[32]

Scepticism about Matienzo's draft outline was not confined to the EDF. Similar concerns started to be raised within the ranks of the UP and their affiliates. Referring to the provision for the appointment of the Emperor's representative in Eritrea, Omer Qadi, whose Independent Muslim League had announced a complete merger with the UP in June 1951, warned that the idea was creating confusion among unionists. The UP, he argued, should either go back to its original demand for unconditional union or commit itself to the implementation of federation. It couldn't support the idea of a representative when the Federal Act did not require Eritrea to accept one. Omer Qadi was also critical of Matienzo's inclusion of that suggestion.[33]

Matienzo explained that, since Eritrean autonomy was placed under the Ethiopian Crown, the presence of the Emperor's representative could only strengthen the bonds of cooperation and spirit of brotherhood that the formula assumed. Eritrea was not being considered as a separate state that would not accept an authority higher than itself. He further complained that party leaders and newspaper editors were attempting to derail the already popularly approved UN resolution.[34]

Matienzo's intervention could not calm the highly charged and combative debate developing within the UP, particularly between Omer Qadi and Gebreyohannes Tesfamariam, chief editor of *Ethiopia*, whose acrimonious pronouncements added to the general public unease over where exactly the federal plan was leading Eritrea. Concerned that such incessant bickering was preventing the public from dealing with the real problems of transition, Weldeab attempted to redirect the people's attention to the British Administration's handling of its responsibilities.

General Drew had been replaced by General Duncan Cumming as Chief Administrator, or head of the Administrative Authority, as the Federal Act referred to it. Cumming, who had served in Eritrea under Kennedy-Cooke during the first years of British occupation, had also been responsible for the territory as an officer of the British Middle East Command. From the outset, Cumming showed no inclination to hasten the process that the Federal Act authorised him to put into effect.

In an article entitled 'But the People Are Still in a State of Limbo', Weldeab accused the Administration of delaying on such crucial matters as establishing a customs union between Eritrea and Ethiopia, putting in place an Eritrean administration, training and inducting Eritreans into the bureaucracy, preparing for the election of a legislative assembly; in short, laying the foundations for the Eritrean Government. After urging Eritreans to move away from the politics of enmity and division and concentrate on pressuring the Administration to carry out its duties, he turned his criticism directly on the UP and *Ethiopia*'s chief editor, Gebreyohannes. Hostility and antagonism, he said, would drag Eritrea back to the days of postponement and uncertainty:

> We have already agreed that federation is the only solution that would bring us together. But, where [in the Federal Act] are we required to accept an Emperor's representative, that we are being coerced to welcome one? Does the Act say that we do not have the right to have our own flag? Why is that right being denied us? Do Eritrean history and our present situation demand and stipulate that Tigrinya is the only tongue destined to be our official language? Why is it being singled out? Let us look at everything through the prism of federation and let that be our guide and destiny. But let us talk face to face, let us see eye to eye; let us dialogue and agree.[35]

All the UP's ferocity was now directed at Weldeab, who was criticised for his audacity in speaking on behalf of a people 'whose wisdom enabled it to see beyond Weldeab's platitudes'. Gebreyohannes opined that a quick political solution was what they needed.[36]

Weldeab's call for peace and dialogue elicited the very opposite response. On 15 August, five bullets were fired at him as he walked past on the other side of Cinema Impero—the sixth attempt on his life.[37] Although Cumming condemned the act some two weeks after it had taken place and urged 'party leaders' to control the actions of their followers, he refrained from holding the UP or the Andinet responsible for the attempt.[38]

In one of his most eloquent and memorable articles, Weldeab declared that he was humbled by the campaign to eliminate him, as if his death, like that of Christ, would be the panacea for all actual or perceived evil. His only regret, he said, was that he was being judged, not by a proper court of law, but by no more than nine individuals who, hiding in the dark, 'were playing with the fate of their people; paying lip service to Ethiopia and its Emperor, while their hearts are filled with manifest self-interest ... and seeking to thrive on the misery of their people'. Up to now, he claimed:

> I have never served or represented the objectives of an alien authority. I am an enemy of slavery, whatever its face or colour. No person, European or African, can ever bind or coerce me into the yoke of slavery. And if anyone dares to kill me for refusing to undertake what I don't feel or believe in, then I too have embraced the courage to die for my political convictions, my country's liberation and the benefits of my brethren.[39]

The attempt on Weldeab's life and his defiant challenge could only add fuel to the controversy over Eritrean autonomy. The more the issue was discussed, the more opponents became entrenched in their respective positions. The EDF's pronouncements, in particular, started to move ever closer to a rejection of the limited powers granted Eritrea by the Federal Act. On 3 October, its secretary general, Ibrahim Sultan, gave the following speech on the occasion of Eid al-Adha:

> We need to realize that, at this time, the hard and difficult road to attain self-government has been laid in front of our people. Yes, in order for our people to join the peoples of the world, and to taste the gifts of liberty, justice and progress provided by the UN, we must struggle to implement the federation between Eritrea and Ethiopia in its true and proper manner ... Any Eritrean who would move to obstruct or derail the internal government guaranteed by the UN, should be made to retreat or be defeated by the sheer sight of our strength and unity.[40]

Obviously, Ibrahim was suggesting that Eritrea would retain its own access to the international community, an opening not provided for by the Act. In the meantime, Matienzo was preparing for his consultations with the general population and paid little heed to Weldeab's ordeal or Ibrahim's suggestions. Indeed, even if he had, there would have been little he could do to accommodate the EDF's liberal interpretation, which could not be done without returning the whole Eritrean issue to the UN General Assembly. But it was an indication of how far away from the Federal Act the independence camp was moving. Not only a sense of unease, as Matienzo recognised, but one of betrayal was taking hold of a large part of the country and, with it, probably also a sense of loss and dismay that the people of Eritrea could be subjected to a fate not of their own choosing. Weldeab Weldemariam expressed this feeling in a poem he published in January 1952, when the British Administration was still stalling in the discharge of its duties. This is how part of it reads in translation:

> Who can stand up to the Englishman,
> The lord of the skies and of the land,
> Yes, the lord of the skies and the lord of the sea
> Who unleashes thunder with his artillery?
> Who can stand up to him except the Almighty?
> Who can stand up to the Englishman?
> He says our case is closed,
> our fate sealed, our sins forgiven,
> But when we watch from the side
> We can't see, our eyes get dimmer,
> We can't walk, our knees buckle.
> We wait for the night to pass,
> But our plight won't end.
> Alohe, Alohe lama sebaktana? (Father, why hast thou forsaken us?)[41]

That section of the Eritrean population that had sought independence was obviously resentful of the UN's federal formula. Soon, it was to grow in size as adherents of union also started to realise the high-handed way in which their fate was being managed. In this initial stage of confusion and disorientation, the EDF's pronouncements and arguments might have looked naive and even spiteful, but they need to be given the serious attention they deserve. Herein lie the antecedents of the story of how Eritrean nationalism survived the quagmire of confusion and mislaid loyalties.

Matienzo's Consultations with Eritreans

On 12 July 1951, Matienzo began his popular consultations by inviting representatives of the various political parties, civic associations, religious establishments, and other community and foreign leaders to meet him. He then toured the country to meet with the inhabitants themselves. He found that public opinion was divided into two opposing camps. Supporters of the EDF were opposed to the Government of Ethiopia's assumption of the mantle of the Federal Government and also to the presence of the Emperor's representative in Eritrea. They wanted Tigrinya and Arabic to be the official languages and Eritrea to have its own flag. UP supporters expressed different preferences, namely, that the Ethiopian Government should become the Federal Government; that the Emperor's representative should not only be allowed into Eritrea, but that he should also be represented within the executive branch of the Eritrean Government; that Tigrinya should become the official language, with Arabic limited to religious and commercial functions; and that the federal (Ethiopian) flag only should fly in Eritrean skies.[42]

The language issue was the most contentious. The ML-Western Province (*teqsim*) insisted that only Arabic be recognised as the official language, with Tigrinya confined to the Tigrinya-speaking areas. Others argued that, since Arabic was a foreign language, Tigrinya and Tigre, both products of the Semitic Geez, should be given the honour jointly.[43]

As G.K.N. Trevaskis observed, the Ethiopian Government, which through its UP agents was campaigning for maximum leverage from the countrywide consultations, did not fully succeed in its endeavours. The EDF, the ML-Western Province and their supporters rejected the Emperor's representation. Although the UP accepted the proposal, many preferred his role to be restricted to naming the Chief Executive of Eritrea. On the issue of languages, although UP supporters rejected Arabic as a national language, hardly anyone backed Amharic to replace Eritrean languages or even stand on a par with them. Ethiopia's gains were, therefore, very limited.[44]

In his concluding report, Matienzo recognised the deep divisions between the political parties and the inhabitants affiliated to them. He noted that they were still faithful to their old principles and loyalties. Nevertheless, his belief in the country's future was strengthened by the spirit of brotherhood and tolerance prevalent among the common people. He concluded that there was general acceptance of the federal solution and a great deal of respect for the Emperor of Ethiopia. He noted that the introduction of civil and human rights by the Federal Act had aroused great hope among the people and that there was a widespread feeling that the cultures, traditions, religious beliefs and languages of Eritrea should be respected.

Matienzo stressed that these aspects had given him hope for the successful outcome of his mission. Apparently, he regarded the issues of the Emperor's representation, languages and the flag as secondary. He simply sidelined them as matters that could be resolved through discussion. They were not, he stressed, such major problems as to require reassessment by the General Assembly. But he did promise to distribute a report on all his findings to the Assembly's members.[45]

On 27 November 1951, Matienzo left for Geneva to draft the Eritrean Constitution in consultation with his legal experts.

British Delays in Federal Act Responsibilities

Article 11 of the Federal Act assigned to the Administering Authority the conduct of affairs of Eritrea during the transition period. In consultation with the UN Commissioner, it was charged with the organisation, as rapidly as possible, of an Eritrean administration; the induction of Eritreans at all levels of responsibility; the convocation of an Eritrean Assembly chosen by the people; and the negotiations on behalf of the Eritrean people of a temporary customs union with Ethiopia. How were these duties discharged?

The Organisation of an Eritrean Administration

Despite the comparatively higher level of secondary and vocational education that they introduced, the British fell short of raising Eritrean standards in the fields of higher management and administration. The oft-repeated excuse that Eritreans were not fit for such positions and for the level of training these posts demanded had become a mantra. Throughout the ten years prior to the arrival of Matienzo, the British Administration made no serious effort, except perhaps in the training of police officers and teachers, to prepare Eritreans for possible self-administration.

The arrival of the UN Commissioner in February 1951 did not change British attitudes and policy. By April, newspapers started to publish public complaints about the delay in nominating an Eritrean advisory body to help prepare for the establishment of the Eritrean Government. The complaints turned to open protests when, in late April, the British declared the Ethiopian day of liberation a public holiday in Eritrea too. Ibrahim Sultan wrote both to Cumming and Matienzo condemning the decision as an infringement on Eritrea's rights under the Federal Act. The fact that the government and assembly of the people of Eritrea had not yet been formed, he argued, did not give the British the right to decide beforehand what holidays Eritreans should celebrate nationally.[46]

Hanti Ertra went further in its criticism of the Administration's declaration:

> This English Administering Authority has not even touched the customs union that should first be put in place. The peace and security that is a prerequisite for the establishment of the Eritrean Government is still manifestly lacking. Eritrean blood is still flowing everywhere like that of sheep and goats. While Eritreans are denied position and responsibility, their affairs are being run by unknown foreigners. At a time when the people of Eritrea are being scattered and hunted down like a herd of cattle without a shepherd, our whole spirit and sense of justice cannot accept or tolerate the declaration of a *fiesta nazionale* on our people's behalf.[47]

Cumming was unmoved by the protests and went ahead to officiate over the federal holiday of Ethiopia's liberation from Fascist Italy. In response to questions as to why he was not moving to lay the foundations of an Eritrean government, he presented a catch-22 scenario that he insisted militated against such an attempt. First, he said, the Eritrean Assembly had to be elected, but that should wait as it might inflame the tensions already existing between the political parties. Besides, there was no Eritrean representative body that could be consulted and, if such a body was to be nominated, Ethiopia should have a say in its composition. Finally, most capable Eritreans were hostile to Ethiopia and would need to be forgiven by its government.[48]

The UP expressed its pleasure on the holiday issue and celebrated along with Cumming, but it proposed the establishment of a public forum or regular gathering to address important issues pending the formation of an Eritrean government. Although the EDF supported the UP suggestion, it accused the British of failing to change their views of Eritrean capabilities. The Administration replied that it wanted to ensure that applicants 'were at least possible material for training' and that it would wait until 'an effort was made to find qualified candidates'.[49]

Thus ended 1951. In January and February 1952, a year after the UN Commissioner's resumption of his duties, the British Foreign Office held a meeting to address the issue. In attendance were two officials of the London office; Brigadier Benoy, the former Chief Administrator for Eritrea; Frank Stafford; and Cumming. Cumming, who had been arguing that, as far as self-government was concerned, Eritreans were years behind their Sudanese neighbours,[50] repeated the same line. Nevertheless, his colleagues thought that the induction of Eritreans should start by June 1952, just three months prior to the date marked for the institution of the Federation. The idea was to name some candidates in April and put them in place by 1 June 1952.[51] It had taken eleven years for the British to give Eritreans the chance to run their affairs from positions of higher responsibility.

The Customs Union

The last part of article 11 of the Federal Act read as follows: 'The Administering Authority may negotiate on behalf of Eritreans a temporary customs union with

Ethiopia to be put into effect as soon as practicable.' According to article 4, the Federation would constitute 'a single area for tax purposes', with 'no barriers to the free movement of goods and persons within the area'. However, the Act specified, 'customs duties on goods entering the Federation which have their final destination or origin in Eritrea, shall be assigned to Eritrea'. After ignoring the issue for over a year, the British Administration met with an Ethiopian delegation led by deputy minister Minassie Lemma to address the topic in Asmera. The BA's financial controller, Arthur Sleep, was also accompanied by two British advisors. No Eritrean national was invited to the deliberations.

The Ethiopians proposed that, to simplify matters and prevent corruption right from the start, Ethiopia would transfer a fixed lump sum to the Eritrean treasury, which would be reviewed every three or five years. This lump sum was to be based on Eritrea's customs revenues for the years 1948–50. However, since Ethiopia's customs duties were much higher than those of Eritrea, it would be willing to increase the lump sum, adding 15% in compensation, provided Eritrea waived the transit charges that it had been imposing.

Even the British representatives were taken aback by the Ethiopian proposals. First, the transit charges that the Ethiopians wanted to be waived formed one of Eritrea's major sources of revenue. Secondly, the proposals appeared to be contrary to the provisions of the Act, the contents of which they could not agree to change. If they were to do so, then the lump sum would have to be calculated on the basis of a detailed assessment of every commodity imported into or exported from Eritrea. Besides, checkpoints would have to be put in place at the border so that there could be no confusion about the destination of the items. Otherwise, the Ethiopian proposals would deny Eritrea its fair share of customs revenues. The Ethiopians stuck to their proposals and the meeting ended without agreement.[52]

In his report, Sleep underlined the great disadvantage that Eritrea would be subjected to if the Ethiopian proposals were adopted. Compared with the projected revenues to the Federal Government, Eritrea's 1948–50 income would be insignificant. Besides, the Ethiopians had deliberately left out of consideration the 1951 revenues, which were higher than those of the previous years. Even then, and in spite of the 15% increase proposed, Eritrea would be at a disadvantage. 'I cannot advise the Government of Eritrea to accept the lump sum,' he concluded.[53]

Arthur Sleep's warning was not heeded. In an exchange of correspondence on the issue, British officials started to argue that article 4 of the Act had not given the Administration a full mandate to decide on behalf of the Eritrean Government. The use of the word 'may' in the provision, as opposed to 'shall', made the assignment optional. Therefore, they suggested that the matter be left for the Eritrean and Ethiopian governments to resolve. In the meantime, a temporary measure could be devised, pending that resolution.[54]

Matienzo was consulted on this. According to Cumming, Matienzo argued that, according to the Federal Act, the whole issue of the services and administration of customs duties was due to fall under the authority of the Federal Government. What had to be obtained were assurances that Eritrea would not suffer financial difficulties in the ensuing complicated calculations to assign revenues due to each government. He further recommended that Ethiopia and Eritrea revise the situation after some years of 'federal experience', when the lump sum proposal might be agreed upon as a convenient solution.[55]

From handwritten side notes in Cumming's report, it seems that some London officials were sceptical as to whether Matienzo had been consulted seriously, since some of his opinions had been given orally. One official went further to warn that, with all the power vested in it, nothing could stop the Federal Government from depriving Eritrea of its fair share of revenues.[56] Commenting on this warning, E.G. Baxter, head of the African Department at the Foreign Office, said that, although it might sound cynical, they should not expect that, with the passage of time, the Federation would continue to operate the way the UN had planned it. They expected the Ethiopians to override the arrangement and, as long as that was done peacefully, Britain would not object.[57]

Ultimately, British officials both in London and Asmera agreed that the Federal Act's wording did not oblige them to decide on a permanent solution to the customs issue. They did, however, agree to cooperate with the Executive Committee of the Eritrean Representative Assembly after the formation of that body during the transition to the Federation.

The customs union was to remain a thorny issue and a unifying factor for Eritreans of differing persuasions throughout the federal period.

Proclamation 121 of 1952

On 28 January, Cumming issued Proclamation 121 of 1952, regulating the first-ever Eritrean elections to convene a representative assembly. Frank Stafford was in charge of the drafting of the law. With the exception of Asmera and Massawa, the British ruled out election by direct ballot on the grounds that no census had ever been taken, no elections ever conducted, and that a large proportion of the population in Eritrea was nomadic and semi-nomadic. Besides, the time constraint did not allow for direct elections to be held. Instead, constituencies created by the Administration would name representatives who would, in turn, elect delegates to function as the 'electoral college' for a constituency. The latter would then be obliged to cast their vote in secret ballots in favour of the candidate they had been delegated to choose.

Candidacy was open only to Eritrean male citizens over 30 years of age; women were excluded. Furthermore, women were excluded from voting as well; that right was reserved for male citizens over 21 years of age.[58] The Administration did not give any reason for its decision. Nor indeed did the UP, the EDF or the women themselves raise a voice in protest at the omission. It was a unilateral decision by the British, who were under no local pressure to disregard half of the population.

When the proclamation was published, one issue stood out as highly controversial and objectionable. In dividing Eritrea into electoral constituencies, it had given more weight and importance to the ethnic and religious composition, rather than the political affiliation, of the population. A constituency had to be composed of 15,000 people to qualify as such. Towns like Keren and Mendefera, which had less than 10,000 inhabitants, thus had to be merged with neighbouring villages to form constituencies for indirect election. In this manner, Eritrea was divided into 68 constituencies arranged in such a pre-planned way that the Assembly seats would be evenly divided between 34 Muslims and 34 Christians.

Three days after the publication of the proclamation, the EDF gave its angry reaction:

> Just like Pontius Pilate, this English Administering Authority is capable of declaring, 'So I have written!' We know, therefore, that whatever we say or write, our utterings and pleas will go unheeded. This English Administration has imposed a law on the election of representatives without consulting, asking or seeking the consensus of the people of Eritrea. It is well known that, for one whole year, we have been writing, begging and crying out for the formation of an Eritrean Council to advise the Administration during this transition period. No one listened to us. Had our brothers [the UP] and the English Authority heeded our pleas, this significant burden would not have fallen on our people.[59]

In subsequent publications of *Hanti Ertra*, the EDF made no secret of its suspicion that dividing Eritrea into ethnic and religious constituencies was aimed at sparking sectarian division and conflict. One such article addressed the people directly:

> The love of your compatriots and your country compel you to be vigilant, lest the dangers of religious and sectarian disunity take root amongst your brethren. It also motivates you to fight with all your means the attempt to replace political differences with religious discord. Of all the instruments and traps at his disposal, this is an enemy's worst tool ... Take note that this is alien thinking being introduced for a purpose. It never existed before in predominantly Muslim or majority Christian areas. Neither is it prevalent now. Understand that this alien idea can throw you into the pit that you have been fighting not to fall into till now.[60]

The UP's reaction was predictably different from that of the EDF. At a February meeting at its headquarters, Tedla Bairu urged his supporters to concentrate more on what type of people should be elected to the Assembly:

> Real and imagined talk and gossip aimed at derailing your purpose and staining your name will come your way verbally and in writing. Throw away this unhealthy talk about sectarianism, religion and provincialism. Shut down this evil spirit that seeks to

> divide you in these historic times ... As has been decided, the people of Mereb Mellash will establish and protect their own internal livelihood. Their aim is to become the children of one great Ethiopia, to bask under its flag, to nestle beneath its Crown and to be herded by one king. Therefore, beware and take note! Long live His Imperial Majesty Haile Selassie I.[61]

The UP went on to launch an open and aggressive campaign against the possible candidature of EDF leaders in the elections. It particularly targeted Ibrahim Sultan and Weldeab Weldemariam, whom it called 'disruptors'.[62] Rather than respond to the UP's attacks, the EDF continued its attempts to engage the Administration on basic issues of the transition period, but to no avail. The Administration was determined to have its way with the elections. An Electoral Commission was formed to oversee the process. According to the proclamation, the Representative Assembly would be instituted for the purpose of ratifying the Eritrean Constitution, whereupon it would be dissolved, and a new legislative assembly elected. For reasons we will come to, the EDF believed that new elections for a legislative assembly would not take place.

This was obviously a time of deep frustration and disappointment for the EDF's leadership and their followers. As we saw in the poem written by Weldeab, the realisation was taking root that the Eritrean matter had not been resolved in the interest of Eritreans. If there was any illusion that the Federation would survive in its UN format, it was dashed in those preparatory stages. The EDF and the independence camp were obviously entering the Federation as an alienated body seeking some way out.

11

THE ERITREAN REPRESENTATIVE ASSEMBLY

Pre-election Political Trends

As the political cleavage in Eritrea changed from unionism versus independence to federalism versus annexation, new styles of behaviour and new types of alliances began to form, especially among the traditional leadership. As they positioned themselves for favours or the restoration of lost rank or property from the incoming Ethiopian administration, old rivalries and jealousies resurfaced to a degree that prompted younger Eritreans to intervene and attempt to shift the focus back to the burning issues of the day.

Weldeab Weldemariam, a constant critic of the old malaise, later contributed to a deeper awareness of the matter by publishing an article which contained the observations of a British official about the sycophancy and selfishness prevalent mostly among *kebessa* traditional leaders of both political persuasions. Eritreans, the official told Weldeab,

> are smart, knowledgeable and quite capable. In this respect, they are not inferior even to Europeans. But they are possessed of a chronic blemish that eats into them like a fungus—and this is called mutual hatred and ill-will. I have served in Akeleguzai, Seraye and now I am in Hamasien. I can say that I know almost all the *mislenes*, village chiefs and elders ... It pains me to see such personalities and educated people hate one another; and compete, affront and belittle each other to such an extent. It often causes me to lose hope. If such obsolete thinking and character is not rid of the heart of Eritreans, they will always be subjected to the will of others. Whenever a *mislene* or an important personality comes to talk to me on matters of administration, he would never leave without telling me some bad things about his fellow villager or provincial. And his gossip and criticisms arise, 99 per cent out of 100, from his own personal grudge and hatred, rather than the benefit of the collective.[1]

Neither Weldeab nor any member of the public responded to these comments, hard as they may have been to swallow. But an awareness of the problem had been growing in the minds of younger Eritreans, who, as early as March 1951, took steps to correct it by establishing a new bipartisan group called Bayto Selam, or the Peace Assembly of Eritrean Youth. Led by former Andinet president Haile Abrehe, and former Shuban activist Mahmoud Ismail, it led a procession of Muslims and Christians to the Muslim and Christian cemeteries in Asmera, where wreaths were laid on the graves of the February 1950 victims of the Asmera riots and healing messages of forgiveness exchanged by the former antagonists.[2] Second, to put a stop to the senseless war of words between EDF's *Hanti Ertra* and *Saut al Rabita*, on the one hand, and the UP's *Ethiopia*, on the other, they brought the editors of the three papers—Weldeab, Yasin Batok and Gebreyohannes, respectively—to the same table and elicited promises of more civilised dialogue, which were soon to break down. Later, they threw a dinner party to honour the 68 elected Assembly members, at which they urged them to discard 'our tears and sorrows ... and to focus on the proper implementation of the federal system ... to ratify the Eritrean Constitution and not to work for rank and glory'.[3]

Bayto Selam, which drew much publicity for the duration of its short life, was a noble attempt by well-meaning young nationalists who sought to enhance 'a spirit of understanding, brotherhood and cooperation between Muslims and Christians' and to urge people 'to come down from the political mountains on top of which they are entrenched, to the open plains where they can sit down and discuss matters of national interest'. It was also an advocacy group that openly criticised Britain for 'dismantling and shipping out Eritrean infrastructure to other countries', for failing to resuscitate the Eritrean economy and for allowing the wanton deforestation of the country.[4]

Bayto Selam was forced to disband when the Administration denied it permission to operate. But many of its members would soon take leading roles in the democratic and nationalist dialogue that it had helped set in motion.

The Elections

As the elections, scheduled for the third week of March 1952, approached, the EDF's distrust of Ethiopia's intentions reached a new level. In November 1951, Ibrahim Sultan visited the American consul, Edward W. Mulcahy, and told him that Ethiopia was already planning the dismantling of the federation at that early stage. The UN and the US should not be standing on the sides while democratic Eritrea was about to be swallowed by Ethiopia, he told Mulcahy. Ibrahim gave his reasons. Ethiopia was unhappy with the activities of Bayto Selam and the new labour movement and with the increasing move of Andinet members to the camp of federalism. That was why it was sending its ministers and high-level officials to Asmera to counter the new trend. Since Ethiopia's moves were directly aimed at destroying the EDF's base, Ibrahim felt justified in planning to travel to Paris to launch an appeal at a UN meeting. The British Administration, and especially Frank Stafford, denied him a travel permit.

Although Mulcahy attempted to assuage Ibrahim's worries by arguing that Ethiopia's obvious desire to be the dominant partner in the Federation could be curbed by the Eritrean Constitution and the Assembly about to ratify it, Ibrahim would not be moved. He was adamantly opposed to the presence of the Emperor's representative in Eritrea, an issue that he expected would be of great contention in the Assembly. Neither he nor his party could tolerate the Ethiopian Government wearing the mantle of the Federal Government. He still thought that separate offices of foreign affairs, defence and customs should be created outside the framework of the Ethiopian Government. The EDF had even written a memo to Matienzo detailing these points.

Mulcahy warned that such obstructive suggestions, and especially the memo, could only frustrate Matienzo's efforts. Ibrahim replied that they emanated from the Eritrean people's desire to accept nothing short of full autonomy within the Federation. In a letter to the State Department, Mulcahy recognised the soundness of many of Ibrahim's points. He also noted Ibrahim's capacity to do all he could to maintain his authority and prestige among his Muslim constituents.[5] In a previous message, he had spoken of rising resentment among the population against the policies of the Amhara, which was growing into an open hatred for Ethiopia.[6]

In the meantime, the EDF was strongly campaigning through its newspapers, *Hanti Ertra* and *Saut al Rabita*, against the British Administration's preference for ethnicity over political affiliation in determining electoral districts. In a series of articles, it attacked Election Proclamation 121 for being regressive and for turning history back to clan, village and *kebila* rivalry from the advanced levels of Eritrean nationalism attained under the leadership of the EDF. It exhorted its readers to answer only to their political beliefs in casting their ballots at the elections.

The UP used Ibrahim's own arguments to accuse him of sowing seeds of division. Gebreyohannes Tesfamariam wrote: 'It was the Eritrean people themselves who demanded that election by the divisive political parties be replaced by the people themselves. Now, individuals like *Ato* Ibrahim are attempting to scale up rugged mountains and climb down slippery slopes to run our elections on the basis of religion. It is indeed very sad.'[7]

In the days preceding the elections, both parties made final appeals to the people. The EDF's message read in part:

> Be aware that this Eritrean Government, your Government, will be elected, established and administered by you. It will not be the subject of any outside authority, nor will it venture to impose its will on you. You are not like the water canal that can be diverted to any direction. Be the master and leader of all events in your country; let no one take advantage of you ... Therefore, the candidates that you will vote for tomorrow should be the ones who will give you liberty and happiness. They should be people who will not be attracted or deviated by money or rank ...

The UP was equally forceful:

> You know that there are Eritrean nationals who, intent on denying love and harmony, work to divide the country along religious, regional and racial lines; all for their own private interest. If these people claim that they have come back to their senses, do not depend on their word and be deceived; demand more proof ... These are testing times when we need cooperation, tolerance and constant reminders to work as one family ... Above all our Emperor Haile Selassie I, who loves and cares for us, has said, 'We have delivered into the hands of our beloved people of Eritrea the right to decide their future.'[8]

Clearly, the tide was turning against the EDF. In a traditional society in which chiefs wielded power and wealth, elections based on ethnicity and religion could only benefit them. The election results of 26 March 1952 bore this out. Of 68 candidates, 66 were announced as winners on election day. Two candidates tied, one of them being Ibrahim Sultan himself. A little-known fellow member of the Rigbat *kebila* called Mohammed Said Feki Ali allegedly won the same number of votes as Ibrahim, *sheik* of the Rigbat, founder of the Muslim League and leader of the independence movement. When Ibrahim went on to win a run-off election a month later and the other tied outcome was resolved, Muslims and Christians shared the 68 seats in even numbers, according to plan.

Even so, it is possible to describe the composition of the Representative Assembly in terms of the already existing political affiliations of its members. The UP became the majority party with 32 seats. With 21 seats, the EDF and its allies came second; and 15 went to the ML-WP. How damaging the ML-WP's split from the ML had been for the independence cause may be discerned from this result. The ML-WP was a British creation aimed at weakening the Independence Bloc and it succeeded in doing just that. Similarly, the religious balance attained was the result of careful planning that gave no chance for voters to cast their ballots on the basis of other considerations. Every step of the way since the beginning of their administration of Eritrea, the British had obstinately denied, forestalled and worked against any inclination by Eritreans to manifest their nationalistic stance.

The elections themselves were generally conducted fairly and efficiently. A few complaints were made mainly by minority groups who felt they had been unfairly merged with larger *kebilas* that did not represent their interests.[9] However, two results caught the attention of the public and the Administration—Ibrahim Sultan's tie with Feki Ali and Weldeab's dismal performance in the election. The American consul Mulcahy could not hide his suspicion of some form of foul play behind the Ibrahim–Feki Ali tie. Some days before the second stage of the indirect elections, Frank Stafford met Mulcahy and told him he had no doubt that Ibrahim was set to win. But, Stafford added, a lot could happen between then and the end of the elections. When the Rigbat election was declared a tie, Mulcahy saw Stafford's hand in the unexpected result. He was sure that Ibrahim had already secured the required votes when Stafford talked to him some days before. By law, electors were obliged to vote for the candidate chosen by a majority of their constituency. The tie could not have come about without some of the electors going against the rule and giving Ibrahim's votes to Feki Ali. In his report, Mulcahy said he failed to figure out how, except for Stafford's intervention, such a change could happen in the space of a few weeks.[10] But as we have seen, Stafford's efforts did not prevail as Ibrahim won the run-off election in May. We will encounter Feki Ali again as a cabinet secretary during the first few years of the Federation.

A more shocking election result for the EDF was Weldeab's poor showing in the central district of Asmera. In a contest that involved several candidates, Weldeab could muster only 135 votes to the winner Tesfamikael Werke's 1,471 and the runner-up Mohammed Aberra Hagos's 633. A couple of lesser-known candidates also beat Weldeab in the final ballot. The UP, which took Weldeab's failure as a judgement on the EDF and a public rebuke of him as a person, could not contain its glee. Its newspaper, *Ethiopia*, tried to dismiss Weldeab as an impostor with the following words:

> This man, editor of the alien paper, *Hanti Ertra*, who claims to have a popular base when he has not; and pretends to have a village of origin when he does not...could not even get a refund for the amount he deposited. One cannot fly without wings. One cannot acquire roots or conjure up an ancestry by belittling native sons and gentlefolk. A boastful flame ends up in the ashes.[11]

Weldeab took his defeat with characteristic calm and humility. In his 1987 interview, he praised the elections for their fairness and even supported the religious balance in the Assembly for giving equal representation to the two major religions. As for his poor performance, he had no one to blame but the EDF itself:

> We nominated two candidates, Mohammed Aberra Hagos and myself. EDF elders assembled at the mosque advised against both of us standing for election, as the enemy would take advantage of the split ... there was no agreement. Tesfamikael Werke won the election; the UP took it. This showed that, although our political programme was the same, there were still remnants of discord amongst us. It was not like that with the UP. Angels may disagree on the way to salvation; devils unite for evil intentions. The UP always formed a common front on most occasions.[12]

Weldeab was not one who suffered personal affronts without giving a fitting response. He reminded the editor of *Ethiopia* that to be elected to an office was a responsibility, not a privilege. Elected officials were there not, 'as the editor often expects, for flattery and gain, but rather to earn the respect and obedience of their electors by dispensing their duties and responsibilities properly ... Failure to be elected to an office should not render a person dishonourable, rootless or a heap of ashes.'[13] It would not take too long for Weldeab to prove his worth.

Assembly Debates on the Draft Constitution

Regardless of the political composition of the Assembly, the fact that Eritrea was finally installing a *bayto* (the Tigrinya equivalent of a parliament or assembly) of its own raised high hopes among the majority of the population. Generally referred to as 'the 68', the members soon became household names. Every newspaper carried articles reflecting the great faith of the people in the 68. Although it was known that, in accordance with Proclamation 121, the Representative Assembly would disband upon ratification of the Constitution and be replaced by a new legislative assembly, people still banked on the good faith of its members to produce a satisfactory result.

On 28 April 1952, the Assembly's clerk, Fergus McCleary, convened its first meeting at which Chief Administrator Duncan Cumming, UN Commissioner Matienzo and the Ethiopian liaison officer Amdemikael Dessalegn gave brief speeches. The following day, 29 April, the Assembly reconvened to elect its officials. Tedla Bairu of the UP stood against *Qadi* Musa Umron, EDF leader from Keren, and won the chairmanship. Ali Rad'ai of the ML-WP became vice chairman, having defeated Saleh Kekia Pasha of the UP. An alliance was obviously being forged between the UP and ML-WP. The Assembly was finally ready for business.

Matienzo presented the draft of his constitutional proposals to the Assembly on 3 May, summarising the principles on which it was based and its salient features. Eritrean autonomy and Ethiopian sovereignty would reconcile the political tendencies of the population. The appointment of the Emperor's representative would not imply intervention in Eritrea's internal affairs. While the principles of Eritrean autonomy, democratic government and respect for human rights were embodied in the draft Constitution, the supplementary safeguards for the various population groups did not imply any form of extraterritorial rights. The Chief Executive, elected by the Assembly, would nominate his own cabinet secretaries. Assembly elections would be conducted by an electoral high commission. The powers of the Assembly, including its right to approve the annual budget, were spelt out. The independence of the judiciary was guaranteed. Provision was made for a civil service commission and an Auditor General.[14]

Matienzo's draft was generally hailed as democratic, progressive and fashioned after the US Constitution. However, it contrasted sharply with the 1931 Ethiopian Constitution under which it was to function. The balance of power it created between the three branches of government would be incompatible with Ethiopia's autocratic system, where all power rested with the Emperor. Whereas the Eritrean Assembly was to be elected by the people, the Ethiopian Senate was appointed by the Emperor and the lower house of parliament selected by the Senate. An independent judiciary in Eritrea could impeach the Chief Executive when legal grounds so demanded; the Ethiopian Constitution shielded the Emperor from any such possibility by declaring his person and dignity 'inviolable'. In addition, the civil liberties guaranteed by the Eritrean Constitution and adopted word for word from article 7 of the Federal Act were granted by the Ethiopian Constitution subject to restrictions imposed by subsequent by-laws and regulations.[15] There were thus two incompatible systems bent on a collision course right from the outset. However, it was not these major issues of constitutionalism and the rule of law that held the representatives' attention. They concentrated rather on those proposals and provisions that directly affected their everyday lives and civil rights.

To the extent that the debates on the draft constitution touched on almost every aspect of Eritrea's culture, laws, economy and society, they provide valuable material for the study of Eritrean society as a whole. That they have not been the object of a separate study has limited the availability of the wealth of information and conventional wisdom contained in them. Here too, we will have to limit ourselves to the four issues that aroused intense debate and revealed latent emotions and loyalties of which many members were probably unaware.

The Issue of Eritrean Citizenship

Whereas article 6 of the Federal Act clearly recognised a 'federal nationality' for all inhabitants of Eritrea, with the exception of foreign nationals, it fell short of according the same recognition to Eritrean citizenship. In a vague sub-article, it added, 'The qualifications of persons acquiring the nationality of the Federation ... [and] exercising their rights as citizens of Eritrea shall be determined by the Constitution and laws of Eritrea'. Assuming that this sub-article recognised Eritrean citizenship by implication, and responding to the overwhelming popular demand for such recognition, Matienzo included two articles on the matter in his draft. In the first provision, the draft proposed that on the basis of reciprocity, all nationals of the Federation would be accorded the same rights in Eritrea as Eritrean citizens. Provided that they satisfied the relevant provisions of the Eritrean Constitution, such federal nationals would have the right to elect and be elected to the Eritrean Assembly and hold administrative offices. The second proposal defined Eritrean citizens as persons who had acquired federal nationality; persons born of one Eritrean parent, or persons who had acquired Eritrean citizenship by law.

To Matienzo's surprise, the reaction from the Assembly members was immediate and fierce. Everyone knew that there was not, and could not be, a 'federal nationality', as no separate federal entity had been created. There could only be an 'Ethiopian nationality', and that was what was being put forward. Mesfin Gebrehiwet, a unionist, set the tone for the discussion when he asked if every federal national (Ethiopian) was being granted Eritrean citizenship. Ibrahim Sultan added that, if that was the case, nothing would prevent federal nationals from coming into Eritrea in great numbers, fulfilling some residential requirements and engaging in acts prejudicial to Eritrea.[16]

In the ensuing explanation, Matienzo seemed to imply that, whereas the word 'Eritreans' referred to 'federal nationals', 'Eritrean citizens' would be those who exercised political rights—the right to vote or stand for election. As an interpretation that would leave out the majority of the population, women and children, who could not vote, the suggestion was quickly drowned in a din of protest. Significantly, the most vociferous advocates for a clear and exclusive definition of Eritrean citizenship turned out to be the unionists. Why, after all the trouble that they had gone to to be Ethiopians, did they suddenly seek to establish an Eritrean identity that would limit, if not rival, Ethiopian supremacy? Mesfin Gebrehiwet, teacher and unionist youth leader, explained:

> The federal plan that we accepted granted us, Eritreans, certain rights. We were not willing to share those rights with unknown people coming in from Wollamo, Wellega or Showa, for that matter. We would suffer consequences. Our land area is limited, not enough to accommodate us, let alone add multitudes from Ethiopia. Besides, accepting the proposition would make us look weak and vulnerable. So, we rose in that spirit. It was not an organised reaction. We did not assign speakers from outside the sessions. It was a spontaneous response.[17]

Many of the UP representatives were traditional chiefs and hereditary *risti* and *gulti* owners with a stake in keeping customary land and property rights intact. It was not surprising therefore that they would be protective of these rights; and, if strengthening Eritrean citizenship guaranteed that protection, they were willing to change their previous stance of submitting to an Ethiopian identity only. Matienzo tried to argue that the Constitution they were adopting was a democratic document that sought to be inclusive; their exclusivist attitude, however, went against that democratic principle.[18]

The Catholic priest *Abba* Habtemariam Nugurru, a unionist from western Seraye, became a leading figure in the debate on Eritrean citizenship. In rejecting the extension of Eritrean citizenship to all federal nationals, he argued, the draft was going far beyond the provisions of the Federal Act. It meant that Eritreans would be obliged to grant land to outsiders. It would not be fair to open up Eritrea for the settlement of potentially large numbers of people.

Other members echoed the *Abba*'s apprehension. *Grazmatch* Teklehaimanot Bokru, later Finance Secretary and an EDF member, strongly objected to the notion that, for Eritreans to be recognised as Eritreans, they needed to be accepted as federal nationals first. *Blata* Habtezghi Okbazghi, representing the Haddish Adi zone of Asmera, added that Eritreans were the owners of centuries-old cultures and traditions that formed the basis of their distinct identity. Rights emanating from such exclusively Eritrean sources should not be open to other federal nationals. Business or commercial activities were acceptable, but political rights should be out of bounds to them.

Matienzo's insistence on a broader interpretation provoked the following response from *Abba* Habtemariam, who provided a deeper understanding of the issue involved:

> It should be clear that Eritrean citizenship will be defined by Eritrean laws and the Eritrean Constitution. An outsider who seeks to be the citizen of a nation has to be subjected to the laws of the citizenship of that country. This is the standard rule. To become English, you apply to the Home Secretary and you abide by the laws of that country. It is the same here ...[19]

Ibrahim Sultan teamed up with one of the senior UP leaders from Akeleguzai, *Azmatch* Beyene Zahlai, to work on the final form of the first provision, which *Abba* Habtemariam redrafted to state that persons eligible for Eritrean citizenship under the auspices of the Federal Act could only obtain that status after fulfilling the relevant requirements of the Eritrean Constitution. That version was adopted.

But the problem was not yet solved. Matienzo's proposal that, 'on the basis of reciprocity, federal nationals be accorded the same rights as Eritrean citizens in Eritrea', seemed a fair proposal to a good deal of the members. It was well known that many Eritreans, some of them in high ministerial and administrative positions, had served in the Ethiopian Government. They naturally saw the proposal as a good thing and even as a window of opportunity for Eritreans seeking employment in Ethiopia. Ibrahim Sultan delivered a famous warning:

> We are forgetting our internal affairs by giving too much attention to Federal matters ... The Federal Act has differentiated between Federal nationality and Eritrean citizenship. If we mix up the two, what will the meaning of our internal autonomy be? What we closed in the previous article, we are now reopening here. If that is the case, we will not be able to challenge the aggression and powerful authority that can push towards us. Do you think that there are free elections and rational appointments across the border? Will Eritreans be able to do in Ethiopia what Ethiopians are being proposed to do here as if there is any freedom there? Rights that Eritreans cannot access in Ethiopia should not be made available to Ethiopians in Eritrea. Let Eritreans protect their homes first, then that of their brothers and neighbours.[20]

Ibrahim's speech aroused deep and conflicting emotions that flared into a heated debate. An irritated Matienzo pointed out that the reciprocity clause was standard practice in federal states. Besides, he had consulted with the Ethiopian authorities, who had assured him that Eritreans would be guaranteed the same rights as Ethiopians in Ethiopia. Mohammed Said Hassano, EDF-Barka, summed up the fears of the majority: 'We are worried because the draft extends political rights to federal nationals. Our wish is that, as regards political rights, there should be a distinction between Eritrea and Ethiopia. Let them have all the other rights on the basis of reciprocity, except political rights. Political rights should be regulated by

Eritrean laws.'[21] He proceeded to amend the draft provision, which the Assembly then adopted. The relevant articles on Eritrean citizenship finally included in the Constitution read as follows:

> *Article 8 Eritrean citizenship*
> Persons who have acquired Federal nationality in Eritrea under the Federal Act ... and have been granted Eritrean citizenship in accordance with the laws of Eritrea shall be citizens of Eritrea.
>
> *Article 9 Rights of federal nationals who are not Eritrean citizens*
> 1. On the basis of reciprocity, Federal nationals who are not Eritrean citizens shall enjoy rights as Eritreans.
> 2. Federal nationals shall enjoy political rights in accordance with the Eritrean Constitution and laws on the basis of reciprocity.

The psychological impact of the enshrinement of Eritrean citizenship in the Eritrean Constitution should not be underestimated. Regardless of the junior position that Eritrea held within the federal set-up, Eritrean identity had made the transition from an old colonial identity to a juridical status. In a unique bipartisan effort, unionists and nationalists had joined hands in shielding it from being thwarted within a 'federal–Ethiopian' identity. Throughout the federal period, school registration documents, job applications, identity cards, licences and marriage certificates for Eritreans had 'Eritrean' tagged to the citizenship boxes. Eritreans, especially the generation that grew up in the 1950s and went on to launch the war of independence, knew no other identity. Subsequent generations emulated their lead. The Eritrean struggle for independence was, in the final analysis, a struggle for national identity. It is in that light that the significance of the Assembly debates should be understood.

The Language Debate

Matienzo's draft on the use and status of languages, which he presented on 8 June, was vague and generalised. It merely stated that all the languages spoken in the country would be used in dealings with public authorities, as well as for religious or educational purposes and all forms of public expression.[22] No provision was made for one or more official languages.

The debate started with amendments proposing that Tigrinya and Arabic be recognised as the official languages of Eritrea. However, any Eritrean citizen would have the right to use any of the other languages for educational, religious or other purposes. The level of non-partisanship manifested with the citizenship issue would not hold this time. After three days of postponement, Weldeyohannes Gebrezghi, UP-Seraye, suggested that the majority of the nations of the world 'had one language, one flag and one crown. There is no one who does not understand Tigrinya in Eritrea; let Tigrinya be the official language. Since Arabic is a religious language, it should be considered alien. It should not be allowed in official functions.'

The reaction was swift and emotional. Controversy threatened to split the chamber along religious lines. Many, like Nasser Abubeker Pasha of the Assaorta, would not accept the idea of Arabic as a mere religious language. 'It is Tigrinya that is confined only to the *kebessa* area; but let us accept it as a compromise.' Some UP members were even more provocative. Hadgembes Kiflom from Akeleguzai suggested that Tigrinya and Amharic be accepted as official: 'Tigrinya for internal affairs and Amharic for federal,' he said. 'We may use Arabic for a limited period, until our brothers here learn Tigrinya.'

Muslim advocates of Arabic took immediate offence. To calm tempers down, the chairman, Tedla Bairu, warned the representatives that hostility within the Assembly would have serious consequences outside. Eventually, with forceful arguments from such prominent members as Mohammed Omer Akito of Denkalia, *Qadi* Ali of the Assaorta and Embaye Habte, UP-Keren, the balance appeared to tilt towards acceptance of Tigrinya and Arabic as official languages.

Noting this, Matienzo announced his willingness to accept the amendment as a compromise solution.[23] Everything seemed set for a positive vote the next morning when *Blata* Demsas Weldemikael (UP-Aba Shawl, Asmera) turned the debate back to where it had started by declaring Arabic out of contention. At that moment, the senior EDF leader and brother of *Ras* Tessema, *Dejazmatch* Berhe Asberom, requested a recess and withdrew from the session with other members, including Demsas. On their return, Demsas declared that he was speaking on behalf of a large number of representatives and that, in the interests of harmony and understanding, he supported Matienzo's new amendment. It was adopted as article 38 of the Constitution by a majority of votes, making Tigrinya and Arabic the official languages.[24]

Apparently, Berhe Asberom, Demsas and their group had withdrawn from the session to strike a deal. Otherwise, an issue which threatened to disrupt the proceedings could not have been resolved with such apparent ease. What exactly happened outside the Assembly?

Issues of the Flag and the Emperor's Representative

The issue of the Emperor's representative in Eritrea was, as we saw, divisive and sensitive nationwide. The Federal Act had not provided for such an appointment and Matienzo had only accepted it under pressure from Ethiopian officials. Consequently, the Assembly debate became highly antagonistic. On 21 May, the Assembly decided to avoid tumult by appointing a committee of twelve members to study the matter and come up with draft proposals for inclusion in the Constitution. It was chaired by *Qadi* Musa Umron, EDF-Keren, and *Melake Selam* Dimetros Gebremariam, UP-Seraye. The discussions within the committee were stormy.[25] According to the Ethiopian author Zewde Retta, UP representatives led by the 'austere' Dimetros Gebremariam went so far as to walk out of the Assembly and threaten to disrupt all proceedings unless the proposal was adopted. The controversy, Zewde said, also spilled over to Asmera itself, where an atmosphere of high tension developed. Only on the intervention of the Emperor himself through his liaison officer and that of Asfaha Weldemikael was the faction led by Dimetros prevailed upon to return to the chamber.[26]

None of the members of the Representative Assembly interviewed for this book would corroborate Zewde's claim. Weldeyohannes Gebrezghi, who was a member of the committee dealing with the matter, was particularly dismissive of Zewde's story:

> We never walked out of the Assembly. And how could Amdemikael [the liaison officer] or Asfaha come to address us in the Assembly? That was absolutely impossible. Neither would we even think of walking out of the Assembly for any reason. We did not do that. I do remember the issues of the flag and the Emperor's representative pulling us apart. There was also a lot of discussion and argument outside the sessions, individual consultations. But nothing like what is being alleged.[27]

Apparently, the only time that a group of representatives left the session was when Berhe Asberom formally asked for a recess during the language discussions. Mohammed Omer Akito was involved in that process. He recollected:

> We insisted that unless the other party accepted Arabic as an official language, we would walk out and throw everything in confusion. We had also made clear that we would not agree to an Emperor's representative. Gradually, the two issues, the language and the representative, became interchangeable. They started to say to us, 'Accept the representative and we will adopt Arabic.' We pained over this. At last, we said, 'If that is our fate, let us, for the sake of the people and their unity, agree to having the representative.' They adopted Arabic. What Berhe and Demsas presented after the recess was what we had agreed on previously.[28]

The agreement was not as automatic as it appears to have been at the beginning. For although the Assembly adopted Arabic on 16 June, debate over the provisions dealing with the Emperor's representative continued until the very end of the month, when the committee examining the issues of the flag and the representative presented its findings to the Assembly. Two problems arose on the scope of the powers and functions attached to the envoy. First was the committee's suggestion that every proposal emanating from the Assembly be presented to the representative for him to determine its compatibility with federal laws and interests. EDF members rejected the proposition as it would give the representative immense powers over the Assembly. The second point was also objectionable to many members as it proposed to allow the representative to make regular contact with the Eritrean executive in order to regulate matters of common federal interest. This too was seen as an opening for Ethiopian interference in internal Eritrean matters. The proceedings reached a deadlock.

In a rare reaction, Matienzo lost his temper. After praising members for dealing with complex issues of democracy, he blamed them for their pettiness on the issue at hand. Did they not realise, he asked, that the Federation was being established under the Ethiopian Crown? Were they doubting the trust that the United Nations had placed in the Emperor, or whether the Emperor would respect the Federal Act?

> You are starting a new life. Do not create problems. Do not belittle the gift granted to you by the United Nations. Come to an agreement with confidence from the heart, not just on paper. The future strength of your people should not be based on negative feelings and the negative handling of problems. It should be based on trust, optimism and a positive attitude.[29]

What Matienzo could not see was that, for both parties, the issues involved were far from petty. They were fundamental to the attainment of their respective visions of Eritrea under the federal set-up. Many of the UP members, though not all of them, did not want to see an Eritrean flag flying alongside the Ethiopian flag for which they had fought for years. For the EDF, a flag would be a symbol of the citizenship and identity they had already secured through hard bargaining. It was the same thing with the Emperor's representative, which the EDF saw as nothing but the undoing of Eritrea's autonomy even before it could be attained.

Here again, a split occurred within the ranks of the UP. Mesfin Gebrehiwet explained why he and fellow UP members like *Abba* Habtemariam stood against an Emperor's representative:

> When we accepted the Federation and swore to upkeep its principles, we wholeheartedly focused on implementing its contents. We started to oppose moves that would weaken the federal format or that would compromise it in any way. Since we saw the presence of an Emperor's representative as a means of weakening the Federation, a few of us came to oppose the proposal.[30]

The other side had equally strong leaders in the persons of Dimetros, Tesfamikael Werke and Weldeyohannes, all from Seraye, and a deadlock ensued. It took days of intense bargaining and arm twisting to break the impasse. There was, moreover, another channel through which the proposal was being promoted. The American consul Mulcahy was of the opinion that ML-WP representatives were, at the time of the debates, in constant contact with their mentor and founder, Frank Stafford. He suspected that they were receiving directions from the British official on every issue, including the question of the Emperor's representation.[31]

The Assembly debates were carried in all the major newspapers. A few days before the final vote on the flag and representation questions, Ahmed Hussein Hayoti, an EDF Assembly member, wrote in both *Saut al Rabita* and *Hanti Ertra*:

> The UN Resolution does not mention an Emperor's representative and, therefore, we cannot accept one. True, his role may be ceremonial, but since his very presence is

> tantamount to interference in Eritrea's internal affairs, we cannot abide by it. As for the matter of the Eritrean flag, already taken care of by Commissioner Matienzo, the role of the Assembly is to merely choose the colour and symbols accompanying it. We hope that they will approve it without any excuses.[32]

On the day of Matienzo's angry intervention, the UP too published its final appeal: 'Let every member of the Assembly clearly understand that the people of Eritrea will neither bargain nor even make the slightest concessions against their Emperor, his Representative or his ancient flag. Yes, nothing, but nothing regarding the Emperor's representative and the flag can ever pass or be sidelined through murky dealings.'[33]

After days of wrangling and rancour, the committee delivered its amendments on 2 July 1952. Four proposals were adopted as a package. The Emperor's representative was to invest the Chief Executive in office in the name of the Emperor, inside the Eritrean Assembly (articles 12 and 2 of the Constitution). The representative was to receive legislation ratified by the Assembly immediately and to consider if it encroached upon federal legislation or involved the international responsibility of the Federation. In that event, he would transmit a request to the Chief Executive within twenty days after the vote of the Assembly for reconsideration (article 14). The representative would promulgate laws approved by the Assembly and transmitted to him by the Chief Executive. The federal flag was to be respected in Eritrea and the flag, seal and arms of Eritrea would be decided upon by law (article 21).

Once these stumbling blocks were removed, the Assembly took little time in disposing of the remaining provisions of the draft. On 10 July, the Eritrean Constitution was approved by the Assembly.

12

THE FEDERATION INAUGURATED

Formation of the Eritrean Government

The British Administration's postponement of the induction of Eritreans into its administration continued to be an issue of bitter popular complaint and resentment. Neither the Federal Act's specific charge nor UN Commissioner Matienzo's continuous reminders would move it towards the installation of a transitional body. The excuse given this time was that the Federal Act did not specify how the Administration was to organise the transition.

On 18 March 1952, Matienzo and his legal advisors met British authorities in London and suggested that an executive committee be appointed by the Eritrean Assembly from within its membership to tackle the problem.[1] It was only after Matienzo's intervention that the Administration decided to act on the matter on 1 April 1952, eleven years to the day after its occupation of Eritrea, and fourteen months after Matienzo's assumption of his duties. The Federation was to come into effect within five months. Since the committee had not been envisaged by the Federal Act, it was not designed to be a formally installed transitional administration. It came, rather, as an afterthought, and Cumming devised it in such a way that it would be answerable to his office, thus denying the Assembly any control over its dealings. It would be there, as it turned out, to fulfil Cumming's bidding. A new article was added to the Constitution (article 97), also as an afterthought, that the decisions of the committee were to remain valid for the future Eritrean Government.

The Eritrean Democratic Front (EDF) objected to this in the strongest of terms. In an article entitled '*Cambiale in bianco*' (Blank Cheques), it condemned the whole exercise as a means for the Administration to do as it saw fit in the final transfer of its powers. It regarded the committee as a mere tool, a messenger with no means of protecting the government on whose behalf it was to enter into binding obligations.[2]

On 8 July, Cumming appeared before the Assembly to declare that administrative responsibility in Eritrea remained with his administration until the Constitution came into effect. Since he could not divest himself of ultimate responsibility, he implied, he could only delegate powers to the committee. More specifically, he proposed to give to the committee the power to enter into contracts and to approve legislation, which would have validity after 15 September. As for the suggestion that article 98 was 'a blank cheque to a body appointed by me', he concluded, 'I trust what I have just said will remove any doubts in your mind.'[3]

On 11 July, Cumming issued the Executive Committee Proclamation of 1952, whose article 4(1) stated that the chairman of the committee would, on behalf of the committee, 'exercise such powers and carry out such of the duties as are now vested in the Chief Administrator, as the Chief Administrator may from time to time direct'. Sub-article 2 read, 'The Chief Administrator may from time to time revoke or modify any direction given under the preceding sub-Article.'[4] On 16 July, the Assembly chose ten of its members to form the Executive Committee under the chairmanship of Ali Rad'ai. Mesfin Gebrehiwet and Weldeyohannes Gebrezghi were among the members chosen.[5]

It was only after the lapse of some time spent in preparation, which meant it had a little over one month until 15 September, that the committee was able to sit for serious work. Both Weldeyohannes and Mesfin confirmed that the sheer volume of the tasks before it and its restricted powers limited its effectiveness. Mesfin expressed himself more clearly:

> I don't remember us rejecting anything. We were not the only committee, by the way. An Ethiopian Committee led by Kifle Ergetu was also in Asmera working separately with the English. They were receiving what powers and property were transferred to them, we were doing the same on the other side. The two committees never met to coordinate our respective tasks ... it was all done by administrative decision and we were not in a position to complain about the allocation of powers or resources.
>
> For example, Eritrean road transport was given to Ethiopia as part of interstate communication. Although all roads were within Eritrea, they were deemed federal because they ultimately reach Ethiopia or Sudan. The same with the railway, which does not touch on Ethiopia, but starts at the port, and ports were federal responsibility. Of course, we asked questions, clarifications, and we argued. But then we also thought that it would be better to accept decisions for the time being and then go for modifications after the formation of the Federation. And, frankly, we were never forceful in our confrontations, no acrimony of any sort. And Cumming always stressed that the Federal Council would correct discrepancies once it was formed after the Federation and we put our trust in the Federal Council. We even thought it would double Eritrean claims.[6]

Brigadier Cumming, aided by Frank Stafford, had his way. By declaring that the transfer of property denoted transfer of possession and not ownership, he assured the committee and the Assembly that the allocations being made would be subject to review and readjustment agreed upon by the Eritrean and Federal governments. No binding means or process was laid down to guarantee that possibility. Thus, roads, railways, ports and airports, local and international, with all the movable and immovable buildings, facilities, assets and land attached to them, went to the Ethiopians. Customs administration, including the part that would deal with the Eritrean share of the duties and revenues, was assigned to the Ethiopians.

As public complaints arose about the high-handed manner in which Eritrean property was freely given without the express consent of the Assembly, Cumming visited that body on 4 September. Not only did he defend his decisions on the railroad, airport, naval base and other issues, but he further told them that he was transferring possession of the choicest Italian villas in Asmera as residences for the incoming federal officials. Thirty more such houses were to accommodate higher officials of the Ethiopian army, whose troops were to be garrisoned in the old Italian camps and barracks at the airport, at Gejeret and Villaggio Genio in Asmera, and in other places throughout the country. Cumming had more to say:

> Clearly, the Representative of the Sovereign of the Federation must have suitable accommodation and it was natural that he should be allotted the former Italian Governor's Palace ... The offices in the immediate vicinity of the Palace have also been allocated to them [federal officials]. I was unable to meet the full requests of the federal authorities either for offices or for houses because I did not wish to reduce unreasonably the number of houses or offices available for the Eritrean Government.

He further insisted that the allocations had been fair and reasonable and rejected accusations that the best houses had been allotted to federal authorities. Since responsibility for the allocation had been placed directly under him without provision for consultation or approval by any other party, he concluded, 'I accept full responsibility for the allocation that has been made.'[7]

The list of allocations that Cumming sent to the Assembly showed the staggering number of buildings and facilities handed over to the Ethiopians. They took over every railway station, every road checkpoint, and every customs office in the country. All post and telecommunications offices and even bungalows on Massawa beach went to them.[8] In short, because of these uncontested allocations, the Ethiopians were given access to even the remotest areas of Eritrea in a manner that could not have been anticipated by the Federal Act. It was a development that would infringe upon Eritrea's enjoyment of its autonomous status and the exercise of control over its internal jurisdiction.

But the blame for this obvious mishandling of the future of a nation and people cannot be placed solely on the British Administration and its uncompromising Chief Administrator. One must wonder why the Assembly as a whole did not object to what many of its members saw as an abuse of power by Cumming and a miscarriage of justice by a departing administration. It was a transition period; the Ethiopian army had not arrived yet, and rural and urban terrorism was still at its lowest levels. Members of the Assembly had the chance to stand their ground and show some mettle. Their objections would certainly have provoked a public outcry and caused the British and the Ethiopians to think twice. It could be that, as Mesfin explained, they were banking on future renegotiations with Ethiopian authorities, which assumed their good faith. Very few realised how naive that line of thinking would turn out to be. Among those who did were Ibrahim Sultan, *Qadi* Musa Umron, Mohammed Omer Akito and six other colleagues who registered their opposition to the British Government and the Executive Committee. Their long list of protests may be summarised as follows:

- We oppose the handing over of the Asmera Palace to non-Eritreans.
- Why are all the best houses being allocated to Ethiopians? They should be given to Eritreans.
- A large number of Ethiopians are arriving in Eritrea to provide federal services; these services are not reserved for them only; Eritreans should also be allotted their fair share.
- Laws that are being promulgated by the King [*sic*] in the name of the Federation should first be seen and approved by the Eritrean Government. We oppose Ethiopian interference in Eritrea's internal affairs.
- Any law that is imposed on a population without its consent can only be dictatorial. We are a democratic country. The Federal Constitution [Ethiopia's 1931 Constitution] should be presented to our Assembly for ratification.
- Ethiopia has assumed full authority over the railway, telegraph and postal administration. This has been done in contravention of the UN Resolution. Therefore, we are set to inform our people that there is no federation and that they can go as they choose. The federation is there in name only.[9]

Like all previous protests, this complaint was shelved. Its significance for the future relationship between Eritreans and the arriving Ethiopian officials should be noted. What Eritreans saw were people from across the border come to replace their old masters, who looked like them in every way except for the colour of their skin. Even the unionists, who had thought they would take over not only federal functions in Eritrea but also higher-level positions in Ethiopia itself, were told that they would be confined to Eritrean affairs in second-rate homes. That was not the deal they had bargained for. According to the US consul Edward Mulcahy, unionist dissatisfaction was becoming visible even among unionist representatives inside the Assembly.[10]

As for the Executive Committee, the most memorable thing that it accomplished was the formulation and ratification of the Organic Laws on whose basis the Eritrean Government was to function. These were the Functions of Government Act, the Administration of Justice Act, the Civil Service Act, the Audit Act, the Advisory Council Act and the Electoral Act. Apart from this, the committee also drafted legislation dealing with provincial administration, employment and appointment processes, police and prisons administration, regulation of the press and the media, collection of taxes, and the administration of justice.

Ratification of the Eritrean Constitution and the Federal Act

The Representative Assembly Turns Legislative

In his draft proposals, Matienzo had determined that, upon adoption of the Eritrean Constitution, the Representative Assembly would act as a legislative body for one or two more years at the most. This was meant to help the country acclimatise itself to its new status and to avoid a potentially contentious election so soon after acquiring its autonomous status. However, to ensure administrative stability and continuity, the term of the Chief Executive would run to four years.

EDF members Bezabih Tesfabruk of the Adi Quala area in Seraye and Ibrahim Sultan proposed that, in order to even out the terms of office of the Assembly and the Chief Executive, the Assembly should continue as the legislature for four more years. This aroused controversy. Unionist Party members wanted new elections as soon as possible, whereas the EDF and its affiliates went along with the Bezabih–Ibrahim proposal. Matienzo tried to explain that the terms of office of the Assembly and the Chief Executive did not necessarily have to coincide. Nevertheless, he would be amenable to any decision of the Assembly, provided that it was not motivated by members' personal considerations.[11] Mohammed Omer Akito, who was at the forefront of the debate for extension, presented a forceful argument that won general support. The amendment was adopted and the Representative Assembly promoted itself to the status of Legislative Assembly. In an interview, Akito explained why he and his colleagues chose that unpopular option:

> We [EDF members] were aware of what was going on. To many of the members, sitting in the Assembly was not representing the people. They took it as personal promotion or tribute, as some kind of access to lordship. If new elections had been held, Ethiopia would have bought many willing sycophants. So many people were after money and rank. And the English encouraged that. We chose the lesser of the two evils. If elections had been held, most of the EDF members would have been removed and whatever little hope there was for Eritrean autonomy would have ended.[12]

The Assembly's decision was criticised by the likes of Omer Qadi, who argued that the Representative Assembly's approval of a constitution drafted by highly qualified legal minds did not give it the kind of experience or legal know-how that a legislature would demand. Initiating and drafting new legislation required legal training, which most of the traditional chiefs occupying Assembly seats simply lacked.[13] Such objections were sidelined and the Constitution was adopted by a unanimous vote.

The Assembly's decision, whatever the real motivation behind it, was to have far-reaching consequences. Proclamation 121 of 1952, the law which provided the basis for the mainly ethnic and religious representation in the Assembly, was now also the basis for the transformed Legislative Assembly—a legal status it was not entitled to hold. The constitutional problem inherent in the decision would manifest itself during preparations for the second parliamentary elections four years later.

The Constitution Ratified

On 11 August, Tedla, Ali Rad'ai, Cumming and Matienzo travelled to Addis Ababa for the ratification of the Eritrean Constitution by the Emperor. In a small ceremony, he signed it into law as he declared, 'We accept, ratify and bless this Constitution and we order our loyal citizens in Eritrea to obey it.'[14] How Ethiopians would regard it was not clear from his brief comment; but he seemed to imply that the federation was an Eritrean affair.

Matienzo expressed his hope that the federal union would progress peacefully and that the Emperor's Government would respect Eritrean internal autonomy and lay the foundations of a federal system. Haile Selassie was vague in his response. He pointed out that the Constitution's adoption and ratification by him and the Eritrean Assembly was by the mutual will of the two parties, not an order or imposition. The people most concerned had accepted the Federation, he added.[15] What exactly he meant here was not clear. Were the people most concerned Eritreans? Haile Selassie did not clarify that either.

Back in Asmera, the Assembly was getting ready to elect the Chief Executive. Because of the alliance between the UP and the Muslim League–Western Province (ML-WP), which, according to American consul Mulcahy, was being forged and actively supported by Brigadier Frank Stafford, the EDF was already out of contention. *Ras* Tessema, the octogenarian leader, had even resigned his Assembly seat. Weldeab, the teacher, journalist and polemicist, could not stand a chance, especially in view of his poor showing in the March elections. That left Ibrahim Sultan. But he too was beset by the problem of internal ML divisions and UP accusations that he was in the pay of the Italians.

Mulcahy, who was in constant contact with Ibrahim, wrote highly sympathetic reports on the man whom he likened to the American fathers of independence and democracy, Samuel Adams and Thomas Paine. Still hopeful of rekindling UN interest in Eritrea's fate, Ibrahim was waging a lone battle for independence. Mulcahy, who also regarded him as incomparable and irreplaceable, expressed his sadness at seeing him reduced to writing desperate articles against a tide that he could not stop.[16] Ibrahim too was thus out of contention.

On 28 August, Assembly members nominated three candidates, Tedla Bairu of UP, Abraha Tessema of the Liberal Unionist Party, and Saleh Hinit, a British Administration functionary. Hinit's name was soon withdrawn as he had not attained the required minimum age of 35 years, Tedla Bairu finally won and became Eritrea's first Chief Executive.[17] Over the following few days, the members elected Ali Rad'ai (ML-WP) chairman and Demsas Weldemikael (UP) vice chairman of the Assembly. The UP–ML-WP alliance had worked effectively.

Ratification of the Federal Act

After appointing four secretaries to his four-seat cabinet, later increased to six seats,[18] Tedla and Ali Rad'ai travelled to Addis Ababa once again for the formal ratification of the Federal Act and the launching of the Federation by the Emperor. On 11 September, they were presented to him. According to Zewde Retta, Ethiopian officials, including the usually moderate Aklilu Habtewold, advised the Emperor to refrain from giving Tedla any special treatment. But, as the amused officials watched from the sides, Haile Selassie went ahead and indulged the Eritreans with a reception worthy of a head of state. At the ceremony, Zewde wrote, one official approached *Tsehafe Te'ezaz* Weldegiorgis and whispered to him, 'It has been said that "If you indulge a Tigrayan excessively, he becomes fastidious and arrogant". Isn't this pomp and fanfare a bit too much for a Hamasien? Can we sustain it?'[19] Weldegiorgis, widely known as Tedla's mentor, replied, 'But then, since we know how to carry a load when we choose and cast it off when we don't, neither today's burden nor tomorrow's consequences bother us much.'[20]

Unaware of the sarcasm even from his mentor, Tedla had his moment with the Emperor. Haile Selassie spoke first: 'When we defended the rights of Eritrea and Ethiopia at the United Nations, we were aware of the high stakes that Eritrea's return would bear upon our Ethiopian citizens. We also understood that, for Eritrea to manage the internal autonomy granted to it, it will need large amounts of money in aid.' Haile Selassie fell short of saying that he was taking over a liability. But shifting his focus to Ethiopia's acquisition of a Red Sea outlet, he promised to support the UN decision and work for the principles of peace and collective security.[21]

After condemning those who sought to give Eritrea a different identity because of its forced colonial separation from Ethiopia, Tedla said in reply, 'The people of Eritrea have now rejected the old politics that used to divide them. They have instead adopted with full volition the Federation resolved by the United Nations and ratified today by Your Majesty. It is my singular duty to express to Your Majesty the Eritrean people's resolve to implement the Federation in word and spirit.'

Haile Selassie was gracious in his lavish praise of Tedla and Ali Rad'ai. He called them 'the first among our new citizens to receive federal citizenship and the first to declare their loyalty to us and our crown', and continued: 'We have noted that when the Chief Executive was chairman of the Assembly, he carried out his duties with efficiency and impartiality. We believe that the chairman of the Assembly will follow the example of his predecessor and run the tasks of the Assembly with due formality and impartiality.'[22]

Tedla and Ali Rad'ai went back to Asmera in the highest of spirits. Considering the woes of office and turn of events that were soon to follow, Tedla's fleeting minutes with the Emperor at the Palace may have been the peak of his achievement.

The Emperor's Representative in Eritrea

Haile Selassie chose as his representative his own son-in-law *Bitweded* (literally, Beloved) Andargatchew Mesai, the husband of his eldest daughter, Tenagne Work. He had previously served as the governor general of the Gondar region in Ethiopia. Whether by coincidence or design, his very first name, which means 'Make them one or merge them', seemed to send a foreboding message of Ethiopia's intentions. Andargatchew was not a stranger to many Eritreans. In 1950–1, he had been involved in a potash extraction contract with the Tigrayan entrepreneur and exile *Blata* Kidanemariam Aberra, who had been working on the potash mines in Denkalia but sought to extend operations into the adjacent Ethiopian reserves. Regarded as a dissident by the Ethiopian Government, Kidanemariam was forced by the Emperor to sign a lopsided contract that would allot 70% of the shares to Andargatchew. A dispute arose when Andargatchew attempted to expropriate Kidanemariam's profits without paying a cent of the value of his own shares. In addition, using Ethiopian influence with the British, he had Kidanemariam arrested on made-up charges.

In a hearing chaired by the Chief Administrator himself, Andargatchew, who was summoned to Asmera to testify, lost the case because of his non-payment of his share of the contract. When deciding in favour of Kidanemariam, Cumming said to Andargatchew, 'How can you claim 70% profit from land you have not even touched? Do you reap crops without sowing in your country? You need to sow seeds first. Case dismissed!'[23] This story made the rounds in Asmera long before Andargatchew's appointment as the Emperor's representative. As we shall see, his reputation for corruption and graft, whether actual or imagined, was to follow him even within his own federal offices.

On 13 September, two days after Tedla's triumphant audience with Haile Selassie, Andargatchew and his princess entered Asmera. Only Andinet youths and schoolchildren accompanied by their teachers were on the streets to welcome him. Asmera residents, especially Muslims, stayed away.[24] In the afternoon of the same day, Andargatchew entered the Eritrean Assembly to administer Tedla's oath of office. With his hand on the Bible, Tedla swore to 'respect the Federation under the sovereignty of the Imperial Crown, loyally to serve Eritrea, to defend its Constitution and its laws, to seek the welfare of the Eritrean people in the unity of its inhabitants bound together by the ties of brotherhood, whatever their race, religion or language, and to seek no personal advantage from office'. After the swearing-in of his four secretaries, what came to be known as Tedla's Government was all set to operate.

Departure of the British and the UN

Goodbye, Britannia

Britain and its representative administrations never accepted Eritrea as a viable nation or the Eritreans as one people. For them, it remained an artificial Italian creation that could be dismantled easily and serve as a trump card in their broader East African and Middle Eastern strategic interests. Their position as caretakers on behalf of the Four Great Powers also gave them the excuse to keep the territory going with the minimum of effort or expense, pending its final fate at the international level. On the other hand, as victors over the Italian colonisers, they felt justified in treating Eritrea as occupied enemy territory and helping themselves to the loot that the Italians had left behind.

If, on the eve of their departure, the British had played a more positive role in charting a course towards a viable federal union with Ethiopia, some of their failings might have been forgotten. As it was, their tardiness in putting the foundations of the Eritrean Government in place and training Eritreans for positions of responsibility; the regressive law that they imposed on the parliamentary elections; the high-handed manner in which they gave away power and property to Ethiopian officials without the consent of Eritreans and beyond the stipulation of the Federal Act; their unilateral decision to invite a fully equipped Ethiopian brigade to replace the departing British battalion: all these could only increase Eritrean resentment. This was especially so as each of these acts of commission or omission was to have dire consequences for Eritreans in the years to come.

In many other ways, however, the British fascinated Eritreans. Their administrative efficiency, their punctual and economical use of time, their decision-making processes, their discipline and respect for hierarchy, even their manner of speech and dress, became things to be emulated by the younger, rising Eritrean intelligentsia. The benefits of democratic government, equality before the law, a free press and freedom of expression, and mutual tolerance in public dialogue were to become rallying points in the forthcoming struggle for independence. Every surviving Eritrean official interviewed for this book—police officer, judge or administrator—claimed to be a product of the British legacy, which had added more finesse to the Italian system, even at the lower levels they occupied of the bureaucratic ladder.

Kegnazmatch Gebremedhin Tessema, later Auditor General of Eritrea, described the foolproof system that Eritrean officials inherited from the British. Everything from the appointment of judges to the filing system followed clearly demarcated procedures. There was no way one could miss a step without incurring responsibility. 'I remember an audit assignment that would only take a week in Asmera, dragging us through six months of drudgery in one Ethiopian province. Even the Italians could not compare with the British in this regard.'[25]

The British are best remembered for their contribution in the field of education, as we have seen. The marked increase in the number of schools and pupils at the elementary, middle and high school levels was remarkable for the time. In his final report, Cumming pointed out that the Eritrean Government was taking over a system of education that had gained broad public support and would grow with its financial capabilities.[26] Health facilities also improved under British rule, with new hospitals and clinics opened in many parts of the country. An Italian medical school produced Italian medical students, most of whom served in Eritrea after returning from further studies in Italy. Qualified Eritrean doctors would not appear until the second half of the federal period.[27] The same positive benefit also applied to the introduction by the British of modern agricultural techniques and general improvements in animal breeding and welfare.

Likewise the promotion of regulated labour relations and the formation of a labour organisation can be credited to the British. By 1952, Eritrean workers had clear ideas about their employment rights and how to negotiate on wages, working conditions, health insurance and other related labour issues. By signing a labour proclamation into law, the British left the working class of Eritrea with the means to fight for its rights. Unemployment in the country was still at high levels, of 30%.[28] Landlessness, caused by the British displacement of Eritrean farmers for the creation of concession farms, was another problem the Eritrean Government would inherit. But from the point of view of social awareness and the crucial role that the labour movement was to play in shaping Eritrea's future, the British labour policy had a positive impact.

Of most immediate concern to the incoming Eritrean Government was the state of the economy and finance. In his last report, Cumming said that Eritrea had racked up a yearly average of £200,000 in debts caused by the high salaries of his British and Italian staff and the high cost of maintaining security in the country. But, although with the departure of the British and the decrease in terrorist activities he expected those problems to improve, he admitted that the Eritrean Government would inherit a £376,000 deficit from the 1950/1 budget year alone.[29] Cumming expected that the problem would be finally resolved once Eritrea started to receive its fair share of the customs revenues yet to be negotiated with Ethiopia. He even predicted that, with the implementation of a more efficient system of tax collection, the Eritrean Government could secure an annual surplus of £60,000.[30]

Cumming ended his comments by lauding Britain's role in bridging the 'racial and religious chasms' in Eritrea. He expected Eritrea to remain 'economically and financially weak [with] little prospect of becoming a viable State ... but her integration with the Ethiopian Empire and the promise of financial assistance from that source should enable her eventually to improve her position'. He called on Ethiopia to be sympathetic and understanding of Eritrea's economic and political weaknesses and to provide wise guidance and material assistance as the 'more happily endowed partner in the federation'.[31]

Cumming's self-congratulatory remarks on Britain's role in bridging the 'racial and religious chasms' in the country could not be backed by evidence. Nor would Eritreans, who till today accuse Britain of having been the main agent of division and economic destruction in their country, accept his claims in good faith. In his poem on the ways of the English, Weldeab may have summarised popular opinion in the following stanza:

> Yes, who can stand up to the Englishman?
> Wives held up in public meetings, can't harvest the crops
> Farmers can't till, merchants can't trade
> Our factories are idle.
> Some want freedom, others Teferi [Haile Selassie]
> Some are laughing, others angry
> Love is in short supply.
> Let us unite in prayers to the Lord
> For His gracious mercy
> So we may own a country.[32]

***

At the stroke of midnight on 15 September 1952, the Union Jack was lowered and replaced by the Ethiopian flag. Beside it was the newly designed blue cloth adorned with green olive branches in the middle, a version of the UN flag, which the Eritrean Assembly had ratified as the country's insignia. Two days later, the British departed from Eritrea after having administered it for eleven and a half years.

Except for the few advisors left behind to assist the Eritrean Government, the British left virtually no trace behind them. No money was left in the government coffers. No building, structure or installation stood to remind people that once they had run the country. No social, political or military link was created to maintain some kind of continuity. No legal avenue was left open for Eritrea to assert its rights under the Federal Act. The British left Asmera as they had come, stealthily. It was as if they wished to erase Eritrea from their collective memory.

Matienzo's Farewell

Anze Matienzo, who was aware of Eritrean concerns over British conduct in the transfer of powers, addressed the issue on 27 August. There had been a public outcry that the UN Commission was standing by as an observer while the British Administration exceeded its powers and responsibility under the Federal Act. Matienzo explained that the Federal Act gave him no specific authority to intervene in the task of the transfer of powers; it was a British assignment. But he had the duty to report the matter to the UN. Ultimately, he said, maintaining the balance between the Federal Government and autonomous Eritrea would depend on a spirit of mutual understanding between the parties. Eritrean participation in the Federal Council and the Federal Government would ensure the maintenance of that balance. He was encouraged by Ethiopia's assurances on the matter.

Referring to the allocation of property to Ethiopia, Matienzo repeated the British claim that it was a temporary transfer of possession as opposed to ownership. It would be open to negotiations between the two governments once the Federation was in place. But, he added, Eritrea's advantages in being linked to an independent state and member of the UN warranted Ethiopia's access to property in Eritrea.[33]

Although Matienzo believed that his message had eased the prevailing tensions, he still expressed his worries over the absence of any guarantees of Eritrean autonomy. The Eritrean Constitution, he wrote, was an adequate document that would enable Eritrea to govern itself as an autonomous state. But to maintain its status required more than a mere document. Both parties had to learn to coexist by respecting each other's areas of authority and responsibility. He repeated his legal consultant's reminder that, if the UN resolution was to be implemented as intended, Ethiopia had to accept and enforce it without reservations. He was encouraged, on the other hand, by the goodwill he had been assured of by the Emperor himself.

Finally, Matienzo urged the UN to appoint a tribunal in Eritrea that would mediate contentious issues that might arise in setting up the Federation. And with that request, he too left Eritrea. Except for the installation of a UN tribunal, whose functions and fate we will deal with later, the UN's exit was no different from that of Britain. With its foreign affairs securely controlled by Ethiopia, Eritrea could only access the world body that had decided its future through the permission of its dominant, senior partner in the Federation. It would take forty years for the UN to revisit the nation that it had abandoned in September 1952.

The Emperor in Eritrea

Emperor Haile Selassie's entry into Eritrea in early October 1952 and his departure in the middle of the month was of such significance that it fully occupied the newly installed Eritrean Government for over six weeks. 'If the British advisors had not helped us,' remembered Mesfin Gebrehiwet, who chaired the reception committee, 'we would certainly not have known how to handle the protocol and ceremony involved.'

Haile Selassie, who chose to come by road, crossed Tigray, prayed at the Church of Mariam Tsion in Axum, and cut the federal ribbon at the symbolic line separating Eritrea and Ethiopia on the Mereb bridge. Waiting on the other side was the welcoming party: Tedla Bairu, his entourage and an honorary police guard, and the Emperor's representative, his princess and federal officials. Since article 11 of the Eritrean Constitution gave precedence to the representative on all ceremonial occasions, it was Andargatchew who stepped forward as the first person to welcome the Emperor across 'the once troubled Mereb River' into Eritrea. Tedla spoke of how the Mereb River was being 'purged of its ages of slavery and bad name and being steered to a new life'.[34] But it was Andargatchew, the Ethiopian representative, not Tedla, the Eritrean Chief Executive, who ushered the Emperor into the autonomous state. A point had been made: any claim to a special status for Eritrea or its Chief Executive had been put aside. Eritrea, which the Ethiopians consistently referred to as 'their returning long-lost province', had passed from Ethiopian hands to Ethiopian hands.

If, as many observers claimed, Tedla felt slighted by the act, he had cause to be. Perhaps with the exception of *Abune* Markos, standing by his side to offer his cross for the Emperor to kiss, Tedla's role in making that day possible had no parallel. The royal treatment that he had received in Addis Ababa just a few days earlier confirmed that to him. Yet he was pushed to the back rows in his own domain and many claim he resented that treatment. It also set his relationship with Andargatchew on a collision course.[35] Tedla would not accompany the Emperor for the rest of his visit, as he was admitted to the military hospital at Kagnew Station in Asmera for an appendectomy. To this day, many believe he actually suffered a nervous breakdown from the shock he received at the Mereb.

Abune Markos was in for a similar jolt. The Emperor had brought with him the Ethiopian Patriarch, *Abune* Basilios, whose subordinate Markos had become. As the Emperor crossed the Mereb, it was the Ethiopian and not the Eritrean cross that he kissed. The same thing happened to the splendidly attired British-trained honorary police guard waiting to give their military salute. 'A contingent of Ethiopian troops ran across the Mereb Bridge, pushed us back to the rails and escorted the Emperor in,' related Captain Kidanemariam, one of the officers in charge of the honour guard.[36]

As he unveiled the plaque commemorating the historic event, Haile Selassie declared that the connection between the two brotherly peoples would be everlasting, blessed and ineradicable. 'Let this sign testify to future generations', read the plaque, 'that the artificial border that has been separating the two countries has been erased and that we have crossed it for the first time.'[37]

People came out in their thousands to welcome Haile Selassie as his motorcade passed through Seraye and parts of Hamasien towards Asmera. It was a genuinely spontaneous reception. His reputation as a man of wisdom and prayer was generally taken at face value by a large number of ordinary Eritreans, who looked up to him for solutions to their unending political and economic problems. He had created an image of himself, carefully groomed through decades, of a benevolent man who stood high above the human weaknesses of his officials and feudal base; a blameless monarch with nothing but the good of his people at heart. In many cases, the image would work for him till the last days of his long reign.

Even members of the EDF and newly federalist-leaning former Andinet activists were inclined to express their trust and guarded confidence in the Emperor.

On 16 September the EDF had announced that, as a gesture of goodwill, it had dissolved itself as an umbrella organisation for the political parties within it. The American consul Mulcahy reported extensively on this and related matters. The EDF's dissolution, he wrote, 'was a gesture to enable followers of Ibrahim Sultan to escape the stigma of being a permanent opposition and psychologically to divorce themselves from their anti-Ethiopian past'. There were, however, rumours that a new opposition party would be formed soon and that

> a small number of Unionists and Liberal Unionists will announce their adherence openly to the new party that will be formed. There seems to be a certain amount of ground for this rumour as evidence of growing dissatisfaction with Unionist leadership, even among the Unionist deputies in the Assembly, has been discernible of late ... such as their direct and successful protest to the Emperor on the excessive number of Amhara officials sent to Eritrea to federal posts and the known opposition of many of them to the appointment of Bitweded Andargatchew Mesai as Representative of the Emperor in Eritrea.[38]

The rumours Mulcahy mentioned were actually based on shifts in loyalty among the younger UP representatives. Mesfin Gebrehiwet and Habtemariam Nugurru were, for example, among those openly advocating federalism, having abandoned their old support for annexation. According to Mesfin, they were attracted by the democratic principles of the Eritrean Constitution, which stood in sharp contrast to the feudal system being imposed upon them. However indirectly, Eritreans had learned enough of democratic ideas in the brief British period to develop a craving for them.[39]

It was a complicated period that conflicted many people. Even the Evangelical Protestant Tedla Bairu, who swore on the Bible to 'respect the Federation under the sovereignty of the Imperial Crown' and to 'defend the Eritrean Constitution and its laws', was put in the awkward position of reconciling two systems in a marriage that could not be consummated.

In the meantime, as a conciliatory gesture, the EDF announced the closure of its paper, *Hanti Ertra*. In its place appeared an independent bilingual *Dehai Ertra* (Voice of Eritrea), later edited by Mohammed Saleh Mahmud and his deputy, Elias Teklu. In its maiden edition, *Dehai* introduced itself as the newspaper of the people; it was meant for all lovers of Eritrea to discuss the country's future. It offered its blessing to the country's newly installed leaders and begged the Creator to guide them in their tasks. 'May they not give a deaf ear to the voice of the people,' it concluded. 'History teaches us that the voice of the people should be freely expressed.'[40]

In other ways, it soon became clear that Haile Selassie's rousing reception was confined to his person. As an alarmed Eritrean public looked on, scores of Ethiopians entered Asmera to take over every conceivable position in the federal offices, leaving no room for Eritrean inductees. The Ethiopian army brigade was already garrisoning itself in all key military installations, and all the villas and houses assigned to the

Ethiopians were being occupied by them. Just as at the Mereb, the Ethiopians had come into Eritrea, not as senior partners in a federal set-up, but as new conquerors. The reaction was immediate and not confined to Eritreans.

The Ethiopian Felasha exile Professor Tamrat Amanuel, a friend of Andargatchew's nemesis *Blata* Kidanemariam Aberra, was standing at the Bar Royal when Haile Selassie's motorcade crossed Asmera's main street (soon to be renamed Haile Selassie Avenue). He called Kidanemariam's assistant, Sahle Gebrehiwet, and said to him:

> What kind of people are you, Eritreans? When you are given the chance to be independent, you choose Ethiopian rule. You prefer to be trampled upon by Ethiopia. What kind of thinking is that? You know, our forefathers used to call your area a military area. You were known as the children of combatants. When they wanted good fighting men, they recruited them from here. When you had salt under your noses, we came from Tigray and Gondar to extract and sell it to you. We even exchange your chickpeas for your salt and sell them to you. Look at you now; you come in multitudes to cheer Haile Selassie. Where do you know Haile Selassie?[41]

Within four days of his visit to Eritrea, Haile Selassie received a joint Muslim–Christian petition accusing what Mulcahy called 'Showan carpetbaggers' of coming to overrun the country. They also opposed the appointment of Andargatchew, the man who had been put to shame publicly in an Asmera court just the year before. According to Mulcahy, Haile Selassie ordered a reduction in the Ethiopian arrivals; but Andargatchew was to stay, a decision that was widely resented.

The arrival of an Ethiopian brigade to replace the departing British battalion in the first week of the Federation also became a cause for broad concern and apprehension over Ethiopia's intentions. Mulcahy wrote that the Showans did not appear to have any understanding of Eritrean feelings; or that they deliberately ignored the Eritrean expectation of a genuine federation as opposed to outright annexation. It had only been four days since the creation of the Federation, noted Mulcahy, and it was difficult to predict how the entire population would receive it. But, in those initial days, mistakes were committed that could have been avoided through tact and careful handling.[42]

Haile Selassie in Massawa

Haile Selassie's biggest prize was, without a doubt, access to the Red Sea. Ever since 1924, when as Crown Prince he first put out his claim to Eritrea and its coastline, he had built a case and international support to justify that claim. With tact and by manipulating history, he managed to convince his people and his sympathisers in Britain and elsewhere that Ethiopia, or Abyssinia before it, had always been a maritime state before colonial intervention. Few realised that the Eritrean coastline had, at least since 1557, been under the control of the Ottomans, the Egyptians, the Italians and the British until the day of his first visit. This is not to imply that Abyssinian kings and warlords never tried to reach the shores of the Red Sea. As we have seen, Subagadis, Wubie, Emperor Yohannes and *Ras* Alula carried out armed campaigns to establish themselves there in the eighteenth and nineteenth centuries. None of them ever succeeded.

There had thus never been any long- or short-term Abyssinian control of the Red Sea before the Turkish occupation to justify the kind of narrative that the Ethiopians imposed on the history of the area. Yet it was a successful campaign, greatly enhanced by Haile Selassie's unheeded warning about the global danger posed by Fascism in 1935–6 and the international sympathy he gained subsequently. More significantly, the narrative became an article of faith, indeed an obsession, for generations of Ethiopians, who, even after Eritrea's independence, still believed that Ethiopia had been robbed of its legitimate access to the sea.[43]

Back in Massawa, Haile Selassie boarded an American ship to cruise around his newly acquired domain. His legal advisor, John Spencer, noted that the Emperor's grave demeanour in no way revealed

> the intensity of his emotions on this occasion marking nearly three decades of struggle for access to the sea. The event was a source too of personal gratification. He was now redeeming before history the mistake [in Ethiopian eyes] made by Menelik II in failing to recover Eritrea after the victory of Adwa. Alluding to my impending departure for New York and the challenges now facing Ethiopia, he said to me, 'When you go, you must remind the Americans that Ethiopia is a young country.' There was no appeal for assistance, no elaboration, just that one injunction. Coming at a moment when Ethiopia, one of the oldest states in the world, was celebrating a reunion marking a political and cultural identity running back many centuries, the paradox and the intensity of the observation caught me by surprise.

As far as Spencer was concerned, Eritrea was secured, and it was the new international dimension and responsibility that came about as a result of Eritrea's addition that was of major concern. The Emperor, Spencer continued,

> had instantly perceived—as his cryptic exhortation to me implied—that with the return of Eritrea, Ethiopia was facing the challenge of growth and development. With an Eritrea possessing a constitution and, in non-tribal matters, a European system of laws, the modernization of Ethiopia's constitutional and legislative structures could not be long delayed. It was decided that a start should be made with bringing the legislative structure up to date before proceeding with constitutional changes. Soon the word came to me to recommend the procedures by which Ethiopian civil, procedural, admiralty and criminal law might be modernized.

Haile Selassie returned to Addis Ababa on 18 October. Only then did the Eritrean Government find the breathing space to attend to its internal administration.

13

THE ERITREAN GOVERNMENT

Structure and Character of the Tedla Administration

Financial constraints would only allow Tedla Bairu to form a cabinet of four secretaries and an all-purpose Office of the Director General to monitor the day-to-day activities of the secretariats of the Interior, Social Affairs and the Economy.[1] The Secretary of Finance maintained a direct link with the Chief Executive, as did Law and Justice until a separate secretariat was created for it. The civil service, later named the Central Personnel Agency (CPA), led by an establishment officer, also remained under the direct supervision of the Chief Executive through the director general.

Staffing the various departments responsible for each secretariat was a major initial problem as many of the relatively better educated and experienced Eritreans had been elected to the Assembly. Tedla obtained the approval of the Assembly to withdraw elected members for his administrative posts, thus opening the way for a by-election for fourteen vacancies.

Tedla adopted the combined Italian and British system inherited by his administration and, despite their lack of proper training in the art of governance, the new appointees took no time in taking charge of their functions. The files of the CPA provide a picture of a loosely regulated system that allowed little opening for illegal or corrupt practices. Despite a few complaints and accusations of partisanship or nepotism, Tedla's tenure was regarded as relatively free from major transgressions, even according to the testimony of some of his chief detractors.[2] We note here, however, that the issue of appointments would always remain the subject of gossip, rivalry and, eventually, open corruption until the hold of the federal system wore out.

Tedla's administration reflected both the conflicts inherent in its awkward position within an unbalanced federal relationship and the conflicted personality of Tedla himself. By all accounts, he was an introvert—reserved, sensitive and secretive. His closest aide, Mesfin Gebrehiwet, gave a description of him that others like Asfaha and Gebreyohannes have confirmed. Tedla, he said, 'was an extremely reserved person who would never let anyone into his most difficult decisions; even the problems that finally did him in, he faced alone. But he was an intelligent man who, under the British, enhanced his Italian education and experience by reading books.'[3]

At 38 years of age, Tedla was still a young man when he came to power. His father, Bairu Ukbit of Gheremi, Hamasien, was a prominent Evangelical Protestant who was as deeply involved with church affairs as he was with the unionist movement. We may assume that Tedla's upbringing and the tendency of the Eritrean Protestant community to lean towards Ethiopia may have been the basis of his Ethiopian sentiments. Tedla's own education in Florence, Italy—he was one of the very few Eritreans to be so privileged by the Italians—entitled him to coveted positions, like teaching in Adwa during Italy's occupation of Ethiopia.[4] But, as we indicated earlier, Tedla was a bundle of contradictions—modern by education and exposure to Western values, but traditional in his political views.[5]

Puzzled by the intensity of his sentiments for Ethiopia, Melles Fre, well-known justice of the Eritrean Supreme Court during the Federation, once asked him what drove him towards the Amhara. 'His response surprised me,' Melles said. 'Tedla said to me, "In time, we will run Ethiopia." I don't think that he had any idea of what the Showans were capable of or of their long experience in political intrigue. Neither was he aware of his own political limitations.'[6]

By swearing on the Bible to uphold the Eritrean Constitution and to protect the Federation, Tedla compounded his contradictions especially in view of his old commitment to outright annexation. This internal conflict played a major role in his political fate and significantly influenced the course of the Federation.

Initial Issues and Problems

A Scandal in Tedla's Cabinet

Tedla's government began with a scandal when 2,000 bundles of *abujadid* cloth and an unspecified amount of sugar disappeared from government warehouses. Saleh Kekia Pasha, representing Hirgigo in the Massawa area, even named certain government officials and businessmen as the beneficiaries of the misappropriation. A shocked Assembly demanded an immediate explanation from the government.[7] Answers by Tedla and his Economy Secretary, Fessehatsion Haile, which sought to circumvent the issue, would not satisfy the general indignation in the Assembly. Furthermore, Assembly members saw Tedla's refusal to appear before them as a deliberate slight, thus setting off the first confrontation between Tedla and the Assembly.[8] 'The Assembly is a legislator and an advisor whose decisions should be upheld and respected,' one member argued. 'If the people, the Assembly and the Government do not work in unison, we will not meet the promises that will calm our people's disturbed hearts.'[9] The mention of 'disturbed hearts' was a reference to public demonstrations against the scandal.

The matter threatened to reach crisis proportions when some lifelong unionists joined in the chorus, thus creating a formidable bipartisan front. [10] But things came to an abrupt end when, fearful of the repercussions of the scandal on the Unionist Party (UP), its top leadership prevailed on Kekia to withdraw his formal complaint. Second, Eritrean Democratic Front (EDF) members suspected that the whole scandal had been staged by the Ethiopians to discredit the Eritrean Government and strangle it in its infancy.[11] Tedla was thus spared his first confrontation with the Assembly. As the UP newspaper aptly put it, 'The case of *abujadid* and sugar, which had started with thunder and lightning, petered off into a trickle.'[12]

Outstanding Issues of Transition

There were, however, other issues that demanded closer contact and cooperation between the legislature and the executive. The Ethiopian birr had replaced the British East African shilling and the unfavourable exchange rate resulted in a reduction in people's buying power. The exclusive assignment of Ethiopians to positions of federal authority also caused deep concern in the Assembly. Moreover, the Ethiopian Government began to issue directives on matters considered within Eritrean jurisdiction. The Assembly wanted to know, for example, on what legal ground the Ethiopian Government had issued a directive regulating transportation on the Asmera–Massawa road, an internal function reserved for the Eritrean Government.[13] It also issued laws and directives in the name of the 'Imperial Ethiopian Government' and not the 'Imperial Federal Government'. Finally, although internal communications—posts, telegraphs and telephones—were an Eritrean responsibility by law, the Ethiopians had taken them over. Assembly members, especially Habtezghi Okbazghi, sent written requests to the Chief Executive to respond in person.[14]

Tedla wrote back to explain that the matter of the Asmera–Massawa road was one of the issues that he expected the Imperial Federal Council to address. Apparently, he had high hopes of the effectiveness of the yet untested council. As for the name of the federal union, Tedla merely referred to Haile Selassie's decree ratifying the Federal Act, according to which the official name of the federal entity would be the Imperial Ethiopian Government. Tedla did not oppose the Emperor's decree. On the matter of internal communications, he agreed with Habtezghi. He wrote, 'Your interpretation of the Federal Act is correct, and it was confirmed by the UN Commissioner and his panel of legal advisors. The Emperor's ratification also gave it legal authenticity. But the details of its implementation require further discussion.'[15]

Another matter of major concern for the duration of the Federation was customs duties. On 22 December, the chairman of the Budget Committee, *Azmatch* Beyene Zahlai, reported that Ethiopia had set Eritrea's share of custom duties for fifteen months at 5,784,145 birr, and that the amount was based on old British accounts that did not remotely reflect the revenues that Ethiopia was collecting after its takeover of Eritrean ports. Beyene, one of the top leaders of the Akeleguzai UP section, voiced his strong opposition to the setting aside of the Federal Act's provision that custom revenues for goods originating from and destined for Eritrea be assigned to Eritrea.

Finance Secretary Teklehaimanot Bokru explained to the Assembly that his efforts to reach an agreement on the customs situation had come to nothing. 'Until this date,' he said, 'we have received 500,000 birr only as our share of customs revenues.' Ethiopia was not even complying with the low rates put in place by the British Administration as a temporary measure until the whole issue was resolved after federation. The true amount should have been twice the amount paid to Eritrea thus far. Teklehaimanot was praised for his efforts, but the problem continued to plague the Assembly's relationship with the Chief Executive and the Ethiopian Government.[16]

Two more subjects occupied the Assembly in the first three months of Tedla's administration: Proclamation 130, establishing the federal courts in Eritrea; and the election of representatives to the Imperial Federal Council.

Proclamation 130 of 1952

The Eritrean Constitution modelled the Eritrean judiciary on the US system. The separation of judicial powers from those of the executive and legislature was guaranteed by the provisions regulating those relationships. Thus, as the court of last instance (article 90–1), the Eritrean Supreme Court was invested with the power of judicial review (article 90–3). It also had the power to pronounce a final verdict in case the Chief Executive was impeached by the Assembly (article 90–6). There were also clear provisions protecting judges from political pressure (article 86), regulating their appointment and work ethic (article 87–8), and defining the powers of the hierarchy of courts from the village level to the Supreme Court.

In Ethiopia, where the courts were subservient to the executive, the Eritrean system was considered undesirable and a bad example. Consequently, Ethiopian officials initiated moves to undermine it even before the implementation of federation by requesting, in July 1952, buildings for federal courts and 'lock-ups' for federal offenders. Although Brigadier Cumming initially argued that the Federal Act did not provide for the existence of federal courts in Eritrea, the British nevertheless included an article in the Administration of Justice Act, declaring that Eritrean courts would not have precedence or superiority over the federal courts to be created in Eritrea. The Eritrean Executive Committee, which discussed this Act, failed to object or note the danger inherent in the British change of mind—an oversight with serious consequences.[17]

The Ethiopians were quick to seize the opportunity created by this omission and, on 30 September, only two weeks after the implementation of the Federation, an Imperial decree establishing federal courts in Eritrea was ready for proclamation. Proclamation 130 of 1952 stipulated that the Ethiopian Supreme Court, with no changes made to its status in relation to the Ethiopian executive, would act as the

Imperial Federal Supreme Court, and the Ethiopian *afenegus* (president of the Supreme Court) would also become the president of the Imperial Federal Supreme Court (article 3). But no separate body named the Imperial Federal Supreme Court was ever created, nor were the structure and functions of the Ethiopian Imperial Supreme Court changed. It was therefore a fictitious name that the Imperial Supreme Court would use, under article 4 of Proclamation 130, to review and overturn decisions of the Eritrean Supreme Court in cases where it deemed such decisions contravened federal laws or interests.[18]

The whole move was a ploy by which to establish a Federal High Court (FHC) in Eritrea to act as a watchdog over the Eritrean Supreme Court and suppress the independence of the Eritrean judiciary. Article 7 of the Proclamation gave to the FHC the power to transfer to its jurisdiction cases that appeared to touch on matters concerning the Federal Act, the Ethiopian Constitution or Ethiopia's international agreements. Eventually, these transfers would know no bounds. Accountable to a ghost Imperial Federal Supreme Court and in contravention of the provisions of the Federal Act, it imposed the Imperial court system inside Eritrea. As we will see, the repercussions would be a major blow, not only to the Eritrean judiciary, but also to the rights and powers of an autonomous Eritrea itself.

Eritrean reaction to the proclamation was swift. In a series of articles published by *Dehai*, it was argued that the powers assigned to the federal courts in Eritrea were so broad that they appeared to allow them to control the Assembly itself. One contributor asked:

> So, what were the discussions and arguments by the Assembly members on the extent of the power and authority to be given or denied to the Emperor's Representative all about? It seems to me that the powers that were specifically denied him by the Federal Act are now coming in through the back door left open by the British in a far stronger and formidable way. This means that the gift of Eritrean autonomy is now meaningless; it is dead. All that work and effort exerted by the United Nations and the Eritrean Representatives is no longer of any value—just because the Ethiopian Government does not want it ... [The Ethiopians] could at least have waited until the arrival of the Imperial Federal Council in Addis Ababa to discuss the matter.[19]

As Ethiopia's aggressive approach gathered momentum, all eyes started to turn to the Imperial Federal Council.

The Imperial Federal Council

Article 5 of the Federal Act provided the following: 'An Imperial Federal Council [IFC] composed of equal members of Ethiopian and Eritrean representatives shall meet at least once a year and shall advise upon the common affairs of the Federation.' It did not give any more details. Presumably, the IFC's specific functions and the weight to be given to its advisory inputs would be determined at the projected meetings.

On 30 October, after a debate on the list of the Chief Executive's nominees, the Assembly agreed on five names. These were Mohammed Omer Qadi of the Independent Muslim League; Tsegai Teferi, a UP member and a public scribe and advocate; Gebremedhin Asihel, a police inspector from Asmera; Adem Mohammed Agdubai, a UP-leaning businessman from Barka; and *Blata* Gebregziabher Gebremikael from the Adi Quala area in Seraye. At the same time, it also selected five citizens to represent Eritrea in the Ethiopian lower house of parliament.[20]

In what appeared to be a deliberate act of pre-emption, the Ethiopian Government chose the same date, 30 October, for publication of Proclamation 130 in its official legal bulletin, the *Negarit Gazeta*. Renegotiation of the draft was at the top of the IFC's agenda, but the Ethiopians blocked that possibility by the proclamation. Other matters of urgency awaiting the IFC were the spiralling price hikes resulting from the currency change from the EA shilling to the birr; Ethiopia's initial refusal to pay Eritrea its fair share of customs revenues; and the complete domination by Ethiopian officials of all federal functions in Eritrea.[21]

For sixteen weeks, the Eritrean members of the IFC waited to be summoned to Addis Ababa for what they saw as the resumption of crucial talks with their Ethiopian counterparts. Coming in the wake of Proclamation 130, the delay caused a visible increase in feelings of apprehension in several quarters. Siraj Abdu, prominent labour leader and a veteran of the Muslim League (ML), reflected the mood within the movement and the party when he wrote:

> Wouldn't it be more appropriate for the Federal Council to have discussed the matter and come to an agreement and then for the federal authority to issue proclamations and orders? Besides, is it right for the Ethiopian Government newspapers and speakers to keep stating that 'Eritrea has joined or been merged to Ethiopia', rather than explaining the true federal relationship? Proclamation 130, which is now our main concern, has authority and superiority over the Eritrean Assembly. It destroys the internal autonomy granted to Eritrea by the United Nations.[22]

After 47 days of nervous waiting, the IFC members travelled to Addis Ababa on 17 December, armed with letters of delegation and a list of 27 topics for discussion from the Assembly and the Chief Executive himself. Proclamation 130 and the unjustifiable assignment of government buildings to Ethiopian authorities topped the government's and the Assembly's concerns.[23] Their arrival in Addis Ababa was a disappointment. The Eritrean delegates to the Ethiopian parliament were given a warm welcome. IFC delegates, according to Omer Qadi, were largely ignored. Referring to himself and his four colleagues in the third person, he explained in a hand-written memoir:

> They went to [Addis Ababa] alright. They were also given their salaries. But they only slept at Itegue Hotel without being engaged in any work or meeting with anyone. No value was given to them ... they should have conferred in Addis Ababa and presented

> their request to His Majesty ... From December 1952 to April 1953, they were unable to accomplish anything ... And so, they returned to Asmera ... Back in Eritrea, they explained both to the CE and the Assembly the major difficulties they had faced and their failure to deliver. The Assembly and the CE panicked. Those who dared to question were branded enemies of Ethiopia.[24]

When the IFC later succeeded in submitting its agenda to the Ethiopian Government, the latter instructed the Eritreans to attend a session of the Ethiopian parliament and argue their case there. The IFC, supported by the newly installed Eritrean members of the Ethiopian parliament, argued its opposition to the illegal Proclamation 130 with a united voice. It was a futile exercise conducted within a venue where the Eritreans were not legally bound to be present. Omer Qadi never explained why he and his colleagues submitted to the Ethiopian parliament. All he said was that 'they had been directed to do so in the memorandum'. Whatever the reason, their action played into the hands of the Ethiopians. After hearing the Eritreans out, the Ethiopian parliament put the matter to the vote. Only the five Eritrean parliamentarians supported the Eritrean motion while all the Ethiopians voted against it. The establishment of the federal courts in Eritrea was thus declared legal as the 'Federal Parliament' had ratified Proclamation 130.[25]

The Eritrean submission to the Ethiopian parliament was a gross mistake. If, as Omer Qadi recalled, it had been made upon instructions in their memorandum, this could only have come from Tedla Bairu, who was, during the same weeks, involved in an argument on the proclamation with several members of the Assembly.

As early as March 1953, Assembly member Bezabih Tesfabruk of the Adi Quala area had asked for government clarification on the legality of Ethiopia's move to establish federal courts in Eritrea. Tedla referred the question to his British legal advisor, Norman Methven, telling him to find some legal ground to prevent Assembly members from raising the issue again as he believed the matter to fall under federal jurisdiction. Methven could not find such legal grounds but suggested the stipulation of an internal rule requiring that matters to do with federal relations not be discussed by the Assembly unless supported by at least ten members and submitted to the government beforehand for its comments.[26] The internal rule was approved by the Assembly and Bezabih's motion was thrown out.

Undeterred by Tedla's interference, the IFC members appealed to Haile Selassie, requesting that the legality of Proclamation 130 be examined by the larger IFC and a panel of legal experts representing both Eritrea and Ethiopia. The Emperor did not respond. Instead, he appointed three judges to head the Federal High Court of Eritrea.[27] On 15 May 1953, the federal courts were formally inaugurated in a hasty ceremony to which Tedla Bairu was invited.

In the meantime, as the other members faded into the background, Omer Qadi continued his lone fight to salvage what remained of the IFC's chances of survival. The collapse of a house started with small signs, he wrote to the government and the Assembly, and since Proclamation 130 put Eritrea's internal autonomy at Ethiopia's mercy and rendered the IFC worthless, 'the Federation is on the verge of destruction'. He went on to ask the following questions. Why has the Eritrean Government become negligent of its capabilities and responsibilities? Why are the Government and the Assembly of Eritrea silent on this issue (Proclamation 130)? Is it because it is not clear to them that the establishment of the federal courts in Eritrea is a high-handed contravention of the Federal Act and Eritrea's internal freedom? Ultimately, whose responsibility is the protection of Eritrea's interests? After posing his questions, Omer Qadi invoked his duty as a member of the IFC and asked every Eritrean citizen to demand a debate on 'this important matter' in the Eritrean Assembly. He also called upon members to voice their opinions on the 'holy rights of our people, the internal freedom of Eritrea, and the life and unity of the Federation'.[28]

On receiving Omer Qadi's letter, Assembly president Ali Rad'ai met with Tedla Bairu and Andargatchew, and all three of them agreed to block any efforts to raise the issue of the federal courts in the Assembly. Three months later, on 27 August 1953, Omer Qadi resigned from the IFC. His letter of resignation stated that the IFC had accomplished nothing of significance and that he saw no value in wasting more of his time as a member. He also declared that he wanted no part in Ethiopian violations aimed at rescinding the Federal Act.[29]

Omer Qadi found no official support or following in his stubborn struggle to turn the IFC into a relevant and effective advocate of Eritrea's federal rights. As the most consistent promoter of 'conditional union with Ethiopia', he was a sincere believer in the success of the federal solution. The personal humiliation and disappointment that he suffered as an IFC member led him to other forms of struggle. But his departure sounded the death knell of the IFC.

Early Public Protests

Since almost all sessions of the Assembly were open to the public, young Asmera residents were always the most enthusiastic attendees. News of the day's proceedings were often spread by word of mouth throughout the town, allowing people to identify issues and generating wide political discussions. Encouraged by the mood in the Assembly, a group of young Asmera residents started to form clandestine groups and post protest pamphlets on public buildings. When the *abujadid* scandal was discussed in the Assembly, they came out in the open, staged a demonstration and demanded a meeting with the Chief Executive. They were led by their spokesperson, Yohannes Teklai, and three colleagues.[30] Most of the demonstrators were former members of Andinet.

To his credit, Tedla met with them, and they presented their multiple complaints to him. They told Tedla that it was not right for *mislenes* (district governors) also to be members of the Assembly, contrary to the separation of powers of the executive and legislative branches of government. Some of Eritrea's administrators were illiterate and incapable of proper communication; they needed to be removed. Police salaries should be increased. The cost of living was too high and needed attention. Appointments to public offices should be based on merit, not on birthright or personal relationships. The Economy Secretary, Fessehatsion Haile, should be removed for his failings, and likewise Assembly president Ali Rad'ai and vice president Demsas Weldemikael for their unfitness for their posts.[31] In an article reporting the encounter, the demonstrators complained that Tedla had threatened them with flogging. 'The Fascists did nothing worse. If the people cannot express their opinions, it means that democracy has disappeared,' they emphasised.[32]

The UP newspaper, *Ethiopia*, responded on behalf of the Chief Executive, arguing that *mislenes* were elected by the people and, therefore, it was not within his powers to remove them from the Assembly. It was true, however, that Assembly duties were taking time away from administrative tasks that required fuller attention. In addition, after flatly denying that Tedla had threatened to flog the demonstrators, *Ethiopia* contradicted itself by admonishing the demonstrators and *Dehai* for exposing the leader for words uttered while he was on 'the verge of anger'.[33]

In fairness, some of the problems, like Eritrea's ruined economy, were hardly of Tedla's doing. But his treatment of the Assembly was of great concern. The Independence Bloc (IB) veteran Fesseha Weldemariam (Gandhi) expressed the prevailing sentiment when, in an article titled 'Decay in the Eritrean Constitution', he criticised Tedla for withdrawing better-educated and more enlightened Assembly members to fill posts in his administration. He also took Assembly members to task for having willingly abandoned the trust of their constituents. If they felt they could occupy both roles, he warned, such a possibility was banned by the Constitution; and their plans and directives would be illegal. After condemning all efforts to weaken the Eritrean Assembly, he blamed the Eritrean people for not using legal channels to defend their rights.[34] Fesseha's words must have touched a nerve, as he was later charged with defamation of the head of government.[35]

Ethiopian Interference and Deepening Confrontation

Andargatchew in Action

Other issues also caused tempers to flare both in the Assembly and in popular circles. On 30 October 1952, Haile Selassie's coronation day, director general Mesfin Gebrehiwet ordered the hoisting of the Ethiopian flag in all business establishments but refrained from according the same status to the Eritrean flag. Immediately, articles demanding Mesfin's resignation appeared in *Dehai*.[36] In the Assembly, *Qadi* Ali Omer and colleagues went further to question the legality of the daily hoisting of the Ethiopian flag at Eritrean government offices.[37] The bitter reaction to Mesfin

Gebrehiwet's relegation of the Eritrean flag was an early indication of the status that the flag was gaining as a symbol of Eritrean nationalism and autonomy.

Another incident that caused a stir on Haile Selassie's coronation day was a speech delivered by Andargatchew, in which he referred to Eritrea as a province of Ethiopia and to Eritreans as 'the children of the Ethiopian Province of Eritrea'. Speaking from the Palace, he avoided the most pressing popular questions regarding the domination of federal offices by Ethiopians and Eritrea's fair share of customs duties. Instead, he went on to enumerate what he called 'His Majesty's gift' to alleviate the economic problems of transition facing the people of Eritrea. Here he highlighted the cancellation of duties on goods entering Eritrea from Ethiopia, the ending of the tax on salt from Eritrea to Ethiopia, the reduction of customs duties on kerosene and industrial naphtha, and the scrapping of duties on the importation of grain from Sudan and other Arab countries into Eritrea. [38] None of these impressed Andargatchew's detractors in the Assembly, who insisted that while salt was an Eritrean product, not only was it expropriated by Ethiopia, but that its new price had made it unaffordable to Eritreans.[39] Nor did his list of 'gifts from the Emperor' have a positive effect on the broader Eritrean claims. At the level of the public, it was Andargatchew's repeated reference to 'Eritrea's merger with Ethiopia' that aroused indignation. In the following weeks, *Dehai* and *Ethiopia* published angry exchanges on the appropriateness of Andargatchew's choice of words—exchanges that were soon to escalate.[40]

In the meantime, it looked as if Andargatchew and his federal colleagues were bent on testing Eritreans' resolve to protect their country's autonomous rights. In December, Andargatchew's office issued a directive requiring foreign residents in Eritrea to register at the federal offices. The Assembly rose in protest. Habtemariam Nugurru of the UP and Berhanu Ahmeddin of the ML presented a joint motion protesting against Ethiopia's 'direct interference in Eritrea's internal affairs'.[41]

British sources indicate that Tedla, who had a spirited talk with Andargatchew on the matter, opposed the Assembly's resolution for having dared to accuse the Emperor's representative directly.[42] *Ethiopia* also expressed its alarm at the unanimous stand of the Assembly. At the same time, it chastised Habtemariam Nugurru and his supporters for their 'misguided thinking' that an Eritrean permit could ever be an adequate guarantee for a foreigner crossing into Ethiopia. It further expressed its dismay at *Abba* Habtemariam Nugurru's change of political direction.[43] The *Abba*, a Catholic cleric at the time, had previously been a strong unionist.

Neither Tedla's opposition nor *Ethiopia*'s hard-hitting criticism would deter the Assembly from pushing forward on the matter. On 5 January, *Qadi* Ali demanded a straight answer to the question whether the Federal Government's directive constituted interference in Eritrean jurisdiction. This time, the Secretary of the Interior admitted that the federal authorities had acted without prior knowledge of the Eritrean Government and that the latter had immediately notified its opposition to the Imperial Federal Government.[44] But nothing that the Assembly or the Government of Eritrea said or did would rescind Andargatchew's directive. Two things were becoming very clear. First, the Assembly's resolutions could be safely ignored; and, second, members of the Assembly who stood up against the Federal Government could become easy targets of abuse by the UP mouthpiece, *Ethiopia*.

Questions on the role of the UP paper in relation to the Eritrean Government began to fill *Dehai*'s columns. A regular contributor, Matewos W, wondered how a mere party newspaper could 'belittle and denigrate Assembly representatives rooting for the rights of the people, as enemies of Ethiopia, as if it is the Government's mouthpiece. The suppression or silencing of representatives committed to our country's welfare and our internal rights will never be allowed by the entire Eritrean population.'[45] *Dehai* and *Ethiopia* appeared to be on a collision course that threatened the fate of one of Eritrea's legacies from the Federal Act—freedom of the press and expression.

A Deepening Confrontation

When *Dehai Ertra* took over the publishing rights of the EDF's defunct *Hanti Ertra*, it had the blessing of Ibrahim Sultan and the ML. Its first two editors were Hussein Said Hayoti and Mohammed Saleh Mahmud, both known ML supporters. Although it was not formally affiliated to any political party or movement, federal and Eritrean officials regarded it as an opposition paper that accommodated opinions critical of their governments.

The press war between *Dehai* and *Ethiopia* intensified after labour leader Siraj Abdu questioned the legality of Proclamation 130 and strongly opposed references to the Imperial Federal Government as the 'Imperial Government of Ethiopia'.[46] *Ethiopia*'s response to Siraj was provocative. 'We would like to state clearly,' it said,

> that the Ethiopian Government, with all its laws, institutions and traditions intact is itself the Federal Government. [*Ato* Siraj] is alarmed by the words 'united', 'merged', and 'mixed' to describe Eritrea's status, in place of the word, 'federated'. But, unless he has forgotten the UN Federal Act, he is merely panicking at his own shadow. *Unione federale* means nothing more than uniting, merging or mixing in an alliance ... *Ato* Siraj's senses are leaving him.[47]

The deputy editor of *Dehai*, Elias Teklu, an emerging polemicist for the opposition, came to his defence. He addressed *Ethiopia* directly:

> The people of Eritrea have, by the will of God, found the king that they had been longing for. Beyond that, are you whining and pining because he [the Emperor] has not come into our midst, snatched our rights away and ruled us with his claws on our throats? If you are indebted to him beyond your means, go settle your dues. Otherwise, to parrot what you have been brainwashed to say in belittling your own brethren and forsaking your country's rights is to go against the laws of nature. Therefore, stop

> whining and work with sincerity; not for money, but for the benefit of your country, Eritrea, and for that of Eritreans and Ethiopians.[48]

The exchange revealed the ever-widening gap separating the two contending sides in Eritrea. As far as *Ethiopia* and its contributors were concerned, Eritrea was already part of Ethiopia, or would soon be with the abrogation of the Federation. *Dehai* and its ever-expanding contributors and readers, on the other hand, were returning to their pre-Federation political stands. As the federal arrangement was a compromise solution that the independence movement had never asked for or willingly accepted, its inauspicious beginning seemed to confirm their worst fears that the UN's formula was a betrayal of their rights. Inasmuch as *Dehai* entertained the resurgence of the language and attitudes of independence, it became a prime target.

Amid all the heated debate, *Dehai* published an article entitled 'People of Eritrea, Speak Up'. Beginning with the oft-repeated claim that Eritrea was economically unviable, the article replied, 'The Eritrea that was supposed to be an economic liability is now denied its own products, which are being whisked away to Ethiopia. The provider is turning into a deprived pauper.' It then used an Amharic saying to accuse the perpetrators of Eritrea's increasing problems:

> *Showana msT wede wsT* [The Showan and the parasite operate undetected from deep inside], so the saying goes. Until they obtain their refined political goals, the Showans appear to be truthful, generous, sympathetic and the lovers of their brethren. However, once their mission is accomplished, neither words nor letters can adequately describe their intrigues. 'Cut down the tree with its own branch' is their principle and they are using a few of our greedy brothers to shackle us inside an iron yoke and reduce us to their eternal slaves. Let us beware today. It will not serve us any purpose to say, 'We did not see this coming,' when things go wrong tomorrow.

The article concluded by urging the people of Eritrea to learn from the experience of their Tigray neighbours, whom the Ethiopian Government had massacred by means of air raids during the first Woyane uprising in 1943.[49]

Dehai had now gone beyond the limits that people in power could tolerate. Deputy editor Elias Teklu was immediately identified as the author, and all anger turned on him. Elias had migrated from Eritrea to Ethiopia in 1940 and returned at the end of the decade to become one of the most determined writers against union or federation of Eritrea with Ethiopia. *Ethiopia*'s response to the above article was aimed directly at him:

> It has been a while since the newspaper *Dehai Ertra* has become the receptacle of filth written in vulgar Tigrinya. And those who write in its columns are mostly worthless people who plundered Ethiopian wealth, and who are disrespected by their own peers ... We cannot expect sense from the likes of this rumbling chaff [Elias Teklu]. These are people who go back to lick their own vomit and break the pot that had fed them—despised individuals with no conscience. Unless we are to consider them

> as unburied corpses, it will be sinful to even put them on a par with the ever-useful beasts of burden.[50]

Elias shot back with equivalent venom, throwing the unlawful enrichment slur back at his accusers:

> We write the truth, and we caution our people from repeating previous mistakes. Yes, we partook in the appropriation of cursed money by saying 'Yes, my lord' long before our four accusers. But not by lying as they did. We toiled for what we earned. But we rejected the bread of plunder and oppression. Instead, we give priority to work for the benefit of our people. The four people who hide their names and praise those who laud Showa and castigate those who criticise it call themselves Eritreans. If they have an inkling of Eritrean brotherhood, they should be offended by the false charges against their own kind ... Aren't they ashamed to accuse me of treason while they are the ones who gave the Great Ethiopia a Judas kiss? Did I collude with Graziani to uncover Amharas and Eritreans from wherever they were hiding and condemn them to be hanged? Did these people think that the time of their exposure will never come?[51]

Elias's reference to Governor Graziani's aides was a deliberate hit at some of the most prominent unionist leaders in Eritrea. Among these were Asfaha Weldemikael, who in October 1952 was appointed deputy representative of the Emperor in Eritrea. He had been the right-hand man of Graziani during the Italian era. *Dejazmatch* Araia Wassie had also served as Graziani's personal interpreter and was poised for an Eritrean cabinet position at this point. *Azmatch* (later *Dejazmatch*) Zerom Kifle was another Graziani man and was the acting president of UP when Elias wrote the article. Thus, like Elias, *Dehai* itself was treading on dangerous ground by taking on these potent forces.

Weldeab Weldemariam, who had distanced himself from political activism after his failure at the polls, immediately saw the precarious direction in which *Dehai* was moving. *Ethiopia* was always the verbal violator, but *Dehai*'s reactions often sought to give as good as it got. It was a confrontation between unequal combatants which Weldeab feared would ultimately harm the broader issue of freedom of expression. An old press warrior and advocate of free speech, Weldeab decided to intervene on behalf of civility. His article in *Dehai*, 'It Is Easier to Govern the World Than One's Tongue', was to be the last of his to grace Eritrean newspapers. He expressed his shock and sadness at the 'venom that was flowing and the flames of fire that were descending' on Eritreans seeking to accommodate themselves to brotherhood and harmony. This kind of destructive language, he advised, was not suitable for newspapers. Criticism was about mutual understanding and advice, not insulting each other in front of thousands of strangers.

> Why are you closing your eyes and hearts when, within your sight, the economic condition of our people is deteriorating, our workers are in deep trouble and despair,

> and the number of our poor and the orphaned is increasing by the day? To proceed with this devastating and destructive press dispute and tear each other up with poisonous fangs is tantamount to slaughtering oneself with a dagger or hanging oneself with a rope ... Let us not listen to those who seek to divert us from the affairs of Eritrea and to place us on the wrong boat. Let the mission or service of each one of us be exclusively over Eritrea.[52]

The last sentence was obviously aimed at the hard-line unionists attempting to place Eritrea on the 'wrong boat'. Ten days after the publication of Weldeab's article, on 13 January 1953, two would-be assassins shot at him in front of the Cinema Impero, and inflicted a near-fatal wound. This was the seventh attempt on his life.[53] Weldeab was a writer whose clear thinking and articulation could easily sway public opinion. It was natural that there would be elements within the Ethiopian and Eritrean governments who wanted to silence him.

The Paper *Dehai* in Danger

On 13 January 1953, Emperor Haile Selassie entered Massawa on a French ship. While he was there, *Dehai* published an open letter by its regular contributor Matewos W:

> To reach this point, the people of Eritrea have been sacrificing their wealth and property for a long time. Today, they expect to be told that they have suffered enough and are immediately entitled to the change they deserve. To say that they will be rewarded in the future is not agreeable to them. Your Majesty, leaving the rest aside, we beg you, at least, to restore all of Eritrea's rights to Eritreans.

Matewos W went on to list the 'rights' that he accused Ethiopia of having usurped. These included the ports, the railway administration, internal transport and communications, and Eritrea's choice administrative and residential buildings. Finally, he demanded that the Ethiopian army, already garrisoned in several locations, should be withdrawn.[54]

There was no expectation that the Emperor would respond to an article in a local newspaper. But Matewos W's demands had been presented to the Emperor in a formal deposition by a significant number of senior Eritrean politicians, including a bipartisan group within the Assembly. The issues also became the main ground for popular disaffection and mistrust of Ethiopian high-handedness. To bring calm to the agitation, Haile Selassie promised to build offices and schools soon. He also announced that Eritreans were welcome as conscripts in the Ethiopian army.

Dehai immediately published Matewos W's response to the Emperor's promise. 'It is not right for us to be happy with a token gift from someone who has taken a million from us,' the article began. Eritreans were demanding agricultural, technological and industrial progress, not the construction of a few buildings. As for conscription, he continued, 'Are we expected to rejoice over the induction of a few

Eritreans into the Ethiopian army? The reward for the brave and heroic people of Eritrea cannot open with this chapter. Did not Italy conscript thousands of Eritreans and throw them into its Somali and Libyan campaigns? Does it mean that the people of Eritrea are grateful to Italy for what it did?'[55]

Such a direct affront to the Emperor, whose dignity was protected as 'inviolable' by his country's constitution, could not be tolerated. *Ethiopia*, as usual, gave a response:

> 'If, in just five months, we have become the beneficiaries of such generosity, we wonder what largesse we are to expect in a year ...' This should have been your [*Dehai*'s] reaction. If it is not in your nature to be grateful, what is to prevent you from expressing a little appreciation and admiration? [With regard to conscription into the Ethiopian army], has not the youth of Eritrea been forced to serve the alien power that you are longing to bring back? Did you then and do you now ever resent those transgressions?

Dehai's editors must have sensed the dangerous direction in which the latest confrontation was leading. The Eritrean Government had its own newspaper, *Zemen*, which had taken over the old British-sponsored *Nai Ertra Semunawi Gazeta*. But the UP newspaper was acting as the officially sanctioned mouthpiece of both the Eritrean and Federal governments. Thus, after Matewos W's affront to Haile Selassie, *Dehai* toned down its habitual forcefulness and Matewos himself called for civility in the exchange. But things had already gone too far. On 7 February, *Dehai* announced that its editors, staff and publisher had been summoned by the police for interrogation. After warning that the incident smacked of the government's dictatorial tendencies, *Dehai* published Elias Teklu's defiant article, 'Let Eritrea Be for Eritreans', in which he aimed his criticism directly at the Government of Ethiopia.

> If Ethiopia is really concerned with the well-being of Eritrea and Eritreans, it should have granted Eritrea's rights to Eritreans. Is it fair to move Eritrean wealth to Addis Ababa to feed Ethiopian children while Eritrean children are exposed to hunger and deprivation in their own land? Freedom means becoming the master of one's own country and property. A people that is surrounded by an army and whose money and products are confiscated cannot be considered free.
>
> Think of it, it was only yesterday that we heard words like 'I am weak, I have no power except prayers' in the great halls of the world. Today, [that same voice] is perpetrating suffering on the innocent people of Eritrea. Our demand is that, if Eritrea and Ethiopia are to be free of faults and blames, Ethiopia should return all of the Eritrean rights that it has taken away.[56]

The words quoted in the article were paraphrased from Emperor Haile Selassie's appeal for help at the League of Nations against Mussolini's invasion of his country. In a regime where the Emperor's name was uttered in whispers, such a bold affront was unthinkable to his officials. The repercussion came abruptly. On 7 March, Elias Teklu issued a second announcement in *Dehai*, informing his readers that he had been charged with an offence for his previous article, 'People of Eritrea, Speak Out', which compared Showans to parasites. He wrote:

> Was it wrong of me to ask the people of Eritrea to speak out? ... Is not the saying *Showana msT wede wsT* [the Showan and the parasite go deep inside] their own ancient proverb? Did I invent it? Are you telling us not to write about what is happening? Are you attempting to bury history? I am referring to the bombs that rained on the great city of Mekele in 1936 [i.e. 1943]. Was that not true? Although you may intimidate me, a common writer, into silence and prevent me from expounding on what I really want to say, the story that time will expose can never be erased ... Whatever the case, the proverb and the atrocities are all their own. God and his creatures are observing that we are being burdened with crimes we did not commit. *Inferh le'eme adleqeleqet meriet* [We will not be afraid even if the world is shaken] is all we can say as we entrust our hopes to God and the truth. Dear readers ... please stay alert lest the democracy that we have attained after a long time disappears piece by piece.

Suspension of *Dehai*

Dehai's lone and stubborn defence of democracy and call for the return of Eritrea's rights received a boost from an unexpected source, the Eritrean Catholic Church's paper, *Veritas et Vita*. In its edition of 1 February 1953, the paper issued an open letter to Emperor Haile Selassie in Italian and Amharic, in which it gave a vivid picture of the alarming direction in which Eritrea was heading in the mere four months between his first two visits. After describing Eritrea as a country whose imports and exports had dried up, whose streets were unsafe and whose factories had turned into graveyards, it urged the Emperor to bring Eritrea back to life.[57]

Once again, *Ethiopia* shot back on behalf of the government, advising the 'monks' to stick to their religious and spiritual calling and stay clear of the misdeeds of others.[58] However, the mood in the country, especially the cities, was too febrile to be affected by such condescending press tirades even if they had government support. The economy, as *Veritas et Vita* pointed out, was already collapsing. The 1952 rainfall had been scanty, and hunger threatened the countryside. This had led to the re-emergence of the *shifta*, beginning in November 1952. Rumours of members of the police force joining the *shifta* and of the Beni Amer of Barka refusing to pay taxes added to the public agitation.[59]

Tedla's reaction to all that happened in these formative months was unclear, as he remained aloof and avoided direct involvement. However, in February, five months after he had taken office, he conducted a tour of all the provinces to explain his government's policies and to respond to his critics. In Akurdet, he accused individuals of seeking to divide the people by exaggerating the economic problems of the country. He told the gathering that his government was their government and that they should not distance themselves from it.[60]

Compared with *Ethiopia*'s editorials and articles, Tedla's words were mild and conciliatory. But the political temperature was already rising and nothing that he said would cool tempers. In its next few issues, *Dehai* kept publishing articles from dozens of contributors pushing for change and democratic rights. A former Andinet member wrote a biting poem in which he asked, 'Did we say "Ethiopia *or* death, or Ethiopia *and* death!"'[61] 'Ethiopia or death!', accompanied by the right thumb facing upwards, had been the slogan of the UP in the 1940s. Andinet youth were now regretting their previous stand.

The authorities had had enough. On Sunday, 22 February, *Ethiopia* published a government statement explaining that officials had been tolerant of the 'lies and propaganda' disseminated by the press. Although the target was the Government of Eritrea, it alleged, the ultimate purpose was to harm the Government of Ethiopia and Ethiopians in general. Eritreans must realise that

> they have rights, without forgetting that they have obligations too. The right of freedom of expression involves the respect of the identity and beliefs of others; and respect for the laws promulgated. Therefore, the Government has decided to hold those who disseminate false propaganda against it accountable. In order to assure the reign of peace in the country and to enable all sides to work in love and harmony for the progress of its economic life, the Government has decided to take stern measures.[62]

Dehai became the first victim of the government's 'stern measures'. After its 26th number on Saturday, 14 March 1953, it stopped publication. Both the editor and his deputy, Mohammed Saleh Mahmud and Elias Teklu, were formally charged with subversion and taken to court. A triumphant *Ethiopia* celebrated the event in an editorial:

> From now onwards, let alone newspaper contributors who can be identified by their signatures, any discourse by any liar that demeans or belittles the Government of Ethiopia or attempts to derail the Government of Eritrea from building its base by spreading poisonous lies meant to frighten people and pit them against each other, will be dealt with mercilessly on the testimony of two or three witnesses. This is the verdict of the people.[63]

Why was *Ethiopia* controlling the government media while the official *Zemen* was standing by? There are indications that the two newspapers were not in tune on some current issues. A week after *Dehai*'s closure, *Zemen* published an article in which it raised the issue of Eritrea's share in federal responsibilities and suggested that the Assembly and the government should confer on the matter. It urged both branches not to abandon the determination of what exactly Eritrea's share should be.[64] In an apparent response to *Zemen*, *Ethiopia* threw the following punch at Tedla's administration:

> A government should act from a position of strength. Yes, we feel that the Government was not being attentive; otherwise, it would have taken note of what was happening. Why was the Government so quiet when people were being invaded by falsehoods and baseless rumours? It is obvious that a government cannot administer through counselling and councillors. The prophets said, 'Show us your strength and come and save us'—*ans'e hailke we ne'a adhnene*—not 'Show us your humbleness'—*ans'e tihtnake*.[65]

Clearly, Tedla was the target here, being put on the spot by the paper of which he had been the founder and first editor for six years previously. Questions were being raised about where Tedla's loyalty lay, and about the relationship between Andargatchew and Tedla and, by extension, the Federal and Eritrean governments. As by-elections for the vacated Assembly seats approached, Tedla's reaction to emerging developments marked the beginning of an erratic path.

14

REVIVAL AND SUPPRESSION OF THE WORKERS' UNION

A Precursor of the Workers' Movement

Around late October 1951, a year before the Federation, the American company Aramco began recruiting Eritrean workers for its oilfields in Saudi Arabia. Three friends, Tsegai Kahsai, Kefela Beraki and Tesfai Zerakristos, were among the first to apply. Examining their names and origin, the company's agents turned them back, explaining that registration was open only to Muslims. Surprised by the affront, the young workers borrowed turbans and *jalabiya* (*djellaba*) from their equally shocked Muslim friends and registered under false Muslim names. They passed the required tests and even learned enough of the Muslim prayers to sail through, but they could not survive the interviews. After consulting with the prominent Muslim leader *Dejazmatch* Hassen Ali, they registered their complaints with the Arab community in Asmera, Aramco, and the American consul Edward Mulcahy. Their words were simple and straightforward.[1] Stressing that Eritrean Muslims and Christians were, above all, 'blood brothers', they accused the Arabs and Aramco of introducing 'new elements of division' at that particularly sensitive time.[2]

In a letter addressed to Tsegai Kahsai, Mulcahy explained that the ban was a result of Saudi Government policy of not allowing any Christians to set foot on the country's soil. Aramco was simply carrying out Saudi orders and had no role or say in the matter whatsoever. Even the US Government did not have any means of changing Saudi policy. The Arab community in Eritrea, which consisted of Saudi, Egyptian, Syrian, Lebanese and Yemeni nationals, expressed their dismay and indignation. But they too could not go beyond promising to appeal, as a community, to the Saudi Government to reconsider its stand.[3] The community had every cause to fear reprisals from young Eritreans already resentful of the privileged position of Arabs.[4]

Every incident in the matter was published and widely discussed in all the newspapers, giving the activists public support and sympathy. Their problem, according to Tsegai, was that they were mostly down-to-earth workers with little formal education and no idea of what to do next. So they sought advice from the more enlightened politicians of the previous decade.

Tsegai Kahsai recalled that the idea of forming a labour organisation came to his attention only when Tsegai Teferi (later *Dejazmatch*), a Unionist Party member and solicitor, told him that the time was ripe for the formation of a workers' union. He had no idea what the proposal would involve.[5] Nor did his colleague Kefela Beraki, who knocked on the door of the appropriate British Administration official. 'You are just individuals,' the latter told him, 'You don't represent workers. If you want me to talk to you about workers, form an association.'[6] Encouraged by such advice, the activists began to plan. In the words of Tsegai Kahsai:

> We decided to call a gathering of the major personalities in the country. We took all precautions to keep the balance between the religious, geographical and political divisions in the country. Since the political problem had been resolved, we wanted to tell them, there now remained the problem of the worker. We needed a law and an organisation. We needed their help to secure one. We would then elect a committee from their numbers to lead us.[7]

It was a naive plan that looked for a solution to the labour problem from the major leaders of the political parties, religious establishments and business community of the 1940s. Weldeab helped them secure Abdella Gonafer's hall, where the Shuban–Andinet reconciliation had been launched the year before. On 28 November 1951, the organising committee of five people was able to bring together over 300 public figures, mainly from Asmera.[8] 'We had neither the experience, the knowledge, nor the courage to address such a gathering of major Eritrean figures of the day,' recalled Tsegai Kahsai. 'Hassen Ali, Tedla Bairu, Abdella Gonafer, Weldeab Weldemariam, Haregot Abbay, *Haj* Suleiman Ahmed ... everyone was there. We were nervous. So we got Tsegai Iyasu, the lawyer, to deliver our speech for us.'[9] Tsegai Iyasu's speech explained the plight of the Eritrean workers by highlighting the almost absolute power of employers. He also presented the issues of wages, health insurance, job security and annual vacations, all unavailable to Eritrean workers. He concluded his talk by begging those assembled to help the young workers achieve their goal.[10]

The idea of a workers' organisation was as new to the people in attendance as it was to the young workers themselves. Many of those invited apologised for having relegated such an important issue to the political wrangling of the previous decade. Some of the businesspeople were amused by the proposition. Haregot Abbay, a major Eritrean businessman, spoke for his peers when he said, 'In time I realise that this organisation will confront and fight the likes of me. But as long as it benefits my brothers and compatriots, I pledge to support it with all my heart and goodwill.'[11]

The Association of Eritrean Labour Unions (as it was initially called), one of the earliest of its kind in sub-Saharan Africa, thus took its first steps at this meeting, at which the organisers requested those assembled to elect a committee of leaders. To their credit, the politicians and businesspeople declined, pointing out that it would be inappropriate to usurp that role from the rightful stakeholders. Some openly argued that the union should be spared the political fragmentation of which they were the embodiment.[12] A committee of ten members led by the initiators of the movement, Tsegai, Kefela and Tesfai, was elected at the meeting. An additional committee of eight advisors was also named; it included the bitter political rivals Tedla Bairu and Weldeab Weldemariam.[13]

As a mass-based movement, independent of the political divisions in the country, the emerging organisation created a site for cooperation of a different kind. Most of its leaders were Andinet activists who had adopted new ideas about democracy and the rule of law, as provided by the Federal Act. They crossed a red line to link up with their former bitter adversaries, the Shuban, in a common cause. Such a dramatic shift in their political loyalties would have a deep impact on the events that followed. But it would not come without a price. In anticipating the dangers looming, *Hanti Ertra* warned,

> No one had been paying any attention to Eritrean workers up till this moment. But from now onwards, the eyes and attention of everyone will focus on the association that is taking its initial steps. However, not all eyes thus levelled on it can wish it well. Eritrean workers, especially the leaders and initiators of the movement, will need to tread their paths with great care.[14]

The Association of Eritrean Free Trade Unions

The Preparatory Stage

After the meeting on 28 November 1951 at the Gonafer hall, the new association faced the daunting task of organising workers and setting up a union. Although the British Administration had given its permission, it did little to help the inexperienced organisers in tackling their main problems—finance, office space, the drafting of a union constitution and choosing the form of the association itself. Employers' support for the union could be only a temporary gesture of goodwill. None of the advisory committee members were readily available to the union because people like Tedla Bairu, Haregot and Tewelde Tedla were members of the Eritrean Assembly and became involved in the ratification of the Eritrean Constitution. Of the remaining members, Weldeab was the best equipped, intellectually and by disposition, to assist the workers, and it was to him that the organisers turned for help.

After the sixth attempt on his life on 15 August 1951, Weldeab's safety had become precarious. He was a targeted man who, by the reckoning of the union organisers seeking his mentorship, could be struck down at any time. He had left his home and family at Geza Kenisha and was sleeping in a hotel near the Cinema Impero. Six or seven workers would surround him whenever he ventured out.[15] With that severe limitation on his personal movement, Weldeab could not be effective in organising workers. Thus, recruiting activists fell on members of the organising committee. Kefela Beraki remembered the verbal abuse and physical blows he received, as a recruiter and Weldeab follower, from bullies under government pay.[16]

There was a reason for the sensitivity over the Weldeab connection. As the workers were grappling with the elementary steps of union organisation, Weldeab was searching for ways of ensuring its viability. To avoid an Ethiopian ban, which he expected might be imposed once the Federation was set up, he helped pave the way for its formation while the British were still in power.

On 28 January 1952, two months after the meeting at Gonafer's hall, Weldeab wrote to Charles Levinson, secretary for East Africa of the International Confederation of Free Trade Unions (ICFTU), informing him that the organising committee in Eritrea was facing stiff government resistance. Ethiopia's opposition to the formation of a labour union would become open after the formation of the Federation on 15 September 1952. Weldeab requested ICFTU's help in pre-empting the impending ban and assistance in the drafting of an appropriate legal framework for the union. The question of including government employees within the union also needed discussion.[17] In reply, Levinson agreed that the union should be formed before the Federation. He also promised professional help in the drafting of a legal framework.[18]

ICFTU's interest on Eritrea had started earlier, when it sent a committee to Asmera in October 1951 and held meetings with British officials and journalists.[19] As editor of *Hanti Ertra*, Weldeab may have made his first contacts with ICFTU at this time. The committee's suggestion to Brigadier Cumming that the union be formed before the Federation seems to indicate that Weldeab or the activists had some influence over it. Cumming agreed to the suggestion but was reluctant to help draft the legal document during his tenure. Instead, he advised ICFTU to seek help from the British Government in meeting Ethiopian objections.[20] In a letter he wrote to the general secretary of the British Trades Union Congress, Sir Vincent Tewson, Levinson advocated the inclusion of Eritrean Government employees in the trade union.[21]

ICFTU's efforts to secure the establishment of the union before the Federation did not bear fruit. Three days after the Federation, Tewson asked Weldeab to update him on the latest developments.[22] For reasons unexplained, the correspondence stopped here. Despite Ethiopian objections, however, the union did come about eventually. We assume that ICFTU's intervention was successful.

Weldeab's involvement with the ICFTU did not please the Ethiopians. He was also in close contact with Sudanese and Italian labour activists, adding to the displeasure of the authorities.

AEFTU Inauguration and the Aftermath

On 16 November 1952, trade union representatives held a meeting where the constitution and programme of the Association of Eritrean Free Trade Unions (AEFTU) was approved. Weldeab Weldemariam was elected president and Siraj Abdu his deputy. Tewelde Tedla, lawyer and member of the Eritrean Assembly, became secretary general, and one of the wealthiest men in Eritrea, Abdella Gonafer, was elected treasurer. The activists Tsegai Kahsai, Kinfe Eliffe and Ibrahim Mahmoud were named advisors. In a follow-up meeting held on 23 November, at which eighteen trade unions were represented, the election and the programme previously approved were ratified. The AEFTU declared its political neutrality; its commitment to improving workers' livelihoods and protecting their rights; and its dedication to Eritrea's growth and progress 'without falling for outside ruses and temptations'.[23]

AEFTU was finally inaugurated on 7 December at the Cinema Impero, with government officials, religious leaders, diplomats and hundreds of workers attending. Weldeab Weldemariam, unanimously elected as president, delivered a speech outlining the AEFTU's programme and objectives. By all accounts, the ceremony went off well. A few days later, *Ethiopia* published an editorial with a veiled message:

> 'Milk me to the tune of the times (*gzie r'iKa Hlebeni*),' so said the cow. Our brothers the workers know the political and economic conditions of our country. It will thus be to their own and their country's benefit to be tactful in what they do. When we express our goodwill in praying that the Almighty, in His wisdom, will lead and direct them, it is with full confidence in their judgement.[24]

It was a warning whose full import became evident with the seventh attempt on Weldeab's life on 13 January 1953, just five weeks after the inauguration of AEFTU. Mulcahy's successor as American consul, Clarence T. Breaux, suspected two people as having been behind the attempt: former Andinet president Gebreselassie Garza, who then held a minor position in the Eritrean Labour Office and who opposed Weldeab's involvement with AEFTU; and Tedla Bairu himself, whom Breaux described as 'intolerant of any form of criticism'. Weldeab's last article in *Dehai*, Breaux said, had aroused the anger of unionists.[25] The Eritrean Commissioner of Police, David Cracknell, also recalled that although the assassins were never apprehended, he suspected Tedla's hand in it. Weldeab's union activism had rekindled the old rivalry between them, and his removal was thus actively sought by the other side.[26] The British consul John Wardle-Smith, for his part, pointed to Ethiopia as the culprit and expressed his doubts whether Tedla, who had issued a strict order for the arrest of the attackers, could also be the instigator.[27]

The question was often asked of Weldeab, why he risked his life yet again for the working people and why the workers, most of them former Andinet activists, chose him as their leader? He responded in one of his interviews that representatives of the workers insisted on his leadership at a time when he had suspended his political activities. But their choice of him, he added, 'had little to do with my personal character or importance. It indicated rather the extent to which the hearts of the Andinet youths had changed. And for that reason, I accepted. At the Cinema Impero, Berhe Andemikael of the bottling company Merenghi, Tsegai Kahsai of the shoemakers and Kefela Beraki of the railway workers nominated me. I was elected unanimously.'[28]

The attempt on Weldeab's life had a tremendous deterrent effect on the pioneering African labour movement, which had started so promisingly. For Weldeab, it was a turning point:

> The last attempt of January 1953 happened after I had established the labour association and been installed as its president. A man called Bahta shot me from behind. He had done it before. The bullet entered my back and exited through my throat. No one, not even the doctors, thought I would survive. But my death had not been willed by God. I was lucky to be released from the hospital fully recovered after five months.

While at the hospital, two suspects were brought to Weldeab for identification; one of them was Bahta. Weldeab refused to point an accusing finger. Kefela Beraki, who was with him at the hospital, asked him why he had done so. Weldeab responded, 'These are mere stone-throwers. If they had brought to me those who sit on comfortable sofas and give orders, I would have identified them. My blood cannot be recompensed by such as these.'[29]

Weldeab was the moving force behind the labour movement and the main advocate of a free press, at a time when *Dehai* was suppressed. It is no surprise that his enemies saw his removal as essential to the effective elimination of both those threats. But his labour supporters would arrange one last stand for their hero.

Worker Response to the Weldeab Shooting

By-elections for the more than a dozen Assembly seats vacated as a result of Tedla's appointments took place on 14 March 1953. With a host of complaints from would-be candidates and constituencies about sectarianism, favouritism and official corruption in the conduct of the election, it was more contentious than the first British-administered process.[30]

Weldeab was recuperating in the hospital when his labour union followers and his old Independence Bloc (IB) and Eritrean Democratic Front (EDF) colleagues registered him as a candidate to fill Mesfin Gebrehiwet's seat in Geza Kenisha. In a district with ten candidates, the reluctant Weldeab won easily. 'At last, people are sympathising with me. I think I am going to die,' he reportedly told a follower while imputing his success to a change of heart among Andinet youth.[31] Weldeab's election was taken as a judgement on both the Tedla administration and federal interference in Eritrean affairs. According to the British consul Wardle-Smith, Weldeab's undisputed victory indicated that the anti-federal sentiment associated with him was spreading. His popularity and his presence in the Assembly would thus 'make him a thorn in the Administration's pillow'.[32] However, the Administration was determined not to tolerate that 'thorn'. On 15 March, as the newly elected members took their oaths in the Assembly, the results of three election districts, including Weldeab's, were put on hold. The American consul Edward Clark reported that the move was a joint Eritrean and federal measure to prevent Weldeab from taking his seat in the Assembly. It had become a hotly debated and much-resented issue among the public.[33]

A few days later, Tedla issued two proclamations cancelling the Keren and Geza Kenisha elections. He ruled that, in the Geza Kenisha district, people who were not eligible for registration had been allowed to vote.[34] According to article 46(2) of the Eritrean Constitution, an election result that was challenged needed to be approved by two-thirds of an Assembly vote; and over half of the membership could form a quorum. Rather than following that procedure, Tedla asked his legal advisor, Norman Methven, to find some legal excuse to annul Weldeab's election. Methven could only come up with a flimsy excuse that had little weight. All the same, Tedla insisted on exploiting the opening. The political atmosphere in Asmera became tense as people expected Weldeab and his followers to stage a principled defence of their rights.[35]

But the means for that defence were no longer available. *Dehai*, the only outlet that could have served the purpose, had already been suspended. Even if it had been available, it is doubtful whether Weldeab would have pushed further than he already had. After seven assassination attempts on his life, he was a defenceless man who had turned down a government permit to carry a gun and who had also been poisoned by a guard assigned to him. He thus chose not to contest Tedla's revocation of his remarkable victory.[36]

Tedla had his way. Even the Assembly failed to come to Weldeab's defence. When a new election was scheduled for the same seat, Weldeab declined to register, sure that the election would be rigged. He told the American consul Clark that his chances of continuing his struggle under these circumstances had already been highly compromised as Ethiopia would not tolerate the democratic rights granted to Eritrea. There was no tolerance of criticism, he asserted, and democracy would be set back a hundred years. He had been summoned to Addis Ababa, where he expected to be told to submit to the Emperor or behave himself. Clark thought that Weldeab's belief in the rights and welfare of his people would not permit him to abandon them and bow to the Amhara. He therefore saw no purpose in going to Addis Ababa. He was considering exile, preferably to Britain, if he could secure the means and a visa.[37]

As Wardle-Smith predicted, Weldeab declined to travel to Addis Ababa. Instead he applied for a visa to leave Eritrea. In a letter addressed to Andargatchew, Ethiopia's representative, he reminded him of the seven attempts on his life and requested a passport to go abroad from where he could help his family. After delays, which included a thorough search of his home, the Emperor granted him permission to stay in Sudan for six months, and then return to Addis Ababa and beg his pardon.[38]

As Weldeab got ready to board the aircraft for Khartoum on an August morning in 1953, police inspector Alem Mammo searched him thoroughly once again. With Colonel Wright, Chief of Police for Asmera and Hamasien, his aide Berhane Demoz, and several officials and well-wishers looking on, Weldeab was asked where he had hidden his documents. 'Inside my head,' was his reply. Then, he said in a loud voice, 'Thanks to the Ethiopian Government, I am leaving this country legally with a passport. After a while, someone will sneak out of here illegally.'[39] It was a pointed reference to Tedla, a prediction that turned out to be prophetic as, thirteen years later in 1966, Tedla 'sneaked out' from his ambassadorial post in Sweden to abandon Ethiopia.[40]

In 1987, Weldeab described his feelings as the aircraft took off from Asmera:

> Liberty; a cruel, unworthy sense of liberty. I had saved myself from death. But I knew inside that it was no liberty. I had betrayed Eritrea; I had left it to save myself. I did not feel fully liberated. I had preferred to die; but then, I was betraying my pledge in order to keep living, to save my physical being. So, I felt liberation on the one hand and betrayal on the other.[41]

Along with Ibrahim Sultan and a great majority of former IB and EDF members, Weldeab's name was associated with Eritrean independence. At no point did they accept the UN federal formula, and their struggle to reverse it met with failure and repression. More than anyone else, Weldeab became the symbol of that struggle for Eritrean independence. His exile turned him into an icon of personal strength and survival, who would be emulated by an increasing crop of younger nationalists and future revolutionaries.

Weldeab's departure was a great blow to the rising labour movement. Police repression and denial of proper legal protection forced the leadership into underground activities and their confinement to a small office in the vicinity of Albergo Italia, which Tsegai Kahsai kept open under the camouflage of a business enterprise. After five years of clandestine work, the union had a final showdown with the government.

Signs of Unrest in Eritrea

Trouble in Massawa and Asseb

The suppression of the union could not deter workers in various sectors from confronting their respective managements to fight for their rights. Ever since the railway strike of 1949, the strike had been adopted as an effective tool of expressing grievances. Besides, economic hardship and political uncertainty were creating an atmosphere of suspicion and stress throughout the country. The Eritrean

Government's inability to stand up to Ethiopia's aggressive stance also gradually eroded people's confidence in their officials.

In early 1954, simmering resentment among workers in Massawa and Asseb came to the surface. The troubles began with rumours that the salt mining companies in both ports were planning to introduce machines to facilitate operations. A workforce already suffering from low pay and, especially in Asseb, high food and fuel prices feared they would be replaced by machines and went on strike in protest. In the ensuing clashes with the police, 25 workers were injured and 257 arrested, and 30 were charged with different degrees of offence and sentenced to imprisonment ranging from three to six months.[42] Asseb now joined Asmera and Massawa as a centre of unrest. Besides its economic disadvantages, worries about its administrative status unsettled the population. Its representative in the Assembly, Mohammed Omer Akito, kept reminding his colleagues and the Eritrean Government to exert a conscious effort to save it from Ethiopian designs. Akito's argument was always that, rather than being administered from far-away Massawa, Asseb deserved its own regional administration as the capital of Denkalia. The Asseb incident was never reported by the government press.[43]

About six months later, Haile Selassie decided to travel from Asseb to Massawa by boat for his third visit to Eritrea. Prior to this, Andargatchew received a message from Abebe Bitew, Ethiopian director of the port authority, warning that four natives of Massawa were planning to carry the Union Jack and stage a demonstration on the day of the Emperor's arrival. He also alleged that a plot had been uncovered involving a group of employees from different companies in the port city to harm the Emperor. A total of eleven suspects were identified by name.[44] Andargatchew did not bother to prove Abebe Bitew's allegations. On the pretext of protecting the Emperor for the duration of his visit, he dispatched a contingent of the Ethiopian army and put Massawa under military control.

At the same time, dock workers in Asseb went on strike over demands for a pay rise. Following negotiations, a 20% increase and a return to work were agreed upon. Overstepping his authority, the Ethiopian military commander in Asseb ordered the businesses concerned to cancel the agreement, which they tried to evade by continuing to make salary payments secretly. Refusing to settle for nothing less than an open and legally recognised pay rise, the workers continued their strike. Because of the tension created, the commander brought 150 Ethiopian nationals (Gurage) from Ethiopia and replaced the striking workers. Their attempt to demonstrate led to a confrontation with the armed soldiers, who fired at the protesters indiscriminately. Three Eritreans died instantly and five were wounded. Reporting the incident for *Dehai* several weeks later, the journalist and eyewitness A. Denkeli wrote: 'The Ethiopian commander of the army in Asseb is intervening and deciding arbitrarily on all internal affairs of the port city. Worse still, the soldiers under his command carry rifles and machine guns at the ready, as if an enemy attack is imminent and they are in active self-defence, thus killing innocent and defenceless Eritreans without any cause whatsoever.'[45]

The British Ambassador to Ethiopia, Douglas Busk, who was notified of the killings by the manager of the Bess company in Asseb, wrote about the incident to his superiors in London.[46] Busk condemned the army action as the result of bad administration and an ignorant form of conflict resolution. He decried the absence of an effective response other than punishment and the lack of any rational handling of such problems. He also noted that Musa Gaas, the Eritrean Administrator of Asseb, who had proposed the pay rise, was entangled in a dispute with the commander, a confrontation that was complicated by Afar hatred for Ethiopia. Busk concluded that, in Ethiopia, a workers' strike was seen not as a manifestation of social discontent but as a 'coup d'état' or an affront to the 'divine right of kings'.[47] As long as Ethiopia remained feudal, strikes and coups d'état would be difficult to separate. He predicted that the time would come when the rulers would regret their repressive ways and future political propagandists would praise the 'Asseb martyrs'.[48]

Back in Massawa, the unrest, which had calmed down owing to Haile Selassie's presence, erupted again after he left. The immediate cause was Ethiopia's attempt to implement a disputed federal directive requiring foreigners to possess a federal ID card. Since Massawans saw this as interference in internal Eritrean affairs, public protests led to yet another confrontation with the army units still in the city. According to Arthur Reid of the UN Tribunal, an unspecified number of people were killed and injured in the ensuing shootings.[49]

15

THE FIRST YEAR OF THE FEDERATION

Tedla's Administration Is Tested

Andargatchew's Speech to the Assembly

In April 1953, the Eritrean Assembly moved to its permanent building, the former Fascist headquarters and today's Ministry of Education, on Asmera's main street. On the 27th of the same month, Andargatchew delivered his first speech from the throne. Most accounts of Andargatchew's rejection of the Federation cite the 1955 speech from the throne in which he declared that no distinction was to be made between 'the affairs of Eritrea and Ethiopia'. But he had already made himself abundantly clear in his maiden address of 1953:

> To begin with, each one of you must know that Eritrea has from ancient times been part of Ethiopia. It used to be called 'the land of Hamasien'. For seventy years, this country had been separated from Ethiopia. However, after a long struggle and bloodshed that has proved its Ethiopian identity to the world, it has united with its mother since Meskerem 1 1945 [11 September 1952]. All Eritreans should realize and believe without any doubt that, as of Meskerem 1, they have merged with their Ethiopian mother, brothers, blood and race ... Because the language [*sic*] 'federation' is alien to our country, there are some who think that Eritrea is separate from Ethiopia. This comes from the lack of knowledge or understanding of the language 'federation'.

Andargatchew then went on to urge the representatives to adopt his definition of federation:

> Starting from Meskerem 1, Eritrea is a domain of Ethiopia ... As part of Ethiopia, it has been given the right of internal administration by the United Nations, ratified by His Imperial Majesty. This is what has been named 'Federation'. There is no name called 'Ethiopia and Eritrea'. There is only Eritrea as a part of Ethiopia. It is completely wrong to make references to 'Ethiopia and Eritrea'. It must be washed out of everyone's spirit ... There are some people who, for their own benefit, desire to live within one Ethiopia without respecting or helping to enforce Imperial Ethiopia's laws and this is neither beneficial nor possible.

Vague as it was, the last sentence seemed to refer to Tedla Bairu, confirming rumours that a rift was growing between them. Andargatchew also set the tone for tackling all the issues and criticisms that Eritreans directed against his Federal Government. After claiming that, on the contrary, the Emperor was being blamed in Ethiopia for partiality because of the special status that he accorded Eritrea, he went on to deny every complaint directed against his office. He placed Ethiopian payments of Eritrea's share of customs revenues at the top of his list and called it 'a gift to Eritrea'. A US grant of $125,000 to the Eritrean Government was also designated an Ethiopian gift. Alleging that Ethiopia had covered Eritrean railway debts of 500,000 birr, he charged that Eritrea had cost Ethiopia 3,700,000 birr in the eight-month association between the two countries. The amount included Eritrea's share of customs duties and excluded the railway revenues Ethiopia had collected since its takeover of that sector in September 1952.

Andargatchew further denied that market prices had increased as a result of the unfavourable currency exchange between the East Africa shilling and the Ethiopian birr and the hike in customs duties. To prove his point, as the American consul Edward Clark commented, he selected seven out of over sixty items that had shown no price change and declared the rumours baseless.[1] Clark noted further that the Ethiopians were well aware of the political discontent and economic malaise in Eritrea and that Andargatchew's speech was a warning that he would employ all the power and authority available to him to suppress opposition.[2]

The president of the Assembly, Ali Rad'ai, who met Tedla Bairu immediately after Andargatchew's speech, was among the first to voice his indignation. He told the Chief Executive that since Ethiopia was unwilling to accommodate Eritrea's rights under the Federal Act, he saw no purpose in continuing in office. He proposed to resign, but Tedla dissuaded him.

Inside the Assembly, where many members were agitated by the content and tone of the speech, Ibrahim Sultan proposed a debate on the matter. Ali Rad'ai blocked Ibrahim's suggestion, citing a technicality, and the discussion never took place. Even Ibrahim refrained from pushing for his proposal, thereby raising the suspicion that Ethiopia's demeanour and aversion to public criticism were instilling fear inside the Assembly and elsewhere in the country.[3] Fear may have been a factor for some of the Assembly members, but, according to Mohammed Omer Akito, there was also a lack of basic understanding of the political process.

> Educated Muslims and Christians were not elected into the Assembly. Western Eritrea sent only traditional *nazirs* who could not read or write even in Arabic. There was one highly educated man in the Assembly, *Abba* Habtemariam Nugurru, whom I will never forget. There was also Teklehaimanot Bokru, but he became Secretary of Finance. The rest were illiterate. Only Yasin Batok and I spoke good Arabic. Ali Rad'ai used to call Arabic 'the language of Akito and Batok'. That was our parliament; it had no real content.[4]

Saleh Musa Abudawd echoed Akito's observation by describing most members as old men 'wrapped in their shawls [*gabbi*] or cloaks covering their noses, peering over them'. For them, politics was a forbidden subject banned by the Emperor. Akito, Said Sefaf of Ghinda'e, Mohammed Berhanu of Mendefera and Saleh Ashekih of Keren, whom he joined, were the young dissenters within the Assembly.[5]

Dehai's closure, Weldeab's exile and the disruption of the labour movement created such a glaring void in the exercise of democratic rights that an atmosphere of resignation seems to have taken hold of the Assembly and Asmera in particular. Confined mainly to Asmera, Massawa, Keren and Asseb, political activity remained removed from the countryside. The British consul John Wardle-Smith was partly right when he said that, as long as the Eritrean farmer harvested a good crop, his cow produced a calf, and his daughter got married, he paid little attention to other events around him.[6] This would change in due course.

The uncertainty also led to shifts in political alliances within the Assembly, with some unionists and federalists changing sides. As Akito repeatedly pointed out, there were some in the Assembly, on both sides, who would sell their souls for rank and money, a weakness that the federal authorities never failed to exploit. Years later, Teklehaimanot Bokru, Secretary of Finance under Tedla, reminisced about the embarrassing display of sycophancy and greed that Eritrean dignitaries staged to outdo each other in the competition for Ethiopian favour. They would go to the Asmera Palace to blacken each other and flatter the Amhara, and in so doing the former confidants of Andargatchew became lowly informants and common spies in the backrooms of the Palace. The Ethiopians easily turned them into 'instruments for weakening and, ultimately, abrogating the Federation'.

As federal interference intensified, so did pressure on Tedla to try to salvage the Federation.[7]

Pressure from Within

A series of seemingly unconnected events and signs combined to create tension between the Eritrean and Federal governments. First, rumours that Tedla's rival for the post of Chief Executive, *Dejazmatch* Abraha Tessema, was planning to take advantage of the political flux became a cause for official concern. Later developments revealed where this would end. Second, the Federal Government was alleged to have threatened groups of Eritreans who sought to appeal to the UN on account of Ethiopian excesses. Third, the Sudanese alleged that Ethiopian agents had approached Muslim businessmen to fund an impending Eritrean annexation.[8] As rumours of annexation reached the ears of the public, Andargatchew panicked. On 22 March, he called Tedla and asked him to proclaim a state of emergency. Tedla was on the verge of obeying when Eritrea's Commissioner of Police, Colonel David Cracknell, refused to consent as no grounds existed for such a measure. Cracknell was convinced that the rumours about annexation had been spread by Italian residents.[9] Added to *Dehai*'s closure and Weldeab's exile, the rumours had the effect of intensifying anti-Ethiopian sentiment.

Cracknell visited Haregot, then director of Internal Affairs, to discuss the situation. As a businessman and philanthropist, Haregot's influence went beyond the sphere of politics. Cracknell explained that he had suspended *Dehai* for its extremist, anti-Ethiopian propaganda, which had upset the Emperor. Haregot did not disagree. He was more forthcoming in expressing his resentment over the behaviour of Ethiopian authorities and the prevailing political situation. Andargatchew and his federal colleagues, Haregot said, were devoid of any understanding of or desire for cooperation. He thought that this emanated from their own inflated sense of self-esteem and authority. As he believed the Emperor was unaware of his officials' behaviour, Haregot sought to press Tedla to meet the Emperor and inform him of the problems. These included the federal authorities' dictatorial directives printed in the newspapers, their unilateral conscription of Eritreans into the Ethiopian army, the choice buildings that they had confiscated, the arrogant tone of their written communications with Eritrean authorities, and, above all, their ineptness, inefficiency and suspicion about everything Eritrean.

On another note, Haregot spoke of a move by the Ethiopians to reorganise the Unionist Party (UP) and turn it into a more potent force by recruiting the old Andinet president Gebreselassie Garza, a disgruntled employee at the Eritrean Labour Office. Haregot did not think that attempts to annex Eritrea to Ethiopia would succeed at a time when anti-Ethiopian feeling was at its peak. He said that the Eritrean Government was determined to implement the Federation, provided the people remained united.[10]

The next morning, Haregot called Cracknell to his office, probably after conferring with Tedla. He told him that, like all Eritrean unionists, he had supported union with Ethiopia, not out of any love for the Ethiopians, but only because it was 'more expedient, a means to an end'. Coming from a unionist leader, Haregot's admission was revealing. He derided the Ethiopian authorities for their 'inefficiency, intolerance and egoism'. The only person within the Federal Government who cooperated with the Eritrean Government was an Eritrean by birth, the deputy representative Asfaha, but he too worked under the thumb of Andargatchew.[11]

From what Haregot told Cracknell, it seems that Tedla's recent federalist leanings were not hidden from the Ethiopians. But nothing that he did or said at this juncture gave any hint of his innermost thinking. On the contrary, his continuous blockage of Assembly proposals and discussions touching on federal trespasses and excesses made him look more like an agent of the demise of the Federation. His colleagues were at the same time becoming more outspoken.

Ali Rad'ai, who had threatened to resign his Assembly presidency, called the British consul Wardle-Smith to his office and confided in him. Working with Ethiopians, he told him, was so difficult that Eritrea was in decline. The Ethiopians were not responding to Eritrean correspondence and were bypassing Eritrean officials at all levels. The Office of the Emperor's Representative was in particular so uncooperative that the Eritrean Government was not accorded due attention and the Federation was not functioning as it should.

Wardle-Smith suggested that the Eritreans were too passive before the Ethiopians and that was because they did not know them very well. 'If you kowtow to them, they will side-line you.' Eritreans were not standing firm in demanding what was rightfully theirs. Ali Rad'ai agreed but stressed that many Eritreans were in agreement that the UN's federal formula had been flawed to begin with. If a hyena and a goat live in the same shed, he told the consul, the result would be obvious. There should have been a UN commission in place to supervise the implementation of the Federation—to put up a fence between the hyena and the goat. That opportunity had been lost. 'What can be done now? All the cards are in Ethiopian hands. Eritreans have no power.'

Wardle-Smith advised that the anti-Ethiopian feeling in Eritrea could lead to the strengthening of the opposition. That could, in turn, provoke Ethiopia to undertake repressive measures. Therefore he suggested that Haile Selassie be told of the activities of his federal officials, so he could put a stop to them.

At the conclusion of their meeting, Wardle-Smith asked why the Eritrean Government was suppressing those Assembly members who stood up on behalf of Eritrea's federal rights. Ali Rad'ai responded that the matter was highly sensitive. Any issue critical of the Federal Government was opposed by Andargatchew, who would ask the Chief Executive to block it. The consul concluded that the Eritrean Government lacked the power to tolerate any form of opposition from the Assembly.[12]

On 2 April 1953, the evening of his meeting with Ali Rad'ai, Wardle-Smith hosted Tedla at his residence and noted from the start that Tedla looked distressed and unsure of himself. His financial advisor, Wilson Heathcote, had submitted his resignation and Tedla had come to ask Wardle-Smith's help in having him change his mind. They then turned to politics and Wardle-Smith asked why the Emperor was not being told of his federal officials' excesses. Tedla expressed his confidence in the Emperor's goodwill and his desire to see the Federation work. It was not working, he said, because the Ethiopian authorities in Eritrea were not fit colleagues or partners. Tedla identified Andargatchew as the main problem but refrained from putting all the blame on him. He himself had just returned from a tour of the provinces where his morale had been boosted by an enthusiastic popular reception. He told his host that his opponents were concentrated in the cities; he had the support of the rural areas.

Wardle-Smith cautioned that the Chief Executive should be wary of popular opinion. The problem, in the consul's opinion, was that Tedla was unable to resolve his differences with the Ethiopians. The issue of Eritrea's share of customs, posts, railways and other revenues should be settled. Those were the people's demands and he needed to show his people that he was fighting for their concerns. He pushed

Tedla to go to the Emperor. Tedla agreed that something had to be done. But, he said, he also wanted to give the Ethiopians time to realise and correct their mistakes. Wardle-Smith thought to himself that he feared Tedla would create any excuse not to do what was necessary.[13]

Tedla also faced criticism from the few advisors left by the British to help the Administration in the economic, financial and legal spheres. It was ironic that the British, who were responsible for the bankrupt economy inherited by the Eritrean Government, should be the main critics of Tedla's prevarication in taking steps to right the situation. The financial advisor Wilson Heathcote had proposed that to improve the Eritrean economy, its fair share of customs revenues should be secured and excessive taxation decreased. But when no steps were taken in those directions, he submitted his resignation. Tedla's dominant role in the government, Heathcote wrote, could not be exaggerated. His secretaries had turned into common clerks who could not decide even on minor issues and the cabinet never met. The Chief Executive took no steps to implement the democratic principles of the Eritrean Constitution. On the contrary, by creating excuses, he closed down the only independent newspaper, thereby curbing freedom of expression; he blocked the Chief Auditor's report from reaching the Assembly; and he vetoed the election of his political opponents. Based on this evidence, Heathcote declared Tedla a weak person who could not carry out his federal responsibility and who was intent on weakening Eritrea in order to speed up the process of annexation.[14]

However, Tedla did make some attempt at taking a firm stand. According to the Finance Secretary, Teklehaimanot Bokru:

> Our main quarrel with the Ethiopians was money. They began to owe us millions of birr. When I first went to Addis, the ministers mocked me. 'Why are you here, *Grazmatch*?' they asked me. I replied, 'To take our share of the customs, port and railway revenues as provided in the United Nations decision.' They teased me, jabbing each other with their elbows. 'Why are you laughing? This is a serious matter and I am here to discuss it seriously,' I protested. They told me to come back after one month.
>
> I went back at the appointed time, but the derision continued. They said to me, 'Has not Eritrea become part of Ethiopia? How can it have its own budget? Ethiopia is the mother and the mother gives and denies as it sees fit. What you are proposing is impossible to even consider.'

When Tedla heard of this, he referred the matter to the Eritrean Assembly, where Teklehaimanot related his encounter with the Ethiopian officials. But a strong Ethiopian lobby at the Assembly, led by the rising UP leader *Melake Selam* Dimetros Gebremariam, took the Ethiopian line, 'a mother gives, and a mother denies', and succeeded in closing the discussion.[15]

A second advisor to clash with Tedla was the Auditor General, Allen Smith. Like Heathcote, he proposed in his report to the Assembly the need for securing customs revenues and decreasing taxation rates. Rather than following procedure and presenting the report to the Assembly, Ali Rad'ai postponed it until after Andargatchew's speech in which, as we saw, he pre-empted the Assembly's discussion. Smith was removed from his position to become the financial advisor; he resigned later and left the country the following year. Next to leave was Norman Methven, the legal advisor, who had been constantly asked to find grounds for blocking matters unwanted by the federal authorities from reaching the Assembly. He too resigned in protest.

The departure of five British advisors between 1954 and 1955 was something that a number of members of the Assembly, especially Dimetros and his core UP group, had been pushing for on the grounds that Eritreans could easily fill their roles at much less expense. In reality, federal officials resented the advisors' adherence to the Federal Act and wanted them out, spreading the rumour at the same time that the Emperor was displeased with their roles.[16] The advisors had stood up for all the demands that the opposition was making and, to that extent, the former's departure was the latter's loss. Clearly, Tedla was being squeezed between two loyalties, with pressure from the federal officials getting the better of him. While in this tight situation, another favour from the Emperor brought him some relief.

Tedla Becomes a Dejazmatch

On 5 May 1953, the anniversary of Haile Selassie's return from exile, Tedla was invited to Addis Ababa to become a *dejazmatch*. This was a high-ranking Ethiopian title, equivalent to a general in the military hierarchy and a step below a duke. All previous higher ranks in Eritrea had been Italian investitures that the Ethiopians did not recognise. Being the first to receive the honour from the Emperor himself conferred a special status on Tedla. Two of the highest awards of the Empire, the Ethiopian Star of Honour and the Ethiopian Great Cordon, also decorated his chest. The Chief Executive was flattered by the Emperor's generosity. As the American consul observed, the honour was meant to exploit Tedla's feelings of loyalty to Haile Selassie.[17]

The Eritrean Assembly in Action and Confrontation

Tedla Addresses the Assembly

It took Tedla nine months after taking office to appear before the Assembly on 22 June 1953. His speech was more descriptive than substantive and avoided the burning issues occupying the Assembly. He acknowledged that people's expectations were not being met and that his government was being blamed for this. But he pointed to the change of currency and the bankrupt economy Eritrea had inherited as the chief causes of the problem. After praising the warm reception he had received on his provincial tours, Tedla enumerated some of the economic and social achievements of his administration by concentrating more on developments in the educational, health, security and trade sectors.[18] On the pressing financial and revenue issues, he told the Assembly that the Federal Council had discussed the matter in Addis Ababa and submitted their views to the Emperor. He explained that communication with the Office of the Emperor's Representative had thus far been oral and needed to be written and formal. A financial committee composed of both Eritreans and Ethiopians had been formed to attend to all issues and it was already engaged in consultation.[19] Tedla called for questions at the end of his speech, but no one stepped forward.

It is difficult to explain why the Assembly, which had consistently demanded his presence, failed to take him to task. Last-minute absences, changes of mind and shifts in position had reduced the level of trust between members. It could be that no one wanted to cause embarrassment. It could also be that members had been bribed to support the government or remain silent. Whatever the reason, it was a missed opportunity that was to tarnish the Assembly's reputation.

There were at least two outstanding issues that Tedla could have been asked about: the status of the port of Asseb and the fate of the suspended *Dehai*. Since Federation, Asseb had been increasingly removed from the control of the Eritrean central government. Commodity prices there, including foodstuffs and fuel, were inexplicably higher than in any other part of Eritrea and Ethiopia, causing the population economic distress. Its administration was steadily slipping away from the hands of the Eritrean Interior Ministry. Rejecting every government excuse, its representative, Mohammed Omer Akito, openly accused the authorities of creating the conditions for the annexation of Asseb by Ethiopia.[20]

The *Dehai* issue was more straightforward. To a question from the Assembly, the Interior Secretary explained that *Dehai* was shut down because its editor had been publishing articles of a subversive nature. A few days before Tedla's appearance at the Assembly, the Supreme Court of Eritrea had dismissed the charges against the editors. Tedla left the Assembly without having to respond to these questions, which had already been put to him in writing.

About a week later, Ibrahim Sultan, who had been silent for several weeks, presented a set of written questions on matters that he said should have been explained by the Chief Executive. These included the usual issues of Eritrea's share of federal revenues; its usurped rights in respect of port, railway and communications administration; appropriate Eritrean participation in the Federal Government; the exact functions of the Federal Council; and Eritrea's proportional membership in the Ethiopian parliament. In a written reply, Tedla asserted that railway, post, telegraph and customs administration was legally Ethiopia's responsibility and that the employment of Eritreans in the lower levels of management ought to be seen as an advantage. As for the proportionality of Eritrean membership in the Ethiopian parliament, he argued that Eritreans constituted one-twelfth of the population of Ethiopia; five representatives in the Ethiopian parliament was therefore more than adequate representation. At a time when Omer Qadi was voicing his concerns about the status of the Federal Council, Tedla refrained from commenting on its activities. He merely pointed out that its main task was to give advice, which 'could be taken or rejected'.[21]

The issue of the Eritrean flag had become highly sensitive. A youth organisation, clandestinely formed, was agitating to uphold its status as the symbol of autonomy and nationalism and to defend its existence. Ibrahim's question referred to the irregular and inconsistent manner in which the flag was being flown at government buildings and on official occasions, a practice that led to public indignation. He proposed a law to regulate its use. Tedla misunderstood the question and responded, 'There is only one national Ethiopian flag and it takes precedence over the Eritrean flag.'[22] Neither Ibrahim nor his opposition colleagues in the Assembly were happy with Tedla's dismissive responses, and they began to regard him as nothing more than an agent of Ethiopian designs to weaken the Federation. Paradoxically, UP annexationists like Dimetros were also unhappy with him, as they saw his occasional moves to uphold the Federal Act as an impediment to their plans.

In the following weeks, the Assembly and the Chief Executive were involved in further confrontations over less controversial issues and proposals. The election proclamation for a new Legislative Assembly was postponed because of disagreements. Strangely, it was the regulation dealing with the death penalty, for which the Assembly proposed public hangings and firing squads to deter potential criminals, that soured Tedla's relationship with that body. Tedla returned the bill for reconsideration, arguing that public executions were barbaric and that they would tarnish Eritrea's name in the eyes of the world. As a progressive stand, Tedla's amendments should have been appreciated by the Assembly. But the opposition, led by Ibrahim, Akito, Bezabih and *Qadi* Ali, seemed to be set on opposing anything that came from him. The ensuing arguments became so acrimonious that Ali Rad'ai adjourned the session for almost one week.[23] This was the moment when Tedla's relationship with the Assembly entered on a collision course.

Consultations of the Joint Finance Committee

As Tedla mentioned in his speech, the Ethiopian and Eritrean joint finance committee held its initial session in May and June 1953. The discussions were wide-ranging as they included new issues like federal taxation; federal duties on wine, alcohol and salt; and the payment of debts left behind by the British Administration and similar impositions that the Eritreans felt were burdensome. However, the issue of Eritrea's share of customs revenue immediately became the focal point.

The Eritreans suggested that in order to determine Eritrea's share as stipulated in the Federal Act, the exact quantity of commodities destined for and originating from Eritrea must be known. For this, they proposed setting up checkpoints at Adi Quala and Senafe, the Eritrean towns on the two main roads linking the two countries. The Ethiopians rejected the proposal. Instead, they claimed, Ethiopia was spending 38 million birr for the upkeep of the Ethiopian army stationed in Eritrea, and since the army was defending the Federation, Eritrea must carry its share of the expenses. As the Eritreans asked for time to consider the matter, the Ethiopians further proposed the merger of the industrial excise tax, a move that would put Eritrea's right of internal taxation in jeopardy. The Eritreans rejected the proposal. The Ethiopian demands did not stop there. The Federal Government had inherited a debt of £980,000 from the British Administration, they claimed, and they believed that Eritrea should cover its share of that cost too. The Eritrean response was that the Ethiopian demands assumed that Eritrea was benefiting from its association with Ethiopia and asked for evidence to prove it.

If anything, all existing evidence pointed in the opposite direction. Ethiopia had been stalling on the payment to Eritrea of even its revenue shares under the temporary British plan. That amounted to 4,627,316 birr a year, payable in three-month instalments. By March 1953, Eritrea had received 1,200,000 birr, only half of what was due to it for the previous six months. As a result, its cash deposits had dwindled to a mere 200,000 birr.[24] Unable to pay salaries to government employees, Tedla had to operate on an austerity budget and, as a result, he and his cabinet colleagues volunteered to cut their salaries in half for the first year.[25]

As the suspicion grew that Ethiopia sought to impoverish Eritrea into submission, the Ethiopian committee's financial advisor, Stanisław Kirkor, voiced his surprise at Eritrean resistance,[26] and argued that it was a beneficiary of the arrangement especially from trade and industrial revenues and that it had the capacity to pay the proposed amounts. The British consul Wardle-Smith disagreed. He pointed out that trade and production in Eritrea had been limited to beer and salt and the climate for investment was non-existent. Kirkor, Wardle-Smith noted, was working to bankrupt Eritrea.[27]

The Ethiopians also tried to put pressure on Eritrean officials to submit. Minassie Lemma, the head of the Ethiopian committee, expressed his anger towards Tedla Bairu, who, he said, had refused to sign a permanent agreement on the settlement of the customs revenue problem. According to a British diplomat, Minassie's open talk about Tedla indicated that the Ethiopians harboured reservations about the Chief Executive.[28] But Tedla stood his ground. Indeed, Ethiopian disregard of the Federal Act was so blatant that he had no other choice but to oppose. Customs duties had been raised significantly, but Ethiopia was the sole beneficiary. The Eritrean public were in open complaint over what it saw as the pillage of their country.

In his general report for 1952/3, the financial advisor Allen Smith estimated that Ethiopia owed Eritrea 2,037,933 birr for that fiscal year alone. Smith urged the Eritrean Government to fight hard for the rectification of the problem.[29] The

Assembly too was preoccupied with the matter. In December 1953, the finance committee, led by Beyene Zahlai, gave the following report:

> The amount of 5,784,145 birr set aside for payment of 15 months of customs revenues (4,627,316 per year) for commodities originating from and destined to Eritrea falls far short of the actual amount due to Eritrea. The above figure is based on the duties imposed by the British Administration. Since the current federal duties are much higher, Eritrea's share should increase proportionately. Nine per cent of the customs revenues levied on commodities originating from and destined to Eritrea should be paid to the Eritrean Government. This is the main source of revenue for the Eritrean Government.[30]

Tedla and his Finance Secretary, Teklehaimanot, were credited for their fight on the issue, but Ethiopian intransigence would not allow them any success. In the meantime, patience was running low in several quarters of the country.

The First Anniversary of the Federation

As the first anniversary of the Federation approached, rumours of an impending annexation of Eritrea by Ethiopia created a new atmosphere of apprehension. Speculation by all the foreign consuls in Eritrea of trouble by the opposition also made the rounds, adding to the tension already in place. Concern about Ethiopian disregard of the Federal Act and the Eritrean Constitution was voiced by other sources as well. On 16 April 1953, UN Secretary General Dag Hammarskjöld's representative, the Canadian Arthur Reid, opened the UN Tribunal in Asmera to follow up on the implementation of the Federation and Somalia's trusteeship under Italy. His duty was to report to the Secretary General on any shortcomings in the transfer of powers.

In June, Reid received a notable complaint from the Swede, Judge Hans Nordström, president of the Federal High Court in Eritrea, who cited three areas where the Federal Act was being overridden. First, Eritrean litigants were bypassing Eritrean courts to sue in the federal courts, thereby extending the latter's jurisdiction into non-federal cases. Second, he told Reid that the federal courts promulgated by Proclamation 130 had been set up outside the framework of the Federal Act and their authority could therefore be legally challenged. Third, Nordström thought that the British Administration had acted beyond its mandate under the Federal Act when it passed railway and internal Eritrean communications into Ethiopian jurisdiction. Nordström had already notified federal officials and the Swedish Government of his concerns. He thought the UN too should be informed. Reid communicated the message to his Secretary General.[31] But no response came.

The opening of the UN Tribunal in Asmera gave rise to hopes of a renewal of UN involvement in Eritrea. Little did people know that Arthur Reid's mandate was limited to registering discrepancies in the apportionment mainly of material property between the federal partners. But his office was besieged by Assembly members, political activists and even government functionaries complaining about the status and fate of the Federation. The first anniversary of the Federation thus arrived in the middle of this period of high emotion and uncertainty.

Federation Day should have been celebrated on 15 September, the date on which it had come into effect. At Ethiopia's insistence, it was moved to 11 September or St Yohannes Day, the Geez (Ethiopian) New Year, when a huge national Orthodox Christian event is observed in both Eritrea and Ethiopia. This was a smart move meant to submerge the Federation within a day of traditional song and dance performances and family get-togethers. People celebrated their traditional feast, giving little attention to the lukewarm gathering in front of the Assembly building, where Andargatchew made a subdued speech stressing the oneness and indivisibility of Ethiopia. Fessehatsion Haile spoke on behalf of the Chief Executive.[32] Throughout Eritrea, the message of the Federation was muted.

Fessehatsion gave the speech because Tedla had chosen to go to Addis Ababa. According to Zewde Retta, he went there for a repeat of the honour he had received the previous year and to stay away from Andargatchew and his deputy, Asfaha. As a protégé of the Minister of the Pen, Weldegiorgis, he also hoped that he would be granted Imperial financial assistance; little did he know that the former strongman's days were already numbered. Uncharacteristically, Weldegiorgis referred the matter to the Finance Minister, Mekonnen Habtewold, Aklilu's brother. Mekonnen advised Tedla to change his request from financial assistance to the opening of an agricultural college in Eritrea.[33] Zewde also claims that, in a private meeting, Tedla told the Emperor that he was unable to work with Andargatchew and his deputy and that he requested they be replaced. Haile Selassie replied, 'As long as we are around, your work will never be compromised. No antagonist will ever attack you. The representative's case and your responsibilities will be weighed appropriately and be handled accordingly in the future.'[34] This vague promise from the master of ambiguity apparently pleased the embattled Tedla.

At the Imperial celebration of the New Year, Tedla was given a place of honour and delivered a speech that included his request for an agricultural college in Eritrea. The Emperor granted it,[35] but the agricultural college never saw the light of day. Before going home with vague promises, Zewde Retta relates, Tedla was visited at his hotel by Eritrean-born officials of the Ethiopian Government who urged him to work for the success of the Federation and reminded him that the Federation would strengthen Ethiopia and that it would not pose a challenge to the Emperor's power. Zewde claims that this advice was one of the factors that pushed Tedla towards the federalist cause.[36] Assuming that Zewde's conclusion has some truth to it, how much of a federalist was Tedla? The test was coming soon.

Ibrahim Sultan and the Opposition

On the day of the New Year and Federation celebrations, the Emperor's representative, the consuls of the US, Britain, France and Italy, and Arthur Reid received an identical unsigned petition. Its contents may be summarised as follows: Ethiopia should return all the authority it had usurped to Eritrea. The jurisdiction of the federal courts in Eritrea was to terminate immediately. The undisciplined soldiers of the Ethiopian army who were abusing and harassing Eritrean women were to return to Ethiopia. The Emperor's representative was to stop intervening in internal Eritrean affairs. Should these demands not be met, the pamphlet concluded:

> We will stand against the Government of Haile Selassie, which allows no individual freedom to human beings. Trusting in God, we have decided to stand against this government for the sake of our country and its honour. When we notify you of our resolve, it is with the belief that the United Nations will come up with a solution to our problems.[37]

Although it was written in Tigrinya, most of the consuls suspected that Ibrahim Sultan, who was then re-emerging after a period of relative silence, was the behind-the-scenes instigator, while the front people were newly converted federalists of the Andinet party.[38] Cracknell noted that the disintegration taking place within Andinet was significant. The slogan among the Andinet, he said, was no longer 'Union or death' but rather 'Federation or death!'[39] Highly placed Eritrean Government officials, both Muslims and Christians, were openly voicing their opposition to the Ethiopian Government.

According to the American consul Clark, Haregot was constantly expressing resentment towards Ethiopia. The Secretary of the Economy and Tedla's occasional deputy as Chief Executive, Fessehatsion Haile, was also in league with Haregot. In fact, Fessehatsion's dispute with the deputy Ethiopian representative, Asfaha, over who should take precedence at a small public gathering became a public manifestation of the simmering conflict between the two governments.[40]

In the middle of this, Ibrahim Sultan of the Muslim League (ML), Mohammed Omer Qadi of the Independent Muslim League, and Ahmed Abdelkader Bashir of the National Muslim Party wrote an appeal to the United Nations. Besides the points raised earlier by an anonymous petitioner, they added the rights denied Eritrean Muslims as an additional complaint. ML-WP was the only Muslim organisation that did not sign the appeal.[41]

Although the Eritrean Government refrained from arresting the signatories, they were summoned by security officials and questioned before being allowed to proceed with their petition. Reid duly transmitted the message to the UN. According to his own testimony, none of his transmissions received any UN attention. He also informed the Secretary General of signs and talks of imminent annexation that were of concern even to UP leaders. The UN remained silent.[42]

Nevertheless, the Muslim leaders' appeal became the object of a series of attacks by the UP paper, *Ethiopia*, which characterised them as people possessed with 'religious malaise' who sought to 'wipe out the name Ethiopia from Eritrea and, if possible, even from the world at large'.[43] It condemned the petitioners for working towards a return to the 'terrible' divisive politics of the 1940s, and called for peace and religious harmony.[44] Emboldened by the paper's editorial tone, some contributors began to submit inflammatory articles attacking Muslims and warning that Christian 'love, humility and tolerance' had its limits.[45] *Zemen*, the Eritrean government paper, stepped in and published a piece by a respondent whose voice of reason and moderation reflected the attitude of the silent majority:

> If there had not been love, humility and tolerance between Eritrean Muslims and Christians, they would have been like those from Asia to Africa who have found no remedy to their religious fighting and have become the playground of aliens. Eritreans would not have been able to reach this level of freedom and brotherhood. The love and tolerance between Muslims and Christians of the past twelve years is a cause to rejoice, not to regret or be embarrassed about.[46]

Did Tedla Bairu give benign support to the opposition? Ibrahim and his fellow petitioners were not detained as they might have been under other circumstances. Instead, they were allowed to telegram their complaints to the UN. The article in *Zemen* was also diametrically opposed to the line taken by the advocates of annexation. The signs were there, albeit vague, but Tedla remained aloof, silent and secretive throughout the weeks following his anniversary visit to Addis Ababa. Strangely, though, at a time when he could have won sympathy, he became entangled in a matter that was to damage his reputation and negatively affect his hold on power.

The Case of Abraha Tessema and His Brothers

Abraha Tessema, Tedla's rival for the post of Chief Executive in the previous election and the leader of the Liberal Unionist Party, had been lurking on the side until his name started to reappear around April 1953. The British consul Wardle-Smith, who was in constant contact with him, reported that Abraha and his followers had started to campaign against Tedla and that the campaign had a religious and regional aspect. Tedla was an Evangelical Protestant from Hamasien; Abraha was Coptic Orthodox from Akeleguzai. Adding to their previous union versus independence struggle, the old rivalry was reignited. Tedla's resentment of Abraha heightened when word reached him that Ethiopia was developing a keen interest in the latter.[47]

The rumours turned out to be true: Abraha confirmed to Wardle-Smith that he had been summoned to Addis Ababa for unspecified reasons. The consul noted that Abraha was worried on two counts. First, since the Emperor was unhappy with Tedla, he might be asked to form an opposition group to operate under the Emperor's instruction, though Abraha would not accept this. Second, he might be offered a position in Ethiopia in order to remove him from Eritrea; Abraha did not want that either.[48]

What happened in Addis Ababa was not clear, but the overtures that Andargatchew, his federal officials and even the princess were making to Abraha and the Tessema family were there for all to see. Tedla's supporters soon started their own counter-propaganda against Abraha. In their March meeting, Haregot told Cracknell that Abraha had been doing incalculable damage to Eritrea by introducing 'sectarian politics', though he did not give any specifics.[49] The allegation and attendant suspicion and ill-feeling, which could potentially damage the relations between the two regions, Akeleguzai and Hamasien, thus persisted until the strange incident of 14 October 1953.

Late that evening, at about 10 pm, two men, Iyasu Tessema, brother of Abraha, and a well-known Andinet hitman, Mikael Welela, were arrested as they exited the Cinema Odeon in Asmera. Iyasu had a pistol and Mikael a hand grenade in their possession. They were immediately charged with an attempt to assassinate the Chief Executive. Although Tedla's motor car was parked outside, he was nowhere inside or in the vicinity of the cinema. Abraha himself and his son Asberom were arrested as accomplices the next day. Four days later, the Eritrean Assembly voted to condemn the act and to allow police authorities to arrest a third brother and one of its members, *Azmatch* Gebrekidan Tessema, *Ras* Tessema's replacement in the Assembly.[50]

As shock waves reverberated throughout Eritrea, Tedla's supporters sang his praises as a magnanimous leader who had risen above political differences to reinstate his would-be assassins to positions of responsibility. *Ethiopia* condemned the alleged 'ungrateful plotters to eternal reprimand'.[51] However, on the third day of Abraha's arrest, Cracknell met with Attorney General Methven. Both agreed that the available evidence showed that the incident had been staged by Tedla and his supporters in order to discredit the Tessema family.[52] As additional evidence linked Mikael Welela to Tedla, the suspicion grew that he had been planted to discredit Iyasu Tessema.[53]

Abraha, Gebrekidan and Asberom were released after two months of detention, two days before their scheduled court appearance on 21 December. Their case was formally dismissed on that date.[54] Iyasu's case likewise turned out to be a farce when the original charge was dropped for lack of evidence and his sentence for illegal possession of arms was rescinded by the Supreme Court.[55]

It was all a badly scripted drama that embarrassed Tedla and tainted his credibility. Following his release, Abraha met Wardle-Smith and Clark, and vowed to fight for the restoration of the honour and position of his family. He then described Eritrea's existing problems and included some predictions that in hindsight seem prophetic:

- Tedla has become the stooge of the Emperor.

- The absence of freedom of the press is denying the formation of political opposition to Tedla.
- Opposition should have come from the Assembly, but the members are a flock of sheep; for this reason, annexation by Ethiopia will come gradually and Eritrea will become a mere province of Ethiopia.
- People will then realise that they have been condemned; they will rise against their masters and a civil war will follow. This will take many years.
- There is no opposition today because Eritreans are hopelessly divided by religion and race. Muslims, Copts, Catholics and Protestants will not stand together on one political platform; but one day, when they are annexed by Ethiopia, they will understand that they have returned to colonial rule. This will make them unite against Ethiopia.[56]

Abraha's legal battle to restore his name and that of his family never succeeded. Neither the Eritrean courts nor the Federal High Court would accept a criminal charge against the Chief Executive, and he was unsuccessful with a civil suit.[57] The real loser, however, was Tedla. The incident brought into public view his intolerance of any form of internal opposition and his dictatorial tendencies. They were to determine his relations with the Assembly and the public at large and limit his effectiveness in his looming confrontations with Andargatchew. The new challenges of 1954 came with Haile Selassie's third visit to Eritrea starting in February.

Haile Selassie's Third Visit and His Tax Reprieve

Haile Selassie's third visit took him deep into the Western Provinces of Eritrea. From Keren through Akurdet and Barentu to Tesseney, he made speeches, prayed in churches, stopped at mosques, and distributed gifts to the throngs of people welcoming him. In Keren, an old UP leader whom the Emperor later dubbed *Dejazmatch* Idris Lijam claimed to speak for the province when he complained of the doubling and trebling of taxes imposed on the people because of Eritrean and federal dues. He begged the Emperor to act on the matter before leaving Eritrea. On the same day, the Emperor, the Chief Executive and the Assembly received a petition addressed to the Emperor and signed by 105 *nazirs* (district chiefs,) *umdas* (village chiefs) and *sheiks* of the entire province, denouncing Idris Lijam's plea as dishonourable and demanding that it be disregarded. Idris Lijam, said the petition,

> can only represent himself. He has compromised and depreciated the government functions and services that we are responsible for. Above all, the audacity with which he dared to do so in front of Your Majesty surprises us ... If the issue of over-taxation is to be discussed, it should be within the Eritrean Government and the Assembly ... His request contravenes the Eritrean Constitution and Eritrea's autonomy, which is equipped with the ability to handle such simple matters.[58]

1. *Ras* Weldemikael Solomon

2. *Ras* Alula

3. Degiat Bahta Hagos

4. Eritrean askaris amputated by Menelik's order after the Battle of Adwa, 1896

5. Ferdinando Martini

6. Top, Kennedy-Cooke meets Abdelkadir Kebire May 1941; bottom, Stephen Longrigg with Eritrean leaders, 1942

7. The Partitioners, from the top, Douglas Newbold, Hugh Boustead and Frank Stafford

8. British Administrators of Eritrea, top left, J.M Benoy; right, F.G Drew; bottom, Maj. Gen. D.C. Cumming

9. Eritrean leaders of the defunct Tigray-Tigrigni movement, left to right Weldeab Weldemariam, Tessema Asberom, Seyoum MaaSho and Abraha Tessema

10. Samples of the Eritrean infrastructure dismantled and sold off to foreign countries

11. The Unionists, clockwise from top left, Gebremeskel Weldu, Abune Markos, Tedla Bairu and Beyene Beraki

12. Founders of Al Rabita Al Islamiya, clockwise from top left, Mufti Ibrahim Mukhtar, Ibrahim Sultan, Suleiman Ahmed and Hassen Ali

13. Leaders of Eritrea for Eritreans, clockwise from top left, Tessema Asberom, Weldeab Weldemariam, Seyoum Maasho and Abraha Tessema

14. Abdelkader Kebire, major proponent of Eritrean unity and independence, VP of Al Rabita and first martyr of the Eritrean independence movement

15. Funeral Ceremony for victims of August 1946 by Sudanese troops

16. Assassinated leaders of the independence movement, clockwise from top left, Kahsai Malu, Abdelkader Jaber, Vittorio Longhi and Berhe Gebrekidan

17. Ibrahim Sultan's final appeal before a UN committee rejecting the proposed federal merger of Eritrea with Ethiopia

18. Haile Selassie ratifies the Federal Act

19. Awate's surrender to Col. David Cracknell, 1951

20. Eduardo Anze Matienzo, UN Commissioner in Eritrea, 1951–1952

21. The Ethiopians, clockwise from top left, Haile Selassie, Andargatchew Mesai, Aklilu Habteweld and Abiy Abebe

22. Col David Cracknell, first Commissioner of Eritrean Police Force, 1941–1954

23. Leaders of the Eritrean Assembly, clockwise from top left, presidents, Ali Rad'ai, Idris Mohammed Adem and Hamid Ferej; vice presidents, Weldemikael and Dimetros Gebremariam

24. Editors of the EDF newspaper, *Dehai Ertra*, Mohamed Saleh Mahmud, left, and Elias Teklu, right

25. Asfaha Weldemikael, Second Chief Executive of Eritrea, 1955–1962

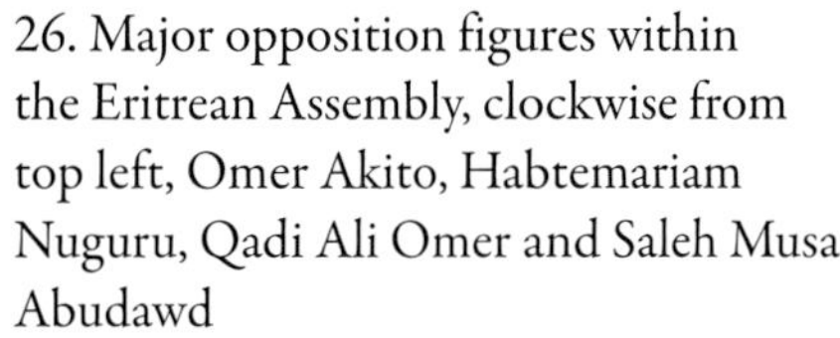

26. Major opposition figures within the Eritrean Assembly, clockwise from top left, Omer Akito, Habtemariam Nuguru, Qadi Ali Omer and Saleh Musa Abudawd

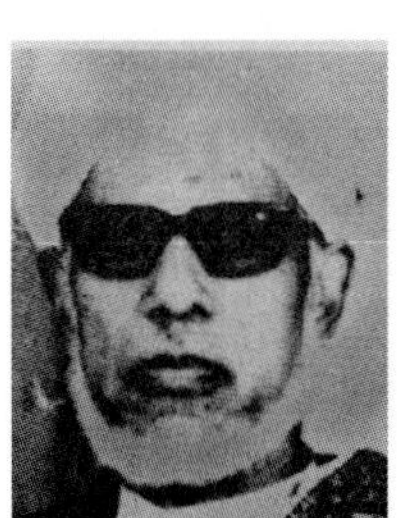

27. Tiku'e Yehdego, student activist, Haraka leader and martyr of the Eritrean armed struggle

28. 1958 nationwide workers' strike in Eritrea marking the end of the first phase of the political struggle

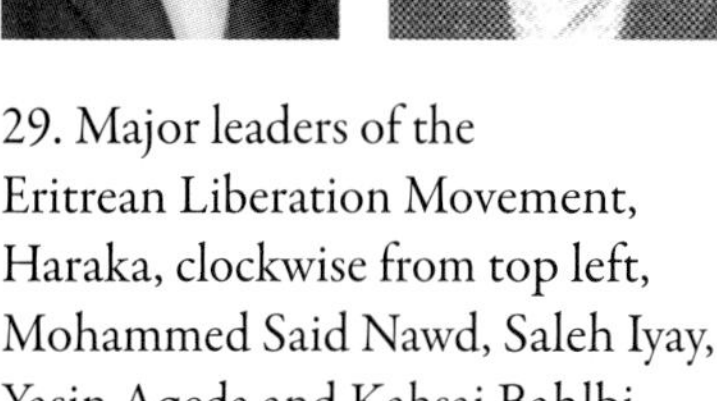

29. Major leaders of the Eritrean Liberation Movement, Haraka, clockwise from top left, Mohammed Said Nawd, Saleh Iyay, Yasin Aqeda and Kahsai Bahlbi

30. Founders of the ELF, left to right, Osman Saleh Sabbe, Idris Mohammed Adem and Idris Gelaydos

31. Hamid Idris Awate

32. Veteran fighters of the ELF, formerly soldiers in the Sudanese army, clockwise from top left, Mohammed Idris Haj, Abu Tayara, Omer Ezaz and Osman Abu Sheneb

33. The triumvirate of annexationists, clockwise from top left Asfaha Weldemikael, Dimetros Gebremariam, Tedla Uqbit; with Emperor's Rep, Abiy Abebe

34. Haile Selassie's pre-annexation carrot and stick speech, 1962, Asmara

35. Asfaha's annexation Assembly speech

36. Haraka annexation protest placard by Weldemikael Abraha

As Haile Selassie left the Western Provinces without committing himself, a group of elders also claiming to represent the peoples of the highlands and lowlands met with him. They told him that their people had no other income beyond what they eked out of their respective trades. Taxation had doubled over the past year and new forms of taxation were in the pipeline. 'Your Majesty is the only one who can relieve us of this catastrophe,' they concluded.

A few days later, Haile Selassie convened a meeting at the Asmera Palace where Andargatchew and Tedla were present and where the elders repeated their plea. Andargatchew read out the Emperor's response:

> You have said what experts had already come to realise that Eritrea is not economically viable. Since you know your condition best, no additional evidence is necessary. But administration is as one manages it. *Just as it is impossible to walk if the shoe does not fit, administration too can be a problem if it is beyond the people's capacity*. It is true that, because your condition is of concern to us, we have been refraining from imposing the federal tax on you. We have been covering all your federal expenses from the Imperial Treasury. [Emphasis in the original]

The words were broadly interpreted as a direct reference to Tedla, indicating that his days were numbered.[59] But the Emperor also emphasised that Eritrea was economically unviable and its form of administration, presumably its internal autonomy, was beyond its abilities and needs. In his concluding remarks, he said, 'Since an act of grace reaching out to all of you is before us, we are willing to share your debts. We will, therefore, pay your expenses of the current year. When we do this, we keep in mind that we are also handling the bigger expenses of port, school and other major works of construction.'

It was not a good day for Tedla Bairu. All the same, he had his say:

> Ever since I accepted my administrative duties, I never troubled anyone with requests for financial help; the people know this. [My purpose] was to motivate people to appreciate the price of freedom and to develop the habit of self-reliance. But since Your Majesty has given this order based on people's request, I humbly thank you on behalf of the people of Mereb Mellash.[60]

Coming from Tedla, this was a bold statement. He was, in effect, distancing himself both from the request for tax relief and from Haile Selassie's reprieve, which he accepted as a fait accompli. According to Zewde Retta, Tedla had actually told the Emperor to ignore the request at an earlier private meeting where Asfaha Weldemikael, the deputy representative, had pressed for Imperial intervention.[61]

The Assembly was in recess throughout these events. On 13 February, 29 members held a meeting and requested an extraordinary session of the Assembly to discuss the tax relief. Tedla refused to comply, and the Assembly's reaction was to wait until the start of its regular session on 15 March. In the meantime, the government printed Haile Selassie's statement on the relief and distributed it as a proclamation throughout the country. In addition, following Haile Selassie's tour, Andargatchew travelled to Nakfa and Karora on the Sudanese border of the northern Sahel province without clearing it with the Eritrean Government. Both the reprieve and Andargatchew's unilateral decision to distribute it publicly and conduct the tour aroused protests in the province. In Sahel, there were calls for court action against those who had initiated the request for tax relief, and fears that since Haile Selassie had paid their taxes, he would claim ownership of the country. It was a widespread feeling that obliged the newspaper *Ethiopia* to issue a disclaimer on behalf of the Emperor, whose motive, it declared, was pure sympathy for his people's plight and not political gain.[62]

Tedla after the Tax Reprieve

About a week after Haile Selassie's departure from Eritrea, Cracknell sought a meeting with the 'worried and apprehensive' Chief Executive to tender his resignation. In a blunt exchange, Cracknell told Tedla that his support among police officers, most of whom were federalists, and among people in general had dwindled. He gave his reasons for so concluding: Tedla's failure to provide a policy for standing up to the Federal Government; his reluctance to counter Ethiopian domination and protect his people; his recent failure to hold public meetings and his tendency, since May 1953, to refuse to meet with or listen to anyone; the measures he had taken against his political antagonists: Weldeab's condemnation, the harassment of Ibrahim Sultan and his followers, the 'assassination plot' by the Tessema family; his failure to use the police force in stopping Gebreselassie Garza and his uniformed followers from bullying people; and, finally, his nepotism and partiality in his most recent appointments, such as his recent choice of ten officials from his own province of Hamasien.

Provoked by Cracknell, Tedla became more forthcoming. He agreed that a clearer policy needed to be presented to the Assembly or directly to the people. He had thus far left the people to identify their desires and inclinations by themselves. Before Federation, he said, the people were driven by political propaganda and foreign money. As far as he was concerned, it was foreigners who were benefiting from the Federation, not Eritreans—a statement that was then the current slogan of the annexationists. Cracknell asked how he planned to maintain a balance between his oath to protect the Eritrean Constitution and Ethiopia's undisguised disregard of it. Tedla replied that he never shirked from respecting the Constitution. For that reason, Andargatchew's intrigues had placed him in an unfavourable position. For such a man to be the Emperor's representative, he said, was a tragedy. He described Andargatchew as a person with no sense of public responsibility or direction and whose only intention was to satisfy his private ambitions.[63]

On 8 March, Wardle-Smith met with Tedla upon Cracknell's suggestion. By then, an ugly confrontation between Eritrean police and Ethiopian army contingents in Massawa had been stopped before deteriorating into open fighting. The Asseb killings had also taken place, and the Assembly was still in recess. Wardle-Smith pointed to the troubles at the two ports, especially Massawa, which was becoming the centre of conflict between federalists and annexationists. The Eritrean Government needed to clarify its position, as the federalists were acting without any sense of direction, while the other party was well organised and well guided. Besides, Ethiopia's abrasiveness and its attitude of superiority were creating ill-feeling among the population. Wardle-Smith feared an eruption of violence.

Tedla again put the blame on Andargatchew, who, he said, was behaving as if he owned Eritrea. He defended Haile Selassie as a lover of the Eritrean people, who knew exactly how they felt. Wardle-Smith disagreed. The Emperor was welcomed by huge crowds every time he came, but he could not enter into the people's feelings. On the contrary, the consul felt that Eritreans hated Ethiopian officials and were not happy at all.

Acknowledging his difficult situation, Tedla blamed the representative and his followers for coming between him and the Emperor, in whom he had great faith. The consul insisted that the Eritrean people lacked leadership and that they were the least informed about their government's plans and policies. They saw that their government was dominated by Ethiopians and, as long as it chose to remain quiet, the situation would not improve. Just as he had told Cracknell, Tedla replied that he was planning to declare his policies in public. Wardle-Smith urged him to do so. He further pushed the Chief Executive to release press statements exposing Ethiopian excesses and to reveal his feelings to the Emperor.[64] But Wardle-Smith did not believe Tedla would carry out his plans. The irony was that the British would now pose as defenders of Eritrean rights. Of all the factors that had put Eritrea in its untenable position, theirs had been the most decisive. What exactly they stood to gain from their new role was difficult to assess.

16

ASSEMBLY, SUPREME COURT AND FEDERAL COURT CHALLENGES

The Supreme Court and Dehai's Reinstatement

When the Police Commissioner ordered the closure of *Dehai*, its editors could have continued publication until ordered to stop by the appropriate court. Instead, they chose to comply and avail themselves of article 90(3) of the Eritrean Constitution, which provided that laws and orders perceived as unconstitutional could be challenged in the Supreme Court. The president, Sir James Shearer, accepted the appeal.

Shearer interpreted article 30 of the Constitution, which allowed residents of Eritrea the right to express their opinions 'through any medium whatsoever (press, speech, etc.) and to learn the opinions expressed by others', in the broadest sense. He held that newspapers were protected against censorship and arbitrary suppression. Under normal circumstances, the country's laws against libel and defamation were sufficient to redress cases where the honour or reputation of others was at stake. Only in emergency situations where public order and security were endangered was pre-publication censure, censorship or the closure of a publication permitted. Even then, the Chief Executive was required to seek Assembly approval within twenty days of the order being issued. Furthermore, that special power came to an end with the ending of the emergency situation.

Shearer stressed that freedom of the press was the foundation of Eritrea's democratic system. No well-informed, intelligent electorate could grow without access to diverse political opinions freely expressed. That was why the Constitution included a provision restraining the government from arbitrary intervention. To the government's argument that the *Dehai* editors could still express their opinion in the other available newspapers, Shearer replied that *Dehai* was the mouthpiece of the opposition and it was unthinkable that its editors, contributors and readers could be accommodated by an antagonistic party. He therefore rescinded the ban on *Dehai* and ordered its reinstitution on 19 August 1953.[1]

It took seven months of government delay and red tape for *Dehai* to make its actual comeback on 5 March 1954. In its editorial '*Dehai* Reopens', it stated that, had the Eritrean Government not been based on democratic principles, *Dehai* would have been condemned to death and hanged in public. It continued:

> A people without a free press cannot claim to be free. What kind of freedom can people possess if they cannot express their benefits and disadvantages through speech and writing? We will not be far from the truth when we say that people who cannot discuss their problems and preoccupations live, not in freedom, but in slavery. We invite those who belittle the laws of democracy that are reigning in the world today to correct their views ... A free press helps the Government more than it does the people. Why? Because it can easily gather from newspapers whatever is hidden from it in the people's minds.[2]

Dehai's return, though brief, is important for understanding the events of those crucial months. The Abraha Tessema case, the troubles in Massawa and Asseb, and the rebellion in the Eritrean Assembly would have remained obscure had *Dehai* not exposed them. It is to the last-mentioned event that we now turn our attention.

Rebellion in the Eritrean Assembly

Assembly Reaction to the Tax Reprieve

15 March 1954 was the date of the opening of the second session of the Eritrean Assembly. Before then, on 13 February, 29 members of the Assembly had signed a petition to the Chief Executive demanding an extraordinary session for the 22nd of the same month to discuss increasing interference by federal officials in internal Eritrean affairs.[3] Tedla ignored the request.

At the opening ceremony, Andargatchew gave his annual address from the throne—a self-righteous speech that went largely unnoticed even in *Dehai*'s columns. Assembly discussions started with Berhanu Ahmeddin of the Muslim League (ML) proposing a motion to thank the Emperor for the tax reprieve. Werede Beyin of the Unionist Party (UP) seconded the motion but added in an amendment that the 'irresponsible' individuals who pretended to represent the people of Eritrea be condemned. Berhanu and Werede had agreed to share the motion beforehand.

Ibrahim Sultan rejected Berhanu's motion of gratitude to the Emperor. He also criticised Werede's amendment as it failed to raise the broader issues of Ethiopian interference in Eritrean affairs, which he described as follows:

> The pamphlets that were distributed throughout Eritrea were meant to expose the poverty and weakness of the Eritrean Government. Besides, the Representative's visit to Nakfa and Karora was not appropriate. By doing so, he is passing the limits and considering the Eritrean Government, which is allowing these deeds to happen in silence, as non-existent.

> Dear members, it is essential that we protect our internal Government, ensure that Ethiopia is restrained from interfering in our internal affairs and that the Representative respects our Constitution. I have no doubt that you recognize the problems that our country is in ... Defending our rights is our duty. If you want to be thankful for your doom, go ahead and be thankful. There will be no doubt, however, that by doing so, you will be harming your country and putting its future in jeopardy.

Ibrahim's speech triggered an intense discussion the like of which had not been seen in the Assembly before. Bipartisanship extended both ways, with UP and Eritrean Democratic Front (EDF) members switching sides in support of or against the motion as amended. Idris Mohammed Adem of the Muslim League-Western Province (ML-WP) expounded on Ibrahim's call for a discussion of Ethiopian interference. The Ethiopian representative Andargatchew's distribution of pamphlets, he said,

> violates and trespasses on the jurisdiction of the Eritrean Government and seems intent on creating havoc and overturning it. Therefore, I reject the first part of the motion and accept the amendment provided that the distribution of the pamphlets is stopped, and His Excellency the Representative is told to terminate the political campaigns that he is undertaking inside Eritrea's internal administration.

Mohammed Said Hassano, ML Barka, rejected the motion in its totality. Characterising the pamphlets and Andargatchew's tour as 'poisonous', he exclaimed:

> Where is the Government of Eritrea? Where is its internal autonomy? Where is the Constitution that was ratified by the Emperor? Where is the Assembly? I do not support the motion to punish those who asked for the reprieve. Why? Because we see some members of the Assembly and the Government going to the Representative to beg. I would not blame the common people if they did what some of our members are doing ... the Representative's office has taken over the office of the CE. Eritrea has become another Ethiopian province, devoid of a Constitution and internal autonomy.

The strongest words came from *Abba* Habtemariam Nugurru (UP):

> I speak in praise of independence and those who stand for it ... Let us put the activities of the Representative on the side and scrutinize ourselves, blame our Assembly. Let us put the blame on this sick and emaciated Government of ours, which has lost its internal rights. The harm that has befallen Eritrea is attributable to the weakness of the Eritrean Government. This is because it has been conducting itself by overriding the Constitution, violating human rights and the rule of law. Is this democracy or fascism?[4]

For two days, supporters and opponents of the motion were locked in a furious debate on whether to expand the topic into a resolution on Ethiopian intervention in general. Fearful of a negative outcome for the government, Ali Rad'ai interrupted the session at least five times on the pretext that arguments were becoming hostile. In fact, those recesses were used by UP leaders to pressure Werede to withdraw his amendment. He complied on the second day of debate, thus effectively taking the agenda off the Assembly floor.[5]

Five days after the closure of the debate, Mohammed Omer Akito raised another issue. 'Why', he asked, 'was the extraordinary meeting demanded by 29 members of the Assembly for 22 February overlooked?' Article 49 of the Constitution obliged the government to comply with the Assembly demand. This time, the Assembly agreed to form a committee to examine the matter.[6]

Public Pressure on the Assembly

While the Assembly was engaged in its debate, the public, especially members and supporters of the ML, put pressure on their representatives. This had begun as early as 14 March 1953, the day of the suspension of *Dehai*. On that day, its Arabic edition, *Saut al Eretria*, published a petition to the UN Tribunal signed by 116 youths of the ML demanding the restitution of Eritrea's rights. They also complained that the Muslim population was being discriminated against both by the Federal and Eritrean governments. Their appeal to the UN came, they said, in the wake of the government's failure to heed their requests.[7]

On 28 February 1954, the ML called a huge meeting where hundreds of leaders and members gathered behind the Grand Mosque of Asmera. The feeling that Muslims were being relegated to second-class citizenship was becoming part of the public complaint against the administration, and Muslim activism was on the rise. The stated aim of the meeting was to assess the condition of Muslims in the country and to narrow the widening gap between the government and the Assembly.[8] Writing about what he called 'The Islamic Conference of Eritrea', *Dehai*'s editor Mohammed Saleh Mahmud described it as focused on bringing people together and helping create peace and harmony among contending political parties and persuasions.[9] The Tigrinya section of *Dehai* too attested to the nationalistic decisions of the meeting. It summarised them as follows: Oppose Eritreans who, for pecuniary or other benefits, are becoming instruments in the abrogation of the Federation and in particular hold legally accountable those in government positions of responsibility working for similar ends. The Assembly committee set up to examine the matter should begin its investigation by scrutinising the Assembly and the government. Should Eritrean rights not be protected by the Emperor, avail ourselves of the right to appeal to the body that gave us our freedom, the United Nations.

In its concluding remarks, the conference stated:

> By disrespecting the Assembly, isn't the Government also disregarding the people? Does it not realize that the people have absolute power over the Government? Why then is it not concerned over the loss by the people of Eritrea of all their rights and the subsequent damage that they are suffering? The Assembly needs to think hard. If it does not act on this issue, the people will use their civic powers over members of the Assembly.[10]

Such public pressure never went unheeded in the Assembly. But, as we have seen, questions on the Asseb killings and Ethiopian interference in Eritrean affairs were consistently ignored by the government, and from October 1953 on, the Chief Executive refused to respond, even in writing, to the Assembly's demands. Beginning at the end of January 1954, the Assembly bombarded the government with a series of demands for explanations to their previous questions. Invoking relevant articles of the Constitution, they tried to compel the Chief Executive to give adequate answers. Besides the issues stated above, concern had arisen over a new campaign for immediate integration with Ethiopia, by people claiming to represent the province of Hamasien. Some Assembly members demanded legal action against the group.[11]

In the middle of this potentially explosive stand-off, the UP's Dimetros Gebremariam and his followers attempted to shift the Assembly's attention by proposing the recognition of a single Ethiopian citizenship throughout the Federation. For the likes of Ibrahim, Akito and Idris Mohammed Adem, this was a continuation of the campaign for immediate union. They led a furious debate that defeated the Dimetros attempt. On 11 May, *Qadi* Ali Omer presented a motion that marked the start of the Assembly's open challenge to Tedla's administration. His proposal may be summarised as follows: The Chief Executive should address the Assembly on the violation of Eritrea's Constitution and its internal autonomy. If the Eritrean Government was unable to protect its own rights, the Assembly should immediately notify the Emperor to secure his protection of the Eritrean Constitution and the Federal Act. If this was not forthcoming, the Assembly should request the United Nations to send a commission to Eritrea.

Qadi Ali was the first representative to raise the possibility of an appeal to the UN. However, as his proposal was about to be debated, Tedla came to the Assembly to deliver his second annual report. Dwelling on minute details of government expenditures and advances in the fields of education and health, he made another unimpressive performance. Even *Zemen* commented that the details were too long to fit into its columns.[12] Without wasting more time on Tedla's report, the Assembly went back to *Qadi* Ali's pending proposal.

The Making of a Resolution

As the members of the Assembly mulled over the deadlock with the Chief Executive, their president, Ali Rad'ai, who had thus far frustrated all their attempts to challenge the federal and Eritrean authorities, set off a strange process. The source of this story is a letter that Assembly member Said Sefaf later wrote to Andargatchew in June 1954. On 13 April 1954, Ali Rad'ai called Said Sefaf of Ghinda'e, one of the five young activists led by Akito in the Assembly, and said to him, 'Why don't you, the Muslim League faction, stand up for Eritrea's rights against the excesses of the Federal Government?' He then handed the surprised Sefaf a written statement instructing him to rewrite it in line with the Assembly format. It called for condemnation of the federal authorities for meddling in internal Eritrean affairs. Sefaf's colleagues, Akito, Abudawd, Mohammed Berhanu, Saleh Ashekih and Tekeste Gebrekidan of Deki Dashim in Hamasien, agreed to the proposal but expressed their doubt whether it would obtain the three-fourths majority vote of those present required for its passage. Ali Rad'ai sent his assurances that he had secured the agreement of all the representatives from the lowlands and Hamasien province.

Through the involvement of one of Tedla Bairu's own brothers, Menghistu Bairu, the deal between the lowlanders and the Hamasien representatives was sealed. Sefaf and Werede Beyin were assigned to pursue the process to the end. Ali Rad'ai's original plan was to send the resolution directly to the UN, but Sefaf and Werede thought it would be more appropriate for it to be addressed to the Emperor, which idea he accepted. The two colleagues then collected the signatures of 41 members, including eight Christian members from Hamasien, one from Seraye and one from Akeleguzai. The rest were Muslim.[13]

On 22 May, in a prearranged procedure, the Seraye representative, Yehdego Gebrerufael, moved to support the empowerment of the committee examining federal intervention. Abudawd proposed an amendment:

> However, we condemn the Government's policy statement where it attempted to corrupt the faith of the people's representatives and Government authorities in contravention of the letter and spirit of the UN's Federal Act of December 1950. We also condemn their continuous intervention in the affairs of the Eritrean Government, thereby impeding its proper functions.
>
> We further order that, in order for him to take the necessary steps for the implementation of this decision, the Sovereign of the Federation, His Imperial Majesty, be informed about our present situation.
>
> Should the appropriate steps not be taken within 20 days, we order the Eritrean Government to present this decision at the United Nations.[14]

After a hot debate, the motion carried with 33 votes for, 7 against and 10 abstentions; two-thirds of the 50 members present supported the motion. The vice president, Demsas Weldemikael, and seven of his fellow Hamasien unionists also voted for the resolution. Since eight of the absentees had already signed the petition, *Dehai* gave the total number of supporters as 42, but printed a list of 41 names.[15] To ensure international attention, Ali Rad'ai had invited Arthur Reid of the UN Tribunal, who procured a copy and duly transmitted it to the UN. All the consuls in Asmera received copies of the resolution and some British newspapers reported the event as a significant development. Given the time and circumstances, it was a bold move.

The Office of the Emperor's Representative was not idle while this was taking place. One source asserted that eleven Muslim members had been offered 1,000 birr each to withdraw their support. Another 26,000 birr was disbursed from the Palace for the same purpose. Dimetros was also known to have prepared a pre-emptive resolution calling for immediate union. None of these moves succeeded.[16] *Ethiopia* printed a series of articles criticising Ali Rad'ai and even casting a dark shadow over Tedla's administration for allowing the issue to be raised in the Assembly. Ibrahim Sultan bore the brunt of the newspaper's anger for the role he played in distributing the resolution to the UN and to the consulates in Asmera. 'Just because some irrational people write to the UN', wrote the paper, 'does not mean that it will give them any serious consideration.'[17] This time *Ethiopia* was right.

UN and Federal Government Reaction to the May Resolution

Although the role of the UN Tribunal in Asmera was limited to the registration of chiefly non-political complaints arising from the implementation of the federal system, Arthur Reid had, from the start, informed UN Secretary General Hammarskjöld on political issues as well. What prompted Reid to do so was mainly the deep trust that Eritrean officials bestowed on him, as if he were a commissioner with powers to protect Eritrea's rights and interests. Even high officials like Feki Ali and Haregot confided in him.

Reid thus kept reporting Eritrean fears that the UN and the Four Great Powers were abandoning the country to the mercy of the Ethiopians. In a series of letters to Hammarskjöld's executive assistant, Andrew Cordier, Reid reported every event that he deemed relevant. These included Cracknell's conversations with Haregot and Tedla, the strife between Eritrean police and Ethiopian army units in Massawa, and Eritrean fears of annexation as a 'fait accompli'. Furthermore, at the instigation of the Italian and British consuls, Reid reported their governments' concerns that Ethiopian disregard for the Federal Act was leading to unrest in the country and that the UN should show some signs of interest in the matter.[18]

Silence from the UN office put Reid in a difficult situation. His office had become the centre of Eritrean complaints and appeals. In the week of the Assembly resolution, he met with Andargatchew, Tedla and their colleagues. His meetings with Justices Shearer and Nordström were especially revealing, as they were of the opinion that the conflict between the federal courts and the Eritrean Supreme Court would eventually have to be resolved by UN intervention. Nordström, Justice J.A. Clarence Smith and the Assembly clerk Fergus McCleary were all urging him to inform the UN of the need to establish a UN body that would arbitrate on the rising tensions.

On 19 March, Reid informed Tedla of his intention to send a proposal to the UN. Tedla approved the move and McCleary volunteered to provide all relevant Assembly questions that needed to be clarified. As he proceeded, Reid cautioned that the UN might not approve of the initiative, but he went ahead nonetheless, suggesting that the UN should establish a neutral court to arbitrate the conflicts.[19]

On 5 April, Andrew Cordier wrote back to Reid. He warned him not to show any sign of UN interest in the Eritrean case. The issue of federation between Ethiopia and Eritrea had ended to the satisfaction of the General Assembly and the subject has been closed. Therefore, he saw no way for the UN to show an interest in Eritrea and the union. Despite the decisive role that the UN had played in drafting the Eritrean Constitution and the creation of Eritrea as an autonomous unit under Ethiopian sovereignty, the matter had 'moved out of its agenda'. The only way that the UN could show an interest in Eritrea, Cordier stressed, would be if the General Assembly entered it as a topic on its agenda on the instigation of a member of the UN.

After rejecting Reid's suggestion that the UN's legal department investigate the matter, Cordier commented on the consuls of the Great Powers in Asmera—British, American and French—pushing for UN intervention. If they were genuinely concerned about Ethiopia's undoing of the federal arrangement, their governments should decide to consider the matter serious enough to deserve the General Assembly's immediate attention. Should they do so, the UN would accept the case. Cordier ended his message by warning Reid not to exceed his functions as registrar of the UN Tribunal and to avoid the slightest conflict of interest.[20]

By June, Reid was busy closing down the Tribunal and leaving Eritrea. As the only means of communication with the UN open to them, Eritreans, particularly members of the Assembly, clamoured around him. They wanted to know the UN's reaction to their May resolution and to all the petitions they had been sending to the Secretary General. They refused to listen to Reid's appeal that he was a mere registrar, not a UN representative. They insisted on UN representation in Eritrea for the survival of the Federation and handed him an appeal to the world body in which they wrote:

> As we understand it, and in relation of the conclusive remarks of the UN Commissioner, the rights of the people of Eritrea are being overridden at the Federal level. The United Nations is the one and the best venue where the unjust, and the Ethiopian Government has become unjust, are controlled and checked. We therefore request that you transmit to the United Nations our appeal that, for the people of Eritrea to attain their goals, a centre is set up to responsibly connect their situation and livelihood with the United Nations.

Akito, *Qadi* Ali, Said Sefaf, Idris Mohammed Adem, Saleh Ashekih and Bemnet Tessema were among the signatories of the petition. In New York, Reid handed the petition and the list of 41 members of the Assembly who had signed the May resolution to the UN. Cordier did not respond. On Reid's covering letter, we find two annotations from Cordier—an exclamation mark beside Reid's claim that he had told the petitioners of his limited powers, and the order 'File—no action'.[21]

The Office of the UN Secretary General had actually gone back on an earlier instruction, given on 9 March 1953, that Reid could transmit public complaints flowing to his office. He had been specifically authorised to open every message to the UN and pass it on as he deemed necessary. Reid reflected on the treatment he had received for having followed instructions: 'After having received confidential reports from me for one year and a half; and after receiving adequate warnings of the possibility of a return to bloodshed and the abrogation of the Federation, the Office of the Secretary General made me a *bouc émissaire* [scapegoat] by appearing to have no knowledge of acts overriding the Constitution in Eritrea.'[22] That was the end of the United Nation's interest and involvement in Eritrea. It was to reopen the 'Eritrea file' that it had closed, thirty-seven years later, under entirely different circumstances.

Before he left Eritrea on 21 June, the authorities threw a farewell party for Reid. He asked Andargatchew what action he had taken with regard to the Assembly's resolution of 22 May. The *bitweded* told him that he considered the procedure adopted by the members illegal and therefore did not send it to the foreign minister. Reid insisted that he should, as he had already sent his copy to the UN Secretary General. Andargatchew was not moved. Reid observed that, by his refusal, Andargatchew blocked the Ethiopian Government from any knowledge of the Assembly resolution.[23]

It would be naive to believe that Andargatchew acted alone on the matter. For at the same time, a concerted effort was being exerted to further weaken the federal base, and this brought Tedla's relationship with Andargatchew into open confrontation. But, in the contest for supremacy, Andargatchew was already gaining the upper hand, not only over the administration, but over the Assembly as well.

About one week after the Assembly's May resolution, Ali Rad'ai called Said Sefaf to his office and said to him, '*Bitweded* Andargatchew has accused me of sponsoring the resolution. Please relieve me from this distressing situation by signing these statements;' and he handed him two letters. Sefaf did not mention the contents of the statement, but from his letter of apology to Andargatchew, we assume that Ali Rad'ai wished to solicit signatures of apology from those who had voted for the resolution. Said Sefaf mentions only Mohammed Berhanu of Mendefera as having signed together with him.[24] On the other hand, according to Saleh Musa Abudawd, Sefaf's change of heart caused a rift in the cohesion of the Akito group.[25]

The fallout from the resolution spelled doom for Ali Rad'ai and a little favour for Sefaf, leaving Tedla's fate in the balance.

Tedla and Andargatchew at Loggerheads

After almost eighteen months of a stand-off between them, the conflict between the Chief Executive of Eritrea and the Emperor's representative came to the surface in February 1954 over a land dispute between the original settlers (*deqebat*) and latecomers (*ma'ekelai aliet*) in Damba-Seharti village in southern Hamasien. An old dispute originating from 1934, it had been settled in favour of the *deqebat* by previous Italian and British courts. Claiming their continuous relegation to second-class treatment as a human right violation, the *ma'ekelai aliet* appealed against the previous colonial decision to the Federal High Court (FHC) in Eritrea. Although, consistent with his principled stand, Justice Nordström rejected the appeal, his two colleagues on the bench allowed it in a majority judgment. The Government of Eritrea, which was the respondent, was thus summoned to defend its case in court. In its reply, the government objected both to the appeal and to the summons, and the Attorney General, A.A. Canner, refused to appear before the court. The court then handed down a summary decision ordering the Eritrean Government to pay 26,500 birr by 18 February in compensation to the Damba appellants.

Through his deputy, Fessehatsion Haile, Tedla objected to the court order as a violation of the Federal Act and the Eritrean Constitution. The Eritrean Government, he contended, could not go against its own Constitution and suggested that the matter be referred to the Emperor for final arbitration.[26] Without waiting for an answer, the FHC dispatched another letter to the Eritrean Government ordering it to make a payment of 26,584.27 birr by 18 April. Should it fail to do so, the amount would be deducted from the Eritrean Government account at the State Bank of Ethiopia.[27]

Tedla wrote back in anger. By intervening in a case that was beyond its jurisdiction, the FHC was creating unrest in the village and elsewhere. He appealed for patience pending an Imperial decision. A legal tug of war followed between Canner, who stood his ground, and Andargatchew's legal advisor, Edgar Turlington; the latter insisted that, since the Supreme Court of Ethiopia was also the Supreme Federal Court, the FHC was within its right to hear the case. He also pushed Andargatchew to order the bank deductions.[28]

Andargatchew suddenly turned democratic by arguing that, as a fundamental provision of the Federal Act and the Eritrean Constitution, human rights violations were a matter of concern to the federal courts. Besides, given the fact that Eritrea had merged with Ethiopia under the Federation, 'Neither I nor the Federal Court can justify refusal by one of His Majesty's subjects to appear before the Federal Court and respond to its questions ... I therefore urge you to agree that the case be heard at the Federal High Court.'[29]

On 15 June 1954, Tedla felt compelled to write directly to the Emperor. After summarising the history of the long-standing land dispute in Damba, he wrote:

> The Government of Eritrea has reasons for rejecting the payment of the amount in question. The main reason being that the Federal High Court has no jurisdiction over the matter ... This is why it has refused to appear before the court ... In addition, the Court itself had set a precedent by denying an appeal to a similar case from Dekemhare ... The President of the Court has also ruled along the same lines, but he was overruled by his colleagues at the bench. Therefore, the issue of whether the Damba case constitutes a human rights violation is for the Eritrean courts to decide and not, under any circumstance, the Federal Courts.

Tedla stressed that the Government of Eritrea would not pay the amount and warned that the matter was becoming a security concern.[30] As the Emperor's response took time, the crisis escalated. Tedla stood firm in his contention that the FHC's intervention could only be justified in cases that touched on the functions and authority of federal matters and federal officials.[31] Andargatchew lost his patience and went on an open offensive. He wrote to Tedla:

> I know that there is a feeling among Eritrean officials that the Federal Government is usurping Eritrean powers. There is no doubt that such a wrong sentiment is prevalent because Eritrean authorities are harbouring an attitude of non-recognition of the Imperial Federal Courts ... These authorities should have set the example for others not to consider the Federal courts as alien ... We know from recent history that even the enemy [Italy] could not separate the people of Eritrea, who are, by race and history, and from one corner to the other, Ethiopian. No one but you can get rid of this provocative spirit that has been created to pit brother against brother.[32]

Andargatchew in effect accused Tedla of spreading a negative attitude in the country towards the FHC. But simultaneous developments that alienated Tedla from his home base could not have been hidden from the *bitweded*; hence, the confident manner in which he decided to attack him so directly. As the antagonists awaited the Emperor's final say, and at a time when he needed all the support that he could muster in his ongoing battle against the Emperor's representative, Tedla's relationship with the Assembly took an irreversible turn for the worse.

Defiance in the Eritrean Assembly and the Final Closure of Dehai

Dehai made its reappearance after its year-long suspension with a virtual noose around its neck. Its retrospective coverage of events such as the Abraha Tessema case and the Assembly's opposition to Haile Selassie's tax reprieve, which had been covered up in its absence, did not go down well with the authorities. But new articles also raised temperatures in the federal offices. Under the editorship of the ultra-unionist and hard-hitting polemicist Teweldeberhan Gebremedhin (Zekios), *Ethiopia* targeted *Dehai* with sarcasm and outright insults surpassing anything ever seen before. Even *Zemen*'s continuous intervention on behalf of civility and its characterisation of abusive language as 'the weapon of fools and the ignorant' could not temper the vitriol.[33] *Dehai Ertra* was nicknamed 'Dahya [Arabic for "ruin"] Ertra'. Every bad word in the book, from 'weakling' to 'barking mad dog', was showered upon its contributors. True, *Ethiopia* wrote in one piece:

> just as there is eternal struggle between saints and devils, so there shall be between believers and traitors. Until we eliminate the race of traitors from our country, these minions are sure to deny us the progress we deserve. Our Lord Jesus Christ said to the weeping women, 'Weep for yourselves and your children, do not weep for me'; so it

> is with these worms whose fate is '*dahya*' [destruction]. Let them cry for themselves. Eritrea means nothing to them, as they mean nothing to Eritrea.[34]

Towards the end of July 1954, *Dehai* let its readers know that the psychological warfare directed against it and its contributors was being accompanied by physical threats. 'If one who rightfully claims to be the master of his own land is subjected to elimination and incarceration, then where is the freedom and brotherhood?' it asked. 'Is it so difficult for them to live in love and peace that they have opted for sabotage and the ways of slavery? The pain from the fascistic persecution being planned for the lovers of Eritrea will not be limited to the few victims alone. It will affect the whole population. People of Eritrea, reflect on this!'[35]

Five days after this article appeared, the Deputy Advocate General of the FHC opened criminal proceedings against *Dehai*'s chief editors, Mohammed Saleh Mahmud and Elias Teklu, as well as the editor of the Arabic section, *Saut al Eretria*, Alamin Ali, and the publisher, Tipografia Fioretti. They were charged with 'subversive political activities aimed at endangering the unity of the Federation and dismantling it'. The group was further accused of forming the core of a political party whose aim was to separate Eritrea from Ethiopia and cause bloodshed in the country. Two articles were cited as proof of subversion—the first one for complaining about the unequal treatment of Muslims, and the second for alleging that the Ethiopians had colluded with Britain to confiscate Eritrean property.[36]

On 6 August 1954, *Dehai Ertra* breathed its last with its issue no. 50. Its editors' expectation of a public protest, particularly from ML members, never materialised. Support came from the Assembly when it met to discuss the budget ten days after *Dehai*'s closure. Twenty-five Muslim members demanded a change of agenda to discuss the issue of *Dehai* and 'the intervention of Ethiopian officials into the internal affairs of Eritrea, which was compromising its internal autonomy'. They notified the Assembly president that, in order to prepare a petition to this effect, they would not attend the morning session of 17 August. Although Assembly rules allowed members to be absent for a purpose, Ali Rad'ai took advantage of their non-attendance to close the Assembly for two more days for lack of a quorum.

On 19 August, Ali Rad'ai reopened the Assembly but insisted that only the budget could be discussed. By then, 29 Muslim members of the Assembly had signed a petition to the Emperor requesting his intervention to stop 'the agitating activities of Ethiopian authorities over Eritrea and Eritreans and their interference in internal Eritrean affairs'.[37] A few days after this, the remaining four Muslim members joined their colleagues, and all Muslims in the Assembly, except Ali Rad'ai, signed the petition.

Rather than using this initiative as a basis for strengthening his position, Tedla took it as a direct affront to his authority, and in a decision that had no factual or legal justification, he availed himself of the powers under article 48(5) of the Constitution to order the suspension of the Assembly for twenty days, as of 20 August. Haile Selassie chose to give his response both to Tedla and to the rebel representatives on 10 September, the day after the Assembly's reopening. Andargatchew called the Assembly to his Palace to read out the verdict; 29 of the signatories refused to attend.

In his terse reply, Haile Selassie expressed his disappointment at the actions of a 'few members who were obstructing progress'. He stressed that federal officials did not overstep their constitutional powers and that the FHC was established in accordance with the provisions of the Federal Act. Opposing the FHC, he warned, was tantamount to opposing the Federal Act. Therefore, he concluded, 'We urge you to understand us when we say that the protection within our entire Imperial domain of our people's possessions with a firm hand [foundation] is both our function and prerogative.'[38] With these seemingly polite Imperial words, the FHC was confirmed as the supreme legal power in Eritrea. Probably fearful of reprisals or out of deference to his prestige, the opposition within the Assembly desisted from further confrontation with the Emperor. Tedla was, instead, seen as the main obstacle.

In the meantime, lack of evidence to support the charges against *Dehai* and the editors caused the court case to drag for several weeks. Judge Nordström was removed from the case and his deputy, the Lebanese judge G.N. Debbas, spent time shuttling between Asmera and Addis Ababa in consultation over the legal issues of the case. In the middle of the confusion, the remaining amenable judges found procedural loopholes to finally decide on the closure of *Dehai Ertra*. Mohammed Saleh Mahmud and Elias Teklu were each handed prison terms.[39]

That contested decision silenced the voices of independence, federalism and, in general, the right of free expression in Eritrea. It was obvious that Ethiopia was setting all pretences aside and was pushing for annexation.

Tedla's Speech on the Second Federal Anniversary

On 11 September, the day after Haile Selassie's verdict on the FHC, Andargatchew and Tedla appeared before the Eritrean Assembly building to deliver their annual addresses at the joint Geez New Year and Federation Day celebrations. Tedla's speech gained immediate and widespread attention. Continually referring to Eritrea as 'Mereb Mellash', Tedla argued that the only justification for Eritrea's federal status was that it had come back to Ethiopia after a spell of colonial separation, and not because it was Ethiopia's equal. If, in implementing the Federal Act in letter and spirit, 'we forget that we are a part of Greater Ethiopia; if we do not believe in our Ethiopian identity, we will be undoing our Federal laws. The Federal Act is, in letter and spirit, the union of Ethiopians.'

It was an opaque speech, dotted with contradictions. After vehemently denying that Ethiopia had confiscated Eritrean property, he stepped back to admit that some outstanding federal issues were being discussed in an Ethiopian spirit, 'like, for example, unsettled talks about the Federal Courts and others'. This indicated that he had not fully accepted or grasped the Emperor's word that the FHC had neither overstepped its constitutional limitations nor been instituted contrary to the provisions of the Federal Act. As if to maintain a balance between his federal leanings and total loyalty to the Emperor, Tedla showered unbridled praise on the Emperor. 'My highest wish', he declared, 'is for the people of Mereb Mellash to be the right hand of His Majesty the Emperor.' In a barrage of attacks, he condemned religious and regional sectarians who dreamed of power at the expense of a failed Federation. He concluded:

> Love and compassion are not a sign of weakness; patience and contemplation are not proof of fear. Let me forward a suggestion before wrapping up my address. Many ask, 'What is *Dejazmatch* Tedla's thinking about our country's current situation?' I am serving our country and His Imperial Majesty by dispensing the heavy responsibility bestowed upon me with diligence and without going back on my oath. The day of greatest happiness for me will be when, after close inspection and deliberation, the people of Mereb Mellash choose full union over federal union.[40]

Haile Selassie was quick to accord Tedla's suggestion the meaning he had been looking for. According to Zewde Retta, on the very next day, 12 September, Haile Selassie assembled his ministers and crown councillors and said to them that Tedla had 'fearlessly and without hesitation expressed his genuine Ethiopian desire to dissolve the Federation'. He called for a discussion of that possibility. Earlier that day, his head of protocol, Endalkatchew Mekonnen, had angered the Emperor by declaring in a press conference that Tedla had merely expressed a wish, not a proposal of action, to the Eritrean Assembly. Foreign Minister Aklilu supported Endalkatchew's position. 'I have been studying Tedla ever since he became Chief Executive and he has been seeking the preservation of the Federation rather than its dissolution,' he told the gathering. Since he was merely appeasing his unionist critics, a speech by him could not determine the survival of the Federation.

Haile Selassie did not readily accept Aklilu's reasoning. 'Tedla has started a fire,' he said. 'He had never said, "I would be happy if the Federation was to be dissolved." Our trusted servants in Asmera have assured us that Tedla's suggestion can stir the people up ... We need to be prepared for the eventuality of the people coming out into the open against the Federation.' Three of the aristocrats, crown councillors *Ras* Kassa and *Bitweded* Endalkatchew Mekonnen, and the Emperor's son, Prince Mekonnen, pressed for immediate action. They argued that there could not be a halfway Federation. If Tedla stood in the way, he could be replaced by the likes of Asfaha for more effective results.

Aklilu refused to give in. Dissolving the Federation, he argued, could provoke international condemnation and even economic sanctions against Ethiopia. He advised patience and caution. Weldegiorgis, the virtual prime minister, helped

Aklilu here and added that the Emperor's representative and his deputy should be told to restrain themselves from their overzealous quest for immediate union. He much preferred that Ethiopia make administrative reforms in order to meet the new challenges that eventual union would bring.

After denying that he had given any instructions to his officials in Asmera to speed up union, Haile Selassie adopted Aklilu's suggestion with the following instructions:

> Since politics is unpredictable, one cannot forecast what tomorrow has in store for us. We shall see how this matter plays out in the future, as you, Aklilu, shall too. In the meantime,
>
> 1. Until such time that Eritreans make it known to us that they prefer their country to be administered within Ethiopia, the function of the Federation should continue in its present form,
> 2. Weldegiorgis's suggestion that we should be ready for the challenges of administering Eritrea in case Eritreans so decide is an excellent idea. Form a ministerial committee under your chairmanship and study the matter.[41]

Public Involvement in Assembly Confrontations

Tedla gained nothing from his half-hearted speech but a veiled rebuke from the Emperor. According to Zewde Retta, the Emperor later wrote to him, 'It is all fine to talk of the Federation but not all that is wished can be realised through a fine speech. You should have known beforehand that to put your words into practice, much prior work had to be done.'[42] But it was on the home front where Tedla's administration was losing face and credibility.

In about June 1954, Tedla demanded the dismissal of two Supreme Court judges, the Italian Ruolo and the British O'Hanlon, charging them with being uncooperative. The Supreme Court president, Sir James Shearer, refused to obey, and it was only after the intervention of the British consulate in Asmera and the embassy in Addis Ababa that he withdrew the order. Even Andargatchew charged him with violation of the principle of the separation of state powers sanctioned by the Eritrean Constitution. The worst part was the rumour that the judges' sole 'fault' had been their refusal to prosecute Abraha Tessema and his brothers.[43]

Tedla also applied great pressure on two other judges of the Supreme Court, Justice Bruna and the Eritrean Justice Melles Fre, to reinstate an old Italian law that conferred extra-judicial powers on law enforcement agencies. Known as article 10 of the Police Ordinance (*articolo dieci*), it gave the police the power to hold suspects indefinitely without a court order and to deny permission for and disband public meetings. As we shall see, it was to be the most feared instrument of suppression throughout the federal period. These issues marred Tedla's relationship with the Supreme Court and, particularly, with that great defender of Eritrea's federal rights, Sir James Shearer.

Another embarrassment for Tedla came with appointments he made to replace Colonel C.W. Wright, the British officer who had succeeded Police Commissioner Cracknell. To do this, he promoted four Eritrean inspectors (majors)—Menghistu Habtezghi, Alem Mammo, Seyoum Kahsai and Tedla Ukbit—to the rank of lieutenant colonel and assigned them to various positions. Andargatchew refused to approve the appointments on the ground that the small Eritrean force did not need so many officers of that rank and, if they were to be granted, such dispensations were the Emperor's prerogative. Tedla revoked the appointments hastily and reassigned his appointees to civilian functions, a switch that one of them, Tedla Ukbit, refused to accept, with significant consequences for the officer's future career and even the Federation's fate. The whole event made Tedla Bairu look weak and inconsequential.

It was at this time that he made a controversial speech. On 13 September, the day after Haile Selassie's Crown Council meeting, the Assembly convened to discuss the budget. However, angry and agitated members disrupted proceedings by demanding a debate on the meaning of Tedla's words of 11 September. Suddenly, the Assembly vice president Demsas Weldemikael announced that, at the request of members, whom he did not identify, he was suspending the session for twenty days until 4 October. No one except Tedla had the power to issue such an order. The Assembly representatives disbanded.[44]

According to Akito, 'At this point, we realised that the Assembly was no longer the forum from which to fight for Eritrea's rights. We decided to take our case to the public.'[45] One week after the Assembly's second suspension, the Muslim League ignored the ban on unauthorised gatherings and called a meeting in Keren, which over 2,500 of its members and supporters attended. Their message was simple—a pledge to keep their opposition peaceful and non-violent, and a demand for change in government policy towards Muslims in general and their demands in particular. Should their demands not be met to their satisfaction, they reserved the right to appeal to the Emperor and from there to the United Nations. They expressed the confidence that their Christian brothers would join them in their struggle.[46]

Pressure for action also came from unexpected sources. Since Assembly meetings were open to the public, a group of regular Andinet activists had fallen under the influence of Akito and his group in their bitter struggle to uphold the Federation and defend the Eritrean Constitution. They were equally swayed by Ibrahim Sultan, *Qadi* Ali Omer and Habtemariam Nugurru, with whom they had frequent discussions outside the Assembly building. According to Tesfai Reda'e, who later became the leader of the group, it was particularly attracted to Akito, whom he described as 'a fearless man whose arguments were most convincing and often delivered with force'. From him and his younger colleagues, but also from Ibrahim Sultan and Habtemariam Nugurru, he recalled, 'we learned how the Federation had been a betrayal of the real aspirations of the people of Eritrea. With their advice and encouragement, we decided to form an organisation that would fight for the preservation of the Federation.'[47]

During *Dehai*'s brief come-back, Tesfai Reda'e had submitted articles praising the opposition in the Assembly as patriots with a place of honour in Eritrean history.[48] Another article, by Abraha Hagos, a defector from Haile Selassie's army recruits, objected to the formation of a Mahber Tegaru or Association of Tigrayans, following the former Mahber Amharu or Association of Amhara, under the sponsorship of the Palace in Asmera. By infiltrating the old Andinet party, these groups were turning it into an Ethiopian-dominated gathering. Abraha's warning to the Amhara was to stay clear of internal Eritrean affairs or suffer the consequences of an Eritrean backlash.[49] Both writers were dismissed from their employment and briefly imprisoned for their articles and for participation in labour strikes by railway workers.

On 5 September 1954, Tesfai, Abraha and several former Andinet operatives established what they called the Eritrean Federalist Youth Association (better known as the Federalisti), camouflaged as a religious gathering. None of the workers had the education, knowledge or experience to articulate their group's policy and programme. All of that was summarised in the oath they took on signing up for membership: 'From this moment, under the shelter of our blue flag adorned by a wreath of green olive branches, which is guaranteed to fly all over Eritrea by our Constitution, we Eritreans pledge to stay true to our Constitution and to its objectives by raising the slogan of "Eritrea for Eritreans".'[50]

With those simple words, the first post-Federation grassroots political organisation was created. The lawyers Mohammed Omer Qadi and Weldeab Weldemariam's personal friend and assistant Yohannes Tsegai agreed to provide them with legal advice where needed. With the banning of free speech and suspension of the labour movement, the Federalisti attempted to fill the gap created by the absence of organised popular activities. As we shall see later, perhaps more than any other group or party in Eritrea, the Federalisti played the biggest role in establishing the flag of the autonomous Eritrea as the expression of Eritrean nationalism and independence. Significantly, too, the opposition within the Assembly, muted and alienated, found an informal means of spreading its views and disseminating information on Assembly proceedings.

17

THE FALL OF THE TEDLA GOVERNMENT

The Federal Officials on the Offensive

Step-by-Step Encroachments

Despite reports by European consuls in Asmera of Ethiopian intentions to annul the Federation, Haile Selassie, on a visit to Britain at the end of 1954, praised the UN federal decision as 'a great accomplishment that I believe will live in our history. This Federation proved to be beneficial both to Eritreans and Ethiopians.'[1] No one in Britain challenged the Emperor's assertion. Emboldened by such Great Power acquiescence, the Ethiopians created new opportunities to further encroach on Eritrean autonomy. On the administrative front, the step-by-step severance of Asseb from the centre at Massawa continued by means of a takeover of Eritrean functions by Ethiopian military and port officials. The volume of trade and customs revenues through Asseb had jumped dramatically from its 1943–50 levels, but without any benefits for Eritrea. Despite Assembly protests, Asseb had virtually fallen under Ethiopian control by the beginning of 1955.

The Ethiopians also trespassed systematically on other areas of exclusive Eritrean jurisdiction. Chief among these was the Education Department. By means of a series of what were called 'Imperial grants', schools, hospitals, churches and mosques were constructed throughout Eritrea. As early as 1954, Amharic was introduced as a mandatory subject in all Eritrean schools, from the fourth grade up. Under the pretext that the Federal Government needed to monitor the schools it had constructed as well as the Ethiopian teachers assigned to Eritrea, a federal Director of Education was appointed to Eritrea. Like the federal courts, he soon became instrumental in 'Ethiopianising' Eritrean education. Federal health, labour and religious affairs officials also added to the already large number of Ethiopian officials settled in the autonomous region.

The thorny issue of Eritrea's share of customs revenues dragged on with no visible solution. In November 1954, Tedla dispatched a high-level Eritrean delegation composed of secretaries Fessehatsion (Economy), Teklehaimanot

(Finance) and Haregot (Law and Justice) for discussions. They came back empty-handed and frustrated by yet another Ethiopian dismissal.[2]

Perhaps most telling in its impact on Eritrean sensitivities was the treatment that the Imperial Federal Council (IFC) was subjected to. At the beginning, Haile Selassie had appointed five Ethiopian officials led by the prominent *Blata* Mers'e Hazen Weldekirkos to represent Ethiopia on the council. In May 1955, he put all pretence aside and assigned three Eritrean dignitaries and two Ethiopian officials from Andargatchew's own staff to represent Ethiopia, thereby making a mockery of the whole intention behind the creation of the IFC. Of the ten positions on the council, eight were assigned to Eritreans, five representing Eritrea and three Ethiopia. The two Ethiopians were already deeply involved in the dismantlement of the Federation.[3] As far as Ethiopia was concerned, the Federation was an Eritrean affair whose problems would be discussed within Eritrea and resolved by the Emperor's representative. This was a matter that Eritreans did not take lightly.

These seemingly disconnected acts of Ethiopian interference further emboldened Andargatchew to take steps to silence Eritrean opposition by targeting Ibrahim Sultan. In May 1955, the Federal High Court charged Ibrahim with the federal offence of 'having insulted the head of a foreign government', an offence punishable under article 38 of the Federal Offences Proclamation of 1953.[4] The 'insult' was a passing remark that Ibrahim had made on a Sudanese official at a time when Sudan was yet to gain its independence and had no head of state. Nevertheless, Ibrahim was forced to appear before the federal court and received a two-year term of imprisonment pending the outcome of his appeal to the Imperial Supreme Court in Addis Ababa. In a blatant dismissal of the concept of parliamentary immunity to which the Eritrean courts adhered strictly, the Eritrean Assembly was informed of Ibrahim's case on 11 May, 27 days after he had appeared before the court and was summarily sentenced. Ibrahim achieved some relief in Addis Ababa, where the Ethiopian Supreme Court reduced the judgment to a suspended sentence, which allowed him to return to his legislative duties.

Such manifest disregard of Eritrean rights and sensitivities had a deep impact on ordinary Eritreans. As a consequence, labour unrest plagued various industries and enterprises in the first part of 1955. *Shifta* activities increased dramatically in the Western Provinces. Under the excuse that old sentiments of annexing the western part of Eritrea to Sudan might be rekindled, the Ethiopian Government stationed its 2nd Army Division in Asmera, with large regiments garrisoned at Akurdet and Tesseney. The whole country was thus placed under virtual Ethiopian military control.[5]

Andargatchew's Speech from the Throne

At the opening meeting of the 1955 session of the Eritrean Assembly, Andargatchew repeated his list of Imperial 'gifts' of the previous year in the form of schools, hospitals, churches and mosques, and the debts Ethiopia was incurring because of Eritrea. He then launched a scathing attack on what he termed 'the cleavages in thinking' dividing the country. He dismissed claims of the suppression of free speech as baseless; denied that Eritrean property had been looted and confiscated by federal authorities; and rejected the Assembly's resolution of 22 May 1954 on federal intervention in Eritrean affairs. On the last-mentioned point, he said,

> My colleagues and I have not understood, and it has not been explained to us, why it is claimed that the Office of the Representative has been 'corrupting the faith' of your colleagues by interfering in your affairs. Whatever it is, as far as the Office of the Representative is concerned, there is not, nor can there be, anything internal or external. The Eritrean case is entirely the concern of Ethiopia and the Emperor. What affects Eritrea negatively or positively cannot but harm or benefit Ethiopia.

With Tedla listening on one side, Andargatchew turned his focus to the Eritrean administration. 'Although we recognise that Eritrea has the right of internal administration, if there is no good administration and good management, Ethiopia in general and Eritrea, in particular, cannot be the beneficiaries. We are toiling to deliver peace and prosperity for the people of Eritrea.'[6] By all accounts, Andargatchew, whom Christopher Clapham describes as 'a Shoan nobleman with a hectoring manner and no connections with the area',[7] was poorly qualified to lecture the Assembly on parliamentary matters. He was an impatient overlord on a mission to do away with every vestige of Eritrean autonomy and, therefore, he viewed all the institutions and legal instruments guaranteeing that status as stumbling blocks to be removed. His implication that, for the Assembly to be considered mature and experienced, it had to accept him as the deliverer of all the 'blessings for Eritrea' was a mindless statement whose consequences he was unable to weigh.

The impact of his message on Eritreans was hugely negative. To Eritrean nationalists who had always seen the Federation as a betrayal of their cause and their demands for freedom, it reinforced their old position. To Federalists who still hoped to see the system work, it was a crushing blow. Even die-hard unionists bridled as Andargatchew moved to 'Ethiopianise' the Andinet party through systematic infiltration by young Tigrayan and Amhara residents of Eritrea, as we shall see in due course.

Urban Unemployment, Labour Strikes and Shifta Upsurge

Labour Strikes

The mass departure of Italian medium and small-scale businesses in the 1950s added to the intractable problem of unemployment in Eritrea. Even among those with guaranteed employment, the issue of low wages became a major source of labour unrest, especially in Asmera, Massawa and Asseb.[8] During the week of Andargatchew's speech alone, three substantial strikes rocked Asmera, two by the employees of Merenghi Bottlers and Melotti Brewery for higher pay and work insurance, and the third by employees of the Public Works Department. The last was significant as it involved the government directly and was nationwide. When government employees joined their fellow workers in solidarity, and stone-throwing incidents brought in the security forces, the issue acquired a political tone.

Although Tedla personally got involved and attempted to persuade workers to return to work, the strike continued in defiance and only ended when the government submitted to some of the workers' demands.[9] Federal officials viewed the PWD strike as an indulgence on the part of Tedla's administration. There were no labour unions in Ethiopia at the time and strikes were unthinkable. The Ethiopians were concerned that the Eritrean labour movement might set a bad example for Ethiopian workers, and the federal authorities wanted to see an end to these distractions.

Upsurge in *Shifta* Activity

1954 and 1955 saw an upsurge in *shifta* activity on a scale reminiscent of the late 1940s. In March and April 1955 alone, major raids and robberies by different *shifta* bands disrupted trade and transportation on the roads to Massawa, Keren, Dekemhare and Tsorona in southern Eritrea.[10] *Shifta* raids were carried out with such impunity that even urban centres like Mendefera, Barentu and the outskirts of Asmera were not spared. Most significant of these was the incident on 28 June 1955 at Mai Shehaiti, on the Hazemo Plains of Akeleguzai. Here, 60 armed Saho *shifta* under the leadership of Osman Haji Nasser and others ambushed a police patrol of thirteen officers. Osman Haji Nasser had been a member of the old Muslim League (ML)-supported Assaorta bands of Ali Shum and Omer Alula. As a result of the ambush, six policemen were killed. Their commander, a sergeant, was captured alive but soon executed by the rebels. The *shifta* lost only two men.[11]

What Eritrean officials found most shocking was the level of support that the *shifta* received from the population at large. As early as April of that year, the newspaper *Ethiopia* had been demanding the deployment of the Ethiopian 2nd Division to deal with the problem. Colonel Wright, Cracknell's successor as Commissioner of Police, who suspected that Ethiopia was actively supporting the *shifta* upsurge to discredit the Eritrean Government, ruled out the proposal. Wright, whose suspicion was reinforced by the freedom with which Tigrayan *shifta* crossed over the Mereb to loot at will, told the British diplomat E.D. Howes that he had no doubt about his conclusions.[12] Moreover, General Merid Mengesha's 2nd Division stood on the sidelines as the *shifta* raided the countryside unchecked. Like Wright, Eritreans generally saw Ethiopia's lack of interest in the *shifta* issue as a deliberate omission.

The big loser in this disruptive game was the Eritrean Government and, particularly, the Chief Executive. Through *Zemen*, the government issued a series of individual and collective appeals to the *shifta*'s conscience that went unheeded.[13] It was only then that Tedla moved to find a lasting solution to the problem. Unfortunately for him, it became intertwined with other matters that compromised his intentions.

The Government in Crisis

The Assembly and Tedla in Open Conflict

There were three groups of people in the Assembly—supporters of outright union, advocates of independence or the preservation of the Federation, and traditional *mislenes* and *nazirs* with little understanding of what was going on. 'There were many who understood only the procedural article for closure of debate, so they could go home,' as Akito put it. Tedla's problem was that he could not gain the support of any one of these diverse groups. Because of his aloof and dismissive nature, each group saw him as an obstacle to its specific objective. This led to a strange and unexpected realignment of forces within the Assembly. There was, for example, an expectation that Andargatchew's last speech from the throne might evoke a violent reaction from the opposition in the Assembly. That failed to materialise, resulting instead in the creation of a bipartisan force against Tedla.

The confrontation blew up when Unionist Party (UP) Assembly members, particularly their virtual leader, Dimetros Gebremariam, began to openly defy Tedla by opposing a number of his budget proposals.[14] Dimetros, who had thus far been the main force behind the frustration of every proposal of the opposition to protect Eritrea's rights, was considered Tedla's and Andargatchew's man in the Assembly. His sudden turn against Tedla thus gained him some friends, especially federalists like Habtezghi Okbazghi and Bezabih Tesfabruk and a few ML members like Mohammed Said Hassano.

In the week between 8 and 14 June, the Assembly met only once to ratify Tedla's proposal on the payment of taxes for the fiscal year 1954. For the rest of the week, lack of a quorum was given as the reason for the disruption of all sessions. In reality, the representatives were busy holding group and private consultations to build a common front against Tedla. On 16 June, Tedla made a pre-emptive move when Assembly vice president Demsas announced that the Chief Executive, in consultation with Assembly president Ali Rad'ai, had closed the Assembly for yet another twenty days. Beyond citing article 48(5) of the Constitution as his authority, he gave no reason for his decision. Assembly secretary McCleary had advised Tedla to be cautious before he made the decision, but Tedla explained that he needed time to prepare his counter-move.[15]

It turned out that the plotting Assembly members were at a loss as to how exactly to confront the Chief Executive. But they could easily identify Ali Rad'ai as Tedla's hatchet man, and all the secret meetings and discussions of the previous week were about removing the president. Tedla's pre-emptive measure was taken to protect his ally in the Assembly.

On the same day, 41 members signed a petition demanding that the Chief Executive convene an extraordinary meeting of the Assembly. The government refused on a procedural technicality and, to add insult to injury, the Chief Executive departed for Addis Ababa, leaving the representatives in a state of limbo. Angry and frustrated, Eritrean Democratic Front (EDF) leaders *Dejazmatch* Berhe Asberom, brother of *Ras* Tessema, and *Qadi* Ali Omer led a smaller group of representatives to the Supreme Court and handed Sir James Shearer another petition. This time, they accused Tedla of a series of 'unjustifiable' closures of the Assembly, of nepotism and favouritism in his award of government positions, and of general inefficiency. They demanded his impeachment under article 75 of the Constitution. But Shearer turned down their demands on the grounds that they had not presented adequate evidence to prove the allegations. Besides, even if they had, he would not discuss the case with them as he would have to adjudicate it, if finally allowed.

Abudawd was in the group, and his vivid description of what happened next reveals the confusion and naiveté among the representatives. They crowded the large hall on the ground floor of the court and agreed that they had three choices. First, apologise to Tedla and beg him to reopen the Assembly; second, go public and expose Tedla's misdeeds against the Assembly; or, third, appeal to the Emperor. In their state of confusion, they chose to appeal to the Emperor.[16]

That same morning, 21 June, the petition rejected by Shearer, duly signed by 41 Assembly members, was telegraphed to Emperor Haile Selassie. Shearer had indicated to the representatives that their case would stand a chance if they bolstered their allegations with more substantive evidence. In their fear of losing their Assembly seats and indeed the Assembly itself, they sought a fair judgement from the Emperor, whom many still considered committed as sovereign to the federal cause.

Tedla's Counter-move

Tedla came back from his trip to Addis Ababa three days before the Assembly was to reopen on 6 July. Since Weldegiorgis had been ousted as Minister of the Pen by then, it was not clear with whom he had met or what he had accomplished in the Ethiopian capital. The same afternoon, on 3 July, he called a press conference. 'We are taking measures unusual for peace times in order to put an end to the acts of vandalism pervading this country,' he told the journalists. With these words, he announced that his administration was issuing Proclamation 1 of 1955 to Protect the Security of the Population. Besides imposing severe punishments on the active *shifta*, it provided for extreme measures against individuals, groups or 'associations' deemed supportive of or sympathetic to the *shifta* or other illegal groups. It gave to the Chief Executive, the security department and the police force extraordinary powers in carrying out their newly expanded responsibilities. To explain his decision to close Assembly meetings, he said that 'evil and self-serving people' were taking advantage of the situation 'to disrupt the livelihood of the people' and that it was his responsibility to fulfil his mission 'under the leadership of my Emperor and for the benefit of our country'.[17]

As always, Tedla's press conference raised more questions and doubts than clarifications. By defining the word 'associations' as 'races (tribes), clans, self-help groups or managements, districts, towns and villages', the proclamation extended its scope beyond the *shifta* menace into all walks of Eritrean life. The suspicion that Tedla's real intention behind the proclamation was to target and silence his political opponents, both within the Assembly and among the public, tarnished his image even further.

Proclamation 1 of 1955 was published on 5 July. The next day, the Assembly met to resume the regular session interrupted by Tedla's latest closure. At 9.45 am, Demsas came into the chamber to announce that the Chief Executive, in consultation with the president of the Assembly, had decided to close the body for an additional twenty days. In his message of closure, Tedla wrote, 'In order to avoid the fearful consequences of the worrisome disagreements within the Assembly and to protect the country's peace, I have come to realise that there is one way open to me—to close the Assembly in accordance with article 48(5) of the Constitution. I hope that we will not be obliged to take similar measures in the future.'[18]

An uproar accompanied Demsas's hasty exit from the Assembly. Angry members demanded that Assembly clerk Fergus McCleary chair a meeting at which they proposed to pass a vote of no confidence in the president, Ali Rad'ai. McCleary declined to do so because he had no constitutional authority to convene the Assembly. In the meantime, helmeted police troops encircled the Assembly building. Director general Mesfin Gebrehiwet gave the order for the representatives to be forcibly removed from the chamber and for all the committee rooms to be sealed. No formal or informal meetings were to be held within the premises. McCleary met Tedla and attempted to reason with him. Since the representatives were calling for Ali Rad'ai's resignation, he told him that it was an internal matter for the legislature. The Chief Executive's actions would be seen as interference and the Supreme Court would so determine should they take their case to it. Tedla relented and called off the proposed police action.[19]

Nevertheless, he stuck to his decision to close the Assembly. On the same day, *Zemen* announced that the Chief Executive was scheduled to address the public at the Cinema Capitol on the following day, 7 July. The representatives for their part had not been idle all morning. Before Demsas's announcement of the closure of the Assembly, 44 of the 46 members in attendance voted to remove Ali Rad'ai from his presidency. When McCleary handed the Assembly decision to Tedla, his terse two-sentence reply, which he sent three days later, read: 'Your message on the President of the Assembly, listing the names of 44 members of the Assembly and signed by them, has reached me. Its contents are unacceptable both to the provisions of the Constitution and the Assembly's standing procedures.'[20]

Having anticipated Tedla's response, the representatives held their own press conference on 7 July, hours before Tedla's address at the Cinema Capitol. Here, they accused Ali Rad'ai of having compromised the Assembly and subjected it to the 'undignified subordination to the personal and often dictatorial interests and points of view of the Chief Executive'. Two-thirds of the members voted to remove him and decided to replace him with a representative of their choice. They also gave a list of the actions harming the functioning of the Assembly and the country at large owing to the Assembly president's total submission to the will of the Chief Executive. In addition, the representatives accused Tedla of nepotism in his official appointments and attacked Proclamation 1 of 1955 as a 'fascistic law' aimed at promoting his family interests and dealing with persons opposed to his 'dictatorial system', and as intended to be used for his benefit in the coming elections.[21]

Tedla's Address at the Cinema Capitol

On 7 July, Tedla addressed a packed audience at the Cinema Capitol. It was a rambling speech full of inconsistencies and ambiguities. He praised his administration for running a non-partisan government free of religious or sectarian considerations. He gave a ringing defence of Ali Rad'ai, whom he characterised as a man essential for the preservation of religious harmony in the country. His closure of the Assembly to maintain Ali Rad'ai in his position was meant, he said, for the good and unity of the country. Since he didn't have a prepared text to refer to, he kept jumping from one subject to another. In an emotional moment, he spoke of the pure love and faith that attracted 'the people of Mereb Mellash' to Ethiopia. He described the 'Muslims of Mereb Mellash' as 'Ethiopian Muslims' who are 'proud like us of their Ethiopian identity ... and are aware that Ethiopia is not the *risti* of Christians alone'. He ended his speech with words of praise for the Emperor and his own parents. 'I would much prefer to run errands for His Majesty, my Emperor, staying close to him and under his shelter. Thanks to my parents, I can be useful in a variety of ways,' he concluded.[22]

Although Tedla's speech was published in full in all the newspapers and distributed as a pamphlet, it never made the impact he had expected. On the contrary, as the British consul Howes put it, his public defence of Ali Rad'ai against the Assembly was seen as meddling in the affairs of the legislature. Beyond that, no one seems to have taken any notice of the contents of the speech.[23] Nor did Tedla's praise of the Emperor bring any dividend for him at the Asmera Palace. Just before his speech, the rebel representatives had gone to Andargatchew to present their case to him and inform him that their telegram had been sent to the Emperor. Andargatchew advised them to wait for the Emperor's response and then saw them off.

Just a little over a year earlier, the Assembly had overwhelmingly voted to condemn Andargatchew's interference in internal Eritrean affairs. Consumed by their indignation over Tedla's high-handedness, they were now, perhaps unwittingly, placing the Assembly's fate in the hands of Andargatchew, the man broadly suspected of being the behind-the-scenes force manipulating the crisis in Ethiopia's favour. This was the time when the priest Dimetros was busy establishing a printing press for an Orthodox Church-supported organisation called Mahber Hawaryat (Association of the Disciples). As a major financier of the project, Andargatchew had developed a close working relationship with Dimetros, leading many to conclude that the crisis in the Assembly was the product of a collusion between the two politicians. As the British consul put it, Ethiopia needed the crisis in order to make a case for immediate union by depicting Eritrea as a nation incapable of administering itself.[24]

In the middle of the confusion, Tedla adopted a business-as-usual attitude and, on 11 September, he travelled to Adi Qeih in Akeleguzai to campaign for the strict implementation of his banditry proclamation. He was received with a degree of pomp and ceremony that must have eased his worst fears. In his speech, he ordered all the *shifta* in the area to lay down their arms within the following fifteen days. He warned of the dire consequences to the *shifta*, their families and government officials who failed to cooperate with the provisions of the proclamation.[25] The question was: would Tedla's power last till his own fifteen-day deadline?

The Removal of Tedla Bairu

On 14 September, Ali Rad'ai was summoned to Addis Ababa. The following day, Andargatchew followed him. On the 19th, ten members of the Assembly also received the same call and boarded an aeroplane. Only two of them, Dimetros and Bemnet Tessema, were known Unionist Party members; the rest, except for Idris Mohammed Adem of ML-WP, were all Eritrean democratic Front (EDF) leaders from the ML or the Shuban al Rabita. Berhe Asberom represented the old Liberal Progressive Party (LPP).[26] We need to ask why such known fighters for Eritrean independence, who had staged a spirited struggle for the Eritrean Constitution and the country's autonomous rights, expected to find justice from the Emperor. Akito described the thinking behind the move:

> Tedla was so sure of the Emperor's affection for him that he thought he had become a mini-king. He wanted to bypass Andargatchew and deal with the Emperor directly. But Andargatchew was the Emperor's representative and would not let Tedla bypass him. This was the source of their quarrel. Tedla's disagreements with the Assembly incapacitated him. He could reach the Emperor only through Andargatchew who had his own men and agents, mainly Dimetros within the Assembly. Dimetros loved Ethiopia and Ethiopians.
>
> Tedla believed that Haile Selassie loved him so much that he would never be tired of him. He fought against us to please him. He even went as far as disregarding the Constitution and that is when we took him to task. When he realised his fault, he feared the Emperor's wrath and told us he could not present our demands to the

> Emperor. 'You do it yourselves,' was what he told us and that's how the ten of us travelled to Addis Ababa.
>
> We told Haile Selassie, 'This man is interfering in the affairs of the Assembly. If the Assembly is independent, you are the protector of the Eritrean Constitution ... We request that you protect the Constitution.'

Akito admitted that the decision to take the matter to Haile Selassie was controversial among Eritreans of various stripes. Many expressed concern that, despite all his faults, Tedla's removal would spell the death of the Federation. The delegates' answer, according to Akito, was:

> Why shouldn't we go? We lay all responsibility on Haile Selassie's head. It is either that or let Tedla play as he pleases, closing and reopening the Assembly with impunity. The Constitution does not allow him to do that. Haile Selassie is the Constitution's guarantor. If he wants to do away with it, let him do that and suffer the repercussions. Our thinking at that time was that our move was correct because Tedla was planning to do as he saw fit; even give Eritrea away to Ethiopia.

The delegates were still in Addis Ababa when Tedla received his summons. Akito narrated what happened:

> Haile Selassie said to Tedla, 'The members of the Assembly do not want you and my people in Eritrea do not want you. You may resign.' Tedla asked, 'Does this mean that you are telling me to step down?' 'We did not elect you,' responded the Emperor, 'It was the Eritrean Assembly that elected you. Go and talk to them.' It was all Tedla's doing. He wilfully entered into a trap and Haile Selassie seized him by the neck.[27]

On 24 July, Tedla, Ali Rad'ai and the ten Assembly delegates took the same flight back to Asmera. On the same day, Ali Rad'ai tendered his letter of resignation as president of the Assembly. The next morning, members of the Assembly led by Berhe Asberom attempted to reopen the suspended session in defiance of Tedla's order. According to Zewde Retta, they did so on the strength of Haile Selassie's encouraging words during their meeting. 'Even we cannot shut down the parliament in this manner,' the Emperor said, 'let alone Tedla. Since we have ordered its reopening, go back to your work.'[28]

When McCleary informed Tedla of the new development at the Assembly, he replied that he had not received any notice from the Emperor on the illegality of the closure. He was, however, aware that newspapers were commenting on the issue. He then ordered the Eritrean and Ethiopian flags to be flown at the entrance of the Eritrean Assembly but still declined to consent to its reopening.[29]

It is difficult to assess what Tedla's state of mind was in those nervous days after his meeting with Haile Selassie. By refusing to reopen the Assembly just a day earlier than its due date, he went against the Emperor's bidding. But even more strange was a letter that he wrote to Ali Rad'ai after the latter's resignation. In recognition of his past excellent services, he told Ali Rad'ai, he was appointing him Secretary of Social Affairs.[30] Ali Rad'ai came back with polite words of gratitude and a humiliating message to Tedla. 'When I was honoured to meet the Emperor,' read the message, 'he told me that my services will be needed at the official level. For this reason, I am obliged not to accept your kind offer at this time.'[31]

On 28 July, the Assembly met to elect a replacement for Ali Rad'ai. In a contest between Idris Mohammed Adem, ML-WP, and Mohammed Said Hassano, ML-EDF, the former was elected with 51 votes for and 16 against. 28 July was also Tedla Bairu's last day in power. In a letter to the president of the Assembly, he gave 'reasons of ill health' for leaving. He wished the Assembly the best of luck and notified the Emperor of his decision.[32]

As he left for Addis Ababa on the morning of 30 July, *Zemen*, which had been singing his praises a few days earlier, dismissed Tedla's excuse of ill health. It claimed that, in his farewell meeting with his staff, Tedla had revealed that the real cause for his departure was his opposition to union with Ethiopia. If this was so, the paper commented sarcastically:

> then His Excellency *Dejazmatch* Tedla Bairu has departed a hated man by his own constituents and totally unacknowledged by the other side. His position had not been as simple as many had thought. It was never easy to reconcile two ways of thinking ... But he would have avoided blame if, before resigning, he had assembled elders and social leaders to impart to them his ideas on mending and reconciling the country's problems; and to clearly state his proposals on the way forward.[33]

A second article had a field day in making fun of the Tedla–Ali Rad'ai exchange about the latter's appointment as Secretary. 'Was he appointing him for that one day between 27 and 29 September?' the paper scoffed, 'or was he doing it on behalf of the incoming Chief Executive?' The article also rebuked Ali Rad'ai for going public with a private Imperial 'promise' made to him, probably in reply to his own appeal.[34]

Except for some grumblings from Tedla's fellow residents of Hamasien who saw his departure as a defeat, no one came to Tedla's public defence. Even the Hamasien ripple soon ended when a group claiming to speak on behalf of the province rejected the sentiment.[35] Thus, Tedla exited the scene friendless and unheralded. Of all the unionists who had delivered Eritrea to Ethiopia, Tedla was the most effective and useful. Yet, like Gebremeskel Weldu and *Abune* Markos before him, his usefulness had come to an end.

In Addis Ababa, Haile Selassie sent him to the Ethiopian Senate, or 'the Garage', as it was known, being widely regarded as the receptacle for undesirables. In the 1960s he served as ambassador to Sweden before abandoning this position to join the Eritrean Liberation Front, reportedly as vice president to one of his former enemies in the Eritrean Assembly, Idris Mohammed Adem. We find no record of what Tedla accomplished in that capacity. He died in 1982.

PART THREE

THE ROAD TO THE ERITREAN REVOLUTION

18

ASFAHA WELDEMIKAEL, CHIEF EXECUTIVE

The Rise of Asfaha Weldemikael

The morning of 8 August 1955 was set for the election of the new Chief Executive. Mohammed Omer Akito described his part in the process as follows:

> As I entered the Assembly building, Bemnet Tessema stopped me at the entrance and took me aside. 'Listen Akito,' he said to me, 'I am going to nominate Haregot for Chief Executive. Please second me. Otherwise, Asfaha will be elected and Eritrea will be doomed.'
>
> To tell the truth, I had never liked Haregot—his character, his actions, not even his face. Asfaha was a knowledgeable, humble person. I used to respect him, but this was politics. For the Federation, Haregot was preferable. Asfaha meant Ethiopia and Haile Selassie. I said okay reluctantly. Bemnet was a Protestant from Hamasien. He was a unionist. He did not want Asfaha, neither did I.

Inside the Assembly, Asfaha was the first to be nominated by none other than *Qadi* Musa Umron, one of the founders and the leader of the Muslim League (ML) in Keren. It was strange, to say the least, that a committed fighter for independence would nominate an equally committed annexationist to become Chief Executive. Unless, as Akito intimated, the opposition was daring Haile Selassie to proceed with annexation and face the repercussions, it was a move hard to understand.

The Ethiopians had been campaigning for Asfaha's election by acclamation, and that was what they were expecting until Bemnet Tessema rose to nominate Haregot. Akito described what happened next:

> I was so disgusted with my Assembly colleagues that I left my assigned seat and was sitting at the back with the invited authorities. When Haregot was nominated, I kept quiet for a while. No one dared second Bemnet's nomination. They were about to declare the acclamation when I raised my hand and shouted out my support. I could see Dimetros's dark face from where I was. It got as black as his black overcoat. If I had not seconded the nomination, Haregot's political life would have ended and they would have declared the vote as agreement to annexation. That moment, I knew that I would be in trouble with Asfaha and the Ethiopians.[1]

Asfaha won the election by 48 to Haregot's 18 votes, with one abstention. After taking the oath of office and pledging to protect the Federation, Asfaha told the representatives that his well-publicised candidacy had given rise to speculation on the future of the Federation.

> By casting your votes for me, you have made it clear where your inclinations and priorities lie ... All of us, especially I, know the intense love for Eritrea and Eritreans that has dwelled in the heart of our own Emperor Haile Selassie I. It is better that we leave all that is beneficial to Eritrea in the hands of our blessed Emperor. Standing up individually to do for Eritrea one thing or the other may be beyond our capabilities. And, in truth, if we have the honesty and ability to assess our people's real thinking, we can see and hear how much the Ethiopian people of Eritrea love Haile Selassie I, the symbol of their freedom. Their spirit itself is self-evident. It needs no interpreter.[2]

Asfaha was clear and unequivocal about his aims and intentions right from this, his maiden speech as Chief Executive. If the federalists and independence-seekers among the representatives listening to him had had other expectations when one of their leaders nominated him, they were in for a shock.

But who exactly was Asfaha Weldemikael? Born in 1914 to a prominent Catholic family in Segeneiti in Akeleguzai, Asfaha graduated from the Catholic *seminario* in Keren, thus obtaining educational qualifications far above the fourth grade mostly available to his peers. His love for Ethiopia, he claimed, was instilled in him by Eritrean clerics with a biblical adulation for Ethiopia and its Emperor.

Before the Italian invasion of Ethiopia, he served as an *aspirante* (cadet) and interpreter at the political offices in Asmera and the Italian consulate in Gondar. Impressed by his service and loyalty, the Italians sent him to Italy in 1936 as a translator of confiscated Ethiopian documents under the supervision of the prominent scholar Enrico Cerulli. In 1937, following Governor Graziani's excessive reprisals in response to an assassination attempt against him, Asfaha was chosen to liaise between 500 Ethiopian noblemen and high officials exiled to Azinara (a Sardinian island).[3] More than anything else, Asfaha reminisced, their plight awoke resentment against Italy and strengthened his Ethiopian resolve.

Back in Ethiopia after Graziani's removal, Asfaha was assigned as aide and personal interpreter to General Nasi, who chose Asfaha to spearhead his policy of pacification by opening a dialogue with the patriots fighting Italy in the countryside. In the process, Asfaha met and befriended the patriots Abebe Aregay, Mesfin Sileshi and others, whom he also served, in his own words, 'by taking on the role of a double agent'.

Although British forces captured Addis Ababa from the Italians in May 1941, General Nasi's resistance from his stronghold in Gondar kept them at bay until November of that year. As his personal interpreter and aide, Asfaha, now a *fitawrari,* stayed with Nasi through thick and thin during the war. When Ethiopian officers accompanying British troops captured him at his office, he had every reason to fear that he would be shot summarily. Instead, he was presented to the Crown Prince

Asfawossen, Haile Selassie's heir, who praised his services to the patriots and to the people of Gondar and Gojam during their nine months of isolation and ordeal. To Asfaha's consternation, the Crown Prince pardoned his loyalty to the Italians and recommended him to the Emperor. Promptly, the Emperor appointed him director general in the Crown Prince's administrative region of Wello.[4] Through this generous act, Haile Selassie gained the total and unquestioning loyalty of a lifelong Eritrean servant. In 1996, some months before his death, the half-paralysed and bedridden Asfaha spoke of Haile Selassie as if he were still in the presence of the monarch—in hushed undertones. 'His Majesty used to say of me, "Asfaha did a lot for Ethiopia while under the Italians. He is an Ethiopian-Eritrean, not an Eritrean-Ethiopian."'

Soon, Asfaha became one of the founders and prime movers of the Addis Ababa-based association for union between Eritrea and Ethiopia and, eventually, its president. He was an effective instrument in the transfer of irredentist ideas from Ethiopia to Eritrea. From his offices in Mekele and Adi Grat in Tigray, he used his deep knowledge of Ethiopian history and culture to train Eritrean cadres for the Ethiopian cause. An attractive speaker and refined conversationalist, he was as adept at quoting from the Bible as from Dante and Victor Hugo. When Haile Selassie appointed him vice representative under Andargatchew in 1952, he knew exactly what to expect in return.

Tedla Bairu's ouster from power put Haregot Abbay at the forefront of the candidacy for Chief Executive. With the likely support of the Hamasien, ML and federalist votes, he could easily have been elected. But opposition to Haregot came from Ali Rad'ai and his ML-WP faction in the Assembly, who approached Andargatchew to demand that Asfaha be released from federal duties to stand against Haregot. The matter went to the Emperor for his decision and, according to Asfaha, 'His Majesty asked, "Is it possible? How can an Ethiopian be Chief Executive of Eritrea?" He used to call me "an Ethiopian-Eritrean". They told him that it was possible since I was an Eritrean by birth and the Eritrean Constitution allowed it. "So be it, then. Who can serve us better than Asfaha?" is what I heard he said.'[5] Every effort was exerted to persuade Haregot to withdraw his candidacy and so make way for Asfaha's election by acclamation. It was Haregot's refusal to give in that led to the election process already described.[6]

One thing to note here was that Asfaha's tenure as the Emperor's vice representative in Eritrea did not terminate upon his election as Chief Executive. Since no new appointment was made to fill it, it was assumed that Asfaha would cover both posts, a situation not allowed for by the Eritrean Constitution and the Federal Act.

Initial Attempts at Appeasement and Annexation

As soon as he took office, Asfaha paid a courtesy visit to *Mufti* Ibrahim Mukhtar, an erudite scholar in his own right, who was the recognised force behind the Muslim

League of Eritrea. His reputation as a nationalist was also sustained by his principled advocacy of independence before the UN Commission of Inquiry and his support of a bicameral Assembly to represent the nation and the diverse population during the Matienzo discussions.[7]

Astutely, Asfaha told the *mufti* that he was worried that some Eritreans might seek to invite foreigners to compromise Eritrea's interests. He had thus come to the *mufti* for advice on religious affairs and his prayers and support. Ibrahim Mukhtar responded that his faith and position demanded that he pray and give advice on matters of interest to the people. However, he expressed his concern that the UN resolution and the Constitution of Eritrea were not being implemented in either the letter or spirit. 'I fear that Eritrea's rights will be assaulted,' he told the Chief Executive. 'I will give my advice to the extent of my capabilities, but it is only if you dispense justice and fairness that you will gain the support of the people.' 'Don't ever worry that the people's rights will be compromised,' Asfaha said as he rose to leave. 'It is unthinkable that I will give up my rights to serve a non-Eritrean.'[8]

Ever after that meeting, Asfaha and the *mufti* did not see eye to eye on major issues. In December 1960, they clashed on Asfaha's unconstitutional interference in the appointment of judges to the Sharia courts.[9] In 1961, the *mufti* was accused of the 'treasonable' act of allegedly having given an interview to various newspapers in Saudi Arabia exposing Ethiopia's disregard for the Federal Act and the Eritrean Constitution, thereby 'disseminating lies highly damaging to Ethiopia'. Asfaha even formed an investigative committee led by himself to interrogate the *mufti*, who denied all the charges.[10] After Asfaha's attempt to appease Muslims through the *mufti* failed on their first encounter, he turned his attention to his mission of annexation.

Asfaha never saw Eritrea's federal status as anything more than an irritating obstacle on the way to full unity. 'It was nothing better than a municipal authority,' he told this writer. 'We never asked for it. They did it to protect the Italians in Eritrea. We did not command the sea. We did not control the railways; economically we had nothing. It stood for a while because His Majesty loved us and supported it. Otherwise, it was a vacuum.' With this attitude, Asfaha could not contain his enthusiasm for too long. As soon as he named his cabinet secretaries—two unionists, two Al Rabita members and two technocrats—he solicited the support of Gebreyohannes, now a cabinet secretary, and the Assembly member Dimetros to send a four-point proposal for a vote in the Assembly. The four points included the adoption of Amharic as Eritrea's official language, the scrapping of the Eritrean flag and of Eritrea's coat of arms, and the appointment of the Chief Executive by the Emperor rather than through election by the Eritrean Assembly.[11]

Rather than putting the proposals to a vote as instructed, the Assembly president Idris Mohammed Adem realised that constitutional issues were at stake and referred the matter to Assembly clerk Fergus McCleary, who sent them on to the new Attorney General of Eritrea, the American F.F. Russell. Russell advised that the first three points could be passed by a two-thirds majority vote in the Assembly. The fourth proposal on the appointment of the Chief Executive by the Emperor contravened article 16 of the Eritrean Constitution, and thus required an amendment of that provision and of the Federal Act.[12] Asfaha's proposals aroused the opposition of Assembly members. The ML faction even sent messages and telegrams both to Asfaha and Haile Selassie voicing their indignation and threatening to appeal directly to the UN. Asfaha relented for the time being.

In May 1956, he garnered the support of some Assembly members and presented another set of proposals to Andargatchew for approval by the Emperor. His intention was to follow this up with a final vote in the Assembly. Zewde Retta, citing Ethiopian documents, summarises Asfaha's new proposals as follows: The Eritrean Chief Executive was to be appointed by the Emperor from among representatives nominated by members of the Assembly for one term only and the position was to alternate between a Muslim and Christian candidate every four years. When the Emperor appointed a Christian as Chief Executive, a Muslim president of the Assembly would be elected by the Assembly, and vice versa. When the Assembly president was a Muslim or Christian, the vice president would be from the other religion. Since the Chief Executive was appointed by the Emperor, he would be directly responsible to the Emperor; the Office of the Emperor's Representative would thus become redundant and therefore would be eliminated.

Without digesting the full content of the proposals, Andargatchew hurried to Addis Ababa for the Emperor's review. As customary, Haile Selassie called Aklilu and his crown advisors for discussion. To the Emperor's displeasure, Aklilu turned the proposals down line by line on the basis that they contravened the letter and spirit of both the Eritrean Constitution and the Federal Act. If the Emperor was to appoint a candidate nominated by the Assembly, his role would be a mere formality, devoid of any political leverage. He also noted that the removal of the Office of the Emperor's Representative from Eritrea would disturb the existing constitutional balance in the country. Furthermore, Ethiopia's adherence to the federal arrangement could encourage the Somalis, still under Italian trusteeship, to take Eritrea as a model and seek a similar future.

It was at this juncture that Andargatchew understood that his own position was being threatened by Asfaha's proposals. Gasping '*O mon Dieu, protège-moi des mes amis* [Oh my God, protect me from my friends],' he quickly aligned himself with Aklilu to oppose the package that he had promoted so enthusiastically moments earlier. When the committee, led again by defence minister Abebe Aregay, also accepted Aklilu's line, Haile Selassie gave in but not without blaming Aklilu for his constant stand against annexation of Eritrea and chastising his son-in-law for bringing to him ideas he had not digested earlier. He reminded the committee that Asfaha's efforts always derived from his genuine beliefs.[13]

Fundamental Changes in the Federal Arrangement

The Ethiopian Constitution of 1955

It had been obvious from the beginning that Eritrea's democratic laws would force Ethiopia to change or amend its feudal constitution of 1931. But other internal factors also demanded such a change. To modernise his administration and decrease his dependence on Ethiopia's feudal and Orthodox hierarchy, Haile Selassie recruited a crop of young, mostly Western-educated Ethiopians who began demanding some fundamental changes.[14] Thus, on the twenty-fifth anniversary of his accession to the throne, he 'granted' the 1955 Revised Constitution to his people.

In its first article, the document, which made no mention of the Federal Act, the Federation or Eritrean autonomy, declared that the Imperial Ethiopian State, which constituted all 'the regions, seas and islands', would be included within the 'sovereign Crown of Ethiopia' whose sovereignty over the regions was indivisible. All citizens of the Imperial Ethiopian State, including those who lived abroad, were collectively declared Ethiopian citizens. It was a carefully crafted provision meant to leave no room for any suggestions of an Eritrean citizenship, which as far as the 1955 Constitution was concerned no longer existed.

There were many differences between the two constitutions and their principles were incompatible in practically every aspect. The Revised Constitution retained the supremacy of the Emperor as sovereign almost word for word as in the 1931 original. He still appointed the members of the Senate and all the judges to the various levels of the Ethiopian judicial system. Whereas the Eritrean Chief Executive could be subject to impeachment for offences he might commit, the Emperor's very honour and person was inviolable and above any legal accountability. In other words, the separation of powers between the three branches of government, which the Federal Act assumed would prevail in the federal set-up, was totally obliterated.

The only novelty introduced in this area was election to the lower house of parliament by universal suffrage and the recognition of the right of women to vote and stand for election, a provision sorely missing in the Eritrean Constitution. Even here, since the resolutions and laws proposed by the house had to be ratified by the Haile Selassie-appointed Senate and the Emperor himself, its powers were limited. Of particular significance to Eritreans were the limitations imposed on the fundamental freedoms—of speech, press, movement—guaranteed by the Eritrean Constitution and the Federal Act. The Revised Constitution did include every conceivable human and civil right in its articles. However, they were all made subject to subsequent decrees, regulations and legal notices that would, in practice, compromise their enjoyment by the population.

The repercussions of the submersion of an essentially democratic constitution within the legal framework of an absolute monarchy would soon become evident.

Administrative Changes in Eritrea

In April 1956, Asfaha issued two executive orders eliminating the Office of Director General and creating the new administrative region of Asseb. As indicated previously, the Office of the Director General, thus far occupied by Tedla's aide Mesfin Gebrehiwet, was responsible for the implementation of the Civil Service Act, one of the organic laws of the Government of Eritrea. Except for some reports of nepotism and religious bias in a few appointments, Tedla's administration had never been criticised for working outside the requirements and legal framework of the Act. The Civil Service Commission, which was chaired by the Chief Executive, was directly supervised by the director general and run by an officer answerable to him.

Documents of the Civil Service Commission preserved at the RDC clearly show the efficient and independent manner in which it operated during the Tedla period. When Asfaha came to power, one of his first targets was Mesfin Gebrehiwet, who was dismissed from his job. Soon afterwards, the Office of the Director General was eliminated by Order no. 25 of March 1956. With this move, the civil service lost its independence under the Act. As a replacement, Asfaha created an office called Chief of Cabinet of the Chief Executive. According to the British consul, the function of the Chief of Cabinet was to implement the orders and priorities of the Chief Executive. Like Tedla, Asfaha became notorious for ignoring his cabinet secretaries in making important decisions. This enabled him to sideline the Civil Service Commission and turn the Chief of Cabinet into his private secretary. Consequently, government appointments, promotions and dismissals were made on the whim of the Chief Executive, reducing the commission and its officer to a rubber stamp of his decisions.[15] The Civil Service Act thus became the first of the organic laws to be done away with.

At this time, another administrative change was taking place in Asseb, which, as capital of Denkalia, had been under the regional administration of the Red Sea province based at Massawa. By Order 27 of 5 March 1956, Asfaha created a seventh administrative province with Asseb as the capital.[16] The reason he gave was that the distance between the two ports created insurmountable communications and administrative problems. The real reason was Ethiopia's desire to control Asseb through Asmera, with Asfaha's approval and cooperation. This marks the start of Ethiopia's overt moves to physically separate Asseb from the rest of Eritrea and completely control the port.[17] *Sheik* Musa Gaas, former district chief, was appointed senior divisional officer for the Asseb and Denkalia province.

Changes in Assembly and Police Force Leadership

The Rise of Dimetros Gebremariam

On 24 September 1955, the federalist-leaning Habtezghi Okbazghi opened a debate in the Assembly for the removal of vice president Demsas Weldemikael, whom he accused of having obstructed the process of deposing Ali Rad'ai and facilitating Tedla Bairu's various suspensions of the Assembly. Of the 46 members present, 42 supported him in his motion. Demsas was forced to step down.

Immediately, Habtezghi nominated arch-unionist Dimetros Gebremariam to replace Demsas. No other candidate was put forward, and 'the Priest', or 'Rasputin' as the Asmera public nicknamed him, was elected by the same margin, 42 of the 46 members present. There were two abstentions on both counts. Strangely, it was the federalists and former members of the Eritrean Democratic Front (EDF) who were behind his election.

Born in September 1900 in Mai Chew, near Areza, on the western escarpment of Seraye, Dimetros obtained his traditional religious education from senior clerics in various monasteries and sanctuaries in Eritrea and Ethiopia. He was ordained a priest in 1922, an investiture that was later ratified by the Coptic establishment in Alexandria in 1929.[18] By the accounts of all his peers, Dimetros was a bright young priest endowed with an impressive natural intelligence. 'But he was unlettered—*analfabeto*—in modern education,' one of his colleagues said. 'His natural intelligence helped him to grasp facts and make political decisions. His *vantaggio dall'ignoranza* (advantage of ignorance) enabled him to pursue his decisions, right or wrong, with bullish determination.'[19]

In the 1920s, *Dejazmatch* (later, *Ras*) Kidanemariam of Areza, the dean of the Italian-appointed district chiefs of the colony, had employed Dimetros as an aide. In his spacious court, the chief behaved like a little monarch, holding public hearings, throwing banquets, accepting and dispensing gifts, granting favours and meting out punishments. Dimetros added the art of traditional feudal administration and justice to his already considerable knowledge of Orthodox religious dogma and the Scriptures. It did not take him long to rise to the position of spiritual confessor and administrative aide to the ageing chief.[20]

In the 1940s, when he became the leader of the Unionist Party, Kidanemariam was already a frail octogenarian, and it fell to his assistant, Dimetros, to represent him in the party's activities both in the Seraye province and nationwide. He made his mark there and, in 1947, was elected to the central council of the Unionist Party. No candidate contested his election to the Eritrean Assembly in 1952.

Dimetros's political influence was greatly enhanced by the reform movement that he initiated in the early 1950s. Led by the ultra-conservative *Abune* Markos, the Orthodox Church had been losing touch with the mass of its Eritrean followers. Its youth movement, the Fenote Berhan, was particularly ill-organised, ill-equipped and too confined to the Asmera area to win over Eritrean youths, who were exposed to foreign-imported religions of various denominations. Even Orthodox priests began defecting to the new religions.[21]

In 1951, a grassroots initiative opposed to Markos's plans to reduce the number of saints' and fast days and curtail the authority of monasteries over churches, turned into a reform movement when Dimetros was asked to guide it. This led to the formation of Mahber Hawaryat, or Association of the Disciples. In the fierce and highly divisive conflict that arose between Markos and Dimetros, the latter gained the full support of Andargatchew and the Ethiopian Government to override Markos's old powers. At the inauguration of Mahber Hawaryat on 5 July 1953, Dimetros said, 'Our Orthodox religion has not been effective in spreading its spiritual and evangelical principles. We find ourselves in an inferior position in this respect. We therefore urge all concerned to reconsider what existed in light of what ought to exist for the enhancement of our religious system.'[22]

Dimetros's reform campaign turned Mahber Hawaryat into one of the most efficient and feared religious organisations in the country. Its highly aggressive drive to revive and expand the Orthodox faith led to the building of churches in deeply Muslim areas and even the conversion of some Kunama people to the faith. In this controversial endeavour, Dimetros secured the friendship of Andargatchew, with whom he formed a business partnership for the establishment of a Mahber Hawaryat Printing Press. It was to be a source of great revenue for the Mahber and also for Andargatchew.

When Dimetros became vice president of the Assembly, he accumulated formidable political and spiritual power and influence. A gift to Ethiopia and its Emperor, he was second only to Asfaha (some say his equal) in his unquestioning belief in the justness of the unionist cause.

Tedla Ukbit, Commissioner of Police

We saw in Chapter 16 that Tedla Bairu's appointment of four police inspectors to the rank of lieutenant colonel was rejected by Andargatchew and that one of them, Tedla Ukbit, refused to accept a new civilian appointment. Like many of his British-trained fellow police officers, Tedla Ukbit leaned towards unionism before the coming of the federal solution, which he later adopted. According to his long-time secretary and confidant Kinfe Tesfagabir, he was still a federalist when he spent months unemployed owing to his spat with Tedla Bairu.

During this period of uncertainty, Dimetros and Asfaha befriended Tedla and worked on drawing him to their side. When Asfaha became Chief Executive, he appointed Tedla, who had already returned to active duty at headquarters, as Commissioner of Police to replace the departing Colonel Wright. He was given the rank of lieutenant colonel. Kinfe Tesfagabir describes the reconversion of Tedla Ukbit to the unionist cause:

> Whereas previously he used to support federation because, as he put it, 'it protects us from Arabs and Muslims', he started to relax his federalist stance when he became Commissioner. 'The question is', he would say to me, 'how do we save the people from this political dilemma? Sooner or later, the Arabs and the Muslims will swallow us.'

> But then, he did not know the Amhara, neither did he trust them. '*Quale e il male minore*—which is the lesser evil?' he would muse. Slowly, unionist propaganda started to win him over. 'Why is total union resented so much?' he began to rationalise. 'Eritreans are holding the most important positions in Ethiopia. If we are smart enough, there is no reason why we should not lead Ethiopia.' This was his greatest miscalculation.[23]

Born in 1924 in the Seraye village of Adi Mengonti, Tedla served as an orderly for Italian officers, 'for whom I washed mules', he told a group of Eritrean workers later in the decade.[24] He was still in his teens when he was inducted into the Eritrean Police Force set up by the British in the early 1940s. Like Dimetros, he was endowed with a natural sharpness and sense of purpose that quickly made him stand out among his peers. His fearless, almost reckless pursuit of what he thought was right, Kinfe imputed to the same *vantaggio dall'ignoranza* that was often used to describe Dimetros.

It did not take long for Tedla to distinguish himself as an effective and efficient police officer and to climb to the most senior levels that Eritreans could reach. In 1951, the British Administration sent him and three other inspectors to Great Britain for specialised police training.[25] Upon his return, Tedla was promoted to the rank of major and was a senior officer under Commissioner Wright when Tedla Bairu's appointments debacle interrupted his progress. His return to duty placed him in the best position to replace Wright as Commissioner, to which position Asfaha duly appointed him.

Tedla Ukbit's character, behaviour, efficiency and pursuit of justice in the style of Victor Hugo's Inspector Javert are the stuff of legend in Eritrean oral history. An ascetic, lonely man, he was perfectly suited for his post. Incorruptible and frugal in his daily life, he could alternate between compassion and generosity, on one hand, and cold-heartedness and cruelty, on the other, all at the same time, according to Kinfe and other colleagues.[26] Through the force of his personality and his organisational skills, he created a security system and intelligence network that slowly turned Eritrea into a virtual police state. The endless volumes of intelligence and police sit-rep reports stacked at the RDC are testimony to the kind of minute scrutiny that the Eritrean public was subjected to. The private lives of politicians and social leaders, even those loyal to the Ethiopian cause, are preserved there for anyone to see.

Tedla had a weakness for power and privilege, which Haile Selassie recognised and fully exploited to devastating effect for the Eritrean cause. With Asfaha and Dimetros, Tedla Ukbit formed the triumvirate of annexationists whose combined powers put almost every aspect of Eritrean life in the hands of Haile Selassie and his Empire.

Haile Selassie's General Amnesty

When Tedla Bairu proclaimed the Banditry Act, he hoped for a decisive result that would salvage his hold on power and show that he could score major successes by himself. That, as we saw, turned out to be an illusion. The Ethiopians knew that Tedla's days were numbered and chose to refrain from backing his initiative. On the contrary, suspicions mounted that Ethiopia was not only encouraging the *shifta* upsurge but also using it to push Tedla out and replace him with Asfaha. Ethiopia had in fact been sending the message that the intractable *shifta* problem could only be solved through its direct intervention, a proposal that neither Tedla nor the Assembly was willing to allow.

Before becoming Chief Executive, Asfaha, who always argued that the guarantees of individual freedom had come to Eritrea fifty years ahead of their time, advocated direct Ethiopian military intervention, collective fines and the public hanging of culprits in recalcitrant villages, to solve the *shifta* problem.[27] At the same time, the top Ethiopian military officer in Eritrea, General Merid Mengesha, aired the same views. He told the British Embassy official in Addis Ababa J.E. Killick that 'it was sad' that Eritreans were unable to control the *shifta* and equally sad that they did not solicit Ethiopian help in the matter.[28] Based on such utterances and the Ethiopians' general attitude towards the *shifta* problem, Killick concluded that Ethiopia actually had a stake in the continuation of the problem.[29] It was not surprising, therefore, that Tedla Bairu's offer of amnesty to the *shifta* failed to produce any meaningful result.

It was only after Tedla's resignation that the Ethiopians made their intervention. On 7 August, the eve of the election for Chief Executive, Emperor Haile Selassie issued a proclamation declaring amnesty for surrendering *shifta*. It was a smart move. Asfaha was his personal choice as Chief Executive, and the Emperor was clearly indicating that more than a solution to the problem would follow if he was elected. However, other considerations may have prompted the intervention. Although most of the *shifta* (many of them Tigrayans crossing the border) were common robbers, there were many among them like the Saho Ahmed Ali and Osman Haji Nasser who raised social issues and had become folk heroes. The Ethiopians may have sensed the dangers of an armed rebellion born of the *shifta* presence.

Haile Selassie's amnesty, whose duration was three months, produced immediate results. But as the *shifta* surrendered from different corners of the country, a dreadful incident took place at the old monastery of Debre Bizen, some fifteen kilometres east of Asmera. On 20 August 1955, three Saho-speaking armed men killed six monks and novices peacefully working on a monastery plot. It was a callous act whose senselessness and cold-bloodedness shocked Muslim and Christian alike.[30]

The Bizen incident gave the government the excuse to go back on Haile Selassie's general amnesty and hold those involved in the actual killings accountable for the deed once they were in government hands. Thus, not only the killers at Bizen, but those who had led the battle against the police at Mai Shehaiti were charged with murder. Osman Haji Nasser and his rebel friends who had surrendered on condition of a fair trial were tried with the Bizen killers and, after a drawn-out court case, were publicly hanged with eleven other condemned *shifta* between 22 and 24 December 1958.

The implications of Haile Selassie's amnesty were more far-reaching than the mere handling of the *shifta* problem. As a reinforcement of Tedla's Banditry Act, it reintroduced the terrible Italian-era law of arrest and detention without due process, article 10 of the Police Ordinance (*articolo dieci*). No guarantees were available to protect the population from arbitrary arrest even in cases unrelated to the *shifta*. Secondly, although Sovereign of the Federation, Haile Selassie did not have constitutional authority under the Federal Act or the Eritrean Constitution permitting him to assume such a role. On the surface, his action may have looked positive as it helped curb a major security problem. But, in reality, it was one more step towards totally ignoring Eritrean claims to autonomy and sidelining its law-making procedures and prerogatives.

The impunity with which the Ethiopian Government went about its policy of intervention did not go unnoticed or unopposed by Eritreans in the Assembly or the public.

Attempts to Revive the Opposition

Ibrahim Sultan and His Followers

The events described above became a cause of deep concern to the former Independence Bloc–EDF members, especially the ML and the federalists. Their former unity was beginning to crumble. Their priorities and political choices suffered from a lack of coherence and clear deliberation. They had initiated Tedla's removal and some of them actively supported Asfaha's accession to power; yet they were the net losers. Above all, elections to the second legislature were fast approaching, and all indications were that the chances of any one of them being elected or re-elected to the Assembly were getting slimmer.

In this atmosphere, Ibrahim Sultan and his colleagues attempted to revive the Muslim League by convening a congress on 2 December 1955. The congress's resolutions, whose main points are listed below, were signed by Ibrahim and delivered to Emperor Haile Selassie and all the foreign consuls in Asmera. In the introductory note, they warned that 'unless pending issues are resolved through brotherly and friendly dialogue in accordance with the UN resolution and the Eritrean Constitution before the termination of the current Assembly, negative consequences harmful to both governments will gestate in the minds of the population'.

They went on to enumerate the demands of the congress: Members of the Federation should receive their fair share of internal communications revenues.

Eritrea's share of federal expenditures should be clearly determined and made known. Customs revenues were to be allocated in accordance with article 6(3) of the Eritrean Constitution. Eritreans were to duly participate in all federal functions—defence, foreign affairs, finance and external communications—and Eritrean functionaries were to be appointed by the Government of Eritrea. All federal passports should be issued, not by the Imperial Ethiopian Government, but by the Imperial Federal Government of Ethiopia and Eritrea. All laws proclaimed by the Federal Government should be submitted to the Eritrean authorities for their comment. The activities of the members of the Federal Council and the five Eritrean members of the Ethiopian parliament should be made public. Serious efforts should be made to improve the economic conditions of the people. Since unity of the people was the precondition for the peaceful development of the country, equality should be enhanced. Muslim rights should be observed in education, employment and commerce. *Dehai Ertra* and its editor, Elias Teklu, were to be pardoned and allowed to operate again.[31]

The resolution was sent to Haile Selassie while he was on yet another of his numerous visits to Eritrea. Every visit was now being treated like a fresh arrival, with flags adorning streets and public places, shops and businesses shutting down, schoolchildren lining the way, and women beating drums and ululating in staged celebrations. This time, the Emperor was on a charm offensive, travelling to Keren, Akurdet and far-away Nakfa by car, making speeches, holding councils, distributing *abujadid*, and handing out fruit, candy and coins to eagerly awaiting children.

In Massawa, he inaugurated the Ethiopian Naval Academy, where he said, 'We are happy to be opening the first naval school in the history of Ethiopia, a thousand years after the termination of our naval forces.' It was an inadvertent admission on his part that, contrary to his persistent claims, Ethiopia (and Abyssinia before it) had had no form of control over the Red Sea. 'From now on,' he told the cadets, 'the sea is your country and Ethiopia your home.'[32]

In Asmera, he similarly opened the Haile Selassie Secondary School, funded and administered by the Ethiopian Government. 'Remember', he instructed the students gathered in front of him, 'that you are studying in this school and that we are placing our hopes in you to develop the unity and knowledge required for the protection and honour of the ancient history of Ethiopia.'[33]

While he was basking in the warmth of staged welcoming parties, flattery and sycophancy, he received the ML resolution but was in no mood to entertain it. A terse 'We have received your petition' was all the response that Ibrahim and his colleagues received. The matter was ignored.

The Entrenchment of the Opposition

Following Ibrahim Sultan's attempt to revive the ML, his supporters began to take the message to the grassroots at every available opportunity. The most notable was the effort exerted by the indefatigable *Qadi* Ali Omer, Assembly representative of the

Assaorta. On 19–21 April he gave a series of sermons at the Asmera Grand Mosque in which he decried the corruption of his fellow representatives. In one sermon, he told a packed audience that the members of the Assembly were going back on their oaths:

> [In] other parts of the world, parliamentarians face grave danger and even sacrifice their lives for liberty and flag. Praise be to Allah, we gained our independence without much martyrdom. But we need to see it through to consummation. I know of eleven Muslims and seventeen Christians who have betrayed us. And you, if you cannot protect your languages, you are not Muslim. Let me give you an example. When you lodge an application to the government, you don't use Tigrinya or Arabic. You pay money to have it written in Amharic or Italian. This shows that you are cowards. I am the representative of 10,000 people, and I am advocating their rights without any fear. Beyond this, I should just resign.[34]

That week, *Qadi* Ali, along with three founding members of the Federalist Youth Association, which we will discuss shortly, were summoned to police quarters and given strict warnings about their activities.[35] But this would not deter the Eritreans who were increasingly concerned by persistent rumours that the Eritrean flag was about to be removed.

In Keren, veterans of the ML and the Shuban took the resistance a step further. In line with its reputation as incubator of the independence movement in the 1940s, Keren was showing signs of reviving its old tradition. Activists known as 'the Group of 11', operating clandestinely, began securing the attention of the security forces, as CID reports clearly show. On 27 April 1956, members of this group led scores of Kerenites to a hall and held a meeting. Spurred by rumours of the impending removal of the Eritrean flag, many of them unfurled it at the meeting and started to make angry speeches.

Idris Hummed Tsa'edui, a veteran of the ML, told the gathering, 'Our flag, recognised by the UN and ratified by the Emperor, could never be abolished by a few men elected by ourselves who are seeking to sell us.' The director of the Keren schools, the prominent teacher *Sheik* Saadadin, reminded his audience that the flag was common to Muslims and Christians, young and old, rich and poor. It needed to be protected by all acting in unison. 'Don't be afraid, be brave,' he said. 'Allah helps the brave. Dying for your country is like living forever.' The strongest speech was made by Idris Nor Adem of the Shuban, who waved a copy of the Eritrean Constitution as he spoke:

> What I am waving at you is our guarantee, our shelter. If your roof is taken away, you will find no protection from the sun and the rain ... This document has the support of 68 nations of the world and the ratification of the Emperor. Therefore, Eritrea must exist. People without a flag cannot claim to be free ... Although the Palestinians have been uprooted from their homes, they are respected wherever they go because

> they have a flag. And in Sudan, they attempted to depose Al Azhar. Men and women opposed the attempt. In fact, the women forced their husbands to act by refusing to serve them meals. This way, the people of Sudan returned Al Azhar to power. If we are not men enough, can't we emulate our women?[36]

Security forces disrupted the meeting, but no arrests were made for the moment. Over the following days, CID informants reported the formation of a new group calling itself Eritrean Islamic Solidarity.[37] With police harassment and mass arrests, groups like this had little chance of surviving long enough to leave their mark.[38]

Federalist Opposition

In Chapter 17, we described briefly the formation of the Federalisti on 5 September 1954. Predictably, their objectives of protecting the Eritrean Constitution and flag immediately placed their leaders and members, along with their lawyers Omer Qadi and Yohannes Tsegai, on the government's blacklist. Not only was their application for legal recognition denied, but Tesfai Reda'e, the Association's president, was attacked by men under the cover of darkness and left for dead with a broken arm.

For the Federalisti, whose membership had risen to between sixty and eighty youths by 1955, the Eritrean flag symbolised the very essence of Eritrean identity. Any act that appeared to downgrade the status of that banner prompted them to react. In 1955, when only the Ethiopian flag decorated Asmera streets to welcome Haile Selassie, Tesfai Reda'e and Gebremikael Begatsion confronted the newly appointed mayor of Asmera, *Dejazmatch* Hagos Gebre, for an explanation. The mayor drove them out of his office. The next morning, government and security officials were surprised to find the Eritrean flag hoisted alongside the Ethiopian flag on the most visible public buildings and main streets of Asmera. 'We worked on this the whole night under the cover of darkness,' Gebremikael explained.[39]

Fearful of a court process that might end up favouring their legal recognition, security forces chose to subdue the Federalisti through psychological harassment and physical harm. After the incident with the mayor, Tesfai Reda'e was taken to a police station and, without any formal charge being made, beaten up again in a manner that shocked friends who took him into their care.[40] But it was not only the police who were chasing the Federalisti. The faction of the Andinet led by the Tigrayan Alemseged Teferi was increasingly becoming a powerful organ of repression, and it took on the group with a vengeance. Abraha Futur, the man who mused 'Did we ask for "Ethiopia *or* death" or "Ethiopia *and* death"?' in a poignant poem, accompanied the motorcade of the visiting Marshal Tito of Yugoslavia through the streets of Asmera on a bicycle flying the Eritrean flag. It had been banned from exhibition anywhere along Tito's path. A few days later, Alemseged Teferi's thugs took Abraha Futur to the vicinity of Medeber, Asmera's artisan centre, beat him up and strung him up on a tree. Friends in hot pursuit, including labour leader Berhe Andemikael, rescued him as he gasped for breath.[41]

Police reports show security surveillance over Federalisti tightening in April 1956. In one of these, Tesfai Reda'e and Abraha Futur are mentioned as the main planners behind a plot to assassinate the Interior Secretary, Araia Wassie; Dimetros; and the Seraye senior divisional officer, Laine Kidanemariam. Along with them, Tedla Bairu's brothers, Menghistu and Manna, were listed as co-conspirators. The report also indicated that the suspects were followers of Haregot and Demsas.[42] No evidence supported the allegations and the Federalisti interviewed for this book denied any links between Haregot and Demsas and their organisation. Obviously, the Asfaha administration was attempting to criminalise the Association and, by this means, build a case against the Chief Executive's potential rivals, Haregot and Tedla Bairu.

On 9 May 1956, as several Federalisti met in a hideout, a police sergeant had them all arrested. Three days later, they were taken to court and charged with three offences—defamation of the government (article 509); operating without an official government permit (article 207); and convening a meeting without the required police clearance or knowledge (article 15 of the Police Ordinance, the old Fascist Italian law revived by Tedla Bairu's Banditry Act). In a long-drawn-out legal process that lasted until mid-1957, the case against thirteen leaders of the Eritrean Federalist Youth Association (EFYA) was pursued through the court hierarchy as far as the Supreme Court. Here, Chief Justice Shearer and his consenting justices, Melles Fre and O'Hanlon, ruled that articles 207 and 509 of the Police Ordinance, cited in the indictment, were incompatible with the Eritrean Constitution, and dismissed most of the charges.[43] The third charge of non-compliance with article 15 was also dismissed, and all the accused were subsequently set free.

The case of the Federalisti became a cause célèbre chiefly because all of the accused were Andinet activists working against the very objective for which they had once fought. Secondly, the defeat of the government in the courts of law exposed the Asfaha administration's repressive nature. Harassment of the lawyer Omer Qadi forced him to escape Eritrea for Egypt. His assistant, Yohannes Tsegai, an employee of the British consulate, also became the victim of a deliberate hit-and-run car incident that left him with a physical disability.[44]

Above all, it was the constitutional issues and the Eritrean flag's status that concerned the public most. Friends and relatives of the accused packed each court session, and whatever was uttered inside the courtroom was soon relayed in every household, workplace, bar and *suwa* (beer) house in town. Although banned from all activity as a group, the Federalisti's influence in taking the political struggle a step higher became evident when many of its members assumed important roles in the next stages of the independence movement.

The Masjid Committee

In April 1956, Asfaha's desire to please the Emperor and draw Eritreans into Ethiopian cultural values backfired in a way that he had not foreseen. Previously, on 7 March, he had declared 9 March, the Prophet Muhammad's birthday, a public holiday for Muslims only.[45] Christians were not to observe the occasion. In the middle of the month of Ramadan, which coincided with Lent the following April, Asfaha issued Proclamation 96 to regulate Eritrean public holidays. To the traditionally observed Good Friday and the official Ethiopian Liberation Day on 4 and 5 May, respectively, he added a feast called *ma'edot*, on Easter Monday, to extend the holiday weekend. *Ma'edot*, he reasoned, was a public holiday in Ethiopia and it had to be observed in Eritrea too for the sake of uniformity.[46]

The month of Ramadan ended a week after Easter Sunday. As Muslim leaders met to discuss their reaction to the insensitive proliferation of Christian holidays and the manner in which Asfaha handled the religious balance, so delicately guarded by past generations, the newly appointed Asmera mayor, Hagos Gebre, ordered the closure of shops on Easter Monday. In a quick reaction, one of the founders of ML, *Fitawrari* Mohammed Aberra Hagos, gave a sermon at the Grand Mosque in which he urged his audience to disregard the mayor's order as it was reminiscent of 'Emperor Yohannes IV's crusades to baptise Muslims'. He followed this with a week-long campaign to persuade Muslim Jeberti and Yemeni business owners to disregard the mayor's order.[47] Other Muslim leaders led by the Assembly member Berhanu Ahmeddin also confronted the mayor on the matter. '*Lascia perdere tutti*—let it all pass' was all he gave them for an answer.[48]

At this stage, Asfaha added fuel to the fire by declaring only one day, the first day of Eid al-Fatr, as a Muslim public holiday, just a week after the long Easter weekend.[49] Muslim anger blew up and they reacted by forming what they called the Muslim Mosque Committee. As its initial act, the committee ordered the closure of all the mosques in Asmera and banned the traditional public observances and ceremony at the Grand Mosque, which were always attended by the Emperor's representative and the Chief Executive. Alarmed by the committee's decisive action, Asfaha condemned it as the 'work of a few individuals'.

Some weeks later, the committee gave its written response through Ibrahim Sultan. It expressed its sadness at Asfaha's characterisation of the decision to close down the mosques as the 'work of a few individuals', when all those who attended the mosques in Asmera had participated in the decision. It then pointed out that the mosque incident was only the tip of a deeper set of complaints, which it presented point by point.

1. To avoid further misunderstanding, Proclamation 69 should be rescinded and the observance of national holidays determined after due consideration.
2. In accordance with article 38 of the Eritrean Constitution, Arabic and Tigrinya should be officially used in all government departments, offices and schools.
3. The Eritrean flag, which was accepted by the people of Eritrea, approved by the UN and ratified by the Emperor, should be hoisted on all public occasions.

4. In accordance with article 31, Muslim students should be instructed in Arabic. Since there was Muslim resentment on this issue, Arabic teachers should be imported from abroad.
5. Since there was no law to satisfy the requirements of a new Legislative Assembly, and since Election Proclamation 121 of 1952 was outdated, the government should promulgate a new election law in accordance with article 96 of the Constitution.
6. Police should observe the law and operate in accordance with article 19 (which compelled government officials to function within the duties determined for them by law).
7. Eritrean Muslims should be appointed to higher government posts and the right of educated Muslims to be considered for appropriate job opportunities should be respected.[50]

Like all previous demands and petitions, this committee's deposition was shelved. With new elections to the Eritrean Assembly pending, the government and federal authorities were busy preparing for that crucial event.

19

THE WEAKENING OF THE LEGISLATURE

Controversy over the Size of the Supreme Court

Asfaha had for long been complaining about the Supreme Court and its president, Sir James Shearer, for their defence of the Federal Act and the Eritrean Constitution. Fearing British sensitivities, the Ethiopians discouraged Asfaha and Dimetros from driving him out of the country. Of more concern to them was the trust and confidence that the federalists and the independence movement were developing towards the court and the supremacy of the rule of law, as well as the due process that it represented. The authorities saw this as a bad habit to be nipped in the bud.

To circumvent Shearer's dismissal or the direct curtailment of the court's powers, Asfaha moved to weaken it without tampering with its substantive authority. Article 89 of the Constitution fixed the number of members of the Supreme Court from three to seven. Asfaha proposed to raise the number of judges to nineteen and asked the Assembly for its approval. Shearer, who received a copy of the proposal for comment, confronted Asfaha and told him that such a proposal could come only from the Supreme Court (article 89(1)). Even then, the change could not be made without amending article 89(1) of the Constitution. Asfaha quickly withdrew his proposal and went for another option.[1]

In his annual report to the Assembly on 2 March 1956, he pointed out that court cases were amassing without any resolution because district administrators, the *mislenes* and *nazirs*, were denied their traditional judicial powers. To rectify this, he proposed to the Assembly that not only *mislenes* and *nazirs*, but also lower-level administrators, like village and market chiefs, be invested with judicial authority. He laid out a procedure whereby their decisions could be appealed against in the regular courts in relatively shorter periods of time.[2]

Shearer realised that the new proposal was a circumvention of the one he had rejected. This time, he had no legal basis to intervene as Asfaha presented it as an administrative measure. The only way he could deal with it was if someone challenged its constitutionality, which no one did. Of the 68 members of the Assembly, 28 were *mislenes* and *nazirs* subject to the Chief Executive's appointment and dismissal. As judges, they did his bidding, thus indirectly compromising the independence of the judiciary while reinforcing his influence on the Assembly. Shearer noted: 'The Assembly will turn into a rubber stamp that will readily sign into law any proposal presented to it by the Executive.'[3]

As Shearer predicted, the Assembly approved the proposal, which also provided that any appellate bench in Eritrea had to consist of a panel of three judges while sitting in session. This meant that the Supreme Court, which had at least four panels, including the criminal, civil, commercial and Sharia benches, would need twelve or more judges to carry out its appellate duties. In other words, Asfaha gave Shearer no choice but to accommodate his proposal by asking the Assembly for an amendment of article 89(1).

The implications of this smart move by Asfaha were far-reaching. By nominating his own men to the Supreme Court and having them confirmed by an amenable Assembly, he sought to break its backbone. There would be little chance of cases not favoured by him succeeding at the Supreme Court. Yet, in spite of its success in the Assembly, the stiff resistance to the new rule by members of the opposition still cast doubts on its implementation. Regardless of this uncertainty, Asfaha and his supporters turned their attention to the forthcoming elections, fully confident of their newly acquired powers.

The Ouster of Idris Mohammed Adem

As we have seen, the Representative or Constitutional Assembly elected in accordance with Proclamation 121 of 1952 voted to turn itself into the first Legislative Assembly. According to rule, it should have disbanded to allow for a new election proclamation and fresh elections to a new Assembly. At the beginning of 1953, an attempt was made to rectify the anomaly when a proclamation left behind by the British was presented to the Assembly. The draft, which provided for the formation of an Electoral Commission to take over the absolute powers that Proclamation 121 had given to the Administering Authority, aimed to limit government intervention in the election process. However, the Assembly failed to approve it. The excuse given was that, to determine the size and number of electoral districts, a census needed to precede the proclamation. A committee was set up to study the matter. No action was taken on the subject until mid-1956.

In June 1956, a move to rescind the 'defunct Proclamation 121' was similarly rejected by the Assembly on the basis that the census requirement had not been met and that it was impossible to resolve the matter so close to the second round of elections. Supporters of the 1952 draft let their chances go by, and as a result Proclamation 121 would apply to the new elections as well.[4] Muslim League (ML) members of the Assembly saw the rejection of the draft law as the prelude to a death sentence on Eritrean autonomy. On 5 June, they handed a petition to Justice Shearer demanding the repeal of Proclamation 121 and its replacement by the 1952 draft election law. Shearer consulted the newly appointed Attorney General of Eritrea, the American F.F. Russell. Russell shrugged off the petition by telling the Chief Justice that the Eritrean Government had decided to carry out the elections in accordance with Proclamation 121.[5]

Incidentally, Russell's appointment to Asmera was shrouded in mystery. He was recruited in the US and signed his contract of employment with the Ethiopian ambassador there. His arrival in Asmera was unannounced. From there he flew to Addis Ababa and met with Andargatchew, Aklilu and, briefly, with the Emperor. Upon his return to Asmera, he was introduced to Eritrean officials as advisor to both the Federal and Eritrean governments, and when Norman Methven left, he became the Attorney General of the autonomous government. The American consul, who was also not informed about Russell's employment, thought the whole affair was a brazen act meant to show who was the real master in Eritrea.[6]

Following Russell's response, Shearer wrote to Asfaha advising him that, although Proclamation 121 was not repealed, it would still be a contravention of article 45 of the Constitution.[7] He suggested that the Chief Executive seek legal counsel, which Asfaha did by consulting with Russell. Russell's advice to Asfaha startled Shearer. The American acknowledged that Proclamation 121 was in contravention of the Constitution, but it would not matter, he assured the Chief Executive, as there would be no way for the Supreme Court to intervene.[8]

Unable to swallow Russell's opinion, Shearer shared his letter to Asfaha with Assembly president Idris Mohammed Adem, an enemy of Proclamation 121. Idris, in turn, made 1,000 copies of the letter and distributed them far and wide to Assembly members as well as citizens whom he felt should be informed. This added to his accumulating troubles with Andargatchew and his office, from where talk of removing him started to circulate.

As Asmera became abuzz with news of Idris's impending dismissal, his supporters attempted to take urgent steps to keep him in his post. In early June, Akito and Omer Qadi pleaded with Shearer to provide them with the legal protection they needed to call for a massive demonstration against Idris's removal. As Chief Justice, Shearer could give no such commitment. In the same week, about 150 people, including fourteen Assembly members led by *Qadi* Ali, Akito and Berhanu Ahmeddin and joined by the prominent Muslim leaders *Haji* Suleiman Ahmed, *Haji* Imam Musa and Ahmed Basaad, met at Abune Petros Square. Calling themselves 'representatives of the people', they sent their demands to the Chief Executive highlighting their concern over Idris's fate.

The same evening, sixty of them held a spirited debate where the call for liberty and a public demonstration of protest figured prominently, and a committee was elected to organise the demonstration.[9] At the same time, Keren held its own meeting which came up with the same call for demonstrations.[10] Both were not to be.

The Interior Secretary, Araia Wassie, who had planted his agents among the activists, issued a ban on the demonstrations. It was the first time in the federal period that Eritreans had ventured on an organised civil campaign.

Nevertheless, clandestine meetings continued in Keren, Massawa and Asmera. Keren was emerging as the centre of political dissent with the Friday *salat* (prayers) providing the pretext for secret discussions and for organisation within and outside the mosque. Police reports in those weeks consistently pointed to Idris Tsa'edui and Osman Hajai in Keren, Ahmed Beshir in Massawa, and the lawyer Gebrelul Gebreyesus in Asmera, as the prime suspects behind the protests. Omer Qadi was named the overall organiser.[11]

All these moves to hold protests would not deter the federal and Eritrean authorities from forging ahead with their plan to remove the president of the Assembly. Andargatchew's office was particularly active in recruiting, bribing and threatening Assembly members for the purpose. Many of them responded by absenting themselves from the sessions, thus denying a quorum for the first half of June 1956 when debate on the budget formed the official agenda. After three failed sessions, an irritated Idris scolded his colleagues by telling them that, regardless of what else was at stake, the budget needed to be discussed. 'I cannot understand why you cannot do that and then move on to whatever is on your minds.'[12]

On 13 June, the Federal Office was able to assemble enough members to make a quorum. The budget, which was approved with little debate, was followed by a motion to remove Idris by none other than a fellow Barka member, Osman Abdulrahman. Since there was no debate on the matter, it fell to a vote, and 43 of the 50 members in attendance voted for Idris's removal. Only 7 opposed it.[13] Why would Osman Abdulrahman go against Idris, a fellow dissenter? According to the British consul Howes, Andargatchew had promised some ML members that if they supported Idris's removal, he would not insist on the enlargement of the Supreme Court and the related amendment to the Constitution. His offer was a quid pro quo.[14]

As *Sheik* Hamid Ferej, also from Barka, took over the presidency, Idris turned into an instant hero. On the morning of the election, Idris's supporters gathered at the entrance of the Assembly building, raising fears of violence or a demonstration. Police action was only averted upon the intervention of the Assembly clerk Fergus McCleary. Unlike Tedla's and Ali Rad'ai's resignations under official pressure, Idris's removal came despite widespread Assembly and popular protest and his refusal to resign under duress. Many even started to dub him the successor of Ibrahim Sultan, a designation that Idris was quick to capitalise on.

As the American consul Richey pointed out, Ethiopia was the ultimate loser in the Idris affair. Idris Mohammed Adem moved on to other forms of struggle, culminating in the formation of the Eritrean Liberation Front at the beginning of the 1960s.

The Election Proclamation at the Supreme Court

In May 1956, members of the ML filed a suit at the Supreme Court seeking the repeal of Proclamation 121 as a defunct law rendered inoperable by article 45 of the Eritrean Constitution. The court accepted the suit as a case of first instance, thereby opening the chance of an appeal against its decision. Five, instead of seven, judges sat on the bench. Omer Qadi argued the case for the plaintiffs.

At the beginning, three judges, Shearer, Melles Fre and F. Ostini, leaned towards agreeing with the plaintiffs. The remaining two, Gebrehiwet Mebrahtu and Hamid Abu Alama, held that the matter of the constitutionality of the proclamation did not concern the court as issuing a new election law was the prerogative of the Chief Executive. The Assembly, on the other hand, had failed to enact the 1952 draft law on two occasions. There was, therefore, no justification for the court to try the matter.[15]

The majority opinion was about to prevail when, according to Shearer, Ostini was called to the Office of the Emperor's Representative and changed his mind 'at the last minute'. He joined the minority.[16] The ML lost its case on 23 June. By this date, the lawyer Omer Qadi, who was the subject of police harassment for his involvement with the Federalisti, had left Eritrea to seek justice abroad. Taking advantage of his absence, Asfaha moved to pre-empt a possible ML appeal. In late July, he issued three legal notices specifically citing Proclamation 121 as the basis for his authority. He designated 5 September election day, named election officials and determined the electoral districts to which they would be assigned. He also ordered a census to be taken in Asmera and Massawa, where elections were to be held by direct ballot.[17]

It was only after the issuance of the legal notices that Ibrahim Sultan lodged an appeal against the Supreme Court decision of 23 June. Unfortunately for the appellant, Shearer had gone to England for vacation and his deputy, O'Hanlon, took over his role. The other judges were the same as in the first instance. In addition to the previous arguments against Proclamation 121, Ibrahim, who argued the case himself, demanded the repeal of the three legal notices announced by the government on the grounds that they were based on a defunct proclamation. He also tried to appeal to the judges' conscience. After describing the Assembly as a collection of chiefs who chose Proclamation 121 in order to 'keep their privileges and respective positions', he said, 'All I am asking of this court is the observance and enforcement of the Eritrean Constitution ... Today, the whole population of Eritrea, and because this process is being reported by the press, the world is watching this court ... Honourable Court, would you not believe that such a law stands against the Federation and the Constitution of Eritrea?'

Ibrahim pointed out that, should elections be carried out under the controversial law, a highly unhealthy and oppressive atmosphere would prevail throughout the country. Arbitrary arrests and open harassment by the police over matters related to the projected elections were already taking place. Such illegal acts, he concluded, would surely frighten off a population for whom free elections were still a new experience.[18]

Appearing on behalf of the government, Russell rebutted every one of Ibrahim's points. Since the Assembly had failed to promulgate a new election law in its four-year existence, no other law was available except Proclamation 121. In such a situation, the Chief Executive was left with no choice but to conduct the election with what rational means was available to him and Proclamation 121 provided just this. In the situation, the constitutionality of the proclamation or the fact that it was defunct did not really matter.[19]

It was indeed strange that an American lawyer would take such a position against a constitutional provision fashioned after the American concept and practice of free elections. Once again, the court split into two. O'Hanlon, Abu Alama, Gebrehiwet and Ostini joined to render Melles in the minority. Shearer was still in England. The majority ruled that, in the absence of a new law and in the face of the Chief Executive's decision to set the election in the following three weeks, the court had no means of forming an electoral commission. Neither could it order the Chief Executive or the Assembly to issue a new proclamation. Although the majority admitted that Proclamation 121 was in fact defunct, holding the election at the set time was a constitutional priority that had to be met regardless of whether the existing election law satisfied some provisions of the Constitution. Accepting the Chief Executive's designation of Proclamation 121 as a rational legal instrument, they rejected Ibrahim Sultan's appeal.

In a dissenting opinion, Melles Fre pointed to the majority's contradictory logic. A defunct law, he intimated, should not be discussed by a court of law. To give it life just because the Chief Executive deemed it rational was unacceptable. He warned that a precedent 'binding and prejudicial' to future elections was being put in place. Nevertheless, after agreeing that the court had no legal authority to give directions to the Chief Executive on the matter, he left it to the discretion of the Chief Executive to opt for an acceptable solution.[20]

Asfaha's triumph at the Supreme Court opened all the avenues for him to conduct the 1956 elections as he deemed fit.

The 1956 Elections

Prelude to the Elections

Even before colonial times, administrative promotions and demotions by parties in power had been a source of unending rivalries, petty intrigues and jealousies among traditional leaders, especially at the district levels. Both the Italians and the British used this effectively to pit one *mislene* or *nazir* against the other. Very often, such individual ill-feelings trickled down to the extended families and followers of the contenders, thus providing fertile ground for rulers to exploit for political gain.

Having mastered feudal tactics from his proximity to the Ethiopian aristocracy, Asfaha, aided by his Interior Secretary, Araia Wassie, set out to reshuffle the district administrators to suit his aim of filling Assembly seats with his own hand-picked candidates. By coincidence or by design, *shifta* activity resurfaced and surged after a lull following Haile Selassie's general amnesty. In an intense campaign carried out by Araia Wassie throughout the country, the government announced the reinstitution of Tedla Bairu's Banditry Proclamation, which included collective punishments on villages suspected of *shifta* sympathy or aid. 'Promotion comes with responsibility,' he often told his administrators. 'Your duties are not confined to hearing litigants. You are also charged with following up anti-social activities among the people and reporting them to the police. The Government will then be able to determine those who deserve further promotion.'[21]

Such a broad interpretation of Tedla's proclamation enabled Asfaha's government to target political activists, whom it could easily characterise as 'anti-social', and detain them without recourse to due process, as permitted by the Banditry Act. Moreover, recalcitrant administrators could likewise be removed for non-compliance and replaced by more amenable ones. Consequently, by July 1956, just one month before the elections, Asfaha removed several disagreeable *kebessa mislenes* and replaced them with his own friends and followers. At least eight of the latter were either members of the Assembly who had not been *mislenes* previously or were already registered as candidates for the forthcoming election.[22] Thus, even before the September elections, the Assembly began filling up with pro-annexation district administrators.

Accompanying this blatant disregard of the principle of the separation of powers was police harassment and relentless surveillance of everyone conceived to be even remotely connected to political activities or activists. Hundreds of CID dossiers labelled *Movimenti delle Persone Politicanti* were filled with the stories, often embarrassingly intimate and detailed, of the major personalities of the time. Past friendships, extramarital affairs, business activities and malpractices, even family secrets of respectable persons were all carefully noted in them. In those pre-election days, such information was used to threaten people who considered standing for election.

The Canadian judge J.A. Clarence Smith later provided some concrete examples of how the police interfered by discouraging or removing unwanted candidates before the election date. In Mendefera, the police arrested several candidates on flimsy excuses and kept them in detention as the campaign proceeded. They were released when Dimetros, claiming to act on their behalf, persuaded them to withdraw their candidacy in return for their freedom. Clarence Smith was in no doubt that Dimetros must have pre-planned the whole plot. He also cited another example where a candidate was stopped by police in Senafe and told to sign a document ordering him not to talk to anyone in the town. When he refused, they arrested him for contravention of an old Italian law, recently revived, providing for the arrest of anyone disobeying police orders. Since Proclamation 121 barred anyone with a police record from running for the Assembly, the man's candidacy was revoked.[23]

Perhaps the most celebrated case was that of Fesseha Weldemariam (Gandhi), a prominent leader of the Independence Bloc (IB) and the Eritrean Democratic Front (EDF). A native of Tse'azega, in the vicinity of Asmera, he was arrested one day before registration as a candidate on the grounds of illegal possession of arms. The charges were proved false and he was released four days later, only to be told that the registration date had expired. Undeterred, Fesseha and his supporters applied for registration in his area of residence in Asmera. This time, Commissioner Tedla Ukbit himself warned Fesseha that undesirable persons like him were not wanted in the Assembly and demanded the withdrawal of his candidacy. Fesseha refused and was arrested again on the same charges as well as additional ones connecting him to the *shifta*. It was only upon a successful plea for habeas corpus and the subsequent dismissal of his charges by the Supreme Court that he was able to stand for election and finally win.[24] His supporters dubbed him 'Gandhi' for his ordeal and legal battles, a nickname that remained fixed to him as long as he lived.

Election Results

Election returns came in on 7 September, two days after election day. With the exception of three electoral districts where the results were inconclusive and also of the Asseb returns, where Akito's election was disputed by the Chief Executive, 64 results were uncontested. According to Clarence Smith, only four results went contrary to Asfaha's plans[25]—those of Fesseha Weldemariam in Asmera, Osman Hindi in Massawa, Mohammed Said Hassano in Barka, and Mohammed Omer Akito in Denkalia. We will treat Asfaha's objection to Akito's election separately.

Consistent with Proclamation 121, Eritrea's eight provinces were divided into six electoral districts based on the ethnic and religious composition of their population. The exceptions were Asmera and Massawa, which constituted two additional districts for direct balloting. Thirty-one candidates were declared elected unopposed. The only districts where every seat was contested were Hamasien, Asmera and Massawa.[26]

Ibrahim Sultan could not run as he was still serving his two-year suspended sentence for his alleged 'insult of a foreign head of state'. Idris Mohammed Adem, under constant police scrutiny and harassment, also decided not to run. Similarly, two prominent opposition members of the first legislature, Bezabih Tesfabruk and *Sheka* Teklemikael, withdrew their candidacy in favour of Asfaha's hand-picked cronies. Akito's friends Batok, Ashekih and Sefaf stayed away.

Of those who did run regardless of the consequences, Abudawd lost to a unionist. Perhaps the most daring and vocal of the opposition leaders, *Qadi* Ali, was declared defeated with not even a single vote in his favour. Considering his enormous influence among the Assaorta and the Muslim community in Akeleguzai, few doubted foul play. Even unionist members who showed slight deviations towards the opposition were not spared. Werede Beyin, who moved to condemn those who had asked for the Emperor's tax reprieve; Bemnet Tessema, who nominated Haregot to run against Asfaha; and Beyene Zahlai, chairman of the Budget Committee who pushed for full payment of Eritrea's customs dues, were declared defeated. The last-mentioned, a prominent unionist, was defeated by Asfaha's own uncle.

Of former EDF, ML and LPP members who were returned either unopposed or by election, many had either tempered their opposition or shifted position in Asfaha's direction. These included members of the Tessema family;[27] Habtezghi Okbazghi and Berhanu Ahmeddin, district chiefs of Haddish Adi; Geza Berhanu of Asmera; and many others. To gain support within the Tessema family, Asfaha restored the traditional administrative and judicial positions and privileges to the family that Tedla Bairu had withdrawn. In this manner, Asfaha made sure that a majority of seats in the Assembly were occupied by *mislenes*, *nazirs* and district judges responsible to him also as government employees.

On 12 September, when the three inconclusive results were resolved,[28] 67 members of the second legislature were sworn in. Akito was left out. Hamid Ferej and Dimetros won back their positions as president and vice president of the Assembly, unopposed. Ferej praised Asfaha's role in the running of a 'democratic election'. Dimetros predicted that the second elections would show better results as, unlike the British-sponsored previous one, it was an 'all-Ethiopian affair'. He called it 'the beginning of our liberation, where the people of Eritrea have shown their civility and unity, gentleness and responsibility; and maturity and capability'.[29]

On the same day, Berhanu Ahmeddin, founding leader of the ML, rose to nominate Asfaha Weldemikael, whom he described as 'the beloved of his people and His Imperial Majesty and a man blessed by his parents', to continue as Chief Executive. The former federalist Habtezghi Okbazghi seconded the nomination. Asfaha, already promoted to the lofty rank of *dejazmatch* by the Emperor, was elected unopposed. Three days later, he and his newly appointed six secretaries took their oaths of office in the presence of *Bitweded* Andargatchew. The secretaries were Araia Wassie (Interior); Ali Rad'ai (Social Affairs); Tesfayohannes Berhe (Finance); Omer Hassano (Law and Justice); Gebreyohannes Tesfamariam (Economy); and Ibrahim Hummed Arey (Public Works).

In his acceptance speech, Asfaha chastised those who had expected the elections to turn violent. 'But the Emperor's grace protected us, and the Ethiopian spirit that has settled among Eritreans by the will of God has shown what they are made of.' He continued:

> Some months ago, I said to this Assembly that this thing called 'democracy' was not a notion that we adopted from a foreign land. I said that we Ethiopians are endowed with democracy by our very nature. We need to go no farther than the process of this election to verify my claim. I would, therefore, like to thank our people of honour and dignity for their patience, sense of direction and superior spiritual strength.[30]

Asfaha and Andargatchew had every reason to feel triumphant as they left the Assembly building. It was an extraordinary session with a limited agenda. Its regular sessions were due to be resumed on 6 March 1957. Before the Assembly disbanded, however, a proposal that appeared to come from outside the house suggested that the opening session of the Assembly be moved from 6 March to 23 October (Geez) to coincide with the Emperor's coronation day. Fifty-one attending members voted to change the date unanimously.[31] This was the first decision of the mostly hand-picked members of the Assembly.

On 5 September 1956, the returning officer of the Southern Denkalia district had announced that Akito had won the race with 16 out of a total of 26 electoral votes. Asfaha refused to acknowledge Akito's election, and it was left pending for 49 days until 24 November. On this date, he sent a message to the Assembly, already in session since October, charging partiality on the part of the returning officer and the police constable responsible for the electoral ward. He further charged that the sixteen delegates alleged to have voted for Akito had written to assure him that they had actually voted for his rival. Above all, rather than attaching the candidates' photographs to the side of the ballot boxes, as was the rule, the returning officer had simply leant the pictures against the boxes. Asfaha considered this as a major omission warranting cancellation of the election result. He told the Assembly that the illegal act had created resentment among the electorate and that it was contrary to the relevant provisions of the law.[32]

It turned out, however, that Asfaha had hidden a letter addressed to him in person by Akito's sixteen supporters protesting against the claim that they had voted for his rival. 'Our conscience demands that we make it known to Your Excellency that the election was conducted with freedom, trust and a healthy spirit. *Sheik* Mohammed Omer Akito is the man who was elected with our full trust. It is only just that you approve his election on behalf of the Government.'[33] But Asfaha would not relent. By invoking article 46(2) of the Constitution, he asked the Assembly to put the Akito case to the vote. If over half the members voted against him, he would be barred from his seat but would have recourse to an appeal to the Supreme Court. Only two of the members, Fesseha Weldemariam and Osman Hindi, took a firm stand in opposition. Strangely, Akito's former opposition friends, Asmerom Weldegiorgis and Habtezghi Okbazghi, led the argument to keep him out on the ground that the placement of the candidates' photos on the side of the ballot box constituted a breach of election rules sufficient to declare the result invalid. Forty-two members agreed with them, seven opposed and one abstained. Akito took his case to the Supreme Court of Eritrea.

The court did not take much time to reject the Assembly's reasons for invalidating the results. More importantly, the judges accepted the letter, duly signed by the sixteen pro-Akito voters, as proof of his indisputable victory. In a split decision due to a technicality, the majority ruled that Akito had convinced the court that nothing of substance had taken place to invalidate his election. They therefore ratified his election and recognised his right to resume his seat.[34] We note here that the court refrained from ordering the Assembly to accept Akito into its ranks. It opted for a statement or recommendation instead of an outright order.

By this time, the Assembly had gone into recess and Akito presented his court decision to Assembly president Hamid Ferej through the clerk McCleary. Dimetros's opposition blocked the appeal from progressing any further. In the meantime, McCleary decided to allow Akito to receive his salary, which he did from February till the Assembly's reopening in August. This too was strenuously opposed by Dimetros and his followers, who threatened to remove McCleary from his position. McCleary was forced to withdraw Akito's salary.[35]

Armed with his Supreme Court document, Akito presented himself at the Assembly on the day of its reopening after the recess. Policemen and Assembly messengers blocked his entry at the gate. What followed is best described in Akito's own words:

> For four years, I stayed in Asmera without employment or salary. I went hungry and broke. For four years, I refused to go to Asseb. On every morning of its sessions, I presented myself at the Assembly only to be forcibly turned back on each occasion. That was my life for four years. Why did I do that? Because I was the one who was lawfully elected. I had the Supreme Court decision in my hand. If I left Asmera for Asseb, even for a visit, Asfaha and Dimetros could claim that I had abandoned my seat and easily replaced me in a by-election. I stayed put in Asmera to deny them that chance. I did not make it into the Assembly neither could they replace me.[36]

Just as the Supreme Court refrained from ordering the Assembly or Asfaha to accept Akito's election, Asfaha too would not deny the court's recognition of Akito's right to his seat. He was content with the Assembly's decision to keep Akito out, a situation that the Supreme Court was powerless to rectify.

Akito was a man of indomitable will, unassailable integrity and a fearlessness matched by few of his peers. His clear insight and biting sense of humour remained intact until his death as a nonagenarian in 2010. He was a nationalist for whom nation-building remained an intriguing process. In his three major interviews with this writer, he often paraphrased Massimo d'Azeglio's famous quote, saying, *L'Eritrea è fatta. Restano da fare gli Eritrei*—Eritrea is made; what remains is to make Eritreans. Nation-building would not be an easy task.[37]

He relinquished his seat in 1960 when he declined to run for a third term. Fearful of his influence in Denkalia, Asfaha confined him to Asmera by appointing him to a minor position at the government printing press, sandwiched between the St Mary's Mental Hospital on the top and the Regina Elena (today's Orotta) Hospital at the bottom of the eastern slope of Forto Hill. Asked where he was working, he once quipped, *sotto i matti, ma sopra i malati*—below the crazy but above the sick. It was a statement that many people adopted as an apt description of Eritrea's awkward state in those times.[38]

The Akito case was also a triumph for Asfaha over the Supreme Court. When he could not win it over, as he had done with the Assembly, he found a way to use his Assembly loyalists to circumvent its prerogatives. But there were still other areas of potential resistance that his administration had to deal with in its drive for complete union.

Some Issues of Significance in 1957

The Banditry Act

The effectiveness of Haile Selassie's general amnesty lasted no more than one year. By mid-1957, Asfaha was blaming administrators and 'a *shifta*-sympathising, uncooperative public' for the resurgence of brigandage. Even Ethiopian *shifta* were encouraged to cross over by 'your spinelessness', he told a gathering of Hamasien administrators. He warned that he would garrison police contingents in renegade villages and charge them with responsibility for their upkeep.[39]

Asfaha was particularly angry with *kebessa mislenes* who were openly defying his orders to punish villages identified as sources or centres of *shifta* activity. In September 1956, he suspended *Azmatch* Mirach Gudum of Liban in western Seraye for disregarding a fine of 10,000 birr imposed on villagers in his administrative district.[40] In Dembelas, another *shifta* stronghold in Seraye, Asfaha not only suspended the *mislene*, *Azmatch* Naizghi Semere, but also stationed a cavalry unit there whom villagers had to feed and provision.

Such arbitrary acts inevitably aroused the resentment not only of the district administrators but also of the provincial officials, who increasingly felt that Asfaha and Dimetros were using the *shifta* pretext to remove disobedient *mislenes* from their traditional positions. There was also the feeling that the incursions from Ethiopia were part of a larger pretext for Ethiopian interference. Seraye senior divisional officer *Azmatch* Beraki Habtezghi actually fell out with Asfaha for refusing to remove the Dembelas *mislene* from his post.[41] The acrimonious exchange between Asfaha and Beraki became known to the public and was taken as an indication of cracks within the Eritrean administration.

Encouraged by ineffective government control, the *shifta* became more daring by the end of 1957. Even the outskirts of Asmera were no longer beyond their reach. As Asfaha attempted to rationalise the *shifta* upsurge as a temporary problem caused by economic hardship resulting from a poor rainy season, the Ethiopians pushed for more drastic measures. Thus, Kumilatchew Belete, an official in Andargatchew's office, proposed that, since Tedla Bairu's Banditry Act had proved ineffective, the property (*risti*) of the outlaws and their extended families should be confiscated and handed over to the government.[42] If anything provoked Eritreans to banditry, it was tampering with their rights to land. After his long tenure in Eritrea, Kumilatchew could not have been unaware of that fact.

Squeezed between the increasingly resentful district administrators and the Ethiopians, Asfaha sent his Banditry Act of 1957 for approval by the Assembly. The Act made a distinction between armed looting confined to foodstuffs and armed robbery that went beyond that. The minimum punishment for the former ranged from five to ten years, while all other categories of robbery were to receive stiffer sentences, including death for recidivists and murderers. More controversial, however, were the provisions of the Act referring to the families, villages and *kebilas* perceived to be related to the *shifta*. Every family was made liable for the payment of 50 birr for every month that one of its members remained a *shifta*. Any unexplained absence by a village or *kebila* member was taken as ground for arrest unless contrary evidence proved the absentee's innocence. Where a robbery was reported and the culprit not discovered, every family head within a radius of ten kilometres from the place of robbery was made liable for compensating the victim.

Chief Justice Shearer, who was not consulted over the Act, opposed it on several counts. It made no provisions for appeal against any of the sentences. Although collective fines were an accepted method of traditional punishment, Shearer regarded its revival as contrary to the rule of law established by the Eritrean legal system. He particularly rejected the decision to hold family heads within a ten-kilometre radius of the scene of a crime responsible for an act they might have had nothing to do with. What if a *shifta* travelled 30 kilometres a day and robbed wherever he went? Where would the radius end, he wondered. Shearer doubted that such a law would rally the people against the *shifta*. He thus declared it unconstitutional and voiced his regret that people might be too fearful of the government to challenge the Act in the Supreme Court, where he would be willing to hear the case.[43]

As the security situation worsened, the Secretary of the Interior, *Dejazmatch* Araia Wassie, undertook a unilateral initiative to solve the *shifta* problem by making individual arrests and consulting with Addis Ababa directly to challenge Asfaha's weakened position. Suspicion that Araia's aggressive behaviour arose from his own ambition to replace Andargatchew or Asfaha prompted the former to return from an extended visit to Addis Ababa, to convene a top-level meeting in Asmera.

With both Asfaha and Araia in attendance, Andargatchew severely criticised all forms of insubordination to Asfaha and announced that the Chief Executive's role would henceforth include the functions of the Emperor's vice representative and that 'his orders should be obeyed instinctively'. Araia was forced to resign his secretarial post and was later exiled to Gondar in Ethiopia as mayor. The British consul Peter Pares rightly described Asfaha's combined federal and Eritrean powers as 'one more nail in the coffin of Eritrean autonomy'.[44]

Elections to the Ethiopian Parliament

In February 1957, the Ethiopian Government announced its schedule for national elections to its Chamber of Deputies. Unlike the Eritrean elections, these were to be conducted by universal suffrage and allowed women to vote and stand for election. Eritrea, whose representation was raised from five to thirteen members, was to participate in the elections at the level of the thirteen Ethiopian provinces.

On 27 February, a petition signed by 500 members of the ML and sent to the Emperor voiced opposition to the terms of Eritrean participation in the elections. The petition read partly as follows:

> – Eritrea and Ethiopia are two states united federally under your Imperial Crown. According to the law, neither of them is an internal part of the other.
> – The Central Government which presides over the said two states ... has not been, we believe, legally constituted to this day.
> – [Out of ten members of the Federal Council] nine are Eritreans and only one Ethiopian, and this is a violation of article 5 of the UN Resolution and article 7 of the Eritrean Constitution, which provides that the IFC shall be composed of equal numbers of Ethiopians and Eritreans.
> – In the preamble to the Ethiopian Electoral Law, it is stated that 'Eritrea is a part of the Ethiopian Empire' and that the people of Eritrea 'proceed to elect their representatives in the Ethiopian Chamber of Deputies'. We believe that the said proclamation is in violation of the UN Resolution and the Eritrean Constitution. Because Eritrea is an autonomous government in its legislative, executive and judicial affairs, Eritrea is by no means a part of Ethiopia to participate in its elections ...
> – As voters we can participate in the Federal Legislative Council of the Central Government ... if it is established according to the law. We will never participate in the Ethiopian Legislative Council as it is in violation of the UN Resolution and the Eritrean Constitution as well as a suppression of the rights of Eritrea in its consideration as an internal part of Ethiopia ... Therefore, we vehemently beg Your Majesty to reconsider para. 3 and above ...[45]

The immediate result of such opposition was most visible in the Asmera and Hamasien region, where registration was weakest. In a meeting with the administrators of the area, Asfaha expressed his disappointment at the poor showing. 'Others shed their blood to obtain this right that we are taking for granted,' he told them.

> Some urban gossip-mongers say that they have written to the Emperor and that they are awaiting his reply. I have seen their petition and it deserves no response ... Just yesterday, they were demanding direct, as opposed to indirect, elections. Why are they now rejecting the direct elections granted by the man who protects the rights of human beings, His Majesty, our Emperor?

Concentrating more on urban opposition, Asfaha gave a stark warning that warmongers would be dealt with severely. He warned: 'The government's sword will be unsheathed over the heads of warmongers. I urge you to counsel your friends and relatives lest you regret their punishment ... May God protect me from being forced to make decisions that may create a rift between me and you, my people.'[46]

In spite of Asfaha's aggressive approach, registration for the elections continued to be lukewarm. Seraye province, where registration was said to be highest, showed 28,000 potential voters complied, far fewer than the expected number. By July, not one Muslim presented himself or herself as a candidate in the entire provinces of Hamasien, Seraye and Akeleguzai.[47]

To cover up the embarrassing situation, the government exploited a provision in the Ethiopian election law that required only one-year residence for citizens to be able to vote in a district. Thus, Ethiopian army personnel who satisfied the residence requirement registered en masse to raise the total number considerably. It must be recalled that the main point of contention in the Assembly discussions on the citizenship issue had been whether non-Eritrean federal citizens should be barred from participation in the internal political processes of Eritrea. Objections from various parts of the country were not only ignored, but even seasonal workers crossing from Tigray to Eritrea were made eligible for registration on the basis of false residence claims.[48]

By August, the government was expressing its satisfaction that even in Asmera and Hamasien, where the resistance was strongest, up to 28 per cent of eligible voters had registered. Consul Pares, quoting the *Mufti* of Eritrea, Ibrahim Mukhtar, found that practically no Muslim in the region had participated in the whole exercise. His American counterpart, Richey, who also toured the Western Provinces, found that the boycott extended beyond Asmera to the Tesseney area.[49]

The elections took place in mid-September. Of the sixteen candidates in Asmera, two were women, Aregash Kassa and Tsehaytu Berhe (Gual Zinar), both famous figures, bar owners and prominent members of the Unionist Party. No Muslim entered the race. Furthermore, except for two candidates in Akeleguzai, no other Muslim stood for election in all the three *kebessa* provinces. It was, overall, a low-key election in which in spite of the government's expressions of satisfaction, voter turnout was far below the desired level. Women's participation was especially minimal. Since most of the candidates were known unionists or protégés of the leaders of that party, the elections provided no cause for excitement. Only in Barentu was small-scale disturbance reported due to some irregularity.[50]

Fourteen candidates, eight Christians and two Muslims, were finally elected. Except in a few cases, most of the results went the way that Asfaha and Dimetros had planned.[51] But it was a partial election in which, as we saw, the larger public and the great majority of women did not participate. Not only that, but on 19 October fifteen Muslim leaders led by *Haji* Imam Musa and *Haji* Suleiman Ahmed sent petitions to the UN Secretary General and to Haile Selassie. The telegram sent to Haile Selassie, and copied to Asfaha and the UN Secretary General, read as follows:

> Most respectfully,
>
> Further to our previous telegram to Your Majesty and following Art. 30 and 35 of the Eritrean Constitution, we beg to inform Your Majesty that the fourteen members

> elected by the minority in Eritrea according to the laws and constitution of Ethiopia to participate in the Ethiopian Chamber of Deputies is contrary to Art. 5 of the United Nations Resolution and Art. 7 of the Eritrean Constitution, and it is neither an election to the Federal Legislative Council in which we had asked to participate nor an election carried out according to the laws of the Eritrean Government. Therefore, their participation in the Ethiopian Legislative Council is illegal, and said members do not represent Eritrea but themselves.[52]

The petition itself went unheeded.

20

POLITICAL AND SOCIAL STRUGGLES AT HOME AND ABROAD

Attempts from Abroad

Weldeab Weldemariam in Cairo

Weldeab's life in Sudan and Egypt would make a fascinating study of a nationalist in exile. After his utter disappointment with Eritrean politics of the previous decade, colonised Sudan of 1953 appeared to him to be a land of law, order, civility and goodwill. 'There are no dark forces here who plot and execute at night, no laying down of traps and nooses for mutual destruction,' he wrote to his friend and aide Yohannes Tsegai.

Even in the safety of exile, the threat of bomb blasts and pistol shots often haunted him. Andargatchew's relentless efforts to have him deported first from Sudan and later from Egypt, where he moved in early 1954, added to his worries. Yet, in spite of all the actual and imagined harassment, he continued to seek a way to resume his struggle for Eritrean independence. When he arrived in Cairo, he wrote: 'I asked the Egyptians to help me resume my work, to allow me to speak to the people of Eritrea. "Ethiopia is preparing to abrogate the UN Federal Resolution," I appealed to them. "I beg revolutionary Egypt to help me speak against this move before Ethiopia carries it out." They ignored my pleas.'

For Weldeab, the following three years were a period of deep anxiety. With the closure of *Dehai*, his sources of information about Eritrea became limited to the rare and guarded messages that Yohannes Tsegai could smuggle out. Yohannes himself was, at the time, a hunted man due to his involvement with the Federalisti. Although in time Eritrea became a blurred image in Weldeab's mind, he never lost his sense of purpose or of the justness of his cause. Ironically, indications or rumours of imminent annexation would not alarm him or throw him into despair. On the contrary, he expected it to happen at any moment. Haile Selassie, he wrote,

> is obliged to decide one way or the other—grant liberty or tighten the noose on Eritrea ... But Eritrea is lethal. It may be chewed up and swallowed, but I don't think

> that it will be digested into flesh and blood. He realizes this. With every passing day, the people are distancing themselves from him. Notions of independence and liberation are taking root. There certainly is the idea of 'putting a stop to all that' (*bisogna stroncare*).

At the same time, Weldeab expressed his disdain for the Eritrean authorities dancing to Haile Selassie's every tune and seeking favours. When Tedla fell and was replaced by Asfaha, he condemned their lack of conscience and outdated and ignorant political and administrative style. 'This is not the age of propaganda,' he said, 'it is rather the age of openness where nothing remains under cover for 24 hours.' On the contrary,

> their façade and clever words are immediately exposed, and their architects put to shame. Just because people submit to them in fear of their wealth and power, they feel that they are governing and leading. They do not want to know how much the people disdain and hate them. They will harden their hearts until a storm they cannot stop descends upon them ... Those who seek to thrive by shackling people under the yoke of oppression never heed the behest of the prophets; they would rather change their words, go back on their promises and try to survive by deceiving themselves and the people.

While in the midst of this embittered period of waiting and uncertainty, his ordeal came to a sudden end sometime in early March 1956.[1] He remembered the incident as follows:

> Mohammed Fayek, who was responsible for the radio programs of the National Guidance Department, called me to his office and said, 'You will address your people by radio. Do you want that?' and I replied, 'In Tigrinya there is a saying that translates, "Butter poured over *shiro* satiates me". I can start today if you so allow.' I used the opportunity to full effect.[2]

Radio Cairo had been broadcasting to Africa in Amharic, Swahili, Afar and Arabic before it allowed Weldeab to broadcast in Tigrinya and Safi Imam Musa, the son of activist nationalist leader *Haji* Imam Musa, to do the same in Arabic. In the beginning, the Eritrean programmes were limited to world news, and topics on literature, science and technology. However, with the intensification of the Suez crisis in mid-1956, and Ethiopia's involvement, over Egypt's objection, as part of a US-sponsored conference to resolve the crisis, Gamal Abdel Nasser took punitive measures against the country. Ethiopian Airlines was denied permission to fly over Egypt, and Weldeab's messages about Eritrean independence were allowed to intensify. In addition, Islamic teachers from Al Azhar University were sent to Ogaden and Somaliland to campaign for the independence of the two territories. Given as well the economic problems inflicted by the closure of the Suez Canal, Ethiopia had no choice but to come to some compromise with Egypt.[3]

Everyone agrees that Weldeab's broadcasts played a pivotal role in raising Eritrean consciousness and further enhancing Eritrean nationalism, especially amongst *kebessa* youth. He was a refined writer with a mastery of the Tigrinya language that is still largely unequalled. He was a lover of parables and proverbs that gave charm and authenticity to the content of his addresses. His evangelical faith and deep knowledge of the Bible and the Geez language kept him close to the mass of Christian people, and his familiarity with the Quran also found him acceptance with the Muslim population. As Enrico Mania puts it, his late-afternoon broadcasts, which coincided with the end of the working day, left Asmera streets empty. Every household with a radio, a rare possession at the time, would be packed for the '*appuntamento con Weldeab*'. In a short time, added Mania, Weldeab's messages became 'legendary', and 'although he was hitting hard, his language was refined, his themes focused, and his advocacy stressed truth and reality'.[4] Few now remember the contents of those broadcasts, but every worker, student and political activist interviewed for this book was in no doubt that he or she was greatly influenced by those words. According to the Tigrayan writer Alemseged Abbay, Weldeab was followed even in Tigray, where some of his proverbs and parables are still quoted.[5]

As Weldeab's influence spread with increasing force and speed, the Eritrean Government's counterattacks shifted to Radio Cairo and the Egyptian Government. In a series of articles in *Zemen*, the Egyptian radio station was accused of 'indulging thieves and carpetbaggers seeking to destroy the peace and brotherhood of the country'. The Egyptian Government 'has employed Eritreans only in name and is attempting to destabilise this island of peace and security, good behaviour and correctness, and of love and harmony'.[6] Once again playing the religious card, *Zemen* warned: 'If they are under the illusion that, by creating a rift between Eritrean Muslims and Christians, who are Ethiopians, they can revive their dream of acquiring the Western Provinces, they are gravely mistaken.'[7]

Weldeab was branded a traitor who would sell his country, and Ethiopia launched a diplomatic offensive to stop his broadcasts and have him deported back home. Aware that the government's efforts to neutralise his messages were meeting with failure, Egypt intensified its propaganda campaigns both in Eritrea and the Ogaden. Ethiopia, for its part, decided to take advantage of its membership of the committee on the Suez Canal to win over Nasser's support. Since the Egyptian leader was at the same time promoting his version of African unity and the organisation of the 'non-aligned' movement, Ethiopia sought to utilise that angle, too, for better effect.[8]

According to Weldeab, the process of negotiations between Ethiopian and Egyptian diplomats directly affected his broadcasts. 'They would suspend my programme whenever they seemed to reach agreement on issues of strategy but allow me to continue if they disagreed. This happened on three different occasions.' At last, when Aklilu met Nasser as part of the Suez committee, he promised him that Ethiopia would desist from supporting anything that would harm Egypt and even expressed his willingness to share the classified information of the committee, provided Egypt was willing to come to some agreement. Weldeab reported what happened next, as told to him by the Egyptian authorities:

> 'So, what are your demands?' asked Abdel Nasser. Aklilu replied, 'Our main demand is the closure of the Tigrinya programme of Radio Cairo.' They told me that Nasser laughed. 'We thought you would be after something bigger. Why is this so important to you?' 'You wouldn't know, but we do. That is our main precondition.' The Ethiopians stuck to their demand and had my programme closed down permanently.[9]

Weldeab's broadcasts lasted a total of about nine months. They stopped in early 1957. In that short period of time, his message reached thousands of Eritreans, especially the youth. Many believe that in those dire times, Weldeab kept the hope and flame of independence alive. His name acquired legendary proportions, a status that his subsequent, often difficult and controversial life within the Eritrean revolutionary movement would not diminish.

Mohammed Omer Qadi and His UN Appeal

Omer Qadi, whom Weldeab described as 'a man of courage and principle', was hunted and harassed by the Eritrean security forces. His court defence of the Federalisti had also not helped his situation. On 12 June 1956, when he was waiting for a visa for a pilgrimage to Mecca, Police Commissioner Tedla Ukbit summoned him to his office. That very day, he later wrote to his fellow lawyer Yohannes Tsegai, 'I had heard that the Federal Government was concocting a plot to discredit me and condemn me to detention ... Upon the advice of knowledgeable friends, I decided not to fall into their trap. I did not want to suffer our friend Ibrahim Sultan's fate—languish in the federal courts and finally apologise for an offence never committed.' [10]

Omer Qadi identified the Interior Secretary, Araia Wassie, as his main tormentor, and on 13 June he secretly left Eritrea for Sudan 'in order to deny them the satisfaction of my arrest'. It took him six months to reach Cairo, where he immediately linked up with Weldeab and started to work on an appeal to the UN. By coincidence, UN Secretary General Dag Hammarskjöld was on a visit to Cairo at the time, and both men got the chance to meet him and hand him a draft of their appeal. Omer Qadi was surprised to find the UN chief highly informed about Eritrea. But Hammarskjöld told them that he was powerless to make any intervention as the matter was more the concern of the Four Powers than the UN.

Refusing to be discouraged by Hammarskjöld's polite rejection, Omer Qadi expressed confidence that the appeal to the UN would culminate in the formation of a UN commission of inquiry that would forestall Ethiopia's inevitable move towards annexation following the 1957 Ethiopian elections.[11] For months, he worked with Weldeab on the document, detailing the injustices committed against the people of Eritrea. They particularly denounced the UN's 'federal solution' as an imposition that Eritreans had been forced to accept in order to avoid Ethiopian annexation or the partition of the country. They also catalogued Ethiopia's high-handed trampling on Eritrean rights under the federal arrangement.[12]

In the meantime, fourteen Eritrean members of the Muslim League (ML) forwarded a petition to the UN and the Emperor demanding that a UN commission be sent to Eritrea to 'investigate and examine the application of the United Nations Resolution ... because presently the Resolution is not wholly applied and Eritrea finds itself in a serious economic hardship'. In a reference to Omer Qadi, the petitioners affirmed their support for 'whoever defends before the floor of the General Assembly the rights of Eritrea'.[13] Some of the petitioners, particularly *Haji* Suleiman Ahmed and *Haji* Imam Musa, would pay a high price for the affront, as we shall see.

Omer Qadi travelled alone to New York when Weldeab was denied an American visa. Upon arrival there in November 1957, he immediately entered the halls of the UN and started to distribute the document that he and Weldeab had prepared so painstakingly. The Ethiopian delegation took prompt action as Omer Qadi was just beginning to reach out to world representatives. The Ethiopian Ambassador met him and Weldeab described their encounter:

> The ambassador and his colleagues saw the document and said to Qadi, 'Mr Omer Qadi, why are you doing this? Why don't you present your grievances directly to the Emperor? Why are you exposing Ethiopia and discrediting the Emperor in front of strangers? This is a simple matter that you as Eritreans and us as Ethiopians can set right. Why go to this extent?' They softened him up with nice words.

Apparently, Qadi was as susceptible to deception as he was bold and courageous. He took the ambassador's words at face value, pocketed a letter of introduction from him to the Emperor, discontinued his mission and headed straight back to Cairo. He met Weldeab the same day and told him that, since his name was included in the letter, they should travel to Addis Ababa together. Stunned by his colleague's naiveté, Weldeab tried to talk him out of his plans:

> 'Omer, you are making a mistake,' I told him. 'You should not be doing this. They tricked you into it. They will jail us and kill us. If not, they will not spare us in other ways, have no doubts about this. I am begging you to change your mind. Don't go to Ethiopia. As long as we are alive and our voices are being heard, we can be of some value to our country. If we enter Ethiopia, we will benefit neither ourselves nor our country. I am begging you to regret this.'
>
> 'You have become the servant of the Egyptians,' he chided me. 'You have stopped being an Eritrean.' I would not let him go at that. 'You must be tired. Take a rest; I will come back to you tomorrow.' I went back to him the next day. He was gone.[14]

Omer Qadi was well received in Addis Ababa, where he was granted a brief audience with the Emperor. Aklilu too met with him and gave him some verbal promises. He returned to Asmera on 6 January 1958 to a hero's welcome from his followers.

The Fate of Omer Qadi and His Followers

As soon as Omer Qadi returned to Asmera, his house became the centre for visits from the political luminaries of the day. Ibrahim Sultan, *Haji* Suleiman, *Qadi* Ali, Mohammed Berhanu of Mendefera, Idris Mohammed Adem, Teklehaimanot Bokru and Akito were among the most frequent participants in the discussions that took place there. Asmera soon buzzed with the rumour that a UN commission of inquiry would shortly be sent to Eritrea. Should this materialise, Omer Qadi would lead a delegation to reopen the Eritrean case at the General Assembly. A CID report of the time noted that 'serious and animated group discussions between Muslims and Christians' were spreading throughout Asmera and that 'Omer Qadi's name and reputation was on the rise'.[15]

Encouraged by all the attention, Omer Qadi went to Massawa on 21 January to meet with and organise supporters in that port city. On his return to Asmera, the director of the Interior, Zerom Kifle, called him to his office and accused him of creating 'subversive and anti-nationalist propaganda'. In defiance, he went to Ghinda'e the following day on a similar mission. Trouble started when he and a bus full of his supporters attempted to travel to Keren two days later. In those weeks, Keren was on the boil with public demonstrations and secret meetings. As Omer Qadi was being awaited with intense expectation, the government intercepted his bus at Adi Teklezan, over 40 kilometres north-west of Asmera, and escorted him back to the capital.[16]

Several significant developments preceded or accompanied Omer Qadi's initiative. First, the students' strikes of the previous year, which we will discuss next, left a deep mark on the political mood of the country. Second, some members of the disbanded Federalisti had moved on to revive the suspended Workers' Union and were secretly working with former leaders of the Independence Bloc (IB), the ML and the Liberal Progressive Party (LPP). Third, from the end of 1957, the Workers' Union began reorganising itself to discuss a labour law drafted by the government. Last, but most important, signs of unrest due to the country's unrelenting economic problems made the government nervous about the timing of Omer Qadi's activities.

On 26 January, a day before Haile Selassie's scheduled visit to Massawa, an estimated 700 inhabitants took to the streets to demand the lifting of the ban on Omer Qadi. When security forces stopped Qadi from travelling from Asmera to address his followers, a group of supporters from Akurdet, Asmera and other towns sent telegrams of protest to the Emperor.[17] On 10 February, members of the ML and the Federalist Association met at Qadi's residence and agreed to present their views to the Emperor in person. Ibrahim Sultan typed up the decision and delivered it to Haile Selassie.[18]

The most significant incident of those months took place in Keren. Word came that after Massawa, the Emperor was scheduled to visit Keren. The town's residents, who were still smarting from Omer Qadi's ill-treatment at Adi Teklezan, decided to carry anti-Ethiopian placards and confront the Emperor at Halib Mentel, some fifteen kilometres from Keren. When he did not turn up, the youths distributed their pamphlets and staged a demonstration, at which the police arrested four persons.[19] The demonstrations turned violent when parents joined in to protest against the unaffordable bail set for their children. Police retaliated with tear gas and live ammunition, wounding up to seventeen people. In a show of solidarity, Keren businesses closed their shops. The protests spread to Akurdet and Tesseney, where shops remained closed from 2 to 6 March 1958.[20]

As it happened, the beginning of March coincided with the scheduled start of the workers' strike. It was thus a highly charged month of defiance and protest. Taking advantage of the mood in the country, the leaders of ML and the Federalisti, who met secretly, sent a joint telegram to the Emperor. Of significance was that, unlike the previous petitions which were mainly signed by ML members, it included Christian opposition leaders, thus heralding the development of nationalist cooperation across the religions. The telegram read as follows:

His Imperial Majesty Sovereign of Federation,
Addis Ababa

Most respectfully and in accordance with paragraph seven Federal Act and Art. 22(J) Eritrean Constitution we forward following petition.

1. Situation in Eritrea became grave needs Your Majesty's urgent attention.
2. Federal Court in Eritrea keeps Mohammed Omer Kadi who returned from United Nations under Your Majesty's patronage under investigation in order to proceed against him.
3. Eritrean Government is using fearful means against population result of which at Agordat many persons imprisoned some tribe Chiefs removed from traditional public functions. At Keren police by using firearms 12 persons wounded and about hundred persons imprisoned consequently Western Province is in general strike for protest.
4. We think these facts are for revenge for complaint presented by these population to Your Majesty during your last visit to Eritrea as the same revenge is taking place against Mohammed Omer Kadi he having delivered complaint to United Nations on behalf of Eritrean people.

However, these facts contradict Federal Act and Eritrean Constitution and Human Rights.

It needs intervention of Your Majesty to put right being the situation very seriously grave as Your Majesty is guarantor of Human Rights over all the area of Federation. We humbly beg your gracious reply to our request and accept our sincere greetings and thanks.

Eritrean Muslim League
Ibrahim Sultan

Imam Musa (Haji)
Idris Mohammed Adem
Yasin Jemal
Mohammed el Hassen
Hamid Hamdan
Omer Akito
Saleh Musa

Partito Giovanile Federalisti Eritrei [Federalist Youth Party of Eritrea]
Teclehaimanot Bucru
Tesfai Redda
Tesfazghi Haile
Zemicael Ogbanchiel
Berhe Andemicael
Abraha Hagos
Gerezgher Ualabzghi
Abraha Futur
Tzeggai Yasu

Asmera, March 5, 1958[21]

The composition of names in the list was a clear indication that new alliances were being forged in Eritrea. Here were ML, LPP, and Federalisti youth leaders (most of the last-mentioned former Andinet activists) working in league with their Shuban counterparts. The dangers inherent in such a development could not escape the government's notice and it moved to halt it. In mid-March, *Haji* Imam Musa and *Haji* Suleiman Ahmed were arrested along with ten followers on orders from the Federal High Court (FHC). Initially, Omer Qadi was required to report to the court every morning. However, on 25 March, he too was arraigned for leaving the country without a proper permit, making written and verbal contacts with foreign governments, and disseminating defamatory material on Ethiopia both in Sudan and Egypt. A total of eighteen people were arrested within the week.[22]

The arrest of Imam Musa, an octogenarian, and Suleiman Ahmed, brother of *Mufti* Ibrahim Mukhtar, provoked the indignation of Asmera Muslims. On 4 April, which fell in the month of Ramadan, Muslim leaders ordered the suspension of religious services in all the mosques. Although they bombarded Haile Selassie and his federal officials with telegrams of protest and threats of open confrontation, the FHC ignored their pleas and went ahead with its proceedings.

The trial itself was highly confrontational and acrimonious because of the defence lawyer Gebrelul Gebreyesus's aggressive style of advocacy. But this would not save the defendants from their fate. On 30 April, the court found Omer Qadi guilty of defaming Ethiopia and handed him a ten-year prison sentence. About a month later, Imam Musa and Suleiman Ahmed were sentenced to four years each in prison. Even the lawyer Gebrelul was not spared. Charging him with 'spiteful and abrasive' behaviour before the FHC, he was handed a three-month sentence of imprisonment and his licence was revoked. In October 1958, Haile Selassie ordered the reprieve of Imam Musa and Suleiman Ahmed. Omer Qadi languished in jail for many more years.[23]

Omer Qadi was the most consistent advocate of conditional union with Ethiopia. Ever since the Bet Giorgis Convention in 1946, he had never deviated from his advocacy of a federal solution for Eritrea and Ethiopia. In his association with Weldeab in Egypt, he remained the federalist, in contrast to Weldeab's quest for full independence. His greatest weakness was the trust that he placed in Haile Selassie's support for his federal plan. With his arrest and persecution, any chance of survival of the UN-sponsored federal arrangement came to an end.

Student Unrest and Strikes

The Student Strike of 1957

In 1955, Haile Selassie inaugurated a first-rate school named after himself at the foot of the Tsetserat, or Forto Hill, of Asmera. With seven other schools (four in Asmera and one each in Massawa, Asseb and Barentu), it was hailed as a great gift from the Emperor to the Eritrean people. A special publication acclaiming the Emperor's generosity issued in 1962 put the cost at over 840,000 birr. Along with the expenses incurred in building the other schools and equipping them with materials and teachers, the Emperor's 'gift' to the country was calculated at over 8 million birr.[24]

Coming amid popular accusations that Ethiopia was several more millions in arrears of payment due to their country, the students of the school were not impressed by the Ethiopian claims. The belief that Ethiopia, not Eritrea, was the beneficiary of the federal set-up had sunk deep into their thinking. With the closure of Italian enterprises and the departure of Italian employers, unemployment and poverty had hit every home, with students often at the receiving end. Resentment thus provoked the youngsters to actively oppose anything to do with Ethiopia. The focal point of their aggrievement and opposition was the introduction of Amharic into the elementary, middle and secondary schools run by the Eritrean Government. The political motive behind the move could not be concealed. An Ethiopian document published later had this to say on the topic:

> The only way that the people of Eritrea can be groomed to love their country and their Emperor and to realise their Ethiopian roots is if the young generation is nurtured through education. Besides, a people can only attain growth and unity if it rallies around one language. If people are united by language, they become a family who care for each other. They will fight to ward off aliens who may covet their country or develop the spirit to resist alien designs that may threaten it.[25]

Popular resentment was not confined to these issues. Ethiopian federal officials—residing in the best villas of Asmera and earning exorbitant amounts compared even with the cabinet secretaries—behaved like masters and conquerors. Moreover, the year 1956 seemed 'destined for the triumphal exaltation of Haile Selassie. The cult of personality of the Emperor became unabashedly obsessive. Every rustle of the leaves was devoted to the Emperor. To His Majesty was devoted the idea, the initiative, the apogee. Thus, the streets, the schools, the hospitals, the institutions bore only one name—Haile Selassie I.'

The Emperor was present at least once or twice in Asmera each year, and every time he came, teams were mobilised to erect arches for his welcome. In Massawa, hundreds of camels and their riders were choreographed for the performance of spectacular shows. Schools and industries were closed, and children and workers made to parade and cheer the monarch and his entourage. 'At the beginning, it was seen as an occasion for stability and deeper affinity between the authorities and the public. The repetition of the ritual of accolades triggered fatigue and discontent.'[26]

In Eritrea, the aura of inviolability that had once surrounded Haile Selassie began to dissipate. Even his closest assistants confided their resentment to the Eritrean officials they could trust. Gebremedhin Tessema, later Eritrea's Auditor General, recalled a conversation that he had with General Mekonnen Deneke, the Emperor's aide-de-camp, who told him, 'The Emperor loves rumour. He ignores information properly assessed and written. He accepts and enjoys gossip scribbled on pieces of paper telling him about people talking behind his back or disobeying his directives. He feels that no one, except him, can create anything. He tries to impress upon us that only he can make people or create work.'[27]

It was at this crucial time in the federal period that Weldeab's broadcasts from Cairo were made and their effect on the students of the Haile Selassie I Secondary School (HSISS) was electric. Every morning, they would come to class fuelled by Weldeab's exhortations of the previous evening. They also actively opposed the directive pressuring them to speak only in Amharic inside the school compound. They resented hoisting the Ethiopian flag every morning and most of them would refuse to sing the official flag song.[28] They also objected to the replacement of an Indian director of the school who understood Eritrean history and sympathised with the Eritrean cause, by someone whom the students saw as hostile.[29]

On the morning of 12 March 1957, the students lined up in their habitual places around the flag post but refused to hoist the Ethiopian flag and sing the accompanying song. Asked for an explanation, a student who could speak Amharic responded, 'This is not our flag.' Rejecting attempts at persuasion by the director and his administrator, the students marched in single file and, boarder and day-student alike, exited the school compound and assembled on the square outside. Negotiations for their return, led by the Interior Secretary, Araia Wassie, and the Chief of Police, Tedla Ukbit, bore no fruit. With each passing day, their demands increased, from the dismissal of the director to the reinstatement of Eritrea's constitutional rights and the Eritrean flag. Neither Clarence Smith, the Attorney General, nor Asfaha himself, who met with their representatives, could persuade the young rebels, most of them between the ages of fifteen and twenty, to return to class.

Popular sympathy lay with the students. Boarding students who slept on the pavement adjacent to the school were offered food, blankets, shelter and pocket money. As the government put pressure on parents to bring their children into line, police action forced them to change venues for planning their actions. On about the sixth week of the stand-off, some submitted to parental pressure and broke the strike to return to classes. A few days later, the strikers entered the school compound with sticks and stones and attacked the strike-breakers, injuring several. Twelve students were arrested by the police.

On 7 May, seven weeks after the start of the strike, about a hundred students marched to the Asmera Central Prison and demanded that they too be incarcerated along with their friends. When told that they could not be put in jail without having committed an offence, they went straight back to their school, jumped over the back fences and broke every window of the building. Laboratories were smashed, the Emperor's huge portrait at the entrance was torn down and trodden upon, and students and staff attacked. With that accomplished, they reassembled at the square near the Central Post Office and peacefully climbed onto police trucks. That evening, 109 students were taken to the Adi Quala Prison, 86 kilometres south of Asmera.[30]

Suddenly, an incident dismissed as a student matter attained national prominence. Within a few days, the matter of jurisdiction over the hearings for their case took a controversial turn. Senbeta Genno, Deputy Chief Prosecutor of the Federal High Court, argued that, since the school was a federal institution, his court should hear the matter. Habtezghi Okbazghi, arguing for the students, refused to let his Eritrean clients be judged outside the Eritrean court system.[31] By coincidence, this legal tug of war was interrupted by the death in Ethiopia of Haile Selassie's second son, Prince Mekonnen. Student impatience over the delays in the proceedings boiled over to other schools and such towns as Keren, Mendefera and Akurdet.[32]

Although Asfaha took personal charge of the case and held open meetings with the students, he could not break their determination. In his handwritten notes on the strike, the Attorney General, Frederick Russell, wrote about Asfaha's worries:

> The CE [Chief Executive] is panicky. He wants to adjourn the matter because of the court mourning for the Duke of Harar. This would hardly appear to the boys in jail as a statesmanlike stroke. The CE had also suggested that my *shifta* Proclamation (no. 1/1955) which I had drafted in June 1955 in order to combat banditry might be invoked in order to be able to put impulsive schoolboys in jail for 3 months and incidentally stigmatizing them as *shiftas*.[33]

In the tenth week of the students' strike, Senbeta Genno prevailed over Habtezghi and began to argue the case against 25 students at the Federal Court. To the 12 initially arrested for damaging the school building, 13 more had been identified as student leaders. The remaining accused, 109 in all, still in Adi Quala, were tried in absentia.

Student Trial at the FHC

On 23 May, Justice Debbas, the deputy president of the FHC, presided over the proceedings.[34] Of the five charges, he dismissed four and directed them to the Eritrean High Court for appropriate jurisdiction. Only one charge, 'assault on a Government (Federal) employee', was invoked against the accused. In a strange twist, however, Debbas announced that the court could not proceed further in the face of the threats and pressure being imposed on the bench and adjourned the trial. Russell, who thought that Debbas 'seemed a bit nervous—that is not the *mot juste* but "harried", "worried" are not correct', concluded that both the Federal and Eritrean governments were attempting to avoid the embarrassment of keeping schoolboys in jail by passing responsibility to the other.[35]

On 27 May, the students of Adi Qeih and Dekemhare joined the strike, extending it nationwide. On the same day, Debbas and his colleagues resumed their hearings. Twenty-one students showed up in court. Eighteen soldiers, many of them armed, and scores of mothers and relatives filled the courtroom. After some legal wrangling, the judges accepted the defence counsel's demand for the release of the youngsters on bail of 100 birr each. Bail was also set at 50 birr each for the 109 Adi Quala internees.[36]

Student unrest subsided when all the prisoners were finally released on 5 June and most of the striking students went back to their classes. But Haile Selassie Secondary School allowed only the strike-breakers back, closing its doors to the rest for the remaining academic year. In addition, the twelve students identified as leaders of the three-month-long unrest were permanently dismissed from the school. We will meet some of them, like Teku'e Yehdego, as activists and revolutionaries in the next stage of the Eritrean nationalist struggle.[37]

The surprising aspect of the student strike was that such a spontaneous event could last for so long and spread throughout Eritrea, unsettling the government to the extent that we have seen. In that sense, it was a first experience for Eritreans. More importantly for the nationalist cause, it produced a crop of activists and leaders who would play an important role in taking the Eritrean independence struggle to a higher level.

The Workers' Strike of 1958

Victimisation of the Eritrean Worker

Tom Killion, who undertook extensive research on the history of the Eritrean workers' movement, has identified several factors that seriously affected their livelihoods in these years. First, their savings in East Africa shillings depreciated greatly when the change to the Ethiopian birr was made on unfavourable terms. Second, the increase in customs duties imposed by the Ethiopian Government on imported necessities pushed prices beyond the reach of the already impoverished workers. Third, Ethiopia's refusal to pay Eritrea its fair share of customs revenues contributed to the worsening economic problems. Fourth, Ethiopia's development of Asseb and its linkage with the Ethiopian hinterland diminished Massawa's traditional role as a communications hub and directly affected trade and industry in Eritrea.[38] In addition, Killion has detailed the personal enrichment of Ethiopian federal officials who entered into partnerships with major Italian investors like the agro-industrialists Barattolo and De Nadai, the Italian-financed electricity company of SEdAO, and CITAO, a major Italian firm responsible for the building of the American base at Kagnew Station in Asmera. Between 1956 and 1960, Ethiopian federal and other authorities became heavy investors in some 400 Italian small and medium-sized enterprises still operating in Eritrea.

Another major source of worker resentment in the mid-1950s was the belief that Addis Ababa was flourishing at the expense of Asmera and other Eritrean towns. As Italian- and Eritrean-owned small factories and workshops closed down, skilled labourers and artisans migrated to Ethiopia, where their trades were in demand. Major construction works like the Haile Selassie Theatre, the Emperor's Jubilee Palace and the Addis Ababa Stadium were designed and constructed by formerly Eritrea-based Italian firms with some Eritrean technical skills. Many of these firms either closed down their businesses to move to Ethiopia or greatly reduced their former capacity, thus compounding the unemployment problem in Eritrea. According to a US consulate report of 1956:

> Eritrea has gained little, if any, economic advantage from the union. Ethiopian investment in the Eritrean economy does not approach that of the Italians or the British ... Most of the conditions which favoured the development of its small industries in the past have disappeared. It appears, therefore, that the more significant growth in the Federation's economy will take place in Ethiopia. With the exception of Asseb, the Federal Government will concentrate development expenditures in Ethiopia.[39]

With only 14,772 Eritreans employed in all non-governmental enterprises, 1956/7 showed great losses in public employment.[40] Compare this with the employment figure of 27,000 Eritreans in 1947. But even the mid-1950s figures were to plummet to 10,000 Eritreans by 1960.[41] The workers' dire situation inevitably led to the resurgence of the labour movement.

The Reorganisation of the AEFTU

In 1953, Tedla Bairu banned the Eritrean Association of Free Trade Unions (AEFTU) following its active role in the election of its wounded president, Weldeab

Weldemariam, to the Eritrean Assembly. In a low-key defiance of that sanction, the AEFTU's treasurer, Tsegai Kahsai, and executive committee members Siraj Abdu, Tewelde Tedla and Tekie Eliffe managed to keep their offices open and retain the records of their general membership.

In spite of the ban, labour unions in Asseb, Massawa and Asmera did not stop presenting their demands or going on strike.[42] But such sporadic and often uncoordinated actions failed to improve working conditions or in any way ameliorate the underlying economic problems. Before disbanding for the 1956 elections, the Eritrean Assembly had sent a labour law based on the Labour Act, one of the organic laws left by the British for the Eritrean Government, for the Chief Executive's approval. Rather than submitting this piece of legislation to the Emperor's representative for ratification, Asfaha shelved the proposal until the end of 1957. He had a reason for doing so.

The law was openly welcomed by labour unionists as friendly and fair to their cause. On the other hand, Italian employers saw it as potentially harmful to their interests and made use of the time accorded them by Asfaha's delay to lobby against it and to dismiss and replace potential activists from among their employees. Fearing that the tide would turn in favour of the employers, workers broke police bans to ask the government's Labour Office for help. The office complied and requested prompt government ratification of the law.[43]

The need to revitalise AEFTU was now obvious. With the prosecution and harassment of the Federalisti, organised political activity was at a standstill. The Federalisti's Association itself, although effective in keeping the flame of protest and nationalist fervour burning, had been unable to grow to more than a hundred members, even at its peak. Apart from government pressure, which stifled its voice and growth, some of its members' ambivalence about the choice between federalism and independence frustrated its more radical elements. Several of the latter, particularly Berhe Andemikael and Zemikael Okbamikael, came to see the revitalisation of the labour movement as the only way to rescue the declining political struggle. They approached Tsegai Kahsai and together launched a clandestine campaign for the reorganisation of the AEFTU.

Lack of experience and probably also personality clashes retarded the task at hand and obliged them to seek leadership from older sympathisers who were not themselves workers. Thus, they named *Cavaliere* Mohammed Ahmed, owner of an advertising agency, as their ad hoc chairman; Assembly member and lawyer Tewelde Tedla, their advisor; and another lawyer named Yishak Teferi, the secretary.[44] The choice of Mohammed Ahmed was to prove controversial as he was an employer and had been known for his close contacts with the Office of the Emperor's Representative.

Contrary to the young workers' expectations, the new leadership failed to carry out their responsibilities. This was 1956, the year of the Assembly elections. Mohammed Ahmed and Tewelde Tedla suspended their union activities to run for Assembly seats. The remaining three also refrained from active participation, preferring to give advice from the side. More damaging to the union's cause was the government's decision to suppress all its activities throughout the election period.

It was only in the autumn of 1957 that the activists, particularly Tsegai and Berhe, were able to resume their mission in earnest. They began by demanding action on the labour law passed by the Assembly, which had been shelved indefinitely by the Chief Executive, but they then faced a frustrating series of fruitless meetings and endless waiting. In a meeting of the representatives of the major labour unions, including the reluctant elderly interim union officials, they formally demanded the implementation of the 1956 labour law. They also communicated to the government that should their demands be rejected, they would call for a general strike for 10 October 1957.

The government reacted by appointing a high-level committee led by Ali Rad'ai, former president of the Assembly and currently Secretary of Social Affairs, to negotiate with the AEFTU's leadership. After weeks of futile appointments and contentious exchanges, Attorney General Clarence Smith informed the expectant workers that they had been promoting a defective legal document. On the instructions of the Chief Executive, he replaced it with an acceptable new draft of 102 articles. He invited the workers to select a committee to study the new draft and submit to him their points of disagreement, if any.

This was not what they had expected from the Canadian lawyer. Rather than pushing the confrontation to the limit, however, they studied the draft and immediately identified article 84 as unacceptable. The article provided that the Chief Executive could withdraw recognition of the workers' organisation 'at any time upon finding that the object of the association has ceased to be the advancement of the interests of its members, or that control of the association has fallen into the hands of a person likely to use that control substantially for another project'.[45] Evidently, the authorities sought to buy time to create an amenable union. Furthermore, Andargatchew's open attack on labour unions in general, as an impediment to capitalist initiative and development, spurred them to forceful action.[46]

On 16 December, about eighty representatives of all the unions assembled to plan their course of action. Mohammed Ahmed stated that the amended draft was likely to be approved by the Assembly and would soon become the law of the land. The representatives saw this as a capitulation and attacked him severely. Tsegai Kahsai, who was vociferous in his criticism, even accused the leadership of treachery. He also suggested that the time for a general workers' strike had come. Berhe Andemikael of the Federalisti further suggested that, if the Assembly failed to deliberate on the original draft by 23 December, they would move towards the general strike in the following week.[47]

Composed as it was mainly of hand-picked annexationists or traditional chiefs with no notion of their parliamentary duties, the Assembly failed to give the draft law the importance and attention it deserved. Lack of a quorum, the most chronic malaise of the second legislature, delayed any consideration of the draft until 18 February 1958, when a committee of seven members was charged to review the draft in the presence of Clarence Smith and present it to the Assembly.[48] As further delays hampered the Assembly's committee, the president, Hamid Ferej, openly pre-empted its review by declaring his support for the new draft.[49]

Worried about the prospect of losing the battle, the labour leaders Tsegai, Berhe and Zemikael decided to approach the Chief of Police, Tedla Ukbit. 'Although he was tough and harsh,' Berhe recalled,

> we banked on his knowledge and respect for the rule of law. We told him: 'You call us stooges of Al Rabita, Nasser and the Arabs. We are none of that. We are simple workers seeking to establish workers' rights. There is a misunderstanding between the Government and us. Let this misunderstanding be laid to rest or condemn us to our old life of slavery under employers and the rich. Help us rise or doom us to stoop in submission.' He asked us if we were planning to go on strike. Scared, we mumbled incoherent replies. But he surprised us with what he said next. 'Listen, I do not support the suppression of the right of workers ... I was myself a swine and horse caterer on the farm of an Italian named Gigi. I know first-hand what a worker's plight and a worker's due is.'
>
> Encouraged by his words, we heaped praises on his frugal and ascetic life and his incorruptibility. We asked him if we could proceed peacefully. Suddenly, he said, 'You may hold your strike.' The Assembly committee was scheduled to discuss the draft on Saturday, May 8. Should the result be in our disfavour, we set May 10 as the day of our general strike.

By his own admission, Clarence Smith had no sympathy for the cause of the labour movement.[50] When he discussed the draft with the committee, he saw no reason to accommodate the union leadership's concerns and recommended only some minor amendments. On 8 May, the committee approved the draft and sent it to the Assembly for a vote. In the accompanying message, Asfaha claimed that the 1956 draft law was defective and that his version corrected those flaws. After assuring the Assembly that he had obtained the agreement of the labour leadership and of employers, he urged the members to protect investors from activities that would hinder them from establishing their enterprises in the country.[51]

In the Assembly, a few members attempted to argue against article 84. But the Assembly passed the draft with forty-four votes. Only three opposed it and one abstained; twenty members were not present. *Zemen* praised the new law as a right and honour only possible under 'Ethiopian freedom'.[52]

The General Strike

The Assembly's vote was announced at 1.30 pm on 8 March. Immediately, the union leadership notified the police that the general strike would take effect on the morning of 10 May, and then spent the rest of the day on planning it. As they parted at 1 am for the night, security forces arrested Tsegai, Berhe and Zemikael and kept them at the Caserma Mussolini (Mussolini Barracks) in the centre of the Asmera main street until 5 pm the following day. Hundreds of workers assembled in front of Caserma Mussolini and forced their release.

On the morning of 10 March, the general strike began with workers gathering at the square in front of St Mary's Cathedral. With the exception of bakeries and the water and electricity supply companies, every enterprise in Asmera closed down for the day. 'Asmera looked barren and crippled,' Tsegai Kahsai recalled. As the gathering filled up the square, a jovial performance of skits and songs depicting worker conditions entertained the crowd. Sixty-eight blindfolded workers groped through the crowd, a pointed reference to the sixty-eight 'blind' Assembly members. Six others with cottonwool stuffed in their ears pointed to the six 'deaf' cabinet secretaries. A limping man on crutches made fun of Asfaha, who suffered from gout.

Surprisingly, the police made no attempt to stop all the workers' banter, mockery and noise. On the contrary, Tedla Ukbit allowed the leaders to rent loudspeakers, and they ascended the platform to make fiery and provocative speeches. This went on until 11 am when Asfaha, accompanied by Assembly president Hamid Ferej, vice president Dimetros and other top officials, arrived on the scene, together with Commissioner Tedla. Asfaha took over the microphones. Tsegai described the moment as follows:

> Asfaha was a refined speaker, a fine orator. But I had never heard him deliver such a bad speech. 'This strike is the work of rogues,' he told us. 'You were offered a law consisting of 102 articles. You approved of 101 and reneged on just one additional provision. Anyone who does this can only be a rogue. I, Asfaha, gave you a law that your fathers and grandfathers never dreamed of. If you load a donkey with a camel's burden, its back will break ...' Angered by his words and condescension, the crowd drowned his voice in an indignant uproar.

What did Asfaha mean by his last utterance? Berhe Andemikael elaborates:

> Asfaha was, in effect, telling us that labour unionism, which did not exist in Ethiopia at the time, was beyond our capacity. 'We are a small entity, an association, not fit to be a government' is what he was saying. In other words, just as a camel's load would break a donkey's back, so would unionism be too weighty for the capabilities of Eritrean workers. The workers felt insulted by those words and started to hurl verbal insults at the CE. Our attempts to calm them down did not work.

Fearful that the crowd might become violent, AEFTU leaders and security officials whisked Asfaha and his companions into the church compound, from where they were taken through the back gates to the safety of their offices. Tedla stayed behind to admonish the crowd for its affront and to order it to disband and the demonstrators to return to their workplaces. The latter made it known that they had no intention of returning to work, choosing instead to remain for further instructions.

Trouble began when police officers started to take bicycles away from the workers and load them on waiting trucks. It was obvious to the leaders that the police sought to provoke a reaction. They thus advised their followers to disband peacefully and claim their bicycles back at a later date. As this was happening, a Jeep full of armed policemen and commandeered by the Asmera police chief, Major Goitom Gebrezghi, arrived at the scene. Minutes later, shots were fired, and pandemonium broke out among the peacefully disbanding crowd. That afternoon, Tsegai, Berhe and Zemikael were arrested and locked up in Caserma Mussolini.

The next day, 11 March, the workers assembled again at St Mary's Square to demand the release of their leaders. Habtemariam Yohannes described what happened next:

> The police came and ordered us to disband. We refused. Mounted troops charged through us and chased us with clubs and lashes. I was running towards the Seyoum Alemayehu filling station when I saw Major Goitom and his armed policemen shooting towards us from a Jeep ... A bullet caught me on the leg. I fell down. Two others also fell by my side. Mercedes trucks were then sent to take us to the hospital. Gebreselassie of Jumbo Glass and a seriously wounded man called Hashela joined us there. No one died from among us.[53]

There are various estimates of the number of workers who died in the police shooting. Some accounts put the casualties at nine; others much higher. According to Osman Saleh Sabbe, tens of workers were killed during the strike.[54] Okbazghi Yohannes put the number at 80 deaths and 500 wounded, while Tom Killion's figures are 9 and 535, respectively.[55] But such claims have proved difficult to establish. Unfortunately, hospital records for the incident are unavailable. Like Habtemariam, all the active participants in the strike could neither identify nor confirm any deaths from the encounter. Nevertheless, the claims raised serious issues over the government's handling of an essentially peaceful demonstration. A police entry for 12 March reported the following:

> Yesterday, the police were forced to use tear gas and live bullets to disperse the crowd and injuries have occurred on both sides. Muslim business owners and shopkeepers have shut their shops and refused to reopen them unless the exact number of deaths and other casualties were made known. This is obviously the advice of the politician Omer Qadi. Their aim is to create the grounds for the UN's intervention. Besides, today, March 12, 1958, at about 10.30 am, Ibrahim Sultan called the hospital from Bar Impero and asked for an account of the dead and wounded. He could not get a tangible reply.[56]

The strike continued throughout the rest of the week. On 11 March, 84 teachers in several Asmera schools went on a two-day solidarity strike.[57] Encouraged by their teachers' move, the students of Prince Mekonnen Secondary School (formerly Scuola Vittorio) were absent from school for a week. Workers in the salt mines, oil depots and other vital enterprises in Massawa also joined the strike. They resumed their work on 16 March only after assurances of a resolution of the workers' demands and the release of the imprisoned leaders.[58]

On the fourth day of the disturbances, and as police repression threatened to grow even more brutal, Assembly representatives for the Asmera constituencies met with Asfaha and bitterly objected to excessive police reprisals.[59] Ignoring their indignation, Asfaha showed them a document allegedly signed by Berhe and Zemikael admitting that they were in the pay of the Egyptian Government. Throughout the week Asfaha and the federal authorities had been blaming 'foreign' intervention as the real cause of the disturbances. Puzzled, the representatives agreed to help the government appease the masses. Berhe swore that neither he nor Zemikael had signed the document and that the government must have forged their signatures.

Nevertheless, the police forced Tsegai, Berhe and Zemikael onto an awaiting Jeep and, despite the detainees' attempts to indicate otherwise, paraded them through town using loudspeakers to announce that an agreement had been reached and that the general strike was called off. At the end of the parade, the three young leaders were returned to their cells, where they languished for the following six months.

The strike and the sound of gunshots lasted until Sunday, 16 March. In the absence of its leaders and planners, it could last no longer. In early April, worker resistance crumbled and the majority started to return to work without achieving any of their demands. Hastening to take advantage of their defeat, the government closed down the AEFTU's offices and confiscated its documents, which were never to be recovered again. On 13 April, Andargatchew signed the very law that had caused the strike.[60] Article 84, which the workers had seen as a death sentence for labour rights and association in Eritrea, thus became the law of the land.

The story of one of the most promising pioneers of labour unionism in Africa ended abruptly. However, as with previous movements, its defeat proved another step forward for the nationalist cause in general. As Okbazghi Yohannes puts it, the issues that drove the workers to strike were only part of the political strife in the country. Referring to the Federalisti and student movements and the Keren riots, he points to the emergence of a new political cohesion that united Muslims, Christians and former Andinet activists.[61] Killion too comes to a similar conclusion. Although defeated, he says, the AEFTU acted as a bridge between the student movement and the Eritrean Liberation Movement. The main force of AEFTU consisted of workers and the Federalistsi. With the inclusion of students in the process, AEFTU created the broad base on which the Eritrean revolution would grow.[62]

Andargatchew, who was in Addis Ababa for the duration of the general strike, dismissed it as the initiative of 'disgruntled individuals who had lost in the 1956 elections'. He also accused some 'inconsequential' foreign journalists and newspapers of having exaggerated its scope and given it coverage it did not deserve. 'We know that there are some who would reap benefits by causing havoc in this Ethiopian province of Eritrea,' he concluded.[63]

The Eritrean labour movement remained banned until 1966, when it was allowed to reorganise as part of the newly formed Ethiopian labour association. Despite the long ban, Eritrean workers never stopped fighting for their rights. Some of their most notable strikes took place between 1960 and 1962.[64]

21

DISMANTLING THE FEDERAL BASE

Economic Decline and Political Unrest

The Aftermath of the General Strike

A few days after the crushing of the general strike of March 1958, Ibrahim Sultan met the American consul Earl Richey and told him that the event had been organised by former Andinet activists opposed to Ethiopia's disregard of the principles guaranteed by the Federal Act. The majority of them had given up all hope of the survival of the Federation and abandoned Ethiopia to form the Muslim League's sister organisation, the Federalist Youth Association, or the Federalisti. He then warned that unless the US used its influence to advise Haile Selassie that his current policy in Eritrea was on the wrong track, the peace and security of his whole empire would be jeopardised.[1]

A few days later, Richey met Asfaha for a long conversation in which he basically paraphrased what Ibrahim had said to him. He also added that the presence of a Bulgarian commercial party in Eritrea, the settlement of Yugoslavs in Asseb, and constant Russian visits to Asmera and Yemen were arousing concern in the US. There was a real possibility of the Egyptians and Russian and Sudanese communists finding an opening to work against US and Ethiopian interests.[2] In reply, Asfaha said that the rights accorded the people of Eritrea by the UN had come to them 300 years too soon. The people did not understand these laws. 'In this regard, the people of Eritrea are children,' he declared. 'Since American democracy cannot work in Eritrea, it is impossible for the Constitution to apply to such a backward people.'

Asfaha denied federal interference in Eritrea's internal affairs. He even rejected the accusation that Eritrea was being deprived of its customs dues. He blamed all the negative rumours on idle people, mostly Muslim, influenced by foreign Muslim forces. To Richey's contention that political repression and the persecution of Omer Qadi and his friends were intensifying Eritrean nationalism, Asfaha gave a typical response. Repression of political parties was justified because Eritreans were incapable of organising and running them; and they would ultimately only serve the interests of foreign forces hostile to Ethiopia and its Western allies. The free press was banned because inept journalists were being used by Italians to print articles that they had not authored themselves and that defamed even the Emperor himself. 'As Ethiopian citizens, it is incumbent upon them to carry out their Ethiopian duties; and it is our responsibility to deter them for the well-being of Ethiopia and ourselves. Eritrea's problem is economic and everything else will be solved with the improvement of the economy.' He suggested to Richey that US investment should replace Italian businesses, which he believed were behind the public resentment on the issues of double taxation and customs duties.

Richey left with the impression that Asfaha had not been truthful to him. Privately, Asfaha had been hoping for a less aggressive Ethiopian drive towards annexation. After the failure of his initial attempts at immediate union, he had realised the strength of the nationalist forces aligned against it and was set on a more measured approach. According to Zewde Retta, Asfaha's ambivalence about the specifics of his new plan created problems with his Ethiopian superiors.[3]

It was an awkward time for the Chief Executive. Because of Andargatchew's extended absence from Eritrea, Asfaha combined the duties of Chief Executive of Eritrea and the Emperor's representative. Laws initiated by him and passed by the Assembly came back to him for ratification. He had become the supreme domestic power, but he could not please his masters enough as he had failed to deliver the trophy that the Ethiopians demanded. This gave rise to the emergence of new enthusiasts seeking to capitalise on Asfaha's perceived laxness with regard to the annexation process.

A Year of Decline and Discord

The year 1958 was one of the worst for the Eritrean economy. Besides the closure of scores of small and medium-level Italian enterprises, rumours abounded that such major businesses as the cement factory and the San Marco Bakery were to be transferred to Addis Ababa. When a number of the biggest industries, including Melotti Brewery, the glue factory in Amba Galliano, the Maderni match factory and the Israeli-run meat processing business INCODE, laid off some of their employees, the prospect of an economic downturn gave rise to an atmosphere of fear and anger in the country.[4] The problem was compounded by a severe drought accompanied by an unprecedented invasion of swarms of locusts, which came in uncontrollable waves from July to October 1958.[5] The government's inability to deal with the calamity and its ineptness in preventing traders from diverting relief food for personal gain exposed it to criticism even from its supporters within the Assembly.[6]

In the absence of political or civic organisations that could channel popular anger and resentment, Eritreans seemed to vent their political differences on each other. In Adi Qeih, the government's decision to dismiss the old *qadi* and Muslim League (ML) leader Ali Omer, and replace him with its own man, caused a rift among

Muslims that threatened to turn violent. It was only resolved on the intervention of Ibrahim Mukhtar, *Mufti* of Eritrea, in favour of *Qadi* Ali.

Sowing religious discord was a strategy that the Federal Government had used from the earlier days of the Federation. In 1953, a memo addressed to Andargatchew revealed the extent to which Ethiopia and the federal authorities were willing to go to provoke religious rancour in Eritrea. The memo contained the following advice:

> The insults to the Federal Government that Muslims and Christians are writing in coordination may poison the minds of our friends. To avoid this, we need to find secret ways whereby Christians and Muslims can develop mutual hatred inadvertently... For example, we can tell the Christians that Muslims are intent on turning them into their slaves by Islamising Eritrea ... and that the Christians cooperating with them are under the pay of Islamic governments. We can similarly tell the Muslims that the few conspirators are paid agents who seek to deny Muslims the great consideration and benefits that Ethiopia has in store for them, and that, otherwise, they have no interest for Eritrea's welfare ... This should be done most secretly, through other mediums.

Authored by Hailu D.K., the suggestion had the backing of Crown Prince Asfawossen and the Imperial Council of Ministers, so the writer claimed.[7]

In 1957–8 there was a sudden proliferation of gossip about a provincial power struggle between Akeleguzai—represented by Asfaha and his Finance Secretary, Tesfayohannes Berhe—and Seraye, led by Dimetros, the Interior Secretary Araia Wassie, and Police Commissioner Tedla. In reaction, a group of Andinet youth from Hamasien organised to take political control and declared that 'As long as provincialism is within us, not only we Eritreans, but Ethiopia and Eritrea, will also be torn apart'.[8] At the same time, reports that *Mufti* Ibrahim Mukhtar was about to launch a movement called the New Revolution (*Nuovo Revoluzione*), and that communist incursions into Eritrea were causing deep concern in the US and Ethiopia, became constant items in security briefings.[9]

While this news from 'unidentified sources' was shaking Asmera and most urban centres, there was a new rise in *shifta* activity in the countryside. Amid this atmosphere of uncertainty and apprehension, clandestine night-time activists often pasted the outer walls of public places, churches and mosques in Asmera, Keren and other major towns with anti-government pamphlets calling for an uprising. A July 1957 pamphlet in Arabic read as follows:

> People of Eritrea,
>
> 1. Live in liberty and die as heroes.
> 2. A people who let their rights slip from their own hands cannot regain them from the hands of others.
> 3. You dumb people! How do you propose to protect your rights and your country? You are not even armed. What will you do if your rulers attack you?

4. You inept people! Don't be the tool of rulers. You have to build your country's future by fire and steel.
5. You weak people! Fear and freedom cannot intermarry. Choose one. Understand the meanings of freedom and liberty.
6. Death to traitors and honour to our country!
7. Long live Eritrea! Down with the unionists![10]

A Split within Andinet

With a major part of the clandestine activists coming from Andinet, the federal authorities could no longer depend on the party's former dedication and enthusiasm. Although old leaders like Gebreselassie Garza and Habtom Araia still occupied the senior positions in the party, defections by younger Eritreans to the federalist and independence camps rendered Andinet, in its current form, of less value to Ethiopia's interests. It was time to change.

Two groups served the purpose. The first one, hailing from the days of the British, was the Association of Tigrayans in Eritrea. Although natives of Tigray, born and raised in Eritrea, formed an important part of the unionist cause, their association had mainly been a self-help gathering until the Federal Office's security chief, Colonel (later *Dejazmatch*) Assegahey Araia, turned it into a spy network to assist the process of annexation. Assegahey's direct links to Haile Selassie's Imperial Palace made his faction the main source of information for the Emperor.

Kumilatchew Belete, Andargatchew's political officer, also sought to direct the Association of Amharas Born in Eritrea, another self-help group that gained legal recognition in 1951, for similar purposes. These associations consisted of religious and church sub-groups scattered across the various districts of Asmera. Concerned about dwindling Eritrean membership of the original Andinet, Gebreselassie Garza and his colleagues agreed to the inclusion of amenable members of the two parent associations in their ranks. A Tigrayan called Alemseged Teferi emerged as the leader and coordinator of the two groups inside Andinet.[11]

In March 1958, Andinet prepared for elections for a new leadership. Prior to this, the Eritreans had split three ways over whether the new leader should come from the province of Hamasien, Seraye or Akeleguzai. Taking advantage of this internal Eritrean squabble, Alemseged Teferi galvanised the support of the Ethiopian faction and presented himself as a candidate against the hitherto unassailable Gebreselassie. Although they had the numerical majority, it became obvious that, because of the provincial split, no Eritrean candidate could stand a chance against the united Ethiopian and dissident Eritrean vote committed to Alemseged Teferi. On 23 March, the election date, Gebreselassie's group blocked the entrance to the Andinet premises. No election could be held that day, and an atmosphere of violence developed,[12] which was to last for over three years. At its peak on 21 September 1959, 200 of Gebreselassie's men faced 80 of Alemseged's and confronted each other at Bet Giorgis. The police had to intervene to avoid bloodshed.[13]

Except for the occasional piece of 'advice' or 'reprimand' from Asfaha, there were no indications that the Eritrean Government was involved in the Andenet developments. It was all a federal affair and its offices used the Alemseged Teferi faction as its new weapon for annexation. All the beatings and harassment perpetrated against the Federalisti and the labour and independence activists can be attributed to this faction. In an undated pamphlet found in the archives of a leader of the faction, Berhanie Mengistie, we find the following warning from the 'Office of the Attack Unit' addressed to the Federalisti:

> We are following you closely ... We know where you are meeting secretly under the guise of a self-help [*ekub*] group. It will be much better for you to stop your evil spirit. Otherwise, we would like to inform you beforehand that we will hunt you down with secret weapons to pass judgement on your lives or to seriously incapacitate you. Our attack group will start its mission at an unspecified time.[14]

During the week of preparation for the workers' strike, another pamphlet attempted to stop it.

> Beloved people of Ethiopian Eritrea, today we hear that a handful of evil people who have been poisoned by the evil thoughts of foreigners are organising an association with neither a base nor material or spiritual cause. We know that its innermost objective is to harm the people. We urge those members of the Association [Andinet] who have joined it without examining its intentions to withdraw immediately. If you fail to heed our advice, we will impose upon you the terrible verdict of patriots.[15]

These were no empty threats. The constant beatings of the Federalisti leader Tesfai Reda'e, and the attempted murder by hanging of his colleague Abraha Futur, indicated that the faction meant business. In defiance, the workers' strike went ahead anyway. Neither Tedla Ukbit's security apparatus nor Asfaha's appeals for moderation could stop the new Andinet's determination and resolve. Eritreans were no longer trusted with the push for annexation; it was becoming chiefly an Ethiopian affair.

The Disposal of the Eritrean Flag

Asfaha (doubling as the Chief Executive and the Emperor's deputy representative), Dimetros (in the Assembly and also the Orthodox Church), and Tedla Ukbit (as Police Commissioner) worked in unison to make every Ethiopian wish appear to be an Eritrean initiative. Except perhaps for Tedla who may have had his own ambitions, perspective and sense of worth, Dimetros and Asfaha turned into submissive agents of their masters while posing as tough decision-makers before their own people.

Although Hamid Ferej was the president of the Assembly, real power lay in the hands of Dimetros. Fesseha Weldemariam describes how Dimetros manipulated the votes of his followers. 'He would point the sharp end of his pencil upwards and his men would vote yes. The opposite direction ensured a no vote. This prearranged practice rendered Assembly debate ineffective and, gradually, passing legislation by "unanimous vote" became the norm.'[16] November and most of December 1958 saw the passing of laws, including the national budget, without debate or a formal vote. Regular absenteeism became the norm; even the quorum requirement was often put aside. Yet, the prospect of immediate annexation eluded its advocates even when the opposition appeared subdued and silent. By this time, the Eritrean Liberation Movement, or Haraka, had already formed abroad and was making initial incursions into Eritrea.

Although oblivious of the new development, Asfaha and Dimetros seem to have opted for gradual instead of immediate union. According to his colleagues and confidants, Dimetros was especially keen on persuading the Ethiopians to prove their good intentions to Eritreans before moving for complete union. Building a dam at Tsebab, on the Anseba River, which would in his opinion turn the plains at the foot of the Keren Heights into a breadbasket, would do the trick.[17]

Paradoxically, according to *Dejazmatch* Gebreyohannes Tesfamariam, Economy Secretary in 1958, Tedla Ukbit took over charge of annexation from his colleagues. Having shaken off the control of the Secretary of the Interior, he invested himself with full powers. 'He did as he saw fit. He could detain people with impunity. He became the prime annexationist.'

In late December, this triumvirate decided to start its phased approach to annexation by removing the Eritrean flag. For weeks before the scheduled date of 14 December 1958, Dimetros, whom the American consul Richey referred to as 'the Ethiopian axe', made the rounds of Assembly members, bribing them with promises of lucrative jobs for relatives, increased salaries and concession licences for themselves, and outright payments in cash. About two-thirds of the members were also district chiefs, *nazirs* and *mislenes* appointed by the Chief Executive and subject to his dismissal. Their position also entitled them to sit and adjudicate in the customary courts. Their combined salary from the three functions was as much as 800 birr at least, a hefty sum by the standards of the day. No one would want to lose that incentive.[18] As rumour of the impending Assembly vote spread, Gebreyohannes met Dimetros for a surprising exchange:

> I said to him, 'Reverend, if you want to merge this country, why don't you just go ahead and do it openly? Why are you going about it in pieces? We are losing our country in morsels. Why?' He replied, 'The Man [Haile Selassie] does not want to see the flag. It makes him feel that we are two separate countries. If we remove it, he may spare our federation ...'

Whatever the real motive, the decision was made to abolish the Eritrean flag. Asfaha knew that this would require amendment of the relevant constitutional provision.

Article 92(2) required that such an amendment could only be proposed by the Chief Executive or a quarter of the total number of Assembly members. Even then, a period of twenty days had to elapse before its presentation for debate and a formal vote. Asfaha sought legal advice on how to avoid the constitutional hurdle and received one from his expatriate legal advisors.

Rather than abolishing the Eritrean flag, he proposed to replace its colours. Article 21(2) of the Constitution provided only for the existence of an 'Eritrean flag and seal to be determined by law'. The blue flag adorned by an olive wreath and branch was not described or defined in that constitutional provision but in later legislation called the Eritrean Flag, Seal and Arms Act of 1952, which the Assembly had ratified. To avoid the constitutional amendment, Asfaha's proposal left article 21 in place and only sought the replacement of the Act by a new one. After arguing that the Eritrean flag was an alien symbol of division, he proposed the following amendment to article 21(3) of the Act: 'The flag of Eritrea shall consist of three bands of equal proportion, the uppermost of which shall be green, the middle yellow and the nethermost red as shown by the specimen flag authenticated by the signatures of the President and Clerk and deposited in the archives of the Assembly.' The amendment did not say that the flag was being abolished or that it was being replaced by the Ethiopian flag. It still recognised the existence of an Eritrean flag, seal and arms. Neither was article 21 of the Constitution tampered with. The only thing that would change was the colour of the flag from blue and green to the tricolour of the Ethiopian flag.

Throughout the week, Eritrean and federal authorities exerted maximum pressure on Assembly members to secure the required quorum. On 24 December, 64 of the 67 members (Akito's seat was still vacant) presented themselves inside the chamber, a record for the second legislature. The motion was adopted.[19] Consul Richey described the scene in more detail.

> So thorough was the work of Dimetros that only two members voted against closure and prearranged debate ... [after which] the amendment was put to an immediate vote and [it] was recorded as if it was adopted unanimously although the acting clerk of the Assembly states that he cannot honestly say that the two members who voted against closure actually voted for passage ... When the vote for passage was called for, pandemonium broke loose as members stood, cheered, shouted, clapped and embraced one another, pulling to their feet those members who appeared reluctant to join in the festivities. No roll call was ever taken ...[20]

It was a clever move on the part of the authorities, who exploited the limitations of the mostly illiterate district chiefs in the Assembly. As popular reaction stayed calm, the Imperial Government and the Emperor kept their distance to give the impression that the Eritrean Assembly was acting on behalf of the people of Eritrea. In actual fact, commented Richey, 'the will of the Imperial Government was done in a display of power politics which is more diabolical than it is clever insofar as the spirit of the United Nations Resolution is concerned'.[21] The abolition of the Eritrean flag was duly promulgated in the official Ethiopian gazette, the *Negarit Gazeta.*

A few days later, Haile Selassie visited Eritrea for the seventh time. As a reward for the removal of the flag, he laid the foundation for the construction of the Zula Dam. He also announced that, in view of the devastation caused by the locust invasion in 1958, he was granting the Eritrean population a tax reprieve for 1958/9.[22] On the day of his departure, Haile Selassie singled out Colonel Tedla Ukbit from among his well-wishers at the airport and handed him a pistol with the Geez initials of Prince Mekonnen Haile Selassie, his deceased and beloved son, engraved on it in gold. This was in reward for the role Tedla had played in the removal of the flag and the silencing of the opposition and for speeding up the process of annexation. Tedla's secretary and confidant Kinfe Tesfagabir was present when this happened, and he later gave the following account:

> His Majesty was courting him by saying, 'You are not a police chief, you are our son.' Finance Secretary Tesfayohannes Berhe, General Abiy Abebe, Andargatchew's replacement, and I were standing side by side when he gave him his son's pistol. Tedla was overjoyed. 'You see, Kinfe,' he said to me later, 'it is just as I told you. It is better to merge with them than to stay on the edges. If customs and the security are in their hands, what is our benefit? It is easier to tackle the Amhara and lead them than to fight the Arabs for independence.' He had very little knowledge of what the Amhara were capable of.[23]

If Tedla had been vacillating between federalism and annexation, Haile Selassie's special treatment secured him at the forefront of the annexation drive. He took command of all security operations and his handling of the opposition became ruthless. This put him at loggerheads with the federal and army security officers, whom he considered usurpers. His favoured position temporarily gave him the upper hand, and even Asfaha and Dimetros had to bow to his bidding. Haile Selassie's behind-the-scenes drive for annexation had found a zealous enforcer.

Further Steps to Dismantle the Federation

Extension of the Ethiopian Penal Code to Eritrea

As part of the process of dismantling Eritrea's rights under the federal arrangement, the Ethiopians decided to remove what judicial independence had been left in the autonomous unit, thereby also putting an end to the democratic tenets of its Constitution. In his book *Eritrea and Ethiopia: The Federal Experience*, Tekeste Negash argues that Eritrean claims to a democratic past and to more advanced political institutions than Ethiopia's were 'a distortion of dangerous magnitude'.

Whatever traces of democracy that may have existed, he concluded, were due to the presence and advocacy of Chief Justice James Shearer.[24]

Leaving aside the polemics of Eritrean institutional superiority over Ethiopia, we need to consider the impact on Eritreans of the rights guaranteed by the Federal Act and the Eritrean Constitution. Shearer's undeniably pivotal role in upholding the principles of the Eritrean Constitution would not have borne fruit without a receptive public ready to act on the available opportunities. Among the events and issues that resonated with the public were freedom of the press, albeit suppressed with the closure of *Dehai*; Ibrahim Sultan's successful but aborted litigation against the defunct Election Proclamation 121; Akito's famous victory over Asfaha's annulment of his legitimate election to the Assembly; the application of habeas corpus to various illegal detentions; and the formation and existence of political parties, labour organisations and civil rights groups. None of these rights and practices were in existence in Ethiopia at the time and, right from the outset, Ethiopian authorities moved to cancel each one in Eritrea. The imposition of the Imperial federal courts on the Eritrean court system was but the beginning of their clampdown. But Eritrea still had its own set of laws that gave its people and courts a measure of independence. Those had to go too.

In 1957, Ethiopia promulgated a new Penal Code drafted by the Swiss lawyer Philippe Graven. Except for the provisions retained from Ethiopia's 1931 Constitution regarding the inviolability and immunity of the Imperial family and related articles, it was a modern legal instrument that satisfied international standards of criminal law. In that sense, it was more advanced than the mixture of customary and colonial laws of Eritrea. We recall that Tedla's Proclamation 1 of 1955 and Asfaha's Security Proclamation of 1957 revived the old article 10 of the Italian Police Ordinance (*articolo dieci*) in order to enforce illegal detentions. In other words, the issue was not the content of the Ethiopian Penal Code but the manner of its imposition on Eritrea, which had its own substantive and procedural laws and enforcement apparatus. Like the federal courts, the Ethiopian Penal Code was neither envisaged nor sanctioned by the UN Federal Act.

As was becoming his practice, Asfaha condemned the old Eritrean laws as fascist in content and origin, and not fit for a government that was democratically constituted. 'Thanks to our Emperor,' he said in his covering letter, 'we have been granted a new penal law by our august Emperor and we need to partake of the fruits it offers.' The proposal declared all previous Eritrean laws null and void. The Assembly adopted Asfaha's motion.[25]

Changing the Name and Seal of the Government of Eritrea

With every success, Asfaha's cleverness grew even more audacious. Six months after the lowering of the flag, he sent two pieces of legislation to further erode the last remaining symbols of federalism. His comments on the first one may be translated as follows:

> In the Constitution, I have noticed a confusion arising from a discrepancy in the wordings of the English and Tigrinya versions. The English version refers to 'Government' and 'Chief Executive'. As you know, a government has an internationally recognised authority and identity. That is not the case with Eritrea. The Federal Act has placed it under the sovereignty of the Ethiopian Crown. Therefore, the word that adequately translates the Eritrean 'Government' is 'Administration'. 'Chief Executive' should also read 'Chief Administrator'.

As far as translation was concerned, Asfaha had a point. The Tigrinya language has yet to find adequate terminology to clearly differentiate between the terms 'state', 'administration', 'government' and 'nation'—all being often used interchangeably.[26] Asfaha banked on the subservience of his men at the Assembly to take advantage of the inadequacies of translation. In order to avoid a constitutional amendment, he argued that the original English version that contained the words 'Eritrean Government' and 'Chief Executive' would be left intact. Since the Emperor had ratified the English version, he also considered it unassailable. What is more, the Assembly had ratified only the Tigrinya text. Although this gave it some legal value, it could not measure up to the status of the original English text and thus could be amended by the Assembly separately from the original. 'We are not seeking the constitutional amendment of the original text. We only need an Assembly decision ... to change the Tigrinya wording,' he added.

There was little discussion on the proposal, and the motion was adopted by acclamation. According to *Zemen*, the applause had hardly died down when a second message from the Chief Executive urged members to change the seal of the Eritrean Government and replace it with one more in tune with its current status as the 'Eritrean Administration'. The new seal, which replaced the olive wreath and branch of the Eritrean Government, was adorned by an image of the Lion of Judah and inscribed with the words 'Conquering Lion of the Tribe of Judah, Haile Selassie I, Emperor of Ethiopia, Eritrean Administration'. Forty-three members voted for the repeal, one abstained; twenty-four were absent.[27]

By means of these acts of undisguised deception, the foundations of the Federation were eroded. The Assembly opened the way to its own extinction and an unopposed annexation.

Elections to the Third Legislature

It was time for elections to the third legislature. In his farewell address to the second, Asfaha had called for the defeat and exclusion of candidates 'who cannot differentiate between village and national politics'. Assembly vice president Dimetros appealed to members to ensure that 'weeds' who 'speak toddler language' should not be readmitted to the Assembly.[28]

In the absence of an Election Commission as required by the Federal Act but never formed after the first election, Asfaha took personal charge of the election. It turned out to be a circus. Independent candidates were blocked either on trumped-up charges or arbitrarily disqualified by provincial officials.[29] Powerful candidates 'kidnapped' consenting electors to secure their votes through lavish parties and bribery. With appeals against such transgressions being decided in favour of Asfaha's selected candidates, his administration secured thirty-six seats unopposed. Except for Denkalia, where the two seats were contested, all twenty-four candidates from the four lowland provinces were unopposed; six from Akeleguzai, five from Seraye and one from Hamasien also sailed through.[30]

Asfaha's high-handedness reached an absurd level in the Tsillima (Dibarua) election. To specifically block the candidacy of Solomon Kahsai, son of the assassinated Liberal Progressive Party leader Kahsai Malu, he issued an amendment to the election law disqualifying any candidate with a police record. Solomon had a record for a minor traffic accident which was already legally settled. Invoking his own amendment, Asfaha ordered election officials to 'take the necessary steps to strike out his [Solomon's] name from candidacy'. His opponent won unopposed.[31] Solomon's exclusion caused an uproar in Tsillima, where ten electors condemned the process as undemocratic and dictatorial, and hundreds of Solomon's supporters rejected the announced result.[32]

Through such undisguised elimination of possible dissidents, Asfaha's administration secured an overwhelming majority in the Assembly. Of the old members of the Independence Bloc and Eritrean Democratic Front, only six survived.[33] But most of these had virtually abandoned their old principles and were, at times, at the forefront of the general rush to please their Ethiopian masters. Henceforth, the Assembly could only become a playground for Asfaha and federal officials.

22

THE ROAD TO THE ERITREAN REVOLUTION

The Eritrean Liberation Movement

The brutal suppression of the student and workers' movements of 1957 and 1958 led to the institution of a police regime throughout Eritrea. Police sit-reps indicate that even high-level government officials were under close surveillance by thousands of informers, nicknamed *qarma* (mosquito or gnat), ubiquitous in every bar, public office or marketplace and on every street corner.[1] In the repressive and stifling atmosphere that prevailed as a result, the transition from peaceful and legitimate opposition to clandestine or open rebellion failed to materialise at the national level.

However, the suppressed opposition found a new voice from an unlikely source—Eritrean exiles in Sudan. On 2 November 1958, a group of young Eritrean refugees founded the Eritrean Liberation Movement (Harakat al Tahreer al Eretria, henceforth ELM or Haraka) in Port Sudan. It is generally agreed that Haraka was the brainchild of Mohammed Said Nawd, a native of Sahel (Nakfa) and a member of the Sudanese Communist Party. The exact identity of those assembled, seventeen in total, varies from source to source. However, all sources agree on eight names as original founders.[2] Prior to establishing Haraka, Nawd had toured Eritrea to find that the 'objective conditions' for revolutionary activity had matured. The idea of forming a movement different from the old political associations came to him, he wrote, when he realised that working with old leaders like Ibrahim Sultan would not be fruitful.[3]

At the November meeting in Port Sudan, the seventeen founders agreed on the organisation's charter, name and a road map for its growth, as drafted by Nawd. It called for unity and the rejection of religious discord as preconditions for independence. It condemned the Eritrean Assembly for collusion with the Ethiopian Government, and the political parties for misrepresenting the people. It also declared that in order to confront these divisive policies and to struggle for full independence, the movement must of necessity be clandestine.[4]

The idea of openly declaring an armed revolution for independence was ruled out in view of the absence, due to Ethiopian repression, of organised political activity inside Eritrea. Besides, since Ethiopia had the backing of the US and the full cooperation of the regime of General Ibrahim Abboud of neighbouring Sudan, the prospect of an armed struggle against such a formidable force was deemed impossible and dangerous.[5] The combination of these factors was what led the founders to make secrecy the basis of their organisation.

Within this context of secrecy and the call for unity, Haraka proposed to put in place 'a secret military force that would spearhead a revolution to change Eritrea's situation'.[6] For Haraka, revolution (al kifah al muselah—the protracted armed struggle) was a long-term strategy that could only come into effect upon the exhaustion of its immediate objective of organising a popular insurrection culminating in a coup d'etat.[7] In his book, Nawd outlines the gradual move towards that objective: the preparatory stage; the educational and growth stage; the stage of preparedness; and the stage of execution of the final coup d'état.[8] The idea was to organise Eritrean members of the government, Assembly and police force both in Eritrea and Ethiopia, and spread its core members throughout Eritrea to arouse popular revolutionary sentiment. When the 'preconditions for the revolutionary coup d'état are satisfied', the Assembly would declare the abolition of the Federation and the police force would overthrow the government in Eritrea. Absolute secrecy in every aspect of the whole process would take the enemy by surprise and ensure final victory. Only if Ethiopia retaliated with full force would a protracted armed struggle begin.[9] With this naive plan, Haraka went into action.

The Growth of Haraka

Haraka's organisation was as ingenious as it was intricate. Seven people who knew each other and met regularly would form a core cell or nucleus. Each member of the nucleus would then organise his or her own cell of seven whose members would be known to him or her alone and they would, in turn, organise further cells of seven people each. This would ensure the proliferation of hundreds of secret cells in a short time. As Awet Weldemichael aptly puts it: 'Clandestine activism became the only way to express popular disapproval of Ethiopian domination and Eritrean ineptitude. Its [Haraka's] inclusive vision appealed to Eritreans disaffected with the schism-ridden political landscape presided over by older politicians. As a result, ELM secret cells quickly multiplied, and its grassroots base swelled.'[10]

There was much in what Haraka preached that aroused revolutionary zeal. Article 4 of its charter, for example, called upon its members to 'follow the ideology that has given light to the progress of mankind ... to upgrade their cultural standards ... and to frequent criticism and self-criticism'. Such non-partisan language drawn from socialist literature was new to most Eritreans, and it fired the imagination of hundreds.

In early 1959, the leadership sent two of its founding members, Saleh Iyay and Yasin Aqeda, to recruit new members inside Eritrea. Iyay, a graduate of the US-sponsored Asmera Technical School, was assigned to the western lowlands and made quick progress especially among students, teachers, government employees, merchants and shopkeepers. After his success in setting up the first cell inside Eritrea at Ali Gidir, Haraka cells burgeoned from there to Tesseney, Barentu, Akurdet and Keren by early 1960.[11]

Initially, Aqeda, an Asmera tailor from the Saho community, was not as lucky. Exposed by a recruit spying for Ethiopia, he was arrested and imprisoned for about nine months. By the time of his release, Haraka had received a major boost when most of the eighteen players of a popular Asmera football team, Adulis FC, agreed to form a single cell.[12] Mostly composed of activists and leaders of the 1957 student movement and led by their coach, Kahsai Bahlibi, and the former student leader and player Tiku'e Yehdego, the Adulis group helped thousands of *kebessa* Christians enlist in Haraka, which was nicknamed 'Mahber Shew'ate'—the Association of Seven—in Tigrinya.[13]

The induction of thousands of Eritreans in Sudan, Egypt, Saudi Arabia, Eritrea and Ethiopia into Haraka cells was a remarkable achievement and a turning point in the progress of Eritrean nationalism. Eritreans bonded within those cells regardless of their religious, regional, linguistic or ethnic origin. Perhaps Haraka's greatest contribution was that by broadening its organisational base it set the bar high for the foundation of a truly nationalist movement at the grassroots level.[14]

The fact that Haraka's clandestine existence could elude Eritrea's tight security network for about three more years is testimony to the level of dedication and determination of its broad membership. Secrecy was an article of faith for Haraka. Everything, from the identity and activities of its leadership to its financial resources and its specific programmes of action, was jealously guarded. But, in time, people began tiring of keeping a secret that seemed to be taking them nowhere. Haraka's failure to transition to an armed struggle, something that was expected of a liberation movement, or to live up to its declared intention of staging a coup d'état, began to erode its foundation.

Haraka's Crisis in Sudan

In 1960, Eritrean soldiers, previously inducted into the Sudanese army during the British period, became important recruits into Haraka. Numbering about eighty men and organised as a contingency force that moved from Kassala to South Sudan, its members established a self-help fund called Sanduq al Keir. If they had any illusion of thriving within the Sudanese army, it was dashed when Sudan became independent in 1956 and they began to suffer discrimination at the hands of the army and government. In 1960, they joined Haraka to form a cell as a regiment and used their Sanduq al Keir to raise funds for the organisation. When they were assigned to South Sudan, the months-long absence of any communication from the Haraka leadership aroused their concern and suspicion.

As Haraka stalled on concrete action, a new organisation, the Eritrean Liberation Front (ELF), which we will discuss more fully in the next chapter, announced its formation in July 1960 and called for an armed struggle for independence. The new organisation naturally caught the imagination of the members of the Sudan army group, whose constant demands for action and openness were frustrated by Haraka's unchanging strategy of secrecy and lack of clear direction.

In an attempt to bridge the gap between Haraka and the ELF, a group representing the soldiers arranged a meeting between Idris Mohammed Adem, now leader of the ELF, and representatives of Haraka. In that November 1960 meeting, Idris spoke like a man of destiny. He told the gathering that he had left Eritrea, where he had served as Assembly president, 'at the behest of the people' and that he and his colleagues in the ELF had the right to sideline the 'suspicious or dubious Haraka movement whose base and leadership' were neither communicative nor known.[15]

Idris's rather superior attitude towards Haraka did not discourage the group from trying to rectify the situation one more time. In 1961, the soldiers were transferred back to Kassala. This time, Haraka sent one of its top leaders, Tahir Fedab, to meet with the committee and the ELF leadership. According to Mohammed Saad Adem, Fedab was uncertain on every issue, from the names of the Haraka leaders, Haraka's military capabilities and source of logistical support, the nature of its alleged contacts with the Eritrean police force, and how exactly it proposed to stage a successful coup. The leadership would reveal itself and provide adequate answers when the time was ripe, Fedab promised.[16]

It was a waiting game that could not be sustained much longer. Soon, Haraka would suffer the consequences of not fulfilling the general demand for the launching of an armed struggle. The situation was even more urgent inside Eritrea, where disaffection and impatience were threatening the cohesion of the cells. In late 1960, Nawd convened a secret meeting inside Asmera, remarkable in its daring in the face of Tedla Ukbit's tight security apparatus. Although Nawd referred to the Asmera meeting as a congress of great significance, his colleagues among the leadership, including Yasin Aqeda and Mohammed Berhan Hassen, dismissed it as just another exercise in futility.

No documents, minutes or written reports of that meeting have survived. But, according to Yasin Aqeda, nothing new came out of the gathering. The main discussion was centred on the already defunct notion of organising the people through incumbent government *mislenes* and *shums*. Its achievement was thus limited to the creation of an inclusive committee to direct the affairs of the organisation within Eritrea. Several activists, including Kahsai Bahlibi of Adulis FC and the former Assembly member Bezabih Tesfabruk, were added to the original team composed of Saleh Iyay, Yasin Aqeda, Mohammed Berhan Hassen and others. Later, in 1962, the addition of Tiku'e Yehdego, Mehari Debessai and Wolday Ghidey, all future figures in the armed struggle, boosted the Christian presence in Haraka.[17]

If anything, the so-called congress only showed that Haraka was sinking deeper within the secret shell in which it had embedded itself. The secret became an obsession, the organisation's *raison d'être*. As its October 1960 statement explained, the 'clandestine way' was essential, as 'mixing up overt and covert procedures is like pouring water on fire and the curiosity to know the names of our leaders will only endanger the secrecy of our organisation ... Haraka is not concerned with individuals and personalities who will always pass on. It is rather committed to the eternal and undying theory and ideology that will pass from one generation to the next.'[18] Such lofty language could not contain or satisfy an impatient constituency demanding action.

Popular Attempts at Peaceful and Armed Rebellion

A Demonstration of Consequence

In his book, *Kab Riq Hfnti* (A Scoop from the Bounty), Tekie Beyene has given an account of a demonstration in September 1960 of which, along with five friends, he was an organiser. Led by Nebyat Negassi, a well-read employee at the Evangelical Printing Press, they approached Tiku'e Yehdego, now a Haraka leader, for confidential advice.[19] On 12 September, the day of Asfaha Weldemikael's re-election as Chief Executive, these students, carrying placards and the banned Eritrean flag, led a few followers out of their hideout. The crowd, which soon grew to approximately 2,000 demonstrators, resisted police attempts to disperse them and reached the Assembly building, where their youthful clamour and enthusiasm were met by the deafening silence of another crowd packed in the street below.[20] When Asfaha's re-election was announced, the crowd, including the demonstrators, left the scene with bowed heads and in total silence. Rather than submission, according to the participants, silence and bowed heads indicated a more grounded resolve to take effective action.[21]

The government could not believe that students hardly out of their teens could beat their tight security control without outside assistance. Over the following two days, the police invoked article 10 of the Police Ordinance to detain seven youths, adding Meswaiti Gebrehiwet and Amanuel Haile to the original five. CID chief Yigzaw Beraki charged them with disrupting the peace and endangering public safety as well as opening an illegal line of communication with foreign diplomats in Asmera.

As Asfaha signed the detention orders, people suspected of having encouraged the youngsters, among them *Dehai*'s former editor Mohammed Saleh Mahmud, the labour union leader Tsegai Kahsai, and Tahir Imam Musa, son of the old Muslim League leader, as well as members of the Federalisti, were arrested.[22] Other young activists were detained too, most notably Kiros Yacob (Tsatse), well known for his bold opposition and numerous arrests and, later, as a martyr of the armed struggle.

Lack of evidence of any outside help seemed to promise the detainees' release when the December 1960 military coup attempt in Addis Ababa aroused further suspicion. As Nebyat Negassi was interrogated about his contacts with Addis Ababa, the government extended the period of detention for another three months. In the meantime, more arrests were ordered. Gebrelul Gebreyesus, the lawyer who defended *Sheik* Suleiman and *Haji* Imam Musa, and Menghistu Bairu, brother of Tedla and a committed nationalist in his own right, were detained under the same rule.[23]

On 24 January 1961, the government bowed to public and parental pressure and released all the detainees. Three of them, Nebyat, Tekie and Kiros, would later participate in the revolution as members of the EPLF. Nebyat and Kiros died on active duty. Tekie went on to serve as Governor of the National Bank of Eritrea and to author and translate several books; he died in April 2019. Amanuel Tesfatsion died in February 2022 in Sweden.

Individual Acts of Violence

On 20 April 1961, two young eighteen-year-old friends, Iyasu Yohannes and Estifanos Zerakristos (Negusse) of Kidane Mehret in Asmera, armed themselves with a pickaxe and knife and tried to enter Asfaha's office. Their attempt failed when, in a scuffle with guards, the pickaxe fell and they were both arrested on charges of attempted assassination of the Chief Executive. During intense interrogation, the two friends swore that they had acted alone in their rejection of the Ethiopian flag and opposition to the illegal removal of the Eritrean flag. Given widespread admiration for the daring and steadfastness of the teenagers, Asfaha was hard pressed to show magnanimity, which, to his credit, he did. They were released without being formally charged or sentenced.[24]

A second daring individual attempt on the Chief Executive's life also came in early 1961. Asfaha, who suffered from gout, had the habit of taking a walk in the vicinity of Campo Cicero, on the northern outskirts of Asmera. One evening, as he was strolling up the Asmera–Keren road with the Assembly president Hamid Ferej, a hand grenade exploded metres away. Unhurt, but in great panic, they both ran back past the football field to take shelter at a nearby shop. A little boy caught in the blast joined them in their escape. Since the perpetrator was never caught, the act remained one of Tedla Ukbit's unsolved mysteries.

In an interview in 2007, Sebhat Aberra, a 29-year-old customs inspector at the time of the incident, revealed to this author that he was the lone actor in the attempt. His claim was corroborated by the shopkeeper and the boy who accompanied the dignitaries in their escape. Having grown up in the home of his uncle, the former Finance Secretary Teklehaimanot Bokru, Sebhat was influenced as a child by the politics of the Liberal Progressive Party and the Independence Bloc, the Federalisti and the labour movement, and by his later membership of a Haraka cell.[25]

The Attempt on Dimetros's Life

On Sunday, 29 October 1961, early in the morning, Dimetros was leaving his house to go to church when a hand grenade exploded near his car in the vicinity of the Albergo Italia. He was unharmed. Five people including the driver and a guard followed the bomb thrower, later identified as Gebremedhin Hailu of Adi Kefelet, south-west of Asmera. As he attempted to escape to Kidane Mehret, he was fired at and immediately surrounded by his pursuers. Refusing to surrender, he drew out a second bomb and set it off in their midst. Apart for the driver, four men were wounded, two severely. A second armed attacker, Yohannes Okbazghi of Zagir, who was wounded in the exchanges, was also captured.[26]

Over the following days, police arrested Sebhat Aberra, the same inspector who had tried to assassinate Asfaha with a hand grenade, and his uncle Girmay Mirach, the son of Liban district chief *Azmatch* Mirach Gudum.[27] *Zemen* explained that Girmay Mirach and Gebremedhin Hailu had failed in their bid for Assembly seats and blamed their defeat on government and official bias and interference. The newspaper further announced that Gebremedhin Hailu, who sustained severe wounds to the limbs and abdomen, died from his injuries.[28] This official explanation was later repeated by the Italian doctor Dante Boveri at the court trial.[29]

However, before *Zemen* published the news, word leaked out of the hospital that, to avoid security investigators, Gebremedhin had torn the stitches off his abdomen with his bare hands and died instantly. The act, probably the first of its kind in the country's recent political history, sent shock waves throughout the land. As Gebremedhin Hailu's reputation catapulted to the heights of heroism, the government turned its attention to more profound motives that would justify such a drastic act.

In a long-drawn-out court case in which the wounded Yohannes Okbazghi and Sebhat Aberra were both the accused and chief witnesses, the government found itself in a legal quagmire. Charges based on Yohannes's testimony were rejected by Judge Tsegai Habtemariam on the grounds that 'the Government's case was based on weak and fragmented evidence that cannot stand the test of the law'.[30] Sebhat Aberra's trial dragged on for months while at the same time he endured interrogation and torture. In a higher court, Yohannes's testimony against Sebhat, given under duress, was again ruled inadmissible. Judge Berhe Beyene (Berhe *Ingliz*) set Sebhat Aberra free on 17 October 1962.[31] Both judges, Tsegai and Berhe, were lauded for their courage.

Gebremedhin Hailu's funeral, which was held on 2 November 1961, was seen by many as a demonstration of protest involving a wide spectrum of the population. Eight buses and scores of private vehicles travelled from Asmera to Adi Kefelet to transport mourners to the occasion. An Ethiopian intelligence report revealed the political meaning of the event. 'The Ethiopian flag that traditionally preceded funeral processions was not flown at this funeral,' it said. 'The attendees are all people suspected of favouring the maintenance of the Federation.' Among the suspects it listed were Haregot Abbay, a cabinet secretary; Bemnet Tessema, prominent businessman; Mesghina Gebrezghi, member of the Assembly; and Melles Fre, Supreme Court justice.[32]

The Ethiopian intelligence report also noted a similar demonstration involving the Ethiopian flag that had taken place about a month previously. On 30 September 1961, Godaif residents of Asmera clashed with the police in protest over the expropriation of their land for the expansion of the Sembel Airport. Two villagers died in the shooting. At their funeral, attended by thousands of people, the report noted that the Ethiopian flag was replaced by a black flag of mourning. 'We have no flag,' the villagers declared, 'and since our dead are martyrs for their land, we will not mourn them.' As a result, no crying or wailing was heard at the funeral and the mandatory traditional mourning period of twelve days was waived. The report concluded: 'This is all part of a trend to oppose the Government by alleging that justice is being denied. Bigger demonstrations over land granted to Italian concessionaires are upcoming and they need to be stopped ... Public protests are growing in Eritrea. We recommend that the Government reconsiders its treatment of the people and sets up a commission to examine the situation.'[33]

Mass Arrests of Haraka Members in Eritrea and Ethiopia

Surprisingly, the Ethiopian security machinery was still unaware of Haraka's existence, at least until July 1961. Only then do we find a security report making a vague reference to 'an Italian- and Arab-instigated dangerous movement named "Eritrea for Eritreans", whose leaders, supporters and the foreign meddlers attempting to create havoc are being searched for appropriate action'.[34] Credit is due to Haraka for eluding Tedla Ukbit and Assegahey Araia's spying networks for over two years of its secret existence. It would not last much longer. In December 1961, nine Eritreans, led by Teku'e Yehdego and including the future minister Weldemikael Abraha, were arrested. The detainees were charged with recruiting people to an association with the object of 'disturbing public security and causing harm to the Government'.[35]

Although no identification of Haraka or Mahber Shew'ate was made, Teku'e's arrest spelt disaster for the clandestine organisation, as he was on the leadership committee of the Asmera cells. However, after police torture and interrogation failed to obtain the desired outcome, Interior Director Zerom Kifle was about to release the detainees when new arrests complicated their case.[36] This time, a complete cell of seven members, which included such future prominent leaders of the Eritrean revolution as Mehari Debessai, Teklai Gebreselassie (Haraka) and Mahmoud Ismail, were caught and identified as having 'established a Mahber Shew'ate'. They were further accused of having sent unsigned letters to Assembly members and 'threatening and terrorising them'.[37]

Within a few months, more and more cells were exposed and arrests of mostly young people, including high school students, filled up Asmera prisons and detention centres. With the extension of the police measures to the Keren and Akurdet areas, where hundreds were incarcerated, Haraka's effectiveness as an organisation virtually came to an end. The arrests were not restricted to membership of the Haraka cells alone. Charges of aiding and abetting 'bandits' also added victims to the congested prisons. Women, children and the elderly were not spared either.[38]

Eventually, the exposure of Haraka cells reached Addis Ababa, where some members broke out of the cycle of inaction. We recall that, underneath the strong Eritrean unionist lobby in Ethiopia, many Eritreans resident in that country had long been averse to the idea. In the 1940s, Eritreans travelled back to their country to warn their fellow nationals of the dangers of joining an Ethiopia that they knew only from a distance. Many stayed to form the Eritrean Independence Party, which Weldeab led for a while and which formed part of the Independence Bloc. Elias Teklu, strong advocate of independence and deputy editor of *Dehai*, was one of their number.

Haraka's appearance in Addis Ababa must be seen within this general context. By 1960–1, the mass migration of Eritrean mechanics, masons, merchants and students to Addis Ababa significantly changed the demographic balance and even the character of the city. For Eritreans, it was an eye-opener. To begin with, they found no trace of the Federation that meant so much to them. Secondly, the mere mention of their identity, as Eritreans, was anathema to Ethiopians, who preferred to call them Tigre (Tigrayan). Besides, many felt that Addis Ababa was growing and modernising at the expense of Asmera and with money originating from Eritrean ports and mines. A combination of such beliefs, no matter how true or untrue they were, made many open to joining Haraka's cells.[39]

However, weary of waiting for the approval of the Haraka leadership's go-ahead for operations, some members started to take their own initiative. This took two forms: pamphleteering and buying arms for launching an armed struggle. On the first count, a group consisting of Barnabas Weldehawariat, Hagos Tesfatsion and Naizghi Kiflu, among others, used the facilities of a Ministry of Health official, Tekle Rosario, to duplicate and smuggle pamphlets into Eritrea. Naizghi, future member of the EPLF central committee and ambassador and minister after independence, took personal charge of the mission but was caught in the act as he distributed pamphlets in Mendefera. That route failed.[40]

The arms smuggling involved more danger and daring. According to Barnabas, an Ethiopian Airlines employee named Gebrai Tekeste smuggled 27 hand grenades inside his TWA carry-on handbag on two separate flights to Asmera. There were no security checks at the time; nevertheless, the act demanded supreme courage. Procurement of the weapons was the responsibility of *Fitawrari* Manna Adhanom, an old Italian *shumbashi* and wealthy merchant, and Mehari Teweldeberhan, a highly successful businessman. Manna, who in addition personally smuggled crates of rifles, ammunition and hand grenades on a truck, had partners in Asmera—former cabinet secretary Mahmoud Omer Ibrahim, Adem Melekin and Menghistu Bairu, a younger brother of Tedla Bairu.[41] Twenty-five hand grenades were delivered to the Awate band by Adem Melekin, as we shall see later.[42]

For a second round, Melekin secured more arms from Addis Ababa and returned home, ahead of thirteen armed men determined to begin an armed struggle.[43] Eighteen more followed in the coming days. Unable to accommodate them or their demand, Haraka leader Kahsai Bahlibi sent one batch to Tesseney, where their numbers and general demeanour aroused security suspicion. They were apprehended and thrown into jail upon arrival.

The group that stayed in Asmera, numbering about seventeen men, were more determined. Mahmoud Omer Ibrahim, Menghistu Bairu and the high school teacher Tekleberhan Zere, who were in contact with the men, could not contain their enthusiasm. In June 1962, all seventeen armed men, led by a worker named Abraha Hagos, left for the Durfo Valley and Mount Re'esi Adi, on the outskirts of Asmera, to force Haraka into armed insurrection. They were a group of highly charged nationalists with no training or experience in what an armed revolution would involve. Although Menghistu and Tekleberhan tried to help them with food and necessities, they soon fell victim to their own inexperience, and Tedla Ukbit's forces hunted down and caught most of them. On 20 June 1962, Tedla himself caught Menghistu Bairu and Tekleberhan Zere red-handed as they waited with weekly supplies for the would-be rebels down the road to Massawa. They were soon joined in prison by Mahmoud, Adem Melekin, the lawyer Solomon Kahsai, whose car Menghistu used to meet the rebels, and Kahsai Bahlibi.

At the subsequent trials, Mahmoud Omer Ibrahim's case was complicated by the discovery on his person of a letter from Idris Mohammed Adem urging him to work with the ELF. The implications of that discovery, especially for Kahsai and Menghistu, were grave.[44] Adem Melekin's contact with Awate's men, to which he admitted under interrogation, would also have landed him in trouble. However, in a celebrated courtroom drama, he removed his shirt to show Judge Tsegai Habtemariam the scars and wounds on his back as evidence of his forced confession. Judge Tsegai dismissed the charges. An appeal court reversed the verdict and sentenced Melekin to twelve years in prison, a term he never served as he had already fled the country. The scrapping of the Federation just five months away meant that all other accused secured early releases.

The Addis Ababa attempt failed with the inevitable arrests of all the activists involved, including *Fitawrari* Manna, Barnabas, Hagos, Tekle Rosario and others. But the city itself continued to be a hotbed for the gestation of Eritrean militancy. In the coming years, Eritreans were to play major roles in the creation and expansion of the Ethiopian labour movement, the radicalisation of the university students' unions, and the popularisation of the strike and public demonstration as means of protest.[45] In the mid-1960s, Kidane Kiflu, Tesfai Gebreselassie, Isaias Afewerki, Haile

Weldense (Deru'e) and Mussie Tesfamikael pioneered the steady flow of hundreds of students from Ethiopian universities into the armed struggle.

Eritreans were also at the forefront of every major student demonstration in the city—the support for Menghistu Neway's attempted coup, the 'Land to the Tiller' demonstrations, the Kolfe concentration camp protests of the 1960s, and many more. Every Ethiopian Airlines aircraft hijacking from within Ethiopia was planned or led by Eritrean radicals.[46] ELF cells throughout the city, especially on university campuses, ensured Eritrean contact, financial contributions and the constant flow of recruits into the organisation. Later, the EPLF's Tihisha group helped to propagate and popularise the new front's objectives during its infancy. Along with the martyr Temesgen Haile, such future prominent EPLF fighters as Teame Beyene, Estifanos Afewerki (Bruno), Ukbai Mesfin, Berhane Abrehe, Amha Kidane, Alem Gidey and Haile Naizghi were major players in the group.[47]

The Demise of Haraka

Haraka's adoption of a supra-religious nationalism stands out as its greatest contribution to Eritrea's history. The memory of its appeal and popularity continues to be held by its surviving original adherents. Its problem lay in the nature and content of its leadership, which, although genuine in its inclusive politics and the maintenance of revolutionary principles, failed to seize the moment of the 'ripe objective conditions' for an armed struggle. The ELF, which branded Haraka communist and anti-religion, soon grew on the basis of its own credentials and at the expense of a Haraka base that was already crumbling.

In early 1965, Haraka sent a small armed contingent, led by a heroic young revolutionary named Mehieddin Ali, into the Sahel district to belatedly involve itself in the armed struggle. An ELF force in the area disbanded the unit upon its arrival, and Mehieddin was killed. Haraka could subsequently survive only as an idea and an appendage of future liberation or political movements. But its legacy as a grassroots organisation that set the Eritrean liberation struggle on an inclusive nationalist path remains etched in the Eritrean revolutionary narrative.

Ibrahim Sultan and Idris Mohammed Adem Exiled

CID reports from 1956–9 indicate that Ibrahim and Idris were among those most followed and harassed by Tedla Ukbit's security forces. Since both had business interests in the Akurdet area, they spent a considerable portion of their time in that region. The administrator of the district of Akurdet at the time, *Balambaras* Mehretab Asfaha, who often met both men on business, later recalled how Asfaha's government put pressure on him to close down their businesses, including agricultural concessions. Ibrahim was especially a marked man. Although trumped-up charges of non-payment of concession rent could not be proved against him, other measures imposed on him and his family members made his life in Eritrea unbearable. His brother too was stripped of his position as *nazir* of the Rigbat.

Mehretab believes that Ibrahim and Idris used their Akurdet business interests as a stepping stone for their eventual exile in Sudan. Ibrahim was, in fact, in the process of securing a government loan when he and Idris disappeared from Eritrea. The exact date of their departure cannot be determined. In his interview with Gunther Schroeder, Idris put it in the month of March 1959 but did not specify the exact day. He said:

> Haile Selassie wanted me to take part in the annulment of the Federation. I refused. After my removal from the presidency of the Assembly, I was asked to be an advisor at the Imperial Palace. I turned down that offer too. They then confiscated my car, my house in Asmera and stripped me of all my medals. I returned to my residence in Akurdet ... When situations turned dangerous for us, Ibrahim and I entered Kassala secretly. There were many Eritrean soldiers in the Sudanese army. We had contacts with them before our departure. Among them were Omer Ezaz, Tahir Salem, Abu Tayara, and Mohammed Idris Haj. They used to send messages to us. We proceeded to Cairo from Khartoum. We did not speak to the Haraka in Khartoum. We asked permission to continue to Egypt, which we procured. We entered Egypt on March 23, 1959.[48]

Predictably, the exile of the two leaders rekindled speculation that a joint Muslim–Christian effort, including Weldeab, would finally result in the fulfilment of Omer Qadi's dream of bringing the UN back to Eritrea. Reports that former Finance Secretary Teklehaimanot Bokru, who was still in Eritrea, had joined them in Cairo raised the excitement to fever pitch.[49] Even the American consul Richey wrote at length on the topic.[50]

The centre of the Eritrean nationalist struggle was shifting to Khartoum and Cairo. In May 1959, Egyptian president Nasser met with both leaders but refrained from granting them the financial support they requested. Later, he made it known that the United Arab Republic, of which he was also the President, would not abandon the Eritrean cause. Italian sources in Cairo also reported that Egypt had reminded the visiting Ethiopian Emperor to 'strictly honour' the international promise made to Eritrea for the protection of the Federation.[51]

Apart from these symbolic gestures, the two exiles could not boast of any immediate breakthrough in their quest for tangible international support. Nor could they attract substantial media attention, which was initially confined to a couple of interviews in some minor newspapers like *Al Shabab* and *Nahdet Afriqya.* For this reason, their activities were confined within the Eritrean exile community in Cairo, whose major event was a demonstration staged on a street where Nasser and Haile Selassie's motorcade was passing. They shouted to Nasser: 'Justice is greater than the affairs of state! Whoever forgets this principle will be judged by Allah!'[52]

In the meantime, the Ethiopians showed their concern about the departures in different ways. According to Richey, the federal security chief Assegahey Araia and Asfaha himself were summoned to Addis Ababa for questioning. In addition, Ethiopian generals Aman Andom, Kebede Gebre and Merid Mengesha were dispatched to Eritrea to assess the security situation there. All this was on top of protestations made by Ethiopian ambassadors over Sudan's and Egypt's decision to harbour the exiles.[53]

Towards the end of 1959, Weldeab joined Ibrahim and Idris, and together they drafted yet another memo to UN Secretary General Hammarskjöld and accredited ambassadors in Cairo. In it, they reminded the world body that, in spite of its disregard for the Eritrean case, they had not given up hope on the UN. If the order, patience and respect for the rule of law shown by the people of Eritrea ran out, it would be morally justified. They therefore urged the UN's involvement before the Eritrean problem threw East Africa into violence and chaos.

They listed Ethiopia's wanton dismantling of the Federation and its reduction to a mere formality. They particularly pointed to the unlawful presence of the Ethiopian army; the appointment of the Emperor's deputy representative as Chief Executive; the fraudulent elections to the second legislature; the imprisonment of Elias Teklu of *Dehai* and of Omer Qadi, Suleiman Ahmed and Imam Musa, all fighters for Eritrea's rights; and, above all, the suppression of the human and civil rights of Eritreans that were guaranteed by the UN's Federal Act. They requested that a UN commission be dispatched to Eritrea to investigate their allegations.[54]

This petition must figure as the last in the series of lawful attempts by Eritreans to re-engage with the UN. Indeed, as the nationalist struggle entered a different phase, it marked the transition to the liberation movement that was then taking shape.

23

THE ERITREAN LIBERATION FRONT

Formation of the ELF in Cairo

The Cairo Students and Idris Mohammed Adem

At the end of 1959, a group of exiled Eritrean students in Egypt met at Jebel Muketem near Cairo to discuss Haraka and the existing situation in Eritrea. Many of the attendees, some of them students at Al Azhar University, who were highly opposed to Haraka's peaceful and secretive mode of operation, played a role in influencing the conclusion of the meeting that Haraka's programme would never bring independence to Eritrea.[1] Previously organised in a self-help association with an Islamic orientation, they attempted to link up with older politicians like Ibrahim Sultan, Weldeab Weldemariam, Omer Qadi and Idris Mohammed Adem, but without any results. Their emerging leader was Seid Hussein, a high-profile militant activist with knowledge of the revolutionary literature on Vietnam, Algeria and the Palestinians, who had also fought in the 1956 war on Egypt's side.[2]

After the failure of their attempts to persuade Haraka leaders to join forces with them in an armed revolution, the students launched a concerted campaign against Haraka. As a result, from Cairo to Kassala, Haraka cells disbanded and most of its members defected to the students' cause. In early 1960, the students received a major boost when Idris Mohammed Adem joined them.[3]

On 7–8 July 1960, a meeting in Cairo discussed the idea of forming a new organisation, charting a programme of action for beginning the armed struggle, and seeking arms for the purpose. While Seid Hussein and the student Mohammed Saleh Hummed were given organisational responsibility, Idris Mohammed Adem was chosen as leader 'for his higher contacts in Cairo and other countries, and his high political profile'. The name Eritrean Liberation Front—Jebhat al Tahreer al Eretria—was adopted out of respect for the Algerian Liberation Front, an inspiration to most of the founders.[4]

Idris Mohammed Adem had very little in common with the Cairo students and their various Islamic, Arab nationalist and Marxist revolutionary leanings. In the politics of Eritrea of the 1940s to 1950s, in which he had been initiated, Islam was never a uniting factor for all Muslims. The Muslim League of the Western Province, to which Idris belonged, had split from the parent Muslim League (ML) in a bid to partition the area from Eritrea. Ethnic and regional considerations played a larger role than religion here. One must also keep in mind that serf emancipation drove the *shumagille* or the ruling classes of Sahel, Barka, Senhit and Semhar away from the ML to the Unionist Party. Islam could not keep them within the ML, which, although composed exclusively of Muslims, promoted and practised an Eritrean nationalist agenda.

In his time as a member of the Eritrean Assembly and later its president, Idris played a major role in defending Eritrea's autonomous rights and its Constitution. Whether those accomplishments and credentials enabled him to rise above the sectarian politics of his past and promote a nationalist cause is a question we shall consider. But those credentials in practice elevated his name to the same level that Ibrahim Sultan had achieved through years of struggle and suffering.

It is not clear at what point Idris accepted the idea of an armed struggle for independence. While still in Eritrea, Hamid Idris Awate had sought his help in his initial efforts to begin armed confrontation. Idris considered the initiative too rash and dangerous and advised against it. By his own account, he had no prior knowledge of the actual beginning of the armed struggle in September 1961. 'When we were abroad, we heard that he [Awate] had gone out to the field. We said, "With no guns, why?" But it was because the Ethiopians were about to arrest him.'[5]

Eritrean Soldiers of the Sudanese Army

In early 1961, when their contract with the Sudanese Government came to an end, a sizeable number of disillusioned members abandoned Haraka for the ELF. Many of them had fought for the British in Libya and Ethiopia and were already hardened soldiers. The induction of this group in the ranks of the ELF had a tremendous impact on its growth and, indeed, the early survival of the armed struggle. However, there was no discernible philosophy or set of values, religious or otherwise, to which they adhered as a group. Mainly composed of rural Beni Amer, Bejuk, Marya, Nara and Blin, they were not insulated by either their military experience in the lowest ranks of the Sudanese army hierarchy or their educational background from the rise of sectarian forces which surfaced over the following years. Besides, when they joined the ELF, it had not yet developed its agenda or constitution. They were, in truth, an amorphous group joining an organisation that had not yet clearly defined itself.

Osman Saleh Sabbe

Osman Saleh Sabbe was one of the most colourful and controversial figures of the Eritrean revolution. Born in 1933 in Hirgigo, south of Massawa, where he went to school, he trained as a teacher in Addis Ababa under the mentorship of Saleh Kekia

Pasha, businessman, educator and former vice president of the Unionist Party.[6] Kekia had big business interests in Ethiopia. While at the Teacher Training Institute in Addis Ababa, Sabbe became involved in an attempt to bring fellow Somali and Ethiopian Harari, Oromo and Gurage schoolmates to a correct understanding of the Islamic faith and practice. Shocked by 'the feudalism, oppression of nationalities, ignorance and slavery perpetrated by the dominant Amhara', he also developed an intense hatred for the 'Abyssinian Kingdom', against which he and his friends vowed to fight.[7]

During the period 1954 to 1957, when Sabbe served as teacher and director at the Hirgigo school, he established a body called Erwa Wesqa (Solid Bonds), which sought to reconcile religious and secular education, but he later transformed it into a political group.[8] On Kekia's death in 1957 and the disruption of the flow of scholarship students to Addis Ababa, Sabbe aroused government suspicion by travelling to Sudan and Egypt to meet with important Islamic figures, Dr Hassen al Turabi among others, on the pretext of developing new sources of scholarship funding through that avenue. Future leaders of the Eritrean armed struggle like Mohammed Ali Umeru and Ramadan Mohammed Nur were the beneficiaries of Sabbe's efforts.[9] By 1959, security harassment made his life in Hirgigo unbearable. He left for Asseb and from there, on 7 February 1960, crossed the Red Sea to Saudi Arabia on a friend's sailing boat.[10]

Idris claims that when Sabbe first met him in Saudi Arabia in January 1961, he was still seeking to use Erwa Wesqa to improve the conditions of Eritrean and Ethiopian Muslims. Idris dissuaded him from that pursuit, arguing that the Eritrean problem was an international matter while Erwa Wesqa's concerns were internal to Ethiopia. Mixing up the two would only damage the Eritrean cause.[11] Sabbe's subsequent praise of Idris's successful diplomatic campaigns and efforts to work with Haraka make Idris's claims plausible. But he was adamant in his rejection of collaboration with older politicians. Ibrahim Sultan, he told Idris, was 'an illiterate, self-serving man who squandered Eritrea's rights and wants to live at its expense'. As for Weldeab, he advised, 'Don't pay any heed to what he says about our office [ELF]. Weldeab pretends to be a nationalist while he is nothing but an extremist Christian (*mesihi mut'asib*).'

Of Sabbe in 1961, when he was 28, we get the picture of an intense activist who saw things in black and white. Just as he conflated Ethiopian and Eritrean Muslims, so did he not differentiate between Eritrean and Ethiopian Christians, whom he collectively referred to as 'Habeshi'. 'Personally,' he wrote, 'I don't believe that Christians will fight for independence. Everything that we do with them should be aimed at neutralising them. Our relationships should be for appearances only (*mujamela*).'[12]

Of all the diverse and often mutually contradictory political and religious forces and dispositions that made up the ELF then, Sabbe was the most categorical in his deliberations and in his adherence to the fundamentals of the Islamic faith. Yet there were also elements of pragmatism in his dealings with the Islamic world even in these early stages, such as his attendance at an Islamic conference in Jerusalem, where he stressed that the ELF would not present itself as an Islamic organisation. He hoped instead to exploit the opportunity to gain international exposure and possible financial and material aid for the ELF.[13] With such a background and with such political and religious views, it was inevitable that Sabbe would affect the course of the Eritrean revolution in a significant way.

The Mejlis al A'ela

Soon after their meeting in Saudi Arabia, Idris and Sabbe travelled to newly independent Somalia where they formed the Somalia and Eritrea Friendship Association, based in Mogadishu. Their stated aim was to internationalise the initiatives already set in place by the Cairo students and exiled politicians like Ibrahim and Weldeab.[14] Sometime after the formation of the Somali–Eritrea Association, a body called Mejlis al A'ela, or Supreme Council, was formed with Idris and Sabbe, later joined by Idris Gelaydos of the Cairo student leadership, as the highest authority in the ELF. No documentation exists on its formation. Later reports simply state that, by the mid-1960s, a seven-man Mejlis was set up and that Mohammed Saleh Hummed, Said Ahmed Hashim, Taha Mohammed Nur and Osman Idris Kiar were added to the original three leaders. According to a 1982 ELF report, right from the outset, secrecy and an intense power struggle between the three top leaders characterised the operations of the Mejlis.[15]

In the meantime, Ethiopia applied pressure on Egypt to halt ELF activities and to deport Eritrean activists from Egypt. On 17 May 1961, angry Eritrean students broke into the Ethiopian Embassy in Cairo and trashed it. In addition to the Arabic media, the BBC broadcast news of the incident, making it one of the first Eritrean items to gain some international attention. Ethiopia condemned both the incident and Egypt's failure to protect the embassy.[16]

The souring of Ethiopia's relations with Egypt was compounded by Somali declarations calling for the establishment of Greater Somalia, which would include the Ogaden, Djibouti and the Somali provinces of Kenya. When the formation of the Somali–Eritrea Association was announced, the Ethiopian press launched into a tirade of vitriol and condemnation that referred to it as a 'friendship of bastards' forged between foreign forces and unworthy Eritreans willing to 'sell their souls' to them.[17]

In November 1949, Ibrahim Sultan had warned the UN General Assembly that the abandonment by the world body of Eritrea's legitimate right to independence would endanger the peace and security of the region. The regional tension that the birth of the ELF brought to the area recalled Ibrahim's prophetic warning.

Hamid Idris Awate

Early Life

The man credited with starting the Eritrean armed struggle for liberation, Hamid Idris Awate, was born between 1911 and 1915 to a rebellious Hafara family of the Beni Amer. His father Idris had escaped Italian rule to raise his family among the Welqait in Ethiopia, from whom Hamid acquired his lifetime penchant for arms and sharpshooting and his knowledge of Amharic. In the 1930s, Awate saw battlefield action in Gondar and subsequently served in Akurdet and Kassala as a corporal in the Italian army. Upon Italy's defeat in 1941, he abandoned his post at Kassala to go back to his village of Hademdemi, where he married and began to raise a family. His confrontation with the British began with his unjustified arrest by a British officer, from whom he escaped by tricking him and relieving him of his gun, and then formed a *shifta* band.[18]

This was in early 1941. Soon afterwards, when the Beni Amer–Hadendowa conflict (1941–5) began, Awate joined Ali *Muntaz*'s forces at the head of his band. After rejecting the British-brokered communal agreement that ended the conflict, he led nine or ten followers to continue the rebellion in the Gash and Barka regions.[19] In 1947, he smuggled his constantly harassed family to the safety of their old refuge among the Welqait, where his band grew to twenty or twenty-five Welqait, Beni Amer and Nara rebels. Between March and April 1948 alone, they carried out four major raids on the Kunama of the Gash River. In one of these, at Tanina, the band killed four Kunama residents, burned down 39 huts and rustled 70 head of cattle.[20]

However, it was his daring raids on police garrisons that earned him a top place on the British Administration's blacklist. In July 1948, a high-profile Sudanese officer, Chief Inspector Mohammed Ali Sikingi, was dispatched to capture him at the head of fifty or sixty members of the elite Field Striking Force. On 27 July, after weeks of relentless and exhausting evasion, Awate's band confronted the force at a place called Koyta-on, near Haikota town, where, from a commanding position, Awate felled Sikingi with a couple of shots.[21] With 1,000 shillings on his head, Awate became the Administration's most wanted *shifta*.

Awate Surrenders

In June 1951, Chief Administrator Cumming sent Police Commissioner David Cracknell to Fanko, 30 kilometres south-west of Haikota, to force Awate, the only *shifta* leader to reject a general amnesty, to surrender. When Cracknell met Awate, the latter subjected him to a tirade of accusations about British failure to preserve peace and about the excesses of tribal chiefs. While bearing Awate's outspokenness with the 'greatest patience', Cracknell noted that Awate was a 'highly strung, intolerant' man, 'deeply infected by political poison'. He wanted to know what the British were doing in Eritrea, wrote Cracknell. 'Were they deliberately ruining the people and depriving them of what little wealth they possessed? Were they breaking down the meagre tribal framework which existed and destroying the customs of the people for some sinister motive?'

Challenged by Cracknell, Awate stated that his clashes with the government could have been avoided and that the killing of Inspector Sikingi grieved him. But it came after 24 days of a dogged pursuit and encirclement from which 'his only escape was the measure he had adopted'. From Awate's hostile attitude towards Ali Rad'ai, who accompanied the Police Commissioner, Cracknell surmised that he was opposed to the ML-WP's proposals for the partition of the Western Province. Cracknell concluded that Awate would be 'a hard nut to crack' and that he was 'undoubtedly a staunch supporter of Ibrahim Sultan'.

Through the good offices of a spiritual leader who apparently broke down 'the political barriers', Cracknell persuaded Awate to surrender. On 31 July, he arrived in Fanko with fifteen of his 59 followers, armed only with four Italian-made guns, one pistol and a few hand grenades, and submitted to Cracknell and a district officer.[22] Cracknell took away most of the guns but allowed Awate to keep a British weapon with fifty bullets. Later, reasoning that he would be more useful as a security supervisor, the Administration appointed him head of security in the Gerset, Hademdemi and Gash areas with six armed men under his command. As Ethiopia awarded rank, administrative posts and judgeships to the other *shifta* leaders, Awate was left in his low-key, unsalaried post in his village.

For about five years after his surrender, Awate virtually disappeared between Hademdemi and the forested banks of the Gash. We hear from him again only in March 1956 when he wrote to the authorities requesting more guns and men for the efficient carrying out of his duties in confronting increasing *shifta* activity.[23] Support for his suggestion by Ali Mihri, senior divisional officer of the Akurdet region, brought strong opposition from Kunama leaders Faid Tinga Longhi and Mohammed Badume Kassu on the grounds that Awate had perpetrated atrocities on their people in his days as a *shifta* and that his appointment would cause more bloodshed.[24]

In July 1957, Awate rejected a humiliating government offer to become part of a salaried patrol unit within a Kunama force of 70 men commanded by the police.[25] His last known contact with the Eritrean Government came in one of his rare visits to Asmera, where he spent most of his time with his peers from the *shifta* era, Gebre Tesfatsion and Gebre's deputy, Zere Debretsion. Noting his frustration and restlessness, both men took the initiative to meet Asfaha and advise him to appoint Awate a *kebila* chief or judge, lest he prove troublesome. Their suggestions were turned down. They turned to Commissioner Tedla, who adamantly told the two men, 'Tomorrow, I will order my men to behead Awate within the week. When they bring it to me, I will call you and show it to you!'

By the time Gebre and Zere returned to Awate, he had already left. 'Later on,' Zere recalled, 'we heard that Awate collected guns and ammunition from his surroundings, killed his horse, attacked and ravaged a police post, and become a *shifta* all over again.'[26]

Awate's Transformation

It was at some point after these events that Awate asked Idris Mohammed Adem to help him organise an armed uprising, a proposal that Idris rejected as impractical and dangerous. At the same time, he was in contact with the spiritual leaders *Sheiks* Mohammed Dawd and Suleiman Mohammed Alamin. Many believe that Mohammed Dawd, grandson and favourite of the spiritual leader *Saidna* Mustafa, greatly influenced the course that Awate took in the following months. As a result of his privileged status, Mohammed Dawd amassed considerable wealth and influence while still in his early twenties. By 1958, at the height of the *shifta* troubles, he had organised his own armed units to defend his surroundings. This brought him into conflict with the government.[27]

According to Gindifil, one of the former Sudan soldiers, Dawd's political opposition to the Federal and Eritrean governments had a religious undertone. Taking the relegation of Arabic to a secondary status in the educational system as an attack on Islam, he had called for Muslim resistance. To this end, he organised seven core units in different parts of the region with Dubuk as the centre.[28] This religious element, according to Gindifil, was what attracted Awate to Mohammed Dawd.

Others argue that Dawd's political orientation was moderate, stressing his nationalism instead. In the early months of the ELF's formation, a delegation was sent to Dawd for his support and blessing. Gesir and Gindifil were among them. Gesir described their utter surprise when, instead of the Quran, Mohammed Dawd handed them a gun and said to them, 'Take this gun and don't say you have no arms and food. The people of Eritrea are with you. As for arms, you can capture them from the Ethiopians. This gun will add to Hamid Awate's collection.' This was proof, Gesir concluded, that Awate and Dawd had come to an agreement on the armed struggle and that religion had not been their prime motive.[29]

By early 1961, hundreds of Haraka members, led by the teacher Mahmoud Mohammed Saleh of Akurdet, were abandoning the organisation and were drawn instead to the ELF and to Awate, whose mocking dismissal of Haraka's plans for a coup as 'a tale of some fancy wishes' was widely known. Amid the break-up of Haraka cells, the widespread arrest of scores of members, and the visit to Akurdet by ELF cadres to draw from the Haraka reservoir, a meeting of great significance for the armed struggle took place in Akurdet in April 1961. Prearranged by *Sheik* Mohammed Dawd in coordination with Awate, it came in response to appeals to Dawd from Cairo students and former Haraka members for coordination and appropriate action. For security reasons, Dawd was represented by his cousin *Sheik* Suleiman Alamin. Awate and Mahmoud were among the attendees.

According to Mahmoud, Awate told the gathering that if there was a serious move to action and 'if you are sure that we can acquire arms, then the right time for the revolution is now'. He needed to know, in detail, the amount and type of arms available and what could be brought in from other countries. The remaining arrangements would be his responsibility. Recruiting fighters in the Gash, Setit, Barka, and even Sahel and Anseba would not be a problem, he told them. 'What I don't know is the *kebessa* and the eastern provinces. We will need people to work and organise there. If arms and the soldiers in Sudan do come ... I will have units ready for action.'[30] Hamid Awate, a *shifta* turned calculating revolutionary leader and planner, must have impressed his audience immensely. It is on record that Awate was in Akurdet on 14 April 1961, ostensibly to request more ammunition for use in defence. He was given only ten bullets by the district administration.[31] Awate used that pretext to attend the Akurdet meeting.

When the Akurdet meeting became known to the government, the authorities decided to arrest Awate. Knowing his elusive ways, they chose tact over direct capture. The senior divisional officer Omer Hassano has left a detailed account of the process. According to his account, Commissioner Tedla sent a letter to Awate telling him that the government was reconsidering his 1956 request for arms and men and inviting him to discuss the matter in person. When Awate refused to go, Hassano sent the district officer of Tesseney, whom Awate met on 31 July. For three days, the district officer attempted in vain to convince Awate that the government was sincere in its desire to make amends. Awate would not be moved. Hassano went to him in person on 2 August at his home, four kilometres from Gerset. At Awate's demand, they met alone the same afternoon.

Awate was suspicious of a plot to arrest him. Hassano invoked his honour and belief in the Almighty to convince him that the police had no knowledge of any crime he had committed and that their invitation was genuine. In the end, Awate agreed to meet the Commissioner on 15 September. As he was waiting for the appointed meeting, Hassano reported, 'with regret, I came to know that he became a bandit and robbed a shop at Ulati village, Hademdemi area, belonging to a Beni Amer tribesman, namely Karar Hummed Mohamed'.[32]

The exact details of Awate's departure from his home vary from source to source. Kidane Hidad, a police criminal investigator in Tesseney, was a member of Haraka and a close friend of Awate from the early 1950s. His account is most plausible. In the days prior to Awate's departure from his village, a *shifta* band led by two men, Ibrahim Mohammed Ali and Omer Kerai, had rustled a large number of cattle belonging to the Israeli meat-packing plant INCODE. Kidane was included in a search team as an investigator. Awate was still at home at this time, and the team met him in the course of routine investigation. Kidane privately asked him if he had been involved in the raid, but Awate flatly denied any such involvement.

Kidane's team was continuing its search and investigation when a police unit, commanded by a Captain Abdelkader, was dispatched to arrest Awate at the end of August. It failed in its mission and, as the coast became clear, Awate came down to his village, divided his property between his two wives, and left the village along with Saleh Mohammed Adem Kirutchai, Hummed Dewhen and Abdu Mohammed Faid.[33] In a 1999 interview, Kirutchai recalled their leader's words on that day:

> He told us that Ethiopia was illegally turning Eritrea into its domain and that it needed people to free it from the fate determined for it by others; people ready to kill and sacrifice themselves for its sake. He then gave Mohammed Faid a Moschetta rifle, and an *Abu Sita* [six-shooter] each for Dewhen and me. He ordered us to lie low in the surroundings until his next call and to avoid the word *tahreer* [liberation] as it might arouse police suspicion.

While still in the Hademdemi area, three of the INCODE cattle rustlers, Ibrahim Mohammed Ali, Omer Kerai and Bereg Norai, joined Awate's group. At the end of August, as Awate's original followers rejoined him, their total number reached ten. The common belief that the Eritrean struggle for independence started with seven men and seven rifles refers to these original seven members, excluding the INCODE rustlers.[34]

Awate was still in his village when word reached his group that a large police contingent was on its way from Akurdet to attack them. Captain Abdelkader, the patrol leader, talked to Haileselassie Weldu about the incident.

> When he saw us from a distance on September 1, 1961, Hamid thought that we were after him. He ran away from us and began his struggle. The next day, September 2nd, we received word that he and his followers had ransacked a shop in Hademdemi, shot bullets into the air and shouted slogans. When I and my company were still there, the Eritrean Government ordered the confiscation of Hamid's property and the incarceration of his family members.[35]

It is often reported that Awate's first shot of the Eritrean revolution was fired against a police unit at Mount Adal. That, as we shall see, came later. Awate's celebrated 'first shot' of the armed struggle was more ceremonial. It took place on 1 September 1961 at Gerset.

Claims that Awate and his followers started the armed struggle under the direction of the ELF cannot be substantiated.[36] Osman Saleh Sabbe may have put the matter to rest when he stated:

> The Eritrean Liberation Front arose among the worker and student communities in the Arab countries of the Middle East in 1960. In the following year, it moved to the mountains of Eritrea after the spontaneous uprising led by the late Hamid Idris Awate on 1.9.1961 at the head of a few fighters armed with old Italian rifles. The Front adopted the spontaneous uprising and evolved during the following years into an organized armed revolution.[37]

The ex-soldiers in the Sudanese army who had been pressuring Awate to accept them in his team were among the first to embrace his 'spontaneous uprising'. However, despite his expressed desire to receive them, he kept insisting that they come to him armed as he saw no point in amassing people without the means to fight. To test their dedication, he also demanded new recruits to come 'with soiled hands—rob a bank, steal a gun'.

In the meantime, aware of the danger that Awate's uprising would pose, the Ethiopians reacted with remarkable speed. Dubbing them *wero bella*—bandits or predators, a term that it was to keep till the end of the armed struggle in 1991—it sent successive armed sorties to wipe out the band in its infancy. Awate found himself engaged in four separate battles against Eritrean police and Ethiopian troops before the ex-soldiers finally joined him. The first battle took place on 26 September at Mount Adal. It was a highly testing conflict in which Awate and his men, although outnumbered and outclassed, showed their determination and fighting spirit. The only casualty they suffered was the capture of Bereg Norai of the INCODE threesome.[38] Police casualties were not reported, but at least two may have been wounded. Once in the safety of his refuge, Awate is said to have told his followers: 'Today, Azanit has given its word. Witness that we and our rulers faced and fought each other for the first time. No more sleeping on a bed from now on!'[39] Azanit, meaning 'herald' or 'harbinger', was his gun's pet name.

The second battle took place on 24 October at about 9.20 am in the Keru area. Here, one of Awate's original aides and followers, Abdu Mohammed Faid, was killed. He is regarded as the first martyr of the Eritrean armed struggle.[40] On 3 December, Awate and his men escaped encirclement at a Greek concession farm in Gurguji, only to be pursued by a police force to a place called Qabat. In the ensuing battle, one police officer was killed and two wounded. Another veteran of the uprising, Mohammed Ibrahim Era, was captured with an Albini rifle and 45 bullets.[41]

The fourth clash took place in Awha al Gedam, in the Keru area, on 9 January 1962, with an Asmera regiment of the elite Police Striking Force. With fifteen men only, Awate's force was outnumbered. Here, Ibrahim Mohammed Senni was killed, making him the second martyr of the revolution. Three more were captured. The police suffered only one casualty.[42]

Awate himself was wounded in this confrontation. As soon as word of this reached Kassala, the ex-soldiers Gindifil, Abu Tayara, Mohammed Idris Haj and Omer Damer hastened to his side with essential medicines and medical equipment. Gesir, who had some medical knowledge, also went along to tend Awate. Together, they took him to the safety of Abilenai Gash Bahr, where they nursed him back to health. Once again, Awate turned down their pleas to remain with him; they returned to Kassala.[43]

It was only after this incident that the first batch of ex-soldiers was able to join the liberation force with an assortment of old weapons and some ammunition. This was in March 1962. Everyone agrees on nine names—Mohammed Idris Haj, Omer Damer, Omer Ezaz, Abu Tayara, Osman Abu Sheneb, Gindifil, Badurai, Jimi'e Adem and Abu Rijla. Seid Hussein was the first Cairo student to join the force sometime later, followed soon afterwards by Mohammed Mai Bietot, Gesir, Osman Saleh, Hamid Ibrahim Tambar and Mohammed Ibrahim. By the time of the arrival of these groups, Awate's force had suffered a total of seven losses, with two killed and five captured. That left him with approximately fourteen fighters. Thus the arrival of the ex-soldiers and the students could not have come at a more opportune time.[44]

The Battle of Balangida Bitama

Awate immediately divided his force of some thirty men into units of which the largest consisted of nine fighters. They were to be led by the ex-soldiers. Arguing that 'if the revolution that we are launching is not cleansed at its inception, it will meet with failure', he dismissed the two former cattle rustlers from the force for objecting to the new appointments. In explaining his harsh disciplinary measure, he told his followers that Eritrea was like a man thrown into a deep pit.

> If we are to emerge from this pit, the 1.5 million people who are now divided by religion, *kebila* and province should resolve their differences and unite as if born from the same womb. There is no country in the world that will help or even listen to us. Our clothing, weaponry and ammunition should all come from the enemy. But let us also note that, unless the *kebessa* join us right now, our struggle will not succeed. Keep this in mind.[45]

On 4 April 1962, after a long walk from the Omal Mountain to a place called Babangida, a police force attacked the rebels. After losing two fighters and killing a policeman, the rebels realised it was no contest and beat a disorganised retreat.[46] The ex-soldiers' first battle as revolutionaries thus ended in failure. When they reassembled at a more secure area, Awate told them that their situation was untenable. They needed an adequate supply of weapons, so he put Omer Ezaz, Abu Tayara and Gindifil in charge of smaller groups and assigned them to different areas in search of weaponry.

As they left for their assigned posts, Awate took five of his old comrades, including Kubub Hajaj, and went back to the Hademdemi–Gerset area. It took the groups from six to seven weeks to collect better guns and ammunition. Some of these were bought from Kassala, while others came through Keren, courtesy of Adem Melekin, as we saw earlier. Idris Mohammed Adem for his part acquired five rifles by means of contributions from Eritrean residents of Saudi Arabia. More confident with their new acquisitions, the group went back to Awate but could not locate him anywhere. After several days of searching and waiting, Abu Tayara said, they were led to Awate's friend and follower Mohammed Faid:

> When we met Faid, we saw Awate's gun and other equipment with him. We asked them where he had gone. At first, they told us that he was moving around in the area. When we insisted on the truth, he informed us that he was martyred. We held a

> meeting immediately. We swore on the Quran to keep his death a secret. We agreed to say that he had gone to Sudan or Cairo or Italy on a mission.[47]

The panic and confusion into which Awate's death threw his followers is not difficult to imagine. Under the temporary leadership of Mohammed Idris Haj, they agreed to reorganise at an appropriate time.

The Death and Legacy of Awate

In an interview with this writer, Cracknell described Awate as a 'thorn in the side' of the British and as a man who had lived by the sword.[48] Awate's policeman friend, Kidane Hidad, agreed that although, when provoked, Awate could be harsh and cruel, he could show great love and sympathy, as he did over the killing of Chief Inspector Sikingi. 'Sikingi was heroic,' he often told Kidane. 'Such a man should not have been wasted in such an unworthy manner. I regret it much. It saddens me deeply ...'

All who knew him closely, including his second wife Asha Osman and his older cousins, remember him as a man of few words, occasional laughter and suppressed emotions who preferred to sit at some distance from his companions with a gun on his lap and his back to the wall.[49] Gesir described his spontaneous reaction to Awate's penetrating gaze: 'Just as you say of him, "Who is this man? Is he a lion? Does he eat people?", he too considered if you were smart or dumb or soft.'

His transition from *shifta* to revolutionary may not be easy to follow in retrospect. But Gesir and one of his closest aides, Kubub Hajaj, separately recalled the remarkable decision taken by him on the discharge of the INCODE rustlers as a good example. In reality, he was not reacting to insubordination in making his decision. But the two men were known robbers, and this was an opportunity for him to cleanse his force of such elements. Incidentally, Ibrahim and Kerai came back to the struggle after Awate's death. Both died, Kerai heroically in Gindifil's raid at Haikota.

Many of Awate's deeds and utterances are often mixed with the myths that have made him into a legend—which Haileselassie Weldu has documented in his excellent portrayal of Awate. The fact is that Awate had special qualities that enabled him to make the transition, indeed the metamorphosis, from *shifta* to revolutionary. True, his excesses as a *shifta*, particularly his devastating raids on the Kunama, did cause resentment. But, as usual with revolutionary leaders, one needs to contextualise the contradictory and controversial aspects of his life.

Awate was an Italian soldier of some consequence, an experience that he took advantage of. He served in Gondar and Kassala and visited Rome, and was thus exposed to different countries and cultures. Contrary to Asfaha's claims that he was too illiterate for a judgeship, Awate was fluent in both written and spoken Italian and spoke Arabic well enough. Besides his native Tigre, he spoke Nara, Kunama, Tigrinya and Amharic. Gesir and others also testified that he always carried with him a transistor radio by means of which he avidly followed world news from Radio Cairo, BBC Arabic, Ethiopia and other regional sources. As Cracknell noted, he was a *shifta* 'infected by political poison'.

Awate died from unknown causes. After having sent his comrades to hunt for weapons, he left, as we have seen, for his home area. On that fateful evening, 28 May 1962, according to Haileselassie Weldu, Awate was with one of his faithful followers, Kubub Hajaj. Here is how Kubub recounted the events of that night to the veteran fighter Tesfai Tekle.

> Awate had the habit of eating three cups of boiled millet a day. That night, I went to give him his nightly portion. 'I will not eat today, I am feverish,' he told me. 'Are you getting old?' I joked. He laughed, 'What are you saying, Kubub?' he asked me and added, 'Take care of my gun. One never knows. Call our comrades here.' I called them.
>
> 'Listen,' he said to us. 'One never knows. In case I die, don't announce my death. My name can serve you for a while. Besides, don't show my grave to anyone.' All of us left him in puzzlement.
>
> He always had the habit of rising at three to four in the morning, performing his morning *salat* and stationing himself at his lookout post. I noticed that he had not risen by four o'clock; I went to wake him up. But he had already breathed his last. We examined him, there was no sign of a snakebite on him. He had not suffered from any noticeable illness, including malaria, over the past days.

True to his request, Kubub Hajaj and his colleagues kept the whereabouts of Awate's grave a secret until they revealed it to ELF officials in 1976.

Awate died too soon to affect the course of the Eritrean armed struggle in any permanent way. But, in his brief period of activity, he learned from his *shifta* experience and grew into a broad-minded nationalist and revolutionary. His vision of religious and regional tolerance and cooperation was more advanced than that of most ELF leaders. His early call for *kebessa* involvement also showed his broad outlook and acute foresight.

Having died only nine months after launching the armed rebellion, he did not live long enough to face the challenges of the expanding revolution. But the legend that he has left is that of an enigmatic figure depicted often in his photos on horseback; an ascetic man of action rather than of words; a larger-than-life presence who appeared to fill more space than his diminutive size allowed. Above all, he was a visionary who left a mantle too large for his immediate successors to wear.

The ELF and the Bergeshish Meeting

After Awate's death, responsibility for the force passed to Mohammed Idris Haj, Abu Tayara and Babikar Mohammed, all former soldiers of the Sudanese army. It did not take long for divisions and misunderstandings to arise, which Sabbe attributed to lack of education and effective organisation, and to immerse the corporals and the force in *kebila* and power politics. Defining the areas of control of each leader and how to share arms captured by a unit were the main issues of contention.

In December 1962, Sabbe was delegated by the Mejlis al A'ela to resolve the tensions within the forces. He assembled 43 fighters in all, who carried only nineteen weapons between them—nine of them non-functional—at Bergeshish in the Gash area, where he advised them to form a collective leadership, which they agreed to. Five units were formed under the leadership of five commanders. Abu Tayara, in charge of the largest group, was overall commander. Ezaz and Mohammed Idris Haj were also awarded lesser commands. The Majlis would transmit its directives through an intermediary, Tahir Salem, stationed in Kassala.

This may be regarded as the point at which the ELF leadership abroad took command of the fighting forces in the field. Militarily, the arrangement worked well, according to Sabbe, who cited three incidents. A few weeks after Bergeshish, Mohammed Idris Haj's unit attacked a police convoy and captured eleven guns. Haj himself died in that encounter. Seven more guns were collected in a second attack sometime later. The most spectacular mission of those early days took place in September 1963 in Haikota. Gindifil and his team hijacked a local bus and commandeered it, driving it to Haikota, where the team took up strategic positions. In a dramatic episode, Gindifil entered the police post pretending to be a deranged man and opened fire. In minutes, the team took over the post and drove their bus to safety, enriched by over forty rifles, two Bren guns and a large supply of ammunition.

On the other hand, Sabbe regretted one aspect of the Bergeshish resolution that he did not take advantage of. Their greatest mistake, he said,

> was that we did not call a congress to establish a legal framework. We only concentrated on the military aspect. We committed a grave mistake. But the forces that we organized expanded fast and, by 1963, were carrying out operations and destroying police stations and garrisons. We were also procuring arms from abroad. At the beginning of 1964, the number of our fighters in western Eritrea grew to about 200 men. Ethiopia began to withdraw some of its distant outposts, allowing us to possess our first liberated areas.[50]

The ELF would suffer from religious and regional divisiveness and conflict resulting from the Majlis's 'regrettable' omissions. But both Haraka's clandestine work and the ELF's successful launching of the armed struggle had already set the Eritrean revolution on a firm footing. Largely unaware of these developments at the initial stages, Asfaha's administration and the Ethiopian Government were still immersed in dismantling the Federation step by step and in pre-empting possible regional and international objections to their annexation drive.

24

ERITREA ON THE EVE OF ANNEXATION

Ethiopia's Courtship of Africa

Ruth Iyob has depicted Ethiopia's image at the turn of the 1960s as double-faced. On the one hand, it projected itself as the champion of the right of colonised Africans to self-determination while its darker face turned to the suppression of the same rights demanded by the peoples of Eritrea and the Somalis of Ogaden. While strengthening its old claims on Eritrea, it also argued that the right of nations to self-determination should exclude nationalist movements within African colonies or independent states, as it would disrupt their national unity. Ethiopia thus skilfully married its own ambitions for territorial expansion with the process of decolonisation already in place.[1]

Besides its troubles in Eritrea, Ethiopia was also apprehensive of Somalia's impending independence. The dream of creating a Greater Somalia, including its own Ogaden region, was being openly promoted by the Somali Youth League and other sympathetic sources.[2] The Afro-Asian People's Solidarity Organization, led by Egypt's Gamal Abdel Nasser, had already voiced its support for the creation of Greater Somalia and for the right of people to liberate themselves from forced associations.[3] At the same time, Kwame Nkrumah of newly independent Ghana formed the All-African People's Conference, a regional organisation that openly rejected colonial borders as geographical definitions of the emerging states.[4] Besides calling for an end to colonial rule in Africa, Nkrumah also championed anti-imperialist and anti-neocolonialist causes and criticised Ethiopia and Liberia, the two countries claiming not to have been colonised by European powers, for not having raised their voices in support of African independence. Haile Selassie's prestige and reputation thus came to be tested at a crucial time in African affairs, an issue of much concern for the monarch.[5]

Beginning in 1958, Haile Selassie used all the advantages at his disposal—his royal stature; the international sympathy that his unheeded warning of a Fascist onslaught had won him in the 1930s; his claim to a share in the British victory over Italy's occupation of Ethiopia; and, of course, the myth of 3,000 years of Ethiopian history and independence. He also had at his disposal a crop of young, Western-educated Ethiopians, led by Aklilu Habtewold, who skilfully applied the considerable diplomatic skills and experience they had accumulated over the previous decade.

To counter the radical line of the Nasser and Nkrumah factions, Ethiopia joined a group of conservative new states like Nigeria, Liberia and the so-called Francophone states, to create the 'Monrovia Group', also referred to as the 'Brazzaville Group', in January 1961.[6] In reaction, Nasser, Nkrumah and their aligned partners joined together to form the 'Casablanca Group'.[7] Three issues separated the two groups: whether to call for immediate African unity under a single leadership, reject neocolonial relationships with former colonial powers, and continue the liberation struggle including armed struggle until Africa rid itself of European colonisation. Under Haile Selassie's leadership, the Brazzaville Group's moderate approach finally won the day.

In 1963, Addis Ababa was chosen as the venue for a heads of states and governments meeting to deliberate on the formation of an African union. In his keynote address, Haile Selassie outlined how the differences between the two contending approaches had been reconciled. First, he strongly supported the principle that no nation could consider itself independent unless all Africans still under colonial rule were accorded their freedom. Second, he suggested that Africa's relationship with the former colonisers should not compromise African honour, but that blame and bitterness be replaced by mutual respect and harmony. Finally, while accepting the necessity of African unity, he proposed a gradual, as opposed to an immediate, union. Even Nkrumah, whose demands were included in the Emperor's proposals albeit in a highly moderated form, was obliged to accept them. The outcome of the meeting was the formation of the Organisation of African Unity (OAU), permanently stationed in Addis Ababa.

As Peter Schwab puts it, although Nkrumah is rightfully recognised as the father of 'indigenous Pan-Africanism', after 1963 Haile Selassie became the wise leader, the elder statesman, of the continent.[8] Using this leverage, Haile Selassie was able to insulate Eritrea from any consideration by the OAU. Total silence on the question of Eritrea was to characterise the OAU's attitude from its inception until Eritrea's independence in 1991. It was a major limitation that the Eritrean liberation movement had to live with and endure throughout its existence.

The American Connection

In the heat of the Cold War between the Soviet bloc and the West, Ethiopia's role in moderating the Casablanca Group's anti-imperialist and anti-neocolonialist stand worked in the interests of the US. This was also the time when, under the leadership of Nasser, Nehru of India, Sukarno of Indonesia and Haile Selassie, the majority of African and Asian states organised themselves into the Non-Aligned Movement, of which the OAU was an adherent. Since the US had more to gain than lose from these developments, there was reason enough for it to be indebted to Ethiopia, one of its most dependent allies in the Red Sea region.

However, Ethiopian–US relations were not as smooth as they seemed. In return for Ethiopia's loyalty and in compensation for its military and intelligence base at Kagnew Station in Asmera, US aid never stopped flowing to Ethiopia, though rarely to the latter's satisfaction. In this period of space exploration, nuclear proliferation and Cold War tension in general, Kagnew Station turned into a crucial intelligence and communications base for the US.[9] As Ethiopia's demands for more aid, especially military aid, became increasingly insatiable, the US refrained from indulging it for fear that it would be used against the people of the region.

The Ethiopians knew how to touch American sensitivities. After a series of warnings to the US that it was 'throwing them into the arms of others', in reference to the offer of substantial aid from the USSR, Haile Selassie visited Moscow in 1959 and came back with a soft loan worth US$100 million. This time the Americans took note. Although they did not believe that Ethiopian posturing would actually translate into an alliance of Imperial Ethiopia with communist USSR, the possibility that Somalia's forthcoming independence might provoke unrest in Eritrea and create opportunities for Soviet intervention was of much concern. Besides, pushing Ethiopia to adopt a position of real non-alignment was not in the US interest.

In July 1960, the Americans agreed to grant $25 million in aid, over half of it military in nature, to Ethiopia. In August, they signed a further agreement that committed the US to training and arming 40,000 troops of the Ethiopian army. On top of that, the agreement included an annual military aid package of $10 million for fifteen years consecutively. Most significant for our story, however, was a clause in the agreement that declared that American interest in the security of Ethiopia was permanent and that it would oppose any activity that put Ethiopia's territorial integrity in jeopardy.[10] Secure in the knowledge of tacit African collaboration and of US support, Ethiopia could now move to its main objective of Eritrea's annexation and the international recognition of its expanded borders.

Attempted Coup in Ethiopia and Eritrean Reaction

On 14 December 1960, when Haile Selassie was on an official visit to Brazil, the commander of his own army of bodyguards, Menghistu Neway, and his brother Germame, Governor of Jijiga, along with Police Chief Tsighe Dibu and the Emperor's chief of security, Workneh Gebeyehu, launched an unsuccessful coup. The Emperor's faltering attempt to modernise Ethiopia had bred discontent within his more progressive bureaucratic and military hierarchy. The failure of the hastily planned coup is generally attributable to four factors. First, the spontaneous public support that the perpetrators expected did not materialise; only students of the

University College of Addis Ababa came out in open support. Second, the ground and air forces stayed loyal to the Emperor, ultimately crushing the coup in the 15–16 December battle in Addis Ababa. Third, seeing the balance of forces tipping towards Haile Selassie, the US denied the coup plotters the crucial backing they needed. Lastly, the Emperor's representative in Eritrea, General Abiy Abebe, secured Eritrea for the Emperor by controlling the loyalty of the army's 2nd Division and the Eritrean police force.[11]

Asmerans became aware of the coup on 15 December when Abiy condemned it over a make-shift air force radio. He ordered all citizens to return to their normal duties and the army and police to keep peace and order.[12] On the next day, as Addis Ababa Radio announced the success of the coup, Abiy dismissed the news as the false claims of a few traitors with no popular following, who had already been defeated by the loyal ground and air forces.[13] That afternoon at 4:30 pm, Haile Selassie and his entourage, which included Chief Executive Asfaha, landed at Asmera airport to a pre-planned welcome. Shops, schools and offices were ordered to shut and people told to line the streets for his arrival. The turnout pleased the Emperor, who hastened to address the nation from Abiy's radio. He expressed his sadness that officers entrusted with high responsibility should betray their duties. He denied their allegation that his own Crown Prince was at the head of the coup and thanked the people of Eritrea for their welcome and loyalty.[14]

By 17 December, coup leaders Germame, Tsighe and Workneh had been killed and Menghistu captured. The plotters' last act was to collectively execute sixteen of Haile Selassie's top officials, including the Tigray Governor, Seyoum Mengesha; the Defence Minister, Abebe Aregay; and the Eritrean former Governor of Adwa, Dawit Okbazghi. Andargatchew miraculously survived by lying motionless beneath a heap of bloody bodies.

On his return to Addis Ababa, Haile Selassie held an international press conference at which he thanked the people of Asmera for their 'enthusiasm and warmth' surpassing all previous welcomes.[15] For a long time, *Zemen* carried news items and articles containing tributes and pledges of loyalty to the Emperor from the Eritrean Assembly and from groups and individuals throughout the country. To all appearances, the people of Eritrea were content with events as they turned out. But Gebreyohannes Tesfamariam, Secretary of the Economy at the time, later disputed the allegation that the Emperor's welcome in Asmera had been as genuine as it appeared. Even the Eritrean welcoming party at the airport came under coercion, he said:

> We were not there willingly, not at all. When they told us to welcome him at the airport and ordered the people to line up on the streets, some of us objected. We argued, 'Soldiers are fighting each other. We don't know who is shooting whom. What if shooting begins when people are on the streets? Do you want us to expose them to a massacre? Who will take responsibility for this?' But there was no unity

> between us. In fact, some of our own colleagues turned around and told Abiy Abebe of our objections. Tedla Ukbit came toting a machine gun and threatened to shoot us all down if we resisted. This is how we went.[16]

The US consul Matthew Looram, who had replaced Edward Richey, also observed that the majority in Eritrea shrugged the coup off as an Amhara internal affair and that their mute reaction did not guarantee Eritrean submission. Should a similar event unfold in Addis Ababa once again, he suspected, elements in Eritrea would learn from the experience and proceed to exploit it.[17]

A Stir in the Assembly

In 1960–1, the hope rekindled by Haraka's clandestine activities and the formation of the ELF began to embolden various sections of the population. According to Nawd, Haraka managed to penetrate the Eritrean Assembly, where the president Hamid Ferej, Osman Hindi of Massawa and Mesghina Gebrezghi of Asmera came under suspicion by the government. But for the most part the Assembly of mostly hand-picked annexationists and traditional chiefs simply waited to put the stamp of approval on Haile Selassie's inevitable declaration of annexation. Torn between these two extreme positions, its members fell victim to harassment from two sources: Andinet and Haraka activists. An Andinet leaflet, signed by 'Brothers Who Won't Betray an Oath', reminded members of the legislature:

> Those who elected you did so to see you realise the long political work aimed at uniting Eritrea and Ethiopia; for you to consummate their Ethiopian wishes and feelings. To be living for eight years under the Federation is regrettable. We have endured the past with a great deal of reservation. Today, if our wish for complete union is not met, we warn you beforehand that the secret plan of a terrible attack on your person will fall upon you.[18]

Coming from an organisation with a history of violence and open support from the Federal Office and its security chief, Assegahey Araia, this was a threat that Assembly members could not take lightly. Soon, however, they were astonished to find a different message lying on their desks inside the Assembly chamber. 'It could only have happened if someone from among us had done it secretly, or one of the Assembly employees,' recalled Assembly member Habtu Tesfamikael. The chilling message, signed by 'The People of Eritrea (for Eritreans)', read as follows:

> Warning!
>
> So, instead of carrying out your responsibility, you are selling your country, your people and yourselves. And you are frightening and silencing those one or two amongst you who will not sell their country and their people. They [annexationists] connived to sell the Eritrean flag. And now they are planning to sell the country for

> their own selfish motives ... But Eritrea's fate is in the hands of its people; it will not be sold by one or two useless persons ... You have sworn in the name of the Almighty that you will serve your people and country freely. The people are now sending you their order and warning that you deliver the rights of Eritrea and its people. Please note the danger that you will face should you fail in your duties. We warn you that you will not see the threshold of your own home.[19]

In the middle of this unsettling time for the Assembly, fifteen members signed a petition demanding the removal from Eritrea of Kumilatchew Belete, a high official in the Office of the Emperor's Representative, for interfering in Eritrean internal affairs. Their request was rejected, but, coming from the supposedly passive body, it caused official concern.[20]

A more serious issue arose when Asfaha's proposed 1961/2 budget showed a deficit of 750,000 birr. Angry members argued that the deficit had been caused by Ethiopia's denial of Eritrea's customs share and a mini-rebellion made the passage of Asfaha's proposal impossible. Recognising the problem he faced, Asfaha left in mid-July for Addis Ababa, where he confronted the Emperor directly on the issue of customs duties. As was his practice, Haile Selassie appointed a committee of ministers and crown advisors.[21] In a later interview, Asfaha, who had been promoted to the rank of *bitweded*, beamed at the memory of his bold confrontation with Aklilu and Yilma Deressa in the presence of the Emperor. He told this writer:

> I reminded them of an Arabic proverb: '"Eat together like brothers, but be accountable like enemies." Let us make an account.' Aklilu and Yilma responded: 'We are fourteen Governorates General. How are we to apportion these customs revenues?' I said forcefully, 'We will not be observers in our own home. It is our right and we are entitled to it.' The main problem, of course, was the power imbalance between us. We were two unequal partners pretending to be peers. Inevitably, the stronger partner was bullying us.[22]

Asfaha went back triumphant when he was awarded one million birr as an Imperial grant for a temporary budget adjustment. With that, the Assembly approved Asfaha's budget proposal, but with the following reservation made by the Budget Committee: 'The Committee, nevertheless, expresses its regret that its recommendations over the past nine years regarding Eritrea's customs dues have not been implemented. Although the Emperor's grant has helped in adjusting the current budget, we urge the Administration to resolve the problem for the future.'[23]

Over the following three weeks, the Assembly became even more embroiled in issues to do with Ethiopia's monopoly over salt mining, which the Assembly considered Eritrea's domain; and with Ethiopia's insistence that Eritrea pay 250,000 birr for the distribution of food aid granted by the US, which had been presented as the Emperor's largesse. Even *Zemen* commented on the fierceness of the debate, particularly referring to Habtu Tesfamikael and Mesghina Gebrezghi as the most forceful.[24] Such an affront from the virtually hand-picked third legislature had not been envisioned by Asfaha and his Ethiopian mentors. The American consul Looram attributed it to the revolutionary wind blowing from Barka. But it would also spur Ethiopia to move more quickly towards annexation. Eritrea, Looram wrote, was 'dying on the vine'.

Ethiopia Tightens Its Grip

Ethiopian Security Takes Over

In the week of the Assembly debates, Ethiopian security activity increased visibly. A memo written by its security officer in Eritrea, Major Taye Metcha, on 2 July, reported to General Abiy Abebe that a difference of opinion on whether the Federation should continue was dividing the Assembly so bitterly that there were fears of public unrest. At the centre of the public discontent were the unpaid customs dues. The memo pointed to students and the unemployed as the main proponents but mentioned Mesghina Gebrezghi, a former unionist, as the instigator, who advised them to demonstrate under the slogan 'We don't want Ethiopia; we are hungry!' The Assembly itself was divided between those advocating annexation through an Assembly vote and those calling for a referendum.

The notion that Eritrea could be self-sufficient, Taye told Abiy, was taking root in Eritrean thinking and 'a huge number of people' supported union in name only; they were actually against it. If this was not stopped in time, the memo stressed, it would be difficult to manage its spread and organisation. Taye then suggested some temporary measures. First, secure through encouragement, persuasion and money the loyalty of those who still believed in Ethiopia's objectives. Second, should the desired aim not be attainable through the Assembly, then plan for a referendum. If the second option was acceptable, then ensure the prior commitment and understanding of the provincial, district and village chiefs.[25]

In the meantime, Assegahey Araia's federal security network had bypassed Tedla Ukbit's domain to penetrate the whole of Eritrea. No one was spared from Assegahey's surveillance. On 2 July 1961 it was reported that Assembly president Hamid Ferej, accompanied by his Assembly colleagues Osman Abdulrahman, Dawd Asfeda and Omer Adem Nashih and two *nazirs* of the area, met with the exiled Ibrahim Sultan near the Sudanese border around Kassala. Ibrahim was said to have urged Ferej to use his position to unite the Assembly in opposition to Dimetros's mission of 'Christianising the Muslim populations of the Nara and Beni Amer'. Based on this information from an alleged participant in the meeting, Taye recommended surveillance be extended to include Ali Rad'ai, Secretary of Social Affairs, and Omer Hassano, Secretary of Law and Justice, people he accused of using their positions as a cover for divisive objectives.

Taye's report was sent to Asfaha one year after it was first created, indicating that although Asfaha was also Ethiopia's vice representative, Ethiopian security withheld information from him too.[26] All indications pointed to Asfaha's loss of his old status. The year 1961 ended with a dramatic surge in manifestations of Eritrean nationalism through individual acts of violence and open defiance. Among them, Looram listed the Assembly affront, the attempt on Dimetros's life, the spread of the *shifta* movement in the west, and news reaching Addis Ababa of popular discontent and the possible existence of a clandestine political organisation.[27]

Obviously, Asfaha was not able to control the political direction that Eritreans were taking. An Eritrean sense of national pride was now being displayed openly. When Ethiopia won the 1962 Africa Cup of Nations on 21 January by defeating Egypt 4–2, Eritreans claimed the victory. Eight of the twelve players fielded by Ethiopia were born and bred Eritreans. Three of the four goals that secured victory were scored by Tekle Kidane, Luciano Vassalo and Italo Vassalo, all Eritreans. The fourth was by the great Ethiopian player Mengistu Worku.[28] The sports writer Teklit Lijam probably reflected the Eritrean mood at the time when he wrote, 'Ethiopia won the Africa Cup by fielding eight Eritreans. In other words, Eritrea won the Cup wearing the Ethiopian outfit. It is said that an Egyptian newspaper wrote, "Eritrea defeated us."'[29] Since Ethiopia has never repeated that triumph of over sixty years ago, the Eritrean claim still persists.

In early 1962, a top-secret Special or Ad-Hoc Directorate in the Emperor's cabinet was set up and charged with planning the road to annexation. The committee gave its final report in June 1962 in the week of serious student unrest in Eritrea. In its introductory note, the report stated that Eritrean Muslim attitudes had gone beyond opposition to annexation, to demands for Eritrea's 'separation' from Ethiopia. Their belief that joining Ethiopia would relegate them to second-class citizenship was leading them to seek support from Somalia and other Arab countries, and, ultimately, to secure the re-engagement of the UN. Furthermore, the report expressed dismay at the significant spread of opposition to Ethiopia among the Christian population that had 'sacrificed so much' for union. Pamphlets detailing 'Ethiopian offences over Eritrea after the Federation are arousing strong hatred over Ethiopia and causing Eritrean unionists to distance themselves from their original stands'. The report continued: 'Many who struggled for union and who feel that they had not been rewarded for their contributions ... are now readily falling for anti-union propaganda.'

Based on this assessment, the Directorate concluded that time for a smooth transition to annexation had run out. It then itemised, in eighteen steps, the steps to a more immediate annexation. Here is a synopsis:

- To arouse Christian communities in Eritrea, spread propaganda linking union between Eritrea and Ethiopia with the Christian religion.

- Appoint to high positions loyal and capable Muslims and neutralise antagonists by co-opting them by means of non-functional appointments.
- Adjust the discrepancy in salary paid to Eritreans and Ethiopians and assure Assembly members of a guaranteed income after annexation.
- Work on Assembly members to support the abolition of the Federation by a unanimous vote; money can play a part here.
- Improve economic, social and living conditions and paint a bright picture of post-federal life through radio and newspaper broadcasts and columns.
- Since *shifta* activity is indicative of maladministration, take steps to eliminate brigands.
- Organise Eritrean workers, teachers and merchants into unions demanding unity with Ethiopia.
- Follow the movement of traitors abroad and enable ambassadors to pre-empt and frustrate their objectives.
- In the event of lack of agreement on the abolition of the Federation, it is possible that internal opposition forces may provoke political warfare, violence and bloodshed. This may enable them to gain the UN's attention and acquire financial and material help from enemies of Ethiopia. To block this possibility, control all exit and entry points, especially through Kassala, Massawa, Asseb and the entire Denkalia coastline.
- Unless we are waiting for the people of Eritrea to come out in the open to express their wishes and grievances, the argument that the Eritrean situation is not grave is not acceptable and should not be taken for granted.[30]

Haile Selassie's Carrot-and-Stick Offensive

As we have seen, the Directorate's recommendations came at a time of widespread demonstrations led by students of the Technical School, Prince Mekonnen School and the Haile Selassie Secondary School. Besides protesting against the removal of the Eritrean flag, seal and the name 'Eritrean Government', the students demanded UN intervention. An unfounded rumour that the UN would review the Federation on its tenth anniversary had been circulating, and the students were demonstrating in support of this taking place.

In preparation for Haile Selassie's planned visit the following June, the authorities used the full police force, including mounted troops, to suppress all demonstrators by the end of May. On 20 June, Haile Selassie received one of the shining African leaders of the era, Ahmed Sékou Touré of Guinea, on a three-day official visit in Asmera, where he treated him with appropriate pomp and ceremony, had him officiate over an air force show, and accompanied him on a tour of the port of Massawa.

By choosing Asmera for Touré's visit, Haile Selassie scored two clever points. First, he sought to court Eritreans with a show of esteem that he would accord their country if they chose union. But his message to Touré was more important. A radical leader with an anti-imperialist outlook, Sékou Touré was a supporter of the right of colonised and oppressed peoples to self-determination. Haile Selassie, who was scheduled to chair the first summit of the heads of African states the following year, feared that Touré, Nkrumah and like-minded leaders would come out in support of the Eritrean revolution. At the time, the Emperor's insistence on the retention of colonial borders was gaining acceptance among the newly emerging African states. What he sought to impress upon Sékou Touré was that, as far as Ethiopia was concerned, colonial borders included Eritrea, the Red Sea coastline and the islands.

The ploy worked for him. In a joint communiqué issued by both leaders, they expressed their support for the independence of still-colonised African countries, called for 'non-interference in the internal affairs of other countries', and expressed opposition to efforts aimed at creating division among African states.[31] Neither Sékou Touré then nor any other African leader thereafter questioned Ethiopia's claim that Eritrea was solely its internal affair. When in 1964 the principle of the retention of colonial borders became enshrined in the OAU Charter, Eritrea's inclusion inside Ethiopia aroused neither African curiosity nor concern, an attitude the regional body maintained until Eritrea's independence in 1991.

After seeing Touré off, Haile Selassie led his entourage to Keren, where he met with the elders and representatives of the Senhit and Sahel regions. It was another charm offensive in which he distributed food, clothes, money, and candy and fruit for children wherever they assembled to welcome him. He promised to build schools and hospitals, and install telephone lines in remote areas. In a slight to Asfaha, who was in the front row of his audience, he instructed the elders and petitioners to reach him in future through his representative, Abiy Abebe.[32]

Back in Asmera the next day, he assembled the senior officers of the Eritrean police force and promoted Colonel Tedla Ukbit to the rank of brigadier general. Four lieutenant colonels, Zeremariam Azazi, Mohammed Nasser, Erdatchew Emeshaw and Menghistu Habtezghi, were elevated to the rank of full colonels. Seven majors and twelve captains became lieutenant colonels and majors, respectively.[33] That was the carrot he offered. The next day came the stick.

On 27 June, the gates of the Asmera Palace were thrown wide open for everyone to attend the Emperor's address. The speech was most memorable for the words he is said to have uttered. Though they were never published, they remain carved in the mind of every generation of Eritreans. 'Ertra merietwa inji hzbua ayasfelgenm'—literally, 'We need the land, not the people of Eritrea.' How the usually astute and reserved Haile Selassie could be so careless in his choice of words, none of the attendees could say. Asfaha Kahsai took it as a slip in an angry and rhetorical speech that revealed his underlying thinking.[34]

Indeed, Haile Selassie was angry. Sticking to the points listed for him by the Special Ad-Hoc Committee of his cabinet, he started by condemning the few renegades who still sought to 'tarnish the history of our forefathers and serve alien forces'. Sixty years of separation from 3,000 years of Ethiopian existence and an artificial border never 'tore our common lives and feelings apart', he said. 'You know very well that the artificial border that was drawn by the designs of men was scrapped by the power of God.'

He strongly denied that Eritrean Muslims would become second-class citizens in Christian Ethiopia and dismissed claims that Ethiopian Muslims were downtrodden. To prove his point, he gave an account of the number of mosques, churches, schools and hospitals built in Eritrea, amounting in outlay to 75 million birr, 'the highest regional investment in the country'. He was going into such details, he underlined, because some 'traitors and liars' claimed that nothing had been done for Eritrea.

After admitting that the security situation was of significant concern, he said: 'We have ordered Lt General Abiy and *Bitweded* Asfaha to work as diligently as Brigadier General Tedla Ukbit has proved in his work and command of the police force.' Asfaha had to bear a second humiliation in as many days. In conclusion, the Emperor said: 'At a time when we are studying ways of uniting with other neighbouring, friendly states, thoughts of separation will only be an obstacle to our progress and an opening for our enemies. You need to realise this. It is a heavy responsibility that we are entrusting you with. May the Almighty who rules over us all guide this behest Himself.'[35]

With that unsettling warning, Haile Selassie went back to his carrot. As the palace grounds cleared of the large gathering, government officials, provincial administrators and prominent traditional chiefs stayed behind for what was apparently a surprise. Thirteen former *azmatches* and *fitawraris*, including Hamid Ferej, were elevated to the lofty title of *dejazmatch*. Eighteen *sheiks* and *kegnazmatches* became *fitawrari*. Nineteen people, including the former *shifta* leaders Asresehey, Hagos and Debessai Dirar, were named *kegnazmatch*. Sixty-two more of lower rank were installed as *grazmatch*. All in all, 112 officials received new titles and a total of 115 were decorated with medals.[36] Asmera wits joked about what they saw as a drama of the absurd. 'Those on the right, *kegnazmatch*; those to the left, *grazmatch*' was how they summarised the whole stunt. (*Kegnazmatch* and *grazmatch* were military ranks for commanders of the right and left flanks in battlefield formation.)

The awards were not as arbitrary as they looked. As Looram noted correctly: 17 'spoilers' from the Eritrean Assembly of 68 members were conspicuously left out from any recognition.[37]

A Campaign for Immediate Annexation

If Haile Selassie's speech was intended to prepare Eritreans for the final act, Tekie Fessehatsion noted, quoting the US consul Looram, 'it did not appear that Eritreans were either ready or willing to be incorporated. Neither a vote in the Assembly nor a plebiscite among the people would bring the union they wanted.' Looram added:

> On subsequent canvassing of key Eritrean figures, however, one sees the other side of the coin which has certainly been covered and mute during this period. Despite all the gimmicks used by the Emperor, the task of the Emperor's representative and that of the Chief Executive will not be an easy one. The fact remains that a favourable vote in the Assembly, the procedure normally considered as the one to be used, cannot be taken for granted. A plebiscite, if remotely honest, would not bring about the desired effect.[38]

After the departure of the Emperor, Asmera was rife with the rumour that Asfaha and Dimetros were stalling on the issue of immediate union. Ethiopia could no longer depend on its old Unionist Party and Andinet bases and, as the special cabinet committee directed, it decided to circumvent them. A campaign, spearheaded by the Asmera Palace's chief of security, Assegahey Araia, and fully supported by Tedla Ukbit, was thus launched to procure signatures for the purpose. Corruption or coercion, whichever was convenient, was applied to great effect. The pressure was more acute on Assembly members who, if they reneged on the Assembly floor, would be held accountable through their prior signature. It was a sinister pre-emptive move that displaced Asfaha's administration, Dimetros's Assembly and the Eritrean population to the fringes of their own affairs.

This writer talked to two prominent former unionists, *Dejazmatch* Weldeyohannes Gebrezghi and *Dejazmatch* Gebreyohannes Tesfamariam, about those crucial pre-annexation months. Weldeyohannes had this to say:

> [Asfaha and Dimetros] worked for the removal of the flag. They did not seek the abolition of the Federation. Tedla Ukbit was the one pushing for abolition and his whole attitude was not quite right. He was going as far as accusing 'the priest and Asfaha' of 'not loving Ethiopia' and threatening to jail them. They appealed to the Emperor, but he was angry with them. That is when they joined the campaign—to hang on to their positions. On the other hand, they were tied to their previous vows to dismantle the Federation. Above all, His Majesty had promised Asfaha that after the Federation, he would be retained as the Governor General.[39]

Gebreyohannes Tesfamariam, former unionist leader of the Asmera–Hamasien region and Secretary in Asfaha's cabinet, met Asfaha to voice his concern about the Palace campaign for annexation:

> '*Bitweded*,' I said to him, 'don't they know that Eritrea is the saviour of the Ethiopian Crown? Don't the Amhara know that the abolition of the Federation will put their Crown in jeopardy? Why do they want to abolish it? Don't they need some advice? Just abolish, with no consent ...?'
>
> 'They will not listen, Gebre, they don't want to. They dream of the abolition only,' he responded.

> I insisted: 'Tomorrow this thing will create for you an international problem. I am not talking about myself but of the consequences tomorrow ... *internazionalmente*.'
>
> 'Leave that to us, it is not your concern ...'

Unhappy with Asfaha's response and the atmosphere of fear and apprehension throughout the country, Gebreyohannes decided to probe further:

> There was no consultation, no mutual trust whatsoever. Imprisonment was rampant for gossip, idle talk ... anything. The fear instilled in every person was hard to fathom. I went to the *bitweded* a second day. I said to him, 'Why are you approving every one of Tedla Ukbit's recommendations for detention? Is it not spoiling our politics in front of the people? Why don't you tell him to stop?'
>
> 'That is Tedla Bairu's law,' he answered. He meant *articolo dieci* [article 10 of the Police Ordinance].
>
> I insisted, 'So? Is it not incumbent upon us to correct it? Can't we do that? What is taking place is inappropriate.'
>
> 'Shall we dismantle it then, Gebre?' he asked me, throwing up his hands like a child. He meant the Federation.

A persistent and confrontational man, well known for his integrity, Gebreyohannes went straight to Abiy:

> 'General, I am here to talk about the Constitution that is in your hands. There is a provision on respect for human rights in that document. But human rights are being disregarded here. You are being blamed for these arbitrary imprisonments of three- to six-month duration.' This was because I believed that they were responsible for the excesses.
>
> 'Can't you tell this to *bitweded*?' he asked me.
>
> I responded, 'I am not here to squeal on the *bitweded*. I am here to charge and challenge him.'
>
> 'Why are you so concerned? How many people of consequence would you say have been imprisoned?'
>
> 'Let us not dwell on the kinds of people being detained. There is a saying in our country, "When the back of a fool is whipped, the heart of the wise sustains a scar." When you let this happen, others will wonder what kind of independence they brought the people. It saddens me. This should not be happening.'
>
> 'I have heard you,' Abiy said and dismissed me. When he told Asfaha of our conversation, a misunderstanding that took a long time to resolve arose between us.[40]

Looram probably talked to the likes of Gebreyohannes, a lifetime unionist who lamented the manner of the Federation's demise, when he canvassed opinions. Along with Asfaha and Dimetros, Gebreyohannes had, as may be recalled, advocated an immediate merger in the early stages of the Federation. Paradoxically, persons from the opposite side, former independence advocates and federalists, some of them from the *Ras* Tessema family, outdid each other in soliciting signatories. *Dejazmatch*

Tesfayohannes Berhe, Secretary of Finance under Asfaha, rationalised the shift in loyalty:

> It was all a done deal. We could not function. I went to Addis Ababa several times on the issue of customs duties. Nothing! It was all a game. They laughed at us; it was depressing. We were neither a Governorate General with defined rights nor an autonomous unit with appropriate dues and status. We were hanging in a state of limbo. So, when the merger talk began, we went along, come what may. I myself agreed. This was when all alternatives had come to a deadlock.[41]

The Akurdet Bomb Attack

On 12 July 1962, Abiy Abebe and Asfaha led their Ethiopian and Eritrean officials on a visit to Akurdet. Their objective was to offset the popularity that the Eritrean freedom fighters were gaining, especially in the Barka region. At 12.30 pm, as the dignitaries assembled in front of the town's administrative building to address the public gathering, two bombs were thrown into their midst. Only one exploded. Omer Hassano, Secretary of Law and Justice; the religious leader *Sheik* Saleh Mustafa; and a policeman died on the spot while five more died the next day. Hamid Ferej, Dimetros, Kumilatchew Belete, the *Zemen* editor Teweldeberhan Gebremedhin (Zekios) and 32 others sustained injuries.[42]

Two men, Abdulrahman Mohammed Musa and Mohammed al-Hassen Hassano, Omer Hassano's nephew, were immediately arrested as the perpetrators. The latter was on the stage with the dignitaries managing the sound system when the explosion went off. Many, including the police investigator Kidane Hidad, still believe in the innocence of the two men, who denied the charges right until their execution years later. At the time, Gindifil, Seid Hussein and a squad had been conducting a reconnaissance inside Akurdet and had even contacted Kidane. It was Gindifil and the ELF who were behind the daring act.[43]

The bomb incident was a great warning for the government. Within two weeks, Akurdet Haraka leader Mahmoud Mohammed Saleh and 36 of his fellow members were arrested. By August, 84 more people had been imprisoned from the environs of Akurdet alone.[44] The arrests spread to Keren, where Saleh Iyay was caught in possession of a duplicator, some arms and hand grenades, and a wad of money. Sixty-six persons were put in prison with him.[45]

In the meantime, despite the imprisonment of the Asmera Haraka leadership, pamphlets 'printed and properly duplicated and written in sophisticated Tigrinya' kept appearing on Asmera streets. As a result, Asmera became the centre of a police campaign to arrest suspects. By September, Mohammed Berhan Hassen of the Asmera Haraka leadership and twenty others had been detained.[46] Except for a few older and established individuals, the detainees were mostly young people, many mere high-school students. Parents invaded government offices to demand their release and to plead that the rule of law be respected.

Pamphlets accusing Ethiopia of starving Eritreans and forcing them into migration called for a fight against annexation. 'A people with a weak leadership falls victim to alien rule,' declared one pamphlet. 'All Eritreans need to show their readiness to die for their country. God will not deliver our country back to us ... If a person is not ready to die for his country, his declarations of love will remain meaningless.'[47]

The whole situation was becoming untenable for both the Asfaha administration and its masters in Addis Ababa. Haile Selassie's patience with the Federation was also running out. The annexation could not be postponed any longer.

25

THE ANNEXATION

Asfaha's Dilemma

Asfaha never failed to claim that he had spearheaded the fight to abolish the Federation, thus saving Eritrea from the threat of Arab nationalism. 'Remember that it was Nasser's picture that was hanging in every Muslim shop in Eritrea, not mine or the Emperor's,' is how he put it to this writer. When Zewde Retta questioned him on the charge that he had succumbed to Haile Selassie's persistent pressure, he gave a guarded response:

> We cannot deny that we accepted his gracious permission and fatherly advice in the implementation of our plans. But we never solicited his guidance on the specific manner of its completion. We have to be believed when we say that he too never interfered in our designs to give us directions. There is a need to correct many people who have come to wrong conclusions on this issue. Haile Selassie I never directly ordered anyone of us to dispose of the Federation.[1]

Citing Haile Selassie's eager rush to abrogate the Federation after Tedla Bairu's emotional outburst for immediate union in 1954 and his own proposal in 1956, both defeated by Aklilu's objection, this writer pressed Asfaha further on the matter. Moreover, if he and Dimetros did not hesitate, why did the need arise for Assegahey's Palace-directed solicitation for signatures? Here is how the conversation went:

Asfaha: Yes, a lot of that happened, it was inevitable. But there was no corruption. In truth, *Melake Selam* [Dimetros] and I maintained that the Federation was untenable and should be terminated. The so-called local autonomy was not there. There was no space for the expansion of economic activities. We were operating with our hands bound. *Sheik* Osman Abdulrahman, from Al Rabita [Muslim League], once said to me, 'We are raising an ogre. Our wives throw away ogres, they don't raise them. Let's get rid of this thing that does not operate beyond Tesseney and Senafe.'

But the actual abolition seemed rushed. It appeared to people that you were being dragged and forced into it.

Asfaha: We did suggest that we discuss it collectively. But Tedla Ukbit was not a man of politics. He was not far-sighted. Melake Selam and I were moving with clear thinking. We were explaining our objectives to Assembly members and provincial elders and gaining their support. They applauded our initiative.

Does that mean that you did not meet with any opposition?

Asfaha: There were those who insisted that we should not tamper with the UN decision. Our response was: 'We are here to bring prosperity to our people. The UN resolution is not bringing about that prosperity. Should we still be tied to it?'

Can we talk more of those who were pre-empting your efforts by campaigning for immediate annexation?

Asfaha: They used to say of us, 'Asfaha and Dimetros advocate union only in front of the Emperor. Power is like candy to them. They are sucking it.' Let me tell you, the people pained for union, they demanded it. Everyone was clapping. There was so much fawning. We never forced them to applaud. We did not! Not that we did not want them to, but we never forced anyone. Yes, Muslims were resisting. The British instilled fear of Ethiopia in their minds. That was a fact. But we persuaded them. We made them accept the King as their own.

Did General Abiy ever put pressure on you?

Asfaha: If there was a clean, elegant person in Ethiopia, it was General Abiy. He never meddled in other people's affairs.[2]

Asfaha's cabinet colleague and fellow unionist Gebreyohannes Tesfamariam did not agree with him about the Emperor's self-restraint in pushing for union. He argued instead that Haile Selassie had from the beginning harassed Asfaha and Dimetros with the demand. The uprising in Barka was the catalyst, Gebreyohannes said, but the Emperor's desire to do away with Federation went back right to the start and its final manifestation was Assegahey's campaign. Assegahey, according to Gebreyohannes,

> was the front man, the cheerleader. He used to mock Eritrean autonomy by joking, 'Even the House of Emperor Yohannes [Tigray] has not been called a Government, let alone this former piece of Ethiopia!' He was from Tigray. One day, he called me to his office. He said to me, 'Gebreyohannes, you know what is being done to bring about immediate unity. Why don't you lead the Hamasien elders and do what Tesfayohannes and Dimetros are doing in Akeleguzai and Seraye?'
>
> I told him that I considered it inappropriate to do so and added, '*Bitweded* Asfaha and *Melake Selam* Dimetros are unionists; why don't you do it the right way, through them? It is not proper for me, as their colleague, to sneak behind them for this. Yes, I am a unionist, but I cannot sabotage the work of the Assembly and the people by leading some elders to the Palace.'

... Dimetros and Tesfayohannes were in fierce competition to see who got first to the finishing line [*traguardo*] of the abolition. Tesfayohannes aborted Dimetros's desire to lead the three provinces to final unity by taking over the Akeleguzai side. Hamasien was also in the race, but Dimetros had the elders in his palm. He led them to sign. I stayed away.

According to Asfaha and Gebreyohannes, the campaign for signatures was even more intense in the western lowlands, where traditional animosity towards Ethiopia was most prevalent and where the liberation struggle was growing. Both mentioned the Keren senior divisional officer Emabye Habte and a man called *Blata* Medhanie as the chief campaigners. Traditional chiefs and religious leaders in particular fell for the propaganda that post-Federation Eritrea would be heaven on earth, that manna would fall from the skies, and that the old *shumagille* privileges would be restored to those serving Ethiopia and the Emperor. Muslims had previously been regarded as enemies; the time had come to remove that stain.

The race gained momentum and became contentious when other Muslim chiefs went along with it. The initiative thus slipped out of the hands of Asfaha and Dimetros. Dimetros had privately wanted Ethiopia to prove its worth by showcasing some real economic advances in Eritrea. But all that he accomplished was the building of churches even in predominantly Muslim areas, leading to accusations of a Christian crusade by Islamic critics.[3] His grand schemes unrealised, he was reduced to a mere campaigner in Assegahey's drive for signatures. Asfaha fared no better, as we will see.

As for the still-enthusiastic Tedla Ukbit, Gebreyohannes had this to say:

General Tedla never fell for money or wealth. He was incorruptible. But they lured him with rank, provincial sentiments and authority, the cause of their later rift. They told him that Akeleguzai had Asfaha, the Chief Executive, to boast about; Hamasien had already had Tedla Bairu. Seraye had not been thus honoured. It is believed that they promised him the Governorship of Eritrea after the Federation and he trusted them. Considering what happened later, I believe it too.

Three Hectic Days

Ethiopia's preparations for the abrogation of the Federation did not go unnoticed by the international community. To begin with, the foreign consuls in Eritrea were always abreast of the situation and, as their reports show, documented events as they happened. On 19 August, the *Washington Post* commented on the cool public reception that Haile Selassie and Sékou Touré had been accorded; the Emperor's threatening speech at the Asmera Palace; the decline of the Eritrean economy and rising unemployment; and Abiy Abebe's use of military force to crush opposition. The article drew a bitter rebuke from the government.[4]

On 8 September, the London *Observer* wrote a highly critical article on the tenth anniversary of the Federation, calling it an 'unhappy birthday'. The journalist, Andrew Wilson, also reported on the high level of unemployment and undisguised dissatisfaction in Asmera, a picture that the authorities dismissed as the propaganda of exiled 'spoilers' in Egypt, Somalia and Sudan. Wilson had asked an Ethiopian Foreign Ministry official, Getachew Mekasha, about possible anti-government demonstrations in Asmera. The latter's response was that 'some Eritreans could indeed demand to be beneficiaries of Ethiopian rights not accessible to them because of the Federation and, in that event, the request had to come from the Assembly'. The response signalled to Wilson that something was afoot. Besides, the existence of an elite army division under the command of the experienced and able General Abiy Abebe further indicated that 'law and order' would soon prevail in Eritrea.[5] By 'law and order', Wilson was obviously referring to the imminent termination of Eritrea's federal status.

In the meantime, Asfaha made one more attempt to salvage his reputation. The Assembly was so pleased by Sékou Touré's visit, he claimed, that many proposed to meet for an hour and vote to terminate the Federation while the Emperor was still in Eritrea. An excited Asfaha took the matter directly to Abiy and together they told Haile Selassie: 'The Assembly is resolute, allow us to terminate the Federation.' Rather than act on impulse, Haile Selassie referred the matter to Aklilu, whose response was predictable. 'If the Federation is abrogated while you are in Asmera, it will appear as if you imposed it yourself. This will expose you to international criticism.' He rejected the request.

Frustrated, Asfaha complained to Abiy that Aklilu's previous objections had put a stop to his earlier attempts to accomplish at leisure what was now being furtively rushed through. Abiy urged him not to hold a grudge against Aklilu, as the latter genuinely believed that the termination of the Federation would create a major internal and external problem for Ethiopia. 'You and I believe that, if Ethiopia's internal unity is consolidated, it will enable us to confront the enemy. Only the future and history will judge who, *Tsehafe Te'ezaz* or we, is right in our contentions.'[6]

Asfaha was not the only person losing patience with Aklilu's line of reasoning. When the Emperor returned to Addis Ababa, he formed a committee that included Abiy, also doubling as the Interior Minister; Merid Mengesha of Defence; Abebe Retta of Health; and Yilma Deressa of Finance. Aklilu, who was the chairman, impressed upon the members that the abolition of the Federation would not strengthen the attachment of Eritreans to an Ethiopian identity. Abebe Retta even scoffed at Asfaha when he said, 'People who dream that Eritreans will feel more Ethiopian when the autonomy granted to them is abrogated suffer from lack of thought and reason.'[7]

In the wake of this latest Aklilu veto, Asfaha and Dimetros collected the signatures of 'all Assembly members' and handed them to Abiy. On 13 November, Abiy flew secretly to Addis Ababa where, according to Asfaha, he conferred for two hours alone with the Emperor. The latter gave his permission for the abolition. Neither Aklilu nor his committee nor the cabinet was made party to this development. It was all sealed between Asfaha, Abiy and Haile Selassie.[8]

Asfaha's claim that every Assembly member signed the document that Abiy took to Haile Selassie is contested by several people. Gebreyohannes agrees that, indeed, a majority had been made to sign at the Palace by consent or coercion. Although he could not give the exact number, he knew that several members refused to comply. In an interview Habtu Tesfamikael, the Massawa representative, produced his Assembly documents and notes of the days leading to 14 November as evidence that not every Assembly member collaborated with Asfaha and Dimetros in their secret machinations. The Assembly reports for 2–14 November reveal the following entries and Assembly activities:

- Friday, 2 November: Assembly reopens after recess and wishes the Emperor a long life and full health on his birthday (the same day, 23 Tikimt, Geez calendar). Adjournment for 5 November. Hamid Ferej has not returned after the Akurdet bomb incident.
- Monday, 5 November: Dimetros presiding. Assembly receives General Auditor's report, new laws and amendments on tax collection, amnesty regulation, and forestry and justice administration.[9] Discussion set for 7 November.[10]
- November 7 meeting postponed for lack of quorum.
- Saturday, 10 November: 46 members present on this date; 21 absent (one member, Mehari Fre of Aba Shawl having died in the interim, the Assembly was reduced to 67 members). Proposal on collection of taxes approved. Committee elected to deal with remaining issues; Werede Beyin, chairman. Adjourned till 12 November.
- 12 November meeting postponed for lack of quorum.
- Tuesday, 13 November: 54 in attendance, Dimetros still in the chair. Long discussion before approval of amendments to the taxation and amnesty legislations. A heated discussion on amendment to the administration of justice bill ends in a deadlock. Assembly adjourns to discuss the issue the following day, 14 November.[11]

On 14 November, *Zemen* reported that Habtu Tesfamikael and three other colleagues had been most active in the debates of the previous day. He himself later recalled that, as far as he knew, the Assembly returned the next day to continue the discussions. His handwritten notes in the margins of the 14 November Assembly agenda show that he was unprepared for what was about to happen later in the morning. The same could be said of his colleagues who joined him in the discussions of 13 November.[12]

According to Asfaha, he did not accompany Abiy both when the latter attended Aklilu's committee and in his private consultation with Haile Selassie on 13 November. Many sources, especially ELF publications, counter-claim that Asfaha,

Dimetros and Tedla Ukbit were summoned to Addis Ababa on 13 November and were specifically ordered to terminate the Federation the next day. This contradicts Asfaha's testimony that only Abiy made the trip and consulted with the Emperor. The Eritrean leaders may well have been summoned and instructed, but no documentary evidence exists to verify this.

We add two more significant remarks about the days leading to 14 November. By the end of the Assembly meeting on 13 November, the number in attendance climbed to 56, as members calling in sick or 'in mourning' were dragged into the Assembly one by one by police and security personnel. The second point relates to the heavy presence and intimidating behaviour of Ethiopian troops on the streets of Asmera. According to Dawit Weldegiorgis, a young officer in command of an army unit stationed on the outskirts of Asmera:

> One week before the vote, my battalion, the 34th, was ordered to march through the city and to camp outside until four days after the vote. I co-commanded one of the companies that ringed Asmera during that time. It was clear from our orders that we were there in case of any trouble from the Assembly or the people. In addition to our battalion, the entire police force, the air force and a detachment of infantry from another part of Ethiopia were all on hand, making their presence felt by marching through the streets and generally being as visible as possible.[13]

On the evening of 13 November, units of the Ethiopian army in full military gear spread throughout Asmera chanting, 'A bullet to anyone who resists.' Asmera residents still remember the fear that the Ethiopian war-chant and the threatening demeanour of the troops instilled in them that night.

The Day of Annexation

In the words of Enrico Mania, the tension on Asmera streets on the morning of 14 November was stretched so thin that one 'could cut it with scissors'. Ethiopian troops with machine guns patrolling the streets in army jeeps 'looked like the conquerors of an enemy city. On every corner, metre by metre, were stationed helmeted agents of the police, guns in hand. The concentration was thickest on the street leading to the Assembly building. The atmosphere gave no hint of a joyous occasion.'[14] By 9.30, most Assembly members had passed through the patrols and checkpoints to take up their seats. Arriving with them were selected guests and Eritrean and Ethiopian government officials, who, according to Asfaha, had no idea why they had been summoned. Some suspected that Asfaha would be elevated to the rank of *ras bitweded*, take over Abiy's post, and give way to the election of a new Chief Executive. Others surmised that the discovery of oil in Eritrea was to be announced.[15]

Several Assembly members have sworn that they had no prior knowledge of the day's agenda. Asfaha's claim that every member was there in full knowledge and with full consent is, therefore, contested. His other contention that all members were present is also not supported by the evidence. Assembly records of the day show that, of the 67 members, 60 were in attendance. Many of them had to be escorted there by the police. Ibrahim Mohammed, well-known football referee and Assembly employee, confirmed that he physically fetched an ailing member from his home in the suburbs of Asmera and carried him up the stairs to the Assembly chamber.[16] President Hamid Ferej excused himself at the last moment with a note to Asfaha telling him, 'Suddenly I was attacked by a sharp pain to my side last night. I may not be there in person, but I am with you in spirit.'[17]

At 10.40, Asfaha, his six cabinet secretaries, Tedla Ukbit and other dignitaries entered the hall. Asfaha immediately began to speak. 'We Eritreans do not know the culture and name of this word "federation". This word does not exist among us as a name or an act. It is rather the evil instrument and destructive dose of poison of external enemies who are attempting to disrupt our unity, block our progress to development and arrest our patriotic zeal.' He stressed that, in view of its alien nature and its harmful effects, the people had been demanding an end to its existence. 'When I present to you the following motion, it is with the belief that as advocates of your people's wishes and nationalist sentiments ... you will approve it with a unanimous vote.' The motion proposed to 'remove and dispose of the name and practice of "federation" from us' and to declare that 'from today forward, we have completely merged into the Administration of our mother, Ethiopia'.[18]

Enrico Mania was the only outside observer present to record his impressions. Asfaha's speech, he wrote, was delivered in an 'imperceptible voice, as if he were praying in secret'. As soon as he finished, before the members even had time to express shock or fear, thunderous applause from the back, where the invited dignitaries were seated, engulfed the hall. It was so loud and rousing that members joined in. Noting that it was a pre-planned stunt to give the appearance of a vote by acclamation, Mania continued: 'The Assembly disposed of the flag, arms and seal of Eritrea by an applause. Applause has grown into an escape from individual responsibility to a collective vote. The Federation that had come at the price of so much violence and difficult negotiations thus ended with one applause, its last breath.'[19]

No formal vote was taken. No one was given the chance to question the legality of the act. Dimetros rejoiced at the elimination of the 'cobweb' that had blurred the vision between brothers. He told members that their acclamation would occupy the first page of their country Ethiopia's annals. He praised God and wished Haile Selassie one thousand more years of sovereign rule. Asfaha gave his concluding remarks: 'We are Ethiopia's head, not its foot. Everything originated with us. We cannot live as an appendage to Ethiopia. Our guarantors are our Ethiopian identity and His Majesty, our Emperor.'[20] With that, he led his entourage of invited guests to a champagne party with Abiy at the Palace.

In 1974, this writer asked *Fitawrari* Yehdego Gebrerufael, representative from Seraye, about the vote by acclamation. He replied:

> I am an old blind man now. Half of my body is already in the grave. I will not lie to you. I had no prior knowledge of Asfaha's agenda on that day. I did not sign any petition for union either. When Asfaha said full union was put into effect, we did not vote. One or two applauded out of fear. Armed soldiers flanked us on both sides and escorted us out of the Assembly hall like a flock of sheep and we scattered to our respective homes.[21]

In 1987, in Kassala, *Sheik* Omer Adem Idris of Barka was asked the same question. He gave a similar reply: 'Asfaha did not put the motion to a vote. Because we were totally confused, we did not even clap, let alone vote. Asfaha's entourage, the officials he invited, were the ones who applauded.'[22]

The next day, 15 November, Haile Selassie issued Order 27 of 1962 terminating the Federation and declaring the Ethiopian Constitution of 1955 the sole law of the land. Not a word of protest or disapproval was heard from the UN or the former Four Great Powers, the guarantors of the Federation. The Assembly, as we saw, was given no time to question the legality of the decision. The only sound of opposition was the faint shots being heard from the fledgling ELF in the western lowlands. They would soon grow louder.

In 1960, the former British political officer in Eritrea, G.K.N. Trevaskis, suggested that 'the temptation to subject Eritrea firmly under her control will always be great' for Ethiopia. He advised, however, that it should desist from falling for that lure, as Eritrean discontent and eventual revolt would affect 'the future of the Federation, and indeed of the whole group of young countries in North East Africa'.[23] Trevaskis's words are often hailed as prophetic by those who believe that the abrogation of the Federation led to the Eritrean revolution. As we have seen, thirteen years earlier, in November 1949 Ibrahim Sultan told the UN committee examining the Eritrean issue that forcing Eritrea to accept a federal solution against its will would lead to an Eritrean uprising for independence with major consequences for the region

Unlike Trevaskis, Ibrahim did not fear a possible Ethiopian abrogation of the Federation, an outcome he and his party took for granted even before its implementation. On the contrary, his objection was to the very idea of the ill-designed and lopsided Federation itself, which he and the whole Independence Bloc saw as an imposition on the people of Eritrea and as a denial of their right to self-determination. He opposed the complete disregard shown to Eritrean nationalism and its subjection to a forced Ethiopian identity and to the interests of regional and international powers.

The political struggles of the people of Eritrea throughout the federal period show that the UN 'federal solution' merely intensified the previous political struggle for independence and helped Eritreans identify themselves as victims of an unfinished process of decolonisation on the African continent. Eritrea's annexation by Ethiopia was thus anticipated. In 1960, when Trevaskis published his book, Haraka was already giving way to the more militant ELF. In 1961, Awate launched the Eritrean armed struggle for independence, and his units already began engaging with the Eritrean police and the Ethiopian army during 1962. By the time of Ethiopia's hasty dissolution of the Federation on 14 November, the ELF had virtually consolidated its leadership of the armed struggle, and the liberation war was already afoot. The argument that Eritreans took up arms because the Ethiopian Government made the mistake of terminating the Federation is thus groundless. It is a misconception that still misleads writers and scholars, mainly Ethiopians and expatriates touting that line, into believing that if the Federation were to be revived, Eritreans would 'come back' to the Ethiopian fold. It was the Federation itself that was at issue, not the manner of its dissolution. That is why the armed rebellion preceded the Federation's abolition.

Finally, an anecdote: *Azmatch* Mirach Gudum, *mislene* of Liban, a well-known wit, was visiting his daughter in Godaif, Asmera, when he received news of the 14 November event in the Assembly. 'Today,' he said, 'Ethiopia has swallowed something it can neither retain nor digest—a ball of black riverbed stone—lomi ityoPya xelim emni ruba wHiTa.'[24] This became one of the most memorable quips on Ethiopia's self-destructive folly in Eritrea.

The Days After

Public Reaction to Annexation

Asmera and, indeed, the whole of Eritrea received the annexation with deafening silence. Being a long-anticipated move, it could not arouse them to spontaneous protest. The threatening demeanour of Ethiopian troops and the low-flying fighter planes on the previous days may also have bullied them into silence. In Addis Ababa, Eritrean members of the Ethiopian parliament must have gathered every ounce of courage when they unanimously condemned the annexation as a violation of a UN resolution. They argued that, rather than abolishing the Federation, Ethiopia should have adopted the model for the remaining thirteen Ethiopian provinces.[25]

Former Eritrean students of the University College of Addis Ababa and Haile Selassie School recall different forms of protest staged by themselves on the days following 14 November. None of these resulted in any major disturbance or any government response. Such passivity in the face of a major transgression by Ethiopia frustrated many Haraka activists, including Kahsai Bahlibi, still languishing in prison. Calls from him and others for some form of protest prompted the Haraka leadership in Port Sudan to send one of its top men, Musa Araho, to organise a demonstration for late December, a little over a month after the annexation. Even though it was certain to fail and despite the likely repercussions, it was thought worth the attempt.[26] Weldemikael Abraha and Nur Abdelhai prepared placards reading, 'Free Eritrea or death!' and calling for UN intervention and popular uprisings, as well as flyers for distribution to the public. Foreign consuls in Asmera were informed of the impending demonstration. The defunct Eritrean flag was also collected in great numbers to be used as the rallying symbol of the protest.

The demonstration itself, which was planned to catch security forces unawares, was stopped by police in plainclothes before it could even cover half the length of Asmera's Haile Selassie (today's Liberation) Avenue. The secret had been leaked and the main organisers, along with dozens of participants, were arrested and jailed.[27] As they awaited their fate, Tedla Ukbit visited them in prison, an encounter all of them recall as highly puzzling. Teklai Gebreselassie (Haraka) described the incident as follows:

> One day, Tedla Ukbit came to the prison and assembled us. 'Why do you choose to place yourselves in jeopardy?' he asked us. 'Where are the big shots who said they would support you? They are now collecting villas and concession farms. You should have told me of your plans. I would have told you what was possible and what was not. You suffered for having not done so. But now, I am setting you free.' He released us with no mention of Ethiopia or Haile Selassie. We had to leave the prison premises physically to believe what he had said.[28]

The Fate of Tedla Ukbit

Tedla Ukbit's post-Federation behaviour deserves some explanation. Throughout the federal period, he had served Ethiopia with characteristic efficiency, dedication and hard work, but always with his highly limited knowledge of the culture and political skills of the Amhara. Barely three weeks after the termination of the Federation, 'when the cheers and tears had subsided' as his secretary Kinfe recalled, former federal officials who had once feared him and approached him with apprehension started to adopt airs of superiority and treat him as a provincial officer with no special status. Taking this as gross interference, he started to disobey direct commands from Addis Ababa and engaged in highly charged arguments with his Ethiopian superiors over the phone.

Asfaha related another dimension of Tedla's predicament. After Federation, Haile Selassie assigned all the major unionists to various positions in Ethiopia and filled the Eritrean administration with former supporters or sympathisers of the Independence Bloc (IB). Tedla was particularly stung by the appointment of Tesfayohannes Berhe, nephew of IB leader *Ras* Tessema, as the Emperor's deputy representative. 'When we were voting for Ethiopia as our country, the Amhara were fixing their seats and power. How can they put Tesfayohannes, a *rabita* [Muslim Leaguer, i.e. Muslim convert], over us?' he told Asfaha upon the latter's appointment as Ethiopian Minister of Justice. Ignoring Asfaha's pleas to calm down, he started to attack the Emperor as 'an old man blinded by power' and to predict that Ethiopia's grave mistakes would lead Eritrea into dysfunction within a year.[29]

Anger led to spitefulness and interference in matters outside his range of duties. When the Emperor's representative, Abiy Abebe, allowed football teams to retain their old provincial names, Tedla banned all football games on the ground that they had become hotbeds of provincial sentiment.[30] His behaviour and work habits also lost their previous consistency. In May 1963, he ordered all police centres in Eritrea to stand ready, an order that lasted three weeks before being withdrawn. He gave no explanation for the directive.[31]

From this point on, his position became unsustainable. Tesfayohannes and his colleagues demanded his removal, a request that Haile Selassie approved. Abiy himself broke the news of his transfer to Addis Ababa, but Tedla would not comply. After shutting himself for several days in his office, he told his secretary, 'We thought we were benefiting our people but we threw them into deep trouble ... we have to correct our mistakes.'[32] He called a meeting of all his senior officers for 4 June 1963.

For days, Tedla refused to respond to Abiy's phone calls. Instead, on the eve of his scheduled meeting, he sent a telegram to all his puzzled provincial commanders in which he wrote: 'The Federation has not been abolished. We will continue with our former functions. Inform your troops and your people of this.' They complied while doubting his very sanity.[33]

The next morning, all senior police officers, including Colonels Zeremariam, Erdatchew and Yigzaw, assembled in the hall of the Asmera police headquarters, across the street from the Asmera Palace. Tedla Ukbit spoke at once:

> We, Eritrean Police, have served our people and governments for 22 years, 12 under the British and 10 under the Federation. During those years, we subjected our people to imprisonment and oppression. They tolerated us because we are their own kith and kin. They would not be as patient if we were alien.
>
> We, the Eritrean Police Force, have not accepted the decision of some 56 members of the Assembly who, by surpassing their mandate, have defeated the federal resolution that the UN put in place after their consultations with the people. From now on, I have decided to resume my functions in accordance with the UN's Federal Act. Please be advised that our people are not to be abused as before. I, General Tedla, will not tolerate any more games on my people. My honour is with my people. I have no honour outside of my people. Do not be afraid of being stripped of your rank. As for me, I have no regard for my status or rank. Relay my decision to your officers. Keep them in place and await my further orders.[34]

Tedla walked the three or so minutes to his office, told Kinfe what he had just done and locked himself in. Immediately, Abiy called out but Tedla would not respond. According to the records of the inquest, Colonel Erdatchew, commander of the Striking Force, hastened from the meeting to inform Abiy of the new development.[35]

Without delay, Abiy dispatched Colonel Kebede Yacob and an army unit to Tedla's office. Kinfe was witness to what followed next:

> Colonel Kebede, a crazy, talkative and conceited officer, came to my office shouting, 'Where is his office?' He bypassed me and burst open Tedla's office. He saw Tedla standing behind his desk with an Uzi pointed at him. He stumbled back in great panic. Colonel Mohammed Nasser was with me in my office and, as we wondered if Tedla was in his right mind, we heard the muffled shot of a firearm. 'Ha! The man just took his own life,' Mohammed Nasser said to me. 'Foolish Amhara, they don't know the kind of man he is!'
>
> Probably after having talked to Abiy by phone, Kebede Yacob came back to our office pushing Zeremariam and Colonel Adem Abdella in front of him. He also forced me to accompany them. When we entered Tedla's office, we found him lying on the floor with the Uzi on his side and a pistol in his hand.

The manner of Tedla's death is still the subject of controversy, with some believing that either Kebede Yacob or the army unit surrounding the headquarters shot him. None of those present at the scene would testify to this at the inquest. The police forensic expert and Dr Cesare Greppi, who recommended an autopsy, called it suicide. Tedla's family, especially his older brother Tewelde Ukbit, turned down the idea of an autopsy, also believing death had been self-inflicted.

Thus ended Tedla Ukbit's controversial life. He was only 39 at the time of his death. On 20 October 1963, a government inquest gave its verdict on Haile Selassie's former 'son' and favourite Eritrean: 'led by the vile notion of being responsible to his own authority alone, it has been confirmed that Brigadier General Tedla Ukbit took his own life by a decision all his own. From the Police CID investigation and the testimony of the medical experts, enough evidence has been gathered to prove that Brigadier General Tedla Ukbit committed suicide.'[36]

A terse report in *Zemen*, already renamed *Hebret* (Union), which did not cite Tedla's rank, announced his suicide a few days after the incident. Despite an official ban on attending his funeral, many of his colleagues and several dignitaries travelled to his native village, Adi Mengonti, to see off the man often considered the best police officer Eritrea has ever produced. He was a tragic figure who woke up too late to his country's predicament.

The Fates of Asfaha and Dimetros

Two months after the annexation, Haile Selassie appointed Asfaha to Minister of Justice; Dimetros, member of the Ethiopian Senate; Gebreyohannes, Minister of State at the Ministry of Posts, Telegraphs and Telephones; and Fessehatsion Haile, chairman of the board of Ethiopian Airlines. He then ordered their immediate transfer to Addis Ababa. Tesfayohannes, as we have seen, took over as Abiy's deputy. Later, in successive appointments, Dimetros was assigned to the management of the property of the Ethiopian Orthodox Church and to the post of *Nebure Ed* of Axum.

Of the four appointees, Fessehatsion turned the position down on the excuse that he had no qualification for a post that required technical knowledge. Reportedly, Haile Selassie praised Fessehatsion for his honesty and rewarded him with a seat in the Senate. By his own admission, Gebreyohannes spent the next four years going in and out of office with a lofty title but with no functions. 'At the office, I used to read newspapers the whole day,' he reminisced. 'It was worse outside. Eritreans received us with sharpened horns, dubbing us "sellers of our country". Our own compatriots subjected us to verbal abuse. *Bitweded* Asfaha's driver returned home because he too was subjected to harassment and got tired of wiping off Eritrean spit decorating the *bitweded*'s car.' In 1965, Gebreyohannes and Fessehatsion begged to return home as advisors to the new representative, Asrate Kassa. Old hands like Hamid Ferej, Ali Rad'ai and Ibrahim Humed Arey joined them in positions of obscurity.[37]

When their unexpected transfers were first announced in January 1963, they often met to try to understand Haile Selassie's thinking. Gebreyohannes's famous comment brought them close to understanding their new reality. 'It is logical,' he told them; 'those of us who fought for our country, Ethiopia, go to Ethiopia. Those who voted for Eritrea as their own [like Tesfayohannes] stay at home.' Even Asfaha, who said to Gebreyohannes, 'His Majesty told us we would stay here to manage the country; does a King lie?', was distressed. Gebreyohannes met Dimetros, who said to him, 'It is unbelievable; they gave their word that all of us would be retained in Eritrea. They even assured us that the Assembly would continue as an advisory body. There was nothing that was not promised.' They agreed that the whole problem emanated from the defective UN resolution, and that they could have done little outside its framework.[38]

The men who decided Eritrea's fate became the victims of their own emotions and misplaced nationalism and loyalties. Gebreyohannes may have spoken for all his like-minded unionists when he stood before the Ethiopian military junta, the Dergue, in the 1970s and boldly told them: 'Our slogan was "Ethiopia *or* death"; you brought us Ethiopia *and* death!' Along with Dimetros, Tesfayohannes and a host of other Eritrean officials of the federal period, Gebreyohannes languished in Ethiopian jails for at least seven years. Haregot Abbay was the only one of the group who was executed by the Dergue.

Asfaha spent less time in prison. In 1996, the bedridden, half-paralysed former Chief Executive talked at length with this writer. The highlights of that four-day interview are as follows:

Was there really no Imperial pressure on you to abolish the Federation?

Asfaha: I personally went to the Assembly, detailed our history and presented the proposal. General Abiy was never a man of intervention. There was no pressure. Dawit Weldegiorgis is a liar. He accused me before the Dergue of stalling on the termination of the Federation. He claimed that the people themselves had pushed for its finalisation. Here in Addis Ababa too, we were being harassed with similar charges. I am one who resents anyone telling me what to do ... I used to reply, 'It is the Assembly, not I that will decide.'

But it was not the Assembly but you who terminated the Federation.

Asfaha: I did not propose termination. I suggested it and asked for the Assembly's approval. Nobody opposed my suggestion ... Later, people tried to reconstruct events. Federation was of no use to us. Our concern was that it would lead to conflict between the two peoples.

But we did come into conflict, in spite of the annexation.

Asfaha: That came later. The Arabs did not want us to live with Ethiopia. The same with the Italians and other foreigners. The main issue was economics. Even today, leaving politics aside, I think there should be economic union. Ethiopia and we cannot live apart economically. That is what I said when I went to vote in the referendum. I said, 'I have always believed in my Eritrean identity. We are Ethiopia's head, not its foot. What has happened has happened. We now need to be watchful of what may follow from Sudan and other Arab countries. It worries me a lot. When we were in power and Nasser was sloganeering, there were those who followed him for religion, at the expense of their country. But I cannot stop Eritrea's independence.' That was what I said.

Did you have any reservations about the way the Federation was disposed of?

Asfaha: It is true that there was lack of capacity [*incapacità*] on the part of Ethiopia. When we came to them of our own will, they committed a big mistake. They should not have removed us. And Tedla Ukbit was politically short-sighted. His chief concern was the maintenance of his position. When I said to him, 'Why don't you congratulate me? I am now the Minister of Justice of Ethiopia,' he answered me, 'We, the wretched ones, fought for their country. When we came to them, he [the Emperor] said, "So you left your seat willingly? Give it to my son-in-law."'

I asked that he be transferred to Addis Ababa with us as Deputy Chief of Police of Ethiopia. They insisted that he was the only one who could keep order in Eritrea. But he was changing his mind from morning to evening. I advised him to take a flight to Addis Ababa and meet with the Emperor. He replied, 'They are not capable anymore,' and left me. Later, he assembled his officers and told them that the Federation had been revived. He went totally against everything that he had done and stood for.

Did you ever regret your role in the dissolution of the Federation, especially now that Eritrea is independent?

Asfaha: There was no time when I considered an alternative for the road I had chosen. It is true that, when we were told to move to Addis Ababa, we all said it was a wrong decision. They could have appointed other Eritreans. I said that what they did was exactly what *Dejazmatch* Abraha Tessema had predicted they would do. His Majesty used to hear me before, but he was getting old by then. I guess that what God willed to happen was inevitable.

The other mistake was staffing Eritrean positions with their own people. They should have thought about the people. When they did appoint Eritreans, they chose the likes of Tesfayohannes, a man who never fought for union. They ignored the old unionists and people did not accept the new officials. In reality, the Emperor was degenerating. Omer Qadi and I never liked each other. But a year after I left, he wrote to the Emperor asking him to reassign me in Eritrea. 'The country is going to ruins' is what he told him. But the Emperor was ageing. Energetic men like Asrate Kassa fed him with rosy pictures of Eritrea which he readily believed. And Aklilu Habtewold was a weak man. He kept Asrate in Eritrea to keep him away from Addis Ababa, where he was his competitor for the premiership. And Asrate kept messing Eritrea up. It was wrong for us to be removed from Eritrea.

Eritrea is free now. What are your thoughts?

Asfaha: May whatever you are planning benefit the people of Eritrea, especially the poor. Governments will come and fall; may the people be blessed; may they find peace. May peace and harmony also descend upon you all. Have faith; lean on God. Ours are a people of faith and religion; respect their beliefs. But the main thing is peace. May the Almighty help you procure peace for the people.

One last question. Many people say that you voted no for independence at the referendum in 1993. How do you respond to them?

Asfaha: Listen, we called for union because we thought that that was what our people wanted. This was what we heard the people say wherever we went. Everywhere, in private and in huge rallies collectively. Especially in the *metahit*. They gave General Abiy and me swords, shields, camels and horses as presents, including the day someone threw bombs at us. The same reception and more was accorded the Emperor. I genuinely believed that to have been the people's will.

We could never in our time think of undertaking the kind of struggle that your generation has just gone through. It could never occur to me that the people of Eritrea would fight for thirty years, pay the sacrifices that they have paid, and emerge victorious. That was outside my range of imagination.

To tell you the truth, I still pain over the separation, especially economic. I don't support that. But who am I to deny the people of Eritrea the freedom that they have earned through so much struggle and sacrifice? I cannot say that to them.

Does it mean that you did not vote no?

Asfaha: I put the card where it belonged.

It was not no?

Asfaha: It was not no.

EPILOGUE

A NOTE ON THE HISTORY OF THE ARMED STRUGGLE FOR INDEPENDENCE

Anything that we can say on the history of the Eritrean revolution, especially the armed struggle for independence, can only be brief, cursory and tentative. At present, Eritrea's revolutionary history is still dominated by contesting narratives, punctuated by partisan and polemical language. The rhetoric of the old revolutionary organisations and their legacy still dictate, not only the historical narratives, but also a great part of Eritrean life and thinking, wherever Eritreans may be. Many of the main actors of the period are still alive and in positions of influence, thus ensuring continuity and sensitivity. Anecdotes about military events and revolutionary accomplishments abound; but the internal dynamics, contradictions and resolutions, advances and retreats, successes and defeats that defined the process still remain shrouded in mystery or are locked up in documents. With the passage of time and the gradual passing away of veterans who could shed light on important aspects of the struggle, historians have dabbled in speculation or built on scanty and unsubstantiated information mostly derived from memory. Adding to the confusion will not benefit the quest for a definitive history of that monumental process.

History is best served when the context within which it takes place is given due consideration. Hindsight or retrospective judgements often result in conflicting narratives that disrupt the flow of history and confuse later generations. The tendency to denounce the other point of view both at the individual and organisational levels did not start with the Eritrean revolution. We recall how, in the 1940s, the intolerance of the Unionist Party (UP) shown towards the independence movement created a toxic political atmosphere in which harassment and physical violence replaced the more moderate and conciliatory politics of earlier in the decade.

Haraka's nationalistic programme and its impressive success in ensuring diversity in its hundreds of clandestine cells seemed to reintroduce dialogue and civility into the independence movement. But the group of exiles who snatched the initiative for an armed struggle away from the vacillating Haraka were an amorphous body with different backgrounds and orientations in contrast with Haraka's more closely knit leadership.

By any standard, the ELF's initiative was a momentous event that took the political struggle to its highest and final form. However, two vital omissions were to affect the progress of the revolution itself. First, the ELF saw itself, not as an evolution or rectification of Haraka, but as its negation, its antithesis. Dubbing Haraka 'communist and anti-religion', it took upon itself the responsibility of sabotaging and, later, virtually destroying Haraka. Losing Haraka's nationalistic and inclusive base left a significant number of its active members out in the cold. It also reinforced the trend within the Eritrean revolution in which dialogue and the accommodation of other points of view became intolerable. Second, in its rush to announce the armed struggle, the leadership gave no time to charting their course towards that objective. Unlike Haraka, which had at least a theoretical road map leading to a coup d'état, the ELF had no defined strategy, philosophy or definite programme.

This point was of more immediate consequence. In the early stages, the ELF's looseness, both in its political principles and organisational structure and discipline, led to the creation of five mutually competing divisions within its fighting forces, roughly representing the ethnic, religious and regional diversity in the country. It was a testing period that threatened to shake Eritrean nationalism to its foundations. In 1967, a reform movement by nationalist and progressive individuals and groups attempted to rectify the situation by calling for an end to the divisions in favour of a united revolutionary army. The defeat of the movement in 1969 led to the emergence of a junta-type group that went on a rampage of repression of its critics and opponents, a move that resulted in the splintering of the ELF.

In the early 1970s, the ELF attempted to purge itself of the old elements of division and re-emerge as a nationalist organisation with an integrated revolutionary army. In the meantime, former ELF splinter groups began working towards a merger that would result in the formation of the Eritrean People's Liberation Forces (later Front) in 1973.

A more testing time both for Eritrean nationalism and for the survival of the revolution itself came when, announcing in a congress of 1972 that Eritrea could only contain one liberation organisation, the ELF set out to destroy the factions of the popular force, thus inaugurating a three-year-long civil war. Considering Eritrea's small population, characterised by an intricate network of kinship ties, the conflict inevitably divided families and pitted siblings against each other. Remarkably, however, the general population refrained from joining in the violence, choosing instead to cross political lines in a persistent call for an end to the war through dialogue and unity. In that sense, the term 'civil war' is a misnomer, as the armed violence never spilled over to involve the people whom the fronts claimed to represent.

Although the war ended in 1975, the bitterness of the experience, and an ever-widening gap in the two fronts' approaches to practically every aspect of the liberation agenda, virtually shut out all possibility of unity. Led by a clandestine

Labour Party that was not so clandestine, the ELF attempted to marry a traditional and conservative leadership with a loose base of conflicting, at times even mutually exclusive, interests. The EPLF, on the other hand, rallied around an effectively clandestine Eritrean People's Revolutionary Party (EPRP) led by a closely knit leadership and a network of strict control over the political, military and social life of the EPLF. Through party cells planted in every unit of the EPLF, the leadership was able to instil a culture of strict discipline, self-sacrifice, self-reliance and the subordination of personal values and desires to those of the collective.

By 1980, the contradictions between the two fronts had reached serious levels of mutual intolerance. In a second round of civil war, the ELF was defeated, disbanded and pushed out of Eritrea a year later. After some ineffective attempts at a military comeback, the ELF succumbed to the internal divisions that had plagued its previous existence and disintegrated into dozens of splinter organisations in exile, each claiming to represent the front. Today, they form part of a fractured diaspora consisting of scores of competing and squabbling opposition groups that have so far failed to pose any meaningful threat to what the EPLF represented and still represents. With the disintegration of the ELF, its history has also fallen into neglect.

The ELF's defeat enabled the EPLF to mould the Eritrean revolution to its nationalist perceptions and principles. Thus, sectarianism of all forms and descriptions was decisively confronted. Religion was considered a matter for the individual, but open expressions of religion were discouraged, if not suppressed. Equality between different languages was manifested in the principle of mother tongue education, still practised over thirty years after independence. All the linguistic and ethnic groups within the front were actively encouraged to develop their own cultures and traditions. The Front's women fighters, who constituted one-third of its membership and a significant percentage of its active combatants and martyrs, were able to open a new chapter in the global fight for gender equality. Uniformity in thinking and conformity to the EPLF's political and military strategy were ensured through continuous political education and criticism and self-criticism sessions to check any possible deviants and deviations. Although a top-down and bottom-up hierarchy was strictly observed and enforced, it was rendered imperceptible by an atmosphere of congeniality and camaraderie between higher-level cadres and the rank and file.

The success of the EPLF lay in its ability to inculcate into the minds of its membership a sense of ownership of everything that it stood for. The leadership's ability to reach out through the party's cells to the smallest and remotest units of the front enabled it to disseminate, gather and control information as it saw fit. Potential political or military crises and setbacks were dispelled through the same lines, sometimes well before they even happened. Obedience to the organisation's rules and orders also became instinctive—'duty first, questions later' was one of the first dictums that a fighter learned in the training camps. This unlikely mix of a sense of ownership with the strict discipline of obedience led to the development of a culture of voluntary submission to authority, whereby fighters developed an aversion to waiting for orders and commands to accomplish a task. The legendary race to martyrdom, 'I go first, you wait', which fascinated the general population, can be attributed to this habit, bolstered by an embedded sense of righteousness and patriotism.

Of great consequence to the writing of the history of the armed struggle was the parallel culture of secrecy and silence, which was also the hallmark of the EPLF's manner of doing things. Information within the organisation was a highly rationed commodity disseminated in accordance with the needs of its various sections. Along with this developed a culture of silence over organisational, departmental and, particularly, individual matters. Talking about oneself, especially discussing one's own role, big or small, in a positive way, was considered boastful and dealt with accordingly. To the extent that this ensured the paramountcy of the collective over the individual, it fitted in well with the EPLF's creed that the masses should take credit for major historical feats and events.

That culture of silence and secrecy is similar to the adherence of police officers of the federal period to the British Official Secrets Act. When this writer pleaded with Colonels David Cracknell, Alem Mammo, Yigzaw Beraki and Berhane Demoz for inside information on police dealings in their time, they invoked the Act as a lifelong commitment, refusing to divulge sixty- to seventy-year-old secrets. A similar commitment to the demands of secrecy about the days of the armed struggle still prevents former fighters, especially commanders of the EPLF, from discussing the more telling or controversial aspects of the front's experiences. The result is that most of the published stories are restricted to anecdotes and reminiscences about specific military or social events that concentrate on the extreme conditions of the struggle and the ultimate sacrifices paid in the quest for independence. Although this forms a core part of the story, it falls far short of satisfying the requirements of a comprehensive history.

The result is that Eritrea's history of the war of independence has become hostage to unresearched works. Apart from a few attempts based on studies inside Eritrea, which shed some light on the period despite the constraints discussed above, most histories are of limited scope and depth.[1] The virtual absence of memoirs written by major figures of the revolution, many of whom have now died, has created a gap in a narrative that already suffers from the scourges of time and memory.[2] History demands thorough research and objectivity. In this age of unhinged social media discourse, imagination and hindsight judgements are obliterating truth and reality. True, there cannot be only one truth or one version of history. But whatever is printed in the name of history needs to be substantiated by credible and incontrovertible evidence—its absence is a glaring gap in most of the written or spoken narratives that clutter the print and the social media.

In the meantime, disparagement of the people, history and culture of Eritrea continues to dominate in conferences, scholarly journals and media outlets, where the Eritrean point of view is rarely, if ever, represented. In 2001, at the end of the 1998–2000 war with Ethiopia, Christopher Clapham, arguing that Eritrean nationalism was an imposition from above, wrote the following: 'As a small, poor, artificial and ethnically fragmented territory, all of whose major population groups spill over its frontiers, Eritrea has always been potentially subject to centrifugal forces, from which it has been protected since independence by an awareness of its military strength. The abrupt collapse of the myth of Eritrean invincibility leaves it in a very vulnerable position.'[3] In 2015, Alex de Waal, whose work focuses on developments in the Horn of Africa, wrote that the survival of Eritrean nationalism was attributable to three factors—'a militarized political culture', 'diasporic and online political "imaginaries"'; and 'obsession with the leader, Isaias Afewerki', after whose departure De Waal expects Eritrea to disintegrate.[4]

The mere dismissal of such catchy and quotable phraseology as unfounded has little effect. They do shape opinions, especially when left unchallenged by fact-based counter-evidence. This book has attempted to tell a crucial part of Eritrea's history. Care has been taken to avoid emotional responses to the type of arbitrary and dismissive judgements quoted above or to becoming involved in the polemics that they invite. This book is mainly about facts, personalities, events and the ever-changing political life of the nation and people. It is especially about the people who, contrary to these and similar opinions, have always maintained a balance between political differences and strife, on the one hand, and dialogue, on the other, by adhering to their ties of kinship, culture and history that cut across ethnic, religious and regional divides, in order to sustain the unity of the country and the base on which Eritrean nationalism has thrived.

It is time that the history of the armed struggle for Eritrean independence holds its own in the historical narratives of Africa. It is a struggle that had to overcome unimaginable odds—division, failure, retreat and international alienation—to attain the ultimate goal of independence. A war of independence is never entirely smooth, rational or blameless. One of the major successes of the EPLF was its acknowledgement and correction of mistakes and excesses. This always went side by side with its iron discipline, enforced by an egalitarian culture and air-tight secrecy.

The rules need to change now. Independence and nationalism, as we are witnessing in our own region, are not a done deal, secured or recognized once and for all. They need nurturing, buttressing and attuning to the times. Eritrea and its people have performed miracles that the world needs to know about. Hopefully, this book may help in achieving just that.

NOTES

PREFACE

1. Bairu Tafla and E. Schmidt, *Discovering Eritrea's Past*, Verlag J.H. Röll, Dettelbach, 2016, p. 17.

INTRODUCTION

1. Alemseged Abbay, *Identity Jilted*, Red Sea Press, Lawrenceville, NJ, 1998, pp. 222–3.
2. Shumet Sishagne, *Unionists and Separatists: The Vagaries of Ethio-Eritrean Relations, 1941–1961*, Tshai Publishers, Hollywood, 2007, pp. 7–8.
3. Ibid., p. 116.
4. Ibid., p. 219.
5. Haggai Erlich, *Ethiopia and the Challenge of Independence*, Lynne Rienner, Boulder, CO, 1986, p. 215.
6. Christopher Clapham, *Transformation and Continuity in Revolutionary Ethiopia*, Cambridge University Press, Cambridge, 1988, p. 206.
7. Patrick Gilkes, 'National Identity and Historical Mythology in Eritrea and Somaliland', *Northeast African Studies*, 10, no. 3, 2003, p. 2.
8. Paul Henze, 'The Question of Eritrea', http://www.africangeopolitics.org/show.aspx?ArticleId=3063, accessed 15 Nov 2007. Henze suggested that Eritrean nationalism was a creation of 'Isaias Afewerki's Marxist EPLF'.
9. Eric Hobsbawm, *Nations and Nationalism since 1870: Program, Myth, Reality*, Cambridge University Press, Cambridge, 1990, pp. 8–10.
10. E. H. Carr, *The New Society*, Beacon Press, Boston, 1951, pp. 2–3.
11. Christopher Clapham, 'War and State Formation in Ethiopia and Eritrea', Paper given at Failed States Conference, Florence, 10–14 April 2001.
12. For details on precolonial Eritrea, see Bairu Tafla and E. Schmidt, *Discovering Eritrea's Past*, Verlag J.H. Röll, Dettelbach, 2016, pp. 66–9 and Appendix II, p. 199; Stephen Longrigg, *A History of Eritrea*, Oxford University Press, Oxford, 1945, pp. 77–83, pp. 103ff; Richard Pankhurst, *The Ethiopian Borderlands: Essays in Regional History from Ancient Times to the End of the 18th Century*, Red Sea Press, Lawrenceville, NJ, 1997, p. 414; Richard Reid, *War in Pre-colonial Eastern Africa*, British Institute in Eastern Africa, London, 2007, p. 84.

13. See Yishak Yosief, *Embiyale Woldu Gomida: Tarik Raesi Weldemikael*, MBY Printing Press, Asmera, 1999; *Negsnet Hagere Medri Bahri (Ertra), Tarik Degyat Hailu Aba Gala*, Semhar Printing Press, Asmera, 2000, for details of the invasions.
14. Bairu and Schmidt, *Discovering Eritrea's Past*, Appendix II, p. 199.
15. Zemhret Yohannes, *Italyawi Megza'eti ab Ertra*, Hidri Publishers, Asmera, 2010, p. 83. The battles of Gundet (November 1975) and Gura'e (March 1976) against the Egyptians; Kufit (September 1885) against the dervishes of Sudan; Dogali (January 1885), Koatit (January 1895) and Senafe (January 1895) against Italy, were all fought inside Eritrea.
16. For details on Weldemikael Solomon, see Yishak Yosief, *Embiyale Woldu Gomida*.
17. Ibid., pp. 106–8.
18. Isaiah Berlin, *The Crooked Timber of Humanity*, Vintage, New York, 1990, p. 245.
19. Zemhret, *Italyawi Megza'eti*, pp. 64–9.
20. For details of the process and impact of the Italian land confiscation policy, see ibid., pp. 102–11. For a discussion on land rights in *kebessa*, see Alemseged Tesfai, 'Communal Land Ownership in Northern Ethiopia and Its Implications for Government Policy', Land Tenure Center, University of Wisconsin, Madison, 1973, pp. 6–14.
21. Yishak Yosief, *Embiyale Woldu Gomida*, pp. 219–20; for a biography of Bahta Hagos, see Gebremikael Germu, *Deggiat Bahta Hagos Segeneiti*, MBY Printing Press, Asmera, 1997.
22. For attempts to rationalise Menelik's 'abandonment' of Eritrea, see Harold Marcus, *The Life and Times of Menelik: Ethiopia, 1844–1913*, Red Sea Press, Lawrenceville, NJ, 1975, p. 176; Bahru Zewde, *A History of Modern Ethiopia, 1855–1991*, James Currey, Oxford, 1991, pp. 12, 113.
23. Marcus, *Life and Times of Menelik*, p. 173. The exact number of casualties in the war vary from estimate to estimate. Wikipedia, quoting Abdusalam Ahmed and Richard Pankhurst, gives the following detailed figures for Italian and Eritrean losses: 6,394 killed, 1,428 wounded and 3,000 captured.
24. A.B. Wylde, *Modern Abyssinia*, 1901, p. 214, quoted in Wikipedia, 'The Battle of Adwa'; Afewerk Gebreyesus, *Dagmawi Atse Menelik*, Rome, 1901 (i.e. 1909), pp. 102–6; Chris Prouty, *Empress Taitu and Menelik II*, Red Sea Press, Trenton, NJ, 1986, pp. 158–9.
25. Raymond Jonas, *The Battle of Adwa: African Victory in the Age of Empire*, The Belknap Press, Cambridge, MA, 2011, p. 237.
26. Ruffillo Perini, *Mereb Mellash (Di qua dal Marèb)*, Tigrinya translation by Vittorio Roncali, Roberto Chiaramonte, Turin, 1997, pp. 24–5.
27. For details of Menelik–Italian collusion against Eritrean rebellion, see Yishak Gebreyesus, *Kidanat Menelikn Talyann ab Mchiflaq Hzbi Ertra, 1897–1907*, MBY, Asmera, 1998.
28. Ibid., pp. 18–20; Zemhret, *Italyawi Megza'eti*, pp. 71–2.
29. G.K.N. Trevaskis, *Eritrea: A Colony in Transition, 1941–1952*, Oxford University Press, Oxford, 1960, p. vii.

30. Bairu Tafla, 'Interdependence through Independence: The Challenges of Eritrean Historiography', in *New Trends in Ethiopian Studies*, ed. Harold Marcus, Red Sea Press, Lawrenceville, NJ, pp. 502, 509.
31. The earliest written law of the *kebessa* is the Higgi Logo Chiwa of the early sixteenth century. The Ser'at Adkeme Melega'e of Seraye; the Adgna Tegeleba of Akeleguzai; the various laws of Hamasien (Habslus-Geremeskel, Shew'ate Anseba, Dembezan, to name a few); the still operative Fithi Megarih and Mehari of the Keren region; and the centuries-old codified laws of the Afar, are some of the codes for the country. For details of selected Eritrean customary laws, see Alemseged Tesfai, *Conflict Resolution in Eritrea*, IGAD Capacity Assessment Study, CPMR in Eritrea, 2001.
32. Berlin, *The Crooked Timber of Humanity*, p. 145.
33. See Zemhret Yohannes, *Italyawi Megza'eti*, pp. 225–89.
34. Ibid., pp. 357–6.
35. Ibid., pp. 218–21.
36. Ibid., pp. 294–302.
37. Ibid., p. 313.
38. Uoldelul Chelati, 'Colonialism and the Construction of National Identities: The Case of Eritrea', *Journal of Eastern African Studies*, 1, no. 2, 2007, pp. 256–76.
39. Zemhret Yohannes, *Italyawi Megza'eti*, p. 314.
40. Ibid.
41. For an interesting analysis on the policy of ethnicity, religion and languages, see Uoldelul Chelati, 'Colonialism and the Construction of National Identities'.

1. THE BRITISH IN ERITREA

1. Richard Pankhurst, 'Italy and Ethiopia: The Emperor Rides Back', *African Quarterly Review*, 11, 1972, p. 45.
2. J. Westwood, *Greatest Battles of World War II*, Bison Group, Lincoln, NE, 1995, p. 60.
3. Ibid.
4. Ibid.
5. Ibid.
6. Colonel Orde Wingate was in charge of the offensive to enter Ethiopia through Galabat and General Cunningham led the forces into Somalia.
7. Westwood, *Greatest Battles of World War II*, pp. 46–7. According to this report, the 4th Division was particularly hard hit, losing nearly 3,000, including several battalion commanders. The number of dead was estimated at 530–550. For an informative section on the British campaign in Eritrea, see Srinath Raghavan, *India's War: World War II and the Making of Modern South Asia*, Basic Books, New York, 2016, pp. 103–21.
8. A. Bruttini and G. Puglisi, *L'Impero tradito*, La Fenice, Florence, 1957.
9. Enrico Mania, *Non solo cronaca dell'Acrocoro,* Stabilimento Fotoliti, Rome, 2005, p. 117.
10. Hailemariam Debena (later Eritrean Accountant General), interview, Asmera, 19 April 1997.

11. David Cracknell, interview, Bridport, May 2002.
12. G.K.N. Trevaskis, *Eritrea: A Colony in Transition, 1941–1952*, Oxford University Press, Oxford, 1960, p. 22.
13. Ibid., p. 21.
14. Weldeab Weldemariam, interview with Gebreselassie Yosef, Ararib, 1987.
15. Mania, *Non solo cronaca dell'Acrocoro*, pp. 120–1.
16. Ibid.
17. Sylvia Pankhurst, *British Policy in Eritrea*, Walthamstow Press, Woodward Green, n.d., pp. 3–4.
18. Estimates of the number of participants vary. Sylvia Pankhurst (ibid.) put it at 3,000–4,000. Weldeab and other participants gave numbers at least double those of Pankhurst.
19. Weldeab interview, 1987.
20. Ibid.
21. Trevaskis, *Eritrea*, p. 23.
22. Mania, *Non solo cronaca dell'Acrocoro*, p. 124.
23. Bollettino Ufficiale della Colonia Eritrea, 'Eritreo', 47,11, 15 Giugno, 1938.
24. Weldeab, interview, 1987.
25. Trevaskis, *Eritrea*, p. 36.
26. FO 371/31608, Stephen Longrigg, Six-Monthly Report on Occupied Enemy Territory, 30 June 1942.
27. FO 371/31608, 27 June 1942.
28. Ibid.
29. FO 196/5/42, 23 June 1942.
30. FO J1437/134/1, 28 February 1943.
31. For a detailed and sound analysis of the thinking behind the committee's proposals and related issues, see Okbazghi Yohannes, *Eritrea: A Pawn in World Politics*, University of Florida Press, Gainsesville, FL, 1991, pp. 60–4.
32. IES 2118, 21 June 1943.
33. FO 35414, 26 March 1943.
34. WO 230/168 71061, 15 June 1943.
35. G.K.N. Trevaskis, *The Deluge: A Personal View of the End of Empire*, I.B. Tauris Books, London, 2019, p. 66.
36. Ibid., p. 70.
37. Ibid., p. 107.
38. Ibid.
39. Ibid., p. 112.
40. Ibid., p. 113.

2. POLITICAL RUMBLINGS IN ERITREA, 1941–1945

1. G.K.N. Trevaskis, *Eritrea: A Colony in Transition, 1941–1952*, Oxford University Press, Oxford, 1960, p. 36.

2. UK Ministry of Information, *The First to Be Freed*, HMSO, London, 1944, pp. 20–1.
3. Stephen Longrigg, *A History of Eritrea*, Oxford University Press, Oxford, 1945, pp. 150–1.
4. Trevaskis, *Eritrea*, p. 38.
5. Sylvia Pankhurst, *British Policy in Eritrea*, Walthamstow Press, Woodward Green, n.d., p. 8.
6. Ibid.
7. IES, J3243/1/1, 24 July 1943.
8. Weldeab, interview, 1987.
9. Trevaskis, *Eritrea*, p. 51.
10. Longrigg, *History of Eritrea*, pp. 148–9.
11. Ibid., p. 151.
12. Ibid., p. 152.
13. G.K.N. Trevaskis, 'The Tribes and Peoples of Northern Eritrea', ch. 1, Trevaskis Papers.
14. Jonathan Miran, *Red Sea Citizens*, Indiana University Press, Bloomington, IN, 2009, p. 174.
15. Ibid., p. 180.
16. Ibid., p. 179.
17. Alberto Pollera, *Le popolazioni indigene dell'Eritrea*, L. Cappelli, Bologna, 1935 [*The Native Peoples of Eritrea*, English translation by Linda Lapin (unpublished)], pp. 119–20.
18. Ibid.
19. FPC Final Report, Appendix 18, IA Part 1.
20. Trevaskis, *The Deluge*, pp. 75–6.
21. For more on Mohammed Tahge, see J. Venosa, *Paths towards the Nation: Islam, Community and Early Nationalist Mobilization in Eritrea, 1941–1961*, Ohio University Press, Athens, OH, 2014, pp. 30ff.
22. Trevaskis, *The Deluge*, pp. 77–8.
23. Ibid.
24. Ibid.
25. Venosa, *Paths towards the Nation*, pp. 30–1.
26. Trevaskis, *The Deluge*, p. 78.
27. Ibid., p. 79.
28. Ibid.
29. Venosa, *Paths towards the Nation*, p. 30.
30. EPLF, 'Socio Economic Study of the Sahel Region', document (unpublished), 1985.
31. Ibid.
32. Venosa, *Paths towards the Nation*, p. 30.
33. Trevaskis, *Eritrea*, pp. 70–1.
34. IES, J3243/1/1, 24 July 1943.
35. Trevaskis, The Deluge, p. 70.
36. Trevaskis, *The Deluge*, p. 118.

37. Trevaskis, *Eritrea*, p. 71.
38. Trevaskis, *The Deluge*, p. 112.
39. Ibid., p. 113.
40. G. Puglisi, *Chi e dall'Eritrea? Dizionario biografico*, Agenzia Regina, Asmera, 1952, p. 281. Some of the disputes that Tessema was able to negotiate successfully included the bloody conflicts between the villages of Tche'alo and Mets'he (1922–3), Robra and Deki Admeqom (1929), and Toru'a and Tsen'adegle (1946), and the armed clashes between the people of eastern Seraye and the Assaorta in 1951.
41. Alemseged Abbay, *Identity Jilted*, Red Sea Press, Lawrenceville, NJ, 1998, p. 223.
42. Ibid., p. 43.
43. Ibid., p. 50.
44. Ibid., pp. 50–1.
45. Yishak Gebreyesus, *Kidanat Menelikn Talyann ab Mchiflaq Hzbi Ertra, 1897–1907*, MBY, Asmera, 1998, pp. 8–19, quoting Martini.
46. Gebru Tareke, *Ethiopia: Power and Protest*, Red Sea Press, Lawrenceville, NJ, 1996, p. 103.
47. *Grazmatch* Seyoum Maasho, interview, Asmera, 1997.
48. Trevaskis, *The Deluge*, pp. 103–4.
49. *Dejazmatch* Ghebrai Teklu was the chief of the district of Engan'a where the town of Dekemhare was located. One of the earliest leaders of union with Ethiopia, he was a powerful rival of Tessema Asberom. At some point in the early 1940s, he briefly succeeded in severing the Dekemhare district from Akeleguzai and joining it to Hamasien. The move was later reversed.
50. Trevaskis, *The Deluge*, p. 107.
51. UK Ministry of Information, *The First to Be Freed*, HMSO, London, 1944, pp. 25–7.
52. FO 371/31608, 11/68/91, H.R. Howe, p. 1.
53. Longrigg, *History of Eritrea*, p. 170.
54. Trevaskis, *Eritrea*, p. 60; Weldeab interview, 1987.
55. Yohannes Tsegai, interview, Asmera, 1997; Qeshi Fessehatsion Eliffe, interview, Ararib, 1987.
56. Trevaskis, *Eritrea*, p. 60.
57. FO 17978 J1012/2, no. 28, RDC ER/FC/23/40–44.
58. *Semunawi Gazeta*, 5/254, 17 July 1947; Asfaha Weldemikael, interview, Addis Ababa, 1996.
59. Asfaha Weldemikael and Gebreyohannes Tesfamariam, interviews, Asmera,1998.
60. Nelson Mandela, *Long Walk to Freedom*, Abacus, London, 1994, p. 247.
61. Basil Davidson, *Black Star: A View of the Life and Times of Kwame Nkrumah*, Westview Press, Boulder, CO, 1989, p. 31.
62. Ibrahim Sultan, interview with Ahmed Haji Ali, Cairo, 1983.
63. Weldeab, interview, 1987.
64. Puglisi, *Chi e dall'Eritrea?*, p. 283; Weldeab, interview, 1987.

65. Trevaskis, *The Deluge*, p. 94. The Admirable Crichton that Trevaskis refers to is a character in a play of the same name by J.M. Barrie about a butler in an aristocratic family who takes over from his masters when they are stranded on an island after a shipwreck. The insinuation is that Tedla was manoeuvring his employers.
66. Of the seven Eritrean irredentists living in Ethiopia that we mentioned earlier, Abraha Weldetatios and Gebremeskel Habtemariam were Orthodox; Lorenzo and Asfaha were Catholic; and Dawit and Kiflezghi were Protestant.
67. Gebreyohannes Tesfamariam, interview, Asmera, 1998.
68. Weldeab, interview, 1987.
69. Ibid.
70. Trevaskis, *The Deluge*, pp. 97–8.
71. Ibid.

3. REFORMS, INTERVENTIONS AND RESISTANCE

1. G.K.N. Trevaskis, *Eritrea: A Colony in Transition, 1941–1952*, Oxford University Press, Oxford, 1960, p. 33.
2. Yeertra Kifle Hager Timhrt Minister, *Yetmhrt Anesasna Edget Achir Tarik*, Asmera, n.d., p. 2.
3. Les Gottesman, *To Fight and Learn*, Red Sea Press, Lawrenceville, NJ, 1998, p. 76. Italo-Eritreans (*hanfets* or half-caste in Tigrinya or *meticci* in Italian) could only be admitted into Italian schools if their Italian fathers recognised their paternity. Even that privilege was withdrawn upon the tightening of Fascist laws in 1938.
4. Memhir Yishak Teweldemedhin was born in 1888. His father, *Qeshi* (Pastor) Teweldemedhin Gebremedhin, was one of the earliest coverts to the Protestant faith. Yishak's younger brother, Ephrem Teweldemedhin, was already the Vice Minister of Foreign Affairs in the Ethiopian government. *Kegnazmatch* Asfaha Kahsai, interview, October 2000.
5. Asfaha Kahsai, interview, Asmera, 8 October 2000.
6. Gottesman, *To Fight and Learn*, pp. 78–80.
7. *ESG*, 256, 3 August 1947.
8. G.K.N. Trevaskis, *The Deluge: A Personal View of the End of Empire*, I.B. Tauris Books, London, 2019, p. 84.
9. On *Blata* Gebregziabher Gilamariam, see Bahru Zewde, *A History of Modern Ethiopia, 1855–1991*, James Currey, Oxford, 1991, p. 107; Zewde Gebreselassie, *Ye Ityopiana ye Ertra Gitcht: Mens'ena Meftihye*, Addis Ababa, 2013–14, p. 112.
10. Edward Ullendorff, *The Two Zions*, Oxford University Press, Oxford, 1988, p. 171.
11. Fesseha Weldemariam, interview, Port Sudan, October 1987.
12. *ESG*, 22, 25 January 1943; *ESG*, 21, 18 January 1943.
13. Ullendorff, *The Two Zions*, p. 168.
14. Harold Marcus, *The Politics of Empire: Ethiopia, Great Britain and the United States, 1941–1974*, Red Sea Press, Lawrenceville, NJ, 1983, p. 9.

15. Zewde Retta, *Yeqedamawi Haileselassie Mengist,* Laxmi Publications, New Delhi, 2012, p. 432.
16. Ibid., p. 437.
17. Ibid., pp. 440–4.
18. Ibid., pp. 438–40.
19. Ibid., pp. 445–6. In 1932, Haile Selassie had sent his son-in-law, *Ras* Desta Damtew, on a friendly mission to the US, where he had requested aid from the US and shared with the President his fears of an impending attack by Fascist Italy.
20. DOS 884.24/112/1/2, 24 April 1943.
21. DOS 884.24/112, 19 June 1943.
22. Zewde Retta, *Yeqedamawi Haileselassie Mengist*, pp. 459–61.
23. Marcus, *The Politics of Empire*, p. 22.
24. J.R. Rasmuson, *The History of Kagnew Station and American Forces in Eritrea*, Il Poligrafico, Asmera, 1973, p. 21.
25. Ibid., pp. 22–3.
26. Wallace Murray memo, quoted by Marcus, *Politics of Empire*, p. 20.
27. Ibid.
28. Johnson, Drake and Piper Inc., *Middle East War Projects*, New York, 1943, p. 22.
29. UK Ministry of Information, *The First to Be Freed*, HMSO, London, 1944, p. 6.
30. Trevaskis, *The Deluge*, p. 98.
31. Sylvia Pankhurst, *British Policy in Eritrea*, Walthamstow Press, Woodward Green, n.d., p. 11.
32. Ibid., p. 13. Those arrested were Inspectors Assefaw Agostino and Gebremariam Gebreyesus and Sergeant Tekleghiorgis Temelso.
33. Ibid., p. 14. The founding member of MFH was *Grazmatch* Zere Bekhit. The other four were *Blata* Fassil Okbazghi, brother of Dawit Okbazghi, Governor of Adwa district and later Deputy Foreign Minister of Ethiopia; *Grazmatch* Tesfamikael Werke, a businessman and major proponent of union; *Blata* Asfaha Abraha; and Araia Sebhatu.
34. Trevaskis, *The Deluge,* p. 99.
35. UK Ministry of Information, *The First to Be Freed*, HMSO, London, 1944, p. 7; Pankhurst, *British Policy*, p. 16.
36. *Dimtsi Ertra*, 20 October 1943.
37. IES, PRO 267/Gen, 7 June 1944.
38. Ibid., 147/7/44, 19 June 1944.
39. Among the members of the committee were Goitom Petros, a diplomat in Ethiopia's service; *Blata* (later *Dejazmatch*) Kiflezghi Yehdego, a judge; the brothers Serekeberhan and Gebremeskel Gebrezghi, both high-ranking officials in the Ethiopian administration; *Fitawrari* Abraha Weldetatios, a close associate of Haile Selassie's secretary, *Tsehafe Te'ezaz* Weldegiorgis; and Dawit Okbazghi.
40. IES, PRO 148/14/44, 19 October 1944.
41. Asfaha Weldemikael, interview, Addis Ababa, 1996.

42. Jordan Gebremedhin, *Peasants and Nationalism in Eritrea*, Red Sea Press, Lawrenceville, NJ, 1989, pp. 127–8.
43. *ESG*, 3/101, 3 August 1944.
44. Ibid., 3/105, 31 August 1944.
45. Ibid., 3/106, 7 September 1944.
46. Ibid., 3/112, 19 October 1944.
47. Ibid., 3/110, 5 October 1944.
48. Ibid., 2/112, 19 October 1944.
49. Ibrahim Sultan, interview, Cairo, 1982.
50. Weldeab, interview, 1987.
51. Ibid.
52. Ibid.
53. Zewde Retta, *Yeqedamawi Haileselassie Mengist*, pp. 482–4.
54. Habtu Ghebre-Ab, *Ethiopia and Eritrea*, Red Sea Press, Lawrenceville, NJ, 1993, pp. 29–31.
55. Ibid., pp. 42–57.
56. John Spencer, *Ethiopia at Bay*, Reference Publications, Algonac, MI, 1987, pp. 174–80.
57. Habtu Ghebre-Ab, *Ethiopia and Eritrea*, pp. 58–61.
58. Spencer, *Ethiopia at Bay*, pp. 181–2.
59. Habtu Ghebre-Ab, *Ethiopia and Eritrea*, pp. 39–40, 41–2.
60. For an account of Aklilu's persistent and well-crafted whirlwind of activity to influence delegates of the Four Powers and members at the conference, see Aklilu Habtewold, *Aklilu Remembers: Historical Recollections from a Prison Cell*, Addis Ababa University Press, Addis Ababa, 2010, pp. 164–72.

4. TOWARDS PARTY FORMATION IN ERITREA

1. G.K.N. Trevaskis, *Eritrea: A Colony in Transition, 1941–1952*, Oxford University Press, Oxford, 1960, p. 38.
2. Sylvia Pankhurst, *Why Are We Destroying Ethiopian Ports?*, New Times and Ethiopia News Books, Woodford Green, 1952, pp. 15–16; G. Puglisi, *Chi e dall'Eritrea? Dizionario biografico*, Agenzia Regina, Asmera, 1952, p. xviii.
3. Ibid., p. 21.
4. WO 230/146 62676, 4 July 1944; WO 230/146 62676, 8 July 1944.
5. FO 371 46116/42626, 13 July 1945.
6. Jordan Gebremedhin, *Peasants and Nationalism in Eritrea*, Red Sea Press, Lawrenceville, NJ, 1989, pp. 71–8.
7. This referred to the *diessa* or village ownership system of land ownership where land was redistributed to village stakeholders every seven years. There were suggestions at the time that the period be extended to fifteen years, considered long enough for farmers to be encouraged to invest on their current share.
8. BMA, Native Advisory Council, Hamasien, 16 April 1946.

9. *ESG,* 4/195, 22 May 1946.
10. Pompilio Mastrandrea (Notary), Rep. no. 15499—Race no. 8306, 3 July 1946, RDC.
11. John Spencer, *Ethiopia at Bay*, Reference Publications, Algonac, MI, 1987, p. 196; Trevaskis, *Eritrea*, p. 67.
12. WO 230/146 62676, 27 February 1945.
13. Ibid., 6 March 1945.
14. *ESG*, 3/130, 22 February 1945.
15. FO 1015/4 CH 62888, 29 November 1945.
16. Ibid., 6 February 1946.
17. Ibid. The signatories to the petition claimed that they were representing 119,400 people from Akeleguzai, including 40,000 Muslims from that province; 85,000 from the western lowlands; 20,000 from Denkalia and the Islands; and 44,000 from the Massawa division.
18. Ibid., 6 February 1946.
19. *ESG*, 4/186, 21 March 1946. The writer, *Blata* Tesfatsion Deres, was the brother of Zerai Deres, the Eritrean who wielded a sword and hurt several Italians on the streets of Rome for allegedly belittling the Ethiopian flag.
20. *ESG*, 4/188, 21 June 1946. The protagonists were Bairu Ukbit, Tedla Bairu's father, arguing for Amharic, and Fessehatsion Haile, future Secretary of the Interior of the government of Eritrea.
21. *ESG*, 4/207, 25 August 1946.
22. Trevaskis, *Eritrea*, p. 67.
23. Ibid., pp. 68–9.
24. *ESG*, 4/206, 8 August 1946.
25. G.K.N. Trevaskis, *The Deluge: A Personal View of the End of Empire*, I.B. Tauris Books, London, 2019, pp. 115–16.
26. Ibid., p. 117.
27. Ibid.
28. Ibid., p. 121.
29. Ibid.
30. Ibid., p. 122.
31. Ibid., p. 123.
32. Ibid., p. 124.
33. Ibid., pp. 124–6.
34. *ESG*, 5/209, 30 August 1946; 5/210, 31 August 1946.
35. Kidane Kelib, interview, Wegret, Eritrea, May 1988.
36. Edward Ullendorff, *The Two Zions,* Oxford University Press, Oxford, 1988, pp. 184–6.
37. *ESG*, 5/210, 5 September 1946.
38. Ibid., 5/240, 5 November 1946.
39. Ibid., 5/217, 24 October 1946; Yohannes Tsegai, interview, 15 May 1996.

40. *ESG*, 5/216, 17 October 1946. Haile Selassie's handout was distributed as follows: 600 EA shillings to each family of the dead, 360 to those permanently disabled, 240 to the seriously wounded, and 160 to those who sustained light injuries.
41. *ESG*, 5/225, 19 December 1946.
42. Ibid., 5/410, 5 September 1946; 5/411, 12 September 1946.
43. Trevaskis, *The Deluge*, p. 127.
44. G.K.N. Trevaskis, *Report on Serfdom*, WO 230/255, S/SE/200, 5 June 1948.
45. Trevaskis, *The Deluge*, pp. 128–9.
46. Ibid.
47. Ibid.
48. *ESG*, 5/209, 29 August 1946; 5/212, 19 September 1946; see also Puglisi, *Chi e dall'Eritrea?*, p. 17.
49. *ESG*, 5/212, 19 September 1946; Trevaskis, *The Deluge*, pp. 130–1.
50. Trevaskis, *The Deluge*, p. 131.
51. Weldeab, interview, 1987.
52. Omer Qadi, 'We Need an Interpreter to Protect the Unprotected Benefits of Our People', *ESG*, 5/216, 17 October 1946.
53. *ESG*, 5/220, 14 November 1946.
54. Jordan Gebremedhin, *Peasants and Nationalism in Eritrea*, pp. 92–4.
55. Weldeab, interview, 1987.
56. Ibid.
57. Weldeab, interview, 1987.
58. *ESG*, 5/222, 28 November 1946.
59. Ibid., 5/223, 5 December 1946.
60. Trevaskis, *Eritrea*, p. 74.

5. ERITREAN POLITICAL PARTIES

1. Ibrahim Sultan, interview, Cairo, 1982.
2. Hassen Ali, in *ESG*, 6 March 1947.
3. Ibid.
4. *Saut al Rabita*, 1/5, 25 March 1947.
5. Ibrahim, interview, 1982.
6. Seyoum Maasho, interview, 1996.
7. G.K.N. Trevaskis, *The Deluge: A Personal View of the End of Empire*, I.B. Tauris Books, London, 2019, p. 132.
8. *Saut al Rabita*, 1/1, 25 February 1947; *ESG*, 5/235, 6 March 1947.
9. *ESG*, 5/236, 13 March 1947.
10. Articles under the names of Weldeamlak Weldedingil and Weldeabzgi Binega were widely believed to have been penned by Weldeab. See *ESG*, 5/227, 9 January 1947; 5/236, 13 March 1947; 5/236, 27 March 1947.
11. *ESG*, Wel Wel, 'Ertra Nmen?', 5/241, 17 April 1947—5/247, 19 May 1947.

12. Ibid., 1/5, 29 May 1947.
13. FPC Final Report, 1A Part 2, 'Eritrea', p. 144.
14. Abdelkader Kebire to Cavaliere Nurhussein, c.1947–8, paraphrased from translation from Arabic by Saleh A.A. Yunis, www.dehai.org, 29 August 1997.
15. *ESG*, 5/227, 9 January 1947.
16. Ibid.
17. Ibid. Al Said Ahmed Hayoti, *Fitawrari* Taha Adem and *Fitawrari* Haregot Abbay were also named secretary general, treasurer and deputy treasurer, respectively.
18. Tedla Bairu, 'Love and Hate', *Ethiopia*, 1/7, 15 June 1947.
19. *Ethiopia*, 1/5, 11 June 1947.
20. Ibid., 1/18, 31 August 1947.
21. The documents were kindly made available to the author by *Grazmatch* Habtu Tesfamikael, one of the founding members of Andinet in Massawa. In 1960, he was elected to the last session of the Eritrean Assembly and was present at the meeting where Eritrea's annexation by Ethiopia was announced.
22. RDC, Habtu Tesfamikael files, Amendment to Party Regulations, UP Youth Association, Massawa, 1949.
23. Ibid.
24. Interviews with Andinet activists Bahta Iyoab, January–February 1998; Zere Debretsion, 20 January 1998, Asmera.
25. Bahta Iyoab, an Andinet unit leader, described cases where he was involved in assassination plots and acts where security forces arrested persons with perfect alibis, thus escaping the law.
26. RDC, Habtu Tesfamikael files, letter to *Fitawrari* Asfaha Weldemikael, vice representative of Emperor Haile Selassie to Eritrea, from *Tsehafe Te'ezaz* Gebreselassie Asbu, *Bashai* Tesfagiorgis Gebretensa'e and others of the UP leadership, n.d.
27. Bahta Iyoab, interview with Yemane Mesghina, January–February 1998.
28. Each of these four districts were led by chiefs allied to *Ras* Tessema, chief of Hadegti. These were *Dejazmatch* Gebrezghi Guangul, the *Ras*'s son-in-law; Maasho Zeweldi of Aret; and *Dejazmatch* Bocru and his son, Teklehaimanot, in Degra.
29. In Tekela, *Dejazmatch* Sebhatu Yohannes of Adi Mengonti led a cluster of independence seekers in the district. He was married to the daughter of *Ras* Tessema's brother, *Dejazmatch* Berhe Asberom. The rest of the district was a unionist stronghold under the leadership of various chiefs such as *Dejazmatch* Mehari Andemeskel of Dibezana. In Adi Quala, the bitter rivalry between *Dejazmatch* Weldegiorgis Kahsai, leader of Eritrea for Eritreans, and *Dejazmatch* (later *Ras*) Haile Tesfamariam was one of the sources of major discord in the town and district. The former's son was also married into the Tessema family. Damba Mitch was under the sway of one of the staunchest anti-Ethiopian leaders and propagandists, *Azmatch* Berhe Gebrekidan.
30. Notable supporters of independence were *Azmatch* Kahsu Milkes, *Fitawrari* Weldeselassie Tessema, *Blata* Gebremikael Beraki and *Bashai* Fesseha Weldemariam, nicknamed 'Gandhi'.

31. Weldeab, interview, 1987.
32. *ESG*, 5/234, 27 February 1947.
33. Ibid.
34. Ibid., 5/244, 5/244, 8 May 1947.
35. Ibid., 2/249, 12 June 1947.
36. Gebremeskel Weldu, 'Ah ... Ahh ... Ah!', *ESG*, 5/242, 24 March 1947.
37. Ibid., 5/249, 12 June 1947.
38. Ibid., 5/253, 10 August 1947.
39. FO 1015/143 6302, 31 December 1947.
40. *ESG*, 5/266, 9 October 1947. The two members of Andinet were Mossazghi Abraha and Asgedom Tekle. The third was *Haleka* (Deacon) Gebremedhin Balai. It is generally believed that the sentences were not carried out and that the perpetrators were later set free.
41. FO 1015/61 62888, 18 June, 1946.
42. G.K.N. Trevaskis, *Eritrea: A Colony in Transition, 1941–1952*, Oxford University Press, Oxford, 1960, p. 78.
43. Ibid., p. 77.
44. FO 1015/143 63021, 31 December 1947; Trevaskis, *Eritrea*, p. 79.
45. *ESG*, 5/257, 7 August 1947.
46. Ibid., 5/258, 14 August 1947.
47. Trevaskis, *Eritrea*, pp. 79–80.

6. THE FOUR POWER COMMISSION OF INQUIRY

1. G.K.N. Trevaskis, *Eritrea: A Colony in Transition, 1941–1952*, Oxford University Press, Oxford, 1960, pp. 84–7.
2. Weldeab, interview; John Spencer, *Ethiopia at Bay*, Reference Publications, Algonac, MI, 1987, p. 197; Trevaskis, *Eritrea*, p. 86.
3. FO 6316 128279 (n.d.).
4. *ESG*, 6/275, 11 December 1947.
5. Spencer, *Ethiopia at Bay*, p. 197; Trevaskis, *Eritrea*, p. 86.
6. FPC Final Report, 1948, Appendix 123, p. 21.
7. Habtu Ghebre-Ab, *Ethiopia and Eritrea*, Red Sea Press, Lawrenceville, NJ, 1993, p. 65.
8. FPC Final Report, 1948, Appendix 123, p. 5.
9. Ibid., p. 21.
10. Ibid., 142–4.
11. Ibid., pp. 96–100. The Ethiopian notables and officials listed in the appeal were Prof. Tamrat, an Ethiopian Felasha scholar exiled to Eritrea because of disagreements with the Haile Selassie government; *Blata* Kidanemariam Aberra, also a Tigrayan exile in Eritrea; *Blata* (later *Dejazmatch*) Kiflezghi Yehdego, a founder of the Unionist Party in Addis Ababa; and Asfaha Weldemikael, future Chief Executive of Eritrea.
12. Ibid.

13. Trevaskis, *Eritrea*, pp. 88–9.
14. WO 230/246 61204, 4 February 1948.
15. Ibid., 5 April 1948.
16. Zewde Retta, *Ye-Ertra Gudai, 1941–1963*, Berhan-na Printing Press, Addis Ababa, 2000, pp. 119–24.
17. WO 230/246, Telegram no. 427/12822/33 CA, 13 April 1948.
18. Ibid., Box 12822 (RDC), 14 April 1948.
19. Ibid., Sir Philip Mitchell to Secretary of State, 2 April 1948.
20. WO 230/246 61204, Box 12822 (RDC), 2 April 1948.
21. Ibid., 5/PA/36/11, 2 July 1948.
22. FO 371/69344, 'Recommendations to the Council of Foreign Ministers', 31 August 1948. See also Okbazghi Yohannes, *Eritrea: A Pawn in World Politics*, University of Florida Press, Gainesville, FL, 1991, pp. 82–8; Trevaskis, *Eritrea*, pp. 83–92.
23. The chief in question was *Dejazmatch* (later *Ras*) Haile Tesfamariam, later president of the Seraye branch of the UP and a bitter rival of *Dejazmatch* Weldegiorgis Kahsai, later president of LPP for the district.
24. G.K.N. Trevaskis, 'A Study of the Development of the *Shifta* Problem and the Means Whereby It Can Be Remedied', FO 371/80876, 13 June 1950.
25. In 1946, the BMA dismissed members of the two most powerful families of the Hamasien—*Ras* Weldemikael of Hazega and *Ras* Beraki Bekit of Arba'te Asmera. One of the chiefs thus dismissed was Asresehey Beraki, brother of the UP leader *Dejazmatch* (later *Ras*) Beyene Beraki. The creation of Italian concessions in 1946 played a big role in galvanising support for the UP in the Hamasien. See Trevaskis, 'The *Shifta* Problem', pp. 24–5.
26. *Grazmatch* Gebrai Meles, interview, Asmera, 1998.
27. Gebreyohannes Tesfamariam, interview, 1998.
28. Jordan Gebremedhin, *Peasants and Nationalism in Eritrea*, Red Sea Press, Lawrenceville, NJ, 1989, p. 110.
29. The BMA actually had some proof that Nega had personal contacts with many of the urban terrorists. For example, the man who was sentenced for having shot Weldeab Weldemariam near his home had visited the liaison officer the day before the incident. Tekola Gebremedhin was targeted for deportation more than once for disbursement of Ethiopian funds for terrorist acts. The steps were never taken. FO 371/63222, 8 November 1947; 13 November 1947; Monthly Political Report, 31 October 1947.
30. Interviews with Gebreyohannes Tesfamariam, 1998; and Asfaha Weldemikael, Addis Ababa, 1996.
31. WO 230/242 61439, no. 36/39, 18 January 1948.
32. Ibid., 26 March 1948.
33. Ibid., 31 March 1948.
34. Ibid., 10 April 1948.
35. Ibid., 13 April 1948.
36. Ibid.

37. Ibid., 3 July 1948.
38. Ibid., 7 August 1948.
39. *Ethiopia*, no. 68, 25 July 1948.
40. *ESG*, 6/310, 12 August 1948. Beyene's utterances were printed in Italian, inside the Tigrinya section of the newspaper.
41. WO230/242 61439, Brig. H.J.M. Flaxman to G.W. Kenyon-Slaney, 16 August 1948.
42. Fessehaye Berhe, interview with Yemane Mesghina, Asmera, 1997.
43. Gebrai Meles, interview, 1997.
44. *Kegnazmatch* Tesfaselassie Kidane, interview, Asmera, 1999.
45. Ibid.
46. Hagos Temnewo, interview, 1997.
47. Gebrai Meles, interview, 1997.
48. RDC, Habtu Tesfamikael files.
49. Spencer, *Ethiopia at Bay*, p. 197.

7. THE ERITREAN CASE AT THE UN GENERAL ASSEMBLY

1. *ESG*, 7/338, 24 February 1949; CRIE, *Terrorism in Eritrea*, Asmera, 1952, p. 21.
2. FO 1015/187, Monthly Political Report, 30 April 1949.
3. Besides Ibrahim, the ML delegation consisted of Abdelkader Kebire, Mohammed Osman Hayoti and Ibrahim Mahmoud.
4. FO 371/3841 J2521, 25 March 1949.
5. FO 371/73787, 2 March 1949.
6. Ibid., J3956, Annexture A, 3 May 1949.
7. Ibid., Annexture B, 3 May 1949.
8. Ibid., Annexture C, 3 May 1949.
9. Ibid., 8 April 1949.
10. Ibid.
11. Ibid., 30 June 1949.
12. Ibid., 4 July 1949.
13. Ibid., 3 May 1949.
14. *ESG*, no. 252, 3 July 1947.
15. *ESG*, 7/349, 12 May 1949.
16. FO 371/73841, Interview in the messages of 8 and 9 February 1949.
17. Ibid., Lascelles to Bevin, 22 February 1949.
18. Okbazghi Yohannes, *Eritrea: A Pawn in World Politics*, University of Florida Press, Gainesville, FL, 1991, p. 91; see also John Spencer, *Ethiopia at Bay*, Reference Publications, Algonac, MI, 1987, p. 201; Harold Marcus, *The Politics of Empire: Ethiopia, Great Britain and the United States, 1941–1974,* Red Sea Press, Lawrenceville, NJ, 1983, p. 84.
19. NSC 19/5, 9 December 1948.
20. Ibid., 19/2, 4 December 1949.

21. Okbazghi, *Eritrea*, pp. 91–3.
22. FO 371/73841, Clutton to Foreign Office, London, 28 March 1949.
23. FO 371/73842, Minutes by Scrivener, 2 May 1949.
24. Okbazghi Yohannes, *Eritrea*, p. 111.
25. Ibid.
26. Ibid., p. 114.
27. Aklilu Habtewold, *Aklilu Remembers: Historical Recollections from a Prison Cell*, Addis Ababa University Press, Addis Ababa, 2010, pp. 181–2.
28. Okbazghi Yohannes, *Eritrea*, p. 115.
29. Ibid., pp. 115–16.
30. The Arab and Muslim states in the committee were Egypt, Iran, Iraq, Lebanon, Pakistan, Saudi Arabia, Syria, Turkey, Yemen and Afghanistan.
31. Okbazghi, *Eritrea*, pp. 122–3.
32. Ibid., pp. 123–4.
33. *The Times*, no. 51378, 11 May 1949.
34. Zewde Retta, *Yeqedamawi Haileselassie Mengist,* Laxmi Publications, New Delhi, 2012, pp. 144–67.
35. Ibid., p. 325.
36. G.K.N. Trevaskis, *Eritrea: A Colony in Transition, 1941–1952*, Oxford University Press, Oxford, 1960, p. 93.
37. *The Times*, no. 51380, 13 May 1949.
38. FO 371/73842, J3052, Minutes by Scrivener, 8 April 1949.
39. Trevaskis, *Eritrea*, p. 93; Okbazghi, *Eritrea*, p. 126.
40. Ibid.
41. WO 230/246, 13 May 1949.
42. FO 1015/187, 31 March 1949.
43. Ibid.
44. Ibid., paras. 862, 869, 30 March 1949.
45. *Luce dell'Eritrea*, 2/77, 13 March 1949.
46. FO 1015/187, Monthly Report, para. 399, March 1949.
47. Ibid., para. 394, 30 June 1949.
48. *Ethiopia*, no. 113, 26 June 1949.
49. FO 371/73844, Minutes by Stewart and Clutton, 7–8 July 1949.
50. RDC, Independence Bloc leaflet signed by Ibrahim Sultan, Seyoum Maasho and Mohammed Abdallah, 24 July 1949.
51. FO 1015/187, BMA Monthly Report, 31 July 1949.
52. FO 1015/187, Bell to Drew, 2 August 1949.
53. In July, sentences of fifteen and ten years' imprisonment were imposed on Andinet leaders Gebreselassie Garza and Habtom Araia, respectively. Anticipation of violence in protest failed to materialise as Andinet and the UP let the incident pass without even token resistance. FO 1015, BA Monthly Political Report, para. 915, 31 July 1949.
54. Ibid.

55. Ibid., para. 973.
56. *Ethiopi*a, 3/127, 15 September 1949.
57. Amare Tekle, *The Creation of Ethio-Eritrea Federation: A Case Study*, University Microfilms, Ann Arbor, MI, 1964, p. 253.
58. Weldeab, interview, 1987.
59. Amare, *Creation of Ethio-Eritrea Federation*, p. 261.
60. FO 321/73842, 8 April 1949; Okbazghi, *Eritrea*, pp. 115–16.
61. Amare, *Creation of Ethio-Eritrea Federation*, p. 267.
62. Ibid., p. 272.
63. Ibid., p. 273.
64. Spencer, *Ethiopia at Bay*, p. 217. According to Spencer, Ethiopia was very unhappy with the composition of the commission. It particularly registered its strong opposition to the inclusion of Zafarullah Khan of Pakistan for having led the drive to send an inquiry commission to Eritrea.
65. Amare, *Creation of Ethio-Eritrea Federation*, p. 275.

8. THE INDEPENDENCE BLOC

1. *Ethiopia*, 3/138, 23 October 1949.
2. FO 1015/187, 31 October 1949.
3. *Ethiopia*, 3/139, 27 November 1949.
4. WO 230/243, '*Shifta* Activity in Eritrea', 7 October 1949.
5. Ibid., 5 December 1949.
6. Ibid.
7. Ahmed Mohammed Seid, interview, 7 March 2000. The same argument was put forward by a veteran of the Eritrean struggle for independence, Omer Adhana of Ad Shuma, who actually had attempted to form an ML armed band only to abandon it as impractical and unsustainable.
8. Abudawd, interview, Asmera, 1999. See also WO 230/243, 4 and 7 January 1950; CRIE, *Terrorism in Eritrea*, Asmera, 1952.
9. *Qeshi* Fessehatsion Elefe, an active unionist in contact with the *shifta*, confirmed this claim. He asserted that he himself had spent time with the *shifta* in the presence of Brans.
10. EPF, Ref. S/4/1/AS/RD, District Police Asmera–Hamasien to Commissioner of Police, 22 May 1951.
11. BAE, Eritrea, Annual Report for 1949, 31 December 1949.
12. *Hanti Ertra*, 1/2, 4 February 1950.
13. Ibid., 1/3, 11 February 1950.
14. Ibid., 1/2, 4 February 1950.
15. *Ethiopia*, 3/148, 4 November 1949.
16. Ibid., 3/148, 4 December 1949.

17. *Hanti Ertra*, 1/2, 4 February 1950. It must be recalled that, when Italy invaded Ethiopia in 1935, it had joined the Tigray and Eritrea dioceses into one. Later, *Abune* Markos had been created archbishop of both dioceses by a synod put together by the Italians.
18. The intended victims were *Blata* Tesfatsion Deres, brother of the celebrated martyr Zerai Deres; *Fitawrari* Gebremikael Beraki of Pro-Italy; and *Fitawrari* Hagos Tesfamariam. *ESG*, 8/380, 15 December 1949.
19. Gebreyohannes Tesfamariam, interview, 1998.
20. *ESG*, 8/381, 12 January 1949; 3/384, 12 January 1950; and following issues. Kidane Habtetsion was still in prison when the British left Eritrea in 1952. Haile Selassie pardoned him on the institution of the Federation.
21. One of the personalities thus kidnapped was *Bashai* Fesseha Weldemariam (Gandhi), a major IB figure. Many of Kidane Habtetsion's colleagues, especially the Tigrayans, insisted on killing him. He was saved upon the intervention of Gebre Tesfatsion, one of the *shifta* commanders.
22. One of these, Tesfatsion Deres, announced his shift from Nuova Italia to the UP in opposition of the presence of 'half-castes' inside IB. See *Ethiopia*, 3/154, 19 January 1950.
23. FO 371/73788, 8 and 9 September 1949.
24. Okbazghi Yohannes, *Eritrea: A Pawn in World Politics*, University of Florida Press, Gainesville, FL, 1991, p. 140.
25. *Ethiopia*, 3/153, 15 January 1950; 3/160, 9 February 1950.
26. Ibid.
27. FO 371/80876, 16 May 1950.
28. FO 371/80872, Stafford to G. Clutton, African Dept, London, 9 February 1950.
29. G. Puglisi, *Chi e dall'Eritrea? Dizionario biografico*, Agenzia Regina, Asmera, 1952, p. 12.
30. G.K.N. Trevaskis, *The Deluge: A Personal View of the End of Empire*, I.B. Tauris Books, London, 2019, pp. 136–7.
31. Okbazghi, *Eritrea*, p. 140.
32. *Sheik* Omer Nashih, interview with the author, Kassala, 4 November 1987.
33. FO 371/80872, Stafford to Clutton, 9 February 1950.
34. FO 371/80871, 16 February 1950.
35. *Ethiopia*, 3/162, 16 February 1950.
36. Seyoum Maasho, interview, 1997.
37. FO 371/80871, 30 January 1950 and 30 February 1950.
38. *Hanti Ertra*, 1/4, 18 February 1950.
39. Wikipedia, 'Public Records Act 1958'.
40. In 2002, Martin Plaut of the BBC and British author Michela Wrong were kind enough to use their connections at the British Foreign Office to locate the document. They were told that the document would be permanently impounded, with no release date stipulated.
41. Mehretab Asfaha, interview, Asmera, 20 September 2006.

42. FO 371/80872, Stafford to Clutton, 30 February 1950.
43. FO 371/80876, Record of Meeting in Sir W. Strang's Room, 6 June 1950.

9. THE UN'S FINAL VERDICT ON ERITREA

1. For more details on the conflict, see FO 371/80879, Findings, Record of the Proceedings of the Court of Inquiry, 1950.
2. Ibid.
3. Ibid.
4. Of the 154 tried, 113 were accused of crimes including theft, public disturbance, possession of arms, murder and arson.
5. Gebreyohannes Tesfamariam, interview, 1998.
6. *ESG*, 16 March 1950.
7. *ESG*, 3/172, 'Those Who Don't Fight Are Angels, Those Who Don't Reconcile Are Devils', 30 March 1950.
8. Ibid.
9. Gebreyohannes, interview, 1998.
10. FO 371/80879, Findings.
11. FO 371/80879, Findings.
12. Seidi Hassen Ali, interview with author, Akria, September 1997.
13. *Hanti Ertra*, 1/5, 25 February 1950.
14. FO 371/80873, Stafford, 'The United Nations Commission in Eritrea: A Summary of its Activities', 12–19 February 1950, quoted by Okbazghi Yohannes, *Eritrea: A Pawn in World Politics*, University of Florida Press, Gainesville, FL, 1991, p. 143.
15. Asresehey was generally seen as the leading *shifta* of the lot. Probably in fear of reprisals, he is reported to have moved his family to the care of Tigrayan district governors inside Tigray, Shire in particular. See FO 371/80873, Extract from SDO Adi Ugri's Report, 21 February 1950.
16. *Hanti Ertra*, 1/2, 1 April 1950.
17. G.K.N. Trevaskis, *Eritrea: A Colony in Transition, 1941–1952*, Oxford University Press, Oxford, 1960, p. 99.
18. Bahta Iyo'ab, interview, 1997.
19. UN General Assembly, Official Records, Fifth Session, Supp. 8 (A/1285), 8 June 1950, pp. 20, 30.
20. Ibid., Berhe to UNCIE, 10 April 1950.
21. *Hanti Ertra*, 1/22, 1 April 1950; see also, *Ethiopia*, 26 March 1950.
22. Okbazghi, *Eritrea*, p. 146.
23. UN General Assembly, Fifth Session, Supp. 8 (A/1285), 8 June 1950, pp. 20, 30.
24. Ibid. In an appendix, the Burmese delegate indicated his preference for a proper federation between Eritrea and Ethiopia. The Emperor would then head a separately instituted federal government as a constitutional monarch.
25. Ibid.

26. FO 371/80876, Cook to Stewart (Foreign Office), 16 May 1950.
27. FO 371/80876, 16 May 1950.
28. *Hanti Ertra*, 1/22, 17 May 1950.
29. FO 371/80875, 15 May 1950; FO 371/80874, 2 May 1950; FO 371/80876, 24 April 1950.
30. FO 371/80876, Cook, Aide-Memoire for H.E. Brusasca, June 1950. Here, Cook claimed that 39 *shifta* had been killed, 29 wounded and 80 captured. At the same time, five Eritrean policemen and five Italians were also killed.
31. FO 371/80877, 23 June 1950.
32. The BMA assumed that the Mossazghi brothers had murdered the Italian and the Greek at a bar in Mendefera. It was later found that the actual killers were Tigrayan *shifta* sent for the purpose by *Dejazmatch* Tsehaye Bissirat, chief of Adyabo, Tigray. BMA's request for them to turn over the killers was turned down by the Ethiopian government, which denied any knowledge of the incident. FO 371/80877, Ambassador Lascelles (Addis Ababa) to Vice Minister Zewde Gebrehiwet, 26 June 1950.
33. FO 371/80877, Monthly Political Report, 11 May–10 June 1950. This old ambition was to be the cause of the 1998 border war between Eritrea and Ethiopia, in which Badme village was to figure prominently.
34. The *shifta* thus executed was Welderufael Abraha, who had killed an Eritrean policeman, a woman and an Italian resident. Public hanging was preferred over a firing squad because the BMA felt that it would instil more fear in potential culprits. FO 371/80877, 'Deterrent Measures Taken against *Shifta*', 4 August 1950.
35. Besides being the chief of Geza Berhanu, *Azmatch* Abdelkader had also been an administrator for *Ras* Beraki Bekit, chief of the Asmera area under the Italians and the father of Beyene Beraki, president of UP. *ESG*, 8/407, 22 June 1950; interview with the *Azmatch*'s daughter-in-law, Seidi Hassen Ali.
36. G. Puglisi, *Chi e dall'Eritrea? Dizionario biografico*, Agenzia Regina, Asmera, 1952, p. 184.
37. Three days after Longhi's death, a bomb believed to have been thrown by his Italo-Eritrean followers landed inside the home of *Dejazmatch* Araia Wassie. Araia, later Secretary of the Interior during the Federation, was one of the founders and prime movers of the UP. Puglisi, *Chi e dall'Eritrea?*, p. 21.
38. *Wehdet Eretria*, 1/19, 26 March 1950; FO 1015/853, Eritrea, Annual Report, 1950, p. 30, para. 174.
39. *ESG*, 8/415, 17 August 1950. Berhe Mossazghi, along with his brother Weldegabriel, had been the terror of Italian nationals, especially after their two siblings had been killed by the Italian police officer Barba. Berhe was reputed to have been directly responsible for the deaths of eleven Italians, a Maltese citizen, a Greek and five Eritreans – three civilian and two policemen.
40. *Wehdet Eretria*, 1/36, 23 August 1950.
41. FO 371/80878, Foreign Office to Whitehall, 28 September 1950.
42. Gebreyohannes Tesfamariam, interview, 1998.

43. FO 70872, 62257, 25 February 1950.
44. Okbazghi, *Eritrea*, p. 152.
45. Ibid., p. 154.
46. Ibid., p. 157.
47. Ibid.
48. Ibid., pp. 156–7.
49. John Spencer, *Ethiopia at Bay*, Reference Publications, Algonac, MI, 1987, p. 233. According to Spencer, Aklilu was actually calling his bluff. Haile Selassie had earlier instructed him that he was to first ask for full annexation of Eritrea and then accept federation in acceptance of the UN's wishes.
50. Ibid., p. 234.
51. Ibid.
52. Ibid.
53. Ibid., p. 169.
54. Ibid., p. 173.
55. FO 1015/527, G. Jebb to Foreign Office, 6 November 1950.
56. Okbazghi, *Eritrea*, pp. 169–70.
57. For the full text of Ibrahim's speech, see UN General Assembly, A/AC.38/L.46, 21 November 1950.
58. The parties Ibrahim listed were the LPP, the Eritrea Independence Party, Nuova Eritrea, the Eritrean Veterans Association and the Italo-Eritrean Association.
59. Amare Tekle, *The Creation of Ethio-Eritrea Federation: A Case Study*, University Microfilms, Ann Arbor, MI, 1964, pp. 326–7.
60. Ibid., pp. 319ff.
61. Ibid., pp. 331–2.
62. Ibid., pp. 334–5.
63. *Ethiopia*, 4/186, 11 June 1950.
64. *Hanti Ertra*, 1/26, 14 June 1950.
65. *Ethiopia*, 4/211, 3 December 1950.
66. *Hanti Ertra*, Special Edition, 5 December 1950.
67. Ibid., 1/51, 6 December 1950.
68. *Hanti Ertra*, 1/55, 3 January 1951.
69. Ibid.
70. Weldeab, interview, 1987.

10. UN RESOLUTION 390-A(V)

1. UN General Assembly, 'Final Report of the United Nations Commissioner in Eritrea', Official Records, Seventh Session, Supplement no. 15 (A/2188), 1952, para. 27, p. 3.
2. For a detailed discussion of the concepts of federation, autonomy, sovereignty and UN recommendations, see Alemseged Tesfai, 'The Role of the Four Great Powers and

the General Assembly of the United Nations in the Federation between Eritrea and Ethiopia', MCL thesis, University of Illinois, Champaign-Urbana, 1972, pp. 46–55.

3. UN Commissioner's Final Report, 1952, para. 198, p. 1952.
4. *Ethiopia*, 4/212, 10 December 1950.
5. Zewde Retta, *Ye-Ertra Gudai, 1941–1963*, Berhan-na Printing Press, Addis Ababa, 2000, pp. 321–2.
6. Ibid., 4/212, 10 December 1950.
7. *Hanti Ertra*, 1/51, 6 December 1950.
8. UN Commissioner's Final Report, para. 29, p. 3.
9. Amdemikael's attempts to woo Matienzo by inviting him to social events and arranging a friendship between their respective wives is well recorded in a series of notes that he addressed to the Emperor. Amdemikael Dessalegn, Memos to Emperor Haile Selassie (handwritten copies), Asmera, 1950–2, RDC, History Project Files.
10. UN Commissioner's Final Report, paras. 39–41, p. 4.
11. Ibid., paras. 42–5, pp. 4–5.
12. *ESG*, 9/435, 4 January 1951; 9/437, 18 January 1951. On 25 December 1950, *shifta* entered the town of Dekemhare and engaged the police in a shootout. Two days before that, another band attacked a police post at Una Minassie, near Adi Segudo, just a few kilometres west of Asmera. Random killings in Ad Ibrahim, in Barka, took the lives of three women and two children. On 1 January 1951, four villagers from Deqi Debat and on 12 January five others near the Mereb were murdered.
13. UN General Assembly, A/2233, UK Final Report, 1952, pp. 7–8.
14. Ibid., p. 6.
15. Ibid., pp. 8–9.
16. Ibid., para. 102, p. 9.
17. Ibid., para. 114, p. 10.
18. Ibid., para. 26, p. 9.
19. The other members of the delegation were the judge Kiflezghi Yehdego, Samuel Gebreyesus, Mohammed Abdallah Medeni and *Azmatch* Ahmed Mohammed.
20. Okbazghi Yohannes, *Eritrea: A Pawn in World Politics*, University of Florida Press, Gainesville, FL, 1991, p. 183.
21. Many of the major leaders, such as Asresehey, Hagos and Gebre, surrendered in Eritrea, while others, particularly the more notorious Tekeste Haile, Debessai Dirar and Weldegabriel Mossazghi, chose to do so to Ethiopian authorities. There, they were received like heroes and offered rank and provincial administrative positions. The same privilege was also accorded those who stayed in Eritrea, where they were appointed to the courts and administrative divisions as judges and administrators.
22. UK Report, 1952, para. 32, p. 10.
23. UN Commissioner's Final Report, 1952, paras. 65–71, pp. 6–7. See also Okbazghi, *Eritrea*, pp. 182–3.
24. UN Commissioner's Final Report, 1952, paras. 69–71, pp. 6–7.

25. Tekie Fessehatsion, *From Federation to Annexation*, Eritreans for Peace and Democracy Publication Committee, Washington DC, 1990, p. 15.
26. Ibid., p. 16.
27. Okbazghi, *Eritrea*, p. 113.
28. UN Commissioner's Final Report, 1952, para. 132, p. 12.
29. *Hanti Ertra*, 2/83, 29 July 1951.
30. Ibid., 2/83, 18 July 1951.
31. *Ethiopia*, 5/246, 29 July 1951.
32. *Hanti Ertra*, 2/85, 1 August 1951.
33. Ibid., 2/86, 8 June 1951.
34. *Ethiopia*, 5/250, 26 August 1951.
35. *Hanti Ertra*, 2/88, 22 August 1951.
36. *Ethiopia*, 5/248, 12 August 1951.
37. *Hanti Ertra*, 2/88, 8 August 1951.
38. Ibid., 2/89, 29 August 1951.
39. Ibid., 2/87, 22 August 1951.
40. Ibid., 2/94, 3 October 1951.
41. Ibid., 3/3, 2 January 1952.
42. UN General Assembly, A/AC.44/R.26/Rev 1, 20 July 1951.
43. Ibid., 44/R.24, 17 July 1951; 44/R.27, 19 July 1951.
44. G.K.N. Trevaskis, *Eritrea: A Colony in Transition, 1941–1952*, Oxford University Press, Oxford, 1960, pp. 116–17.
45. UN General Assembly, A/AC.44/R.53, 22 October 1951, pp. 2–3.
46. *Hanti Ertra,* 2/22, 2 May 1951.
47. Ibid., 2/73, 9 May 1951.
48. FO 371/96721, 16 April 1951.
49. UN Commissioner's Final Report, 1960, para. 730, pp. 66–7.
50. FO 371/96726, Cumming to J.M. Baxter, 30 December 1951.
51. Ibid., 15 January 1952.
52. FO 31/96784, Exploratory and Technical Discussions, 2 April 1952.
53. Ibid., 'Apportionment of Customs Revenues between Eritrea and Ethiopia', 16 May 1952.
54. Ibid., R. Allen to D.C. Cumming, 13 May 1952.
55. Ibid., 30 May 1952.
56. Ibid.
57. Ibid., Baxter to Cumming, 30 May 1952.
58. UK Report, 1952, paras. 152–9.
59. *Hanti Ertra*, 3/111, 30 January 1952.
60. Ibid., 3/114, 20 February 1952.
61. *Ethiopia*, 5/277, 28 February 1952.
62. Ibid., 5/283, 23 March 1952.

11. THE ERITREAN REPRESENTATIVE ASSEMBLY

1. *Hanti Ertra*, 2/104, 12 December 1951.
2. *Ethiopia*, 4/228, 1 April 1951. A Catholic priest, *Abba* Okbamikael, and *Dejazmatch* Hassen Ali of the ML leadership were among the main speakers.
3. Ibid., 3/126, 14 May 1952.
4. Ibid., 5/279, 9 March 1952.
5. DOS, Mulcahy to State Department, 777.00/12-651, 6 December 1951.
6. Ibid., 777.00/11-851, 8 November 1952.
7. *Ethiopia*, 5/277, 26 February 1952.
8. Ibid., 5/279, 9 March 1952.
9. An interesting case involved a Tigre *kebila* (Bejuk) in the same district as two *shumagille kebilas* of the Mensa'e, Abrehe and Shahqan. Although the *shumagille* were the majority, accommodation of *tigre* objection and *shumagille* internal rivalry saw the seat go to an outsider, albeit a *shumagille* of a minor *kebila* that had had no *tigre* (serfs) under it. EPLF, *Cultural Situation in Geleb*, Division of Research, Department of Political Consciousness, EPLF, 1984.
10. DOS 777.00/4F/4-2952. See also Tekie Fessehatsion, *From Federation to Annexation*, Eritreans for Peace and Democracy Publication Committee, Washington, DC, 1990.
11. *Ethiopia*, 5/284, 29 March 1952.
12. Weldeab, interview, 1987.
13. *Hanti Ertra*, 3/120, 2 April 1952.
14. UN Commissioner's Report, paras. 427–35, p. 38.
15. See relevant provisions of the Ethiopian Constitution of 1931.
16. UN General Assembly, A/AC.44/R.61, 19 May 1952 (13th Meeting).
17. *Fitawrari* Mesfin Gebrehiwet, interview, Asmera, 2001.
18. UN General Assembly, A/AC.44R.62, 19 May 1952 (14th Meeting).
19. Ibid.
20. UN General Assembly, A/AC.44/R.65, 21 May 1952 (17th Meeting).
21. Ibid.
22. Ibid., A/AC.44/R.8 (9th Meeting).
23. Ibid., A/AC.44/R.87, 11 June 1952 (32nd Meeting).
24. Ibid.; see also Akito, interview, 2004.
25. UN General Assembly, A/AC.44/R.64, 21 May 1952.
26. Zewde Retta, *Ye-Ertra Gudai, 1941–1963*, Berhan-na Printing Press, Addis Ababa, 2000, pp. 348–9.
27. Weldeyohannes Gebrezghi, interview, 2003.
28. Akito, interview, 2004.
29. UN General Assembly, A/AC.44/R.127, 3 July 1952.
30. Mesfin Gebrehiwet, interview, 2001.
31. DOS 777.000/8-2952, 29 August 1952.
32. *Hanti Ertra*, 3/133, 2 July 1952.

33. Zewde, *Ye-Ertra Gudai*, pp. 348–9.

12. THE FEDERATION INAUGURATED

1. UK Final Report, 1952, paras. 221–2, p. 37.
2. *Hanti Ertra*, 2/132, 25 June 1952.
3. UK Final Report, 1952, Appendix G, pp. 63–4.
4. Ibid., Annexure F, pp. 62–3.
5. The remaining seven members were Haregot Abbay, Idris Mohammed Adem, Teklehaimanot Bokru, Said Sefaf, Mohammed Said Ali Bey, Berhanu Ahmeddin and Embaye Habte. Abraha Tessema and Saleh Hinit were also appointed as advisors. *Andinetn Me'eblnan* (Unity and Progress), 1/20, 19 July 1952.
6. Mesfin Gebrehiwet, interview, 2001.
7. UK Report, 1952, Appendix J, p. 67.
8. Ibid., First Schedule, pp. 69–75.
9. RDC, Acc. 14033, EC/EDM/1, 30 August 1952. The six co-signatories, all ML or ML-WP members, were Ali Omer Osman, Mohammed Bey Abbe, Mohammed Said Hassano, Ibrahim Hummed Ali, Idris Osman Mohammed, and Abdallah Abdulrahman.
10. DOS F79001-0017, 775A.0019-1952, 19 November 1952.
11. UN General Assembly, A/AC.44/R.139, 17 July 1952.
12. Akito, interview, 2004.
13. *Andinetn Me'eblnan*, 1/20, 19 July 1952.
14. *ESG*, 10/520, 21 August 1952.
15. Ibid.
16. DOS F780007-0616, Mulcahy, 'Ibrahim Sultan's Views on Federation of Eritrea', 30 October 1952.
17. *ESG*, 10/522, 4 September 1952.
18. The secretaries appointed by Tedla were *Sheik* Mohammed Said Feki Ali (ML-WP), Interior; *Grazmatch* Teklehaimanot Bokru (EDF), Finance; *Ato* Fessehatsion Haile (Independent), Economic Affairs; and *Sheik* Mohammed Nur Hassen Naib (British administrative assistant), Social Affairs.
19. 'Hamasien', the name of a province, is used here to avoid calling Eritrea by its name. Eritreans were also purposely called 'Tigre' or 'Tigrayan' to discourage their nationalist sentiment. This deliberate attempt to obliterate Eritrea's name continued until the end of Ethiopian rule in 1991.
20. Zewde Retta, *Ye-Ertra Gudai, 1941–1963*, Berhan-na Printing Press, Addis Ababa, 2000, pp. 367–8.
21. *Ethiopia*, 6/333, 14 September 1952.
22. Ibid.
23. Sahle Gebrehiwet, interview, 2006. Sahle Gebrehiwet was an employee of the Tigrayan entrepreneur and political exile *Blata* Kidanemariam Aberra.
24. DOS 775A.00/9-1952, Mulcahy to State Department, 19 September 1952.

25. Gebremedhin Tessema, interview, 23–27 June 2003.
26. UK Report, 1952, para. 42, p. 12.
27. The first Eritrean to qualify as a medical doctor was Kahsai Tesfai, at Edinburgh University in 1957. He and two fellow Eritrean students, Bereket Habteselassie and Tesfalul Tesfai, had been awarded scholarships to Britain from the General Wingate Secondary School in Addis Ababa. Bereket went on to become a well-known lawyer and writer. Tesfalul returned home for health reasons.
28. UK Report, 1952, para. 51, p. 13. In 1952, there were 16,000 regular workers and 7,500 unemployed people in Eritrea. The figures do not include those who had not been registered.
29. Ibid., para. 68, p. 15.
30. Ibid., para. 75, p. 16.
31. Ibid., paras. 286–8, pp. 46–7.
32. *Hanti Ertra*, 3/3, 2 January 1952.
33. UN General Assembly, Seventh Session, Supplement 15, A/2188, paras. 760–4.
34. *Ethiopia*, 6/359, 6 October 1952.
35. Tedla's close confidant and aide, Mesfin Gebrehiwet, was one of the officials who contested this claim. 'If that was the case, Tedla never showed any inkling of it,' he said in his interview. 'But then, he was a very private and secretive person, not given to freely expressing his feelings.'
36. Captain Kidanemariam, who gave this interview, was one of the police officers commanding the honour guard welcoming the emperor. Orotta, Eritrea, 1987.
37. *Ethiopia*, 6/359, 6 October 1952.
38. DOS 775A.009, F7900-0017, Mulcahy to State Department, 19 September 1952.
39. Mesfin, interview, 2001.
40. *Dehai Ertra*, 1/1, 21 September 1952.
41. Sahle Gebrehiwet, interview, 2006. According to Sahle, Professor Tamrat had been charged to write an official history of Ethiopia. Instead, he produced his own version which displeased the Emperor and caused his exile to the British in Eritrea. Where Tamrat's book finally ended up, we have been unable to trace.
42. DOS 775A.009, F7900-0017, Mulcahy to State Department, 19 September 1952.
43. Many Ethiopian scholars and writers have been strongly campaigning for the reversal of some of the terms of Eritrean independence to accommodate Ethiopia's claim over Asseb. It is a campaign that keeps intensifying even after the rapprochement between Eritrea and Ethiopia in 2018, after their border conflict of 1998–2000. See the following literature on the subject: Abebe Teklehaimanot, 'Ethiopia's Sovereign Right of Access to the Sea under International Law', Master's thesis, University of Georgia, Athens, GA, 2007; Getatchew Begashaw, 'Port of Asseb as a Factor for Economic Development and Regional Conflict', http//www.amazon.com.uk/262-4263174-10780527; Andargatchew Tsege, *Egnam Eninager, Twldm Aydenager* (Let Us Speak Up, Lest the Generation Is Confused), Netsanet Publishing Agency, Addis Ababa, 2018, pp. 476–96.

13. THE ERITREAN GOVERNMENT

1. These were Interior, Economy, Finance and Social Affairs with secretaries Mohammed Said Feki Ali, Fessehatsion Haile, Teklehaimanot Bokru and Mohammed Nur Hassen *Naib*, respectively, heading each secretariat.
2. Asfaha Weldemikael, interview, Addis Ababa, 1996. The complaints of favouritism mainly arose from Tedla's appointment of fellow Evangelical Christians to high-level positions. These included Fessehatsion Haile, Secretary of the Economy; Mesfin Gebrehiwet, director general; and Efrem Amanuel and Abraha Gebreselassie to lesser positions.
3. Mesfin Gebrehiwet, interview, 2001.
4. G. Puglisi, *Chi e dall'Eritrea? Dizionario biografico*, Agenzia Regina, Asmera, 1952, p. 280.
5. G.K.N. Trevaskis, *The Deluge: A Personal View of the End of Empire*, I.B. Tauris Books, London, 2019, p. 94.
6. Melles Fre, interview.
7. Eritrean Assembly, Minutes, no. 90, 23 October 1952.
8. Ibid., no. 21, 24 October 1952.
9. Habtezghi Okbazghi in *Ethiopia*, 6/346, 30 October 1952.
10. Ibid.
11. Akito, interview, 2004.
12. *Ethiopia*, 6/346, 30 October 1952.
13. Eritrean Assembly, Minutes, no. 114, 2 December 1952.
14. Ibid.
15. Ibid.
16. *Dehai*, 1/13, 27 December 1952.
17. Ibid., letter from Sir Harry Trusted, 22 September 1952.
18. *Dehai*, Proclamation 130 of 1952, 1/13, 13 December 1952.
19. *Dehai*, 1/10, 22 November 1952.
20. Eritrean Assembly, Minutes, no. 97, 30 October 1952; no. 99, 30 October 1952. The first Eritrean representatives in the Ethiopian parliament were *Bashai* Gebregiorgis Gebre, Said Adum Mohammed, Said Ali Higo Mohammed, Said Ahmed Hayoti and *Qeshi* Gebremikael Tesfalidet.
21. The Ethiopian officials sent to fill federal functions in Eritrea were Seifu Gebreyohannes (Finance), Befekadu Weldemikael (Posts and Communications), Fantaye Weldeyohannes (Interstate Trade), Abebe Bitew (Ports), Teklu Dilnesahu (Customs) and Yakob Zeneyos (Railways). See Zewde Retta, *Ye-Ertra Gudai, 1941–1963*, Berhanna Printing Press, Addis Ababa, 2000, pp. 393–4.
22. *Dehai*, 1/9, 'The Imperial Federal Council and the Representative Assembly', 15 November 1952.
23. RDC, UN Tribunal in Eritrea files, no. 60, Memorandum of Eritrean Representatives of Imperial Federal Council, 7 July 1953.

24. Mohammed Omer Qadi, 'Tarikh Hagerka Mflat' (Knowing the History of Your Country), MS, History Project, RDC, p. 44.
25. Ibid.
26. Eritrean Assembly, Minutes, A/ADM/6, Methven to McLeary, Motions and Questions, 11 March 1953.
27. DOS 775A.31/5-1953, Clark to State Department, 19 May 1953. The judges appointed were the president, Hans Nordström of Sweden; and Matias Hiletewerk and *Dejazmatch* Demoz Hagos, representing the Federal and Eritrean governments, respectively.
28. DOS 775A.21/6-1953, 10 June 1953.
29. Ibid.
30. Yohannes Teklai's three colleagues were Yebio Gebremeskel, Kidane Kelati and Mengis Adhanom.
31. *Dehai*, 1/8, 8 November 1952.
32. Ibid.
33. *Ethiopia*, 6/349, 13 November 1952.
34. *Dehai*, 1/11, 29 November 1952.
35. Ibid., 1/25, 1 March 1953.
36. Ibid., 1/8, 8 November 1952.
37. Eritrean Assembly, Minutes, no. 173, 1 January 1953.
38. *Dehai*, 1/12, 15 November 1952.
39. Eritrean Assembly, Minutes, no. 129, 29 December 1952.
40. See *Dehai*, 1/12, 29 December 1952.
41. Eritrean Assembly, Minutes, no. 129, 29 December 1952.
42. Tekeste Negash, *Eritrea and Ethiopia: The Federal Experience*, Nordic African Institute, Uppsala, 1997, quoting FO 371/102671, BCA to BCAA, 3 January 1953.
43. *Ethiopia*, 6/360, 1 January 1953.
44. Eritrean Assembly, Minutes, no. 133, 5 January 1953.
45. Matewos W in *Dehai*, 1/16, 3 January 1953.
46. *Dehai*, 1/9, 'The Imperial Federal Council and the Representative Assembly', 15 November 1952.
47. *Ethiopia*, 6/351, 23 November 1952.
48. *Dehai*, 1/12, 6 December 1952.
49. Ibid.
50. *Ethiopia*, 6/358, 25 December 1952.
51. *Dehai*, 1/15, 27 December 1952.
52. Ibid., 1/16, 3 January 1953.
53. The seven attempts on Weldeab's life are the following: (1) 15 June 1947, a bomb attack when dining at his home in Geza Kenisha with his wife and two young children; (2) 6 July 1947, a bullet wound inflicted on him as he descended from his car near his home in Geza Kenisha; hospitalised for two months; (3) 4 February 1950, a bomb attack from inside the compound of the Evangelical Church as he drove out; he was wounded on the neck inside the burning car; his wife, Aberash, extinguished the fire and saved her

husband; (4) 1 April 1950, near the Capri Restaurant in Asmera, missed from close range a pistol shot as he walked past with fellow EDF leader Asmerom Weldegiorgis; (5) 23 September 1950, inside a hotel near the Maritime Building in Asmera where he was being protected; poisoned by one of the waiters assigned to serve him; (6) 15 August 1951, near Cinema Impero in Asmera, escaped unharmed from five bullets aimed directly at him; (7) 15 January 1953 at 8 pm, wounded at the corner of Bar Moderna.

54. *Dehai*, 1/20, 24 January 1953; 1/21, 31 January 1953.
55. Ibid., 1/21, 31 January 1953.
56. Ibid., 1/21, 7 February 1953.
57. *Veritas et Vita*, 1 February 1953, in FO 371/102634, 4 February 1953.
58. *Ethiopia*, 6/372, 12 February 1953.
59. DOJ, F790001-0037, Breaux to State Department, 8 December 1952; see also FO 371/102634, 10 February 1952.
60. *Zemen*, 1/28, 20 February 1953.
61. *Dehai*, 1/24, 28 March 1953.
62. *Ethiopia*, 6 March 1953.
63. Ibid.
64. *Zemen*, 1/33, 27 February 1953.
65. *Ethiopia*, 6 March 1953.

14. REVIVAL AND SUPPRESSION OF THE WORKERS' UNION

1. Tsegai Kahsai, interview, 12 December 2002.
2. *Hanti Ertra*, 2/99, 1 November 1951.
3. Ibid.
4. Ibid. In the exchange between the workers and Arab community leaders, a heated discussion led to ill-feelings that threatened to escalate at one point. Weldeab Weldemariam and *Hanti Ertra* had to intervene to calm tempers down. It was after this intervention that the community decided to appeal to the Saudi Government.
5. Tsegai Kahsai, interview, 16 December 2002.
6. Kefela Beraki, interview.
7. Tsegai, interview, 2002.
8. The five organisers were Tsegai Kahsai, Kefela Beraki, Tesfai Zerakristos; Kidane Eliffe, brother of the Bayto Selam leader, Kinfe Eliffe; and *Blata* Yihdego Lemma. The last-mentioned was an elder and not a worker by profession. He was a merchant and a well-known wit sympathetic to the workers' cause.
9. There were two persons called Tsegai Iyasu. One was a worker involved with the organisers of the labour union. The second was a well-known Asmera lawyer who later joined the EPLF for a brief period in the late 1970s. The incident above refers to the latter.
10. *Hanti Ertra*, 2/103, 5 December 1951.
11. Ibid.

12. Tsegai Kahsai, interview, 2002.
13. Besides the three pioneers, the following were elected to the labour leadership: Yihdego Lemma, Mohammed Abdelkader Kiar, Tekie Eliffe, Ibrahim Mahmud, Abdulrahman Zeinu, Ahmed Saad Saleh and Ahmed Adem. Besides Weldeab and Tedla, the advisory committee included Abdella Gonafer, Haregot Abbay, *Haj* Suleiman Ahmed, Adem Kusmullah, Tewelde Tedla (advocate) and *Haj* Ahmed Basaad.
14. *Hanti Ertra*, 2/103, 5 December 1951.
15. Tsegai Kahsai, interview, 2002.
16. Kefela Beraki, interview.
17. Weldeab to Levinson, 28 August 1952, Weldeab Weldemariam Collection, RDC.
18. ICFTU, OR/ML/rb, Levinson to Weldeab, 6 February 1952.
19. *ESG*, 10/478, 1 November 1951.
20. ICFTU, OR/O/E4, Levison to Sir Vincent Tewson, 8 February 1952.
21. Ibid., OR/ML/nf, Levinson to Tewson, 26 March 1952.
22. Ibid., OR/O/PL/kp, Tewson to Weldeab, 18 November 1952.
23. *Dehai*, 1/11, 29 November 1952.
24. *Ethiopia*, 6/354, 11 December 1952.
25. DOS 77SA.00/1-1653, 16 January 1953.
26. David Cracknell, email interview, 18 September 2003.
27. FO 371/102634, Wardle-Smith to Foreign Office, 17 January 1953.
28. Weldeab, interview.
29. Kefela Beraki, interview.
30. For details on such complaints, see *Dehai*, 1/25, 7 March 1953.
31. Berhe Andemikael, interview.
32. FO 371/10264, Wardle-Smith to Busk, 18 March 1953.
33. DOS F790001-0051, 20 April 1953.
34. Ibid., 23 April 1953, reprinting contents of the proclamation from *Il Quotidiano Eritreo*.
35. Ibid.
36. Weldeab, interview, 1987.
37. DOS F790001-0059, Clark, 'Memorandum of Conversation with Weldeab Weldemariam and Arthur Reid', 14 May 1953.
38. Weldeab, interview, 1987.
39. Colonel Berhane Demoz, interview. Berhane was Colonel Wright's aide at the Asmera and Hamasien Police Headquarters.
40. Asfaha, interview; Zewde Retta, *Ye-Ertra Gudai, 1941–1963*, Berhan-na Printing Press, Addis Ababa, 2000, p. 387.
41. Weldeab, interview, 1987.
42. FO 371/102681, Wardle-Smith to Busk, 10 June 1953; see also FO 371/18297, 2 February 1954.
43. Ibid. Wardle-Smith's report and analysis are the only sources available on the Asseb incident.

44. IEG, Ministry of National Defence, file no. 197, Department of Marine, Abebe Bitew to Andargatchew Mesai, 10 January 1954.
45. *Dehai*, 2/32, 2 April 1954.
46. Prior to the Asseb killings, the manager of Bess Company, Wirts, had travelled to Massawa to alert the Emperor, who gave him a letter authorising him to settle the matter peacefully. The killings had already taken place by the time Wirts returned to Asseb.
47. FO 371/108297, Busk to Anthony Eden, 4 February 1954.
48. Ibid.
49. Arthur Reid, Answers to Questions from Bertil Wänström, MS, RDC, History Project Collection.

15. THE FIRST YEAR OF THE FEDERATION

1. *Zemen*, 1/46-47, 27 and 28 April 1953.
2. DOJ, 775A.21/4-3051, 30 April 1953.
3. Ibid., 775A. 21-5-1153, 11 May 1953.
4. Akito, interview, 2004.
5. Abudawd, interview, Asmera, 7 September 1999.
6. FO 371/102634, Wardle-Smith to R. Allen, 27 February 1953.
7. Tekleberhan Zere, interview, Asmera, 16 November 2003. Tekleberhan Zere was a well-known teacher at the Akhrya School in Asmera. A member of the Eritrean Liberation Movement (Haraka) in the 1960s, he shared a cell with Teklehaimanot Bokru, who, as one of the major Eritrean nationalist figures, spent many years in incarceration, at one time with his teenage son, Angesom. Unfortunately, Teklehaimanot, like many of his fellow nationalists, did not leave written documents or memoirs about his life and activities. Tekleberhan's patchy anecdotes about him are the most informative.
8. FO 371/102634, Cracknell report, 21 March 1953.
9. Ibid., Wardle-Smith to R. Allen, 23 March 1953.
10. Along with Gebreselassie Garza, Sahle Andemikael, director of the Girls' School in Asmera was also assigned to help in the strengthening of the UP.
11. FO 371/102634, Cracknell to Wardle-Smith, 23 March 1953.
12. Ibid., Wardle-Smith to R. Allen, 4 April 1953.
13. Ibid.
14. Tekeste Negash, *Eritrea and Ethiopia: The Federal Experience*, Nordic African Institute, Uppsala, 1997, pp. 83–4, quoting FO 371/102365, 6 May 1953.
15. Tekleberhan Zere, interview, 2003.
16. FO 371/102634, Wardle-Smith to Busk, March 1953.
17. DOS 775A.21/5-1153, 11 May 1953, Clark to State Department.
18. Tedla's report showed that the total number of Eritrean students had risen to 14,974, of whom 3,590 were girls, an increase of approximately 1,500 students from what the British had registered. The 456 teachers at all levels was also a marked increase. The statistics only dealt with the 11 schools under government control, leaving out private

schools. In the health sector, Tedla listed 10 hospitals, 103 clinics, 38 doctors and 719 nurses and dressers. The Eritrean labour force stood at 6,754 workers, of whom 439 were foreigners (400 Italian, 19 British, and others), of a total of 18,000 foreign residents, the majority of whom were Italian. As regards the maintenance of law and order, 223 robbers and 29 arms had been captured by security forces.

19. The members of the committee were Minassie Lemma, Deputy Minister of Finance; Legesse Gebre, director general of Customs; Stanisław Kirkor, financial advisor; E. Turlington, legal advisor; and Seifu Gebreyohannes, representing Ethiopia. Eritrean representatives were Finance Secretary Teklehaimanot Bokru; Economic Secretary Fessehatsion Haile; financial advisor Allen Smith; and Attorney General Norman Methven.
20. Eritrean Assembly, Minutes, no. 142, 16 March 1953.
21. Ibid.
22. Ibid.
23. Ibid., no. 189, 9 July 1953.
24. FO 371/102634, Wardle-Smith, conversations with Wilson Heathcote, 19 March 1953.
25. Mesfin Gebrehiwet, interview, 2001.
26. FO 371/102655, Wardle-Smith, 11 June 1953.
27. Ibid., 3 July 1953.
28. Ibid., Ramsden to Foreign Office, 27 July 1953.
29. GOE, Allen Smith, Financial Advisor's Memorandum, Con/Fin/c/1, 14689, 7 December 1954.
30. Eritrea Assembly, Minutes, 20 December 1953.
31. Arthur Reid to Bertil Wänström, 1974, MS, History Project Collection, RDC.
32. See DOS 775A.00/9-2453, 24 November 1953.
33. Zewde Retta, *Ye-Ertra Gudai, 1941–1963*, Berhan-na Printing Press, Addis Ababa, 2000, pp. 401–3.
34. Ibid., p. 404. Zewde Retta, who had full access to Ethiopian documents from that era, produces very interesting anecdotes and secret information of historical value. The problem is that he rarely acknowledged his sources. The quotation from the Emperor is likewise unacknowledged but not outside the range of possibility.
35. Ibid.
36. Ibid.
37. Arthur Reid to Bertil Wänström, 1974, MS, RDC.
38. Ibid.; see also DOS 775A.00/10-2653, Clark, 26 October 1953; Tekeste Negash, *Eritrea and Ethiopia*, p. 85.
39. DOS 775A.00/10-2653, Clark, 26 October 1953.
40. Ibid.
41. Tekeste Negash, *Eritrea and Ethiopia*, p. 85.
42. Reid to Bertil Wänström, 1974, MS, RDC.
43. *Ethiopia*, 7/440, 15 October 1953.
44. Ibid.

45. Ibid., 22 November 1953.
46. *Zemen*, 2/115, 28 November 1953.
47. FO 371/102634, 17 March 1953.
48. Ibid., 10 March 1953.
49. Ibid., Cracknell memo, 22 March 1953.
50. Eritrean Assembly, Investigation Diary, 25 October 1953; see also Eritrean Assembly, Minutes, nos. 239–40. For a comprehensive story, see *Dehai*, 2/35, 23 April 1954. In its brief return to publication early the next year, *Dehai* carried a detailed coverage of the case. The circumstances of its republication will be described in the next chapter.
51. *Ethiopia*, 7/441, 1 November 1953.
52. Cracknell to Alemseged, correspondence, *Dehai Mail*, 28 September 2004.
53. Tekeste Negash, *Eritrea and Ethiopia*, p. 87; DOS 775.31/5-1953, Clark to State Department, 19 May 1953.
54. *Dehai*, 2/35, 28 April 1954.
55. *Zemen*, 2/236, 28 April 1953. Mikael Welela was an Andinet hitman and a convicted felon whom Haile Selassie pardoned during the Federation.
56. FO 371/1/108, 24 December 1954.
57. FHC, Civil Case 29-31/46, 20 September 1955.
58. RDC, Fergus McLeary files, Box 13, Acc. 14210, letter to Emperor Haile Selassie, the Chief Executive and the Eritrean Assembly, 7 February 1954.
59. Zewde Retta, *Ye-Ertra Gudai*, pp. 409–10; *Ethiopia*, 7/457, 11 February 1954.
60. *Ethiopia*, 7/457, 11 February 1954. From his days as secretary general of the UP, Tedla had the habit of referring to Eritrea by its old name, Mereb Mellash. He was to use it more frequently for the remainder of his tenure as Chief Executive.
61. Zewde Retta, *Ye-Ertra Gudai*, pp. 409–10.
62. *Ethiopia*, 7/457, 11 February 1954.
63. FO 371/108196, Cracknell to Wardle-Smith, 22 February 1954.
64. Ibid., Wardle-Smith to Ambassador Busk, Addis Ababa, 8 March 1954.

16. ASSEMBLY, SUPREME COURT AND FEDERAL COURT CHALLENGES

1. Supreme Court of Eritrea, *Voce dell'Eritrea* represented by Mohammed Saleh Mahmud vs Secretary of the Interior and Commissioner of Police, represented by A.A. Canner, 19 August 1953; *Dehai*, 2/30, 12 March 1954.
2. *Dehai*, 2/28, 5 March 1954.
3. Arthur Reid to Bertil Wänström, 1974, MS, History Project Collection, RDC.
4. *Dehai*, 2/31, 26 March 1954.
5. Ibid., 2/32, 3 April 1954. Werede became the object of bitter criticism from both sides. Berhanu Ahmeddin chastised him in the Assembly for abandoning him at the last moment. *Ethiopia* too issued a whole article criticising him for making a distinction between the 'beggars' (the people of Eritrea) and the 'begged' (the Emperor) when they were both parts of the same entity.

6. Eritrean Assembly, Minutes, no. 270, 23 March 1954.
7. *Saut al Eretria*, 14 March 1953.
8. Ibid., 2/28, 5 March 1954.
9. Ibid., 2/30, 19 March 1954.
10. Ibid., 2/36, 30 April 1954.
11. Eritrean Assembly, A/ADM/6/vol. III, 28 February 1954; 25 March 1954; 13 April 1954.
12. *Zemen*, 2/256, 22 May 1954.
13. RDC, *Sheik* Said Sefaf file, Sefaf to *Bitweded* Andargatchew Mesai, Representative of the Imperial Ethiopian Government in Eritrea, June 1954.
14. Eritrean Assembly, Minutes, no. 304, 22 May 1954.
15. *Dehai*, 2/40, 28 May 1954.
16. Clarence Smith to Bertil Wänström, Response to Questionnaire, 1974, History Project Collection, RDC.
17. *Ethiopia*, 8/481, 3 June 1954.
18. RDC, UN Tribunal in Eritrea files, Reid to Cordier, 18 March 1954.
19. Ibid., Reid to Cordier, 20 March 1954.
20. Ibid., Cordier to Reid, 5 March 1954.
21. Ibid., Reid to Cordier, 15 July 1954.
22. Arthur Reid, Answers to Questions from Bertil Wänström, MS, RDC.
23. Ibid.
24. RDC, Said Sefaf file, Sefaf to *Bitweded* Andargatchew Mesai, June 1954.
25. Abudawd, interview, 1999.
26. GOE, EC/LJD/398, 7 April 1954.
27. FHC, Civil Case 7-46, *Balambaras* Zegai Zemou and Others vs The Government of Eritrea, 22 April 1954.
28. IEG, EG LJO/30, Turlington to Andargatchew, 7 April 1954,
29. Office of the Emperor's Representative, no. 324/53/28, Andargatchew Mesai to Tedla Bairu, 20 April 1954.
30. GOE, CON/LJ/5, Tedla Bairu, Memorandum, 15 May 1954.
31. GOE, CON/LJ/5, 21 July 1954.
32. Office of Emperor's Representative, no. 470/53/28, 28 October 1953.
33. *Zemen*, 2/267, 6 June 1954; 2/274, 15 June 1954.
34. *Ethiopia*, 8/486, 20 June 1956.
35. *Dehai*, 2/48, 23 July 1954.
36. IEG, Department of Advocate General vs Tipografia Fioretti and Others, Criminal Case no. 251/46, 28 July 1953.
37. RDC Archives, Box 9, Acc. no. 14069, Telegram to Emperor Haile Selassie, 19 August 1954.
38. *Zemen*, 2/346, 10 September 1954.
39. FO 371/113515, Eritrea Annual Review for 1954, 3/01670. The prison terms for the two editors were never disclosed publicly. According to Elias's brother Abraham,

the accused, who refused to submit to the jurisdiction of the FHC, were subjected to torture and harassment. Finally, Mohammed was imprisoned for two years and Elias for six. Elias's term was longer because the charges against him were more substantial than his colleague's. But both stood their ground till the very end. Upon release from prison, Elias was banished to Ethiopia. Mohammed went on to play a prominent role in the struggle for independence. Abraham Teklu, interview, 2006.

40. *Zemen*, 2/348, 14 September 1954.
41. Zewde Retta, *Ye-Ertra Gudai, 1941–1963*, Berhan-na Printing Press, Addis Ababa, 2000, pp. 434–6.
42. Ibid., p. 237.
43. FO 371/113515, Eritrea Annual Review for 1954; see also Eritrean Assembly, Minutes, no. 333, 14 September 1954.
44. Eritrean Assembly, Minutes no. 333, 14 September 1954.
45. Akito, interview, 2004.
46. Ibid.
47. Tesfai Reda'e, interview, 2002.
48. *Dehai*, 2/37, 7 May 1954.
49. Ibid., 2/48, 23 August 1954.
50. Tesfai Reda'e, Abraha Hagos and Gebremikael Begatsion, joint interview, 2002.

17. THE FALL OF THE TEDLA GOVERNMENT

1. *Zemen*, 2/406, 24 November 1954.
2. Ibid., 2/408, 26 November 1954.
3. Ibid., 2/542, 12 May 1955. *Dejazmatch* Araia Wassie, UP leader and later Interior Secretary; *Dejazmatch* Hagos Gebre, also of the UP, later mayor of Asmera; and the engineer and former Shuban al Rabita activist *Sheik* Mahmud Omer Ibrahim. To these were added members of the Federal Office, Befekadu Weldemikael (chairman) and Kumilatchew Belete.
4. IEG, Federal Deputy Advocate General's Office, file no. 611/1110/1, 11 May 1955.
5. DOS 775A.54/3-1255, Clark to State Department, 12 March 1955.
6. *Zemen*, 2/507, 29 March 1955.
7. Christopher Clapham, *Transformation and Continuity in Revolutionary Ethiopia*, Cambridge University Press, Cambridge, 1988, p. 207.
8. *Zemen*, 2/512, 15 May 1955.
9. Ibid., 2/505, 26 March 1955; and 2/511, 2 April 1955.
10. Ibid., 2/488, 6 March 1955; 2/493, 12 March 1955; 2/504, 25 March 1955.
11. Osman Haji Nasser had previously broken out of the Adi Quala prison, where he had been incarcerated for a dispute with villagers of that area. On taking up arms against the system, he sent a series of letters to the police and the government declaring that his sole aim was to 'rectify the injustices and oppression' suffered by him personally and the people in general. IEG, Police Sit-rep, 220, 27 May 1955.

12. FO 371/113519, 23 March 1955.
13. *Zemen*, 2/564, 1 July 1955.
14. One of Tedla's proposals, the construction of a dam in Zula, was roundly defeated in the Assembly, which diverted the funds involved to a salary increment for the police force. Eritrean Assembly, Minutes, no. 356, 26 April 1955.
15. FO 371/113519, 9 July 1955.
16. Abudawd, interview, 1999.
17. *Zemen*, 2/587, 5 July 1955.
18. GOE, CON/ASMB/2, Appendix A, CE Headquarters, 6 July 1955.
19. FO 371/113519, 9 July 1955.
20. GOE, CON/GSM/2, Tedla to McCleary, 9 July 1955.
21. FO 371/113519, 9 July 1955.
22. *Zemen*, 2/590, 8 July 1955.
23. FO 371/113519, 9 July 1955. People from that period who attended the speech mostly recalled Tedla's wish to run errands for the Emperor and his high praise for the education his parents had given him. Nothing more. See interviews with Hailemariam Debena, Asfaha Kahsai and Mesfin Gebrehiwet.
24. Ibid.
25. *Zemen*, 2/593, 12 July 1955.
26. Ibid., 2/595, 14 July 1955. The EDF leaders included in the ten-man delegation were Ibrahim Sultan, *Qadi* Ali Omer, Mohammed Berhanu, Musa Adem Umron, *Dejazmatch* Berhe Asberom, Mohammed Omer Akito and Said Sefaf.
27. Akito, interview, 2001.
28. Zewde Retta, *Ye-Ertra Gudai, 1941–1963*, Berhan-na Printing Press, Addis Ababa, 2000, p. 444.
29. Eritrean Assembly, A/ACT/17, 25 July 1955.
30. Ibid., nos. 386, 387, 388, 26–27 July 1955.
31. Ibid.
32. *Zemen*, 2/607, 28 July 1955; GOE, CON/2, Eritrean Assembly, Minutes, no. 390, Appendix A, 28 July 1955.
33. *Zemen*, 2/608, 30 July 1955.
34. Ibid.
35. Ibid., 2/614, 7 August 1955.

18. ASFAHA WELDEMIKAEL, CHIEF EXECUTIVE

1. Akito, interview, 2001.
2. *Zemen*, 2/616, 10 August 1955.
3. Notable among those exiles were future ministers and high government officials like *Tsehafe Te'ezaz* Weldemeskel, *Blata* Ayele Gebre, Tesfaye Tegegn, *Blata* Kidanemariam Aberra and *Negadras* Wodajo Ali.
4. Asfaha Weldemikael, interview, Addis Ababa, 1996.

5. Asfaha, interview, 1996.
6. Seyoum Haregot, *The Bureaucratic Empire: Serving Emperor Haile Selassie*, Red Sea Press, Trenton, NJ, 2013, p. xxiii. According to Seyoum Haregot, Andargatchew said to Haregot, 'Are you banking on your wealth for this election?' Haregot replied, 'Not on my wealth, I am banking on the votes in the Assembly.'
7. Nerayo Bahre, 'Mufti Ibrahim Mukhtar's Political Views', 2012, History Project Collection, RDC; UN General Assembly, A/C.44/2R.30, Communication Office of the Mufti, Ibrahim Elmukhtar and UN Commissioner in Eritrea, 25 June 1951.
8. Nerayo Bahre, 'Mufti Ibrahim Mukhtar's Political Views'.
9. Ibid.
10. Ibid.
11. Tekeste Negash, *Eritrea and Ethiopia: The Federal Experience*, Nordic African Institute, Uppsala, 1997, pp. 112–13, quoting FO/113520, BCA to BEAA, 26 October 1955 and 23 November 1955.
12. Ibid., p. 113. Article 16, in conjunction with article 91(1) of the Eritrean Constitution, provided that the Assembly could not amend the Constitution on matters that were contrary to the laws and principles embodied in the Federal Act.
13. Zewde Retta, *Ye-Ertra Gudai, 1941–1963*, Berhan-na Printing Press, Addis Ababa, 2000, pp. 475ff. Included in Abebe Aregay's committee were Aklilu, Minister of the Pen Tefera Work, and his deputy, Gebreweld Engidawork, as well as Andargatchew.
14. Peter Schwab, *Haile Selassie I: Ethiopia's Lion of Judah*, Nelson-Hall, Chicago, IL, 1979, p. 52.
15. FO 371/18744, 10 March 1956.
16. The original six provinces and their capitals were Hamasien/Asmera; Akeleguzai/Adi Qeih, Seraye/Mendefera, Red Sea/Massawa, Senhit/Keren and Barka/Akurdet.
17. American consul Richey also wrote that the creation of the Asseb province was meant to showcase Ethiopia's fair treatment of Muslims. The message was that Somalis would also be accorded similar treatment should they join Ethiopia.
18.G. Puglisi, *Chi e dall'Eritrea? Dizionario biografico*, Agenzia Regina, Asmera, 1952, p. 117.
19. Weldeyohannes Gebrezghi, interview, 2003.
20. *Abba* Teweldeberhan Andemeskel, interview, 29 July 2005.
21. *Qeshi* Mahdere Tesfamikael, interview, 5 January 2005. According to *Qeshi* Mahdere, the conversion of two well-known and respected priests from Seraye, *Qeshi* Asrat Maasho and *Qeshi* Sequar, to the Seventh Day Adventist Mission sent shock waves throughout the Orthodox hierarchy.
22. *Zemen*, 1/66, 10 July 1953.
23. Kinfe Tesfagabir, interview, 2010. Dr Kinfe Tesfagabir is better known to Eritreans as the man who invented the Tigrinya shorthand in the 1950s.
24. Tsegai Kahsai, interview, 16 December 2002; Berhe Andemikael, interview, 2 and 9 October 2007.
25. The three other colleagues were Inspectors Seyoum Kahsai, Rezene Berhane and Zeremariam Azazi.

26. Col. Kifle Gebremikael, interview, 22 August 2008; Captain Mikael Gebrenegus, '*Zweale Yngerka:* Developments and Phenomena after the Abrogation of the Federation', memo to Alemseged Tesfai, October 2010.
27. FO 371/113519, 30 June 1955.
28. Ibid., 27 June 1955.
29. Ibid.
30. *Zemen*, 2/627, 25 August 1955.
31. DOS F790001-0148, Clark to State Department, 3 February 1956.
32. *Zemen*, 3/732, 3 January 1956; 3/733, 4 January 1956.
33. Ibid., 3/737, 10 January 1956.
34. EPF, CID Report, Movimenti delle Persone Politicanti, 19 April 1956, RDC Archives.
35. Ibid., 19 and 24 April 1956.
36. Ibid., no. 120, 27 April 1956.
37. Ibid.
38. For details of the genesis of the political movement in Keren, see Ali Mohammed Saleh, *Tezekrotat Ertrawi Tegadalai*, Dubai, 2007.
39. Interview with EFYA leaders Tesfai Reda'e, Gebremikael Begatsion and Abraha Hagos, 2 October 2002. Most of the information on the EFYA is based on these wide-ranging interviews and on police records of the organisation.
40. Gebremikael Begatsion, interview, 2 October 2002.
41. Berhe Andemikael, interview, 2 and 9 October 2007.
42. EPF, CID Report, 31 March 1956.
43. Supreme Court of Eritrea, The State vs Tesfai Haile, Tesfai Reda'e and Others, Court of Appeals (Criminal), Case no. Rev 65/56, Asmera, 14 January 1958.
44. EPF, CID Report, 26 September 1956; Yohannes Tsegai, interview, 1997. The British consul, who suspected foul play with Yohannes's 'accident', filed an official complaint and demand for an investigation that went largely unheeded.
45. *Zemen*, 3/782, 9/3/1956.
46. Legal notice 362 of 1956, in *Zemen*, 3/831, 3 May 1956.
47. EPF, CID Report, 8 May 1956.
48. Ibid.
49. *Zemen*, 3/835, 11 May 1956.
50. DOS 775A.006-1456, E. Richey to State Department, 4 June 1956. For the Muslim League memorandum, see Appendix, F90001-0176. See also Tekeste Negash, *Eritrea and Ethiopia*, pp. 124–5.

19. THE WEAKENING OF THE LEGISLATURE

1. FO 371/118744, Memorandum by Sir James Shearer, in Howes to Killick, 24 July 1956.
2. *Zemen*, 3/805, 3 April 1956.

3. FO 371/118744, Shearer Memorandum, 24 July 1956.
4. Ibid.; see also Clarence Smith to Bertil Wänström, 28 January 1974, History Project Collection, RDC. One of the IB leaders, Gebrezghi Guangul, chairman of the Election Committee, was at the forefront of the rejectionist move.
5. FO 371/118744, Shearer Memorandum, 24 July 1956.
6. DOS 775A.02A/2-2455, D.I. Schneider to State Department, 24 February 1955.
7. Article 45 provided for the establishment of an electoral high commission by the Supreme Court. It had the responsibility of supervising all electoral proceedings and preventing or putting a stop to irregularities.
8. FO 371/118744, Shearer Memorandum, 24 July 1956.
9. EPF, CID Reports, Araia Wassie to Asfaha Weldemikael, 6 June 1955. *Haji* Suleiman Ahmed, *Haji* Imam Musa and Basaad were to head the committee.
10. Ibid., 8 June 1955.
11. Ibid., no. 170, 31 May 1956.
12. *Zemen*, 3/858, 7 June 1956.
13. Ibid., 3/864, 14 June 1956.
14. FO 371/118744, Richey to Killick, 19 June 1956.
15. Supreme Court of Eritrea, Melles Fre (minority opinion) in the case of *Sheik* Ibrahim Sultan; see DOS 775A.00/9-1065, 10 September 1956.
16. FO 371/118744, Shearer Memorandum, 24 July 1956. Clarence Smith, a judge at the time, confirmed this by revealing that Ostini was subjected to threats at Andargatchew's office. Clarence Smith to Bertil Wänström, 24 July 1956, RDC, History Project Collection.
17. *Zemen*, 3/896, 25 July 1956.
18. DOS 775A.00/9-1065, 10 September 1956.
19. Ibid.
20. Ibid.; see also EPF, CID Reports, 23 August 1956.
21. *Zemen*, 3/758, 5 February 1956; 3/759, 7 February 1956.
22. Ibid.
23. Clarence Smith to Bertil Wänström, Response to Questionnaire, 16 May 1956, p. 4, History Project Collection, RDC.
24. Ibid.; see also Fesseha Weldemariam, interview.
25. Clarence Smith to Bertil Wänström, Response to Questionnaire, 16 May 1956, RDC.
26. Uncontested results reported stood as follows: 5 in Akeleguzai; 4 in Seraye; 12 in Keren; 8 in Akurdet; 2 in Massawa; and 1 in Denkalia.
27. *Dejazmatch* Berhe Asberom, Tessema's brother; *Azmatch* Gebrekidan Tessema, his son; and *Azmatch* Gebrezghi Guangul, his son-in-law, had virtually joined the unionist camp. So had Asmerom Weldegiorgis of Adi Quala, Berhe's son-in-law.
28. *Zemen*, 3/936, 13 September 1956.
29. Ibid.
30. Ibid., 3/939, 16 September 1956.
31. Ibid., 3/340, 18 September 1956.

32. Asfaha Weldemikael, 'The Contested Election of Asseb and Denkalia', 24 September 1956, RDC, file J-ASM/10.
33. GOE, Office of the Chief Executive, CE/ASMB/10, 24 November 1956, RDC.
34. Supreme Court of Eritrea, Mohammed Omer Akito vs Chief Executive of Eritrea, Represented by Attorney General Clarence Smith, 12 February 1957.
35. FO 371/125359 (Appendix), P.R.A. Mansfield, 'Visit to Asmera', 6 June 1957.
36. Akito, interview, 2001.
37. The original quote from D'Azeglio was: *'L'Italia è fatta. Restano da fare gli Italiani'.*
38. Akito, interview, 2001.
39. *Zemen*, 4/1144, 31 May 1957.
40. GOE, INT B1, 25 September 1956.
41. Ibid., 5/INT B1, 9 June 1957. Beraki Habtezghi was removed from Seraye for inviting the suspended Naizghi Semere of Dembelas to a meeting of district administrators in Mendefera. He was moved to a lesser position at State Property.
42. Office of the Emperor's Representative, Kumilatchew to Asfaha, INT 738/4/57, 13 May 1957.
43. Ibid., 20 September 1957. From Consul Pares's conversations with Clarence Smith and McCleary.
44. FO 370/125359, 20 December 1957.
45. Ibid.
46. *Zemen*, 4/1144, 31 May 1957.
47. EPF, CID Reports, 15 July 1957.
48. Ibid.
49. FO 371/125359, 6 September 1957; Richey to Pares, 26 September 1957.
50. *Andinet*, 4/171, 17 October 1957.
51. One celebrated case involved the election of Tesfamariam Yehdego, whose father, Eritrean Assembly member Yehdego Gebrerufael, was one of the signatories of the 22 May 1954 resolution against federal interference in Eritrea's internal affairs. Dimetros and Tesfamariam had a public conflict in at least two election processes in which Tesfamariam prevailed. Gebreselassie Garza's angry condemnation came largely because the candidates who won in Asmera, Tsegai Gebreab and Goitom Beyin, were not particularly well known for their unionist stance.
52. FO 371/125359, 19 October 1957. The author has made some minor spelling and grammar corrections to the original petition, which was written in English.

20. POLITICAL AND SOCIAL STRUGGLES AT HOME AND ABROAD

1. RDC, ER/FG/09/53, Yohannes Tsegai Collection, letter from Weldeab, 2 March 1956. In this letter, Weldeab told Yohannes that he was still waiting for a reply to his request for broadcast rights. In his 1987 interview, he said that the programmes started some time in 1955. With the passage of time, Weldeab may have mixed up the dates. We take the date in the letter as more authentic.

2. Weldeab, interview. *Shiro* is a traditional stew made of ground chickpeas. Butter spread on top of it is considered a treat.
3. John Spencer, *Ethiopia at Bay*, Reference Publications, Algonac, MI, 1987, pp. 288–91; see also Harold Marcus, *The Politics of Empire: Ethiopia, Great Britain and the United States, 1941–1974,* Red Sea Press, Lawrenceville, NJ, 1983, p. 107.
4. Enrico Mania, *Non solo cronaca dell'Acrocoro,* Stabilimento Fotoliti, Rome, 2005, p. 205–6.
5. Alemseged Abbay, *Identity Jilted*, Red Sea Press, Lawrenceville, NJ, pp. 77–8. Weldeab's most quoted words are (in translation), 'Corn grows a beard like a man, but is toted like a baby.' This was in reference to modern Eritrea being governed by backward Ethiopia, according to Alemseged Abbay's interpretation.
6. *Zemen*, 3/927, 1 September 1956.
7. Ibid., 3/928, 2 September 1956.
8. Spencer, *Ethiopia at Bay*, p. 307. This was the time when Nasser's Afro-Asian People's Solidarity Organization and Kwame Nkrumah's All-African People's Conference were in contention. Ethiopia was in another group comprising of Liberia, Nigeria and other former French colonies. Nasser's and Nkrumah's merger into the Casablanca Group eventually led to the formation of the OAU. Haile Selassie played an important role in bringing the diverse parties together, thereby acquiring a leading position in Africa. Ethiopia used this leverage to the detriment of the Eritrean cause.
9. Weldeab, interview, 1987.
10. RDC, ER/FG/01/51, Yohannes Tsegai Collection, Mohammed Omer Qadi to Yohannes Tsegai, 6 June 1957.
11. Ibid., p. 2.
12. RDC, Hist. Fed/110, no. 01682.
13. DOS 777.00/11-157, Richey to State Department (Appendix 1), 1 November 1957.
14. Weldeab, interview, 1987.
15. EPF, CID Report, 14 January 1958.
16. Ibid., 21, 22, 23 January 1958.
17. DOS 775A.00/2-1 58, Richey to Secretary of State, 1 February 1958.
18. EPF, CID Report, 25–6 January 1958; 3–5 February 1958.
19. Ali Mohammed Saleh, *Tezekrotat Ertrawi Tegadalai*, Dubai, 2007, pp. 5–7; DOS 775A.00/3-558, Richey to Secretary of State, 5 March 1958.
20. DOS 775A.00/3-558, Richey to Secretary of State, 5 March 1958.
21. DOS 775.00/3, F790001, 19 March 1958. Note that the petitioners included former Assembly president Idris Mohammed Adem of the ML-WP. Among the leaders of the Federalist Association was Teklehaimanot Bokru, one of the most consistent advocates of Eritrean independence and Finance Secretary under Tedla Bairu.
22. DOS, Telegram no. 15933, Richey to Secretary of State, 25 March 1958.
23. EPF, CID Files, nos. 80, 89, 2 February 1958–10 October 1958.
24. Press Department of the Office of the Emperor's Representative, *Publication Issued to Celebrate the 10th Anniversary of Eritrea's Freedom and Merger with Ethiopia*, Il Poligrafico, Asmera, September 1962.

25. IEG, Ministry of Education and Fine Arts, Assefa Lulseged, Educational Inspector, no. M/14/51, 26 February 1959, p. 5.
26. Mania, *Non solo cronaca dell'Acrocoro*, p. 204.
27. Gebremedhin Tessema, interview, 2003.
28. The song of the Ethiopian flag—'*demun yafesese, lbun yenedede*'—was different from the national anthem—'*Ityopia hoy des ybelish*'. The former praised patriots and wished long life to the Emperor. The anthem put God and the Emperor on a par in uniting patriots and securing liberation.
29. This part is based on interviews with the following active participants of the strike, many of them the leaders: Daniel Haile Manna, Berhe Tesfamariam (Mariano), Teame Gebreyohannes, Dr Belay Ghiorghis (Giorgio), Afewerki Habtu, Daniel Tesfai, Andom Kiflemariam, Gebregziabher Gebremariam, Afewerki Habtu Hailu, Tesfai Gebreab.
30. EPF, CID Report, Movimenti delle Persone Politicanti, 10 May 1957. This document reports that as the students marched to the post office and were trucked to Adi Quala, they shouted political slogans.
31. IES, Frederick Russell, Diary, 12 May 1957.
32. EPF, CID Reports, 24, 25 May 1957.
33. IES, Russell Diary, 22 May 1957.
34. *Cavaliere* Idris Lijam and an Ethiopian named Deneke sat on the bench with him.
35. IES, Russell Diary, 23 May 1957.
36. Ibid., 27 May 1957.
37. Among the dismissed students were Gilamikael Tesfamariam (Mariano), highly acclaimed goalkeeper for the Adulis and the Eritrean and Ethiopian national teams; his teammate Mekonnen Yehdego; Teku'e Yehdego, the highly influential revolutionary; Daniel Haile, later a banker; and Seyoum Tareke, later an international football referee.
38. Tom Killion, 'Workers, Capital and the State in the Ethiopia Region, 1919–1974', PhD thesis, Stanford University, 1985, pp. 359–60.
39. Ibid., quoting US SD OIR 1730, 31 December 1955.
40. GOE, Dept. of Social Services Report, 5/56-5/57, 21 June 1957.
41. Killion, 'Workers, Capital and the State in the Ethiopia Region', p. 363. According to government sources, employment figures improved beyond 1958, when 29,704 were registered. The highest figures were those of 1961—30,892. These numbers were, however, deceptive as they included seasonal employment for cotton-picking and fruit-gathering by the agro-industrial enterprises of Barattolo and De Nadai, respectively. See GOE, Dept of Social Services Report, 14 July 1961, n. 24.
42. The bloody riots in Asseb of January 1954; the Merenghi Bottlers strike of 22 March 1955; the PWD strikes of 22 March 1955; and the Melotti strike of 6 June 1955 are the most notable. For details, see Alemseged Tesfai, *Federeshin Ertra ms Ityopia: kab Matienzo ksab Tedla*, Hidri Publishers, Asmera, 2005, pp. 463–70 and 599–603.
43. GOE, Dept of Social Services, Asfaha Kahsai to Secretary of Social Services, 30 April 1956.

44. Interviews with Tsegai Kahsai, Berhe Andemikael and Araia Hadgu. The other persons named were Assembly member Menghistu Debessai and Kinfe Eliffe, the only active unionist in the group.
45. Killion, 'Workers, Capital and the State in the Ethiopia Region', p. 373.
46. *Zemen*, 5/1277, 10 November 1957.
47. EPF, CID Report 129-130, 17 December 1957.
48. *Zemen*, 5/1360, 19 October 1958.
49. Ibid., 5/1373, 7 March 1958.
50. Clarence Smith to Bertil Wänström, Response to Questionnaire, 14 March 1987, History Project Collection, RDC.
51. *Zemen*, 5/1375, 9 March 1958.
52. Ibid., 5/1356, 9 March 1958.
53. Habtemariam Yohannes, interview, 2004.
54. Othman Saleh Sabby [Sabbe], *The History of Eritrea*, Dar Al-Masirah, Beirut, 1974, p. 246.
55. Killion, 'Workers, Capital and the State in the Ethiopia Region', p. 379.
56. EPF, CID Report, no. 48, 12 March 1958.
57. GOE, Dept of Education, Asfaha Kahsai to Sec. of Social Services, ST/16/494, 18 March 1958.
58. GOE, Labour Office, Massawa, *Sheik* Malik Nasser to Director of Labour, Mass/LO/13/74, 18 March 1958.
59. The representatives at this time were Demsas Weldemikael, Ibrahim Ali Bekhit, Solomon Hailemelekot, Berhanu Ahmeddin, Habtezghi Okbazghi, Fesseha Weldemariam (Gandhi) and Maasho Beyin (*Qeshi*).
60. Killion, 'Workers, Capital and the State in the Ethiopia Region', p. 379.
61. Okbazghi Yohannes, *The United States and the Horn of Africa*, HarperCollins, New York, 1997, p. 158.
62. Killion, 'Workers, Capital and the State in the Ethiopia Region', pp. 379–89.
63. *Zemen*, 5/1384, 23 March 1958.
64. Some of the most notable strikes were those of the SAVA Bottlers of 1960, and the workers and employees of SAIDE at Mersa Gulbub and Cantiera of Godaif in 1961; and that of the employees of the Ethiopian Highway Authority in 1962. GOE, Dept of Social Services, Monthly Report, July 1969–August 1962.

21. DISMANTLING THE FEDERAL BASE

1. DOS 775A.00/3-2558, Richey to State Department, 25 March 1958.
2. Ibid.
3. Zewde Retta, *Ye-Ertra Gudai, 1941–1963*, Berhan-na Printing Press, Addis Ababa, 2000, pp. 484–5.
4. EPF, CID Reports, 21 April 1958; 17 June 1958; 21 June 1958.
5. See *Zemen*, 24 July 1958—9 October 1958.

6. Ibid., 5/507, 6 October 1958. The unionist from Keren, Sefaf Hyabu, expressed harsh words on the provincial governors' failure to stop the conversion of relief food into 'a trade deal'.
7. IEG, Imperial Federal Office, P/C2/128, June 1954.
8. EPF, CID Report, INT/C/12/1321, 26 January 1958.
9. Ibid.
10. EPF, CID Report, 11 July 1957.
11. Tsegai Kahsai, interview, 27 June 2011.
12. EPF, CID Report, 19 May 1958.
13. Ibid.; also see 26 June 1958 entry.
14. EPF, CID Reports, document stamped with the name Berhanie Mengistie, an Ethiopian Andinet activist, n.d.
15. Ibid.
16. Fesseha Weldemariam, interview, 1987.
17. That Dimetros had such a dream was confirmed by his colleague and successor at Mahber Hawaryat, Qeshi Mahdere; his bitter critic, *Abba* Teweldeberhan, formerly head of Debre Merqerios; and *Grazmatch* Shewit, his driver.
18. DOS 775A/1-459, 'Abolishment of Flag of Eritrea', Richey to State Department, 4 January 1958.
19. Ibid.
20. Ibid. Fesseha Weldemariam claimed that members who tried to voice their opposition were forcibly silenced by the majority supporters. His own attempt was interrupted, he said, by a member pulling him down by the sleeve, which was torn off from the shoulder.
21. Ibid.
22. Ibid., 6/1598-1603, 16–27 January 1959.
23. Kinfe Tesfagabir, interview, Fiumicino Airport, 7 February 2010.
24. Tekeste Negash, *Eritrea and Ethiopia: The Federal Experience*, Nordic African Institute, Uppsala, 1997, pp. 144–5. Tekeste has further argued that the claim by Eritreans to a democratic experience was guaranteed by the presence and strong support of Chief Justice Shearer and that it disappeared with his departure in late 1959.
25. GOE, CE/LG/21, Chief Executive to President of the Assembly, 10 November 1959. The laws rescinded by the proclamation were the Decreto Royale no. 1019, 1 June 1936; Ordinamento e Amministrazione dell'Africa Orientale Italiana; Proclamation 98 of 1950; and the Death Sentence Proclamation of 1953. Only two members, Fesseha Weldemariam and Maasho Beyin spoke when the floor opened for debate. There was no mention of what they said. Two of the major leaders of the Independence Bloc, Gebrezghi Guangul and Berhanu Ahmeddin, proposed the adoption of the motion. Of 51 present, 46 members voted for the motion, only 5 opposed; 17 were absent.
26. Tekie Tesfai's English–Tigrinya dictionary highlights the discrepancy. Here, 'government' is translated as *mengsti, mmHdar, gz'at*; 'administration' as *mmHdar*; and 'state' as *kfal mengsti* (part of government). The problem is compounded by the word *hager*, which also means 'state' or 'nation'. *Hagere Ertra* is the State of Eritrea.

27. *Zemen*, 7/1927, 19 May 1960.
28. Ibid., 7/1970, 18 July 1960.
29. Eritrean Administration, INT/A/11, 12 September 1960. In Maria Tsellam, a candidate with popular support was blocked by the order of the Assembly president Hamid Ferej.
30. *Zemen*, 7/2007, 9 September 1960. The unopposed candidate from Hamasien was Werede Beyin, who had openly 'kidnapped' the majority of the electors and secured their vote, thus denying his rival, Tekeste Seleba, even the minimum numbers required to stand for election.
31. Eritrean Administration, INT/A/4, 7078/6576, 20 September 1960.
32. Ibid., AB/Eritrea, 18.5, 7 September 1960.
33. These were *Dejazmatch* Berhe Asberom, *Kegnazmatch* Berhanu Ahmeddin, Osman Hindi, Asberom Weldegiorgis, Mohammed Said Hassano and Gebrekidan Tessema.

22. THE ROAD TO THE ERITREAN REVOLUTION

1. Some of the government and Assembly officials under intense scrutiny were Haregot Abbay, Bemnet Tessema, Akito, Fesseha Weldemariam, Suleiman Ahmed, Imam Musa, Tsegai Kahsai and many more. The so-called Haregot–Bemnet clique that often met at Cinema Roma café was often referred to as 'people of bad faith' or 'evil intentions'.
2. These were Nawd, Idris Mohammed al-Hassen (Genshera), Hassan Alhaj Idris, Yasin Aqeda, Osman Mohammed Osman, Mohammed al-Hassen Denkeli, Habib Gaas and Saleh Iyay. Interviews with Kahsai Bahlibi, Sahel, 1987; Yasin Aqeda, Asmera, 1 June 2006; Idris Genshera, 24–25 November 2004; Saleh Iyay, with Gunther Schroeder, Khartoum, 1988.
3. Mohammed Said Nawd, 'The Eritrean Liberation Movement (Haraka): Truth and History', Unpublished MS, Tigrinya original.
4. Haraka Charter, 1962; see also Tahir Fedab, 'The Eritrean Liberation Movement and Its Historical Progress (1958–1967)', Unpublished MS, RDC, 1993, p. 88; Genshera, interview, Port Sudan, 1987.
5. Adem Mohammed Said, interview, Kassala, 1987. In later years, the Abboud regime actually handed over five Eritreans to the Ethiopian authorities. Adem Mohammed Said identified two of these as Mohammed Shifa and Suleiman Abubaker.
6. Tahir Fedab, 'The Eritrean Liberation Movement and Its Historical Progress', p. 88.
7. Genshera, interview, 2004.
8. Nawd, 'The Eritrean Liberation Movement', p. 44.
9. Ibid.
10. Awet Weldemichael, *Third World Colonialism and Strategies of Liberation*, Cambridge University Press, Cambridge, 2013, p. 59.
11. Iyay, interview, 1988. As a student, Iyay was noted for his refusal to attend the hoisting of the Ethiopian flag in the morning, but standing at the forefront to relish its lowering down every evening.

12. Mohammed Berhan Hassen, *Mnqsqas Harnet Ertra*, Selam Printing Press, Asmera, 2001.
13. Interviews with former club players Berhe Tesfamariam (Mariano), Tesfagabir Shihay and Andom Kiflemariam. An intense sportsman of indomitable courage, Kahsai Bahlibi used to oblige his players to swear an oath of allegiance 'not to promote religious, ethnic or provincial division' before admission into the club.
14. For a discussion on this point based on interviews with veteran Haraka members, see Gaim Kibreab, *Critical Reflections on the Eritrean War of Independence*, Red Sea Press, Trenton, NJ, 2008, pp. 149–50.
15. Mohammed Saad Adem, 'The Eritrean Revolution', Unpublished MS, RDC, Acc. no. 0712. The Haraka representative was Suleiman Abbe.
16. Ibid.
17. Interviews with Mohammed Berhan Hassen and Weldemikael Abraha. Later, in 1962, the addition of Tiku'e Yehdego, Mehari Debessai and Wolday Ghidey, all future figures in the armed struggle, boosted the Christian presence in Haraka.
18. Fedab, 'The Eritrean Liberation Movement and Its Historical Progress', pp. 189–90.
19. Tekie Beyene, *Kab Riq Hfnti*, Hidri Publishers, Asmera, 2009, pp. 2–3; Amanuel Tesfatsion, interview (by phone), Stockholm, 21 December 2019. Besides Nebyat and Tekie, the group comprised Berhe Weldegabriel, Amanuel Gebreyesus and Amanuel Tesfatsion.
20. Ibid., p. 9. Meswaiti Gebrehiwet, one of the organisers, estimated that the crowd numbered much more than 2,000.
21. Tekie, *Kab Riq Hfnti*, pp. 9–10, Meswaiti, interview; Amanuel Tesfatsion, interview.
22. Tekie, *Kab Riq Hfnti*, 26 September 1960.
23. Eritrean Administration, INT/C/2/1076, SDO 775/Vol. IV/154, 26 December 1960.
24. Iyasu Yohannes, interview, Asmera, 23 September 2010. Iyasu soon joined Haraka, migrated to Cairo where he went to school and, later, joined the EPLF. Estifanos went on to become a famous goalkeeper for the San Bernardo and Airlines football teams of Asmera and Addis Ababa, respectively.
25. Sebhat Aberra, interview, 14 September 2007. The shopkeeper, Gerensae, famous in the Villaggio Paradiso area of Asmera, recalled Sebhat following Asfaha and Ferej up to his shop on the night of the bombing. The boy, Aregai Teferi, was an employee of the Water Resources Department of Asmera. They have both since died.
26. *Zemen*, 9/2290, 31 October 1961; interviews with Yohannes Okbazghi (2001), Shewit Desta (1997, 2012), *Qeshi* Mahdere Tesfamikael (2006). See also 'A Short Life History of Melake Selam Dimetros Gebremariam', *Fenote Berhan*, 4/304, September 1988.
27. *Azmatch* Mirach of Liban, perpetually in conflict with the neighbouring village of Habela, had previously been stripped of his position by Asfaha for allegedly being indulgent towards the *shifta* following Asfaha's anti-*shifta* proclamation of 1957. Sebhat Aberra was the chief's grandson.
28. *Zemen*, 9/2291, 1 November 1961.

29. FHC, District Court of Eritrea, Tsegai Habtemariam presiding, 'Ruling on Prima Facie Witness's Account', App. 14-20, Asmera, 27 October 1960.
30. Ibid. Those charged with conspiracy were Tsehaye Abraha, Weldeab's friend and an old LPP activist; and *Azmatch* Tesfai Beraki, a former prominent unionist, also a native of Adi Kefelet.
31. Ibid.
32. IEG, Ethiopian Military Intelligence Report, INT/36/01, 'Ma 0004 sle ato Gebremedhin hailu qebir Tiqimt 24, 1954' (31 October 1961). The remaining suspects were Menghistu Bairu; Tesfai Beraki, former detainee in the case; Tekeste Seleba, former Assembly member; Tsegai Kahsai of the workers' association; and Domenico Bahlibi, director of the Government Printing Press.
33. Ibid.
34. Office of the Emperor's Representative, Security Dept, file no. 543, Taye Metcha to Lt. Gen. Abiy Abebe, 27 July 1962.
35. Ibid., CID/B/20/10/2787, Col. Irdachew Imeshaw to SDO Hamasien, 15 December 1961.
36. Ibid., M/1/AS/137, Chief of Police Asmera to SDO Hamasien, 29 January 1962.
37. Ibid.
38. Ibid., HQ/AG/40F 793, Goitom Gebrezghi to Belai Gebrezghi, 5 May 1962.
39. Ibid.
40. Ibid. Also video interview with Manna Adhanom by Asmerom Habtemariam and Negash Asfaha, Asmera, 18 November 1991.
41. Menghistu Bairu was a remarkable man who was exposed to continuous imprisonment, harassment and torture by Ethiopian security forces until the mid-1970s. For background information on him, see Herui Tedla Bairu, *Eritrea and Ethiopia*, Red Sea Press, Trenton, NJ, 2016, pp. 15–18.
42. Interviews with Tsehaitu Eshetie, Manna Adhanom's sister-in-law, who hid the weapons in her home at Ferrovia, Asmera, 30 April 2013; Adem Melekin with Osman Saleh, Asmera, 8 September 2002. Ali Kerar, Mohammed Idris Haj and Omer Ezaz received the consignment on behalf of Awate.
43. Adem Melekin, interview, 2002.
44. IEG, Ethiopian Military Intelligence Report, INT 36/36/01, M-0018, Taye Metcha, 'Bandit Movement in Asmera and Hamasien', 25 July 1962.
45. See Beyene Solomon, *Fighter for Democracy: The Saga of an Ethiopian Labour Leader*, Publish America, Baltimore, MD, 2010. Beyene, an Eritrean from Tse'azega, was a founder and first president of the Ethiopian Labour Union.
46. The Eritrean Amanuel Gebreyesus led the first Ethiopian Airlines hijacking with the future EPRP leader Berhanemeskel Redda in 1969. The second hijacking of January 1971 was an all-Eritrean affair led by Amanuel Yohannes and included Yohannes Sebhatu, Mussie Tesfamikael and Debessai Gebreselassie (Tiki). The third hijacking, which resulted in the killing of the would-be hijackers by security personnel on the flight, was also organised and led by the EPLF's Amanuel Yohannes. The Ethiopian

revolutionary Wallelign Mekonnen and the Eritreans Martha Mebrahtu and Yohannes Fekadu, among others, perished in the massacre. The only survivor, Tadelech, was wounded.

47. Temesgen Haile, a veteran of the Addis Ababa student movement and prominent activist of the Tihisha group, died in police custody in 1973.
48. Interviews with Idris Mohammed Adem and others by Gunther Schroeder, Khartoum, 1989.
49. EPF, CID Report, 19 March 1959. The entry for 17 March indicates that Ibrahim and Idris had left Eritrea before 13 March. The entry for 19 March reports suspicions that their departure and permission to enter Cairo with little delay had been facilitated by the British consul in Asmera.
50. DOS 775A.00/6-2959, 29 June 1959.
51. DOS 775A.00/5-1459, 14 May 1959; 775A.0011-3059, Claude D. Ross (Cairo), Memorandum of Conversation with Eritrean Nationalists, 30 November 1959.
52. Ibid.
53. DOS 775A.00/4-1759, Richey, 'Defection of Sheiks Ibrahim Sultan and Idris Mohammed Adem', 17 April 1959.
54. Ibid., 775A.00/11-3059, Claude D. Ross, Memorandum of Conversation with Eritrean Nationalists, 30 November 1959.

23. THE ERITREAN LIBERATION FRONT

1. Gelaydos, interview with Gunther Schroeder, Khartoum, January 1988.
2. Solomon Dirar, *Ertrawyan Comando: Qya 18 Deqiq*, Hidri Publishers, Asmera, 1994, p. 11. Seid Hussein was accompanied by Mahmud Haroun and Ahmed Hashim in the airport attempt. In 1975, he was liberated from Sembel Prison in Asmera, courtesy of a daring ELF operation. He was executed by the ELF in 1977.
3. Gesir, interview, 26 October 2007.
4. Taha Mohammed Nur, interview with Schroeder, Rome, 28 May 1988. Those in the meeting were Idris Gelaydos, Idris Mohammed Adem, Mohammed Saleh Hummed, Said Ahmed Hashim, Adem Akte, Ibrahim Idris Bilenai, Seid Hussein, Abdelkader Ibrahim, Mohammed Seid Omer (Anteta), and Taha Mohammed Nur. This list, which can be corroborated for most names, may not be definitive, as other accounts add, subtract or replace some of them.
5. Idris Mohammed Adem, interview with Gunther Schroeder, 15 March 1989, Khartoum.
6. In 1944, Kekia built a school in Hirgigo, where Sabbe and other local children went to learn. It was a secular school which Kekia named after Haile Selassie. After Hirgigo, Sabbe was sent to Addis Ababa, where he enrolled in the Medhane Alem and Teferi Mekonnen schools.
7. *Ustaz* Mohammed Abdelkader Shek, interview with Hassen Saad, 11 March 2013; Othman Saleh Sabby [Sabbe], *The History of Eritrea*, Dar Al-Masirah, Beirut, 1974, p. 248.

8. Sabby [Sabbe], *The History of Eritrea*, p. 43.
9. Ibid.
10. Ahmed Sheik Ibrahim Feres, 'My Struggle in the Eritrean Revolution', Unpublished MS (Arabic original), 1991, pp. 7–8.
11. Idris Mohammed Adem, interview, 15 March 1989.
12. RDC, ELF Collection, ELF/17/122, Sabbe to Idris, 7 November 1961. Sabbe was particularly angry with Ibrahim and Weldeab, whom he also accused of meeting a fortune-teller named Abubeker al Tekuriri, , who had been sent by Haile Selassie to promote the federal idea. 'You crushed the Tekuriri by telling him that you did not leave Eritrea to revive the Federation,' he wrote to Idris. 'I applaud you for that. You have boosted my morale.'
13. Ibid., 12 December 1961.
14. Ibid., 28 October 1961.
15. *Da'eret al Ala'elam* (published by the ELF), 1982.
16. *Zemen*, 8/2178, 18 May 1961.
17. Ibid., 8/8249, 31 December 1961.
18. Haileselassie Weldu, *Hamid Idris Awate*, Hidri Publishers, Asmera, 2018, pp. 34–42. The officer was locally known as Dewdew. When Awate was under Dewdew's custody, Kunama *shifta* attacked his party. Dewdew untied Awate, gave him his own gun and ordered him to join his party against the attackers. Awate took the opportunity to point the gun at Dewdew and make his escape. Awate's family subsequently suffered reprisals until he later moved them to the land of the Welqait.
19. Ibid., p. 51. Awate's initial *shifta* band consisted of Osman Longhi, Hassen Karar, Adem Faid, Idris Mahmoud, Ybet Hamid-Hamjor, Shanin Fakd, Fikak Mahmoud and Assenay Shokon.
20. WO 230/242 61439, 22 June 1948. In the first two raids of 19 March and 15 May 1948, Awate led bands of 16 Welqait and 5 Beni Amer and 27 Welqait and 7 Nara gunmen, respectively.
21. Haileselassie Weldu, *Hamid Idris Awate*, pp. 150–6.
22. RDC, D.D.P. Cracknell, 'Surrender of Hamid Idris Awate', Asmera, 1951.
23. GOE, SDO HQ/70/B, SDO to DO Barentu, 17 March 1956.
24. Ibid., 27 June 1956.
25. Ibid., INT B/7, HQ/AD/S/70/A, 1 June 1957.
26. Zere Debretsion, interview with Yemane Mesghina, Asmera, 20 January 1998.
27. Ibid. Also interview with Mohammed Dawd's cousin, Alamin Sheik Saleh, 28 January 2013.
28. Gindifil and Abu Tayara, interviews, 1989. Besides Dubuk, the centres were Gash, Upper Barka, Lower Barka, Zara, Algheden and Baria (Nara).
29. Gesir, interview. For discussions on the religious issue with reference to Awate, see Awet Weldemichael, *Third World Colonialism and Strategies for Liberation*, Cambridge University Press, Cambridge, 2013, p. 60; J. Venosa, *Paths towards the Nation: Islam, Community and Early Nationalist Mobilization in Eritrea, 1941–*

1961, Ohio University Press, Athens, OH, 2014, p. 205; Haileselassie Weldu, *Hamid Idris Awate*, pp. 239–41.

30. Mahmoud Mohammed Saleh and *Sheik* Suleiman, interviews.
31. GOE, SDO Akurdet, HQ/AD/27/E, Omer Hassano to Secretary of the Interior, 9 September 1961.
32. Ibid.
33. Kidane Hidad, interview, Keren, 19 April 2013. Some accounts credit Kidane with having tipped off Awate about the imminent danger of arrest. Kidane denies the claim. 'I cannot take credit for what I did not do. I did tip and save him on another occasion, after he had left his village and a contingent led by Major Gebrekidan Tesfai was approaching to encircle his group. Not only did I tip him, but I used my Haraka contacts to cut off telephone lines and help him disappear. But this was later.'
34. Apart from the three cattle rustlers, Kirutchai counted the following seven as the pioneers of the armed struggle: Hamid Awate, Kirutchai, Awate Mohammed Faid, Hummed Dewhen, Fagurai Abu Halima, Adem Abu Halima and Abdu Mohammed Faid.
35. Haileselassie Weldu, *Hamid Idris Awate*, p. 274.
36. Ruth Iyob has written that Awate shot his first bullets with thirteen fighters of the ELF, suggesting that he was already a member of that organisation (*The Eritrean Struggle for Independence: Resistance and Nationalism, 1941–1993*, Cambridge University Press, Cambridge, 1995, pp. 104–5). Tekeste Negash says that the ELF brought Awate into its ranks a year after its creation. He also asserts that Idris Mohammed Adem had invoked their common Beni Amer roots to do so and that Awate had taken up arms in protest against Beni Amer land confiscated by the Eritrean and Ethiopian governments (Tekeste Negash, *Eritrea and Ethiopia: The Federal Experience*, Nordic African Institute, Uppsala, 1997, p. 149).
37. Sabbe, *The History of Eritrea*, p. 249.
38. *Zemen*, 8/2266, 26 September 1961; 8/2268, 29 September 1961. Bereg Norai or Osman Bereg was captured with one rifle and fourteen bullets on 26 September.
39. Haileselassie Weldu, *Hamid Idris Awate*, pp. 304–5.
40. *Zemen*, 9/2340, 11 January 1962.
41. Ibid., 9/2314, 6 December 1962. The captured fighters were new additions, not constituting the original veterans. These were Saleh Mohammed Hassen, Osman Idris Haj and Musa Mohammed Musa.
42. Ibid., 9/2340, 11 January 1962.
43. Gesir and Gindifil, interviews.
44. Awate's original revolutionary force consisted of the following: Hamid Idris Awate, Abdu Mohammed Faid (killed), Awate Mohammed Faid, Mohammed Hassen Dewhen, Saleh Kirutchai, Mohammed Ibrahim, Fagurai Abu Halima, Adem Abu Halima, Ferej Mahmoud Badurai, Ali Dawd, Musa Mohammedin, Karar Adem Hasot, Shengerai Amar, Bereg Norai (captured), Ibrahim Mohammed Ali, Mohammed Omer Kerai,

Adem Degaf. As always, names are added and subtracted from this list, but the names above are consistent in most accounts.

45. Gesir and Kubub Hajaj, quoted by Tesfai Tekle, interview, Asmera, 27 May 2013.
46. *Zemen*, 8/2398, 7 April 1962. The fighters who died in this battle were Ibrahim Ahmed Hummed and Ali Delab.
47. Abu Tayara, Interview with Gunther Schroeder, 23 March 1989, Sudan.
48. Cracknell, interview, 2002.
49. In 2005, the author and his research team spent time at Hademdemi, near Gerset, with the Awate family. Several tapes of interviews and conversations were collected on that visit.
50. Sabbe, interview with Gunther Schroeder, Khartoum, 4 April 1983.

24. ERITREA ON THE EVE OF ANNEXATION

1. Ruth Iyob, *The Eritrean Struggle for Independence: Resistance and Nationalism, 1941–1993*, Cambridge University Press, Cambridge, pp. 42–5.
2. J.A. Lefebvre, *Arms for the Horn: US Security Policy in Ethiopia and Somalia, 1953–1991*, University of Pittsburgh Press, Pittsburgh, 1991, p. 97. After having failed in its quest to acquire Somalia or, at least, British Somaliland, Ethiopia was intent on securing the Ogaden by proposing the demarcation of its border with Somalia as it stood before the impending Somali independence in 1960. Its attempts failed when the US sided with Italy as the Administering Authority of the trusteeship of Somalia, to force Ethiopia to sign only a temporary agreement that would not bind the emerging Somali state.
3. Ibid., pp. 96–7; John Spencer, *Ethiopia at Bay*, Reference Publications, Algonac, MI, 1987, p. 307.
4. Spencer, *Ethiopia at Bay*, p. 307.
5. Peter Schwab, *Haile Selassie I: Ethiopia's Lion of Judah*, Nelson-Hall, Chicago, 1979, p. 102.
6. The Brazzaville or Monrovia Group consisted of Ethiopia, Liberia, Congo (Brazzaville), Ivory Coast, Madagascar, Cameroon, Chad, Gabon, Central African Republic, Dahomey, Niger, Upper Volta, Mauritania, Senegal, Nigeria, Somalia, Siera Leone and Togo.
7. The Casablanca Group consisted of Morocco, Ghana, Egypt, the Provisional Government of Algeria, Guinea, Mali and Libya.
8. Schwab, *Haile Selassie I*, p. 108; see also Seyoum Haregot, *The Bureaucratic Empire: Serving Emperor Haile Selassie*, Red Sea Press, Trenton, NJ, 2013, pp. 152–5.
9. At the end of the 1950s, President Eisenhower stated that the US should maintain without any disruption or discontinuity 'our key Kagnew facilities'. Lefebvre, *Arms for the Horn*, p. 103.
10. Ibid., pp. 94–103.
11. Harold Marcus, *The Politics of Empire: Ethiopia, Great Britain and the United States, 1941–1974*, Red Sea Press, Lawrenceville, NJ, 1983, pp. 116–17.
12. *Zemen*, 8/2073, 15 December 1960.

13. Ibid., 8/2074, 17 December 1960.
14. Ibid.
15. Ibid., 8/2078, 21 December 1960.
16. Gebreyohannes, interview.
17. Marcus, *The Politics of Empire*, quoting Looram, p. 153.
18. RDC, Berhanie Mengistie files.
19. RDC, Habtu Tesfamikael files.
20. Tekie Fessehatsion, *From Federation to Annexation*, Eritreans for Peace and Democracy Publication Committee, Washington, DC, 1990, quoting Looram, p. 43.
21. Asfaha interview, 1996. Present at the meeting were Prime Minister Aklilu, Yilma Deressa of Finance, Merid Mengesha of Defence, and Endalkatchew Mekonnen of Trade and Industry.
22. Asfaha, interview, 1996.
23. *Zemen*, 8/2225, August 1961.
24. Ibid.; see also 8/2231, 2232, 2233, 2, 4 and 5 August 1962.
25. Office of the Emperor's Representative, file no. 589, Taye Metcha to Abiy Abebe, 26 August 1961.
26. Ibid., Dept of Security, no. 345/24/80, Taye Metcha to Asfaha Weldemikael, 6 August 1962.
27. DOS 775.00/12-2761, Looram to State Department, 27 December 1961.
28. The remaining five players fielded were Gilya Tesfamariam (Mariano), Berhe Goitom, Kiflom Araia, Asmellash Berhe and Tesfai Gebremedhin. Besides Mengistu, the Ethiopians were Awad Mohammed, Getachew Wolde and Girma Zeleke.
29. Teklit Lijam, *Football in Eritrea*, Francescana Printing Press, Asmera, 2018, p. 200.
30. IEG, His Majesty's Special Directorate, 573/54, Memo by Lt Col. Yirgu Endaylalu, 17 May 1962.
31. *Zemen*, 9/2448, 22 June 1962; 9/2449, 23 June 1962; 10/2450, 26 June 1962.
32. Ibid.
33. Ibid., 9/2451, 27 June 1962.
34. Asfaha Kahsai, interview, 2000.
35. *Zemen*, 9/2452, 28 June 1962.
36. Ibid., 9/2454, 30 June 1962.
37. Tekie Fessehatsion, *From Federation to Annexation*, p. 44.
38. Ibid., quoting Looram to State Department, Airgram A-1, 3 June 1962.
39. Weldeyohannes was variously a director of Trade and Industry and of Law and Justice in the Eritrean Government. He was also a highly successful businessman.
40. Gebreyohannes, interview, 1998.
41. Tesfayohannes Berhe, interview, London, December 1997.
42. *Zemen*, 9/2463, 13 July 1962.
43. Kidane Hidad, interview, 19 April 2013.
44. RDC, Box 127, File no. S/INT/B/7, Vol. III, Acc. no. 15182, pp. 84–92.
45. Ibid., S/INT/B/6, Vol. II, Acc. no. 15179.

46. Eritrean Administration, Office of the Police Commissioner, M/1/KAS/46, 10 and 20 September 1962.
47. *Zemen*, 9/2463, 13 July 1962.

25. THE ANNEXATION

1. Zewde Retta, *Ye-Ertra Gudai, 1941–1963*, Berhan-na Printing Press, Addis Ababa, 2000, p. 494; Asfaha, interview with author.
2. Asfaha, interview, 1996.
3. Shewit Desta, interview, Asmera, 2012.
4. *Zemen*, 9/2486, 16 August 1962.
5. Andrew Wilson, 'Eritrea Is Facing an Unhappy Birthday', *The Observer*, 9 September 1962. Similar article in *New York Times*, 'Unrest Angers Haile Selassie', 8 July 1962.
6. Zewde Retta, *Ye-Ertra Gudai*, p. 496.
7. Ibid., p. 501; see also Asfaha's interview with author.
8. Ibid.
9. Habtu Tesfamikael files, Assembly documents, History Project Collection, RDC.
10. Ibid.
11. *Zemen*, 10/2546, 14 November 1962.
12. Habtu Tesfamikael files, History Project Collection, RDC.
13. Dawit Weldegiorgis, *Red Tears: War, Famine and Revolution in Ethiopia*, Red Sea Press, Trenton, NJ, 1989, pp. 80–1.
14. Enrico Mania, *Non solo cronaca dell'Acrocoro,* Stabilimento Fotoliti, Rome, 2005, p. 223.
15. Zewde Retta, *Ye-Ertra Gudai*, p. 503.
16. Ibrahim Mohammed, interview, 2001.
17. Zewde Retta, *Ye-Ertra Gudai*, p. 503.
18. *Zemen*, 10/2547, 15 November 1962.
19. Mania, *Non solo cronaca dell'Acrocoro*, pp. 225–6.
20. *Zemen*, 10/2547, 15 November 1962.
21. Yehdego Gebrerufael, interview, Iyamo, 1974.
22. Omer Adem Idris, interview, Kassala, 1987.
23. G.K.N. Trevaskis, *Eritrea: A Colony in Transition, 1941–1952,* Oxford University Press, Oxford, 1960, p. 131.
24. Sebhat Aberra, interview, 2007.
25. Seyoum Haregot, *The Bureaucratic Empire: Serving Emperor Haile Selassie*, Red Sea Press, Trenton, NJ, 2013, pp. 21–3. In a conversation with this writer, *Ato* Yekunoamlak Belay, one of the former members of the Ethiopian parliament, confirmed the condemnation.
26. Weldemikael Abraha, interview. The chief organisers who were arrested included Weldemikael Abraha (later minister in post-independent Eritrea), Mahmoud Ismail, Teku'e Yehdego, Musa Araho, Nur Abdelhai, Teklai Gebreselassie (Haraka)—all active participants in the ensuing struggle for independence.

27. Ibid.; see also Mohammed Berhan Hassen, *Mnqsqas Harnet Ertra*, Selam Printing Press, Asmera, 2001, p. 4.
28. Teklai Haraka, interview, Ararib, 1987. Teklai Gebreselassie (Haraka) was one of the pioneers of Mahber Shew'ate. He was a prominent colleague of such veterans as Mehari Debessai, Weldemikael Abraha and Weldemikael Gebremariam. After years of exile, he joined the EPLF in the 1970s. He died of natural causes after independence.
29. Asfaha, interview, 2 September 2006.
30. Teklit Lijam, *Football in Eritrea*, Francescana Printing Press, Asmera, 2018, p. 222; RDC, letter from Mikael Gebrenegus to Alemseged Tesfai, October 2010, p. 3.
31. RDC, letter from Mikael Gebrenegus to Alemseged Tesfai, October 2010, p. 5.
32. Kinfe Tesfagabir, interview, 2010.
33. Colonel Kifle Gebremikael, interview, Asmera, 2008.
34. RDC, Inquest Commission, Kifle Ergetu (chairman), Summary of Inquest, 20 October 1963.
35. Ibid.
36. RDC, Inquest Commission, Statement, 20 October 1963.
37. Gebreyohannes, interview, 1998.
38. Ibid.

EPILOGUE

1. Mohammed Said Nawd, Tahir Fedab and Mohammed Berhan Hassen have each left memoirs about Haraka, based on pure memory, that clash on practically every point. Ruth Iyob's *The Eritrean Struggle for Independence: Resistance and Nationalism, 1941–1993*, Cambridge University Press, Cambridge, 1995; Redie Bereketeab's *Eritrea: The Making of a Nation, 1890–1991,* Repro Economicum, Uppsala, 2000; and Awet Weldemichael's, *Third World Colonialism and Strategies for Liberation*, Cambridge University Press, Cambridge, 2013, albeit a comparative study with East Timor, are some of the exceptions in that they are partially based on research inside Eritrea, and do shed some light on the period, but are clearly constrained by the limitations discussed above.
2. As this book goes to print, one former EPLF leader, Mesfin Hagos, has published his memoir. In view of his present status as an opponent of the Eritrean Government from abroad, his book is bound to arouse controversy. It is too soon to assess the impact that his initiative will have on the overall history of the struggle. Hopefully, it will provoke much-needed discussions and responses. See Mesfin Hagos and Awet Tewelde Weldemichael, *An African Revolution Reclaimed: A Memoir of Eritrean Freedom Fighter Mesfin Hagos*, Red Sea Press, Trenton, NJ, 2023.
3. Christoopher Clapham, 'War and State Formation in Ethiopia and Eritrea', Failed States Conference, Florence, 10–14 April 2001, pp. 10, 13.
4. Alex de Waal, *The Real Politics of the Horn of Africa*, Polity Press, Cambridge, 2015, p. 154.

PRIMARY SOURCES

Archives and Manuscripts

1. Institute of Ethiopian Studies (IES), Addis Ababa
   F.F. Russell Diary

2. Research and Documentation Centre (RDC), Asmera
   British Military Administration (BMA)
   British Administration of Eritrea (BAE)
   Eritrean Administration
   Eritrean Assembly
   Eritrean Police Force (EFP)
   Government of Eritrea (GOE)
   History Project Collection
   Imperial Government of Ethiopia (IEG):
      Ethiopian Military Intelligence
      Federal High Court (FHC)
      Imperial Federal Office
      Office of the Emperor's Representative
   International Confederation of Free Trade Unions (ICFTU)
   Supreme Court of Eritrea
   UK Official Documents:
      Foreign Office (FO)
      War Office (WO)
   UN Four Power Commission (FPC) Reports, including:
      UK Government Report Concerning the Administration of Eritrea
      UN Commissioner's Report
   UN Tribunal in Eritrea
   UN General Assembly, Official Records
   US Official Documents:
      Department of State (DOS)
      Department of Justice (DOJ)
      National Security Council (NSC)

Berhanie Mengistie papers
Eritrean Liberation Front (ELF) collection
Fergus McCleary files
Habtu Tesfamikael collection
Said Sefaf papers
Weldeab Weldemariam collection
Yohannes Tsegai collection

Newspapers

Addis Zemen (official Ethiopian Government paper)
Andinet (mouthpiece of the Unionist Youth Party)
Dehai Ertra (paper representing the views of the Eritrean opposition, 1953–4)
Dimtsi Ertra (paper published by Eritrean unionists living in Ethiopia, from 1944)
Ethiopia (mouthpiece of the Unionist Party of Eritrea)
Fenote Berhan (Eritrean Orthodox Church newspaper)
Hanti Ertra (paper published by the Independence Bloc of Eritrea)
Il Quotidiano Eritreo (official Italian newspaper under the British Administration)
Luce dell'Eritrea or Mebrahti Ertra (published by the Pro-Italy party L'Unità)
Nai Ertra Semunawi Gazeta (*ESG*) (official Tigrinya and Arabic weekly under the British Administration)
New York Times
The Observer
Saut al Rabita (mouthpiece of the Muslim League of Eritrea)
Times of London
Unione e Progresso (paper published by Omer Qadi's Independent Muslim League)

Major Interviews

(Unless otherwise specified, all interviews were conducted by the author)
Aberash Yehdego, 23 April 2004
Adem Melekin, 15 April 2001, by Osman Saleh
Alemash Sebhatu, 31 March 2009
Asfaha Weldemikael, Addis Ababa, 1996
Bahta Iyoab, Asmera, 1997, by Yemane Mesghina
Berhe Andemikael, 2 and 9 October 2007
Cracknell, David, Bridport, UK, 2002
Fesseha Weldemariam (Gandhi), Port Sudan, 24–9 October 1987
Gebrai Meles, Asmera, 1997, by Yemane Mesghina
Gebreyohannes Tesfamariam, Asmera, 1998
Hagos Temnewo, Shambuko, 1997, by Yemane Mesghina
Ibrahim Sultan, Cairo, 1983, by Ahmed Haji Ali

Idris Mohammed al-Hassen Genshera, 24–5 November 2004, by Bahre Goitom
Kahsai Bahlibi, Ararib, 1987
Kidane Hidad, Keren, 19 April 2013
Mehretab Asfaha, Asmera, 2 September 2006
Mesfin Gebrehiwet, Asmera, 2001
Mohammed Idris Arey (Gesir), 26 October 2007
Mohammed Omer Akito, Asseb, 2 February 2004
Saleh Mohammed Adem Kirutchai, Tesseney, 1999, by Osman Saleh
Saleh Musa Abudawd, Asmera, 1999
Sebhat Aberra, 14 and 27 September 2007
Seyoum Maasho, Asmera, 1997
Tesfai Reda'e, Gebremikael Begatsion and Abraha Hagos, Asmera, 2 October 2002
Tsegai Kahsai, Asmera, 16 December 2002
Weldeab Weldemariam, Rome, 1982, by Arefaine Berhe and Ahmed Haji Ali; and Ararib, 1987, by Gebreselassie Yosef
Weldemikael Abraha, Asmera, 23 March 2013
Yohannes Tsegai, Asmera, 1996, 1997
Zere Debretsion, Asmera, 20 January 1998, by Yemane Mesghina

BIBLIOGRAPHY

Abebe Teklehaimanot, *Ethiopia's Sovereign Right of Access to the Sea Under International Law,* University of Georgia, Athens, Ga, 2007 (Masters Thesis)

Afewerk Gebreyesus, *Dagmawi Atse Menelik*, Rome, 1901 (1909 GC)

Aklilu Habtewold, *Aklilu Remembers, Historical Recollections from a Prison Cell,* Addis Ababa University Press, 2010.

Alamin Mohammed Said, *Sewra Ertra: Msguamn Mnqulqualn*, Red Sea Press, Lawrenceville, 1994.

Alemseged Abbay, *Identity Jilted*, Red Sea Press, Lawrenceville NJ, 1998.

Alemseged Tesfai, *Aynfelale: Eritrea 1941-1955,* Hidri Publishers, Asmara, 2001. (Tigrinya Text)

——— "*Communal Land Ownership in Northern Ethiopia and Its Implications for Government Policy,*" Land Tenure Center, University of Wisconsin, Madison, 1973. (Master's Thesis)

——— *Conflict Resolution in Eritrea*, IGAD Capacity Assessment Study: CPMR in Eritrea, 2001.

——— *Ertra: kab Federeshin nab Gobetan Sewran 1956-1962,* Hidri Publishers, Asmara, 2016. (Tigrinya text)

——— *Federeshin Ertra ms Ityopia – kab Matienzo ksab Tedla*, Hidri Publishers, 2005, (Tigrinya text)

——— *"The Role of the Four Great Powers and the General Assembly of the United Nations in the Federation Between Eritrea. and Ethiopia,"* Master's Thesis, University of Illinois, Champaign-Urbana, 1972.

Ali Mohammed Saleh, *Tezekrotat Ertrawi Tegadalai*, Dubai, 2007.

Amare Tekle, *The Creation of Ethio-Eritrea Federation: A Case Study*, Denver, University Microfilms Ann Arbor, 1964.

Amdemicheal Dessalegn, *Memos to Emperor Haile Selassie*, (hand written copies, Amharic), Asmara 1950-1952, (RDC, History Project Files.)

Andargatchew Tsege, *Tewlid Aydenager Egnam En-nager* (*Let Us Speak Up, Lest the Generation is Confused*), Netsanet Publishing Abency, Addis Ababa, 2018.

Bairu Tafla, "Interdependence through Independence: The Challenges of Eritrean Historiography," New Trends in Ethiopian Studies, Red Sea Press 1994.

Bairu Tafla and Schmidt E., *Discovering Eritrea's Past*, Verlag J.H. Dettelbach, 2016.

BIBLIOGRAPHY

Bahru Zewde, *A History of Modern Ethiopia – 1855-1991,* James Curry, 1991

Bereket Amare, *Tarik Senselet Weledotat*, Atlas Printing Press, Asmara, 2019.

Berlin I., *The Crooked Timber of Humanity*, Vintage, 1990.

Beyene Solomon, *Fighter for Democracy: The Saga of an Ethiopian Labor Leader,* Publish America, Baltimore, 2010.

Carr E. H., *The New Society*, Beacon Press, Boston, 1951.

Clapham C., *Transformation and Continuity in Revolutionary Ethiopia,* Cambridge University Press, 1988

——— *The Horn of Africa: State Formation and Decay*, Oxford, 2017.

——— "War and State Formation in Ethiopia and Eritrea," *Failed States Conference*, Florence, 10-14 April 2001.

Davidson B., *Black Star: A View of the Life and Times of Kwame Nkrumah,* 1989.

——— *The Black Man's Burden,* Times Books, New York, 1992.

Dawit Weldegiorgis, *Red Tears, Red Sea Press, Trenton N.J., 1989.*

Ehrlich H., *Ethiopia and the Challenge of Independence*, Boulder, 1986.

——— *Ras Alula,* Red Sea Press, Lawrenceville, 1995.

EPLF Department of Public Administration, *Socio Economic Study of the Sahel Region* (Manuscript), 1985.

Gaim Kibreab, *Critical Reflections on the Eritrean War of Independence*, Red Sea Press, Trenton, 2008.

Gilkes P., National Identity and Historical Mythology in Eritrea and Somaliland, *NE African Studies*, 2003.

Gebremichael Gurmu, *Deggiat Bahta Hagos Segeneiti,* MBY Printing Press, Asmara, 1997

Gebru Tareke, *Ethiopia: Power and Protest*, Red Sea Press, Lawrenceville, 1996.

Getatchew Begashaw, Port of Assab as a Factor for Economic Development and Regional Conflict, http//www.amazon.com.uk/262-4263174-1078052.

Gottesman L., *To Fight and Learn*, Red Sea Press, Lawrenceville, 1998.

Hobsbawm E., *Nations and Nationalism Since 1870*: *Program, Myth, Reality*, Cambridge University Press, 1990.

ICFTUz, OR/ML/rb, Levison to Weldeab, 6/2/1952.

ICFTU, OR/O/E4, Levison to Sir Vincent Tewson (ICFTU HEAD), .8/2/1952.

Johnson, Drake and Piper Inc, *Middle East War Projects*, New York. 1943.

Jonas, R., *The Battle of Adwa, African Victory in the Age of Empire,* The Bellknap Press, Cambridge Mass., 2011.

Jordan Gebremedhin, *Peasants and Nationalism in Eritrea*, Red Sea Press, Lawrenceville, NJ, 1989.

Killion, T., *Workers, Capital and the State in the Ethiopia Region, 1919-1974*, UMI Dissertation Information Service, 1984.

Lefebvre, R., *Arms for Africa,* University of Pittsburg Press, 1991.

Longrigg, S., *A Short History of Eritrea,* Oxford, 1945.

Mandela N., *Long Walk to Freedom*, Abacus, London, 1994.

Mania E., *Non Solo Cronaca dell'Acrocolo,* Stabilimento Fotoliti, Roma, 2005.

Marcus H., *The Life and Times of Menelik 1844-1913,* Red Sea Press, Lawrenceville, 1995.

——— *The Politics of Empire, Ethiopia, Great Britain and the United States 1941-1974,* Red Sea Press, Lawrenceville, 1983.

Markakis, J. and Nega Ayele, *Class and Revolution in Ethiopia,* Red Sea Press, Trenton NJ, 1986.

Miran J., *Red Sea Citizens,* Indiana University Press, Bloomington, 2009.

Mohammed Omer Qadi, *Tarikh Hagerka Mflat (Knowing the History of Your Country)*, Handwritten Document (Manuscript), History Project, RDC.

Mohammed Said Nawd, *The Eritrean Liberation Movement (Haraka): Truth and History*, Unpublished MS, Tigrinya, History roject, RDC.

Okbazghi Yohannes, *Eritrea: A Pawn in World Politics*, University of Florida Press, Gainsville, 1991.

——— *The United States and the Horn of Africa*, Harper Collins, 1997.

Pankhurst, R., *The Ethiopian Borderlands: Essays in Regional History from Ancient Times to the End of the 18th Century,* Red Sea Press, Lawrenceville NJ, 1997.

——— "Italy and Ethiopia: The Emperor Rides Back," *African Quarterly Review*, 1971-72.

——— "Some Historical Aspects of Land Tenure in Ethiopia," *Proceedings in Agrarian Reform,* MLR, Addis Ababa, 1970.

Pankhurst, S., *British Policy in Eritrea*, Walthanstow Press, Woodward Green. (Undated)

——— *Eritrea on the Eve*, New Times and Ethiopia News Books, Woodward Green, 1952.

——— *Why Are We Destroying Ethiopian Ports?*, New Times and Ethiopia News Books, Woodford Green, 1952.

Perini R., *Mereb Mellash (Di Qua da Mereb)*, Tigrinya translation by Vittorio Roncali, Chiaramonte Roberto, Torino, 1997.

Pollera, A., *Le Popolazioni Indigene dell'Eritrea*, Bologna. L.Cappelli, 1935.` [*The Native Peoples of Eritrea,* English Translation by Linda Lapin, (unpublished) p. 119-120.]

Pool D., *From Guerillas to Government*, Oxford, 2002.

Prouty C., *Empress Taitu and Menelik II*, Red Sea Press, Trenton, 1986.

Puglisi G., *Chi e dall'Eritrea? Dizionario Biografico*, Agenzia Regina, Asmara. 1952,

Raghavan, S., *India's War World War II and the Making of Modern South Asia*, Basic Books, New York, 2016.

Rasmuson J.R., *The History of Kagnew Station and American Forces in Eritrea,* Il Poligrafico, Asmara, 1973.

Redie Bereketeab, *Eritrea: The Making of a Nation 1890-1991*, Repro Economicum, Uppsala, 2000.

Reid, A., *Answers to Questions from Bertil Wanstrom* (Manuscript), RDC – History Project Collection.

——— *Correspondence with Andrew Cordier*, UN Tribunal in Eritrea, 18/3/1954.

Reid, R., *War in Pre-Colonial Eastern Africa*, The British Institute in Eastern Africa, London, 2007.

——— *Frontiers of Violence in North-East Africa: Genealogies of Conflicts Since c. 1800,* Oxford University Press, 2011.

Russel, F., *Diary*, (Handwritten Manuscript),12 May 1957, Institute of Ethiopian Studies, Addis Ababa.

Ruth Iyob, *The Eritrean Struggle for Independence: Resistance and Nationalism* 1941-1993, Cambridge, 1995.

Saad Adem, *The Eritrean Revolution* (Manuscript), RDC Acc. No. 0712.

Sbacci, A., *Ethiopia Under Mussolini,* Zed Books, London, 1985.

Seyoum Haregot, *The Bureaucratic Empire*: Serving Emperor Haile Selassie, Red Sea Press, Trenton, 2013.

Spencer, J., *Ethiopia at Bay*, Algonac, Michigan 1987.

Shumet Sisagne, *Unionists and Separatists, The Vagaries of Ethio-Eritrean Relations 1941-1961*, Tshai Publishers, Hollywood, 2007.

Tahir Fedab, *The Eritrean Liberation Movement and Its Historical Progress (1958–1967)*, Unpublished MS, RDC, 1993.

Tekie Beyene, *Kab Riq Hfnti*, Hidri Publishers, Asmara, 2009.

Tekie Fessehatsion, *From Federation to Annexation*, Eritreans for Peace and Democracy Publication Committee, Wash. DC, 1990.

Trevaskis G.K.N., *Eritrea: A Colony in Transition* 1941-1952, Oxford University Press, London, 1960.

——— *Report on Serfdom*, WO 230/255, S/SE/200, 5 June 1948

——— *The Deluge, A Personal View of the End of Empire in the Middle East*, JB Tauris, London, 2019.

——— *The Tribes and Peoples of Northern Eritrea*, (Trevaskis Papers manuscripts), RDC.

UK Ministry of Information, *The First to Be Freed*, His Majesty's Stationary, London, 1944.

——— *Abyssinian The Official Campaigns: Story of the Conquest of Italian East Africa*, His Majesty's Stationery, London,1942.

Edward Ullendorff, The Two Zions, Oxford University Press, Oxford, 1988.

Uoldelul Chelati, "Colonialism and the Construction of National Identities, The Case of Eritrea," *Journal of Eastern African Studies*, 2007.

Venosa, J., *Paths Towards the Nation: Islam, Community and Early Nationalist Mobilization in Eritrea 1941- 1961,* Ohio University Press, 2014.

Westwood, J., *Greatest Battles of World War II,* Bison Group, 1995.

Yishak Gebreyesus, *Kidanat Menelikn Talyann ab Mchiflaq Hzbi Ertra: 1897-19079 (Agreements Between Menelik and Italy in the Suppression of the Eritrean People)*, MBY, Asmara, 1998.

——— *Mederetat (Lectures)*, MBY, Asmara, 2007.

Yishak Yosief, *Embiyale Weldu Gomida: Tarik Raesi Weldemikael, (The Story of Ras Weldemikael Solomon)*, MBY Printing Press, Asmara 1999.

——— *Negsnet Hagere Medri Bahri (Ertra), Tarik Degyat Hailu Aba Gala, (The Story of Dejazmatch Hailu Aba Galla)*, Semhar Printing Press, Asmara, 2000.

Zemhret Yohannes, *Italyawi Megza'eti ab Ertra, (Italian Colonialism in Eritrea),* Hidri Publishers, Asmara, 2010,

——— *Mekete Antsar Italyawi Megza'eti ab Ertra, (Rebellions Against Italian Colonialism in Eritrea),* Hidri Publishers, Asmara, 2010.

Zewde Gebreselassie, *YeItyopiana yeErtra Gitchit Mens'ena Mefthe, (Causes and Solutions to the Conflict Between Ethiopia and Eritrea)*, Addis Ababa, 2015-2016.

Zewde Retta, *YeErtra Gudai, (The Eritrean Case)*, Berhan-na Selam Printing Press, Addis Ababa, 2000.

——— *Yeqedamawi Haileselassie Mengist*, Laxmi Publications, New Delhi, 2012.

INDEX